Sybex's Quick Tour of Windows 95

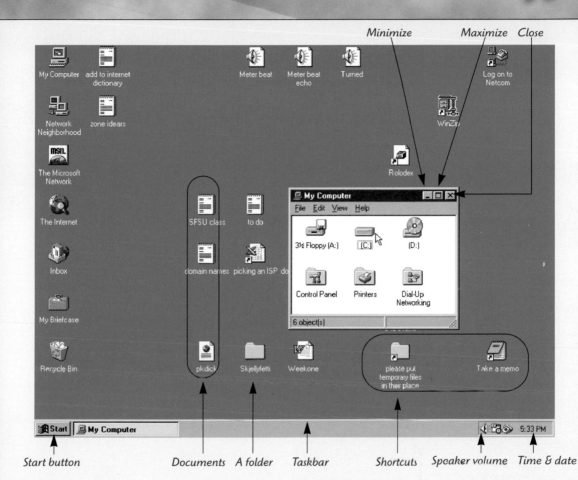

Minimize   Maximize   Close

Start button   Documents   A folder   Taskbar   Shortcuts   Speaker volume   Time & date

The Desktop *is where your programs, files, and shortcuts reside.*

My Computer *allows you to browse the contents of your computer, open folders, open documents, and run programs.*

Network Neighborhood *gives you direct access to other computers (and shared resources, such as printers).*

The Microsoft Network *dials up your connection to Microsoft's online service.*

The Internet *starts up the Internet Explorer, a World Wide Web browser (available only with Plus!).*

Inbox *starts Microsoft Exchange and opens your inbox, so you can see if you have any new mail.*

My Briefcase *is a new feature for keeping documents consistent as you move them between computers.*

Recycle Bin *makes it easy to delete and undelete files.*

The Start button *pops up the Start menu, from which you can run just about every program.*

The Taskbar *displays a button for every running program.*

Create **shortcuts** *on your Desktop for frequently used programs and documents.*

Every window has a **Minimize, Maximize** *(alternating with Restore), and* **Close** *button. The Close button is new; the others just look different.*

FORMATTING A FLOPPY DISK

To format a floppy disk, first double-click the My Computer icon. Put the floppy in the disk drive. Then right-click the 3½ Floppy icon in the My Computer window and choose Format. The Format dialog box appears.

If you want some density other than the standard 1.44MB, click the Capacity drop-down list box and choose another option. To give the disk a label, click in the Label box and type one. Then click Start.

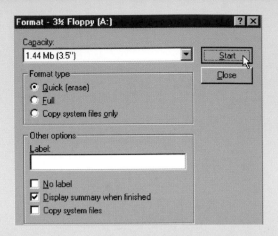

USEFUL KEYBOARD SHORTCUTS

TASK	KEYSTROKE
Get help	F1
Quit a program	Alt+F4
Pop up shortcut menu for selected item	Shift+F10
Pop up the Start menu	Ctrl+Esc
Cut a selection	Ctrl+X
Copy a selection	Ctrl+C
Paste a selection	Ctrl+V
Delete a selection	Delete
Undo the last action	Ctrl+Z
Select all items in window	Ctrl+A
Refresh a window	F5
Open folder one level up from current one	Backspace
Close a folder and all its parents	Shift and click Close button
Rename a selection	F2
Find a file starting with current folder	F3
Delete a selection without putting it in Recycle Bin (be careful!)	Shift+Delete
View a selection's properties	Alt+Enter or Alt+double-click
Copy an icon	Ctrl+click and drag
Create a shortcut from an icon	Ctrl+Shift+click and drag

Sybex Inc.
2021 Challenger Drive
Alameda, CA 94501
Tel: 510-523-8233 · 800-227-2346
Fax: 510-523-2373

SYBEX®

Mastering
Microsoft Access
for Windows 95

Alan Simpson

Elizabeth Olson

Mastering
Microsoft® Access®
for Windows® 95
Third Edition

Alan Simpson

Elizabeth Olson

San Francisco • Paris • Düsseldorf • Soest

SYBEX®

ACQUISITIONS MANAGER: Kristine Plachy
DEVELOPMENTAL EDITOR: Melanie Spiller
EDITOR: Vivian Perry
PROJECT EDITOR: Brenda Frink
TECHNICAL EDITORS: Mike Gunderloy and Tanya Strub
BOOK DESIGNER: Suzanne Albertson
BOOK DESIGN DIRECTOR: Catalin Dulfu
ASSISTANT BOOK DESIGN DIRECTOR: Heather Lewis
DESKTOP PUBLISHER: Dina F Quan
PRODUCTION COORDINATOR: Dave Nash
INDEXER: Ted Laux
COVER DESIGNER: Design Site
COVER PHOTOGRAPHER: Mark Johann

Screen reproductions produced with Collage Complete.

Collage Complete is a trademark of Inner Media Inc.

SYBEX is a registered trademark of SYBEX Inc.

TRADEMARKS: SYBEX has attempted throughout this book to distinguish proprietary trademarks from descriptive terms by following the capitalization style used by the manufacturer.

Every effort has been made to supply complete and accurate information. However, SYBEX assumes no responsibility for its use, nor for any infringement of the intellectual property rights of third parties which would result from such use.

The previous editions of this book were published under the title *Understanding Microsoft Access*.

First edition copyright ©1993 SYBEX Inc.

Second edition copyright ©1994 SYBEX Inc.

Library of Congress Card Number: 95-71898
ISBN: 0-7821-1764-3

Manufactured in the United States of America

10 9 8 7 6

Shareware Distribution

This CD contains various programs that are distributed as shareware. Shareware is a distribution method, not a type of software. The chief advantage is that it gives you, the user, a chance to try a program before you buy it.

Copyright laws apply to both shareware and commercial software, and the copyright holder retains all rights. If you try a shareware program and continue using it, you are expected to register it. Individual programs differ on details—some request registration while others require it. Some request a payment, while others don't, and some specify a maximum trial period. With registration, you get anything from the simple right to continue using the software to program updates.

Copy Protection

None of the programs on the CD is copy-protected. However, in all cases, reselling or making copies of these programs without authorization is expressly forbidden.

To Susan, Ashley, and Alec, as always

Alan Simpson

To Keith, for encouraging me and keeping me sane

Elizabeth Olson

ACKNOWLEDGMENTS

THIS book was a massive undertaking. Many thanks to everyone on the team who stuck with it despite the brutal schedule.

The authors wish to thank Dr. Forrest Houlette for his many contributions to Parts Three, Four, and Five of this book. Way to go Forrest! Writing credits also go to Technical Editor Mike Gunderloy, who put on an additional hat for us by writing Chapter 18.

We're tremendously grateful to the Microsoft support team, who, through the magic of the CompuServe electronic highway, provided fast, helpful responses to our many questions, who listened to our suggestions for improving the product, and who kept us supplied with the latest test software as we raced to meet our deadlines.

Many thanks to Sybex's editorial and production teams for their much-appreciated support. Developmental Editor Melanie Spiller got us started on the right foot. Project Editors Brenda Frink, Abby Azrael, and Val Potter kept things moving smoothly, and Editor Vivian Perry provided careful scrutiny and corrected our writing blunders. We also want to extend our gratitude to Desktop Publisher Dina Quan, Production Coordinator Dave Nash, Indexer Ted Laux, Book Design Director Catalin Dulfu, Assistant Book Design Director Heather Lewis, and to the many others on the Sybex team who made this book possible. A huge amount of thanks go to Technical Editor Mike Gunderloy for his meticulous review and many suggestions for improving this book's technical content, and to Technical Editor Tanya Strub who checked the early chapters for us.

And last, but not least, a million thanks to our families—Ashley, Susan, and Alec Simpson and Keith Olson—for their patience and support through yet another long bout of frenzied book writing.

Contents
AT A GLANCE

CONTENTS

PART THREE   **DATABASE TUNING AND ADMINISTRATION**

PART FOUR   BUILDING A CUSTOM APPLICATION

APPENDICES

INTRODUCTION

WELCOME to *Mastering Microsoft Access for Windows 95*, the book for new and intermediate Microsoft Access users, and for aspiring application developers.

Like Access, this book is geared toward experienced Windows users. That's not to say that you need to be a Windows genius to use Access. But if you're just now making the transition from DOS to Windows, or just getting started with computers, you'll surely want to get your Windows "basic skills" down pat before you start using Access. (Our book, *Alan Simpson's Easy Guide to Windows 95*, can help you do that. It's also published by Sybex.)

Just in case you're wondering, we used Windows 95 exclusively while writing this book; however, Microsoft Access for Windows 95 also runs under Windows NT and we've sprinkled a few notes about Windows NT throughout the text. Readers who are using Windows NT should have little trouble following our instructions, although you may encounter some minor differences along the way.

New to Database Management?

It's not necessary to know anything about database management or programming to use this book. We start at square one in Chapter 1. As for programming—don't worry about it. Programming is definitely in the "not required" category when it comes to using Microsoft Access.

New to Access for Windows 95, but an Old Hand at Access 2.0?

If you're an old hand at using Microsoft Access 2.0, but are trying (or planning to try) Microsoft Access for Windows 95 for the first time, there are several ways to find out what's new.

First, you can flip to the end of chapters in this book to find our "What's New in the Access Zoo?" sidebars, which highlight important new features that relate to the chapter you've selected.

If you have Access 1.*x* or 2.*x* databases that you'd like to use with Access for Windows 95, be sure to check Appendix A of this book for an introduction to points you must consider *before* removing your old version of Access and for information about converting your existing databases.

Finally, you can view online details of what's new. After installing Access, simply open the *What's New* book in the Access for Windows 95 Help Contents, and then explore the many subtopics that appear. Chapter 1 explains how to use the Access online help.

A Focus on Creating Applications

Microsoft Access is a huge product, and nearly every nook and cranny of it is already documented in the online help. In this book, rather than waste paper repeating all of that information, we've opted to focus on two things: 1) general day-to-day use of Microsoft Access, and 2) using Access to create custom Windows applications. To meet those goals, we've organized the book as follows:

Part One   An Overview of Access   This part is for experienced Windows users who are new to database management and/or Access. Here we cover basic skills and concepts, and offer a hands-on guided tour.

Part Two   Creating a Database   This second part of the book covers all the basic Access objects you'll create to manage data: tables, queries, forms, and reports. The information presented here is vital to casual users, to more ambitious application developers, and to aspiring developers.

Part Three   Database Tuning and Administration   Here you'll learn how to personalize Access, speed up databases for optimal performance, administer your databases and use database replication, and take advantage of networking and security features.

Part Four   Building a Custom Application   Most Access users eventually realize that, with just a little more effort, they can turn their database into an easy-to-use "stand-alone" Windows application. Part Four of this book is all about that topic—creating applications.

Part Five   Refining a Custom Application   For application developers who aspire to learn Visual Basic programming and other more advanced application topics, we offer Part Five.

Features of This Book

This book offers several features that will help you learn Access and find the information you need, when you need it. Here are some examples:

- **Notes, Tips, and Warnings**. These provide good ideas, shortcuts, references to related topics, and cautions that point out when you might want to think twice before clicking that mouse!

- **Sidebars**. Sprinkled throughout the book, sidebars provide useful tidbits that will help you work smarter with Microsoft Access or Windows 95.

- **What's New in the Access Zoo?** Designed to help people upgrading from Access 2.0 to Access for Windows 95, these end-of-chapter sections highlight new features discussed in the chapter.

- **Access in an Evening (Chapter 3)**. A hands-on guided tour of Access, designed to give you a feel for working with the program, in just a few short lessons.

- **About Access, Office, and Windows 95 (Chapter 4)**. Highlights common features in Access, Office, and Windows 95, so you can learn Access more quickly and take advantage of integration between Access and other programs in Microsoft Office.

- **CD-ROM Disk**. The CD-ROM disc in the back of this book contains a great multimedia catalog of ready-to-run Access applications that you can purchase separately, as well as demos, shareware, freeware, sample databases, and more. See Appendix B for more information.

Conventions Used in This Book

We use the standard terminology that just about everyone else uses to discuss Access. However, we do use a shortcut method to display a series of commands and/or options you follow to get a particular job done. We always present the commands in the order you'll select them, separated with a ➤ symbol.

For example, the instruction "Choose Help ➤ About Microsoft Access" means "Choose *About Microsoft Access* from the *Help* menu" (using either the underlined keys or the mouse). And the instruction "Choose Start ➤ Programs ➤ Microsoft Access" means "Click on the *Start* button on the Windows 95 taskbar, then choose the *Programs* option from the Start menu, and then choose the *Microsoft Access* option from the menu that appears" (again, using either the underlined keys or the mouse). This approach lets you see, at a glance, the exact sequence of commands you must choose to get a job done. It also helps you remember command sequences that you use often.

We also use toolbar buttons and other symbols in the margin. The toolbars provide a convenient way to perform many common Access operations with a simple mouse click. For example, clicking on the Print button shown at left prints the currently highlighted table, query, form, macro, or module. You'll often see a button in the margin the first time it's called for within a chapter.

 As you'll discover, the Help system in Access is quite extensive. The "info" symbol shown at left marks places in the text that direct you to specific Help topics or other sources for further information.

 Finally, because things don't always go as planned, you'll occasionally need to do some troubleshooting. The "first aid" symbol shown at left marks places where you'll find problem-solving information.

Thank You

Our sincerest thanks go to you for choosing this book. We hope it serves you well. As usual, we welcome comments, criticism, and suggestions. You can reach us at:

Alan Simpson
P.O. Box 630
Rancho Santa Fe, CA 92067-0630
Fax: (619) 756-0159
MSN: CoolNerds
AOL: CoolNerds
WWW: http://www.coolnerds.com/coolnerds
Internet: alan@coolnerds.com
CompuServe: 72420,2236

Elizabeth Olson
P.O. Box 23981
San Diego, CA 92193
eolson@cts.com

PART ONE

An Overview of Access

CHAPTER

1

Getting Started and Getting Around

MICROSOFT Access for Windows 95 is a *database management system*, sometimes abbreviated DBMS. As the name implies, a DBMS helps you to *manage data* that's stored in a computer *database*. The data you manage can be virtually anything, including:

- Names and addresses
- Business contacts, customers, and sales prospects
- Employee and personnel information
- Inventory
- Invoices, payments, and bookkeeping
- Libraries and collections
- Schedules, reservations, and projects

Access Isn't Just for Techies!

Don't worry if you know nothing about databases and don't want to become an expert on the topic. Access *Wizards* can guide you through almost any step, and they can create databases for you automatically. So even if you need to set up something as complex as a system for managing orders, inventory, or assets—or something as simple as keeping a list of contacts and birthdays—Access Wizards can take care of the grunt work while you focus on getting useful information from your computer. You'll have a chance to try Wizards during the hands-on tour in Chapter 3, and in many other chapters of this book.

If you're a technical type, never fear! Access has more than enough to make you happy. It's a full-featured application development system that includes the Visual Basic programming language and other tools for setting up sophisticated applications for yourself and your customers. You'll learn more about these features in Parts Four and Five.

You may already know what kinds of data you plan to manage with Access, and you may already be familiar with other database programs and with the basic concepts of database management. If not, you'll learn more about databases in the next chapter. But whether you're a seasoned veteran eager to start working in Access or a database newcomer wondering where to begin, the first step is to learn how to start Access and use its extensive Help system to coach you along as you work.

Starting Access

To start Microsoft Access:

1. Start Windows 95 in the usual manner.

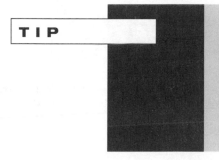

TIP

If you're using Microsoft Office for Windows 95, and have added Access to the Microsoft Office Shortcut Bar, you can start Access by clicking on the appropriate button on the Office Shortcut Bar (see Chapter 4). Or, if you've set up a shortcut icon for Access on the Windows desktop, you can double-click on that icon to start Access. Then skip to step 3 below.

2. Click on the Start button on the Windows taskbar, and then choose Programs ➤ Microsoft Access.

3. After a short delay, you'll sec the Microsoft Access startup dialog box, shown in Figure 1.1. (If you've just installed Access, no list will appear below the Open An Existing Database option.)

4. From here, you can do any of the following:

- **To create a new blank database**, choose Blank Database and then click on OK. The File New Database dialog box will open. (More about this in Chapter 5.)
- **To use the Database Wizard to create a new database,** choose Database Wizard and then click on OK to open the New dialog box. (More about this in Chapter 5.)

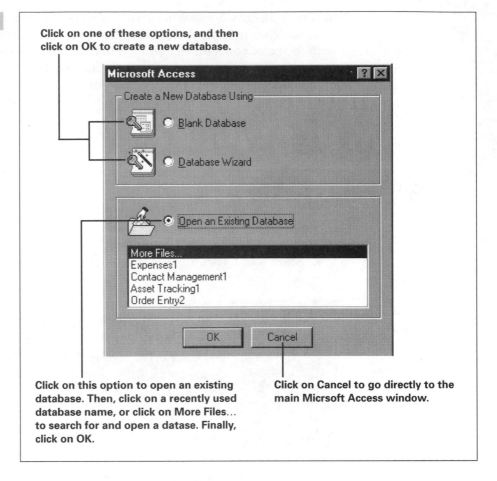

FIGURE 1.1

The Microsoft Access startup dialog box. From here, you can create a new database, open an existing one, or click on Cancel to go to the main Access window.

Click on one of these options, and then click on OK to create a new database.

Click on this option to open an existing database. Then, click on a recently used database name, or click on More Files... to search for and open a datase. Finally, click on OK.

Click on Cancel to go directly to the main Micrsoft Access window.

- **To open an existing database,** choose Open An Existing Database. If a list of database names appears, click on a recently used database name in the list, or click on More Files... so you can look for the database you want to use. Click on OK. See "Opening an Existing Database" later in this chapter for more details.

- **To go to the main Microsoft Access window** (shown in Figure 1.2) without creating or opening a database, click on the Cancel button or press Esc.

N O T E

If Access is customized to bypass the startup dialog box, you'll be taken to the main Access window as soon as you finish step 2 above. We'll explain how to bypass the startup dialog box later in this chapter.

Figure 1.2 shows the main Microsoft Access window that appears when you click on Cancel in the startup dialog box, and anytime you close an Access database.

 Advanced users can learn about optional command-line startup switches for Access in Chapter 15 and by searching the Access Help index for *Startup Options, Command-Line Options*. We'll explain how to use Access Help later in this chapter.

FIGURE 1.2

The main Microsoft Access window that appears when you click on Cancel in the startup dialog box and anytime you close an Access database. You'll also see this window if Access is set up to bypass the startup dialog box.

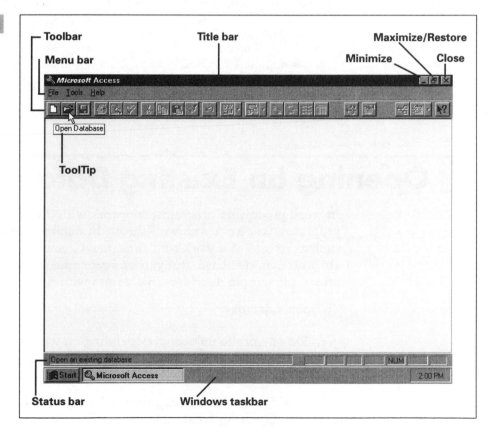

Creating a Desktop Shortcut

A *shortcut icon* makes it easy to launch a program or open a file by double-clicking on that icon on the Windows desktop. To quickly add an icon that will launch the Access program from the desktop, minimize or close any open windows and then...

1. Use Windows Explorer to open the folder that contains Microsoft Access. For example, right-click on the Start button on the Windows taskbar, choose Explore, double-click on the MSOffice folder (it's usually on drive C), and then double-click on the Access folder.

2. Locate the Msaccess program icon, which has a picture of a key next to the Msaccess program name.

3. Hold down the *right* mouse button while you drag the icon to the Windows desktop. Release the mouse button.

4. When the shortcut menu appears, choose Create Shortcut(s) Here.

In the future, you can start Access by double-clicking on the "Shortcut to Msaccess" icon on your desktop. To discover other ways to create shortcuts for Access, look up the *Shortcuts...* topics in the Access Help index or the Windows Help index. (To get Windows help, click on the Start button on the taskbar and choose Help.)

Opening an Existing Database

In word processing programs, you work with documents. In spreadsheet programs, you work with worksheets. In database management systems, such as Access, you work with *databases*. Chances are, you'll want to create your own database. But you can get some practice now by exploring one of the sample databases that comes with Access.

To open a database:

1. Do one of the following, depending on whether you're starting from the startup dialog box, from the main Microsoft Access window, or from the Windows desktop:

   • **From the startup dialog box** (see Figure 1.1), choose Open An Existing Database (this is the default choice).

Organizing the Start ➤ Programs Menu Items

If your Start ➤ Programs menu has too many entries, or isn't organized the way you like, you can rearrange it easily. For the sake of example, let's suppose you want to move Microsoft Access and other Microsoft Office programs from the main Start ➤ Programs menu into a Microsoft Office submenu that looks something like this:

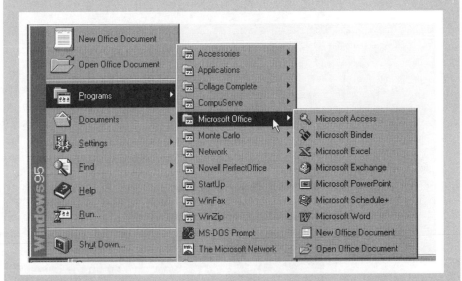

All it takes is a little knowledge of Windows Explorer, and these basic steps:

1. Right-click on the Start button on the taskbar and choose Explore.

2. In the left pane of the Exploring window, click on the Programs folder (it's below the Start Menu folder). The right pane will show the contents of the Programs folder.

3. In the right pane of the Exploring window, right-click your mouse on an empty part of the pane and choose New ➤ Folder from the shortcut menu.

4. Type a new folder name, such as **Microsoft Office**, and press ↵.

5. In the left pane, click on the + sign next to the Programs folder, and then use the vertical scroll bar to scroll the left pane until you can see the new folder you created in step 4.

6. Starting in the right pane, drag the program (or folder) you want to move from the right pane to your new folder in the left pane.

7. Repeat step 6 as needed, and then click on the Close button in the Exploring window.

For more details on customizing the Start menus, choose Start ➤ Help, and click on the Index tab. Then type **Start Menu, Reorganizing** and press ↵. To learn more about Windows Explorer, look up topics below *Windows Explorer* on the Index tab in Help.

Then, if the database name you want to open is shown in the list, double-click on that name, and you're done. If the database name isn't in the list, double-click on More Files…, and continue with step 2. (If no list appears, click on OK and continue with step 2.)

TIP

As usual in Windows, you can choose an option in a list by clicking on it and then clicking on OK (or whatever button carries out the default command), or by clicking on the option and pressing ↵. Or, for quicker selection, try double-clicking on the option you want to choose.

 • **From the main Microsoft Access window** (see Figure 1.2), choose <u>F</u>ile ➤ <u>O</u>pen Database, or click on the Open Database toolbar button (shown at left), or press Ctrl+O. You'll see an Open dialog box, similar to the example shown in Figure 1.3.

TIP

If you've recently used the database you want to open, try this tip for opening the database quickly: Choose <u>F</u>ile from the menu bar, look for the database name near the bottom of the <u>F</u>ile menu (just above the E<u>x</u>it option), and then click on its name or type the number shown next to its name.

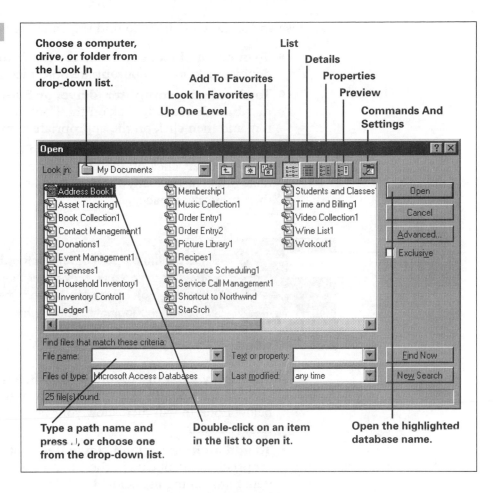

FIGURE 1.3

The Open dialog box

Choose a computer, drive, or folder from the Look In drop-down list.

Add To Favorites

Look In Favorites

Up One Level

List

Details

Properties

Preview

Commands And Settings

Type a path name and press ⏎, or choose one from the drop-down list.

Double-click on an item in the list to open it.

Open the highlighted database name.

Order Entry1

Order Entry1

- **From the Windows desktop,** locate the database using standard techniques in Windows Explorer, My Computer, or Network Neighborhood. When you find the database you want to use, double-click on its name or icon (see the sample icon, shown at left). Or, if you've used the database recently, click on the Start button on the Windows taskbar, choose Documents, and then click on the name of your database in the list that appears. Access will start and the database will open. You're done, so you can skip steps 2–5 below.

2. Use any of these methods to find the database you want to open:

- **To open an object shown in the list *below* Look In,** double-click on the appropriate object icon or name.

- **To choose the computer, drive, or folder where the database is stored,** click on the Look In drop-down list button, and then click on the appropriate item.

- **To open the folder that's just above the currently selected folder,** click on the Up One Level button in the Open dialog box; or click anywhere in the list below Look In, and then press Backspace.

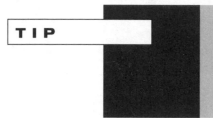

TIP

To find out the purpose of any toolbar button in a window or dialog box, move your mouse pointer to that button and look for the ToolTip near the mouse pointer. See "Using the Toolbars" later in this chapter for more information.

- **To display a list of "favorite" databases and folders,** click on the Look In Favorites toolbar button. The list below Look In will then show your favorite folders and databases only.

- **To add an item to your "favorites" list,** make sure the appropriate item appears in the Look In text box, or click on an item name in the list below Look In. Then, click on the Add To Favorites toolbar button, and choose an option from the menu that appears.

- **To manually enter a drive, directory, and/or file name,** type the appropriate information into the File Name text box at the lower-left corner of the Open dialog box; or, choose an item from the File Name drop-down list.

- **To change the appearance of the list below Look In,** click on the List, Details, Properties, or Preview toolbar buttons as needed.

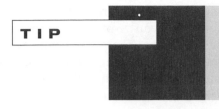

T I P

You can delete, rename, and do other handy operations on items from the Open dialog box. To begin, click on an item in the list below Look In. Then right-click on the item and choose an option from the shortcut menu.

3. If you're choosing the database from the list below Look In, make sure the database name is highlighted in the list (click on it if necessary).

4. If you're on a network and you need to open the database for your exclusive use, select (check) the Exclusive box on the right side of the dialog box. Select the Exclusive option *only* if you're sure you need to prevent other people from updating information in the database (they'll still be able to view the data). Otherwise, leave the check box empty, so that other people can view and update the database as needed.

N O T E

Don't worry. Access automatically makes sure that no two people can update information simultaneously and get the data out of sync. See Chapter 18 for more information about networking and security.

5. Click on the Open button. (As a shortcut for steps 3 and 4, you can double-click on a database name in the list below Look In.)

The database will open, and you'll see either the database window, or a form that describes the database or lets you work with it.

T I P

If the database you're planning to open usually displays a form, but you'd prefer to bypass that form and go directly to the database window, hold down the Shift key while you open the database. This action bypasses the form and any options that are set in the Startup dialog box (Tools ➤ Startup).

➤ As Figure 1.3 shows, the Open dialog box offers many buttons and special features that we haven't mentioned here. If you've played with other Open dialog boxes in Microsoft Office or you've spent some time with Windows Explorer, you'll learn the fine points quickly. For more guidance, click on the ? button in the upper-right corner of the Open dialog box and then click on the part of the dialog box you're curious about. Feel free to experiment!

Opening the Sample Northwind Database

Let's suppose you did a normal Access setup and installed the sample databases. Here's one way to open the Northwind sample database that comes with Access:

1. If you're starting from the Microsoft Access startup dialog box, choose <u>O</u>pen An Existing Database. Then highlight More Files...

Maximizing Your On-Screen Real Estate

The Windows 95 taskbar can take up valuable on-screen real estate that you might prefer to make available to your database objects. Fortunately, it's easy to hide the taskbar temporarily and bring it into view only when you need to. Most screen shots in this book were taken with the taskbar hidden. Compare Figure 1.2 (which shows the taskbar) with Figure 1.4 (which doesn't).

To hide the taskbar temporarily, right-click on any empty spot on the taskbar, choose <u>P</u>roperties, make sure the Always On <u>T</u>op and A<u>u</u>to Hide options in the Taskbar Properties dialog box are checked, and then click on OK. In the future, the taskbar will remain hidden until you move your mouse pointer to the edge of the screen where the taskbar was lurking the last time you used it. (If you don't remember where the taskbar was, move the mouse pointer to the bottom, top, left, or right edge of the screen until it pops into view.)

To display the taskbar permanently again, return to the Taskbar Properties dialog box and deselect (clear) the A<u>u</u>to Hide option. (It's usually best to leave Always On <u>T</u>op checked.) Then click on OK.

(if it's available), and click on OK. If you're starting from the main Microsoft Access window, choose File ➤ Open Database.

2. Use double-clicking to open the MSOffice folder (usually on drive C), then the Access folder below MSOffice, and then the Samples folder below Access.

3. In the list below Look In, double-click on Northwind.

4. If the "welcome" form appears, click on OK to go to the database window.

TIP

There's a shortcut to the sample Northwind database (appropriately named *Shortcut To Northwind*) in the My Documents folder that usually appears when you choose File ➤ Open Database. You can double-click on that shortcut to open Northwind if you prefer.

The various *objects* (a term for database components, such as tables and forms) will appear in the *database window* (see Figure 1.4). You can move, size, maximize, minimize, and restore the database window using all the standard Windows techniques.

What Is a Database, Anyway?

A widely accepted definition of a database is "a collection of data related to a particular topic or purpose." If that sounds a bit stuffy, just think of a database as a general-purpose container for storing and managing information. The information can be anything from names and addresses to details about your business's inventory and orders.

There's more to a database than data. A database also can contain *objects* to help you manage that data, such as forms (for entering and editing data) and reports (for printing data in the format you want). All told, a database can contain any combination of these six types of objects:

Table Tables are the fundamental structures in an Access database because they store the data you'll be managing (see Chapter 6). Within a table, data is organized into fields (columns) and records (rows).

FIGURE 1.4

The Northwind database window with the Tables tab selected

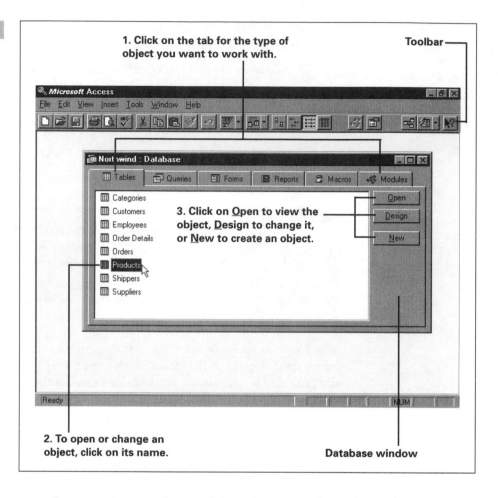

Query A query is a tool for asking questions about data in your tables and for performing actions on data (see Chapter 10). Queries can answer questions such as "How many customers live in Connecticut and what are their names and phone numbers?" You can use queries to combine or *join* data from many separate, but related, tables. A query can, for example, join Customers, Orders, Order Details, and Products tables to answer questions such as "Which customers ordered left-handed farkledorfers, and what is the value of those orders?" Queries also can help you change, delete, or add large amounts of data in one fell swoop. Finally, you can use queries as the basis for your forms and reports.

Form   Forms let you display and enter data in a convenient format that resembles fill-in-the-blank forms (see Chapters 11 and 13). Your forms can be plain and simple, or quite elaborate with graphics, lines, and automatic lookup features that make data entry quick and easy. Forms can even include other forms (called *subforms*) that let you enter data into several tables at once.

Report   Reports let you print or preview data in a useful format (see Chapters 12 and 13). Like forms, reports can be plain or fancy. Examples include mailing labels, lists, envelopes, form letters, and invoices. Reports also can present query results in an easy-to-understand format. For instance, you can print "sales by customer," "receivables aging," and other management information for use in making business decisions.

Macro   A macro is a set of instructions that automate a task you need to do often (see Chapter 20). When you run a macro, Access carries out the actions in the macro, in the order in which the actions are listed. Without writing a single line of program code, you can define macros to automatically open database forms, print mailing labels, process orders, and more. Macros make it easy to assemble a collection of tables, queries, forms, and reports into turnkey *applications* that anyone can use, even if they know little or nothing about Access itself.

Module   Like macros, modules allow you to automate and customize Access (see Part Five). However, unlike macros, modules give you more precise control over the actions taken and they require you to have Visual Basic programming expertise. You may never need to use modules, so don't worry if you're not a programmer.

During the hands-on lessons in Chapter 3, you'll have a chance to create a database complete with tables, forms, reports, queries, and even a simple form module. You'll be astounded at how quickly you can do this when you let the Wizards do all the tough stuff for you.

Working in the Database Window

The *database window* is one of your main tools for using Access. When exploring the sample Northwind database, and when creating databases of your own, you'll use this simple three-step process to work with the objects in your database:

1. Choose the *type* of object you want to create, use, or change using the tabs near the top of the database window. That is, click on the Tables, Queries, Forms, Reports, Macros, or Modules tab.

2. If you want to use or change an existing object, click on its name in the list of objects.

3. Do one of the following:

   - **To create a new object of the type you selected in step 1,** click on the New button near the side of the database window.
   - **To use (or view or run) the object,** click on the Open (or Preview or Run) button.
   - **To change the object's appearance or structure,** click on the Design button.

TIP

As a shortcut for opening (or previewing or running) an object, you can double-click on its name in the database window.

What happens next depends on the type of object you selected, and the type of operation you chose in step 3. We'll say more about the various types of objects in upcoming chapters.

Closing an Object

Regardless of how you open an object, you can use any standard Windows technique to close it. Here are three sure-fire methods:

- Click on the Close (×) button in the upper-right corner of the window you want to close (*not* the Close button for the larger Microsoft Access program window).

- Choose File ➤ Close from the Access menu bar.

- Press Ctrl+W or Ctrl+F4.

Some Access windows also display a Close button on the toolbar, which offers another way to close the object.

If you've changed the object you were viewing, you may be asked if you want to save those changes. Respond to the prompt accordingly.

Uncovering a Hidden Database Window

Sometimes the database window will be invisible even though you've opened a database. If that happens, you can return to the database window (assuming the database is open) by using any of these techniques:

- Press the F11 key.

- Choose Window ➤ ...: Database from the menu bar (where ... is replaced by the name of the database that's open, such as Northwind).

- Click on the toolbar's Database Window button (shown at left).

If none of those methods works, close any other objects that are on the screen and try again. If you still can't get to the database window, you've probably closed the database. To reopen the database, choose File from the Access menu bar, and then click on the name of the database near the bottom of the menu. Or use File ➤ Open Database as discussed earlier in this chapter.

NOTE

When you open some databases, a custom form window will appear, rather than the database window. That's because whoever created that database has turned it into an *application*. Even so, pressing F11 usually will take you to the database window (unless the application designer has disabled this feature). Often you can bypass the initial form window and all the other startup options by holding down the Shift key as you open the database.

Changing Your View of Database Objects

You can use options on the <u>V</u>iew menu, or equivalent buttons on the toolbar, to change the size of objects and amount of detail listed for objects in the database window. Table 1.1 summarizes what's available. In Figure 1.4, for example, we clicked on the List button on the toolbar (<u>V</u>iew ► <u>L</u>ist) to display database objects in a list.

TABLE 1.1: <u>V</u>iew Menu Options and Equivalent Toolbar Buttons

VIEW MENU OPTION	BUTTON	DESCRIPTION
Large Icons		Shows each object as a large icon, with the object name below the icon. Object names initially appear in rows; however, you can drag them as needed.
Sm<u>a</u>ll Icons		Shows each object as a small icon, with the object name next to the icon. Object names initially appear in horizontal rows; however, you can drag them as needed.
<u>L</u>ist		Shows each object as a small icon, with the object name next to the icon. Object names appear vertically, in one or more columns.

TABLE 1.1: View Menu Options and Equivalent Toolbar Buttons (continued)

VIEW MENU OPTION	BUTTON	DESCRIPTION
Details		Shows each object as a small icon, with the object name next to the icon. Object names appear with one object to a line and five columns of detail about each object. The columns list the object's Name, Description, date/time Modified, date/time Created, and object Type. • To resize a column, move your mouse pointer to the vertical divider that's just to the right of the column heading. When the pointer changes to a crosshair, drag the mouse to the left or right; or, double-click on the divider for a snug fit. • To sort by a column (in ascending order), click on the appropriate column header button. To sort the column in descending order, click on the column header button again. • To add a Description to any object, right-click on the object name in the database window, choose Properties, type a Description, and then click on OK.

Note: You can use the View ➤ Arrange Icons and View ➤ Line Up Icons commands on the menu bar (or right-click on a blank area on the database window and choose View, Arrange Icons, or Line Up Icons options from the shortcut menus) to rearrange and line up icons as needed.

Managing Database Objects

The database window lets you do much more than just open objects. You also can use that window to *manage* the objects in a database—that is, to copy them, delete them, rename them, and so on. Here's how:

1. If the object you want to work with is currently open, close it, as described earlier under "Closing an Object."

2. If you haven't already done so, choose the type of object you want to work with (by clicking on the Tables, Queries, Forms, Reports, Macros, or Modules tab on the database window).

3. Click on the name of an object, and then:

   - **To delete the object**, choose Edit ➤ Delete or press Delete, and then click on Yes when prompted for confirmation. To delete the object and move it to the Windows Clipboard (without being asked for confirmation), hold down the Shift key while pressing Delete, or press Ctrl+X (*be careful, there's no undo for this operation;* however, you *can* paste the object from the Clipboard, by pressing Ctrl+V).

   - **To rename the object**, click on the object name again (or choose Edit ➤ Rename), type a new name (up to 64 characters, including blank spaces if you wish), and then press ↵.

   - **To copy the object** into this same database, choose Edit ➤ Copy or press Ctrl+C. Then choose Edit ➤ Paste or press Ctrl+V. Enter a valid object name (up to 64 characters), choose other options as appropriate, and then click on OK. The copy will appear in the list of objects in its proper alphabetical position. (You may need to scroll through the object names to find the copy.) Copying can give you a head start on designing a table, form, report, or other object that should be similar to the object you copied. You can then change the copied object without affecting the original.

   - **To create a shortcut icon on the Windows desktop for the selected object**, choose Edit ➤ Create Shortcut, specify the Location (if you wish), and then click on OK. In the future, you can double-click on the shortcut icon on the Windows desktop to start Access and open the object in one fell swoop.

For another way to create a shortcut to an Access object, size the Access window so that you can see Access and the Windows desktop at the same time (one way is to right-click on an empty place on the Windows taskbar and choose Cascade). Then, if you want to put the shortcut in a folder, open that folder in Windows Explorer, My Computer, or Network Neighborhood. Finally, drag and drop the selected Access object to the desktop or folder. You also can drag and drop tables and queries from the database window to Microsoft Excel, Microsoft Word, and other program windows (see Chapter 4).

- **To print the object,** choose File ➤ Print, or press Ctrl+P, or click on the Print toolbar button (shown at left). Then click on OK from the Print dialog box to print the entire object.

- **To preview the object** to see how it will look when printed, choose File ➤ Print Preview or click on the Print Preview toolbar button (shown at left). When you're done previewing the object, close it as described earlier under "Closing an Object."

- **To export the object to another Windows program,** or to a different Microsoft Access database, choose File ➤ Save As/Export. Complete the dialog box and click on OK.

- **To import or link data from another program or database,** choose File ➤ Get External Data, and then choose either Import or Link Tables. Complete the dialog box that appears, and then click on the Import or Link button.

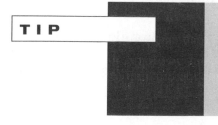

Many of the operations described above also are available when you right-click on an object or right-click on any gray area on the database window. See "Opening Shortcut Menus" later in this chapter for details.

➤ See Chapter 7 for more information about moving and copying objects between databases, or about interacting with other programs. Or search the Access Help index for any of these topics: *Exporting Data…*, *Importing Data…*, and *Linking….*

Using the Toolbars

Toolbars offer timesaving shortcuts to commonly used commands. To use the toolbars:

1. Move the mouse pointer to the toolbar button you want to choose.

2. If necessary, look at the status bar for a description of the current button. Or wait a moment, and a brief description (called a "ToolTip") will appear near the mouse pointer, as shown below.

3. Do one of the following, depending on the type of button you're pointing to (see Figure 1.5 for examples):

   - **For a square (normal) button**, click on the button.
   - **For a drop-down button**, you have two choices. Either click on the picture part of the button to take whatever action the picture shows. Or, click on the drop-down arrow next to the picture and then choose an option from the menu or palette that appears.
   - **For a combo box**, click on the drop-down arrow next to the box and then choose an option from the list that appears; or, click on the drop-down arrow and then type your choice into the text box.

N O T E

If you change your mind about choosing a drop-down button or combo box after you've clicked on its drop-down arrow, click on the drop-down arrow again, or click on an empty area outside the toolbar.

T I P

If the drop-down button opened a palette, you can drag the palette anywhere on the screen. After you detach the palette from its button, the palette remains open and available until you click on the Close button on the palette, you click on the arrow next to the drop-down button, or you close the object you're working with.

FIGURE 1.5

Examples of square (normal) buttons, drop-down buttons, and combo boxes on toolbars. The toolbars shown here appear when you design a form or report. To arrange these toolbars into palette form, we used techniques explained in "Positioning the Toolbar," later in this chapter.

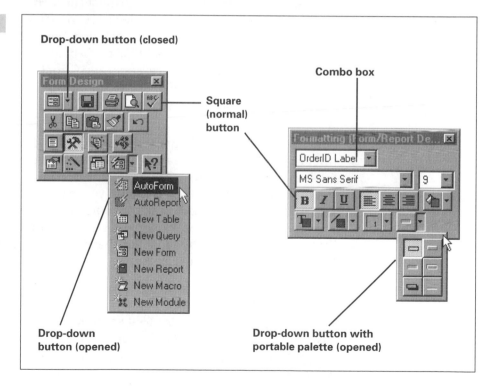

Drop-down button (closed)

Combo box

Square (normal) button

Drop-down button (opened)

Drop-down button with portable palette (opened)

Viewing Toolbars, ToolTips, and the Status Bar

Toolbars, ToolTips, the status bar, and other on-screen features are optional and customizable. If you don't see one of these features in Access, chances are it's just hidden (or turned off).

To display (or hide) the status bar, startup dialog box (see Figure 1.1), and ToolTips:

1. Open any database window. (The Tools ➤ Options and Tools ➤ Startup commands described below are available only when a database is open.)

2. Choose Tools ➤ Options from the Access menu bar, and then click on the View tab.

3. Select (check) an option to display (or turn on) the feature; deselect (clear) the option to hide (or turn off) the feature. For example, select Status Bar, Startup Dialog Box, Color Buttons On Toolbars, and Show ToolTips to display the status bar, startup dialog box, toolbar appearance, and ToolTips described in this chapter.

4. Click on OK.

You also can customize many startup features for the current database (including whether the database window, status bar, and built-in toolbars appear). To do so, choose Tools ➤ Startup. You'll see the Startup dialog box, shown in Figure 1.6. As usual, you can select (check) options you want to turn on, and deselect (clear) options you want to turn off. You also can type text into the text boxes and choose options from the drop-down lists. When you're finished making changes, click on OK. See Chapter 15 for more about personalizing Access.

NOTE Pressing the Shift key when you open the database will bypass any Startup options that you've changed, giving you the default options shown in Figure 1.6.

FIGURE 1.6

This sample Startup dialog box shows default options that work well for most people. Choose Tools ➤ Startup to get here. (The form name *Switchboard* will appear in the Display Form text box if you used the Database Wizard to create a database.)

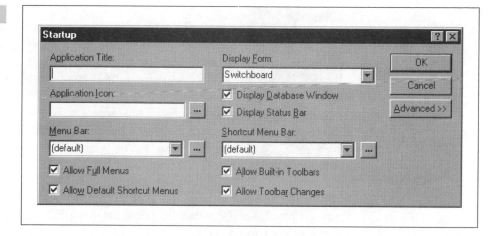

Positioning the Toolbar

By default, the toolbar is *docked* just below the menu bar (see Figure 1.4). You can convert it to a free-floating toolbar, or dock it to some other edge of the screen, by following these steps:

1. Move the mouse pointer to some blank area between buttons (or below or above a button) on the toolbar.

2. Drag the toolbar toward the center of the screen or double-click to make it free-floating (see the example below); or, drag the toolbar to some other edge of the screen to dock it there. To restore a floating toolbar to its previous docked position, double-click on the toolbar's title bar or any empty spot on the toolbar.

N O T E

The Database toolbar (shown above) can be docked at any edge of the screen. However, toolbars that contain a combo box or other buttons that are wider than the standard square buttons can be docked at the top or bottom edge only. The Formatting (Form/Report Design) toolbar, shown in Figure 1.5, is one toolbar that you can dock at the top or bottom edge of the screen, but not at the left or right edge.

When the toolbar is floating freely, you can drag it by its title bar (or by any empty space between buttons) to any place on the screen. Here are some other toolbar tips:

- **To close (hide) the floating toolbar**, click on the Close button on the toolbar's upper-right corner. Or, right-click on any toolbar and click on the toolbar's name in the shortcut menu that appears (shortcut menus are discussed in the next section).

- **To redisplay a hidden toolbar**, choose View ➤ Toolbars, click on the check box next to the toolbar you wish to view, and then click on the Close button in the Toolbars dialog box.

- **To redisplay a default toolbar for the current view,** right-click on any visible toolbar and then click on the toolbar's name in the shortcut menu that appears.

If the redisplay procedures above don't work, choose Tools ➤ Startup, select (check) Allow Built-In Toolbars, and then click on OK. Close and then open the database again. If necessary, choose View ➤ Toolbars to redisplay the toolbar.

N O T E

If you manually show a built-in toolbar, it will appear in every view. If you hide a built-in toolbar from within its default view, it will be hidden in every view (including its default view).

➤ There are many other ways to use and customize the toolbars, as we'll discuss in Chapter 23. But for now, just knowing how to hide, display, and position the toolbar is enough. If you do need a quick reminder or more information on toolbars, search the Help index for *Toolbars*.

Opening Shortcut Menus

Access provides many *shortcut menus* to save you the trouble of looking for options on the menu bars and toolbars. Shortcut menus in the Open and Save dialog boxes also offer handy ways to manage your files and folders without leaving Access.

To open a shortcut menu that's tailored to whatever you want to work with, right-click on the object or place you're interested in; or, click on the object and then press Shift+F10. For example, right-clicking on a table name in the database window opens this menu:

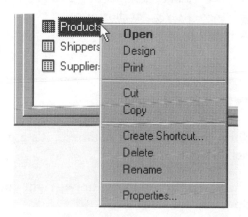

NOTE

If the shortcut menus don't appear when you right-click, choose Tools ➤ Startup, select (check) Allow Default Shortcut Menus, and choose OK. Then close and open the database again.

To select an option from the menu, do one of the following:

- Press ↵ if you want to choose the **boldfaced** option on the menu.
- Click on the option with either the left (primary) or right (secondary) mouse button.
- Type the option's first letter or highlight the option with your mouse, and then press ↵.

To close the menu without selecting an option, press Esc or Alt or Shift+F10, or click outside the menu.

T I P

The term *right-click* means to point at something with your mouse, and then click the *right* (secondary) mouse button. This right-click trick is available throughout Access (and, indeed, throughout Windows). As you work with Windows and Access, be sure to experiment with right-clicking, because you're sure to discover some truly great shortcuts.

Closing a Database

When you're done working with a database, it's a good idea to close it. Any of these methods will work:

- Click on the Close button in the upper-right corner of the database window.
- Go to the database window, and then choose File ➤ Close from the Access menu bar.
- Press Ctrl+W or Ctrl+F4.

As usual, you'll be prompted to save any unsaved work.

NOTE You can have only one database open at a time. Access will automatically close the currently open database if you choose File ➤ Open Database or File ➤ New Database before closing the current database.

Getting Help

One thing we hope to teach you in this book is how to get answers to questions—even if *we* haven't provided those answers. You can achieve this goal easily if you learn how to use Access's plentiful built-in Help. We'll show you how to use this self-help tool next.

Summary of Self-Help Techniques

Table 1.2 summarizes many ways to get and use online Help in Access. Remember that you can use all the standard Windows techniques while you're in the Help system to annotate Help, print a topic, change fonts, and so forth. For more information on those topics, see your Windows documentation or the Windows online Help. Or, experiment by right-clicking in any Help text window and choosing options from the shortcut menu.

TABLE 1.2: Microsoft Access Online Help Options and Techniques

TYPE OF HELP	HOW TO GET IT
View Help Topics	Choose Help ➤ Microsoft Access Help Topics.
Table of Contents	Click on the Contents tab in the Help Topics dialog box.
Search Help	Click on the Index, Find, or Answer Wizard tab in the Help Topics dialog box.
Display a Minimized Help Window	Click on the *? Microsoft Access...* button on the Windows 95 taskbar.

TABLE 1.2: Microsoft Access Online Help Options and Techniques (continued)

TYPE OF HELP	HOW TO GET IT
Answer Wizard	Choose <u>H</u>elp ➤ Answer <u>W</u>izard, or click on the Answer Wizard tab in the Help Topics dialog box. (Often, you also can press F1 to view the Answer Wizard.)
What Is...?	Press Shift+F1 (or click on the ? button on the toolbar or at the upper-right corner of a dialog box), and then click on the command or place you want help with.
Version Number, System Information, Technical Support	Choose <u>H</u>elp ➤ <u>A</u>bout Microsoft Access.
Exit Help	Click on the Close button at the upper-right corner of a Help screen, or press Esc.

Using the Help System and This Book

This book is designed to complement the Help system, not to replace it. Because the online documentation does such a good job of showing you the steps for practically any procedure you can perform in Access, and because many of those procedures won't interest everyone, we've taken a more conceptual approach here—one that should help you work more creatively. That is, instead of presenting hundreds of little step-by-step instructions (as the Help system does), this book deals with larger, more general concepts, so that you can see how (as well as when, why, and sometimes whether) to apply the nitty-gritty details you'll find in the Help system.

From time to time, this book shows an information symbol like the one at left (in fact, you've already seen a few in this chapter). This symbol is a reminder that, once you've learned the underlying concepts and the basic techniques involved in a topic, you can find further details under the Help topics identified next to the symbol.

Looking Up Information

Like a book, the Access Help system has a Table of Contents, which is a great way to learn how to do things. To get to the Help contents:

- Choose <u>H</u>elp ➤ Microsoft Access <u>H</u>elp Topics from the Access menu bar, and then click on the Contents tab in the Help Topics dialog box.

- Or, if you're already in a Help window, click on the Help <u>T</u>opics button near the top of the window to return to the Contents, Index, Find, or Answer Wizard tab you selected most recently.

The Contents lists many options to explore. Figure 1.7 shows the Contents tab with the Getting Help "book" opened. To open or close a *book*, double-click on the book's icon. To open a *topic* (preceded by a question mark icon, like this **?**), double-click on that topic. In Figure 1.8, you see the Help window that opened after we double-clicked on the *Getting Help* book and then double-clicked on the *Open The Northwind, Orders, Or Solutions Sample Databases* topic.

TIP

For a visual introduction to Access, go to the Contents tab, double-click on the *Visual Introduction To Microsoft Access* book, double-click on the Visual Introduction to Microsoft Access topic, and then click on the button next to the topic you're interested in. A large, graphical dialog box will appear. You can click on the <u>N</u>ext and <u>B</u>ack buttons at the lower-right corner of the dialog box to proceed from page to page, or click on the <u>C</u>lose button to exit Help. Many pages in the visual topics also have "hot spots" that you can click on for more information.

Here are some tips for using a Help window (see Figure 1.8):

- **To view Help text that's hidden at the moment,** use the vertical and horizontal scroll bars as needed, or resize the Help window.

FIGURE 1.7

The Contents offers electronic "books" filled with help on many topics. Double-click on books to open or close them. Double-click on topics to open them.

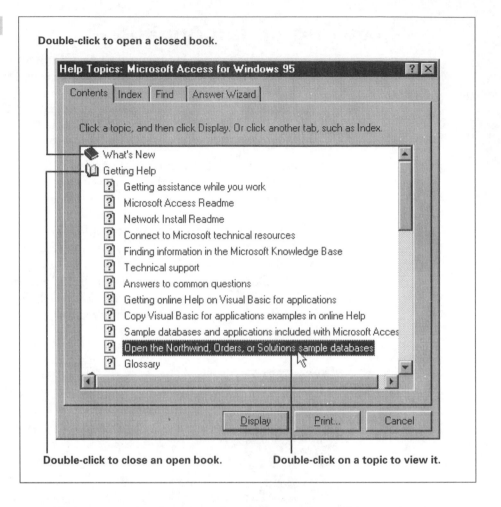

Double-click to open a closed book.

Double-click to close an open book.

Double-click on a topic to view it.

- **To jump to a related topic**, click on the small button next to that topic in the help text. The mouse pointer changes to a pointing hand when you point to a jump button.

- **To see the definition of a term or a button**, click on any text that's underlined with dots (usually in green) or click on a picture of a button. (Click anywhere inside or outside the definition or press Esc to hide the definition again.)

- **To print the current Help window**, click on the Help window's Option button or right-click anywhere in the Help window text, and then choose Print Topic.

FIGURE 1.8

A Help window that explains how to open the sample databases that come with Access

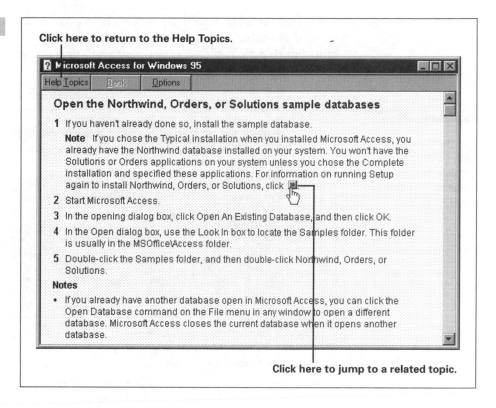

Click here to return to the Help Topics.

Click here to jump to a related topic.

- **To return to the previous Help window**, click on the Help window's Back button.

- **To return to the Help Topics** (see Figure 1.7) from any Help window, click on the Help window's Help Topics button.

- **To make the Help window reappear** if it's minimized or hidden, click on the Microsoft Access For Windows 95 Help button on the Windows taskbar (the button name is preceded by a small ? icon).

- **To close the Access Help window,** make sure it's the active window and then press Esc or click on its Close button.

Help with Whatever You're Doing

Even when you're not in a Help window, you should look at the status bar, preview areas, and any colored text on the screen for hints on what to do next. For example, you'll often see a hint box on the object and a description of available shortcut keys in the status bar, as shown in Figure 1.9 (though that example won't appear until you design a table, as discussed in Chapter 6).

FIGURE 1.9

Hint boxes and the status bar often provide further information about what to do next.

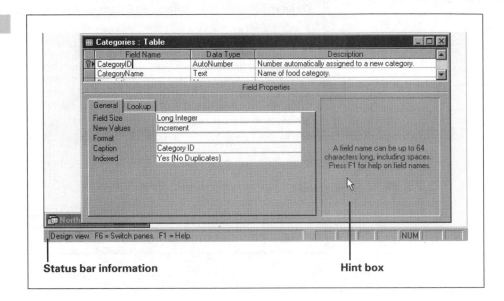

Searching Help

Like any good book, the Help system also has its own index. You can search the index for help with just about any topic. Here's how:

1. Go to the Help Topics window as explained earlier in this chapter, and then click on the Index tab (or the Find tab). Figure 1.10 shows the Index tab's contents after we typed **closing** in the text box.

2. As instructed on the screen, type a word, or select one from the list of topics. Search is not case-sensitive. This step highlights the closest match to your entry in the list(s) below the text box.

3. Click on Display (or double-click on a topic).

Once a Help window opens, you can use any of the techniques described earlier to work with that window (see "Looking Up Information").

FIGURE 1.10

The Index tab after we typed *closing* in the text box

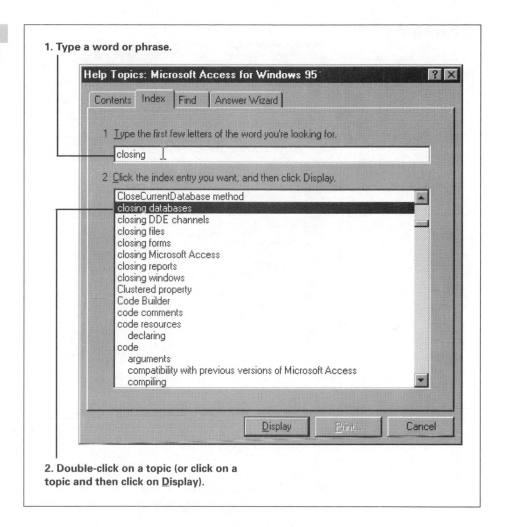

1. Type a word or phrase.

2. Double-click on a topic (or click on a topic and then click on Display).

Asking the Answer Wizard

The Answer Wizard makes it easy to search for information by typing a question. The more specific your question is, the more specific the suggested topics will be. But you don't have to worry about matching a topic name exactly, because the Answer Wizard is pretty forgiving and even quite smart (it *is* a Wizard, after all!).

To use the Answer Wizard, choose <u>H</u>elp ➤ Answer <u>W</u>izard from the Access menu bar, or click on the Answer Wizard tab any time the Help Topics dialog box is open (see Figure 1.11). Type your question, and then press ↵

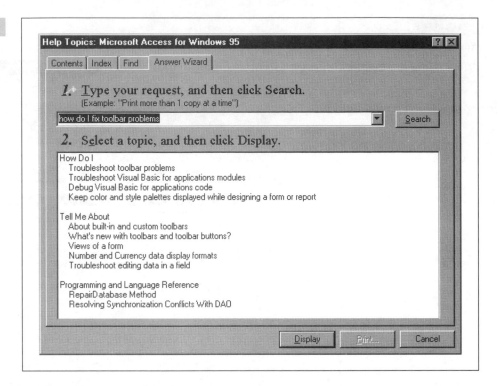

or click on the <u>S</u>earch button. When the list of related topics appears, double-click on the topic you're interested in or click on a topic, and then click on the <u>D</u>isplay button.

In Figure 1.11, we typed **how do I fix toolbar problems** and pressed ↵. The Answer Wizard ignores extraneous words, such as "how do I fix" and focuses on the important keywords, such as "toolbar" and "problems." It then displays a list of topics that seem to answer your question.

Asking "What *Is* That Thing?"

Another way to get quick information is to use "What's That?" Help. This type of help explains what a menu command, button, or dialog box option is for:

1. Press Shift+F1 or click on the Help toolbar button (shown at left). If you're in a dialog box, click on the ? button in the upper-right corner of the dialog box. The mouse pointer changes to a combination arrow and question mark.

2. Click on a button on the toolbar, or select commands from the menus, or click on a place in the dialog box to get help with that particular item.

If you change your mind about using "What's That" Help before choosing a topic, press Esc or Shift+F1, or click on the Help or ? button again to return to the normal mouse pointer.

Here are some other ways to get "What's This?" help:

- In a dialog box, right-click on the option name or button you're curious about and choose What's This?

- In a dialog box, click on or tab to the place you want help with, and then press Shift+F1 or F1.

- In the menus, highlight the option you want help with, and then press Shift+F1 or F1.

Version Number, System Information, Technical Support

Do you need to check the version of Access you're using, to see how much memory and disk space are available, or to find out how to get technical support? It's easy:

1. Choose Help ➤ About Microsoft Access to open the About Microsoft dialog box.

2. Click on the System Info button (for information about your system resources) or click on Tech Support (for details about getting help from humans).

3. Click on the Close and OK buttons (or press Esc) as needed to return to Access.

Getting Out of Help

There are many ways to get out of Help, but the easiest is simply to make sure the Help window is active (click on the window or its taskbar button if you need to), and then press Esc as needed.

N O T E

In addition to the online Help described in this chapter, Microsoft offers many other sources of help for Microsoft Access, Microsoft Office, and other Microsoft products. See Chapter 4 for information about these additional resources.

The Solutions Database

Budding Access developers and power users will be happy to know that Access comes with a sample database named Solutions. This database contains a collection of forms, reports, and interface elements that developers often use to create applications, along with step-by-step instructions for reproducing the examples. You might want to try this database as you read Parts Four and Five of the book, or any time you want to stretch your knowledge about the fine points of Access.

You'll find the Solutions database in the same folder as the Northwind database described earlier. To open it, choose File ➤ Open Database from the Microsoft Access menu bar, type **\msoffice\access\samples\solutions** in the File Name text box, and press ↵. Read the Solutions Intro form (if it appears), and click on OK. Then, select a category of examples, and double-click on the example you're interested in. If the Automatically Display The Show Me Topic For The Selected Example box is checked on the main solutions form, a Show Me window will open with details about how the example was created. To display the Show Me window anytime, click on the Show Me button on the toolbar. Using this database and learning from it are pretty self-explanatory once you've developed some basic Access skills. Feel free to experiment. When you're finished using Solutions, click on the Exit button on the main Solutions form.

Exiting Microsoft Access

When you're done using Access, you should return to Windows before shutting down and turning off your computer. You can exit Microsoft

Access using any technique you'd use with other Windows programs:

1. Go to the database window or to the main Microsoft Access window.

2. Choose File ➤ Exit, or click on the Close button in the upper-right corner of the Microsoft Access window, or press Alt+F4.

TIP To exit Access when Access is minimized, right-click on the Microsoft Access button on the Windows taskbar, and then choose Close.

You'll be returned to Windows or to another open program window. If you want to shut down and turn off your computer now, exit any open programs normally, and choose Start ➤ Shut Down from the Windows taskbar. Next, choose Shut Down The Computer? ➤ Yes and wait until Windows tells you it's safe to turn off the computer. *Then* turn off the computer.

Where to Go from Here

Where you go from here depends on your past database experience:

- **If you're new to Access and to databases**, continue with Chapters 2 and 3.

- **If you're new to Access but know something about databases**, try the hands-on guided tour in Chapter 3.

- **If you're familiar with Access**, flip to the "What's New in the Access Zoo" section at the end of most chapters in this book, including this chapter. For another view of what's new, go the Help Topics dialog box (Help ➤ Microsoft Access Help Topics), click on the Contents tab, double-click on the *What's New* book, and then double-click on a "what's new" topic.

What's New in the Access Zoo?

Many features discussed in this chapter are new to Access for Windows 95. These include:

- The techniques for starting Access follow Windows 95 standards.

- The Open dialog box, which lets you open an existing database, is new and improved.

- The tabs and buttons on the database window are in different places.

- You can drag and drop objects from the database window to your Windows desktop or to a folder in Windows Explorer, My Computer, or Network Neighborhood. You also can drag and drop tables and queries from the database window to Microsoft Excel, Microsoft Word, and other programs (see Chapter 4).

- The database window includes new toolbar buttons and View menu options that let you display database objects as large icons, small icons, a list of icons, and a detailed list (see Table 1.1).

- Toolbars offer drop-down buttons and portable palette buttons in addition to the normal square buttons and combo boxes.

- The online Help is new (and Cue Cards no longer appear). New features include "What's This?" help, an Index, a Find word list, and the Answer Wizard (see Table 1.2).

- Access programming is done with the Visual Basic for Applications programming language, rather than Access Basic.

CHAPTER

2

Understanding Databases

MOST people are accustomed to working with *information*, which is *data* that's organized into some meaningful form. You probably can recognize the information shown in Figure 2.1 as an invoice. You can find the customer's name and address, the products that person ordered, and just about any other information you might want, simply by looking at the invoice. The invoice as a whole presents business information—namely, what happened in a transaction—by meaningfully drawing together various related items of data.

Now suppose you want to store all your invoices on the computer. At first, it might seem simplest to buy a scanner (a device that converts text on paper to a file on a disk) and scan each invoice into a computer file. Later, you could display a copy of the invoice on the screen, and print it. To do that, you wouldn't need a database management system at all. All you'd need is a scanner and a simple graphics program.

Why Store Data?

The problem with the scanner approach is that *all* you can do is retrieve, view, and print the invoices. You can't analyze or reformat the data on the invoice at all. For instance, you can't print mailing labels, envelopes, or form letters for all your customers. You can't analyze your orders to view overall sales.

Why not? Because the computer doesn't have the eyes or brains it takes to "look into" the invoice and "pull out" certain types of information. Only *you* can do that, because you *do* have eyes and a brain.

FIGURE 2.1

A sample printed invoice. You probably can find whatever information you need about the transaction on this sheet of paper, because you recognize different types of information (name, address, products, order total) based on their context.

Invoice

E & K Sporting Goods
1337 West 47th Street
Fridley, NC 28228
USA
Phone: (704) 555-1555 Fax: (704) 555-1556

Invoice Date	8/31/95	*Contact Name*	Shirley Ujest	*Customer ID*	4
Order ID	16	*PO Number*	78	*Ship Date*	2/1/95
Order Date	2/1/95	*Terms*	Net 10 days.	*Shipping Method*	Federal Express

Ship To:	*Bill To:*
WorldWide Widgets	WorldWide Widgets
187 Suffolk Ln.	187 Suffolk Ln.
Boise, ID 83720	Boise, ID 83720
USA	USA
(208) 555-8097	(208) 555-8097

Product ID	Product Name	Quantity	Unit Price	Discount	Line Total
8	Billiard balls	2	$127.45	0.00%	$254.90
2	Football	1	$5.65	0.00%	$5.66

Subtotal	$260.56
Freight Charge	$2.00
Sales Tax	$0.00
Order Total	$262.56
Total Payments	$10.00
Total Due	$252.56

You'll never go wrong with our products along!

Flexibility Is the Goal

If you want the flexibility to display, print, and analyze your information in whatever format you wish, you first need to break that information down into small units of *data*. For example, a person's last name is one unit of data. That person's zip code is another. The name of one product the customer purchased is another unit of data, and so forth.

After breaking the information into discrete units of data, you can use a database management system, such as Access, to analyze and present that data in any way you wish. If each person's surname is a discrete unit of data, for example, you can tell Access to "alphabetize your customers by name" or "find the order for Smith."

You can put the individual units of data into any format you wish, such as mailing labels, envelopes, or invoices.

You Use Tables to Store Data

In Access, you must break *all* your information into data that's stored in *tables*. A table is just a collection of data that's organized into rows and columns. You can put *any* information that's available to you into a table.

Let's forget about invoices for a moment, and focus on storing information about customers. Suppose you have a Rolodex or card file with all your customer names and addresses in it, as shown below. For each customer, you maintain the same pieces of information—name, address, and so on.

Mr. Andy A. Adams
123 A St.
San Diego, CA 91234
    (619) 556-9320

How can you break the information on this Rolodex down into raw data that's neatly organized as a table? Easy. Just make a column for each data element, such as last name or state, and then list the corresponding data elements for each customer in rows, as shown in Figure 2.2.

FIGURE 2.2

Names and addresses, which might once have been on Rolodex cards, organized and typed into an Access table

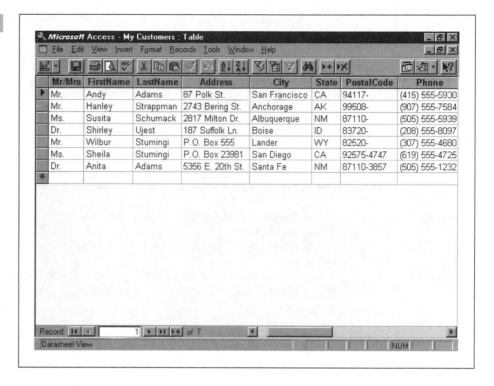

Terminology Time

Now is as good a time as any to get some terminology out of the way, so we can talk about tables and databases more precisely. Here are four terms you'll see often as you work with any database management system:

Table   A table is a collection of data organized into rows and columns.

Field   A single unit (or column) of information in a table. The sample table in Figure 2.2 consists of fields named Mr/Mrs, FirstName, LastName, Address, City, State, PostalCode, and Phone, as you can see by looking across the top of the table.

Record   The set of all data fields for one row of the table. The sample table in Figure 2.2 contains seven filled records: one for a customer named Andy Adams, another for Anita Adams, and so forth.

Database   Contrary to what some people think, a database is not a table. A database is a collection of *all* the tables and other objects (such as forms and reports) that you use to manage data.

We'll tell you more about why a database might contain several tables later in this chapter.

The More Fields, the Better

Looking back at Figure 2.2, you may be wondering *why* we bothered to break the information into so many different fields. Isn't using the three fields Mr/Mrs, LastName, and FirstName, a little excessive?

Not really, because organizing the data into separate fields *now* will make it easier to arrange the data in a meaningful form *later*. Here are ways to arrange the data in the first record of the table shown in Figure 2.2:

Mr. Andy Adams

Mr. Adams

Adams, Andy

Dear Andy:

Andy Adams

Yo Andy!

As you'll see in later chapters, you can rearrange the table columns in any order you wish, and you can use forms and reports to organize table data into any format.

Why Use Multiple Tables?

Earlier we said that a database can contain many tables. So now you may be wondering *why* you'd want to put more than one table into a database.

The simple reason is that it's easier to manage data if all the information about a particular "subject" is in its own table. For example, if you're designing a database to track membership in an organization, you might create separate tables such as these:

All Members	Membership Types and Dues
Committees	Committee Members
Payments Made	Payment Methods
Your Company or Organization	

If you're using Access to manage orders for your company's products, you might use these tables instead:

Customers	Employees
Order Details	Orders
Payment Methods	Payments
Products	Shipping Methods

Remember that these tables are suggestions only. Access really doesn't care *what* type of data you put into tables. All that matters is that you find a way to break the information you need to manage into the tabular fields-and-records format.

TIP

The Database Wizard and Table Wizard can create many types of tables for you automatically. These Wizards break your database into tables, and divide your tables into separate fields with only a small amount of guidance from you. The process is so fast and painless that you'll be creating complete databases in no time. You'll learn more about these Wizards in Chapters 3, 5, and 6.

When to Use One Table

Until you get the hang of it, it's not always easy to decide whether data should go into one table or several tables. But this general rule of thumb always applies:

- If there is a one-to-one correspondence between two fields, put those fields into the same table.

For example, it makes sense to put all the My Customers information in one table, because there's an exact one-to-one dependency between fields. That is, for every one customer, there's one customer name, one address, one city, and so forth.

When Not to Use One Table

Just because you put all your customer information into a single table doesn't mean you should put all the information for an entire business in one table. After all, you wouldn't put all the information for your customers, orders, products, and so forth on one Rolodex card. Likewise, you wouldn't put all that information into a single table.

It makes more sense to put customer data in one table, product data in another, and order data in yet another, because there is no one-to-one correspondence between information about customers, products, and orders. After all, any *one* customer might place *many* orders. And any *order* might be for many *products*. So here we have some natural *one-to-many* relationships between the "subjects" of your tables.

The One-to-Many Relationship

The one-to-many relationship describes a situation in which for every *one* item of data in one table, there may be *many* items of related information in another table. For example, each *one* of your customers might place *many* orders (at least, you hope so!). Therefore, it makes sense to put all your customer data in one table, and data about the orders they place in another table, as shown in Figure 2.3. (In the figure, only the first few fields from each table are shown. Additional information about customers and orders is scrolled off the screen.)

FIGURE 2.3

A one-to-many relationship between orders and customers (any *one* customer might place *many* orders). The CustomerID field in the My Orders table identifies which customer placed each order.

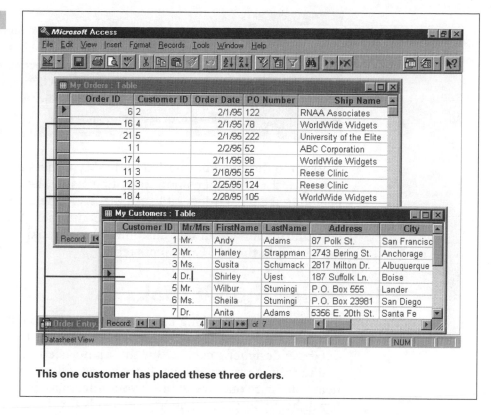

This one customer has placed these three orders.

If we do that, however, we also need a way to determine exactly *which* customer goes with each order. And that's where the *primary key field* comes in.

The Primary Key Field

The primary key field in a table uniquely identifies each record in that table. In the My Customers table shown in Figure 2.3, there is one customer with the ID 4. That table might include other people named Shirley Ujest from other cities. But only one customer has the ID 4. When we added the CustomerID field to the My Customers table, we made it the primary key, so Access would make sure that no two people were given the same CustomerID number.

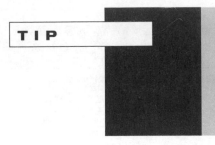

TIP

Your social security number is an example of a primary key field, because it uniquely identifies you on the government's databases. Even though other people in the country may have the same first, last, and even middle name as you, *nobody* else in the country has the same social security number.

Notice too that the information in the My Orders tables is compact. For example, the customer's honorific, first name, and last name aren't repeated in the My Orders table. All the My Orders table needs to get that information is the customer's unique ID number. Access can then dig up any information about that customer just by looking up the corresponding record in the My Customers table.

It's Easier Than It Looks

This business of breaking information down into data in separate tables confuses many beginners, and it has been known to end many a budding database designer's career. But there's no need to throw in the towel if you're feeling uneasy. As you'll see in the following chapters, Access will help you figure out how to break your information into related tables, and it will help you define primary key fields for the tables. So all you really need to understand now is that:

1. Your database is likely to contain several tables.

2. Your tables will use a primary key field to uniquely identify each record in the table.

Where to Go from Here

Remember that the whole reason for breaking information into raw data is to give *you* the flexibility to analyze and display data any way you wish. Once your data is organized into a database on disk, there's no limit to the type of *information* you can glean from that data (Chapters 10 through 14 will explain more about this).

Where should you go next in this book? Here are some suggestions:

- To learn the basics of Access in a hurry, try the hands-on practice in Chapter 3. In just minutes, you'll create a fully functional database—complete with data, forms, reports, and a push-button menu for managing it all.

- To get an idea about how Access and the other programs in the Microsoft Office suite can work together, check out Chapter 4.

- To find out how to create a database for storing your tables, proceed to Chapter 5. (All tables must be stored in a database.)

- To find out how to create tables for data that's all on paper, and not on any computer, see Chapter 6.

- To learn how to manage data that's already on the computer in some database format (such as Access, dBASE, Paradox, SQL, text, and so forth), jump to Chapter 7. You may be able to use that data without creating your own tables from scratch.

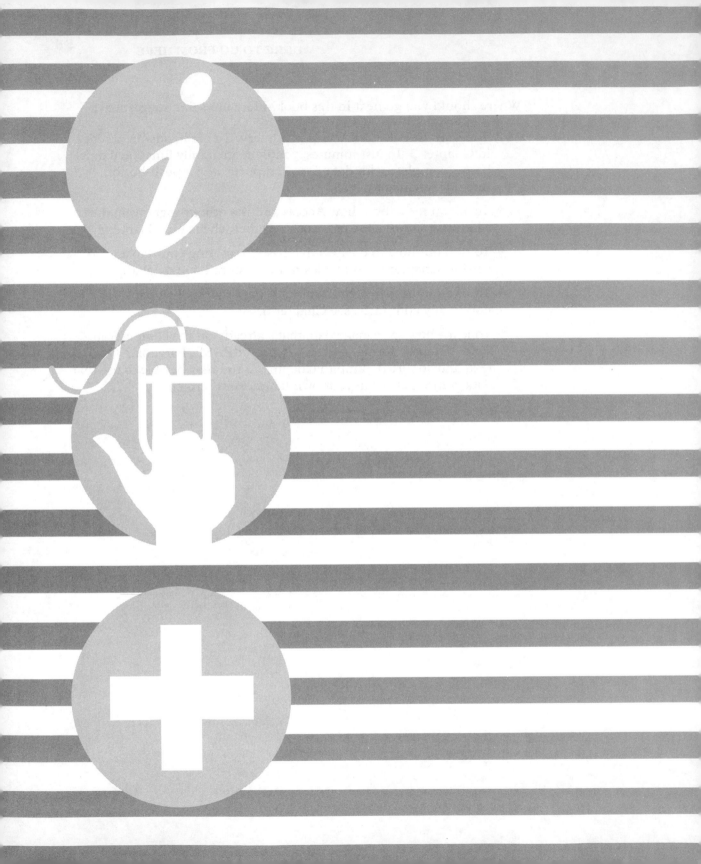

CHAPTER

3

Access in an Evening

THIS chapter offers a hands-on guided tour of Access databases in seven quick lessons. These lessons probably won't make you an Access guru, but they'll give you both the big picture of what Access is all about and direct experience with its most important features.

During these lessons, you'll use Wizards to create an application for managing information about your contacts—complete with data, forms, reports, and a pushbutton Switchboard form that makes the database a cinch to use. You'll also learn how to enter data, sort it in alphabetical order, find specific information, customize forms and reports, isolate specific information by using queries, and tweak the descriptions that appear on the Switchboard form.

TIP

Access offers many automated Wizards to help you set up new databases, tables, forms, reports, and queries in a flash. We strongly encourage you to use Wizards, rather than from-scratch methods to create most new objects, especially if you're new to Access or to database management. Once an object exists, you can tweak it as necessary. This "create it with a Wizard and then refine it" approach is sure to save you time, and it will help you learn Access more quickly.

Before You Start These Lessons

Before you start these lessons, you already should have your basic Windows skills down pat—using a mouse, sizing, moving, opening, and closing windows, using dialog boxes, and so on. Also, you should browse through Chapters 1 and 2 to get an idea of what you'll be doing here.

For best results, give yourself 15 to 30 *uninterrupted* minutes to finish each lesson. If you need to pause after a lesson, see "Taking a Break" at the end of Lesson 1. To resume with the next lesson, see "Returning from a Break."

Lesson 1: Creating a Database and Tables Automatically

The first step to using Access is to start the program and go to the Microsoft Access startup dialog box or the main Microsoft Access window. If you don't know how to do this, see Chapter 1 for help.

Creating an Instant Database

During these hands-on lessons, you'll create a new database (named Address Book Lessons) that can help you manage information about your contacts. You'll use the Database Wizard to create this database. Here goes:

1. If you're starting from the Microsoft Access startup dialog box, choose Database Wizard and then click on OK. If you're starting from the main Microsoft Access window, choose File ➤ New Database from the menu bar.

2. In the New dialog box, click on the Databases tab, and then double-click on the Address Book icon.

NOTE

In Windows 95, file name extensions for registered file types usually are hidden. If you've chosen *not* to hide those extensions, Access and other Windows 95 programs will show them in various dialog boxes. For example, the icon for the Address Book database will be named *Address Book.mdz* when file name extensions are displayed. For more about showing or hiding file name extensions, see Chapter 5. In this book, we'll assume file name extensions are hidden.

3. In the File <u>N</u>ame text box of the File New Database dialog box, type **Address Book Lessons** and then click on Create or press ↵.

> **N O T E**
>
> Access normally looks for and stores your databases in a folder named \My Documents on the disk drive where Access is installed. To change this default location, open any database and choose <u>T</u>ools ➤ <u>O</u>ptions, click on the General tab, and specify a folder name in the <u>D</u>efault Database Folder text box. To return to the default setting, change the folder name in the <u>D</u>efault Database Folder text box back to . (a period). See Chapter 15 for more details.

You'll see an empty database window titled *Address Book Lessons: Database*. After a brief delay, the first Database Wizard dialog box will appear atop the database window, as shown in Figure 3.1. This dialog box tells you something about the database you're about to create.

FIGURE 3.1

The first Database Wizard dialog box appears on top of the Address Book Lessons: Database window.

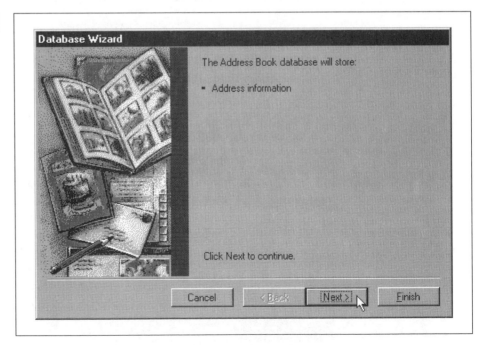

Understanding the Wizards

The Database Wizard will ask you a few questions and then use your answers to build tables, forms, and reports automatically. To use the Wizard:

1. Read the first Database Wizard dialog box, and then click on <u>N</u>ext.

2. The second dialog box, shown in Figure 3.2, asks which fields to include in each table and whether to include sample data

All the Access Wizards work in similar ways, and they have the same buttons at the bottom of each dialog box (see Figure 3.2). Just follow the directions, answer questions, and click on the buttons described below until you finish using the Wizard:

Cancel   Cancels the Wizard and returns to wherever you were before you started the Wizard.

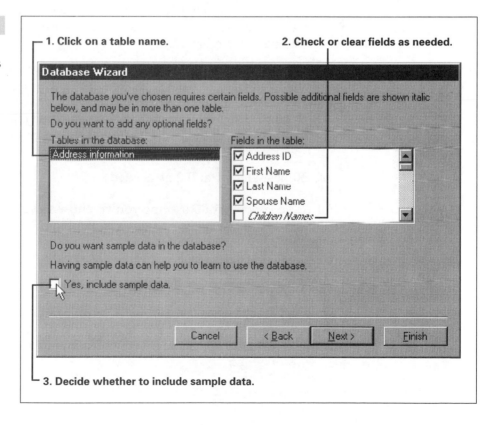

1. Click on a table name.   2. Check or clear fields as needed.

Database Wizard

The database you've chosen requires certain fields. Possible additional fields are shown italic below, and may be in more than one table.

Do you want to add any optional fields?

Tables in the database: Fields in the table:

Address information

- ☑ Address ID
- ☑ First Name
- ☑ Last Name
- ☑ Spouse Name
- ☐ *Children Names*

Do you want sample data in the database?

Having sample data can help you to learn to use the database.

☐ Yes, include sample data.

Cancel   < <u>B</u>ack   <u>N</u>ext >   <u>F</u>inish

3. Decide whether to include sample data.

Back   Returns you to the previous Wizard dialog box.

Next   Continues to the next dialog box.

Finish   Goes straight to the last Wizard dialog box. The Wizard will use default settings for any dialog boxes that it skips. The Finish button is available only when the Wizard has enough information to complete its job.

Choosing Optional Fields for Your Tables

A *field* is a single unit of information stored in a table. *Examples:* a person's name, address, or phone number. When you use the Database Wizard to create a database, all the necessary tables and fields will be defined automatically and you don't have to make any changes. But if you *do* want to include optional fields, or omit fields, here are the steps to follow:

1. In the tables list at the left side of the dialog box shown in Figure 3.2, scroll to and click on the name of the table you want to work with. (In the Address Book database, there's only one table, and it's selected already.)

2. In the fields list at the right side of the dialog box, scroll to the field you want to work with. Then, to include the field, check the box next to its name. To omit the field, clear the check mark from the box. As usual in Windows, clicking on a checked box clears the check mark, and clicking on an empty check box puts a check mark in the box.

3. Repeat steps 1 and 2 as needed.

For these lessons, we'll assume you've chosen the fields that the Wizard suggested initially. That is, *italicized* fields are *not* checked, and non-italicized fields *are* checked.

Including Sample Data

The Database Wizard can add some sample data to your database. Using sample data will help you learn to use the database more quickly, and it will save you time. (You can delete the sample data later.)

We want you to start with some sample data, so please select (check) the box next to Yes, Include Sample Data (see Figure 3.2), and then click on the <u>N</u>ext button to continue to the third Database Wizard dialog box.

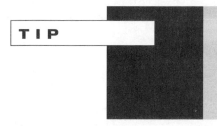

T I P

If you forgot to check the Yes, Include Sample Data box before clicking on the <u>N</u>ext button, it's easy to recover. Just click on the <u>B</u>ack button in the next dialog box that appears, check the Yes, Include Sample Data box, and then click on <u>N</u>ext.

Choosing a Style for Forms

The third Database Wizard dialog box lets you choose a background color and general style for database forms (called *screen displays* in the Database Wizard dialog box). In Figure 3.3, we've selected the Standard style. To choose a style, click on it in the list of styles. The left side of the dialog box will show a sample form that reflects your current choice. Preview any styles you wish, and then choose Standard, the style used throughout this chapter. When you're ready to continue, click on the <u>N</u>ext button.

FIGURE 3.3

The third Database Wizard dialog box with the Standard style selected for forms

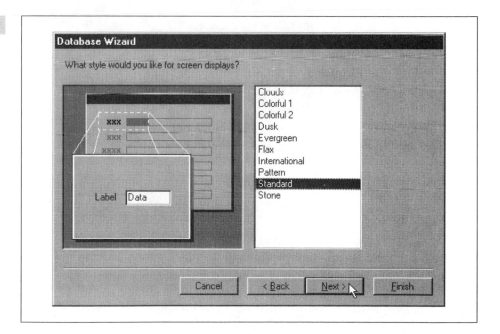

Choosing a Style for Printed Reports

In the fourth Database Wizard dialog box, you'll choose a general style for printed reports (see Figure 3.4). Again, you can click on a style in the list and preview a sample until you find a style you like. Pick a style that appeals to you (or use the Compact style that we chose), and then click on Next.

N O T E

In Chapter 13, you'll learn how to set up your own form and report styles, and add them to the list of predefined styles. You'll also find out how to reformat an existing form or report with a different style.

FIGURE 3.4

The fourth Database Wizard dialog box with the Compact report style selected

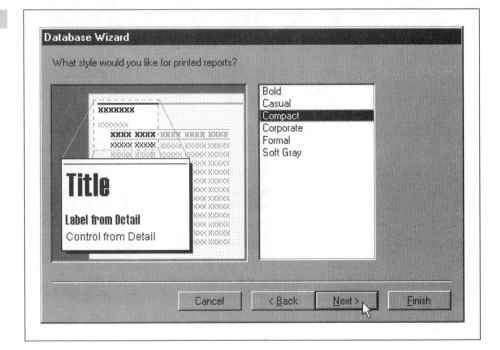

Choosing a Database Title and Adding a Picture

In the fifth Wizard dialog box (see Figure 3.5), you can choose a different title for your database. This title will appear on the Main Switchboard form (which you'll see soon), and on all reports. For now, Address Book is fine, so leave the title unchanged.

You also can include a picture on all reports. Just for grins, add a picture by following these steps:

1. Click on Yes, Include A Picture to check that option, and then click on the Picture button.

2. When the Insert Picture dialog box appears (see Figure 3.6), use the techniques discussed in Chapter 1 to locate the folder named

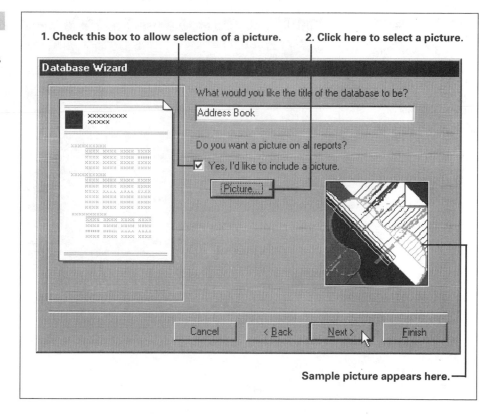

The fifth Database Wizard dialog box lets you choose a title and a picture to use for your database. In this example, we've used the suggested title, and chosen the Music picture from the \MSOffice\Clipart folder.

\MSOffice\Clipart. Assuming you did a standard installation, you can just type **\msoffice\clipart** in the File Name text box and press ↵.

3. Make sure the Preview button is selected (pushed in) on the dialog box toolbar, and then click on a file name in the left side of the dialog box. Each time you click on a file name, a preview of the picture it contains will appear in the preview area. The example in Figure 3.6 shows the Music file name and preview selected.

4. When you're satisfied with the picture you've selected, click on OK. The sample picture will appear in the Database Wizard text box, next to the Picture button.

5. Click on Next to continue to the next dialog box.

FIGURE 3.6

After clicking on the Picture button in the dialog box shown in Figure 3.5, you can search for and preview pictures that will appear on your reports. The list of graphics will depend on which software you've installed and which folder you've chosen to search.

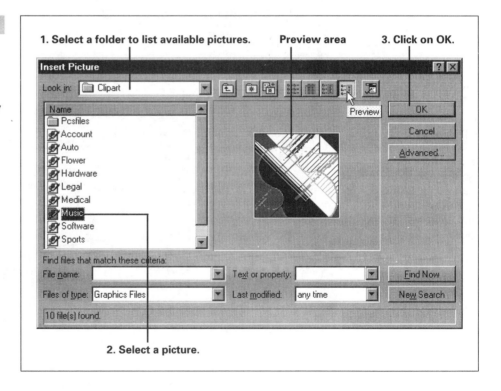

Finishing Up

That's all the information the Wizard needs. In the last dialog box, you have two options:

Yes, Start The Database   Leave this option checked if you want to go to a Switchboard form that lets you start working with your database immediately. Clear this option if you want to go directly to the database window, bypassing the Switchboard. For now, leave this option checked.

Display Help On Using A Database   Checking this option will display online help about using a database. Leaving this option unchecked won't display any extra help. Leave this option unchecked for now.

To create the database with all the choices you made, click on the Finish button now. (If you need to revisit any of the previous Database Wizard dialog boxes, click on the Back button as needed.)

Wait patiently for a few moments while the Database Wizard conjures up an entire database of tables, forms, reports, and other objects. (On-screen bars will keep you informed of the Wizard's progress as it works.) When the Wizard finishes its job, you'll see the Main Switchboard form for your database (see Figure 3.7).

Congratulations! You've created your first Access database. Easy, huh? In the following lessons, you'll learn how to work with and customize your new database.

At Your Leisure

➤ To learn more about databases and tables, see Chapters 5–7 of this book. Or, go to the Access Help Contents, open the *Creating A Database And Working In The Database Window* book, and then peruse the subtopics. Or just skip all that and move on to Lesson 2.

If you want to take a break at the end of this or any other lesson, close your database as discussed next under "Taking a Break." Before you resume a lesson, reopen the Address Book Lessons database, as discussed under "Returning from a Break."

FIGURE 3.7

The Main Switchboard form gives you all the options you need to create and manage Address Book data. Access creates a Main Switchboard form automatically, any time you use the Database Wizard to create a non-blank database.

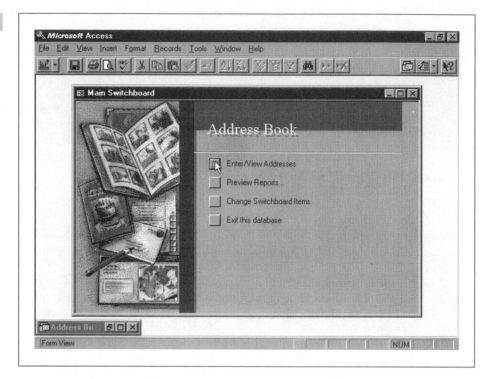

Taking a Break

Anytime you want to take a break at the end of a lesson, do one of these steps to save your work and close the database (*before* you turn off the computer!):

- If you're viewing the Main Switchboard form, shown in Figure 3.7, click on the button next to the last option, Exit This Database.

- If you're viewing the database window (see Chapter 1), choose File ➤ Close from the menu bar, or press Ctrl+W, or click on the Close button on the database window.

Then, if you're done using Access for a while, exit Access by choosing File ➤ Exit from the Access menu bar. If you plan to turn off your computer, exit any other programs that are running, choose Start ➤ Shut Down from the taskbar, and then choose Shut Down The Computer? ➤ Yes in the Shut Down Windows dialog box. When the message tells you it's safe to turn off your computer, go ahead and turn it off (if necessary).

Returning from a Break

To resume with a new lesson after taking a break, use any of the techniques you learned in Chapter 1 to open the Address Book Lessons database and its Main Switchboard form. Here's a summary of the steps:

- If you're at the Microsoft Access startup dialog box and you see *Address Book Lessons* in the list under Open An Existing Database, double-click on that name.

- If you're at the Microsoft Access startup dialog box and Address Book Lessons doesn't appear in the list, make sure More Files... is highlighted, click on OK, and then double-click on *Address Book Lessons* in the list of file names.

- If you're at the Microsoft Access main menu, choose File from the Access menu bar. Then, if *Address Book Lessons* appears near the bottom of the File menu, click on its name. If it doesn't appear, choose Open Database, and then double-click on *Address Book Lessons* in the list of file names.

- If you're at the Windows 95 desktop and you've used the Address Book Lessons database recently, choose Start ➤ Documents ➤ Address Book Lessons.

The Address Book Lessons database will open and the Main Switchboard form will appear (see Figure 3.7).

Some Important Switchboard and Database Window Tips

These tips are worth remembering as you work with the Address Book Lessons database:

- **To open the Address Book Lessons database window without opening the Main Switchboard first,** hold down the Shift key while you open the Address Book Lessons database. You'll be taken directly to the database window.

- **To open the Main Switchboard form from the database window,** click on the Forms tab on the database window, and then double-click on the *Switchboard* form name.

- **To open the database window without closing the Switchboard form first**, press F11, or click on the Database Window toolbar button, or choose <u>W</u>indow ➤ Address Book Lessons : Database from the menu bar.

- **To open the database window when it's minimized on the Access desktop**, click on the database window's Restore button, or double-click on the window's title bar, or press F11.

Lesson 2: Exploring the Address Book Lessons Database

Before you enter any data or print any reports, why not explore the Address Book Lessons database and Switchboard forms a little? Because you asked the Wizard to add sample data, you'll have plenty of places to investigate.

Exploring the Address Book Form

Let's start by exploring the first option on the Main Switchboard (see Figure 3.7):

1. Click on the button next to Enter/View Addresses. You'll see the Addresses form, which lets you review or change information for each contact. Here's what you can do with the buttons at the bottom of this form:

    - **To preview and print a fact sheet** about the contact shown on the form, click on the Pre<u>v</u>iew Fact Sheet button. You'll learn more about previewing and printing in Lesson 4. (For now, click on the Fact Sheet report's Close toolbar button or press Ctrl+W to return to the Addresses form.)

    - **To dial your contact's phone** with your computer's modem, click in the box that contains the phone number you want to dial, and then click on the <u>D</u>ial button. An easy-to-use AutoDialer box appears. (For now, click on Cancel if you've opened that dialog box.)

- **To switch between page 1 and 2 of the Addresses form**, click on the 1 or 2 button, or the PgUp andPgDn key.

2. When you've finished exploring the Addresses form, click on its Close button or press Ctrl+W to return to the Main Switchboard form.

N O T E   In Lesson 4, you'll learn how to add and change data, and use navigation buttons to move from record to record. For now, just take a look at what's available and don't worry too much about changing any data or viewing other records in the table.

Exploring the Address Book Reports

The Main Switchboard's *Preview Reports* option lets you preview and print a variety of reports about your contacts. Here are some steps to try:

1. Click on the button next to Preview Reports. A new Reports Switchboard will appear (see Figure 3.8).

2. If you wish, click on a button to preview one of the reports (the Greeting Card List, for example). Lesson 5 will show you how to work with reports.

3. To return to the Main Switchboard after you're done viewing a report, click on the Close button on the preview window's toolbar, or press Ctrl+W.

4. To return to the Main Switchboard form, click on the button next to Return To Main Switchboard.

Other Buttons on the Address Book Main Switchboard

As Figure 3.7 shows, there are two more options on the Address Book Main Switchboard. Here's what they're for:

Change Switchboard Items   Lets you add, change, and delete prompts on the switchboards and create new switchboards. We'll

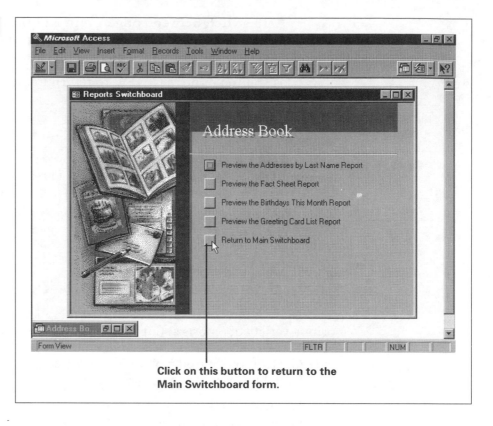

Click on this button to return to the Main Switchboard form.

look briefly at ways to customize the switchboards in Lesson 7. Chapter 21 of this book explains much more.

Exit This Database   Lets you close the Main Switchboard form and the Address Book Lessons database window in one step. You'll be returned to the main Microsoft Access menu.

Lesson 3: Creating and Customizing a Form

An Access form is like a fill-in-the-blanks paper form, except that you fill it in using the keyboard rather than pencil or pen. Our Address Book

Lessons database already has a nice form. But let's go ahead and create a new one for practice:

1. If you've gone exploring, close the Address Book Switchboard form and return to the database window. To do this quickly, click on the Close button in the upper-right corner of any Address Book switchboard form, and then press F11 to restore the database window.

2. In the database window, click on the Tables tab, and then click on the Addresses table name to highlight it.

W A R N I N G The Switchboard Items table contains entries that control the switchboard forms for your database. Do not change items in this table, or your switchboards may stop working correctly. In Lesson 7, you'll learn how to use the Switchboard Manager to maintain this table in a safe manner.

3. Click on the drop-down arrow next to the New Object toolbar button (shown at left, and second-to-last on the toolbar), and then choose New Form from the menu that appears (or choose Insert ➤ Form). In the New Form dialog box, double-click on AutoForm: Columnar. Wait a few moments while Access creates an automatic form.

Access instantly creates the form for entering and editing Address Book data, and names it Addresses (see Figure 3.9). The form contains one *control* for each field in your table.

N O T E A *control* is a graphical object that displays data, performs an action, or makes the form (or report) easier to read. You'll learn more about controls in Chapter 13.

FIGURE 3.9

The automatic form for the Addresses table. To create this form, choose the New Form option from the toolbar's New Object drop-down button and then double-click on AutoForm: Columnar in the New Form dialog box.

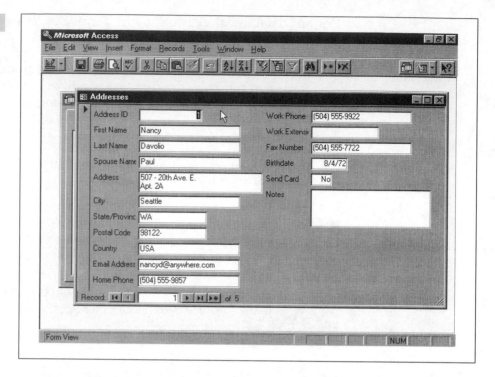

Modifying and Saving the Form Design

The new form is perfectly usable as-is. But chances are, you'll want to tailor the Wizard's instant form to your own personal tastes. We'll show you some basic skills for designing fancier forms. When you finish the steps given below, your form will resemble Figure 3.10.

Whenever you want to change the look or behavior of something in Access, you must switch to *design view.* In design view, you'll see menu commands and toolbar buttons that help you make changes. You also may see a grid, which makes it easier for some people to size and align controls on the form. Let's switch to design view now and move some controls around on the Address Book form:

1. To switch from *form view* to *design view,* click on the Form View toolbar button (shown at left), or choose <u>V</u>iew ➤ Form <u>D</u>esign from the menu bar.

FIGURE 3.10

The Addresses form after changing some field labels, dragging fields to more convenient places on the form, and changing the Address ID field so that the cursor won't land in it during data entry and the field will be dimmed.

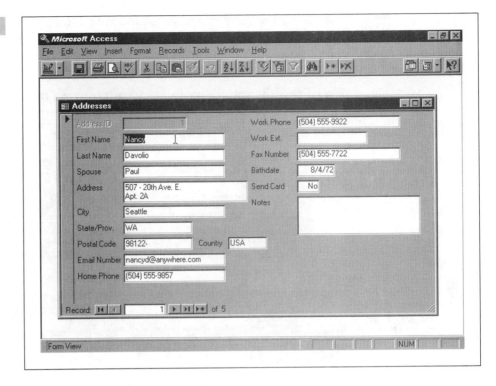

2. To give yourself lots of room to work, maximize the design view window.

3. If the optional tools in design view are covering your form (or are missing), you can hide or show them by choosing options on the View menu. For example, if the Toolbox is in your way, choose View ➤ Toolbox. For this exercise, select (check) the Ruler and Form Header/Footer options on the View menu. Leave the other options unchecked to hide those other tools.

4. Scroll down until you can see the Country control, and then click on the Country control (the empty box just to the right of the Country label). When selected, "move" and "size" handles appear on the control, as shown below.

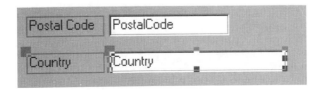

5. Keeping your finger *off* the mouse button, move the mouse pointer to any edge of the control, until the mouse pointer changes to a "move" icon (a hand with all five fingers showing), as shown at left.

6. Press the mouse button (without moving the mouse), and drag the Country control up and to the right, until it's in line with the Postal Code control, as shown below:

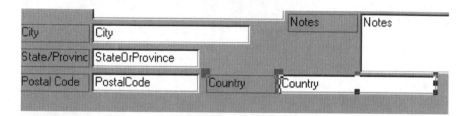

N O T E   These mouse operations may take some practice. If you don't get them right the first time, repeat steps 5 and 6 until you do.

You've now moved the Country control. You can use the same dragging technique to size controls, and to move a label and/or text box independently. Try this technique to move the EmailAddress and HomePhone controls and labels up, to fill in the gap left by the Country field. Always move the mouse pointer to an edge or corner of the control first, until you see the mouse pointer change to the icon that best expresses what you want to do, as summarized below:

     Move all selected controls.

     Move current control only.

     Size diagonally.

Size horizontally.

 Size vertically.

A Few Designer Tips

Here are some quick "designer tips" that might help you further refine the form (you don't need to try them now):

- **To select several controls at once**, hold down the Shift key as you select, or drag a "lasso" around them. (To lasso those critters, start with no control selected and the mouse pointer on the grid or an empty part of the form, not on the control. Then drag a frame around all the controls you want to select.)

- **To select all the controls at once**, choose Edit ➤ Select All, or press Ctrl+A.

- **To deselect one selected control or all selected controls,** click anywhere outside the selection area.

- **To deselect only one of several selected controls,** hold down the Shift key while clicking on the control(s) you want to deselect.

- **To size and align the selected controls**, use the Format ➤ Align and Format ➤ Size commands from the menu bar (see Chapter 13).

- **To make a label fit its text exactly,** select the label, move your mouse pointer to any of the sizing handles, and then double-click on the sizing handle. Or, select the labels you want to resize, and then choose Format ➤ Size ➤ To Fit from the menus.

- **To delete the selected control(s)**, press the Delete key.

- **To undo a change you're not happy with,** choose Edit ➤ Undo, or press Ctrl+Z, or click on the Undo toolbar button.

To change the text in a label (the part that appears to the left of a control):

1. Click on the label text so that selection handles appear around the label.

2. Click inside the selection. An insertion point will appear and the sizing handles will disappear temporarily.

3. Use normal Windows text editing techniques, including these, to change the text:

- **To highlight (select) text,** drag the mouse through that text, or double-click on a word.
- **To position the blinking *insertion point,*** click the mouse or press the ← and → keys.
- **To delete selected text or text at the insertion point,** press Delete or Backspace.
- **To add new text at the insertion point,** simply type it.

4. When you're done making changes, press ↵. The selection handles will reappear around the label.

Try Some Hands-On Designing

Go ahead and try some more hands-on designing now. Don't worry if you don't get *exactly* the results we show—it's OK to make mistakes, and it's OK to experiment.

1. Change the label text for these controls, as follows:

- Change the label for the SpouseName control from Spouse Name to **Spouse**.
- Change the label for the StateOrProvince control from State/Province to **State/Prov**.
- Change the label for the WorkExtension control from Work Extension to **Work Ext**.
- Change the label for the EmailAddress control from Email Address to **Email Number**

2. Resize all the labels on the form so they have a snug fit. The quickest way is to select all the controls (Ctrl+A), and then choose Format ➤ Size ➤ To Fit.

3. Click in an empty area of the form to deselect all the controls.

Next, resize the Country control smaller, so that it doesn't crowd the Notes control. To do this, click on the Country control (the box to the left of the Country label). Move the mouse pointer to the sizing handle at the right edge of that control (the mouse pointer changes to a horizontal two-headed arrow), and then drag to the left until you've sized the control to your liking.

To move the Country control closer to its label, make sure the Country control is selected, and then move the mouse pointer to the sizing handle at the upper-left corner of the Country control (the pointer changes to a hand with one pointing finger). Drag to the left until the Country control is closer to the Country label.

Preventing the Cursor from Landing in a Field

When you enter a new record, Access will assign a value to the AddressID field automatically (you can't change this value). The form will be more convenient to use if you prevent the cursor (also called the *insertion point* or *highlight*, depending on its shape) from landing in that field. To disable the AddressID control:

1. Click on the AddressID control (the box to the right of the AddressID label) to select it.

2. Click on the Properties toolbar button (shown at left), or choose <u>V</u>iew ➤ <u>P</u>roperties. You'll see the *property sheet* on the screen.

3. Click on the Data tab at the top of the property sheet, and then double-click on the Enabled option to change its setting from Yes to No (see Figure 3.11). The AddressID control will be dimmed on the screen.

4. Click on the Close button on the property sheet (or click on the Properties button or choose <u>V</u>iew ➤ <u>P</u>roperties) to hide the property sheet again.

As you'll learn later in this book, *properties* are characteristics of elements in your database, and you can change them anytime. Don't worry too much about properties now.

FIGURE 3.11

The Enabled property for the AddressID control is set to No to prevent the cursor from landing on that control when you use the form for data entry.

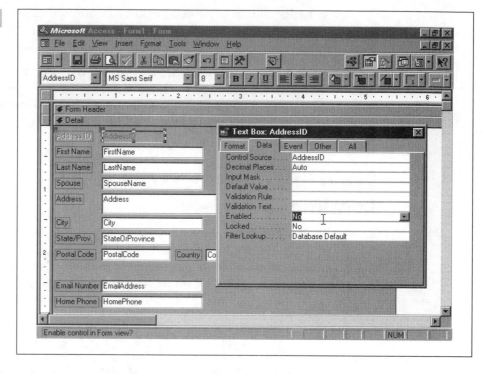

Closing and Saving the Form

None of the design work you've done so far is saved yet, so saving is the next order of business. To save the form and close it:

1. Choose File ➤ Close, or press Ctrl+W.

2. When asked about saving the form, click on Yes.

3. In the Save As dialog box, type **Addresses1** (or just accept the suggested form name) and click on OK.

4. If you wish, click on the Restore button on the database window to restore the window to its previous size.

That's all there is to it! The form name will appear in the database window whenever you're viewing form names (that is, after you've clicked on the Forms object tab on the database window). In the next lesson, you'll open the form and start using it.

At Your Leisure

➤ To reinforce what you've learned, and explore forms in more depth, look at Chapters 11 and 13. Or, go to the Access Help Contents, open the *Working With Forms* book, open the *Basics* book, and then explore any sub-topics that intrigue you. Or, just move on to Lesson 4.

Lesson 4: Adding, Editing, Sorting, and Searching

Your database now contains several *objects*, including a table and two forms. You can use either form to enter some data into the table.

Opening the Form

To open the Addresses1 form:

1. Start from the database window, and click on the Forms tab.

2. Double-click on the Addresses1 form name, or highlight (click on) the name and then click on Open. Your form will appear in *form view* (see Figure 3.10, earlier in this chapter). Notice that the AddressID field is dimmed and the cursor is positioned in the FirstName field. The cursor skips the AddressID field because you changed the Enabled property for that field to No in the previous lesson.

TIP

If you prefer to use the Addresses form that the Database Wizard created for you automatically, either double-click on the Addresses form name on the Forms tab of the database window, or click on the button next to the Enter/View Addresses option on the Main Switchboard form.

Entering Data

If you have a Rolodex or little black book of contacts' names, addresses, and other vital statistics, grab it now. Or, if you don't want to bother with real names and addresses, use the fake one shown in Figure 3.12. Either way, follow these general steps to add some names and addresses to your Addresses table, via the Addresses1 (or Addresses) form:

1. If the table is currently empty, you can skip to step 2 and begin entering data immediately. However, if the table already contains data, you'll need to move to a new, blank record. To do so, click on the New Record button (shown at left) on the toolbar or the navigation bar (see Figure 3.12).

2. Type the person's first name into the First Name field, and then press Tab or ↵, or click anywhere within the Last Name field.

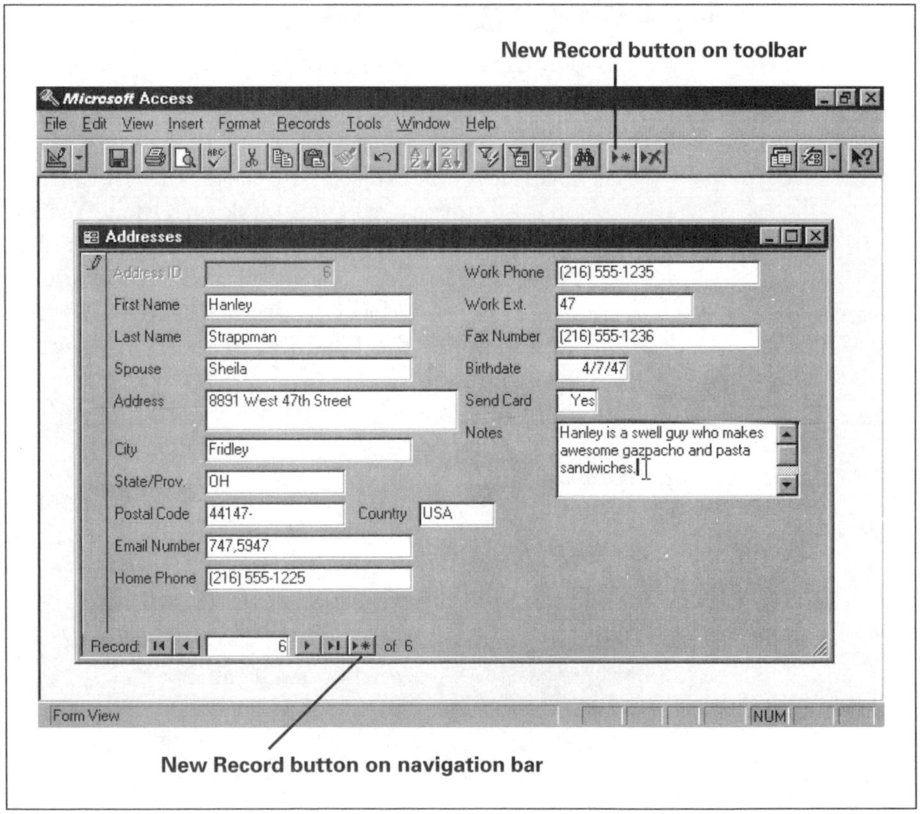

FIGURE 3.12

A new record added to the Addresses table, via the Addresses1 form you created earlier

New Record button on toolbar

New Record button on navigation bar

3. Type that person's surname into the Last Name field, and then press Tab or ↵, or click within the Spouse Name field.

4. Fill in each of the remaining fields, as shown in Figure 3.12. Here are some tips to help you enter the remaining data:

- **To move forward from one field to the next,** press Tab or use the mouse. If the field *doesn't* display a vertical scroll bar and scroll arrows when the cursor lands in it, you also can press ↵ to move to the next field. (The Address and Notes fields include vertical scroll bars and arrows.) If the field *does* display a vertical scroll bar and scroll arrows when the cursor lands in it, pressing ↵ will end the current line of text and move the insertion point to the start of the next line *within* the field.

- **To leave a field empty,** press Tab to skip it, or click on the field you want to type in next.

- **To enter Postal Codes,** type the numbers only. The form automatically displays a hyphen after the first five digits. *Example:* When you type **441471234** in the Postal Code field, Access changes your entry to **44147-1234**.

- **To enter telephone numbers,** type the numbers only. The form automatically displays parentheses around the area code, and a hyphen after the exchange. *Example:* When you type **2165551225** in the Home Phone field, Access changes your entry to **(216)555-1225** as you type.

- **To enter birthdates,** omit slashes between the numbers for the month and day if the numbers have two digits. If the numbers for the month and day have only one digit, type a slash to move to the next part of the date. Access will insert slashes in the field automatically. *Example:* When you type **121595** in the Birthdate field, Access automatically changes your entry to **12/15/95** as you type. To enter the numbers for an April 7, 1947 birthdate, type **4/7/47** or **040747**.

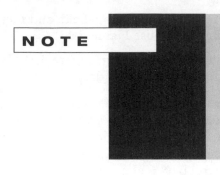

NOTE It doesn't hurt to enter the punctuation in the postal code, telephone number, and date fields, but it does take extra work. Data entry shortcuts, such as automatically inserting parentheses and hyphens in telephone numbers, are controlled by Input Mask properties in the table or form design. See Chapters 6 and 13 for more details.

5. After filling in the last field (Notes), press Tab to move to the next blank record.

6. Repeat steps 2–5 to fill in more names and addresses. For practice, enter at least three. If possible, include some entries that have the same State/Province.

Making Changes and Corrections

If you're an experienced Windows user, you'll probably find that editing text in an Access form (or the datasheet view) is similar to typing and editing text in any other Windows program. But even if you're not experienced, these techniques can help you fix typing mistakes:

- **To delete text at the highlight or insertion point position**, use the Backspace and Delete keys.

- **To move to the next field**, press Tab. To move to the previous field, press Shift+Tab. To move to any field in the form, click on that field.

- **To switch between** *navigation mode* **and** *editing mode*, press F2. You're in navigation mode when you use the keyboard (Tab, Shift+Tab, and ↵) to move to another field; in this mode, the field's contents will be selected, and anything you type will *replace* what's already in the field. When you switch to editing mode, you can *change* (rather than replace) what's already in the field; in this mode, the blinking insertion point replaces the selection highlight. You can press F2 anytime you need to switch from one mode to the other.

- **To move to other records,** use the navigation bar at the bottom of the window (see Figure 3.13). Or press Page Up and Page Down to scroll up and down through existing records.

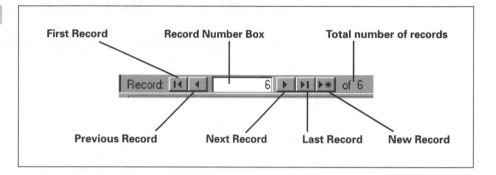

First Record   Record Number Box   Total number of records

Record: |◄ ◄   6   ► ►| ►* of 6

Previous Record   Next Record   Last Record   New Record

> **N O T E**   In the Addresses form created by the Database Wizard, Page Up and Page Down display the first or second page of the Address form, respectively. Pressing Page Down when you're on the second page of the form takes you to the second page of the next record. Pressing Page Up when you're on the first page of the form takes you to the first page of the previous record (if any).

- **To switch to** *datasheet view,* where you can see all the data that you've entered so far, click on the drop-down arrow next to the Form View toolbar button (shown at left, and the first button on the toolbar), and then choose Datasheet View; or, choose View ➤ Datasheet (see Figure 3.14). You can make changes and corrections in datasheet view, if you wish—it's not necessary to switch back to form view.

- **To resize columns in datasheet view,** move the mouse pointer to the vertical line at the right edge of the column header for the column you want to resize, and then drag the line to the left or right. Or, for a snug fit, double-click on the vertical line that's just to the right of the column name.

FIGURE 3.14

The sample table in datasheet view. We resized the columns to fit snugly around the data.

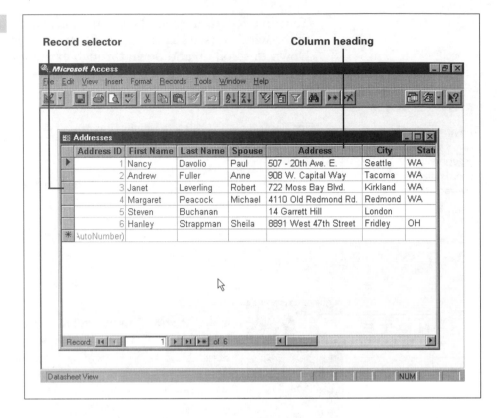

Record selector   Column heading

- **To move an entire column in datasheet view**, move the mouse pointer to the column name in the header, click the mouse, and then drag the column to the left or right.

- **To switch to form view**, click on the drop-down arrow next to the Form View toolbar button, and then choose Form View; or, choose View ➤ Form.

NOTE

If you click on the Form View toolbar button (instead of clicking on the drop-down arrow next to that button), you'll switch to the view that's shown on the button. For example, clicking on the Form View button when you're in form view takes you to form design view. Clicking on the Form View button when you're in form design view takes you to form view.

- **You can't change the contents of the AddressID field**, and there's no reason to. In fact, you can't even move the cursor into that field.

- **To move to a new, blank record**, click on the New Record button on either the toolbar or the navigation bar (see Figures 3.12–3.14).

- **To delete a record**, click on the record selector at the left side of the record and press Delete. Or, click anywhere in the record you want to delete, and then click on the Delete Record toolbar button (shown at left). When prompted, click on <u>Y</u>es if you're sure you want to delete the record, or click on <u>N</u>o to retain the record. **Warning:** Once you click on <u>Y</u>es to delete the record, it's gone for good!

Don't Save Each Record

In case you're paranoid about losing your work (which certainly is understandable!), rest assured that as soon as you finish filling in (or changing) a record and move to another record, Access saves that record to disk. The only record that isn't saved is the one you're editing at the moment. (This unsaved record is marked at the left with a pencil icon.)

Sorting and Filtering

After you've put at a few records into your table, you can unleash Access's real power. Let's begin by sorting (alphabetizing) the records:

1. If you're in form view, switch to datasheet view. To do so, choose <u>V</u>iew ➤ Data<u>s</u>heet from the menu bar.

2. Click on any person's surname to move the cursor into the Last Name column.

3. Click on the Sort Ascending toolbar button (shown at left), or choose <u>R</u>ecords ➤ <u>S</u>ort ➤ <u>A</u>scending. Or, right-click and then choose Sort Ascending from the shortcut menu.

Instantly, your records are sorted (alphabetized) by surnames. You can follow steps 1 through 3 to sort on any field in your table. Try it and see.

Now suppose you only want to see contacts who live in Washington (or whichever state you want to look for). Here's a quick way to filter out those unwanted non-Washington contacts, temporarily.

1. Put the cursor in any State/Province field that contains WA (for example), and be sure not to highlight any text in the field.

2. Click on the Filter By Selection toolbar button (shown at left), or choose <u>R</u>ecords ➤ <u>F</u>ilter ➤ Filter By <u>S</u>election. Or, right-click on the field and choose Filter By Selection from the shortcut menu. (If you prefer to see all records *except* those for your Washington contacts, right-click and choose Filter Excluding Selection instead.)

The non-Washington records will disappear temporarily. To put the records back in their original order and display the hidden records again, choose <u>R</u>ecords ➤ <u>R</u>emove Filter/Sort; or, right-click and choose Remove Filter/Sort from the shortcut menu.

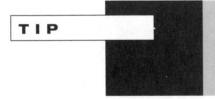

T I P

You can sort and filter records in form view or datasheet view. However, we suggest using datasheet view because it's easier to see the results from there. See Chapter 9 for more about sorting and filtering.

Finding a Record

Suppose you've added hundreds, or even thousands, of names and addresses to your Addresses table. Now you want to look up a particular contact's address or phone number. Here's the easy way to do that:

1. Switch to form view or datasheet view (choose <u>V</u>iew ➤ <u>F</u>orm or <u>V</u>iew ➤ Data<u>s</u>heet).

2. Click in the field you want to search (in this example, click in any Last Name field).

3. Choose <u>E</u>dit ➤ <u>F</u>ind, or press Ctrl+F, or click on the Find toolbar button (shown at left). You'll see the Find In Field dialog box.

4. In the Find What text box, type *exactly* the last name you're look-ing for. (Don't worry about upper/lowercase, but do spell the name correctly.)

5. Click on the Find First button. The Last Name field of the first re-cord that has the requested name will appear highlighted on the screen. (If Access didn't find a match, a message will appear; click on OK to clear the message.)

6. If several people in your table have the same last name, and you want to find each one in turn, click on the Find Next button as needed. When Access tells you it has finished searching, click on OK.

7. When you're done searching, click on the Close button in the Find In Field dialog box.

Remember: Computers Are Dumb!

If your search doesn't find what you were expecting, remember that the computer isn't smart and it can't read your mind. You *must* click on the field you want to search before starting the Find command and typing the text you want to search for. (For example, if you click on the Address field, and search for *Strappman*, you'll get no match.)

Likewise, if you type a first name such as *Steven* into your table and then search for *Stephen*, Access won't find the correct record. *Steven* and *Stephen* are similar enough for *you* to say "Yeah, that's a match." However, Find isn't smart enough figure out that Steven and Stephen sound alike, and it certainly won't know if you want to match either name.

NOTE

Filter by Form, Advance Filter/Sort, and queries let you search for text that's similar to text that you enter. For example, you can tell Access to find a First Name *like* "*St*en.*" This statement will match records that contain Steven or Stephen in the First Name field. See Chapters 9 and 10 for details.

Closing the Form or Datasheet

When you're done playing with the data, close the form or datasheet view:

1. Choose File ➤ Close, or press Ctrl+W.

2. If you're asked for permission to save your current work, click on Yes if you want to save any filtering or other changes to the table or form; click on No if you want to discard those changes.

Don't worry if you're *not* asked for permission to save your work—Access will ask *only* if you've altered the form or datasheet view. All the names and addresses you typed are stored safely on disk for future reference.

At Your Leisure

 ➤ If you'd like to explore the topics described in this lesson on your own, skip to Chapter 9. To explore the topics online, go to the Help Contents, open the *Finding And Sorting Data* book, and then investigate the subtopics shown. Or, move ahead to the next lesson now.

Lesson 5: Creating and Printing Reports

In this lesson you'll create, preview, and print a set of mailing labels. These mailing labels will be a nice addition to the Birthdays This Month, Fact Sheet, Addresses by Last Name, and Greeting Card List reports that the Database Wizard created for you automatically.

Preparing Mailing Labels

Let's prepare a report that can print names and addresses on standard Avery mailing labels. Here are the steps:

1. In the database window, click on the Tables tab, and then click on the Addresses table name.

2. Click on the drop-down arrow next to the New Object toolbar button (shown at left, and the second-to-last toolbar button), and then choose New Report (or choose <u>I</u>nsert ➤ <u>R</u>eport from the menus).

3. In the New Report dialog box, double-click on Label Wizard.

NOTE   If you forget to choose a table (or query) in step 1, you'll need to choose one from the drop-down list in the New Report dialog box.

4. In a moment, the Label Wizard dialog box will ask *What label size would you like?* Under Label Type, choose Sheet feed if you'll be using a laser (or other sheet-fed) printer to print labels. Otherwise, choose Continuous (if you'll be using a dot-matrix printer to print labels).

5. In the same dialog box, scroll to and click on the appropriate Avery label size, and then click on <u>N</u>ext.

TIP   The Avery label number and label dimensions are printed on the box of labels. If you don't have labels already, just pick Avery number 5095 or some other 2-across size.

6. When asked about font and color, choose any options you want to use. The Sample text at the left side of the dialog box will reflect your current choices. Click on the <u>N</u>ext button to continue.

7. Use these techniques to fill in the Prototype Label box, making it look like the example shown in Figure 3.15:

- **To add a field to the label,** click in the Prototype Label box where you want the field to appear. Then double-click on the field in the Available Fields list, or click on the field and then click on the > button. The field will appear in the Prototype Label box.

FIGURE 3.15

Fields from the
Addresses table
arranged for printing
on a mailing label

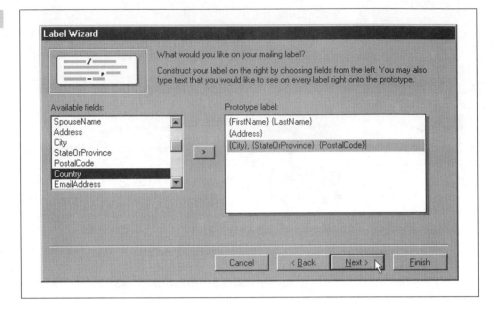

- **To add a space, punctuation mark, or other text,** click
  where you want the space or text to appear (if the insertion
  point isn't there already), and then press the appropriate
  key(s) on your keyboard.

- **To start a new line on the prototype label**, click on the
  next line in the Prototype Label box or press ↓ or ↵.

- **To delete a field or text,** position the insertion point in the
  Prototype Label box where you want to start deleting, and
  then press the Delete or Backspace key as needed. Or, select
  text with your mouse or keyboard, and then press Delete or
  Backspace.

8. When you're done filling in the Prototype Label box, click on
Next.

9. When asked which fields you want to sort by, scroll down to
PostalCode in the Available fields list, and then double-click on
that field name. (If you prefer to sort by LastName and
FirstName, double-click on those field names instead.) Click on
Next to continue.

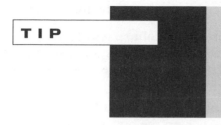

TIP If you accidentally double-click on the wrong field(s), click on the << button to clear all the fields, and then double-click on the correct field(s). To clear just one field, click on that field in the Sort by list, and then click on the < button.

10. Click on the <u>F</u>inish button in the last dialog box, and wait a few seconds.

The Wizard will create a report with names and addresses formatted for the label size you specified. When the Wizard is done, you'll see a preview of the labels on the screen.

Closing and Saving the Report

You'll learn more about how to preview and print the report in a moment. But first, save the report and close the report preview window. To do so, choose <u>F</u>ile ➤ <u>C</u>lose or press Ctrl+W. (If you click on the Close toolbar button by accident, you'll be taken to design view. Just press Ctrl+W to return to the database window quickly.) Your report format is saved with the name Labels Addresses, as you can see by clicking on the Reports tab in the database window.

Don't Reinvent the Wheel!

Keep in mind that Access has saved the report *format*, not its *contents*. So even if you add, change, or delete addresses in the future, you *do not* need to re-create the reports to print the data. Whenever you print a report, Access automatically puts the table's current data into the report's format.

Previewing and Printing a Report

Previewing and printing a formatted report is a snap. Here are the steps:

1. Make sure your printer is ready. If you want to print on mailing labels, load the labels into the printer.

2. To see the list of available reports, do one of the following:

- **If you're starting from the database window,** click on the database window's Reports tab. You should see the names of the reports the Database Wizard created, plus the one you created.

- **If you're using the Main Switchboard form** in your Address Book application, click on the button next to the Preview Reports option. You'll see options for printing reports created by the Database Wizard. (Later in this chapter, we'll show you how to add your new Labels Addresses report to this list of options.)

3. To preview the report, do one of the following:

- **If you're starting from the database window,** click on the name of the report you want to print (for example, Labels Addresses), and then click on the Preview button on the database window; or just double-click on the report name. You also can choose File ➤ Print Preview from the menu bar.

- **If you're starting from the list of reports** on the Reports Switchboard, click on the button next to the report you want to view.

TIP
To print a report from the database window without previewing it first, click on the report name you want to print, and then choose File ➤ Print ➤ OK.

4. The report will open in Print Preview mode, with sample data shown. (Maximize the window if you wish.) Here are some tricks you can use to view your report:

- **To zoom in and out** between 100 percent magnification and a full-page view that fits on your screen, move the mouse pointer into the report area and click the mouse, or click on the Zoom toolbar button (see Figure 3.16). Click the mouse or on the Zoom button again to return to the previous size.

- **To zoom to various magnifications,** choose options from the toolbar's Zoom Control drop-down list. Or, right-click in the report area, choose Zoom from the shortcut menu, and then choose a magnification. Or, choose <u>V</u>iew ➤ <u>Z</u>oom options from the menu bar.

- **To display multiple pages at once,** right-click in the report area, choose Pages, and then choose a page layout. Or, choose <u>V</u>iew ➤ P<u>a</u>ges options from the menu bar. Or, click on the toolbar's One Page and Two Pages buttons.

5. When you're ready to print the report, choose <u>F</u>ile ➤ <u>P</u>rint (or press Ctrl+P) and then click on OK in the Print dialog box that appears. Or, to bypass the Print dialog box, click on the Print toolbar button (shown at left).

FIGURE 3.16

The Preview mode toolbar

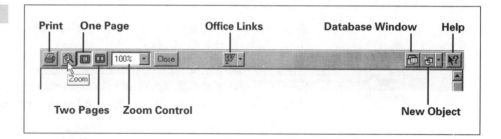

NOTE

The Print dialog box lets you choose a printer, print the report to a file, select a range of pages to print, and specify the number of copies and collation method. The <u>S</u>etup button in that dialog box lets you change the margins and layout for the report.

6. To return to the database window or the Reports Switchboard form, click on the Close toolbar button.

At Your Leisure

➤ If you want to learn more about reports before moving on to the next lesson, skip ahead to Chapters 12 and 13. Or, go to the Access Help Contents, open the *Working With Reports* book, and then explore the subtopics shown.

Lesson 6: Using Queries

You can use *queries* to isolate certain fields and records of data in a table, to sort data into alphabetical or numeric order, to combine data from several related tables, and to perform calculations on data in tables. In this lesson, you'll use queries to set up a simple list that shows specific fields and specific records in the Addresses table, in sorted order by last name. Then you'll change the query to show records for everyone in the table.

Creating a Query

To create a query from your Addresses table:

1. Starting from the database window, click on the Tables tab, and then click on the Addresses table name.

 2. Click on the drop-down arrow next to the New Object toolbar button (shown at left, and the second-to-last toolbar button), and then choose New Query (or choose <u>I</u>nsert ➤ <u>Q</u>uery from the menus).

3. In the New Query dialog box, double-click on Design View. Figure 3.17 shows the query design window that appears.

N O T E   It's often easiest to use the Simple Query Wizard (and other query Wizards) to speed up the job of creating queries. But for the query you'll be designing next, the from-scratch method is a little faster and it gives you practice using the query design window.

Choosing Fields to View

To fill in the design grid, you first choose the fields you want to work with, in the order you want them to appear. Follow these steps now to add the

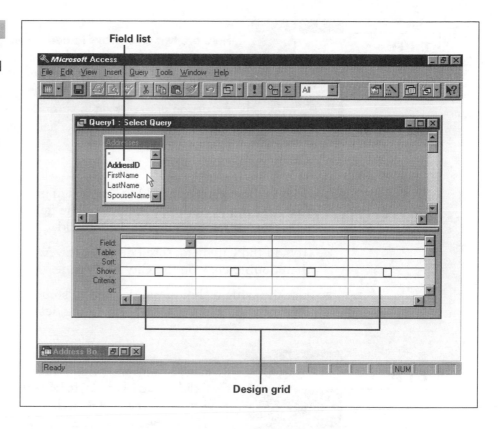

The query design window shows the field list for the Addresses table in the top pane and the design grid in the bottom pane. By default, Access creates a Select Query (one that lets you select specific information from your tables), which is why the window's title bar displays Query1 : Select Query.

LastName, FirstName, City, StateOrProvince, and HomePhone fields to the grid:

1. Maximize the query design window so you can see more columns in the design grid at once.

2. To add the LastName field to the design grid, double-click on that field in the Addresses field list near the top of the window. The Last Name field will appear in the first blank column of the design grid. The Table row in that column will show the name of the table the field comes from, and the Show row will include a check mark to tell Access to display that field when you run the query.

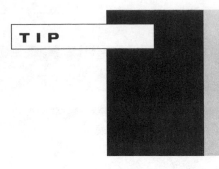

> **TIP**
>
> Here are two other ways to add a field to the query design grid: 1) Drag the field name from the Addresses field list to the appropriate column in the design grid; or 2) Click on the Field box in the appropriate column of the design grid, click on the drop-down arrow that appears, and then choose the field name you want to use.

3. To add the FirstName field to the design grid, double-click on that field in the Addresses field list. The field will appear in the next (second) column of the design grid.

4. To add the City field, scroll down in the Addresses field list, and then double-click on the City field name.

5. Use the same techniques described in step 3 to add the StateOr-Province and HomePhone fields to the design grid.

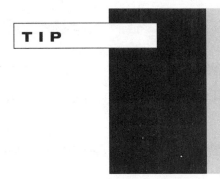

> **TIP**
>
> If you add the wrong field to a column of the design grid, click in the Field box for that column, click on the drop-down arrow, and then choose the correct field name from the list. To delete a column in the design grid, move the mouse pointer just above the field name in that column (until the pointer changes to a black ↓), click the mouse to highlight the entire column, and then press Delete.

Figure 3.18 shows the five fields in the query design grid.

Choosing Records to View

Suppose you want to view the list only for people who live in Washington. To do so, type **wa** (or **WA**) into the Criteria row under the StateOr-Province column. Here's how:

1. Click in the Criteria box that's underneath the StateOrProvince column.

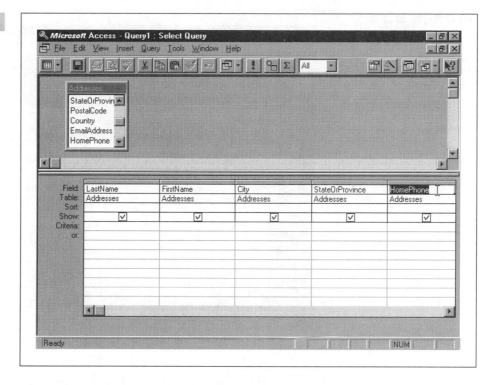

FIGURE 3.18

Five fields—LastName, FirstName, City, StateOrProvince, and HomePhone—added to the query design grid

2. Type **wa** or any state that you've stored in the table (see Figure 3.19). Don't worry about typing exact uppercase and lowercase letters.

3. Press ⏎. Access automatically adds quotation marks around the text you typed and moves the cursor to the next column.

Choosing the Sort Order

Let's sort the list by last name and then by first name within identical last names. To do this, you tell Access which fields (columns) to sort by and whether you want to sort in Ascending (A–Z) order or Descending (Z–A) order. Here are the steps:

1. Use the horizontal scrollbar to scroll the design grid back to the LastName column, and then click in the Sort box below the LastName column. Then, click on the drop-down arrow that appears and choose Ascending from the list.

This query will display the LastName, FirstName, City, StateOrProvince, and HomePhone fields of records that have Washington (wa) in the StateOrProvince field.

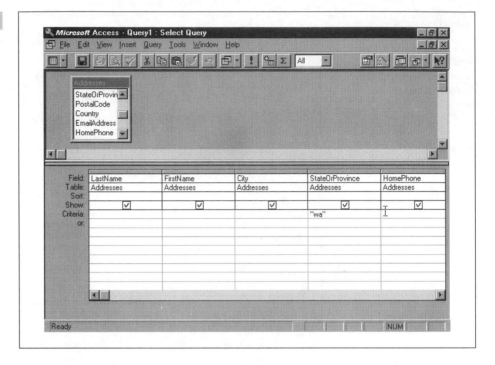

2. Click in the Sort box below the FirstName column, click on the drop-down arrow, and then choose Ascending. Figure 3.20 shows the query design window after you complete this step.

TIP

If you choose the wrong column to sort by, click on the Sort box below the appropriate column, click on the drop-down arrow, and then choose Not Sorted.

Because the LastName column appears to the left of the FirstName column in the design grid, records will be alphabetized by people's last names. The FirstName field will act as a tie breaker, meaning that records with identical last names will be alphabetized by first name.

Running the Query

Running the query is a snap. To try it, click on the Run toolbar button (shown at left), or choose Query ➤ Run from the menus.

FIGURE 3.20

This query will sort the query results by last name and first name within identical last names. Because the Criteria for StateOrProvince is set to "wa" (Washington), the query results will show data for people in Washington only.

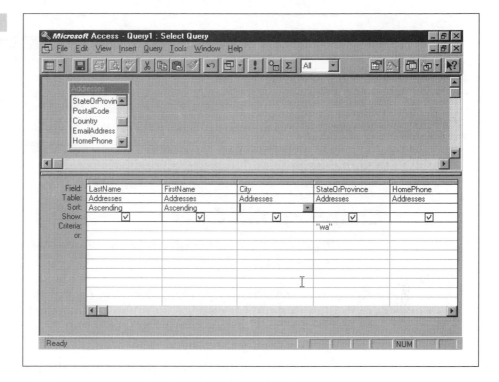

The query results will appear in datasheet view, and will show only the Last Name, First Name, City, State/Province, and Home Phone columns, and only the people in Washington, alphabetized by last name and first name (see Figure 3.21). All the data is *live* and you can change it the same way you change any data in datasheet view.

NOTE

You might have noticed that the column headings (or *captions*) shown in Figures 3.14 and 3.21 don't exactly match the field names. For example, the field name for a person's surname is *LastName*; however, the column heading shows *Last Name* (with a blank space between words). These column headings are controlled by the *Caption* property in the table or query design. Chapter 6 explains how to change table properties, and Chapter 10 delves into changing properties in a query.

FIGURE 3.21

The query results appear in datasheet view. In this example, we restored and resized the query results window to frame the results nicely.

Changing the Query

Changing the query to display an alphabetized list of *all* the records in the table is easy. Try it now:

1. To switch back to the query design window, click on the Query View toolbar button (shown at left, and the first button on the toolbar), or choose View ➤ Query Design. Maximize the query design window, if necessary.

2. Delete "wa" in the Criteria box below the StateOrProvince column. To do this quickly, select (drag your mouse through) "wa" and then press Delete.

3. Run the query again (click on the Run toolbar button).

Now the datasheet view resembles Figure 3.22. Because you removed "wa" (Washington), the query results show all records in the table—not just the people from Washington.

FIGURE 3.22

The datasheet after removing "wa" (Washington) from the StateOrProvince field of the query design, running the query again, and restoring and resizing the window

Last Name	First Name	City	State/Province	Home Phone
Davolio	Nancy	Seattle	WA	(504) 555-9857
Fuller	Andrew	Tacoma	WA	(504) 555-9482
Leverling	Janet	Kirkland	WA	(504) 555-3412
Peacock	Margaret	Redmond	WA	(504) 555-8122
Buchanan	Steven	London		(71) 555-4848
Strappman	Hanley	Fridley	OH	(216) 555-1225

Record: 1 of 6

Just for grins, print a quick copy of this list now by choosing File ➤ Print ➤ OK or by clicking on the Print toolbar button.

Saving and Reusing the Query

You'll probably want to see an updated list sometime later, perhaps after you've added, deleted, or changed some records. Rather than re-creating this query each time, you can save it and reuse it anytime. To save the query now:

1. Click on the Save toolbar button (shown at left), or choose File ➤ Save.

2. Type a valid Access object name (such as **Addresses PhoneList Query**), and then click on OK.

3. Close the Select Query window (press Ctrl+W). The query design and datasheet will disappear, but your query will be saved.

TIP You can save the query design from the design window or the datasheet window—the steps are the same. You also can save the design when you close the window. If you're asked about saving changes, click on the Yes button and enter a query name if prompted to do so.

To run a saved query, go to the database window (press F11 if necessary), click on the Queries tab, click on the query you want to run (Addresses PhoneList Query in this example), and then click on the Open button on the database window. Or, just double-click on the query name. The query will run on the latest data in your table. (If you wish, close the datasheet window and return to the database window.)

NOTE To change the query design instead of running the query, click on the Queries tab on the database window, click on the query you want to change, and then click on the Design button on the database window.

At Your Leisure

> To learn more about queries, see Chapter 10. Or, open the Access Help Contents, open the *Working With Queries* book, open the *Creating A Query* book, and then explore the subtopics that appear.

Lesson 7: Customizing an Application

Now you've created several database objects—a table, a form, a report, and a query. But those objects aren't put together in a way that allows people who know nothing about those objects to use the database easily. To make your database extra easy to use, you can add these objects to the "turnkey" *application* that the Database Wizard created for you automatically. In this lesson, you'll learn some techniques for doing just that.

Adding Command Buttons to a Form

Let's begin by adding command buttons, like those shown in Figure 3.23, to the Addresses1 form you created in Lesson 3.

1. Starting from the database window, click on the Forms tab, click on Addresses1, and then click on the <u>D</u>esign button on the database window. You'll see the form design window, where you can modify the form. Maximize the form design window to give yourself some room to work.

2. You'll need to increase the height of the Form Header in order to put the command buttons there. To do this, move the mouse pointer to the bottom of the Form Header section until it changes to an up/down arrow crossed by a bar (shown at left). Then drag the horizontal line at the bottom of the section downward. For this example, make the Form Header about .75-inch high (look at the vertical ruler, which is marked in .25-inch increments, as you resize the form header).

FIGURE 3.23

Command buttons that you'll add to the Addresses1 form in this lesson. The Database Wizard used similar techniques to add the Pre*v*iew Fact Sheet and *D*ial buttons to the Addresses form that it created automatically.

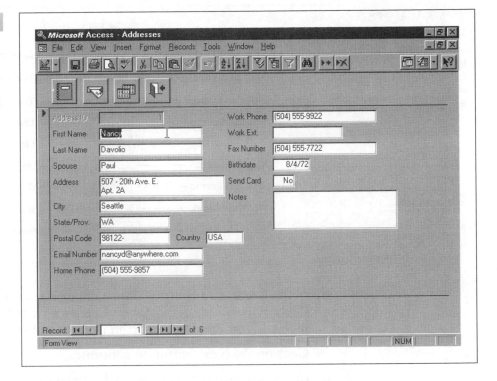

3. You'll use the *toolbox* (shown in Figure 3.24) to create the command buttons. If the toolbox isn't visible, click on the Toolbox toolbar button (shown at left), or choose *V*iew ➤ *T*oolbox.

4. When the toolbox appears, make sure the Control Wizards button is selected (pushed in). You can drag the toolbox anywhere you want it on the design window.

NOTE   If the property sheet or another tool is blocking your view in the form design window, hide that tool by choosing its name from the *V*iew menu.

5. To create a command button, click on the Command Button tool in the toolbox, and then click where you want the upper-left corner of the button to appear on your form. In this example, click on the left edge of the Form Header (see Figure 3.23).

FIGURE 3.24

The toolbox lets you create new objects on a form.

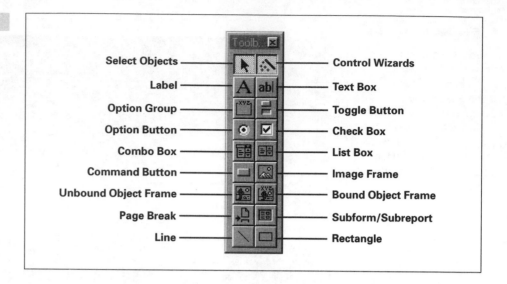

Select Objects —————— Control Wizards

Label —————— Text Box

Option Group —————— Toggle Button

Option Button —————— Check Box

Combo Box —————— List Box

Command Button —————— Image Frame

Unbound Object Frame —————— Bound Object Frame

Page Break —————— Subform/Subreport

Line —————— Rectangle

6. In the Command Button Wizard dialog box that appears, click on Report Operations in the Action Categories list (first column), and then click on Preview Report in the Action list (second column).

7. Click on the <u>N</u>ext button to continue.

8. In the next dialog box, click on Addresses By Last Name in the report names list. (The Database Wizard built this report automatically when it created the Address Book Lessons database.) Click on the <u>N</u>ext button.

9. In the next dialog box, click on <u>N</u>ext to accept the suggested button picture.

10. When asked about a name for your button, type **Addresses by Last Name Button** and click on <u>F</u>inish.

The button appears on the form, as shown below. You can't test the button yet, because it works only when you're in form view (you're in design view now). Before testing that button, you'll add three more.

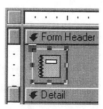

T I P To move a button, drag it to a new location. If you want to bypass "grid snap" while moving or sizing an object, hold down the Ctrl key while you're dragging.

Creating the Button for Mailing Labels

Follow these steps to add a second button to your form:

1. Click on the Command Button tool in the toolbox, and then click slightly to the right of the command button you just created.

2. In the next Wizard dialog box, click on Report Operations and Preview Report in the two columns, and then click on Next.

3. Click on Labels Addresses in the list of available reports, and click on Next.

4. In the next Wizard dialog box, select (check) Show All Pictures. Then scroll up to Mailbox (the pictures are listed in alphabetical order, by picture name) and click on that picture name. This step will put a picture of an envelope going through a mail slot on the button.

5. Click on Next.

6. Type **Labels Button** and click on Finish.

Creating the Query Button

Follow these steps to add a button that will run the query named Addresses PhoneList Query:

1. Click on the Command Button tool in the toolbox, and then click slightly to the right of the "mailbox" command button you just created.

2. In the next Wizard dialog box, click on Miscellaneous and Run Query in the two columns, and then click on Next.

3. Click on Addresses PhoneList Query in the list of available queries, and click on Next.

4. In the next Wizard dialog box, click on <u>N</u>ext to choose the suggested picture.

5. Type **Addresses PhoneList Query Button** and click on <u>F</u>inish.

Creating the Close Button

The final button will make it easy to close the form. To create it:

1. Click on the Command Button tool on the toolbar, and then click just to the right of the last button at the top of the form.

2. Click on Form Operations in the first column, click on Close Form in the second column, and then click on the <u>N</u>ext button.

3. In the next Wizard dialog box, click on <u>N</u>ext to accept the default Exit picture.

4. In the next Wizard dialog box, type **Exit Button** and click on <u>F</u>inish.

5. Save your work by clicking on the Save button on the toolbar, or pressing Ctrl+S.

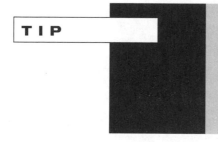

TIP

To align buttons or other objects on the form, select the objects you want to align, and then choose F<u>o</u>rmat ➤ A<u>l</u>ign and an appropriate alignment option. To set equal horizontal spacing between objects, select the objects, and choose F<u>o</u>rmat ➤ Hori<u>z</u>ontal Spacing ➤ Make Equal. See Chapter 13 for more information.

Adding Visual Basic Code to a Form

Next you'll learn how to add some Visual Basic for Applications (VBA) code to your form. Please don't think that programming is something you *have* to do in Access. You can create very powerful Access applications with no programming whatsoever. This little experiment with Visual Basic serves mainly as a way to get your hands dirty, so you can see how programming with VBA works.

Follow these steps (carefully!) to add some programming code to your form now:

1. Click on the Properties toolbar button, or choose <u>V</u>iew ➤ <u>P</u>roperties, to open the property sheet.

2. Choose <u>E</u>dit ➤ Select Fo<u>r</u>m. The property sheet displays the properties for the entire form.

3. Click on the Event tab on the property sheet, and then scroll down to the On Open property. You'll add some code to maximize the Addresses1 form window anytime you open the Addresses1 form.

4. Click in the On Open text box, click on the Build (...) button that appears, and then double-click on Code Builder. A module editing window will appear, with the cursor positioned on the blank line between the Private Sub Form_Open and End Sub statements.

5. Press the Tab key, and then type *exactly*:

```
DoCmd.Maximize
```

as shown below. Be careful to type the text correctly—there's no margin for error when you're writing program code.

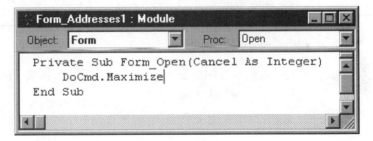

6. Choose <u>F</u>ile ➤ <u>C</u>lose (or press Ctrl+W) to return to the form design window. Notice that [Event Procedure] now appears as the On Open property.

7. Next, scroll down to the On Close property of the property sheet. You'll add some code that restores the previously displayed window to its original size anytime you close the Addresses form.

8. Click in the On Close text box, click on the Build (...) button that appears, and then double-click on Code Builder. A module editing window will appear, with the cursor positioned on the blank line between the Private Sub Form_Close and End Sub statements.

9. Press the Tab key, and then type *exactly*:

DoCmd.Restore

as shown below.

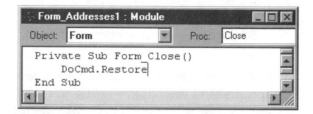

NOTE This DoCmd.Restore command restores a window to its previous size. For example, if you open the Addresses1 form from the database window, the database window will reappear at its previous size when you close Addresses1. Likewise, if you open Addresses1 from the Main Switchboard (as explained later), the Main Switchboard form will reappear at its previous size.

10. Choose File ➤ Close (or press Ctrl+W) to return to the form design window.

11. Choose File ➤ Close ➤ Yes to save and close the modified form.

You'll return to the database window (press F11 if necessary).

Customizing the Switchboard Form

The Switchboard form that the Database Wizard created when you set up the Address Book Lessons database provides buttons and options that make it easy to update and report on information about your contacts. Since you've gone to the trouble of setting up some new forms and reports, you'll probably want to add them to the switchboard. You also might want to change the names of options that appear on the switchboard.

To begin, open the Main Switchboard form, and then click on the button next to Change Switchboard Items. Or, choose Tools ➤ Add-Ins ➤ Switchboard Manager from the menu bar. You'll see the Switchboard Manager dialog box, shown in Figure 3.25.

FIGURE 3.25

The Switchboard Manager lets you create new switchboard pages, edit existing pages, delete pages, and choose a default switchboard page.

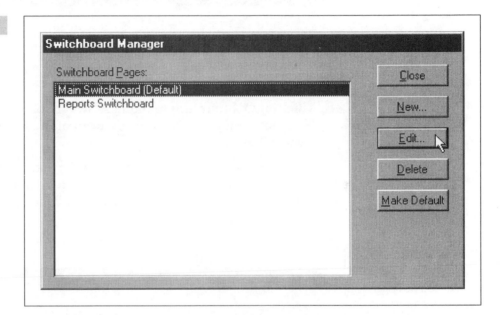

Adding the Addresses1 Form to the Main Switchboard

Follow these steps to add your new Addresses1 form to the Main Switchboard Page:

1. In the Switchboard Manager dialog box, click on Main Switchboard (Default) in the Switchboard Pages list, and then click on the Edit button. The Edit Switchboard Page dialog box will appear (see Figure 3.26 for a completed example).

2. Click on the New button to open the Edit Switchboard Item dialog box.

3. In the Text box, type **Enter/View Addresses1**.

4. Click on the drop-down list button next to the Command box and choose Open Form In Edit Mode. A Form box will appear.

5. Click on the drop-down list button next to the Form box and choose Addresses1. The completed Edit Switchboard Item dialog box looks like this:

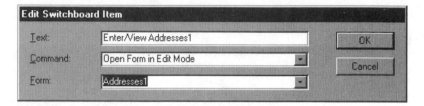

6. Click on OK to return to the Edit Switchboard Page dialog box. Your new entry appears at the bottom of the Items On This Switchboard list.

7. To move your new item to the top of the list, click on that item, and then click on the Move Up button four times. Figure 3.26 shows the completed Edit Switchboard Page dialog box.

FIGURE 3.26

The Edit Switchboard Page dialog box after you add a new item and move it to the top of the list

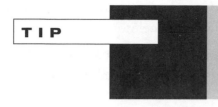

T I P If you want to remove the old Enter/View Addresses option from the list, click on that item in the Items On This Switchboard list, click on the Delete button, and then click on Yes to confirm the deletion.

8. Click on the Close button to return to the Switchboard Manager dialog box.

Changing the Option Names on the Reports Switchboard

We think the options for printing reports on the Reports Switchboard are a bit verbose, and maybe even somewhat wordy. If you agree, follow these steps:

1. Click on Reports Switchboard in the Switchboard Pages list, and then click on the Edit button. Here's what you'll see:

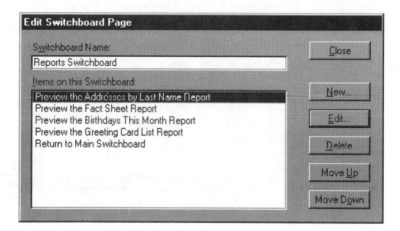

2. Click on the first item in the Items On This Switchboard list, and then click on the Edit button. The option name will be highlighted in the Text box.

3. Replace the selected text with **Addresses by Last Name Report.** To do this quickly, select *Preview the* (and the space after *the*) and press Delete. Then click on OK.

4. Repeat steps 2 and 3 for the second, third, and fourth items on the switchboard, using the guidelines below:

- For the *second* item, change the Text to **Fact Sheet Report.**
- For the *third* item, change the Text to **Birthdays This Month Report.**
- For the *fourth* item, change the Text to **Greeting Card List Report.**

Now add the new Labels Addresses report to the list of items on the Reports Switchboard:

1. Click on the New button to open the Edit Switchboard Item dialog box.

2. In the Text box, type **Mailing Labels Report**.

3. Click on the drop-down list button next to the Command box and choose Open Report. A Report box will appear.

4. Click on the drop-down list button next to the Report box and choose Labels Addresses.

5. Click on OK to return to the Edit Switchboard Page dialog box. Your new entry appears at the bottom of the Items On This Switchboard list.

6. To move your new entry up a notch, click on the Mailing Labels Report item, and then click on the Move Up button once. The Edit Switchboard Dialog box will resemble the example shown below:

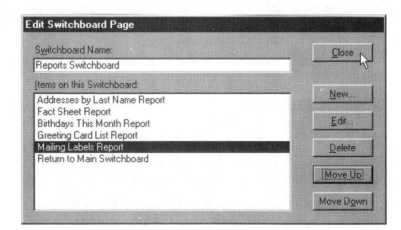

7. Click on the <u>C</u>lose button twice to return to the database window.

Putting It All Together with Startup Commands

When you open a database, Access looks for certain startup commands and executes them automatically. You can customize your database by choosing startup commands that hide the database window, go straight to a specific form, and more. The Database Wizard took care of setting up the essential startup commands for you automatically. But let's customize those startup commands, just for practice:

1. With either the Main Switchboard form or the database window visible, choose <u>T</u>ools ➤ Start<u>u</u>p. Or, with the database window visible, right-click on any tab, and choose Startup from the shortcut menus. You'll see the Startup dialog box (a completed example appears in Figure 3.27).

2. In the A<u>p</u>plication Title box, type **Address Book Lessons**. (This title will appear on the Access title bar anytime the database is open and on the taskbar.)

3. Make sure *Switchboard* appears in the box below Display <u>F</u>orm. (You can use the drop-down list below Display <u>F</u>orm to choose any form that's available for the Address Book Lessons database; however, using Switchboard gives you the most flexibility.)

FIGURE 3.27

The Startup dialog box after we filled in the Application Title

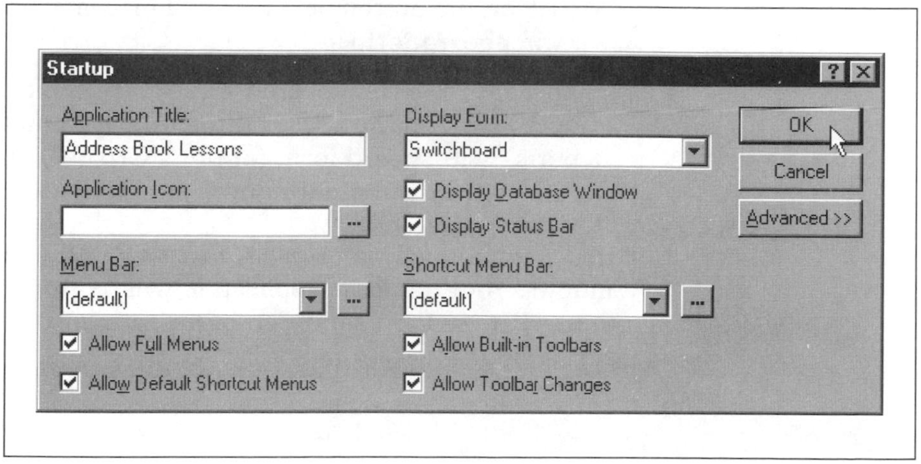

4. Click on OK. The new application title immediately replaces *Microsoft Access* in the window's title bar.

N O T E The Main Switchboard form automatically minimizes the database window when you open the form; therefore, you don't need to clear the Display Database Window check box in the Startup dialog box.

Testing the Application

Now you're ready to test the whole thing. Follow these steps to close and then reopen the database:

1. Choose File ➤ Close, or press Ctrl+W, until the Main Switchboard form and database window disappear.

2. To open the database you just closed, choose File from the menu bar, and then choose Address Book Lessons.

The Main Switchboard form will open, and you'll see the text Address Book Lessons in the Access window's title bar. Now you can explore the Address Book Switchboard form to your heart's content. When you're finished, do one of the following:

- To close the Main Switchboard form *and* the database window, click on the button next to Exit This Database on the Main Switchboard form.

- To close the Switchboard form but leave the database window open, click on the Close button on the Main Switchboard or Reports Switchboard form (or press Ctrl+W), and then press F11 to display the database window.

When you're done using Access, choose File ➤ Exit, and you'll return to Windows. Your database application will be stored safely on disk for future use. To use the application in the future, start Access, and open the Address Book Lessons database.

At Your Leisure

➤ To learn more about creating applications, see Parts Four and Five of this book.

There's More Than One Way to Create Turnkey Applications

As you've seen, there's more than one way to automate your work and to create turnkey applications with Access. For example, you can use a Switchboard form, which Access sets up anytime you use the Database Wizard to create a database. You also can add command buttons and Visual Basic programming to forms, as you did for your Addresses1 form. And, you can use combinations of these and other techniques that you'll learn about in Parts Four and Five of this book. Your application can be as simple or as sophisticated as you wish, depending on your requirements and your expertise. It's all up to you!

Where to Go from Here

Congratulations! You've just created your first Access database, and your first custom Access application. The steps you followed to set up the Address Book example also work for more than 20 other applications that Access can create automatically.

If you'd like to build a fancier application now, use the Database Wizard to create an Order Entry database (*with* sample data, of course). We'll use the Wizard-generated Order Entry database—with some tweaks to the Wizard-supplied data—to illustrate key concepts throughout this book. Alternatively, you can copy our sample Order Entry database from the CD-ROM disc supplied with this book (see Appendix B for details). Having your own Order Entry database to experiment with as you read will make learning Access easier and more fun.

What's New in the Access Zoo?

You've just taken a look at many of the features that make Access for Windows 95 so much easier for beginners to learn and use than Access 2.0 was. These features include:

- Database Wizards that can create more than 20 turnkey applications, complete with sample data.

- More convenient filtering methods, including Filter by Selection.

- The Visual Basic for Applications (VBA) programming language, which replaces Access Basic.

- The Switchboard Manager (Tools ➤ Add-Ins ➤ Switchboard Manager), which lets you create and customize switchboard forms without programming or macros.

- The Tools ➤ Startup feature, which lets you define how a database will behave when you open it—again, without programming or AutoExec macros.

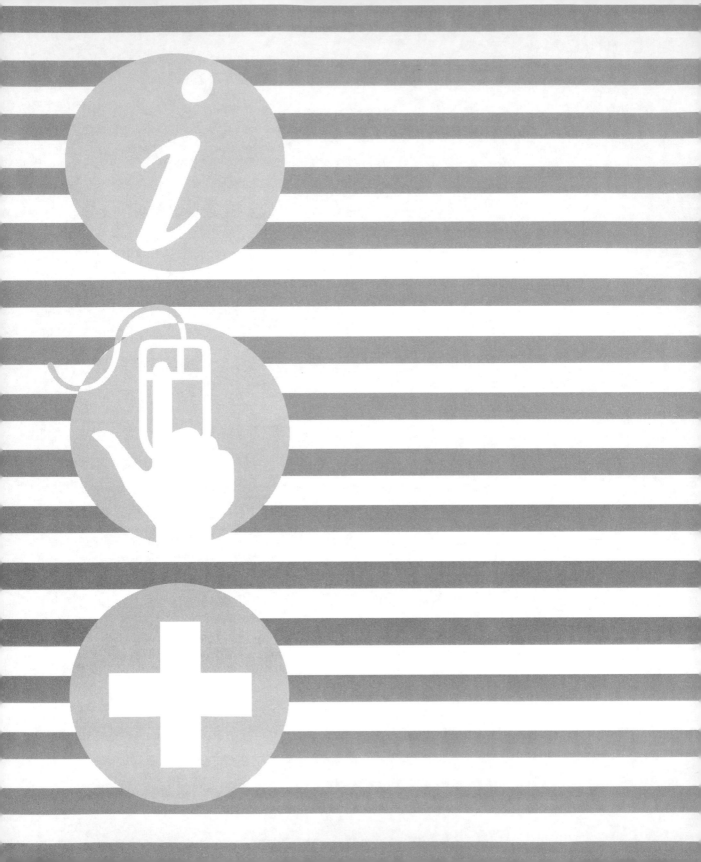

CHAPTER

4

About Access, Office, and Windows 95

MICROSOFT Access for Windows 95 is tightly integrated with Windows 95 and Microsoft Office for Windows 95. In this chapter, we'll highlight the most important integration features, and point you to places where you can get more details. If you're completely new to Access and Microsoft Office, you might want to skim through (or even skip) this chapter, and then come back to it when you find yourself asking "How can I make the most of what I know about Windows 95 and Office for Windows 95?" and "How can I make the most of my Access data?"

Making the Most of Windows 95 and Access

Microsoft Access is designed from the ground up to fully support features in Windows 95. Listed in alphabetical order below are some of the most important Windows 95-like features that you'll find in Access.

32-Bit Application Microsoft Access for Windows 95 is a 32-bit application, which means that it runs in its own protected computer memory area. For this reason, Access won't grind to a halt if some *other* program on your computer decides to misbehave. Access also takes advantage of the multi-threading capabilities of Windows 95, something programmers will appreciate; therefore, the Jet database engine, Microsoft Access, and modules written for Visual Basic for Applications all run in separate threads. (On high-end Windows NT machines, multi-threading allows several CPUs to cooperate on a single Access application at the same time.)

Briefcase Replication Access for Windows 95 takes advantage of the Windows 95 Briefcase feature. This lets you work remotely with replicas of your database and later merge the changes back into your master databases. Any design changes made to the master databases also will be propagated to the replicas. Replication is ideal for managing remote changes to data and balancing the load over a network. See Chapter 17.

Database Explorer The database window in Access for Windows 95 looks and acts a lot like Windows 95 Explorer, as well as windows that appear when you open My Computer or Network Neighborhood. To view database objects as large icons, small icons, a list, or a detailed list, choose options on the View menu, or click on appropriate Database toolbar buttons, or right-click on an empty area inside the database window and choose View options from the shortcut menu. To arrange icons by name, type, creation date, or modification date, choose options on the View ➤ Arrange Icons menu, or right-click on an empty area inside the database window and choose Arrange Icons options from the shortcut menu. See Chapter 1 and Figure 4.1.

Long File Names and UNC Paths Like all programs designed for Windows 95, Microsoft Access for Windows 95 supports long file names and universal naming convention (UNC) paths. UNC paths let you refer to files on a remote computer by supplying the computer name, rather than permanently mapping a drive letter to the remote computer. For example, an Order Entry database file located in the My Documents folder on drive C of a computer named Hanley might have a tongue-twisting UNC name of *\\Hanley\c\My Documents\Order Entry.mdb*.

Plug-and-Play Screen Resolution Plug-and-Play screen resolution lets you change your screen resolution on the fly. To use it, minimize Microsoft Access and any other programs that are covering the Windows 95 desktop. Next, right-click on any empty area of the desktop, and choose Properties. Finally, click on the Settings tab in the Display Properties dialog box, use the slider control below the Desktop Area option to set the screen resolution you want to use, and then click on OK. Respond to any prompts that appear, and then click on the Microsoft Access taskbar button to return to Access.

Shortcut Menus Windows 95-style shortcut menus are available throughout Access. Simply right-click on the place for which you want to see a shortcut menu, and then click on (or right-click on) the shortcut menu option you want to use (see Figure 4.1).

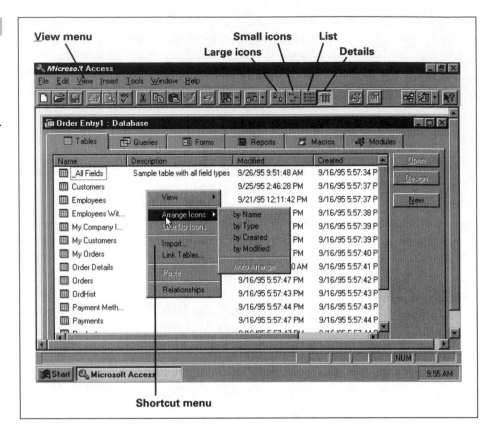

Special Effects Access for Windows 95 and its forms and reports can display the same sunken, raised, etched, chiseled, shadowed, and flat special effects you often see in Windows 95 programs and dialog boxes. See Chapter 13 and Figure 4.2.

Windows 95 Look and Feel Access for Windows 95 uses all the standard Windows 95 controls you've grown to love, including tabbed dialog boxes, option buttons, drop-down lists, command buttons, and new check mark-style (✓) check boxes. So once you've mastered Windows 95 skills, working with Access will seem easy and natural. Figure 4.3 shows a typical Access for Windows 95 dialog box.

Windows 95 Shortcuts Creating a desktop shortcut to any Access object is similar to creating shortcuts in Windows 95. Simply drag and drop an object from the Access database window to your desktop, and then

FIGURE 4.2

An Access for
Windows 95 form that
uses various Windows
95-style special effects

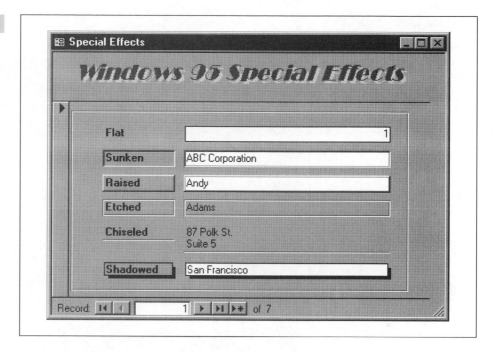

use the dropped object as you would any shortcut. For example, double-click on the shortcut to start Microsoft Access and open the associated object; or right-click on the object to open a shortcut menu (see below) that offers a host of possibilities for working with the object. See Chapter 1.

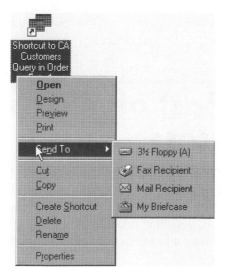

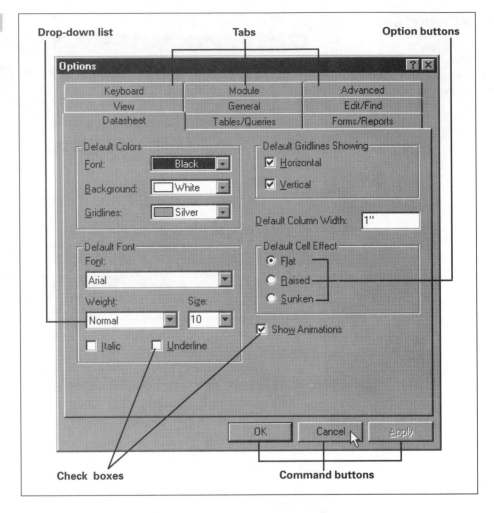

Making the Most of Microsoft Office and Access

Microsoft Access for Windows 95 shares many common features with other programs in the Microsoft Office for Windows 95 suite, especially Microsoft Excel and Microsoft Word. So if you've installed all or part of Microsoft Office, you can take advantage of these common features immediately. We'll take a look at some of these shared features next. Later in this chapter, we'll discuss convenient ways to share data between programs in Microsoft Office.

The Microsoft Office Shortcut Bar

The Microsoft Office Shortcut Bar, shown below, is installed automatically when you install Microsoft Office for Windows 95. You can use the Office Shortcut Bar to launch and switch between programs, to open files, and more. It's fully customizable, so you can tailor the ShortcutBar to do just about anything except brew your coffee and wash the cup.

Displaying and Hiding the Office Shortcut Bar

The Microsoft Office Shortcut Bar usually appears at the upper-right corner of your desktop. If it doesn't appear, click on the Start taskbar button, and then choose Microsoft Office Shortcut Bar from the Start menu. Or, click on the Start taskbar button, choose <u>R</u>un, type the command line "**\MSOffice\Microsoft Office Shortcut Bar.lnk**" (with the quotation marks), and then press ↵.

Handy Ways to Use the Office Shortcut Bar

Here are some things you can do when the Office Shortcut Bar is visible:

- **To find out what an Office Shortcut Bar button is for,** move your mouse pointer to the button. A ToolTip will appear near the pointer to explain the button's purpose.

- **To choose a button on the Office Shortcut Bar**, click on the button.

- **To display the Office Shortcut Bar as a floating palette of buttons,** move the mouse pointer to any empty area between buttons, and then drag the bar toward the middle of the screen.

- **To dock the floating Office Shortcut Bar** at the upper-right corner of the desktop, double-click on the Office Shortcut Bar's title bar.

- **To open the Control Menu for the Office Shortcut Bar**, click or right-click on the Office Shortcut Bar's Control-Menu icon, and then choose any of the options shown below:

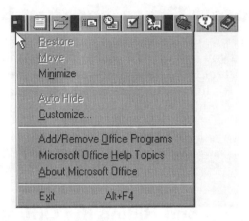

- **To choose or hide bars on the Office Shortcut Bar,** right-click on an empty area between buttons on the bar, and select (check) or deselect (clear) the name of the bar you want to display or hide, respectively.

- **To switch to another bar on the Office Shortcut Bar** when multiple bars are selected, click on the button for the bar you want to use.

- **To customize the currently selected bar on the Office Short-cut Bar,** right-click on an empty area between buttons on the bar and choose Customize, or double-click on an empty area between buttons. Then choose an appropriate tab from the Customize dialog box (see Figure 4.4), complete the dialog box as needed, and then click on OK.

- **To quickly add an Office Shortcut Bar button that will** launch a program (including Microsoft Access), or open a document or folder, select the bar that should contain the new button. Next, use Start ➤ Find, or My Computer, or Windows Explorer to locate the program, document, or folder name you want to add as a button. Then drag the program, document, or folder name to any button on the Office Shortcut Bar (when the mouse pointer displays a small + sign, you've hit the right spot on the Office Shortcut Bar and can release the mouse button). Your new shortcut button will appear at the end of the Office Shortcut Bar.

FIGURE 4.4

The Customize dialog box for the Office Shortcut Bar after we clicked on the Buttons tab. (Don't worry if the Customize dialog box on your own computer differs slightly from this example.)

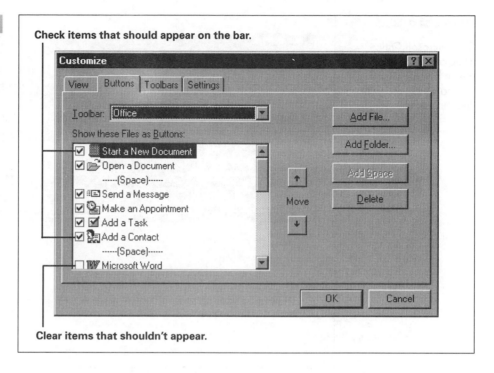

Check items that should appear on the bar.

Clear items that shouldn't appear.

- **To quickly remove a button from the Office Shortcut Bar**, right-click on the button and choose Hide Button.

- **To exit the Office Shortcut Bar**, click or right-click on the Control-Menu icon at the top-left edge of the Office Shortcut Bar, and then choose Exit.

 For more details on using the Microsoft Office Shortcut Menu Bar, see your Microsoft Office documentation; or, click or right-click on the Control-Menu icon at the top-left edge the Office Shortcut Bar, and then choose Microsoft Office Help Topics.

Common Bars

Common menu bars and toolbars appear throughout the Microsoft Office suite, so you won't have to waste time hunting for options you use often. Figure 4.5 shows the Microsoft Excel, Word, PowerPoint, and Access program windows opened on the desktop. Notice the similarities among their menu bars and toolbars.

FIGURE 4.5

The Microsoft Office suite offers common menu bars and toolbars to speed your learning process.

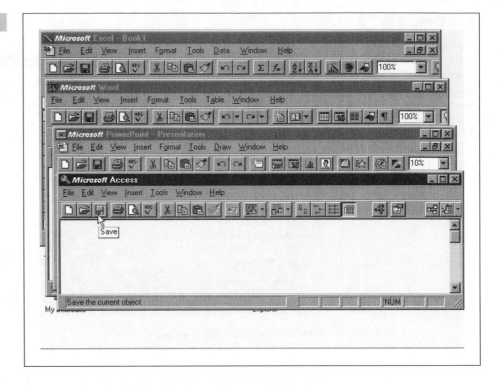

Common Dialog Boxes

Many dialog boxes—including New, Open/Import, Page Setup, Print, and Save—work the same way, regardless of which Microsoft Office program you're using. In Figure 4.6, for example, you see the Open dialog box for Microsoft Word. Figure 4.7 shows the very similar Import dialog box for Microsoft Access.

Common Office Tools

You'll also find common tools that work in identical (or similar) ways throughout Microsoft Office. Table 4.1 briefly describes each tool and tells you which Microsoft Office programs offer it.

FIGURE 4.6

An Open dialog box
in Microsoft Word

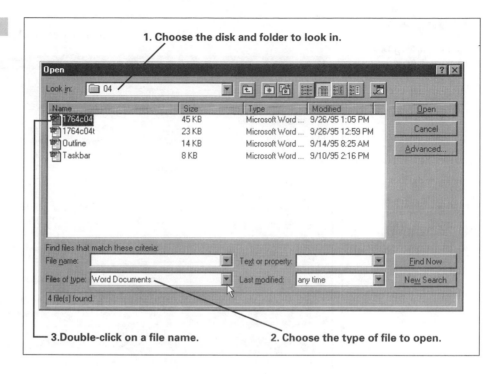

1. Choose the disk and folder to look in.

3. Double-click on a file name.

2. Choose the type of file to open.

Tapping the Microsoft Knowledge Base and More

Every Microsoft Office program offers many sources of help. For example, you can look in the *Getting Results* book, the Answer Wizard, the Help Index, the Help Contents, and the Readme file that come with most Microsoft Office programs. But that's not it by a long shot! You also can get in-depth technical help on a variety of Microsoft products from these resources (which are listed in alphabetical order):

- **Microsoft Download Service (MSDL).** The MSDL is a bulletin board service that contains Microsoft Software Library (MSL) articles and support files for you to download to your computer. Using your modem, dial (206) 936-6735 in the United States, or (905) 507-3022 in Canada.

FIGURE 4.7

An Import dialog box
in Microsoft Access

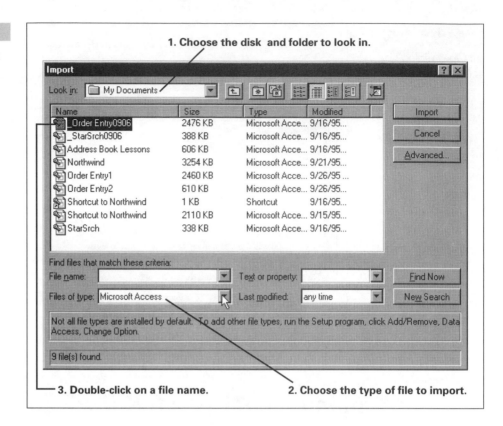

1. Choose the disk and folder to look in.

3. Double-click on a file name.

2. Choose the type of file to import.

TABLE 4.1: Common Microsoft Office Tools

FEATURE	WHAT IT DOES	MENU OPTION OR SHORTCUT	WHERE YOU'LL FIND IT
AutoCorrect	Corrects typing errors automatically.	Tools ➤ AutoCorrect	Access, Excel, PowerPoint, Word (Chapter 9)
AutoFormat	Formats a document automatically.	Format ➤ AutoFormat	Access, Excel, Word (Chapters 11, 12, and 13)
Export/ Save As	Saves objects with a new name or format.	File ➤ Save As/Export or File ➤ Save As or File ➤ Export	Access, Excel, Exchange, PowerPoint, Schedule+, Word (Chapter 7)

TABLE 4.1: Common Microsoft Office Tools (continued)

FEATURE	WHAT IT DOES	MENU OPTION OR SHORTCUT	WHERE YOU'LL FIND IT
Format Painter	Copies the appearance of one control or selection to another.	Format Painter toolbar button	Access, Excel, PowerPoint, Word (Chapter 13)
Import/Link	Imports or links data from other programs and formats.	File ➤ Get External Data ➤ Import, or File ➤ Get External Data ➤ Link Tables, or File ➤ Open, or File ➤ Import	Access, Excel, Exchange, PowerPoint, Schedule+, Word (Chapter 7)
Insert	Inserts date and time, page number, picture, object, and more (depends on program).	Insert menu options	Access, Excel, PowerPoint, Word (Chapters 8 and 13)
Options	Customizes default settings.	Tools ➤ Options	Access, Excel, Exchange, PowerPoint, Schedule+, Word (Chapter 15)
Print	Prints objects and documents (some programs also offer a preview feature).	File ➤ Print (Ctrl+P) or File ➤ Print Preview	Access, Excel, Exchange, PowerPoint, Schedule+, Word (Chapter 9)
Properties	Displays and changes properties of the active document or database.	File ➤ Database Properties or File ➤ Properties	Access, Excel, Exchange, PowerPoint, Word (Chapter 5)
Send	Sends the active document or object using electronic mail.	File ➤ Send	Access, Excel, Exchange, PowerPoint, Word (Chapter 7)
Spell Check	Checks for and replaces spelling errors.	Tools ➤ Spelling (F7)	Access, Excel, Exchange, PowerPoint, Word (Chapter 9)

- **Microsoft Fast Tips.** This service offers recorded or faxed answers (in English) to common technical problems, and lets you order catalogs, Application Notes, and popular articles from the Knowledge Base (KB) via fax or mail. Call (800) 936-4100 from any touch-tone telephone.

- **Microsoft Knowledge Base (KB)** on America Online, CompuServe, GEnie, Internet (via World Wide Web, FTP, or Gopher), Microsoft Developer Network, Microsoft TechNet, and The Microsoft Network. The KB contains a comprehensive set of articles (updated daily) with detailed answers to how-to and technical support questions, and lists of bugs and fixes. From the World Wide Web and Gopher sites, you can do full-text searches of KB articles and download files automatically.

- **Microsoft Press publications.** Microsoft Press offers development kits, resource kits, and a variety of books about Microsoft products and related technologies. Call (800) MSPRESS or (800) 677-7377.

- **Microsoft Software Library (MSL)** on America Online, CompuServe, GEnie, Internet, Microsoft Developer Network, Microsoft Download Service (MSDL), Microsoft TechNet, and The Microsoft Network. Here you'll find a collection of binary (non-text) files, including device drivers, utilities, Help files, and technical articles for all Microsoft products.

- **Microsoft TechNet and Microsoft Developer Network (MSDN) CD-ROMs**. These subscription services offer KB, MSL, and other information on CD-ROM. To subscribe to these services, call (800) 344-2121 for Microsoft TechNet or (800) 759-5474 for MSDN.

- **Online support forums** on America Online, CompuServe, GEnie, Internet, and The Microsoft Network. Online support forums are frequented by end-users, third-party developers, and Microsoft support staff who can answer many of your questions quickly.

You can reach the KB and MSL at these Internet sites:

- Microsoft World Wide Web, at www.microsoft.com

- Microsoft Gopher, at gopher.microsoft.com

- Microsoft FTP, at ftp.microsoft.com (supports anonymous logon)

You can reach the KB, MSL, or Microsoft forums from CompuServe:

- To reach the KB, type **GO MSKB** at any ! prompt; or, choose equivalent menu options from your CompuServe navigation program.

- To reach the MSL, type **GO MSL** at any ! prompt; or, choose equivalent menu options.

- To reach the Microsoft forums, type **GO MICROSOFT** at any ! prompt; or, choose equivalent menu options. To reach the Microsoft Access forum directly, type **GO MSACCESS**; or choose equivalent menu options.

To reach the KB from America Online:

- Choose Go To ➤ Keyword, and type **Microsoft** in the Enter Word(s) box. In the Microsoft Resource Center, click on Knowledge Base.

To reach the KB from GEnie:

- Type **m505** at the GEnie system prompt.

To reach the KB from the Microsoft Network:

1. Log on to the Microsoft Network.
2. Click on the Start button on the Windows taskbar, and then select Find ➤ On the Microsoft Network.
3. Type **Knowledgebase** in the Containing text box and then click on Find Now.
4. Double-click on the topic that appears.

 ➤ For more information about all the resources mentioned above, look up *Technical Information* and its subtopics in the Help Index of any Microsoft Office program. If you're a member of The Microsoft Network, you can connect to many of these resources by choosing Help ➤ The Microsoft Network from any Microsoft Office program's menu bar.

Sharing Access Information with Other Office Programs

Imagine having to retype all the names and addresses that you've painstakingly stored in your Access database—just to send form letters from Microsoft Word. And who in their right mind would want to retype data stored in Excel worksheets after deciding that a database table offers a more efficient way to store that information? None of that tedium and wasted effort is necessary when you use Windows 95 technologies and the integrated Microsoft Office suite. In the next few sections, we'll summarize ways to transfer information to and from Access, and point you to places in this book where you can get more details.

NOTE   If you get messages about difficulties in starting programs or establishing links between programs, chances are that not enough memory is available to complete the job you're trying to do. To solve this problem, respond to any messages that appear, and restart your computer (Start ➤ Shutdown ➤ Yes). Then launch only the program or programs that absolutely must be in memory at the same time, and try the operation again. If you still have problems, you may need to install more memory on your computer. (Access itself requires about 12MB of memory, and you'll often need at least 16MB to perform tasks that involve multiple Office programs.)

Using Import and Export

You can use file *import* or *link* techniques to create an Access table from data stored in an external file, such as an Excel worksheet. To get started, go to the Access database window and choose the File ➤ Get External Data ➤ Import or File ➤ Get External Data ➤ Link Tables commands.

To convert data in an Access table (or other object) for use in another program such as Excel or Word, use the *export* feature. After exporting the

Access data, you can start the other program, open the file you created, and use it normally. To start exporting data from Access to another format, go to the database window and click on the table, query, form, or other object that contains the data you want to export. Then choose File ➤ Save As/Export.

 ➤ Chapter 7 explains how to create Access tables from files stored in these formats: Access, Excel, Paradox, text files, dBASE, FoxPro, Lotus 1-2-3, and ODBC databases. There you'll also learn how to export data from Access to these formats: Access, Excel, Paradox, text, dBASE, FoxPro, Lotus 1-2-3, Rich Text Format, Microsoft Word Merge, and ODBC databases.

Using OLE

Windows 95 OLE technology offers many ways to share selected data or entire files between Microsoft Access, Microsoft Office, and other Windows programs. Chapter 8 provides step-by-step instructions for using these techniques to put data into Access tables, including OLE fields. But let's take a quick peek now at what's available.

Using the Clipboard

The cut-copy-and-paste technique offers a versatile way to exchange selected data between programs. If possible, the original formatting is preserved when you complete the paste operation. (When you paste rows from a Microsoft Access datasheet to another program, the field names also come along for the ride.)

In a nutshell, the cut-copy-and-paste procedure is as follows:

1. Select the object you want to move or copy using the standard selection methods for the program you're copying or moving from.

2. Choose Edit ➤ Copy (Ctrl+C) or Edit ➤ Cut (Ctrl+X), or click on the Copy or Cut toolbar button if it's available. Your selection will be copied (if you chose Copy) or moved (if you chose Cut) to the Windows Clipboard.

N O T E The Windows Clipboard is a scratchpad area in your computer's memory. Each time you copy or cut a selection to the Clipboard, the new selection replaces the previous contents of the Clipboard. Data on the Clipboard usually stays around until you exit Windows.

3. Start the target program and open the document, table, or other object where the copied or moved data should appear. Then put the cursor where the data should appear.

4. To paste the data from the Clipboard, do one of the following steps, and then answer any prompts that appear.

- Choose Edit ➤ Paste (Ctrl+V) or click on the Paste toolbar button.
- Choose Edit ➤ Paste Special (if available), complete the Paste Special dialog box, and then click on OK.
- In Access only, choose Edit ➤ Paste Append to add records to the end of the table shown in the current datasheet or form.

The pasted material will appear on your screen.

Using the Insert Menu Commands

You also can use commands on the Insert menu to insert all or part of an object into the current document, presentation, OLE Object field, or other object. The steps for inserting and the appearance of the inserted data depend on which program you're using when you insert the data, which Insert command you choose, and which type of data you insert.

Here, for example, are the steps for inserting Access table data into a Microsoft Word document. The inserted data becomes a standard Word table that's independent of the original Access table.

1. Start Microsoft Word and open the document that should contain the Access table data.

2. Choose Insert ➤ Database, and then click on the Get Data button.

3. In the Open Data Source dialog box, choose MS Access Databases from the Files Of Type drop-down list, and then locate and double-click on the database you want to use.

4. In the Microsoft Access dialog box, click on the Tables or Queries tab, and then double-click on the table or query that contains the data you want to insert into the document.

5. If you wish, click on the Query Options button to select fields and values to insert. Click on the Table AutoFormat button to choose a format for the inserted data.

6. Click on the Insert Data button, complete the Insert Data dialog box that appears, and then click on OK.

Figure 4.8 shows the screen after we inserted the Employees table data from our sample Order Entry database into a Microsoft Word document. In this example, we chose the Classic 2 Table Autoformat style and hid the table gridlines (Table ➤ Gridlines).

In most Office programs, you can use the Insert ➤ Object command either to insert a new object that you create on the fly, or to insert an existing object that's stored in a file. Chapter 8 takes you through the steps for inserting objects into OLE Object fields in Access, so we won't repeat

FIGURE 4.8

Here we used the Insert ➤ Database command to copy the Employees table data from our sample Order Entry database to a Microsoft Word document.

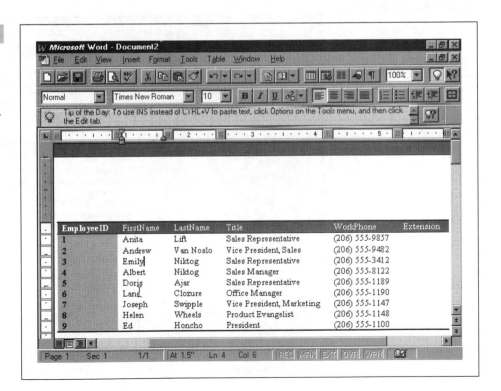

them here. (The steps for inserting an object are similar whether you start from Access, Excel, Exchange, PowerPoint, or Word.)

If the program can do so, it will show the inserted data with its "real" appearance; otherwise, the inserted data will appear as a "package" icon. In Figure 4.9, for example, we inserted the bitmap file named arcade.bmp from the \Windows folder into the Word document from Figure 4.8. Next to the bitmap file, we inserted the Address Book Lessons sample database. Notice that the bitmap file appears as a picture, but the Address Book Lessons database object appears only as a package icon, because Word can't display an entire database at once. To open either inserted object for viewing or editing, simply double-click on the object's picture or icon. When you're done working with the inserted object, do one of the following:

- If the object opened within the main program window, click outside the object. The hashmarks and sizing handles around the

FIGURE 4.9

The Microsoft Word document window after we used Insert ➤ Object commands to insert a bitmap file and an Address Book Lessons database into the document

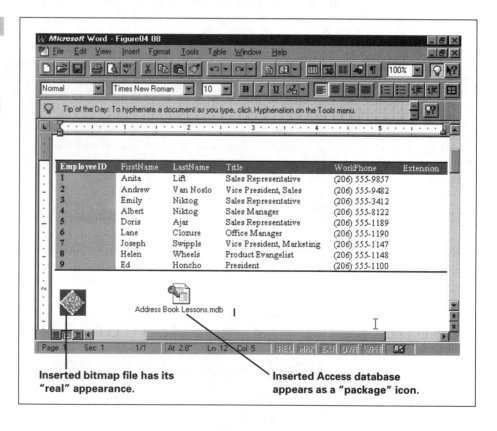

Inserted bitmap file has its "real" appearance.

Inserted Access database appears as a "package" icon.

object will disappear and the main program's tools and menu bar will reappear.

- If the object opened in a separate program window, choose File ➤ Exit from the object's program window. You'll be returned to the main program window.

Dragging and Dropping

The drag-and-drop technique offers a convenient way to copy or move selected data from one open program to another. You can't drag and drop between all Windows programs, but a little experimentation should quickly reveal what's possible. Figure 4.10 shows the basic drag-and-drop procedure. Here's how to reproduce that example:

1. Start Microsoft Word and Microsoft Access, and then open a Word document that contains some text and an Access table that contains an OLE Object field. Next, tile the programs vertically on the screen by right-clicking on an empty area of the windows taskbar and choosing Tile Vertically from the shortcut menu.

FIGURE 4.10

In this example, we dragged and dropped selected text from a Word document to an OLE Object field in an Access table. In datasheet view, the copied text in the OLE Object field appears simply as *Microsoft Word Document*; in a form, however, the copied data will look much as it does in Microsoft Word.

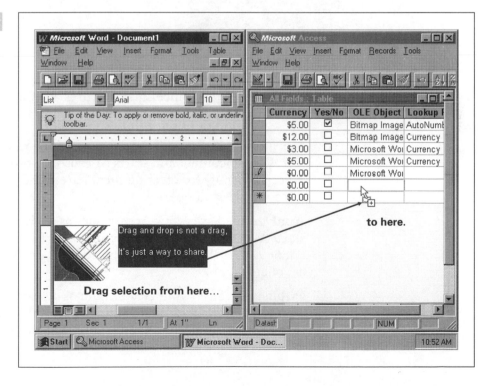

2. In the Microsoft Word document, select the text you want to copy to the Access OLE Object field.

3. Hold down the Ctrl key while dragging the selected text from the Microsoft Word window to the OLE Object field in the Microsoft Access window. When the mouse pointer reaches its destination, release the mouse button and Ctrl key. (These actions will *copy* the selected text to the OLE Object field. To *move* the selection, rather than copy it, do not hold down the Ctrl key while dragging.)

Using OfficeLinks in Access

The OfficeLinks feature in Microsoft Access provides a nifty way to copy Access data to other Microsoft Office program formats and to immediately start the appropriate Office program. To use OfficeLinks, select a table, query, form, or report from the Access database window, and then choose options on the Tools ➤ OfficeLinks menu or the OfficeLinks drop-down toolbar button (shown below).

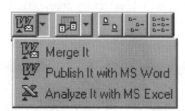

Chapter 7 covers the OfficeLinks features in more detail, but in case you're curious now, your options are:

Merge It Merges your Access data with a new or existing Microsoft Word document and starts Microsoft Word. This feature is especially handy for creating form letters and mailing labels from Access tables and queries.

Analyze It Saves your Access data as a Microsoft Excel file and starts Microsoft Excel. This feature is perfect when you need to examine Access data with the sophisticated analysis features that Excel offers.

Publish It Saves your Access data as a Microsoft Word Rich Text Format (RTF) file and starts Microsoft Word. Use this feature when you want to dress up your Access data or mix it with word processing text and pictures.

Using Access Data from Microsoft Excel

Microsoft Excel and Microsoft Access have a special relationship with one another, because they both can interpret and display data in a tabular row-and-column format. Excel offers several ways to use Access data without ever leaving Excel itself.

NOTE   Chapter 14 explains how to create PivotTables, which are special Excel objects that are embedded within an Access form. To create and use PivotTables that display Access data, you must start from Access, not Excel.

Converting a Worksheet to an Access Table

You can import the current Excel worksheet to an Access table in a new or existing database. After you complete this procedure, the Excel worksheet and imported table will be independent of one another (that is, changes to the worksheet in Excel won't affect the Access table, and vice versa).

To begin the process, open the worksheet you want to convert (in Excel, of course). Then:

1. If your worksheet contains any blank rows, delete those rows. Then put the cursor into any cell within the worksheet.

2. Choose <u>D</u>ata ➤ Con<u>v</u>ert To Access.

3. When prompted, choose whether to convert the data to a <u>N</u>ew Database or an E<u>x</u>isting Database whose name you supply, and then click on OK.

After a brief delay, the Import Spreadsheet Wizard (described in Chapter 17) will guide you through the remaining steps, and your new table will appear in the Tables tab of the Access database window. You can then use the table as you would any normal Access table.

Creating an Access Form or Report from an Excel Worksheet

You also can create an Access form or report for use with the current Excel worksheet. The resulting form or report will reside in the Access database, and the Excel worksheet will be *linked* to a new Access table in that database (that is, changes you make in Excel will update the linked table in Access, and vice versa).

To create the form or report, start from Excel and follow these steps:

1. Open the worksheet you want to view with the form or report. If your worksheet contains any blank rows, delete those rows. Then put the cursor into any cell within the worksheet.

2. To create a form, choose Data ➤ Access Form. To create a report, choose Data ➤ Access Report.

3. If your worksheet isn't already linked to an Access database, you'll see a Create Microsoft Access Form or Create Microsoft Access Report dialog box (an example appears below). Choose whether to store the form or report in a New Database or an Existing Database whose name you supply, choose whether the worksheet has a Header Row or No Header Row, and then click on OK. If you choose to create a new database, the new database will have the same name as your Excel file.

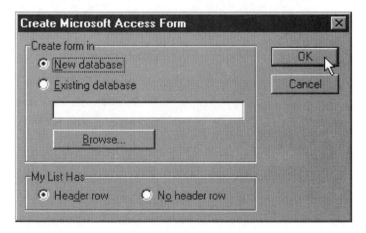

4. When the Form Wizard or Report Wizard takes over, follow its instructions and complete the remaining steps.

Your Excel table will be linked to the Access database, and your new form or report will appear in the Forms or Reports tab of the Access database window and on the screen.

From Access, you can use the linked table and form or report normally. To use the form or report from Excel, click on the View Access Form or View Access Report button that appears near the right edge of your worksheet (see Figure 4.11).

NOTE

From Access, you can add records to linked Excel worksheets and change records, but you cannot delete them. From Excel, you can add and delete worksheet rows and change cell data as you would in any normal worksheet.

FIGURE 4.11

A sample Microsoft Excel spreadsheet named Employees, after we used the Data ➤ Access Form and Data ➤ Access Report commands in Excel. To view the Access form or report without leaving Excel, click on the View Access Form or View Access Report buttons, respectively.

Click on these buttons on the Excel worksheet to view the data from within an Access form or report.

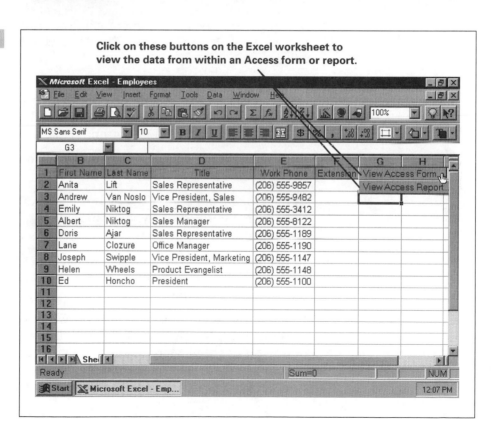

➤ To learn more about the AccessLinks add-in program that creates Access forms and reports (or to find out what to do if the <u>D</u>ata ➤ <u>A</u>ccess Form and <u>D</u>ata ➤ A<u>c</u>cess Report commands don't appear in Excel), look up *AccessLinks Forms And Reports* in the Excel Help Index. See Chapter 7 for more about linking and using Excel worksheets in Access. Chapter 11 explains how to use the Form Wizard, and Chapter 12 covers the Report Wizard.

Using Access Data from Microsoft Word

As we mentioned earlier, you can start from Access and use the Office-Links feature to merge Access data with a new or existing Microsoft Word main document. You also can start from Microsoft Word and merge data from an Access table or query into a form letter, mailing label, envelope, or catalog main document. Here's one way to do the job:

1. Starting from a blank document window in Microsoft Word, choose <u>T</u>ools ➤ Mail Me<u>r</u>ge. The Mail Merge Helper dialog box will appear.

2. In the Mail Merge Helper dialog box, click on the <u>C</u>reate button and select the type of main document you want to create (Form <u>L</u>etters, <u>M</u>ailing Labels, <u>E</u>nvelopes, or <u>C</u>atalog). When prompted, click on the <u>A</u>ctive Window button.

3. In the Mail Merge Helper dialog box, click on the <u>G</u>et Data button, and then choose <u>O</u>pen Data Source.

4. In the Open Data Source dialog box, choose MS Access Databases from the Files Of <u>T</u>ype drop-down list. Then locate and double-click on the database you want to use.

5. In the Microsoft Access dialog box, click on the <u>T</u>ables or Queries tab, and then double-click on the Access table or query that contains the data you want to use.

6. Respond to any prompts that appear. When you reach the main document window in Microsoft Word, use the Insert Merge Field button on the Mail Merge toolbar to insert the merge fields that contain the data you want to display, type any text that should appear between fields, and press ↵ after inserting fields as needed.

Figure 4.12 shows the document window after we added fields and some text for a form letter.

7. To start the merge, choose <u>T</u>ools ➤ Mail Merge (or click on the Merge Helper button on the Mail Merge toolbar), and then click on the <u>M</u>erge button; or, click on the Mail Merge button on the Mail Merge toolbar; or click on the <u>M</u>erge button in the Mail Merge Helper dialog box. Complete the Merge dialog box (shown below), and then click on <u>M</u>erge. Word will merge the latest data from your Access table or query with your main document and output it to the location you specify in the Me<u>r</u>ge To drop-down list.

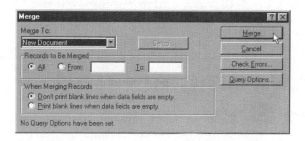

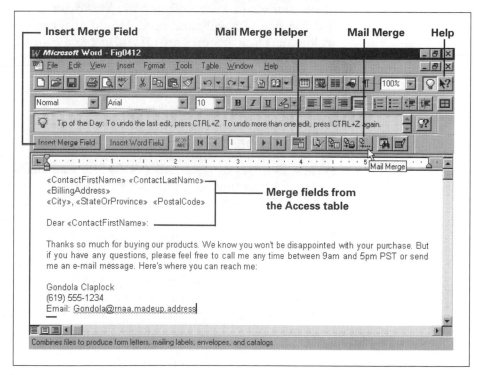

FIGURE 4.12

A sample form letter that uses fields from an Access table

8. When the merge is complete and you've printed the results, close the merged results file without saving it (if you merged to a new document). Save your main document (File ➤ Save) and close it if you wish (File ➤ Close).

The next time you want to merge your main document with the latest Access data, just open the main document in Word (File ➤ Open), and repeat steps 7 and 8 above.

 ➤ If you need help setting up merge fields on your main document, click on the Help button on the Standard toolbar in Microsoft Word, and then click on the Insert Merge Field button on the Mail Merge toolbar. Or, look up *Mail Merge* and its subtopics in the Microsoft Word Help Index.

For Programmers and Techies Only

Two features in Microsoft Access, Microsoft Office, and other programs for Windows 95 will dazzle and delight programmers and application developers. These features are *OLE Automation* and *Visual Basic for Applications*. For a *Readers' Digest* condensation of what this means to you, please read on.

About Visual Basic for Applications (VBA)

Visual Basic for Applications (VBA) offers a consistent programming language for building programs across Microsoft Office, and it replaces the Access Basic language that came with Access 2.0. The beauty of VBA is that you can reuse code written for Access in Microsoft Excel, Visual Basic, or Project with only minor changes.

 ➤ Chapter 25 introduces you to VBA. For online help with the language, look up *Visual Basic* and its subtopics in the Access Help Index. Or, go to the Access Help Contents, double-click on the *Visual Basic For Applications* book, and then explore the additional books and subtopics that appear.

About OLE Automation

OLE Automation is a standard technology that programs use to expose their OLE objects to development tools, macro languages, and other applications that support OLE Automation. From Access, you can use VBA to manipulate OLE Automation objects. You also can use OLE Automation to manipulate Access objects from other programs, such as Microsoft Excel.

 ➤ We'll introduce you to OLE Automation in Chapter 27 of this book. For more information on the topic, look up *OLE Automation* and its subtopics in the Access Help Index.

Where to Go from Here

This chapter has introduced you to the many ways that Microsoft Windows 95, Microsoft Access for Windows 95, and other programs in the Microsoft Office for Windows 95 suite can work together to help you get the most from your Access data. In the next chapter, you'll learn how to create instant databases and ready-to-use applications with just a few clicks of your mouse.

What's New in the Access Zoo?

Some data sharing features such as import and export, OLE, and Office-Links were available in Access 2.0 (although they weren't as easy to use as they are in Access for Windows 95). However, practically everything else covered in this chapter is new and well worth a look.

PART TWO

Creating a
Database

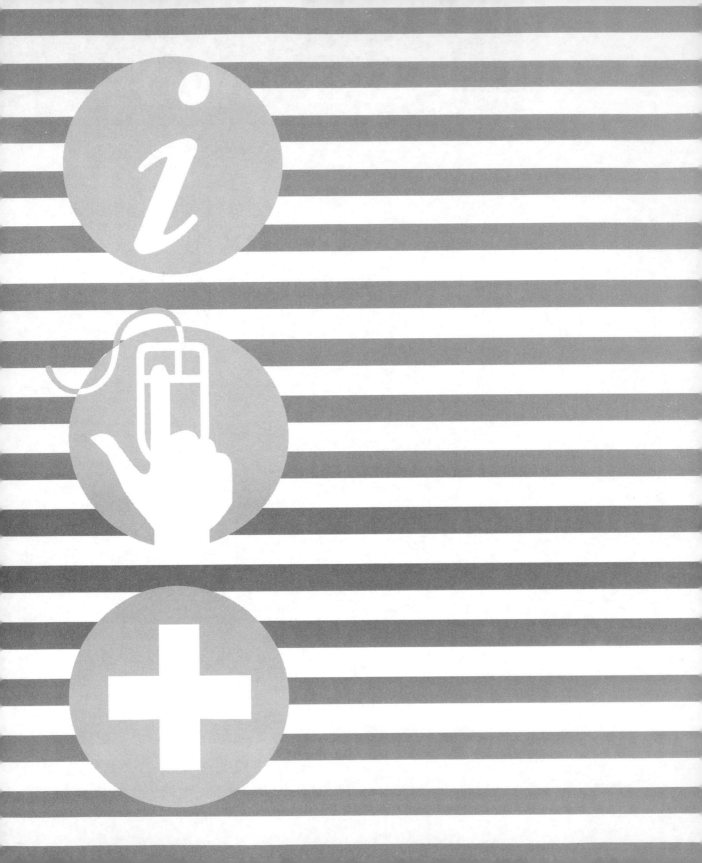

CHAPTER

5

Creating a Database and Application

IT'S terminology time again! An application is a computer-based system that lets you perform useful tasks, such as managing orders, accounts receivable, product inventory, and other types of information. A turnkey application makes it easy to enter and use information with the turn of a key; that is, without worrying about how everything is put together behind the scenes. And an Access database is a file that holds all the objects for a single application, including the tables, forms, reports, queries, modules, and macros. In this chapter, you'll learn how to create databases and more than 20 different turnkey applications.

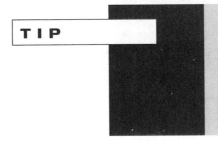

NOTE If you haven't tried the hands-on lessons in Chapter 3, you should do so now. Those lessons take you through creating a database and turnkey application and give you practice using Access Wizards.

TIP After creating your database, you can use the Database Splitter Wizard (Tools ➤ Add-Ins ➤ Database Splitter) to split it into one file that contains the tables, and another that contains the queries, forms, reports, macros, and modules. A split database can be faster to run over a network. See Chapter 18 for details.

A Database Is Not a Table

If you're an experienced "*x*BASE" user, you might think the term *database* is synonymous with the term *table*. However, Access follows the more formal database terminology in which *database* refers to all the data, plus all the objects you use to manage that data.

Remember that you *don't* need to create a new database each time you want to create a table or some other object. Instead, put all the tables and objects that make up a single application into *one* database. That way, objects that belong together will be stored in the same database.

Getting Started

The first step to creating any application is to set up the database file. It's often best to start with a blank database if you plan to import or link most of your tables from data stored in other computer files (see Chapter 7), or you're a developer who prefers to create most database objects from scratch.

Beware! Starting with a blank database can be more work than starting with a Wizard-created database of predefined objects. Taking the from-scratch route usually involves these general steps:

1. Create the blank database (see "Creating a Blank Database" in this chapter).

2. Create, import, or link the tables (see Chapters 6 and 7).

3. Create data entry forms (see Chapters 11 and 13).

4. Enter data using data entry forms or datasheet view (see Chapter 8).

5. Create additional forms, reports, and queries as needed (see Chapters 10–13).

6. Use programming techniques, form buttons, macros, and other tricks to assemble the objects into a turnkey application (see Parts Four and Five).

If you plan to let Access Wizards create your database and application automatically, your work is done almost before you start. In fact, you often can get by with just three main steps:

1. Use the Database Wizard to create a database and a turnkey application (see "Creating a Database with the Database Wizard" in this chapter).

2. Enter data (see Chapter 8).

3. Print reports as needed (see Chapters 3 and 9).

Of course, you might need to tweak the turnkey application throughout its lifetime. The rest of this book will show you how.

TIP

By studying the sample applications created by the Database Wizard, you can more quickly learn techniques for designing and customizing your own applications. For example, you can study database objects in design view to find out what makes those objects tick. You also can study the relationships among tables in the database, using techniques discussed in Chapter 6.

Creating a Blank Database

To create a blank database:

1. Do one of the following:

- If you're starting from the Microsoft Access main menu, choose File ➤ New Database, or press Ctrl+N, or click on the New Database toolbar button (shown at left). You'll see the New dialog box, shown in Figure 5.1.

- If you're at the Microsoft Access startup dialog box (see Chapter 1), choose Blank Database and click on OK. The File New Database dialog box, shown in Figure 5.2, will open. Skip to step 3.

FIGURE 5.1

The New dialog box lets you create a blank database (General tab), or any of more than 20 pre-defined turnkey applications (Databases).

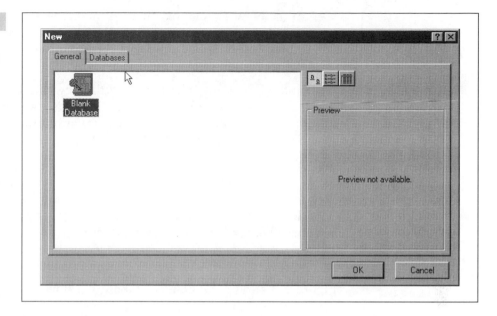

FIGURE 5.2

Use the File New Database dialog box to choose a name and location for your new database. You also can create new folders and delete unwanted databases from this dialog box.

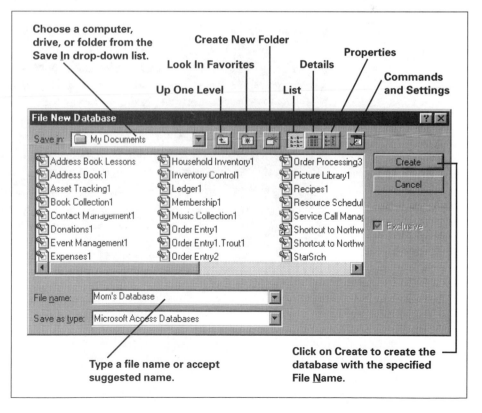

Blank
Database

2. In the New dialog box, click on the General tab (if it's not selected already), and then double-click on the Blank Database icon (shown at left). The File New Database dialog box will open (see Figure 5.2).

3. In the File Name text box, type the new database file name (or accept the suggested name). Your file name can be any length, and it can include spaces and most punctuation marks. Examples: Order Entry, My Videotape Collection, Mom's Database.

4. Access usually suggests that you save the database in a folder named My Documents on drive C. To save the database to a different drive or folder, choose that drive or folder from the Save In drop-down list. For more details, see "Using the File New Database Dialog Box" later in this chapter.

5. Click on the Create button.

Figure 5.3 shows the blank database window that appears next. From here, you can start adding new tables, as explained in Chapter 6.

N O T E

Access databases have the file extension .mdb. However, this extension—like that of most other files on your computer—usually is hidden from view. To show file extensions in dialog boxes that display file names, right-click on the Start button on the taskbar and choose Explore (or double-click on My Computer on the Windows desktop). When the Exploring or My Computer window opens, choose View ➤ Options, click on the View tab in the Options dialog box, deselect (clear) Hide MS-DOS File Extensions For File Types That Are Registered, and click on OK. Close the Exploring or My Computer window.

FIGURE 5.3

The database window
for a new blank
database named
"Mom's Database."

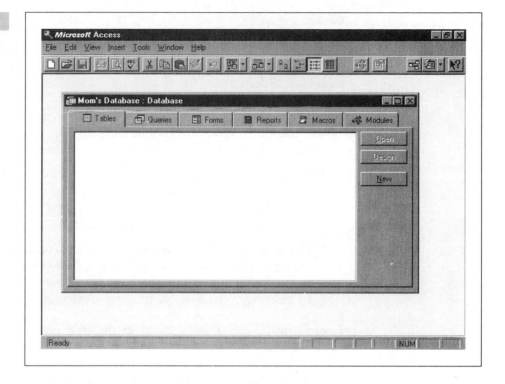

Using the File New Database Dialog Box

The File New Database dialog box (see Figure 5.2) is similar to the Open
dialog box described in Chapter 1, and the easiest way to learn about
this dialog box is to experiment with it. These tips will help you choose a
location and file name for your database:

- **To choose the computer, drive, or folder where the database
  should be stored,** click on the Save In drop-down list button,
  and then click on the appropriate item.

- **To open objects shown in the list below Save In,** double-click
  on the appropriate object icon or name.

- **To open the folder that's just above the currently selected
  folder,** click on the Up One Level toolbar button in the dialog
  box; or click anywhere in the list below Save In, and then press
  Backspace.

TIP

To find out the purpose of any toolbar button in a window or dialog box, move your mouse pointer to that button and look for the ToolTip near the mouse pointer.

- **To display a list of "favorite" databases and folders,** click on the Look In Favorites toolbar button. The list below Save In will then show your favorite folders and databases only.

- **To create a new folder within the current folder,** click on the Create New Folder toolbar button. In the New Folder dialog box that appears, type a folder name, and then click on OK. Open (double-click) the new folder if you wish.

- **To manually enter a drive, directory, and/or file name,** type the appropriate information into the File Name text box at the lower-left corner of the File New Database dialog box; or, choose an item from the File Name drop-down list.

There's much more you can do in the File New Database dialog box. Here are some things to try:

- **To change the appearance of the list below Save In,** click on the List, Details, or Properties toolbar buttons as needed.

- **To explore the current folder** (in Windows Explorer), control folder sharing, display folder properties, and more, right-click on an empty area in the list below Save In, and then choose options from the shortcut menu.

- **To display or change properties** for an item selected in the list below Save In, or control the order in which file names are listed, or map a network drive, click on the Commands And Settings toolbar button and choose a menu option.

- **To manage an existing database file** (for example, cut, copy, delete, rename, or view its properties), right-click on that file in the list below Save In and choose an appropriate option from the shortcut menu.

When you're finished using the File New Database dialog box, click on Create (to create the database shown in the File Name text box), or click on Cancel (to return to Access without creating a database).

Creating a Database with the Database Wizard

Chapter 3 explains how to use the Database Wizard to create a turnkey application for managing address information. Here's the Cliff's Notes version of the steps to follow for creating any of more than 20 turnkey applications in Access:

1. If you're at the Microsoft Access startup dialog box, choose Database Wizard and click on OK. If you're at the main Microsoft Access window, choose File ➤ New Database from the menu bar, or press Ctrl+N, or click on the toolbar's New Database button.

2. In the New dialog box, click on the Databases tab (see Figure 5.4), and then scroll to the icon for the type of information you want to manage. When you've found the icon you want to use, double-click on it.

FIGURE 5.4

The New dialog box with the Databases tab selected.

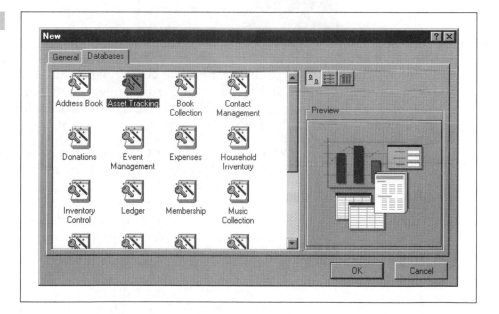

3. The File New Database dialog box will open (see Figure 5.2). In the File Name text box, type a database name (or accept the suggested name). If necessary, choose a drive and folder from the Save In drop-down list. Finally, click on the Create button.

When you complete step 3 above, an empty database window will appear briefly, followed by the first Database Wizard dialog box. Here's how to finish the job:

1. Read the description of the new database in the first Database Wizard dialog box, and then click on Next.

TIP

You'll find standard buttons at the bottom of each Wizard dialog box. These include Cancel (cancels the Wizard and returns to wherever you were before you started the Wizard), Back (returns you to the previous Wizard dialog box), Next (continues to the next Wizard dialog box), and Finish (goes to the last Wizard dialog box and assigns default settings for any dialog boxes you skip).

2. In the second Database Wizard dialog box (see Figure 5.5), use the guidelines below to choose which fields to include in each table and to tell the Wizard whether to include sample data. When you're finished, click on Next to continue with the third Wizard dialog box.

- **To choose a table to work with,** click on the table's name in the tables list at the left. Then, in the fields list at the right, select (check) the fields you want to include, and deselect (clear) fields you want to omit from the table. Optional fields are shown in italics. Required fields are checked initially and shown in normal (roman) type. (You won't be allowed to clear required fields.) Repeat this step as needed.

- **To include sample data,** select the box next to Yes, Include Sample Data. To omit the sample data, deselect that box. Including sample data can help you learn to use the database more quickly. Once you've played with the database a bit,

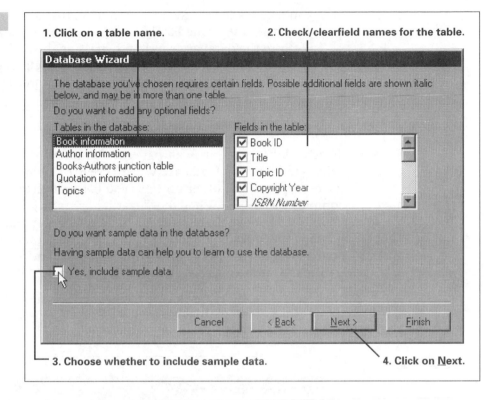

FIGURE 5.5

Use the second
Database Wizard
dialog box to choose
which fields to include
from each predefined
table and whether to
include sample data.

1. Click on a table name.   **2. Check/clearfield names for the table.**

Database Wizard

The database you've chosen requires certain fields. Possible additional fields are shown italic below, and may be in more than one table.

Do you want to add any optional fields?

Tables in the database:

Book information
Author information
Books-Authors junction table
Quotation information
Topics

Fields in the table:

☑ Book ID
☑ Title
☑ Topic ID
☑ Copyright Year
☐ *ISBN Number*

Do you want sample data in the database?

Having sample data can help you to learn to use the database.

☐ Yes, include sample data.

Cancel   < Back   Next >   Finish

3. Choose whether to include sample data.   **4. Click on Next.**

you can delete the sample data; or, delete the database itself, and create a new one without sample data.

3. In the third Database Wizard dialog box, choose a background color and general style for database forms (also called screen displays). The left side of the dialog box will show a sample form that reflects your current choice. Click on the Next button to continue.

4. In the fourth Database Wizard dialog box, choose a style for printed reports. Again, the sample area will reflect your choice. Click on Next to continue.

5. In the fifth Wizard dialog box, you can specify a title for your database and pick a picture for use on reports. (See Chapter 3 for pointers on choosing sample pictures.) After making your selections, click on Next to go to the last dialog box.

6. In the last dialog box, choose whether you want to start the database after the Wizard builds it. If you check Yes, Start The Database,

you'll be taken to a Switchboard form that lets you work with your database immediately; if you clear this option, you'll go directly to the database window, bypassing the Switchboard. You also can choose whether to display online help about using a database. Again, refer to Chapter 3 if you need more details.

7. Click on the Finish button to create the database and its turnkey application form, named Switchboard.

That's all there is to it. Wait patiently for a few moments while the disk drive whirls and the Database Wizard creates an entire database of tables, forms, reports, and other objects (you'll see progress bars as the Wizard completes its tasks). When the Wizard finishes its job, you'll either see the main Switchboard form for your database or the database window, depending on your choice in step 6. Figure 5.6 shows the sample Switchboard form for the Book Collection database, and Figure 5.7 shows the Tables tab on the database window for this same database.

Now you're ready to explore your new database and fill it with useful information.

FIGURE 5.6

The Switchboard for a Book Collection database created by the Database Wizard

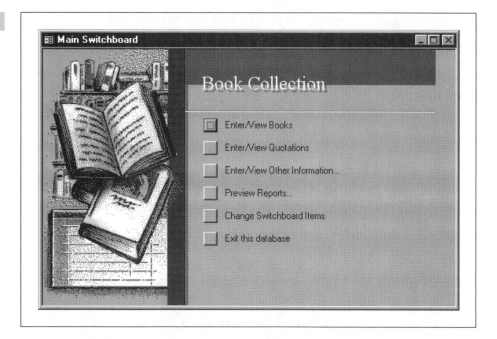

FIGURE 5.7

The Tables tab of the database window for the Book Collection database

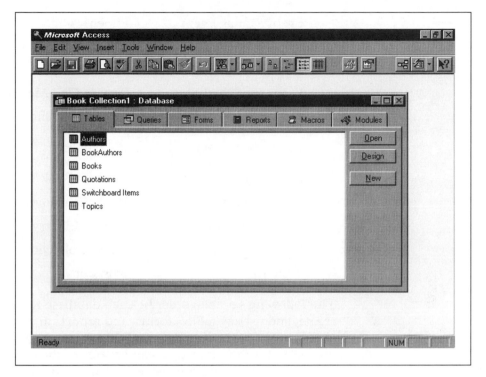

 The next section explains a little about each database that the Wizard can create automatically. For information on three other sample database applications that come with Access, look up Sample Databases And Applications in the Access Help Index. Not sure how to navigate the database window? See Chapter 1 for help. Finally, refer to Chapter 3 for pointers on perusing a new turnkey application.

About the Sample Databases

If you already have an application in mind, there's a good chance that Access can set it up for you automatically. The Database Wizard can create these business and education databases...

Blank Database	Asset Tracking
Contact Management	Donations

Event Management	Expenses
Inventory Control	Ledger
Membership	Order Entry
Resource Scheduling	Service Call Management
Students and Classes	Time and Billing

...and these personal and household databases...

Blank Database	Address Book
Book Collection	Household Inventory
Music Collection	Picture Library
Recipes	Video Collection
Wine List	Workout

The following sections describe each database the Database Wizard can create, and list key tables, forms, and reports in each database. (Pay special attention to the Key Reports listed, because they give you clues about the kind of information you can get out of the database.) The brief descriptions presented here can help you decide which databases you can use right out of the box, and which you can use as a starting point for your own custom databases.

Rather than listing every table, form, and report in each database, we've described key objects only. In general, it's best to use the Switchboard forms—and not the database window—to maintain data, fill in forms, and print reports in these databases. Certain reports, such as invoices and purchase orders, aren't listed in the Key Reports sections below, because you must click on a button on a form in order to preview and print those reports properly. You'll find an asterisk followed by the type of report printed—for example, (*Invoice)—next to the names of key forms that have special "Preview/Print" buttons.

TIP

You'll also find these databases—complete with sample data—on the CD-ROM disk that accompanies this book. See Appendix B for details.

Blank Database

Blank
Database

This is the database for Access application developers and other people who wish to create objects from scratch, or who want to import or link objects from other computer databases (see Chapter 7).

> **Key Tables**   None.
>
> **Key Forms**   None.
>
> **Key Reports**   None.

Address Book

Address Book

Use the Address Book database to keep track of names, addresses, phone numbers, and other vital statistics. Chapter 3 took you on a step-by-step tour of this database and showed you how to customize it.

> **Key Tables**   Addresses.
>
> **Key Forms**   Addresses.
>
> **Key Reports**   Addresses By Last Name, Birthdays This Month, Fact Sheet, Greeting Card List.

Asset Tracking

Asset Tracking

Use the Asset Tracking database to track information about your company's assets. Great for businesses that own valuable stuff!

> **Key Tables**   Asset Categories, Assets, Depreciation, Employees, Maintenance, Status.
>
> **Key Forms**   Asset Categories, Assets, Employees, Status.
>
> **Key Reports**   Assets By Category, Assets By Date Acquired, Assets By Employee, Depreciation Summary, Maintenance History.

Book Collection

Book
Collection

Bibliophiles, students, teachers, and librarians will love the Book Collection database, which lets you keep track of your favorite books, authors, and quotations.

> **Key Tables**   Authors, Books, Quotations, Topics.
>
> **Key Forms**   Authors, Books, Quotations, Topics.

> **Key Reports**   Quotes By Author, Titles By Author, Titles By Topic.

Contact Management

Contact
Management

Everyone who hands you a business card or buys you lunch is a potentially valuable contact. Use the Contact Management database to record information about your contacts, track phone calls you make to them, and dial calls automatically using your computer's modem.

> **Key Tables**   Calls, Contact Types, Contacts.
>
> **Key Forms**   Contact Types, Contacts.
>
> **Key Reports**   Alphabetical Contact Listing, Weekly Call Summary.

Donations

Donations

Charitable organizations, non-profit corporations, and starving book authors can use the Donations database to track contributions and fund-raising campaigns.

> **Key Tables**   Contributors, Donation Campaign Setup, Pledges.
>
> **Key Forms**   Campaign Information, Contributors.
>
> **Key Reports**   Campaign Summary, Pledge Listing, Unpaid Pledges.

Event Management

Event
Mangement

Managing administrative details for large events such as seminars, training classes, meetings, and concerts is a snap with the Event Management database.

> **Key Tables**   Attendees, Employees, Event Types, Events, Fee Schedules, My Company Information, Payment Methods, Payments, Registration.
>
> **Key Forms**   Attendees (*Invoice), Employees, Event Types, Events, Fee Schedules, My Company Information, Payment Methods.
>
> **Key Reports**   Attendees Listing, Sales By Employee, Sales By Event.

Expenses

Expenses

Filling out employee expense reports is easy when you use the Expenses database to do the job. Throw those tedious paper forms in the recycling bin, and fill out those expense reports quickly on your computer.

Key Tables   Employees, Expense Categories, Expense Details, Expense Reports.

Key Forms   Expense Reports By Employee (*Expense Report), Expense Categories.

Key Reports   Expense Report, Expense Rpt Summary By Category, Expense Rpt Summary By Employee.

Household Inventory

Household Inventory

Perfect for insurance purposes, the Household Inventory database helps you keep a room by room inventory of every valuable item in your home. (Be sure to keep a backup copy of this database in your bank safety deposit box or some other place that will be secure in case a natural—or unnatural—disaster strikes.)

Key Tables   Categories, Household Inventory, Rooms.

Key Forms   Categories, Household Inventory, Rooms.

Key Reports   Inventory By Category, Inventory By Room, Inventory By Value, Inventory Details.

Inventory Control

Inventory Control

The Inventory Control database offers everything you'll need to manage your company's product inventory.

Key Tables   Categories, Employees, Inventory Transactions, My Company Information, Products, Purchase Orders, Shipping Methods, Suppliers.

Key Forms   Categories, Employees, My Company Information, Products (*Purchase Order), Shipping Methods, Suppliers.

Key Reports   Product Cost Comparisons, Product Purchases By Supplier, Product Summary, Product Transaction Detail.

Ledger

Ledger

Use the Ledger database to maintain a chart of accounts and transactions against each account.

> **Key Tables** Account Types, Accounts, Transactions.
>
> **Key Forms** Account Types, Accounts, Transactions.
>
> **Key Reports** Account Summary, Summary By Account Type, Transaction Listing.

Membership

Membership

The Membership database is perfect for organizations that must track information about members, committees, and dues payments.

> **Key Tables** Committees, Members, Member Types, My Organization Information, Payment Methods, Payments.
>
> **Key Forms** Committees, Member Types, Members (*Invoice), My Organization's Information, Payment Methods.
>
> **Key Reports** Alphabetical Member Listing, Committee Members, Invoice, Listing By Membership Type, Outstanding Balances.

Music Collection

Music Collection

If you're a music fan with many recordings in your library, you can use the Music Collection database to store information about your albums/CDs, favorite recording artists, and the locations of your best-liked music.

> **Key Tables** Music Categories, Recording Artists, Recordings, Tracks.
>
> **Key Forms** Music Categories, Recording Artists, Recordings.
>
> **Key Reports** Albums By Artist, Albums By Category, Albums By Format, Tracks By Album.

Order Entry

Order Entry

If your business processes orders from customers, you'll want to try the Order Entry database, which has all the tools you need for managing customer, product, order, payment, and shipping information.

Key Tables Customers, Employees, My Company Information, Order Details, Orders, Payment Methods, Payments, Products, Shipping Methods.

Key Forms Employees, My Company Information, Orders By Customer (*Invoice), Payment Methods, Products, Shipping Methods.

Key Reports Customer Listing, Receivables Aging, Sales By Customer, Sales By Employee, Sales By Product.

Picture Library

Picture Library

Photography buffs can use the Picture Library database to list and describe pictures on each roll of film in your library. Great for tracking the thousands of shots you took at the Louvre!

Key Tables Photo Locations, Photographs, Rolls Of Film.

Key Forms Photo Locations, Rolls Of Film.

Key Reports Photographs By Date Taken, Photographs By Film Roll, Photographs By Location, Photographs By Subject.

Recipes

Recipes

If you use the Recipes database, you'll never have to wonder where you stashed your recipes for Cheez Whiz a la Orange and Twinkies Au Gratin. This database makes planning, shopping for, and whipping up nourishing meals such as these easier than ever before.

Key Tables Food Categories, Ingredients, Recipes.

Key Forms Food Categories, Ingredients, Recipes.

Key Reports Recipe Details, Recipes (Sorted Alphabetically), Recipes By Category.

Resource Scheduling

Resource Scheduling

Use the Resource Scheduling database to schedule the use of company resources such as meeting rooms, cars, overhead projectors, airplanes, and other equipment, and to assign each resource for use with a certain customer at a specific time.

Key Tables Customers, Resource Types, Resources, Schedule, Schedule Details.

Key Forms Customers, Reservations, Resources Types, Resources.

Key Reports Resource Schedule, Resources By Type.

Service Call Management

Service Call Management

Service companies that send technicians to customer sites can use the Service Call Management database to track customers, employees, work orders, invoices, payments, and more.

Key Tables Customers, Employees, My Company Information, Parts, Payment Methods, Payments, Workorder Labor, Workorder Parts, Workorders.

Key Forms Employees, My Company Information, Parts, Payment Methods, Workorders By Customer (*Invoice).

Key Reports Finished Workorders In House, Revenue Entered By Employee, Sales By Month, Unfinished Workorders, Workorder Summary.

Students and Classes

Students and Classes

Teachers and school administrators will like using the Students and Classes database to track students, classes, assignments, and grades.

Key Tables Assignments, Classes, Departments, Instructors, Students.

Key Forms Classes, Departments, Instructors, Students.

Key Reports Class Listing By Department, Class Results Summary, Results By Assignment, Results By Student, Student Schedules, Students.

Time and Billing

Time and Billing

The Time and Billing database can help consultants, lawyers, and other professionals who bill their time by the hour to manage their businesses more efficiently.

Key Tables   Clients, Employees, Expense Codes, My Company Information, Payment Methods, Payments, Projects, Time Card Expenses, Time Card Hours, Work Codes.

Key Forms   Clients (*Invoice), Employees, Expense Codes, My Company Information, Payment Methods, Time Cards (*Time Sheet), Work Codes.

Key Reports   Client Billings By Project, Client Listing, Employee Billings By Project, Project Billings By Work Code.

Video Collection

Video Collection

The Video Collection database can help film and television aficionados avoid being buried in the brown tape of a large video library. Use this database to store information about videotaped programs and movies.

Key Tables   Actors, Program Types, Video Programs, Videotapes.

Key Forms   Actors, Program Types, Videotapes.

Key Reports   Alphabetical Program Listing, Program Listing By Actor, Program Listing By Type.

Wine List

Wine List

Oenophiles rejoice! The Wine List database can help you keep your wine cellar inventory under control. Never again will you confuse that mellow Muscat Canclli with a fine Fume Blanc, and you'll always know the vital statistics of each precious bottle.

Key Tables   Wine List, Wine Purchascs, Wine Types.

Key Forms   Wine List, Wine Types.

Key Reports   Wine By Type, Wine by Vintage, Wine By Vintner.

Workout

Workout

Tracking each activity in your exercise regimen and each day's progress toward physical perfection is no sweat with the Workout database.

Key Tables   Exercise Types, Exercises, Units, Workout Details, Workout History, Workouts.

Key Forms   Exercise Types, Exercises, Units, Workout History, Workouts.

Key Reports   Exercise Listing By Type, Workout History By Exercise, Workout Stats By Month.

Changing the Database Properties

You can view, change, and define properties for your database by choosing File ➤ Database Properties from the menu bar, or by right-clicking on the database window's title bar (or any gray area on the database window) and choosing Database Properties. Figure 5.8 shows the database properties for an Order Entry database that we created with the Database Wizard. Here's what the tabs in the dialog box are for:

General   Displays general information about the database.

Summary   Displays and lets you change summary information (see Figure 5.8).

Statistics   Displays file statistics, including date created, modified, accessed, and printed.

Contents   Lists all the tables, queries, forms, reports, macros, and modules in the database.

Custom   Displays and lets you add and delete custom properties that can help you find a database quickly.

Click on the appropriate tab in the Properties dialog box, and then view and change the properties as needed. When you're finished, click on OK to return to the database.

Why customize database properties? Because you can use them later to find a database if you've forgotten its file name or location. To look for and open a database based on its properties, choose the File ➤ Open... commands in Microsoft Access, Word, or Excel. When the Open dialog box appears, click on the Advanced button, specify the properties you want to look for in the Define More Criteria area of the dialog box, and then click on the Find Now button.

FIGURE 5.8

The database properties for the sample Order Entry database, with the Summary tab selected

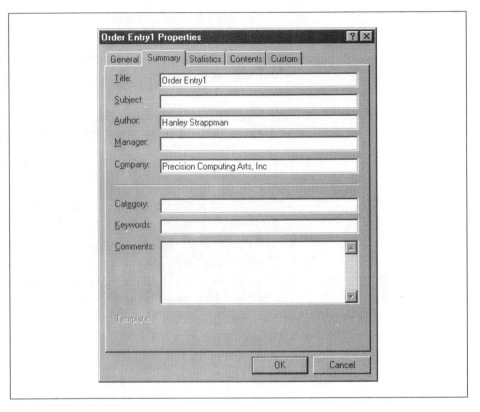

 ➤ To learn more about database properties, search for the Properties, Database topic and its subtopics in the Access Help Index. For details about searching for specific database properties in the Open dialog box, look up Advanced Find Dialog Box in the Help Index.

Where to Go from Here

Once you've set up a database, you can start using it. For your next stop, go to the following chapters in this book:

- If you created a blank database and none of your data exists on a computer already, continue with Chapter 6.

- If you created a blank database and some or all of your data exists on a computer already, continue with Chapter 7.

- If you used the Database Wizard to create a database, continue with Chapter 8.

What's New in the Access Zoo?

Creating databases is easier and more flexible now than it was in Access 2.0. Major improvements include these:

- The Database Wizard lets you create complete applications in nearly two dozen categories, from Asset Tracking to Workout.

- The File ➤ Database Properties command lets you display and change database properties.

- The File New Database dialog box lets you specify a new database name and location, create folders, and manage database files.

Creating
Access Tables

ALL the data you want to manage with Access must be stored in tables. If the data you want to work with is already stored in a computer database somewhere, you probably can use Access to get at it, as Chapter 7 explains. But if the data exists on paper only, or it isn't available yet, or it's in a format that Access can't import or link, your first step is to structure tables that will store the data. This chapter is all about creating tables.

NOTE If you used the Database Wizard to create a database, you can skip this chapter and continue with Chapter 8 to learn more about entering data into your tables. You can always return to this chapter later if you need to add, change, or delete table fields.

 ➤ If you'd like to review or dive more deeply into topics covered in this chapter, go to the Access Contents, open the *Creating, Importing, And Linking Tables* book, and then explore the subtopics. For hands-on practice with creating and opening a database and its tables, see Chapter 3.

Creating the Database

If you haven't done so already, you must create a database to store your tables, as explained in Chapter 5. If you have created a database already, be sure to open that database (see Chapter 1).

NOTE Remember, a table is *not* the same as a database. A database can contain any number of tables. So don't create a new database each time you want to create a table. As long as your new tables are related to other tables in the current database in some way, you should continue to add those new tables to the current database.

Using the Table Wizard to Create Tables

Want a table in a hurry? Then follow these steps for using the Access Table Wizard:

 1. In the database window, click on the Tables tab, and then click on the <u>N</u>ew button. Or, click on the drop-down arrow on the New Object toolbar button (shown at left) and choose New Table. Or, choose <u>I</u>nsert ➤ <u>T</u>able. You'll see this New Table dialog box next:

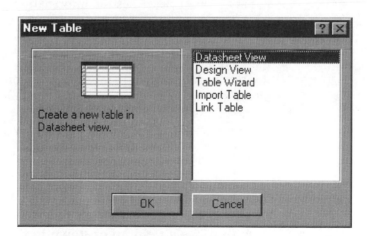

2. Double-click on Table Wizard. You'll be taken to the Table Wizard dialog box, shown in Figure 6.1.

FIGURE 6.1

The Table Wizard dialog box will help you create a table.

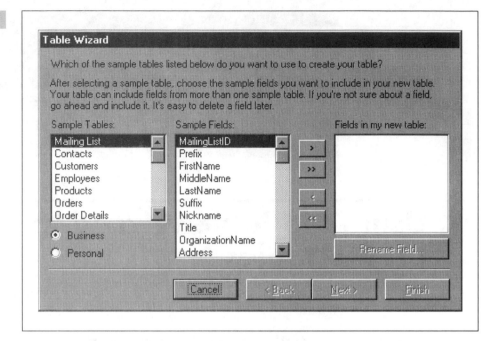

3. Choose either Business or Personal from the option buttons.

4. Scroll through the list of tables, and then click on the sample table name that best describes the information you want to store (Mailing List, Contacts, Customers, or whatever).

5. For each field you want to include in the table, click on a field name in the Sample Fields list, and then click on the > button (or double-click on a field name). Or, click on the >> button to copy all the sample fields to your table. The field names will be copied to the Fields In My New Table List in the order you specify. Here are some ways to manage the Fields In My New Table list:

   - **To delete a field**, click on that field in the Fields In My New Table list, and then click on the < button.

   - **To delete all fields in the Fields In My New Table list**, click on the << button.

   - **To move a field up or down in the list,** first delete that field from the Fields In My New Table list. Next, in the Fields In My New Table list, click on the place where the field should appear. Finally, double-click on the appropriate field name in the Sample Fields list.

- **To change a field's name,** click on that field in the Fields In My New Table list, click on the Rename Field button, type a new name for the field, and then click on OK.

T I P

As for all the Wizards, you can click on the <u>B</u>ack button to back up to a previous dialog box, <u>N</u>ext to continue to the next dialog box, <u>F</u>inish to zip to the finish line, and Cancel to exit the Wizard without creating the table. Always look at each Wizard dialog box carefully for previews, tips, and other information that will help you decide what choices to make and what to do next.

6. When the Fields In My New Table list contains the fields you want to include in your table, click on the <u>N</u>ext button.

7. The next dialog box suggests a name for the new table. You can leave this name unchanged (if a table with this name doesn't already exist in the database), or type a new name. See the sidebar on "Object Naming Rules" for details about how to name tables and other objects.

8. The dialog box that asks for a table name also asks what you want to do about assigning a primary key. You have two options:

    - **To have Access make the decision for you** (the easiest method), select Yes, Set A Primary Key For Me, and click on <u>N</u>ext.

    - **To make your own decisions about the primary key,** select No, I'll Set The Primary Key, and click on <u>N</u>ext. In the next dialog box, choose from the drop-down list whichever field will be unique for each record. You'll also need to tell Access which type of data the primary key field will contain (numbers that Access assigns, numbers that you enter when you add new records, or numbers and/or letters that you enter when you add new records). When you're done choosing primary key options, click on <u>N</u>ext.

NOTE If you're not sure about how to handle primary key fields just now, don't worry about it. Select Yes, Set A Primary Key For Me in step 8 and click on Next. You'll learn more about primary keys later in this chapter, under "Setting a Primary Key."

9. If there's already at least one table in your database, you'll be asked to specify whether your new table is related to other tables in your database. Here's what you can do:

   - **If you're not sure about the table relationships,** click on Next to continue with the next dialog box for now. You can define relationships later, if necessary, when you understand more about them. "Defining Relationships Among Tables," later in the chapter, explains relationships and shows how to define them anytime.

   - **If you do know which relationships you want to define** between the table you're creating and another table that already exists in the database, click on the related table in the list, and then click on the Relationships button. In the next dialog box, tell Access how your new table is related to the existing table, and click on OK. Repeat this step until you've defined all the relationships you want, and then click on Next.

10. In the last dialog box (which displays a checkered flag), tell the Wizard what to do after creating the table. Then click on the Finish button to create the table.

You'll be taken to the table design window, or to the datasheet view, or to a form, depending on your choice in step 10. To return to the database window now:

   - Choose File ➤ Close from the Access menu bar, or click on the Close button on the window that appears, or press Ctrl+W. If you're prompted to save your changes, click on Yes or No, as appropriate.

Object Naming Rules

Access gives you considerable freedom when assigning names to tables, table fields, forms, reports, queries, macros, and modules. Still, it will complain if you don't follow the naming rules, which are as follows:

- The name cannot be the same as any other object of the same type within the database. For example, you can't have two tables named MailingList; however, it's OK to have one table named MailingList1 and another named MailingList2.

- You cannot give a table and a query the same name.

- When naming a field, control, or object, make sure your name isn't the same as the name of a property or other element that Access is already using. This is especially important if you're writing Visual Basic code.

- The name can be up to 64 characters, including spaces. However, the name cannot start with a space.

- The name can include any combination of letters, numbers, and spaces.

- The name can include punctuation characters, *except* a period (.), an exclamation mark (!), an accent grave (`), or brackets ([ ]).

- If you plan to write programs for use with your database, avoid using spaces in object names. For example, use *CustomerInfo* instead of *Customer Info* (for a table name) or *LastName* instead of *Last Name* (for a field name). Programming is easier when the object names do not include spaces.

- The name cannot include control characters (ASCII 00 to ASCII 31).

- When naming fields, avoid choosing names that are the same as built-in Access function names or property names. Strange things may happen if you do.

For more about naming rules, look up *Naming Rules* in the Access Answer Wizard, and then double-click on appropriate subtopics. For a complete list of Microsoft Access specifications, look up *Specifications* in the Access Answer Wizard, and then double-click on *Look Up Microsoft Access Specifications* under *How Do I*.

NOTE When you use the Table Wizard to create a table, Access automatically sets up *input masks* for certain fields (such as those that store telephone and fax numbers, postal codes, and dates). Input masks make data entry easier by controlling where data is entered, what kind of data is allowed, and how many characters you can enter. There's more about input masks later in this chapter.

We'll talk about the table design window and ways to change a table's structure later in this chapter. But first, let's look at ways to create a table without a Wizard. The process begins with planning a table from scratch.

Planning a Table from Scratch

Instead of using the Table Wizard to create a table, you can plan and create a table from scratch. Your first step is to decide which fields to include in your table. If you're working from a fill-in-the-blank paper form, this task can be easy. Generally speaking, you can create one field for every "blank" on the fill-in-the-blank form. An accountant, for example, might create a table that has a field for each blank on a Federal 1040 tax form. There's one catch to this one-blank, one-field approach: You generally *should not* include fields that contain the results of calculations. Why not? Read on.

Do Not Include Calculated Fields

Access can perform instant, accurate calculations on any data in your table, and then display the results in queries, forms, and reports (which you'll learn about in upcoming chapters). So, for best results, *do not create* fields that store the results of a calculation. Here are the potential problems with storing calculation results in the table:

- You risk printing faulty totals or results that aren't based on up-to-the-minute data.

- You're wasting disk space. After all, there's no need to store what Access can calculate on-the-fly for you.

- You'll need to do the calculations yourself. Unless you're some kind of human calculator, doing the calculations yourself is a waste of time and can lead to errors.

In short, tables should contain raw data only—just the numbers you'll need to base calculations on later—and not the results of any calculations.

Creating a Table without Using a Wizard

Follow these steps to create the table from scratch, without using the Table Wizard:

1. Click on the Tables tab on the database window, and then click on the <u>N</u>ew button. Or, click on the drop-down arrow on the New Object toolbar button, and choose New Table. Or, choose <u>I</u>nsert ➤ <u>T</u>able.

2. Double-click on Design View in the New Table dialog box that appears next.

NOTE   Chapter 8 explains how to define fields simply by entering data into a blank datasheet; it also explains how to add, rename, and delete fields from datasheet view.

You'll be taken to the table design window (see Figure 6.2), where you tell Access which fields will go into the table.

FIGURE 6.2

Use the table design window to define the name, data type, and properties of all fields in a table.

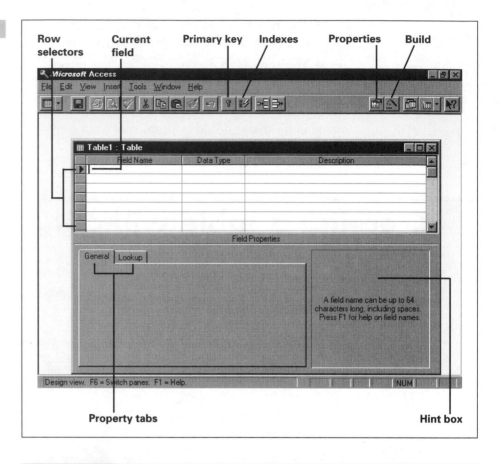

> **TIP**
>
> You might want to use the Table Wizard to set up a table that's almost like the one you want. Then, right-click on the table name, choose Design, and use the techniques described in this chapter to tweak the table structure to perfection.

Defining a Table's Fields

Next you must define the fields in your table, by following the steps below. As you define the fields, glance at the hint box in the table design window for guidance. (You also can press F1 for more information as you follow each step.)

1. In the Field Name column, type a field name (up to 64 characters including blank spaces). Field names must follow the rules given earlier in this chapter (see the sidebar titled "Object Naming Rules").

2. Click on the Data Type column next to the field name, and select the appropriate data type from the drop-down list. (See "Choosing Appropriate Data Types" below for more information.)

3. Click on the Description column, and type a description of the field (a description is optional, but very helpful). This description will appear on the status bar later, when you're entering data.

4. If you wish, click on the General or Lookup tab in the Field Properties area and set properties for the field you're defining. See "Setting Field Properties" later in this chapter.

5. Repeat steps 1–4, putting each field definition on its own row, until you've defined all the fields in your table.

When you've finished defining the table's fields, save the table structure as discussed shortly, under "Saving a Table Structure."

TIP

If you prefer to let a Wizard guide you through setting up a field, click in the Field Name column where you want the new field to appear. Then, right-click and choose Field Builder from the shortcut menu or click on the Build toolbar button (see Figure 6.2). The Field Builder will guide you through the remaining steps.

Choosing Appropriate Data Types

Access can store different types of information in different formats. So when you're defining a table without a Wizard, you must think about what type of information will be stored in each field.

To define the data type of a field, click in the Data Type column next to the field name, and then click on the drop-down list button that appears.

You'll see the list shown below, and you can select a data type by clicking on it. Table 6.1 summarizes the data types you can choose.

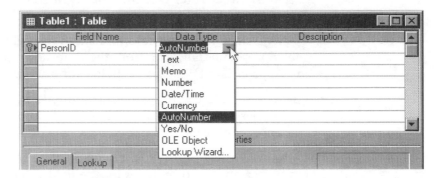

TIP

Be sure to assign the Text data type—rather than the Number data type—to fields such as telephone numbers, fax numbers, postal codes, and e-mail addresses. Unlike the Number data type, the Text data type lets you enter punctuation characters and letters, as in these examples: *(520)555-5947* for a telephone or fax number; *73444,2330* or *Hanley@RNAA47.com* for an e-mail address; *85711-1234* or *H3A3G2* for postal codes.

TABLE 6.1: Access Data Types

DATA TYPE	STORES
AutoNumber	A number that's assigned automatically, and never changes again. *Tip:* Use the New Values property on the General tab to control whether numbers are assigned incrementally or randomly.
Currency	Dollar amounts.
Date/Time	Dates (e.g. 12/31/96) and times. *Tip:* Use the Format property on the General tab to control the appearance of the date.

TABLE 6.1: Access Data Types (continued)

DATA TYPE	STORES
Lookup	Values that come from another table, a query, or a list of values you supply. *Tip:* Use the Lookup tab properties to define a lookup field, or choose the Lookup Wizard data type to set up the lookup field automatically.
Memo	Large bodies of text up to 64,000 characters in length.
Number	True numbers such as quantities. *Tip:* Use the Field Size, Format, and Decimal Places field properties on the General tab to control the size and appearance of numbers.
OLE Object	Any OLE object such as a picture, sound, or word processing document.
Text	Any written text up to 255 characters in length, numbers that you won't be using in arithmetic calculations, and certain "number-like" codes such as zip codes, phone numbers, or product codes that contain letters, hyphens, or other nonnumeric characters.
Yes/No	A "true" or "false" value only. *Tip:* Use the Format property on the General tab and the Display Control property on the Lookup tab to control the appearance of the field's contents.

To learn more about how to decide what data type to use for fields in a table, click in the Data Type column on the table design window and press F1. Or, search for *Data Types* topics and subtopics in the Access Help Index.

Defining Field Properties

You can change a field's properties (characteristics) using options on the General and Lookup tabs below the Field Properties area in the table design window's lower pane. Different data types offer different properties.

WARNING The Field Properties area of the table design window shows the field properties for only one field at a time. Check to make sure the ➤ symbol on the row selector is pointing to the appropriate field name in the upper pane before you change properties in the lower pane.

To set a property for a field, follow these steps:

1. Select the appropriate field in the table design window's upper pane.

2. Click on the appropriate tab (General or Lookup) in the Field Properties area in the table design window's lower pane.

3. Click in the box next to the property you want to set.

4. Do any of the following:

   • Type a value for the property.

   • Click on the drop-down arrow (if one appears) next to the property and click on an option in the list that appears. For properties that offer a drop-down list, you also can double-click on the appropriate property box to cycle through the available values for that property.

   • Click on the Build (...) button if one appears, or right-click on the field and choose Build, for help in setting the property.

 ➤ You can get immediate help as you define field properties by pressing F1. You also can search for *Fields, Properties* in the Access Help Index.

Important General Field Properties

Here (in alphabetical order) are the most important field properties on the General tab (we'll get to the Lookup properties later in this chapter):

Allow Zero Length   If Yes, the field will accept an "empty string" as a valid entry, even if the Required property is set to Yes. That empty string will appear as two quotation marks with nothing in between ("") when first typed into the field; those quotation marks will disappear when you move the cursor to another field.

Caption   Lets you define an alternative name for the field, to be used in datasheet view and as labels when you create forms and reports. The caption offers a handy way to make your datasheet columns and labels more readable when field names do not contain spaces. *Example:* If you've named a field *LastName*, specify that field's Caption property as the more readable text *Last Name*.

Decimal Places   Lets you specify the number of digits to the right of the decimal separator in a numeric field. Choose "Auto" to have the Format property determine the number of decimal places automatically.

Default Value   Lets you define a value that's automatically inserted into the field; you can type a different value during data entry, if necessary. (See Table 6.2 for examples.) The default value for a Text field is the empty string; for a Number or Currency field, it's 0.

Field Size   Lets you specify the maximum length of text allowed into the field, or the acceptable range of numbers. The default size for text is 50 and for numbers is Long Integer, although you can change these settings by choosing Tools ➤ Options, clicking on the Tables/Queries tab, and changing values in the boxes under Default Field Sizes (see Chapter 15).

TABLE 6.2: Examples of Default Values You Can Assign to a Field in the Default Value Property

DEFAULT VALUE	FILLS FIELD WITH
=Date( )	Today's date (use the Date/Time data type)★
=Now( )	Current date and time (use the Date/Time data type)★
0	The number zero (use with Number and Currency data types)
Yes	A "true" setting (use with Yes/No data type)
No	A "false" setting (use with Yes/No data type)
CA	The letters CA (for a Text field that defines the two-letter state abbreviation for California, used in the United States)

★ Use the Format property on the General tab to determine the appearance of the field's contents.

NOTE Access *doesn't* pad text that's shorter than its allotted width to fill out the rest of the field. Hence, there's no disk consumption penalty for making the size of a Text field wider than it needs to be. However, a smaller maximum field size can conserve memory and speed up processing.

Format   Lets you define the appearance of data in the field.

Indexed   Lets you choose whether to index this field, and whether to allow duplicates in the index. See "Defining Indexes," later in this chapter for more details.

Input Mask   Lets you define a pattern for entering data into the field. For help with creating the mask for a text or date/time field, click on the Build (...) button after selecting this property. The Input Mask Wizard will guide you through each step. You also can press F1 for help when the cursor is in the Input Mask property box.

Required   If set to Yes, the field cannot be left blank.

Validation Rule   Lets you create an *expression* that tests data as it comes into the field, and rejects faulty entries. (See Table 6.3 for examples.)

TIP In addition to specifying a validation rule, you can limit the entry in a field to values from another table. To do so, you can: 1) define relationships between tables; 2) define lookup fields; 3) create a drop-down list in a form. We'll explain the first two methods later in this chapter; Chapter 13 discusses the third method.

Validation Text   Defines the error message that will appear on the screen when faulty data is entered into the field. When writing the validation text, it's best to indicate which field is invalid, so the user can more easily understand what's wrong during data entry. (See Table 6.3 for examples.)

TABLE 6.3: Examples of Validation Rule Expressions and Validation Text for Error Messages

VALIDATION RULE	POSSIBLE VALIDATION TEXT	HOW IT LIMITS ENTRY
>0	The Unit Price must be greater than 0.	Disallows 0 or negative number in a Number or Currency field.
<>0	A Rating of 0 is not acceptable.	Allows any negative or positive number, but not zero.
Between 1 and 100	The Rating must be between 1 and 100.	Accepts only numbers in the range of 1 to 100 (inclusive) in a Number or Currency field.
>=Date( )	Sorry, no Order Date backdating is allowed!	Allows only today's date or later dates in a Date/Time field.
>=#1/1/96#	Sorry, First Payment date must be January 1996 or later.	Prevents dates earlier than January 1, 1996 in a Date/Time field.

TIP To test all your validation rules against existing data in the table, choose Edit ➤ Test Validation Rules ➤ Yes.

Setting a Primary Key

A *primary key* is a field (or fields) that uniquely identifies each record, much as a license plate uniquely identifies each car on the road. When you define a primary key, you tell Access to do three things:

- Make sure no two records in the table have the same value in the field (or fields) that define the primary key.

- Keep records sorted (ordered) by the entries in the primary key field.

- Speed up processing.

A primary key can be just one field, or it can consist of two or more fields. When two or more fields define a primary key, Access doesn't consider records to be duplicates unless the combined contents of all the fields in the primary key are identical.

N O T E No field that is part of a primary key can ever be left blank during data entry.

To set a primary key in your table design:

1. Select the field you want to use as a primary key by clicking on the row selector button to the left of the field name. Or, if you want to select multiple fields, hold down the Ctrl key and click on the row selector for each field you want to define.

2. Click on the Primary Key toolbar button (shown at left). Or, choose <u>E</u>dit ➤ Primary <u>K</u>ey from the menu bar. Or, right-click on the highlighted row selector and choose Primary Key.

The field(s) you've set as the primary key will have a key icon in the row selector, as shown below.

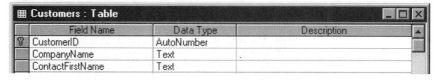

If you change your mind about assigning a field as a primary key, just repeat the two steps above.

Defining Indexes

You can add an index to a field as a way to speed up sorting and searching on that field. Not all data types can be indexed, but any field that has a property named Indexed at the bottom of the General field properties tab is a candidate for indexing. Each table in your database can have up to 32 indexes.

NOTE If the field's data type allows it, the field isn't a primary key, and the field name starts or ends with *ID, key, code,* or *num,* Access will create a Yes (No Duplicates) index automatically. To specify which field names will trigger an automatic index, choose <u>T</u>ools ➤ <u>O</u>ptions, click on the Tables/Queries tab, and then edit or replace text in the AutoIndex On Import/Create box. See Chapter 15 for more details.

Be aware that indexes can slow down data entry and editing a little, because Access must update the index whenever you add or change data. So you should index only the field(s) that you're most likely to use for sorting and searching. (To save you time and trouble, the Database Wizard and Table Wizard set up indexes on appropriate table fields automatically.)

To add or remove an index on a field:

1. Click on the name of the field you want to work with.

2. Click on the General tab under Field Properties.

3. Click on the Indexed property if it's available, click on the drop-down arrow next to Indexed, and then click on one of these options:

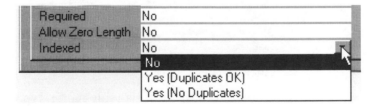

When defining a field as an index, be sure to choose Yes (Duplicates OK)—rather than Yes (No Duplicates)—unless you're absolutely sure that no two records in the table should have identical values in that field. To remove an index from a field, set the Indexed property to No. You'll see examples of indexed fields later in this chapter.

WARNING The primary key automatically gets an Indexed property of Yes (No Duplicates). You can't change that setting unless you remove the primary key on that field.

TIP You can view and change the index name, field name, sort order, and index properties for all the table's fields at once, if you wish. To do so, choose View ➤ Indexes from the menu bar, or click on the Indexes toolbar button (see Figure 6.2).

Saving a Table Structure

Once you're (reasonably) satisfied with the fields in your table, you can close and save the table structure. Here's how:

1. Choose File ➤ Close from the menu bar, or press Ctrl+W, or click on the Close button in the table design window. You'll probably see a dialog box similar to this one:

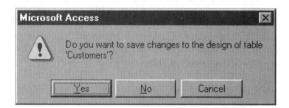

2. Click on Yes.

3. If you're prompted for a table name, type the name you want to assign to the table (up to 64 characters, including blank spaces), and then click on OK.

4. If you haven't defined a primary key, you'll see this dialog box:

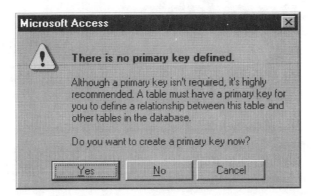

5. If you're not sure how to answer, we suggest that you click on <u>Y</u>es and let Access create a primary key for you. (Access will create a field named ID with the AutoNumber data type.) Your database usually runs faster if every table has a primary key.

You'll be returned to the database window, where you can see the new table name on the Tables tab.

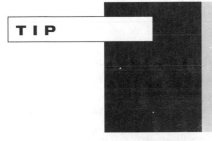

TIP

You can save the table structure without closing the table design window first. Just click on the toolbar's Save button, or press Ctrl+S, or choose <u>F</u>ile ➤ <u>S</u>ave anytime you're in the table design window. Access will save the changes you've made so far, and you'll remain in the table design window.

WARNING

When you save tables, forms, reports, queries, and other objects in your database, the database will increase in size. To make the current database smaller, you must compact the database. To get started, close the database, choose <u>T</u>ools ➤ Database <u>U</u>tilities ➤ <u>C</u>ompact Database, specify the database to compact from, and then choose a database name to compact to. See Chapter 17 for more details.

Opening a Table

After you've created a table, you can open it anytime:

1. In the database window, click on the Tables tab.

2. Click on the name of the table you want to open. Then...

   - **To open the table for entering or editing *data*,** click on the <u>O</u>pen button or double-click on the table name.
   - **To view or change the table's *design* (structure),** click on the <u>D</u>esign button.

You also can open or design a table by right-clicking on its name in the database window and then choosing Open or Design from the shortcut menu. The shortcut menu for tables also offers other handy options— Print, Cut, Copy, Create Shortcut, Delete, Rename, and Properties—for you to explore. To find out the purpose of any option on the shortcut menu, point to that option with your mouse and look at the status bar for a brief description; then, if you need more details, press the F1 key.

Switching between Design and Datasheet Views

Once the table is open, you can switch quickly between *datasheet view* and *design view*. The differences between the two views are:

- **In datasheet view,** you typically work with the table's contents (data). However, you also can make some changes to the table's structure (more about this in Chapter 8).

- **In design view,** you work with the table's structure only (field names, data types, properties), not its contents.

To switch views while a table is open, click on the Table View toolbar button:

 Switch from datasheet view to design view

Switch from design view to datasheet view

You also can switch to design or datasheet view by choosing View ➤ Table Design or View ➤ Datasheet from the menu bar. Or, click on the drop-down arrow next to the Table View toolbar button and then choose Design View or Datasheet View.

Why Two Views?

You will use datasheet view to add data to your table, as explained in Chapter 8. Figure 6.3 shows some names and addresses typed into a table named Customers. In datasheet view, field names appear across the top of the table, and none of the underlying structural information (such as data types and properties) is visible. If some fields are scrolled off the right edge of the window, you can use the horizontal scroll bar at the bottom of the window to scroll left and right through the fields.

FIGURE 6.3

The Customers table in Datasheet view

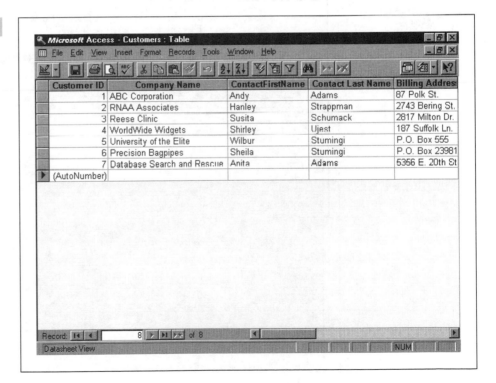

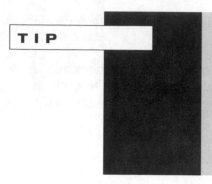

TIP

When adding data to a table that includes an AutoNumber field (such as the CustomerID field shown in Figure 6.3), Access usually will number records sequentially, starting with 1 (1, 2, 3, and so forth). You can use the trick described under "Changing the Starting Value of an AutoNumber Field" near the end of this chapter to change the starting number for your table's records (1001, 1002, and so forth).

In design view, you can see and change the underlying table structure. Field names are listed down the left column, and the data type, description, and field properties are presented. None of the table's data is visible in design view. Figure 6.4 shows the same Customers table in design view.

FIGURE 6.4

The Customers table in design view

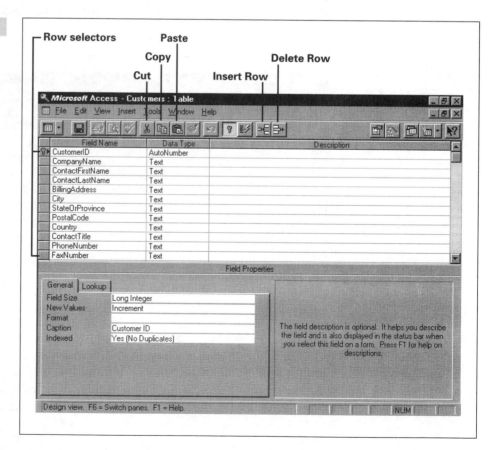

Modifying the Table Structure

Here are some techniques you can use to change a table's structure in design view:

1. Open the table that you want to modify in design view (or switch to design view if you're in datasheet view). Then:

    - **To change a field's name**, data type, description, or properties, use the same techniques you used when creating the table structure.

    - **To insert a new field into the structure**, move the cursor to where the field's new row should appear, and then click on the Insert Row toolbar button (shown at left), or press the Insert key, or choose Insert ➤ Field from the menu bar.

    - **To delete a field from the table structure**, move the cursor to the row that contains the field you want to delete, and then click on the Delete Row toolbar button (shown at left). Or choose Edit ➤ Delete Row from the menu bar.

    - **To undo an accidental insertion or deletion**, click on the Undo toolbar button (shown at left), or choose Edit ➤ Undo..., or press Ctrl+Z.

WARNING   Do not rename or delete fields without carefully considering the effect of doing so. Queries, forms, reports, and other objects that rely on the presence of certain fields won't work properly if you rename or delete those fields.

Selecting Rows in Design View

While you're in table design view, you can select rows (that is, fields) to manage:

- **To select one row,** click on the row selector to the left of the field you want to select. The row will be darkened (highlighted), as shown below:

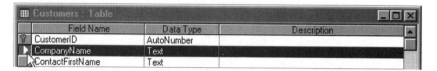

- **To select multiple adjacent rows,** drag the mouse pointer through the row selectors of all the rows you want to select. Or, click on the selector for the first row you want to select, and then Shift-click on the selector for the last row you want to select.

- **To select multiple non-adjacent rows,** Ctrl-click on the row selector for each row you want to select.

- **To deselect selected rows,** click on any Field Name, Data Type, or Description box.

- **To deselect one selected row** in a group of selected rows, Ctrl-click on the row you want to deselect.

After selecting one or more rows, use these techniques to manage them:

- **To move one selected row,** click on its row selector again, but this time hold down the mouse button and drag the selection to its new location.

- **To copy the selection,** choose Edit ➤ Copy, or press Ctrl+C, or click on the Copy toolbar button. Next, click on the row selector for the empty row where you want to put the copy, and then choose Edit ➤ Paste or press Ctrl+V (or click on the Paste toolbar button). Finally, *rename the copied field, because no two fields in a table can have the same name.*

- **To delete the selection,** press the Delete key.

- **To insert blank row(s) above the selection,** press the Insert key.

Saving Changes Made to a Table Structure

After changing the table structure, you can save those changes in any of these ways:

- Switch to datasheet view or close the table design window (File ➤ Close). If asked whether you want to save the new structure, click on Yes if you want to save the changes, or No if you don't want to save them.

- Choose File ➤ Save, or press Ctrl+S, or click on the Save toolbar button (shown at left). You'll remain in the table design window.

If the table already contains data, and your design changes will affect that data, a message will warn you of the change. Here's an example:

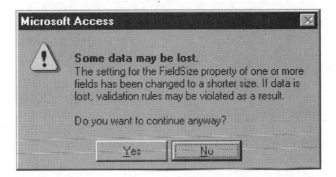

Read the warning carefully, and then click on the appropriate command button.

Moving, Copying, Deleting, Renaming Entire Tables

It's easy to copy, delete, and rename entire tables from the database window. The techniques are explained in Chapter 1, under "Managing Database Objects."

Changing Properties of an Entire Table or Object

You can change the overall properties for a table or other Access object. For example, you can add a Description that will appear in the database window. Here's how:

1. Go to the object's design view window or click on the appropriate tab on the database window and then click on the object's name. Different properties are available, depending on whether you start from the design window or the database window; however, you can change the Description property by starting from either window.

2. Choose <u>V</u>iew ➤ <u>P</u>roperties from the menu bar, or click on the Properties toolbar button (shown at left). Or, if you're starting from the database window, right-click on the object name and choose Properties.

3. Complete the Properties dialog box that appears.

More Database Window Tricks

It's easy to view an object's Description from the database window: Choose <u>V</u>iew ➤ <u>D</u>etails, or click on the Details toolbar button, or right-click on an empty area inside the database window and choose View ➤ Details.

You can sort objects in the database window by name, description, date created, date modified, or type. Any of these techniques will work:

• If you're viewing the database window in detail (<u>V</u>iew ➤ <u>D</u>etails), click on the column heading you want to use for sorting. For example, click on the Name column heading to sort objects into ascending (A–Z) alphabetical order by object name. Click on the column heading again to sort the objects in descending (Z–A) alphabetical order.

• Choose <u>V</u>iew ➤ Arrange <u>I</u>cons, or right-click on an empty area in the database window and choose Arrange Icons. Then choose By Name, By Type, By Created, or By Modified.

Tables in the Order Entry Database

Throughout this book, we'll often refer to the Order Entry database, which we created using the Database Wizard described in Chapters 3 and 5. If you haven't created a sample Order Entry database yet, you might want to do so now. Feel free to use the sample data the Wizard provides, your own data, or a combination of the two. Having this database available on your own computer will make it easier for you to follow the examples in this book.

Figure 6.5 shows the tables that make up the completed Order Entry database and describes them briefly. We'll give you more details about these tables in the sections that follow.

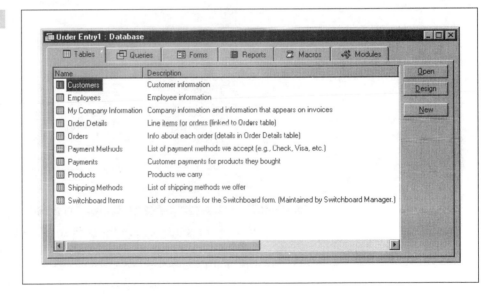

The Customers Table

The Customers table is an important table in the Order Entry database because it stores name and address data for customers. Figure 6.6 shows this table's field names and data types.

Changing Your Screen Display Size

Most figures in this book are shown with the Windows Desktop Area set to 640 by 480 pixels. However, we chose a Desktop Area of 800 by 600 pixels for some examples (such as Figure 6.5) that don't fit on a 640 by 480 screen. To change the Desktop Area on your own screen (if your monitor supports such changes and you're running Windows 95), minimize or close the Access program window (if it's open), right-click on an empty area on the *Windows desktop* (not the Access window), choose Properties, click on the Settings tab, drag the Desktop Area slider to the appropriate setting, click on OK, and then answer any prompts that appear.

FIGURE 6.6

The Customers table structure in the Order Entry database

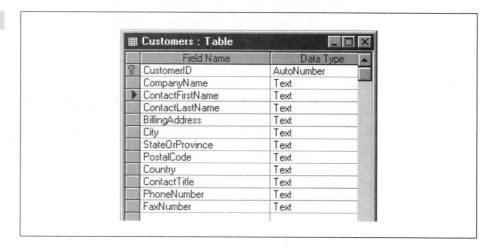

Customers Primary Key and Index

The primary key in the Customers table is the CustomerID field. It's an AutoNumber field, which means that new entries are assigned an ID number automatically as they're added to the table. Furthermore, that number will never change (because the value in an AutoNumber field can't change), and no two entries ever have the same ID number. Like all primary key fields, CustomerID is indexed and duplicates aren't allowed.

NOTE The New Values field property on the General tab offers you two ways to assign values to AutoNumber fields. The default choice, Increment, increases the field's value by 1 for each new record. To assign *random* long number values to new records, choose the Random option instead. Only one AutoNumber field is allowed in each table.

About Validation and Input Masks

Many people assign input masks, the Required property, and other restrictions to certain fields. For example, if you explore the General properties of the Customers table, you'll notice that input masks are defined for the PostalCode, PhoneNumber, and FaxNumber fields, as described below:

PostalCode   The input mask *00000\-9999* allows you to enter zip+4 codes without typing a hyphen. *Example:* You type **857114747**, and the input mask changes your entry to 85711-4747.

PhoneNumber   The input mask *!\(999") "000\-0000* lets you enter phone numbers without having to type the parentheses around area codes, or the hyphen after the exchange. *Example:* You type **6035551234**, and the input mask changes your entry to (603)555-1234.

FaxNumber   The input mask *!\(999")"000\-0000* is the same one used for the phone number.

NOTE If you need to omit the area code when entering phone or fax numbers that have the *!\(999")"000\-0000* input mask, use the mouse or your keyboard to skip the area code portion of your entry.

You might want to remove these input masks if you want your own database to handle international names and addresses. Requiring a particular pattern, or an entry at all, can prevent the entry of addresses in foreign lands. In fact, we don't even *know* the postal code or telephone number format used in Zimbabwe or Mongolia. Do you?

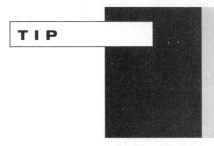

T I P

Restrictive field properties can make data entry frustrating or downright impossible. When you're first designing a table, avoid making the field properties too restrictive. For example, don't require entries unless you *absolutely* need them. You can always make the table more restrictive after you've worked with it for a while.

The Products Table

The Products table stores information about products sold by the business that uses the database. Its structure appears in Figure 6.7. The ProductID field is the primary key in the Products table, to ensure that each product the business sells has a unique identifying code.

FIGURE 6.7

The Products table structure in the Order Entry database

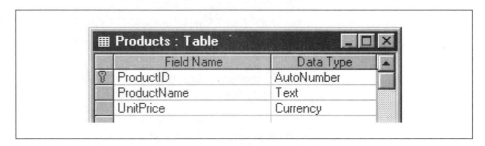

The Orders Table

The Orders table tracks all orders placed. Ordering information is divided into two tables (named Orders and Order Details), because there is a natural one-to-many relationship between a given order and the number of details (or line items) that go with that order (see Figure 6.8).

FIGURE 6.8

There's a natural one-to-many relationship between an order and the number of items ordered (sometimes called **order details** or **line items**). Therefore, information about orders is split into two separate tables. In the Order Entry database, those tables are named Orders and Order Details.

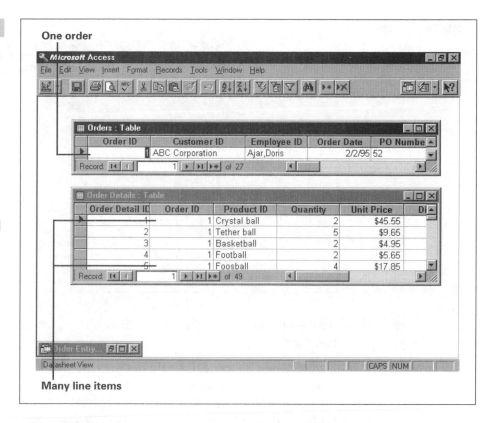

One order

Many line items

NOTE

The Order Entry database comes with an Orders By Customer form, which lets you enter and display data from several tables at once. You'll learn how to create similar data entry forms in Chapters 11 and 13.

Figure 6.9 shows the structure of the Orders table. The OrderID field is the primary key, and is defined as the AutoNumber data type so that orders are numbered automatically as they're entered into the table. The fact that OrderID is an AutoNumber field will have implications for the Order Details table (as you'll learn shortly).

The CustomerID field in the Orders table plays two important roles. First, it's an example of a field that uses *Lookup properties*. In this case, the CustomerID field in the Orders table looks to the CustomerID field in the Customers table for a list of possible values. Lookup fields can make

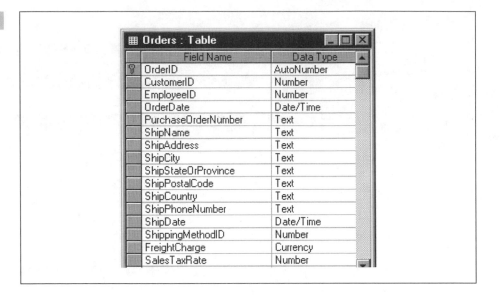

data entry quick and error free (there's more about lookup fields later in this chapter).

Second, the CustomerID field in the Orders table relates the Order to the CustomerID field in the Customers table, thereby ensuring that our database includes a valid customer record for each order placed. In the Customers table, CustomerID is an AutoNumber field. In the Orders table, the CustomerID field *must* have the Long Integer property for Access to match records correctly. A similar relationship exists between the OrderID field in the Orders table and the OrderID field in the Order Details table. (See "Defining a Relationship When One Field Is an AutoNumber" near the end of this chapter.)

Other interesting fields in this table include:

EmployeeID   A lookup field that lets you choose which employee sold the order.

ShippingMethodID   A lookup field that lets you choose a valid shipping method for the order.

SalesTaxRate   A number that's displayed in Percent format. A validation rule for this field requires entries to be less than 1 (<1) and displays an error message (validation text) if you enter a value greater than or equal to 1. *Example:* If you type **.065** into the

SalesTaxRate field, Access displays a value of 6.5%. If you type **6.5** into this field, Access instead displays the validation text error message "This value must be less than 100%."

The Order Details Table

The Order Details table stores one record for each line item of an order. Its structure is shown in Figure 6.10. In this table, the OrderDetailID field is defined as the AutoNumber field type and as the table's primary key.

The OrderID field in the Order Details table relates each Order Details record to the appropriate record in the Orders table, which ensures that each line item belongs to a valid order. OrderID is the foreign key to the AutoNumber primary key field named OrderID in the Orders table. This field is indexed, with duplicates allowed, so that each order can have many line items.

FIGURE 6.10

Structure of the Order Details table in the Order Entry database

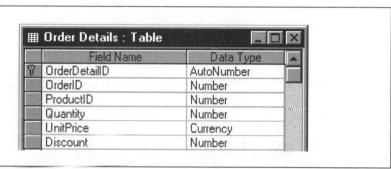

NOTE

Foreign key is a fancy term for table field(s) that refer to the primary key field(s) in another table. When the primary key has an AutoNumber data type, the foreign key field *must* be assigned the Number data type with the Long Integer field size. (See "Defining a Relationship When One Field Is an AutoNumber" near the end of this chapter for more details about foreign keys.) For other data types, the foreign key and its related primary key must have *exactly* the same data type and size.

Other interesting fields in the Order Details table include these:

ProductID   A lookup field that lets you select a valid product from the Products table.

Discount   Like the SalesTaxRate field in the Orders table, this field is displayed in Percent format and must be less than 1.

The Employees Table

The Employees table stores employee information. Figure 6.11 shows this table's structure. Notice that the EmployeeID field is both an AutoNumber field and the table's primary key. The WorkPhone field is defined with the usual input mask for phone numbers.

FIGURE 6.11

The structure for the Employees table

The structure for the Employees table

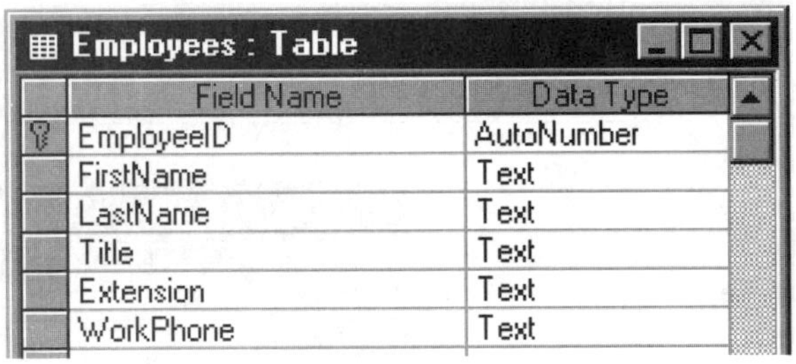

The Payments Table

The Order Entry application uses the Payments table to track which orders have been paid, how much of the order was paid, when the payment was made, and so forth. Figure 6.12 shows the structure for this table. Here, the PaymentID is an AutoNumber field and the primary key for the table. Other interesting fields include the following:

OrderID   Ties the payment to an order in the Orders table, and it is indexed (with duplicates OK).

PaymentDate   A Date/Time field that has an input mask of *99/99/00*, which lets you enter dates such as 2/2/95 in any of these ways: **020295, 022/95, 2/2/95**.

FIGURE 6.12

The structure for the
Payments table, which
keeps track of
customer payments

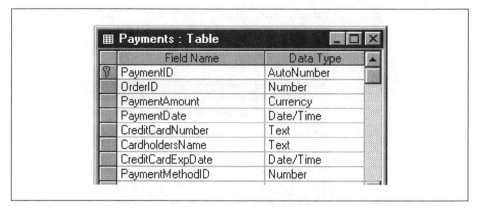

CreditCardExpDate   A Date/Time field that has the same input mask as PaymentDate.

PaymentMethodID   A lookup field that lets you choose a valid payment method from the Payment Methods table.

Other Tables in Order Entry

Order Entry uses two other small tables—Payment Methods, and Shipping Methods —which provide lookup information for the main tables already described. The structures for these two tables are shown below:

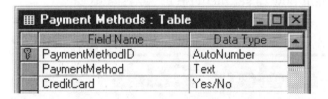

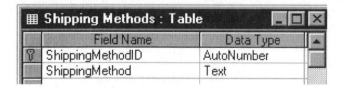

Finally, the table named My Company Information is used to define standard text and default settings for invoices. Its structure is shown below:

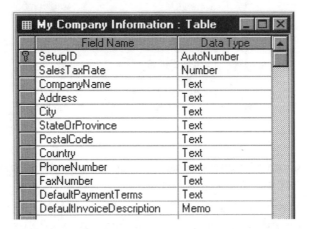

In the My Company Information table, several fields have input masks that we've already described. The SalesTaxRate field has a validation rule and text that will make Access reject entries greater than or equal to 1. The PostalCode field has a 00000\-9999 input mask, and the Phone-Number and FaxNumber fields have the !\(999")"000\-0000 input mask.

We've mentioned lookup fields many times in this chapter. Now we'll explain how to set them up in Access tables.

About Lookup Fields

You can create *lookup fields* that speed up and simplify data entry in a table's datasheet or in a form. As the name implies, the lookup field *looks up* values from another place, and then automatically fills in the value you select. The source data can come from any of these places:

- A table that has a primary key field.

- A query (or SQL statement) that displays specified columns and data from a table.

- A fixed list of values that you enter when you create the field.
- A list of all the field names in a table.

For example, when entering data into the Order Details table, you can look up and fill in a ProductID field by selecting a value from a drop-down list. Figure 6.13 shows the ProductID field in the Orders form after we clicked on its drop-down arrow. To fill in (or change) the ProductID, we just click on an entry in the list.

FIGURE 6.13

The ProductID lookup field (shown here on the sample Orders form) lets you look up and fill in the ProductID with a click of your mouse. The data for this lookup field comes from the Products table.

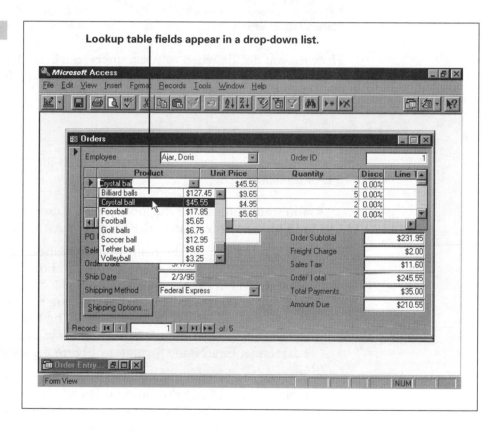

NOTE   In datasheet view, a lookup field always appears as a combo box, even if you've set its Display Control property to List Box in table design view. But when you add a lookup field to a form (such as the Orders form shown in Figure 6.13), Access automatically uses the Display Control property to decide whether to create the control as a combo box (which has a drop-down arrow that you must click to see the list) or as a list box (which shows the list itself, without a drop-down arrow).

How do you decide when to use a query, a table, a list of values, or a list of field names to display source data for your lookup field? The following sections offer some answers to this question.

Use a Query When...

It's best to use queries or SQL statements to display the list of values in a lookup field when...

- You want columns in the lookup field's drop-down list to appear in a specific order (such as PersonID, LastName, FirstName).

- You want to display the results of calculations, or to combine data from several fields into a single column. For example, a query or SQL statement makes it easy to display a customer or employee name as "Ajar, Doris" instead of showing the name in separate LastName and FirstName columns. (The EmployeeID field in the Orders table and Orders form displays employee names in LastName, FirstName format, as Figure 6.13 shows.)

- You want to restrict the lookup field's values to selected rows in a table. Suppose your Products table includes discontinued products that aren't available for sale. A query that filters out discontinued products offers a perfect way to display product names in the lookup field while preventing anyone from entering an order for discontinued products.

- You want changes to data in the query's source table(s) to be reflected in the drop-down list *and* in the lookup field that uses the query.

In a nutshell, queries and SQL statements offer the best way to make the lookup field display exactly what you want it to. They're also more efficient than using tables alone. You'll learn how to create queries in Chapter 10.

N O T E

An *SQL statement* is an expression that defines an SQL (Structured Query Language) command. Access uses SQL statements behind the scenes to interpret any queries you create in the query design window. SQL statements typically are used in queries and aggregate functions, and as the record source for forms, reports, list boxes, and combo boxes that Access Wizards create. For more about SQL, look up *SQL Statements* and its subtopics in the Access Help Index.

Use a Table When...

You can use tables to display the list of values in a lookup field when...

- Columns in the table are arranged in the order you want them to appear in the lookup field's drop-down list during data entry.

- You don't know how to create a query or SQL statement, or you don't want to bother.

- You want changes to data in the source table to be reflected in the drop-down list *and* in the lookup field that uses the table.

Use a List of Values When...

Occasionally, you might want to use a list of values when the list won't change often and it doesn't need to be stored in a table. Such a list might be handy for honorifics or salutations. Keep in mind that changes to data in the value list will be reflected in the drop-down list, but *not* in any records you added to the lookup field before you changed the list value.

Use a List of All Field Names in a Table When...

This method is useful mainly to application developers. Suppose you're designing a data entry form for a user who knows little about Access, and that user wants the option to sort the table's records by any field he or she chooses. To do this, you could add a combo box or list box lookup field that displays all the fields in the table. Then, place a control for that new field on your form, and attach to the control's On Update property a macro or event procedure that sorts the data by whatever field the user selects from the combo box or list box.

NOTE If you want the user to sort by specific fields only, use a list of values that contains the sortable field names, rather than a list of all field names in the table. The list of values method is preferable if the table you're planning to sort contains non-sortable field types, such as Memo or OLE Object fields.

If all this sounds like gobbledygook right now, don't worry about it. There are plenty of ways to use lookup fields without knowing about macros, event procedures, On Update properties, and the like. If you're curious about using such techniques, see Chapters 20 and 25.

Setting Up a Lookup Field

Access offers two ways to set up a lookup field. First, you can use the Lookup Wizard, which guides you through the process step by step. Second, you can use the Lookup tab in the Field Properties area of the table design window to define the lookup field manually.

With the Lookup Wizard...

When you're first learning how to set up lookup fields, you might want to stick with the Lookup Wizard. Here's how use it:

1. Switch to the design view for your table.

2. Move the cursor to the empty row that should contain your new lookup field. You can leave the field name blank because the Lookup Wizard will assign a field name for you.

3. Click on the Data Type cell next to the blank field name, click on the drop-down arrow, and then choose Lookup Wizard. The Lookup Wizard will take over.

4. In the first Lookup Wizard dialog box, choose whether to get values from an existing table or query, or whether to type the values you want. Click on the <u>N</u>ext button.

TIP

As usual, you can click on the <u>N</u>ext button to move to the next step, the <u>B</u>ack button to back up to the previous step, and the Cancel button to bail out early.

5. Complete the remaining dialog boxes that appear, reading each one carefully, and clicking on the <u>N</u>ext button to move ahead. Be sure to choose or define column names in the order you want to see them in the drop-down list during data entry. Keep these questions and answers in mind as you work through the Lookup Wizard dialog boxes:

- **Which columns do you see in the drop-down list during data entry?** By default, the columns will appear in the order you chose them in the Lookup Wizard (though you may need to use the scroll bars to see them all); however, the primary key column usually will be hidden. You can change this default behavior in the Lookup Wizard dialog box that lets you adjust column widths. To do so, uncheck the Hide Key Column box; or hide any column by dragging (to the left) the vertical line next to the column name until the column disappears; or reposition any column by clicking on its column name and then dragging the name to the left or right.

- **What relationships are created behind the scenes?** If data for your new field comes from a table, the Lookup Wizard creates a relationship between the current table and the table whose data you're looking up. The field you're creating becomes the foreign key in that relationship. This behind-the-scenes action will ensure that you don't accidentally delete the lookup table or lookup fields without first deleting the relationship.

- **What values appear in the table after you choose an item from the drop-down list during data entry?** The *first* column you leave visible will appear in the table.

- **What values are actually stored in the new field when data comes from a related table?** If you've chosen to hide the related table's key column, the new field will store values from the *primary key field* of the related table. If you've chosen *not* to hide that table's key column, the field name you select in the second-to-last Lookup Wizard dialog box controls which data is stored in the new field. (This dialog box asks you to choose a field that uniquely identifies the row).

- **What values are actually stored in the new field when data comes from a query or a list of values you type in?** The field name you select in the second-to-last Lookup Wizard dialog box controls which data is stored in the new field.

- **What name is assigned to the new field?** If data for your new field comes from a table or query, the Lookup Wizard gives the new field the same name as the primary key of the related table or the first field of the query, and it sets the new field's Caption property to whatever name you choose in step 6 below. If data for your new field comes from a list of values you typed in, the Lookup Wizard uses the name you assign in step 6 for the field name and leaves the Caption property blank.

6. When you reach the last dialog box, type a label to use as the caption for your new field (if you wish), and then click on the <u>F</u>inish button to finish the job. Respond to any prompts that appear

In addition to handling all the details described in step 5 above, the Lookup Wizard also fills in the Lookup properties for you automatically. To see these properties for yourself, go to the table design window, click in the row that contains your lookup field, and then click on the Lookup tab in the table design window's Field Properties area.

With the Lookup Properties Sheet...

Of course, you can define Lookup field properties without a Lookup Wizard, as follows:

1. Switch to the design view for the table.

2. If you haven't done so already, specify the Field Name and Data Type for your lookup field.

3. Click on the Lookup tab in the table design window's Field Properties area.

4. Click in the Display Control property box, click on the drop-down arrow that appears, and then choose either List Box or Combo Box.

5. Complete the remaining properties in the Lookup property sheet (see the next section for details).

Figure 6.14 shows the Lookup properties for the EmployeeID field of the Orders table. Figure 6.15 shows the query that's "behind" the SQL statement shown in the Row Source box of Figure 6.14. And Figure 6.16 shows the results of running that query (we ran this query, so you can see the relationship between the query results and the Lookup properties). See Chapters 3 and 10 for more about queries.

Important Facts about Lookup Fields

You'll have great success with setting up lookup fields if you remember these points:

- If you plan to use a table or query to supply values for the lookup field, that table or query must exist. (When using the Lookup tab, rather than the Lookup Wizard, you can create a query on the fly, by clicking in the Row Source property box and then clicking on the Build (...) button that appears. See Chapter 10 for more about queries.)

- If you're using a table to supply values for the lookup field, that table must have a primary key.

- You can hide a column in your drop-down list by setting its width in the Column Widths property box to zero (0 in).

The Lookup properties for the EmployeeID field of the Orders table

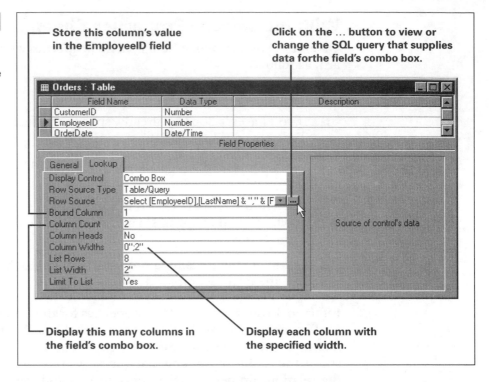

Store this column's value in the EmployeeID field

Click on the ... button to view or change the SQL query that supplies data for the field's combo box.

Display this many columns in the field's combo box.

Display each column with the specified width.

The query behind the SQL statement for the Row Source property shown in Figure 6.14. To display this query, we clicked in the Row Source box on the Lookup properties tab, clicked on the Build (...) button that appeared, and widened the second column in the query design grid.

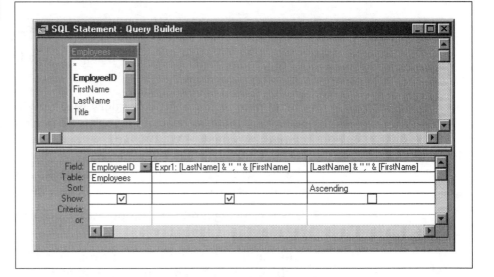

FIGURE 6.16

The results of running
the query shown in
Figure 6.15

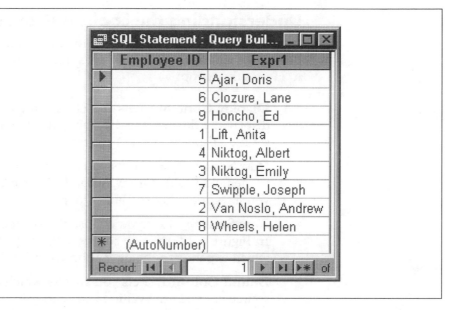

- The *first* column in the drop-down list is always the one you see in the lookup field (unless you've hidden the column by setting its column width to 0; in this case, the column you see is the first one that isn't hidden).

- The value that's actually stored in the lookup field is the one that's specified as the *bound column* (more about this shortly). The data type of the lookup field must be compatible with the bound column, regardless of what you see in the field during data entry.

N O T E

The last two points above can be confusing. The easiest way to keep them straight is to remember that the first (unhidden) column controls *what you see* when you scroll through the table in datasheet view. The bound column controls *what actually is stored* (what you get) in the lookup field.

With these points in mind, let's take a closer look at the properties on the Lookup tab in the table design window.

CHAPTER 6

Understanding the Lookup Properties

At first glance, the property sheet for the Lookup tab might seem rather daunting (see Figure 6.14). But it's not bad once you know more about it. Here's the scoop:

Display Control   Lets you choose the type of control used to display the field on the datasheet and forms. (For lookup fields, set the Display Control property to List Box or Combo Box.)

Row Source Type   Lets you choose the type of source for data in the field (Table/Query, Value List, or Field List). Generally, you'll want to choose Table/Query.

Row Source   Lets you choose the source of the control's data. In Figure 6.14, the row source is the SQL "Select" statement, which expands to the query shown in Figure 6.15.

Bound Column   Lets you specify which column in the row source contains the value to store in this lookup field. The data type for the field must be compatible with values in the bound column. For instance, if the bound column stores numeric values (such as EmployeeID values), the data type for the lookup field also must be numeric (Number, Currency); if the bound column stores long integer values, the data type for the lookup field must be either Long Integer or AutoNumber.

Column Count   Lets you specify how many columns to display. The example in Figure 6.14 tells Access to display two columns (however, the first column is hidden because its Column Widths setting is 0).

Column Heads   Lets you choose whether to show the column headings. By default, no column headings appear. To show column headings, change the setting to Yes.

Column Widths   Lets you specify the width of each column shown in the drop-down list. In Figure 6.14, the first column width is 0 (hidden), and the second column is 2 inches wide. When typing the column widths, use a semicolon (;) to separate each column's width specification; you can omit the unit of measurement ("). For example, if you type **0;2** in the Column Widths property box, Access will change your entry to **0";2"** when you move the cursor out of the Column Widths box.

List Rows   Lets you specify how many rows to display in the drop-down list at once (the default is 8).

List Width   Lets you specify the width of the entire combo box. (A List Width of *Auto* tells Access to calculate the width automatically.)

Limit To List   If set to Yes, only values shown in the drop-down list are allowed during data entry. If set to No, Access allows entries that aren't shown in the drop-down list.

 ➤ For immediate help as you define Lookup properties, click in the appropriate property field and press F1.

Defining Relationships among Tables

You can define all the relationships among your tables at any time. There are several advantages to defining the relationships early on (before you add much data):

- When you open multiple related tables in a query (see Chapter 10), the related tables will be joined automatically, saving you a few extra steps.

- Access will create some needed indexes automatically, to make your related tables perform more quickly.

- You can define *referential integrity* relationships between tables when joining them. Referential integrity ensures that the relationships between records in related tables remain valid, and can prevent problems from occurring when you try to delete or change a record that's related to records in another table. *Example:* Referential integrity can ensure that every Orders record has a corresponding record in the Customers table (thus, every order can be traced back to a customer). It also can prevent you from deleting a customer record if outstanding orders remain for that customer.

To define relationships among existing tables:

1. Close any open tables so that only the database window is visible.

 2. Choose Tools ➤ Relationships from the menu bar, or click on the Relationships toolbar button (shown at left), or right-click anywhere on the database window and choose Relationships. The Relationships window appears. (It will be empty unless you've previously defined relationships among your tables.)

 3. To display tables for which you want to define relationships, click on the Show Table toolbar button (shown at left), or right-click on an empty part of the Relationships window and choose Show Table, or choose Relationships ➤ Show table from the menu bar. You'll see a dialog box similar to this one:

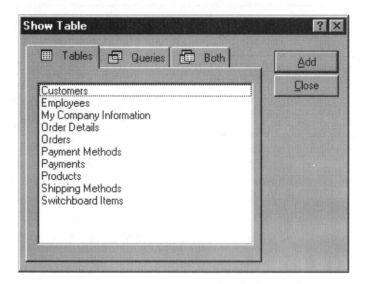

4. To add a table or query to the Relationships window, click on an appropriate tab (Tables, Queries, or Both) in the Show Table dialog box. Then, click on the name of the table or query you want to add, and click on the Add button; or double-click on the table or query name. To add several tables at once, use the standard Shift-click and Ctrl-click techniques to select the tables, and then click on the Add button.

5. Repeat step 4 until you've added all the tables and queries for which you want to define relationships. Then click on the <u>C</u>lose button.

6. Relate the tables as explained in the next section.

Figure 6.17 shows tables from the Order Entry database that are good candidates for relating. We've arranged and sized the tables, but haven't shown the relationships among them.

T I P   To tidy up the Relationships window anytime, move the tables by dragging their title bars, and resize the tables by dragging their borders.

Tables from the Order Entry database added to the Relationships window. The relationships among the tables haven't been defined yet.

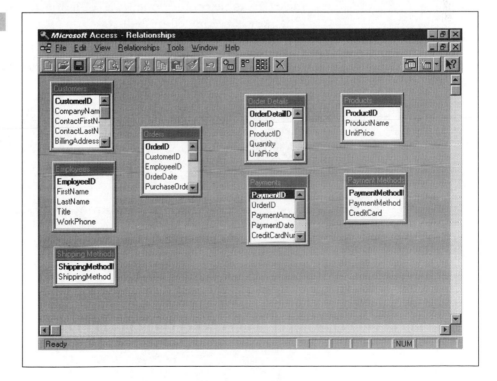

N O T E   If you created the Order Entry database with the Database Wizard, all the relationships among the tables will be defined for you automatically, and the window will look more like Figure 6.18 than Figure 6.17 (although you'll certainly need to rearrange the tables to straighten out the spaghetti appearance of the lines between them).

Relating Two Tables

To define the relationship between any two tables in the Relationships window:

1. Move the mouse pointer to the primary key field in the *primary table* (the table on the "one side" of a one-to-many relationship). That key is boldfaced in the list.

2. Drag that field name to the corresponding field in the related table (that is, drag it to the appropriate *foreign key*).

T I P   You can drag from the foreign key field in the related table to the primary key field in the primary table. The results will be the same.

3. When you release the mouse button, you'll see a dialog box similar to this one:

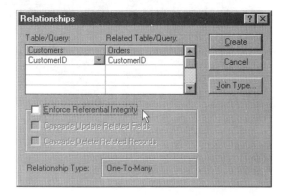

4. If you want to enforce referential integrity between the two tables, select (check) the Underline{E}nforce Referential Integrity box. Then, if you wish, tell Access how to handle changes and deletions in the primary table:

- If you want *changes* to the table on one side of the relation to automatically carry over to the related table, select (check) the Cascade Underline{U}pdate Related Fields check box.
- If you want *deletions* in one table to carry over to the related table, select the Cascade Underline{D}elete Related Records check box.

NOTE In order to define referential integrity between tables, the matching field from the primary table must be a primary key or have a unique index, the related fields must have the same data type (or be AutoNumber and Long Integer), and both tables must be stored in the same Access database. For more details about referential integrity rules, go to the Relationships dialog box and press the F1 key.

5. If you want to change the type of join between tables, click on the Join Type button, choose the type of join you want to use, and then click on OK. (If in doubt, don't make any change. You can always define the relationship in a query, as discussed in Chapter 10.)

NOTE *Join* is a database term that describes the correspondence between a field in one table and a field in another table. There are several types of join, though the default join (called an *equi-join* or *inner join*) works fine for most situations. To learn more about joins, search for *Joins, Defining Types For Tables* in the Access Help Index.

6. Click on the Underline{C}reate button to finish the job.

Access shows the relationship between the two tables as a join line connecting the related fields. The appearance of the line indicates the type of join you've chosen and whether you're enforcing referential integrity. In the example below, the thick, solid bars in the join line indicate that referential integrity is enforced between tables. The small 1 indicates the table on the "one side" of this relationship; the small infinity sign indicates the table on the "many side" of this relationship.

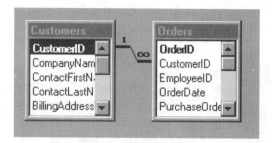

You can repeat steps 1 through 6 above to define the relationships between as many pairs of tables as appropriate in your database. Figure 6.18 shows all the relationships between tables in the Order Entry database, as the Database Wizard defined them.

In the Order Entry database, referential integrity with cascaded updates and deletions is enforced between these tables: Customers and Orders, Orders and Payments, Orders and Order Details, and Products and Order Details. To make data entry more flexible, referential integrity *is not* enforced between these tables: Shipping Methods and Orders, Payment Methods and Payments, and Employees and Orders.

WARNING

When you're first designing a database, don't go hog wild with setting up relationships between tables. If the relationships between tables are too strict, data entry can be cumbersome. It's easy to add or remove relationships later if you need to, so don't worry too much about defining every possible relationship. Start conservatively, add a few sample records, and then decide whether the relationships should be more restrictive or less restrictive.

FIGURE 6.18

The Order Entry Relationships window, showing all relationships the Database Wizard defined

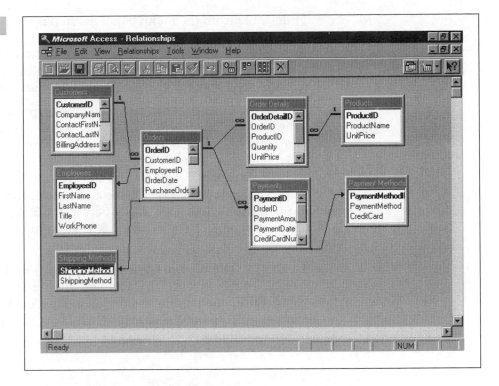

More Tips for Using the Relationships Window

Here are some other tips for using the Relationships window:

- **To show tables that are directly related to a selected table**, click on the table and then click on the Show Direct Relationships toolbar button (shown at left). Or, right-click on the table you're curious about, and choose Show Direct Relationships. Or, click on the table and choose Relationships ➤ Show Direct.

- **To show all tables and relationships that are currently defined for the database**, click on the Show All Relationships toolbar button (shown at left). Or, right-click on an empty area in the relationships window and choose Show All Relationships. Or, choose Relationships ➤ Show All from the menu bar.

- **To hide a table that you've added to the Relationships window**, click on the table you want to hide. Then press Delete, or right-click and choose Hide Table, or choose Relationships ➤

Hide Table from the menu bar. This step does not delete the table from the database, and it doesn't delete any relationships defined for the table; it just hides the table from view. (To add the table to the view again, click on the Show Table toolbar button, double-click on the appropriate table name, and click on Close.)

- **To clear all tables from the Relationships window,** choose Edit ➤ Clear Layout, or click on the Clear Layout toolbar button (shown at left). When asked for confirmation, click on Yes. The Relationships window will be empty. Again, no tables or relationships are deleted, but your work toward tidying up the Relationships window *will* be lost. To see all the tables and relationships again, right-click on any empty part in the Relationships window, choose Show All Relationships, and then tidy up the window as needed.

- **To change the design of any table** shown in the Relationships window, right-click on that table and choose Design Table. When you're finished changing the table's design, click on the design window's Close button or press Ctrl+W; you'll return to the Relationships window.

Printing the Relationships Window and other "Unprintable" Things

Alas, there's no way to print the Relationships window directly. Your best bet is to set up the window the way you want it, and then press Alt+Print Screen to capture the screen to the Windows Clipboard. Then start the Paint applet (Start ➤ Programs ➤ Accessories ➤ Paint), and choose Edit ➤ Paste or press Ctrl+V. Finally, print the image from Paint by choosing File ➤ Print ➤ OK.

Saving the Relationships Layout

When you use the Relationships window to add, change, or delete relationships, the relationships are saved automatically; however, changes to the window's layout are not. Therefore, any time you're happy with the appearance of the Relationships window, you should save the layout. There are many ways to do this: Choose File ➤ Save, or press Ctrl+S, or click on the Save toolbar button (shown at left), or right-click on an empty part of the Relationships window and choose Save. If you want to save the layout and close the Relationships window in one step, choose File ➤ Close, or press Ctrl+W, or click on the window's Close button; then click on Yes when asked about saving your changes.

After you've defined all the relationships among your tables, close the Relationships window (choose File ➤ Close). If you're asked about saving changes, click on Yes.

Redefining (or Deleting) a Relationship

If you later discover that you've made a mistake while defining the relationships among your tables, you can follow the same steps presented under "Relating Two Tables" to return to the Relationships window and view existing relationships. Then:

- **To change the relationship** between two tables, double-click on the thin part of the join line, and then make your changes in the Relationships dialog box. Or right-click on the thin part of the join line and choose Edit Relationship from the shortcut menu. Or, click on the thin part of the join line and choose Relationships ➤ Edit Relationship from the menu bar.

- **To delete the relationship** between two tables, right-click on the thin part of the join line that you want to delete. Then choose Delete Relationship from the shortcut menu. Or click on the thin part of the join line, and then press Delete or choose Edit ➤ Delete. When prompted, click on Yes to confirm the deletion.

 ➤ For more examples and information on defining relationships between tables, open the Microsoft Access Contents, open *Creating, Importing, And Linking Tables,* open *Defining Relationships And Setting Referential Integrity Options,* and then explore the subtopics. You also can search the Help Index for *Relationships...* topics and subtopics.

Important Tips for AutoNumber Fields

AutoNumber fields are great timesavers in Access. But you must understand how they work in order to use them effectively. To help you get the most from using AutoNumber fields, we'll first explain how to set a starting value for AutoNumber fields. Then, we'll explain how to define a relationship between tables when one field's data type is AutoNumber.

NOTE

AutoNumber fields aren't always the best choice for assigning meaningful identifiers, such as customer numbers because you can't delete or change AutoNumber field values. Furthermore, the autonumbering sequence will contain "holes" where you've deleted records. For example, if you've entered three customer records, the AutoNumber fields will have the values 1, 2, 3. If you then delete the customers whose AutoNumber fields are 2 and 3, the AutoNumber field for the next new customer will have the value 4. Sometimes this will be desirable, and sometimes it won't.

WARNING

If the table for which you're changing AutoNumber field values contains data and that table is involved in a referential integrity relationship you may lose records from related tables (if cascaded deletes are allowed), or you may not be allowed to do step 13 below (if cascaded deletes are not allowed). Therefore, you should do the steps in the next section *only* if your related tables are empty (or contain only a few records that you don't care about).

Changing the Starting Value of an AutoNumber Field

Suppose you want to use an AutoNumber field to uniquely identify each customer in a table, bumping each new customer number by 1. However, you want the numbering to start at some number other than 1, such as 1001 for 4-digit ID numbers or 10001 for 5-digit numbers. Here's how to do that:

1. Open, in design view, the table that contains the AutoNumber field. (Make sure the AutoNumber field's New Values property on the General tab is set to Increment.)

2. Choose File ➤ Save As, enter a new name (such as _Temp), and then click on OK. (Make sure the title bar of the table design window reflects this new name.)

3. Change the data type of the AutoNumber field from AutoNumber to Number, and make sure its Field Size property is set to Long Integer.

4. Switch to datasheet view, and click on Yes when prompted for permission to save the table.

5. Type the starting number you want to use for the AutoNumber field, *minus 1*. (You also must enter a value in any Required fields you've defined.) In the example below, we assigned the first customer an ID of 1000, so that our customer numbers for "real" data will begin at 1001.

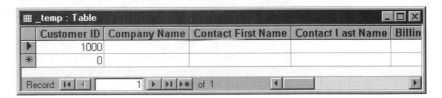

6. Close the temporary table (press Ctrl+W).

7. In the database window, highlight the name of that temporary table, and choose Edit ➤ Copy.

8. Choose Edit ➤ Paste.

9. In the Table Name box, type the name of the *original* table (Customers in our example)

10. Click on the Append Data To Existing Table option button.

11. Click on OK to complete the copy.

12. In the database window, double-click on the name of the original table (Customers in our example) to view its contents. You should see both the original record(s) (if any) and the newly numbered one(s), as shown below.

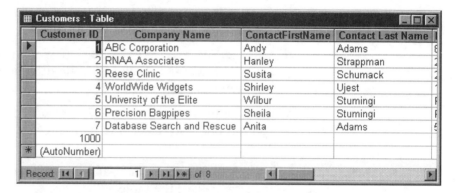

Customer ID	Company Name	ContactFirstName	Contact Last Name
1	ABC Corporation	Andy	Adams
2	RNAA Associates	Hanley	Strappman
3	Reese Clinic	Susita	Schumack
4	WorldWide Widgets	Shirley	Ujest
5	University of the Elite	Wilbur	Stumingi
6	Precision Bagpipes	Sheila	Stumingi
7	Database Search and Rescue	Anita	Adams
1000			
(AutoNumber)			

Record: 1 of 8

13. If the table doesn't contain old records, skip to step 15. Otherwise, move the record(s) with the old numbers to the Windows Clipboard. To do this, drag the mouse pointer through all the record selectors, *except* the selector for the new record you just added, choose Edit ➤ Cut (or press Ctrl+X), and then click on Yes.

14. Now paste the records back into the table by choosing Edit ➤ Paste Append ➤ Yes. The new records will start with the next available AutoNumber value (1001 in this example).

15. Click on the record selector for the empty temporary record (1000 in this example), press Delete, and then click on Yes to delete the record.

16. If the table was empty after you finished step 15 and you plan to compact the database that contains the table (see Chapter 17), add at least one new record to the table. Adding this new record will prevent the compacting operation from resetting the value for the next record added to 1 more than the previous value (effectively undoing your efforts in the above 15 steps).

17. Close the table and click on <u>N</u>o if asked about keeping the data on the Clipboard.

18. Now highlight the name of the temporary table (_Temp), press Delete, then click on <u>Y</u>es as needed to delete it.

NOTE This procedure will work *only* if the temporary table's starting number (e.g., 1000) is at least one higher than the highest AutoNumber field value that's currently stored in the table you're renumbering.

Any new record that you add to the table will be numbered starting at one more than the last record currently in that table.

Defining a Relationship When One Field Is an AutoNumber

When you define a relationship between two tables, where the primary key on the "one" side of the relationship is an increment AutoNumber field, the foreign key (that is, the corresponding field on the "many" side) *must be* the Number data type with its field size set to Long Integer. Figure 6.19 shows an example.

NOTE You also can match a Replication ID AutoNumber field with a Replication ID Number field. For information about replication, see Chapter 17, or look up *Replication* in the Access Answer Wizard.

The reason for this requirement is somewhat technical, but basically it's because Access stores AutoNumber field data as four-byte numbers. Only a foreign key that's exactly the same four-byte number will match the primary key. Setting the field size property of a number to Long Integer ensures that a four-byte number will be stored in the field.

FIGURE 6.19

When the primary key on the "one" side of a relationship is an AutoNumber field, the corresponding field on the "many" side must be a Long Integer.

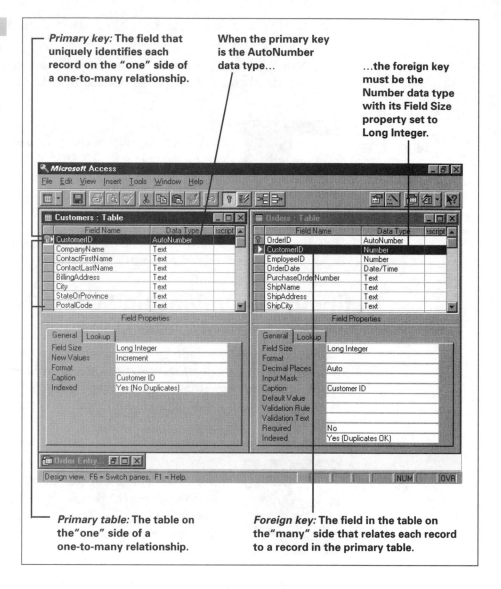

Primary key: The field that uniquely identifies each record on the "one" side of a one-to-many relationship.

When the primary key is the AutoNumber data type...

...the foreign key must be the Number data type with its Field Size property set to Long Integer.

Primary table: The table on the "one" side of a one-to-many relationship.

Foreign key: The field in the table on the "many" side that relates each record to a record in the primary table.

If you forget to set the property of the foreign key to Long Integer, you won't be able to define a relationship between the tables. Or worse yet, if you add data to both tables without defining a relationship first, and then try to access related records from both tables, the results will be incorrect and *very* confusing.

This is just one of those picky little things you need to remember about Access. If you forget, and problems arise much later down the road, you might not think to check the field properties in the tables until you've spent 20 hours on hold with technical support and pulled out all your hair.

Documenting Your Tables and Database

It's often handy to have a printed copy of information about your table structures when you start developing other objects in your database. Chapter 17 covers these "database administration" tools in detail. But here's a quick preview of techniques for the curious:

- **To print design information about any database objects** (including tables or the entire database), choose Tools ➤ Analyze ➤ Documentor, or click on the drop-down arrow next to the Analyze button on the database window's toolbar and choose Documentor.

- **To view or change database properties,** choose File ➤ Database Properties, or right-click on the database window's title bar or any gray area on the database window and choose Database Properties.

- **To print the table design window or the Relationships window,** use standard copy/cut-and-paste techniques to copy the screen to the Windows Clipboard, paste the Clipboard contents into Windows Paint, and then print the results. See the sidebar titled "Printing the Relationships Window and other 'Unprintable' Things" earlier in this chapter.

Analyzing Your Tables and Database Performance

Two Access Wizards can help you optimize your tables and improve database performance. You'll learn about both of these in Chapter 16. But for now, here's a summary of what's available:

Table Analyzer Wizard Analyzes any table you choose and lets you split it into related tables, if necessary. To get started, choose Tools ➤ Analyze ➤ Table, or click on the drop-down arrow next to the Analyze button on the database window's toolbar and choose Analyze Table.

Performance Analyzer Wizard Analyzes relationships, tables, queries, forms, reports, macros, modules, or all objects, and provides suggestions for making the selected objects work more efficiently. To use this Wizard, choose Tools ➤ Analyze ➤ Performance, or click on the drop-down arrow next to the Analyze button on the database window's toolbar and choose Analyze Performance.

Where to Go from Here

In this chapter, you've learned how to design tables using both the Table Wizard and various from-scratch methods. Where should you go from here?

- To learn how to import or link existing data into your tables, see Chapter 7.

- To learn more about entering data into your tables, see Chapter 8.

What's New in the Access Zoo?

Access for Windows 95 has many improved features for creating and managing tables. These include:

- A revamped Table Wizard, which can create tables for you automatically.

- An enhanced table design window that offers new field properties.

- A Lookup Wizard and lookup properties, which let you set up fields that take their values from other tables and queries or from a list of values. During data entry, you can select the values from a drop-down list.

- Fields with the AutoNumber data type can have automatic values assigned incrementally or randomly.

- An enhanced Relationships window lets you define relationships between tables and change any table's design on the spot.

- New and improved Wizards for documenting and analyzing databases and for splitting one large table into related tables (see Chapters 16 and 17).

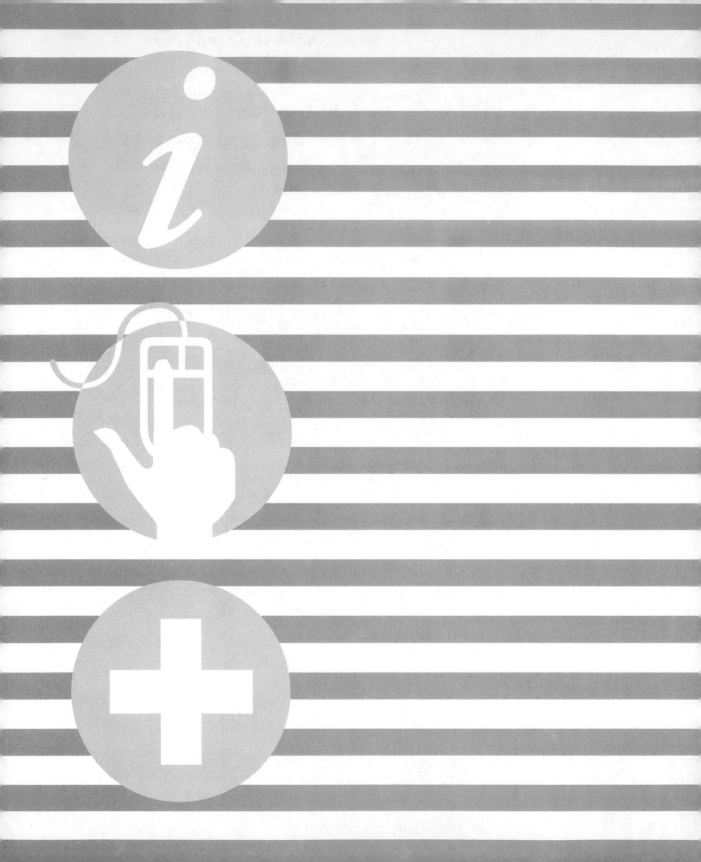

CHAPTER

7

Linking, Importing, and Exporting Data

YOU'LL want to read this chapter if you already have data on your computer that you want to pull into Access, or you've created an Access database and want to export its data to another program.

 Most procedures described in this chapter for linking, importing, and exporting data are quick and easy to use. However, a few fine points can be tricky, especially if you're working with ODBC, Paradox, or dBASE database files. Luckily, there's lots of online Help available. Choose one of these topics from the Access Help Index to get going quickly:

- Importing Data From Other Programs And Formats.
- Exporting Data To Another File Format.

NOTE See Chapter 4 for other ways to share data among Microsoft Office programs.

Link, Import, Export: What's the Difference?

Access gives you several ways to share data with other programs:

Link   Lets you directly access data in another computer database. Any changes you make via Access will affect the original database as well as the Access database. That is, you'll be working with *live data*.

In previous versions of Access, linking was called
attaching.

Import   Lets you make a separate copy of data from other programs and file formats into an Access table. Changes you make
via Access *will not* affect the original data.

Export   Lets you copy data *from* an Access table *to* some other
program or file format, such as Microsoft Word or Excel, or even a
separate Access database. The exported data is an entirely separate copy that *isn't* linked to your original Access data in any way.

Automating Import and Export Procedures

You can use a macro or Visual Basic procedure to automate importing, linking, and exporting certain types of data. Here are the macro and Visual Basic actions you'll need to use:

TransferDatabase   Lets you import or export data between the
current Access database and another database. See the *Transfer-
Database Action* and *TransferDatabase Method* topics in the Access
Help Index.

TransferSpreadSheet   Lets you import or export data between
the current Access database and a spreadsheet file. See the *Transfer-
Spreadsheet Action* and *TransferSpreadsheet Method* topics in the Access Help Index.

TransferText   Lets you import or export data between the current Access database and a text file. See the *TransferText Action* and
TransferText Method topics in the Access Help Index.

SendObject   Lets you create Microsoft Excel (*.xls), Rich Text
Format (*.rtf), or MS-DOS Text (*.txt) output from a table, query,
form, report, or module, and then send that output in an electronic
mail message. See the *SendObject Action* and *SendObject Method* topics in the Access Help Index.

Parts Four and Five of this book introduce macros and Visual Basic.

After importing or linking data from another program into Access, you can use that data as though you had created it in Access originally. For example, if you import or link a Paradox table into your Access database, you can open that table and use it as you would any Access table.

Similarly, you can use exported Access tables in other programs, just as though you had created the exported data in the other program originally. Thus, you can export an Access table to Paradox format, fire up Paradox, and then open and use the table as you would any other "native" Paradox table.

N O T E   *OLE* is a technology that offers another way to combine information from separate programs. However, OLE lets you share *objects*, rather than *data*. We'll talk about OLE in Chapter 8.

Interacting with Other Databases

You can import or link data from any of these database formats:

- dBASE III, III+, IV, and 5.

- Paradox versions 3.*x*, 4.*x*, and 5.0.

- Microsoft FoxPro versions 2.0, 2.5, 2.6, and 3.0.

- Open Database Connectivity (ODBC) databases, including Microsoft SQL Server. You'll need a properly installed and configured ODBC driver.

- Databases created with the Microsoft Jet database engine, including Microsoft Access (versions 1.*x*, 2.0, 7.0) and Microsoft Visual Basic.

- Databases kept in Microsoft Excel worksheets, versions 5.0 and 7.0.

NOTE

Btrieve and Oracle 7.x support won't be available when Access is released. When it is ready, the Btrieve ISAM will be obtainable from Microsoft Product Support Services (PSS), CompuServe, and the Microsoft Network. The Oracle driver will be included in a service pack. Please check those sources for details.

Before you bring data from one of these other formats into an Access database, you need to decide whether to link to that data or import your own copy of it. Table 7.1 lists some points that can help you decide.

TABLE 7.1: Differences between Imported and Linked Tables

IMPORTED TABLE	LINKED TABLE
Copied from the external table to your open database. (Requires extra disk storage.)	Linked to your open database. No copies are made. (Conserves disk storage.)
Use when you no longer need to have the original application update the table.	Use when you still need to have the original application update the table.
Converted to Access format and works exactly like a table you created from scratch.	Retains its original database format, but "acts like" an Access table.
You can change any properties, including the structure, of an imported table.	You can change some properties, but you can't change the structure of a linked table.
Access can work faster with imported tables.	Access may work more slowly with linked tables.
Deleting the table deletes the copy from your open database.	Deleting the table deletes the link only, not the external table.
Access translates certain data types of the original table to Access data types.	No data type translations are necessary.

Where You'll See Imported/Linked Tables

When you import or link data from another database, Access treats the data as it would one of its own tables. But, for linked tables, you'll see special icons in the database window indicating that the data is not originally from Access.

In Figure 7.1, we linked Access tables named Expense Categories, Expense Details, and Expense Reports (from another Access database), a Paradox table named Biolife, and a dBASE 5 table named Grades to an open Order Entry1 database. We also imported a table named Sales from a Microsoft Excel worksheet. Notice that the icons next to the linked

FIGURE 7.1

Linked tables are indicated by special link icons.

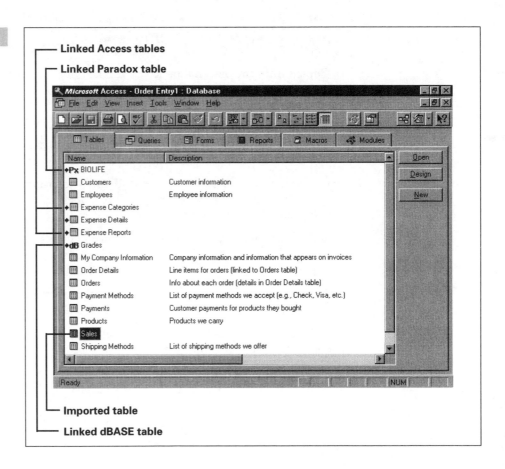

tables include an arrow symbol to indicate a link to the external tables; however, the icon next to the Sales table looks like any other Access table icon.

Importing or Linking a Table

Here are the general steps for importing or linking tables. The exact procedures will depend on the type of data you're importing or linking. Refer to the appropriate section below for more details.

1. Open (or create) the database you want to import or link the table to and switch to the database window if it isn't visible.

2. Do one of the following, depending on whether you are importing or linking:

   - **To *import*,** choose File ➤ Get External Data ➤ Import, or right-click on the database window (the shaded part, not a table name) and choose Import. Or, click on the Tables tab on the database window, click on the database window's New button, and then double-click on Import Table in the New Table dialog box.

   - **To *link*,** choose File ➤ Get External Data ➤ Link Tables, or right-click on the database window and choose Link Tables. Or, click on the Tables tab on the database window, click on the database window's New button, and then double-click on Link Table in the New Table dialog box.

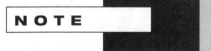

NOTE You cannot delete rows from linked Excel tables or text files.

3. In the Files Of Type drop-down list, choose the type of data you want to import or link. For example, click on the drop-down list button next to Files Of Type, and then click on Paradox to import or link a Paradox table.

4. Locate the file name you want to import or link, and then click on it in the list below Look In. Figure 7.2 shows a typical Link dialog box; the Import dialog box is similar.

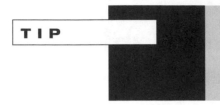

TIP
The techniques for locating drives, folders, and files in the Link and Import dialog boxes are the same ones that work in the Open and File New Database dialog boxes (see Chapters 1 and 5, respectively).

5. Click on the Import or Link button, or double-click on the file name you want to import or link.

FIGURE 7.2

A Link dialog box for linking an Excel table

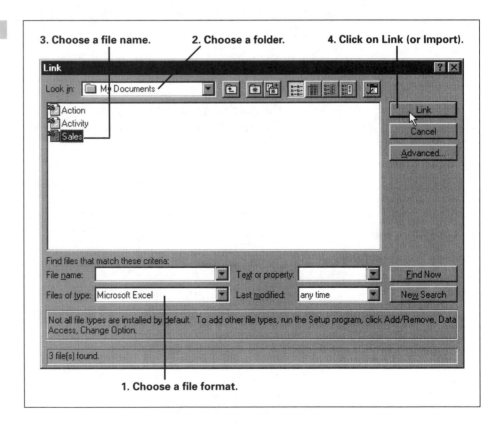

3. Choose a file name. 2. Choose a folder. 4. Click on Link (or Import).

1. Choose a file format.

6. Respond to any additional prompts and dialog boxes that appear.

- If you're linking a dBASE or FoxPro table, you'll be prompted to choose one or more existing indexes to associate with the table. Choosing indexes will speed up access to the linked table.

- If you're importing or linking a table from Paradox or a SQL database, you may be prompted for a password. This password is set in the external program, and is different from an Access user password.

N O T E

Passwords of linked tables are stored in your database so that you can open the table later, simply by double-clicking on it in the Access database window. Be aware that the database password is stored in an unencrypted form. If you need to protect sensitive data in the linked table, it's best to implement user-level security, rather than using a database password. (See Chapter 18 and the Help Index topic *Linking Tables, Password-Protected Databases.*)

7. If you see a message that the operation is complete, click on OK.

8. If the Import or Link dialog box remains on your screen, you can repeat steps 3–7 until you've imported or linked all the tables you want. When you're done, click on the Close button as needed.

 ➤ For more help on importing and linking tables, go to the Access Help Contents, open the *Creating, Importing, And Linking Tables* book, open the *Importing Or Linking Tables* book, and then double-click on an appropriate topic. You also can look up topics and subtopics under *Importing Data...* and *Linking Data...* in the Access Help Index.

Importing or Linking Paradox Tables

Access can import or link tables (.db files) from Paradox version 3, 4, and 5. The steps are:

1. Start from the Access database window and choose the Import or Link command. (Two easy starting points are to choose the File ➤ Get External Data commands on the menu bar, or right-click on the database window and choose Import or Link Tables from the shortcut menu.)

2. From the Files Of Type drop-down list, choose Paradox.

3. Locate the file you want to import or link, and then double-click on it in the list below Look In.

4. If you're prompted for a password, type the password that was assigned to the table in Paradox and then click on OK.

5. When you see the message that the operation is complete, click on OK.

6. Repeat steps 3–5 as needed. When you're done, click on Close.

 ➤ Having trouble? Perhaps the following will help:

- A linked Paradox table must have a primary key (.px) file if you intend to update it through Access, and that file must be available or Access won't be able to link the table. Without a primary key, you'll only be able to view the linked table, not change it.

- In general, any ancillary file that Paradox maintains for a table (such as a .mb file for memo fields) should be available to Access.

- Because Access can't open OLE objects stored in a linked or imported Paradox table, no OLE fields will appear when you open the table in Access.

- When linking a shared Paradox table that resides on a server, you must set the ParadoxNetPath key in the Windows registry to the path of the Paradox.net or Pdoxusrs.net file. Furthermore, if you're using Paradox version 4 or 5 to share data in your workgroup, you also must set the ParadoxNetStyle key to "4.x." For Paradox version 3 tables, set this key to "3.x" (the default is "4.x").

For more details about importing and linking Paradox tables, look up *Import Or Link A Paradox Table* in the Access Answer Wizard. See topics under *Registry* or *Registry Editor* in the Access Help Index for details about using the Registry Editor.

WARNING Making changes incorrectly in the Registry Editor can produce unexpected results in Access. Be sure to back up all or part of the registry before making changes in the Registry Editor. See the topic *Backing Up The Registry* in the Registry Editor's Help Index for details.

Importing or Linking dBASE and FoxPro Files

Access can import or link tables (.dbf files) from dBASE III, IV, and dBASE 5, and FoxPro 2.0, 2.5, 2.6, and 3.0. Here are the basic steps for importing or linking a dBASE or FoxPro table:

1. Start from the Access database window and choose the Import or Link command.

2. From the Files Of Type drop-down list, choose dBASE III, dBASE IV, dBASE 5, Microsoft FoxPro, or Microsoft FoxPro 3.0.

3. Locate the file you want to import or link, and then double-click on it in the list below Look In.

4. If the Select Index Files dialog box appears, double-click on the index file you want to use. Repeat this step until you've specified all the index files associated with the .dbf file you chose in step 3, and respond to any other prompts that appear. When you're done, click on the Close or Cancel button.

5. When you see the message that the operation is complete, click on OK.

6. Repeat steps 3–5 as needed. When you're done, click on Close.

When linking dBASE or FoxPro files, keep these points in mind:

- To improve performance later, you can have Access use one or more existing dBASE index files (.ndx or .mdx) or FoxPro index files (.idx or .cdx). The index files are tracked in a special information file (.inf) and are maintained automatically when you update the table through Access.

- If you use dBASE or FoxPro to update data in a linked .dbf file, you must *manually* update the associated indexes; otherwise Access won't be able to use the linked table.

- Do not move or remove any .ndx, .mdx, or .inf files that Access is using, or Access won't be able to open the linked table.

- To link tables on a read-only drive or CD-ROM drive, Access must store the .inf file on a *writable* directory. To specify this directory, you must specify the path for the .inf file in the Windows Registry.

 ➤ For more about updating, look up *Import Or Link A dBase or FoxPro Table* in the Access Answer Wizard. See topics under *Registry* or *Registry Editor* in the Access Help Index for details about using the Registry Editor.

Importing or Linking SQL Tables

If everything is properly set up, you can use Access and Open Database Connectivity (ODBC) drivers to open tables on Microsoft SQL Servers and other SQL database servers on a network. Here are the basic steps for linking or importing SQL database tables:

1. Start from the Access database window and choose the Import or Link command.

2. From the Files Of Type drop-down list, choose ODBC Databases.

3. In the SQL Data Sources dialog box, double-click on the SQL data source you want to use. (If necessary, you can define a new data source for any installed ODBC driver by clicking on the New button and following the instructions that appear. After creating the new data source, you can double-click on it to continue. Alternatively, you can manage your ODBC data sources by double-clicking on the 32bit ODBC icon in Control Panel.)

4. Complete the remaining dialog boxes that appear, clicking on OK as needed to proceed (these dialog boxes depend on the data source you chose). For example, you may be prompted for the following:

- Your login ID and password.
- Whether you want to save the login ID and password (if you're linking).
- The tables you want to import or link.
- The fields that uniquely identify each record.

5. When you're finished importing or linking, click on Close.

 If you're having trouble with the importing or linking procedure, consider these points:

- Before connecting to a SQL database, you must install the proper ODBC driver for your network and SQL database. You can find information on this procedure by looking up the *Installing Drivers* topic in the Access Help Index.

- Access includes the ODBC drivers for Microsoft SQL Server, Access, Paradox, dBASE, FoxPro, Excel, and Text. Before using any other OBDC driver, check with its vendor to verify that it will work properly.

- If you'll want to edit a linked SQL table, that table usually must contain a unique index. If no unique index exists, you can create one by executing a data-definition query within Access. For information on data-definition queries, open the *Microsoft Jet SQL Reference* book in the Access Help Contents, open the *Data Definition Language* book, and then double-click on the *CREATE INDEX Statement* topic.

- If the SQL table's structure changes after you link it, you'll need to use the Linked Table Manager to refresh your link to the table (see "Using the Linked Table Manager" later in the chapter), or delete and recreate the link.

- If an error occurs while you're importing, linking, or using a SQL table, there may be a problem with your account on the SQL database server or the database itself. Please contact your SQL database administrator for assistance.

➤ For more about the subtleties of importing and linking SQL tables, look up *Import Or Link A SQL Table* in the Access Answer Wizard.

Importing or Linking Other Access Databases

Normally you'll want to store all the tables, forms, reports, and other objects that make up a given application in a single Access database. But in a large company, different departments might create their own separate Access databases. Fortunately, it's easy to import objects (tables, queries, forms, reports, macros, and modules) or link tables from other unopened Access databases into your open database. Then you can use the objects as if they were part of your currently open Access database. This is much easier than using copy-and-paste to copy several related objects at once. Also, linked tables make it easy for many users to share a single copy of their data over a network.

N O T E You can import just the structure or both the structure and data of Access tables. If you intend to import objects (forms, reports, queries, and so forth) for use with tables in the open database, the name and structure of the tables in the open database must match the name and structure of the tables originally used to create the objects you're importing.

To import objects or link tables from an unopened Access database:

1. Start from the Access database window and choose the Import or Link command.

2. From the Files Of Type list, choose Microsoft Access.

3. Locate the Access database you want to import or link, and then double-click on it in the list below Look In.

4. If you're linking, you'll see the Link Tables dialog box shown in Figure 7.3; skip to step 6. If you're importing objects, you'll see the Import Objects dialog box shown in Figure 7.4; continue with step 5.

FIGURE 7.3

The Link Tables dialog box

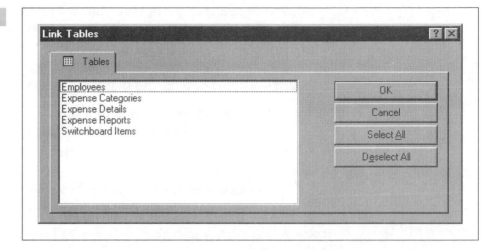

FIGURE 7.4

The Import Objects dialog box after clicking on the Options button

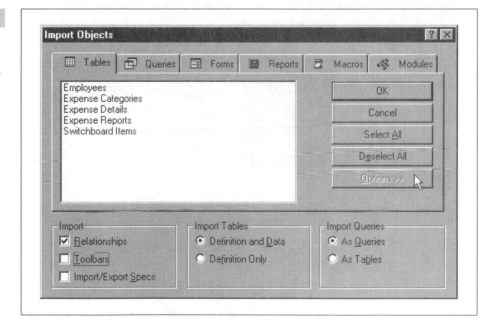

5. If you're importing objects, click on the tab for the type of object you want to import. As Figure 7.4 shows, your options are Tables, Queries, Forms, Reports, Macros, and Modules. For additional import options, click on the Options button (see Figure 7.4), and

then choose any of the options shown. (For help with the options, click on the ? button at the upper-right corner of the Import Objects dialog box, and then click on the place you need help with.)

6. Use any of the following techniques to select the object(s) you want to import or link, and then click on OK to continue.

- **To select all the objects of a particular type in one fell swoop**, click on the Select <u>A</u>ll button.

- **To deselect all the selected objects**, click on the D<u>e</u>select All button.

- **To select one object** that isn't selected yet, or to deselect an object that is selected, click on its name.

Access will import or link all the objects you selected and return to the database window.

TIP

The opposite of importing or linking a database is splitting it—a trick that can make your database run faster over networks. You can use the Database Splitter Wizard (<u>T</u>ools ➤ Add-<u>I</u>ns ➤ <u>D</u>atabase Splitter) to split a database into one file that contains the tables, and another that contains the queries, forms, reports, macros, and modules. See Chapter 18 for details.

Another Reason to Use Wizards

It turns out that objects created with Access Wizards are perfect candidates for linking or importing into other Access databases that also contain objects created with those Wizards. For instance, if the Database Wizard or Table Wizard was used (with default settings) to create Customers tables in two Access databases—Order Entry and Service Call Management, for example—those tables will have the same structure in both databases. If you then import into the Service Call Management database a report that was designed to print the Customers table in the Order Entry database, that report should work perfectly on the Customers table in the Service Order Processing database.

Using Linked Tables

After linking a table from another database, you can use it *almost* like any other Access table. You can enter and update data, use existing queries, forms, and reports, or develop new ones. So even if the data resides in separate programs on separate computers, Access can use the external table almost as if you had created it from scratch in your open database. The only real restrictions are that you can't change the structure of a linked table, and you can't delete rows from a linked Excel table or text file.

NOTE   After *importing* a table from another database, you can use it *exactly* like any other Access table. Access will never know that your imported table wasn't originally one of its own.

Setting Properties of Linked Tables

Although you can't add, delete, or rearrange fields of a linked table, you can set some table properties, including the Format, Input Mask, Decimal Places, and Caption. You change these properties in the table design view (see Chapter 6). In the database window, you can right-click on the table name on the Tables tab, choose Properties, and change the Description property.

TIP   Anytime you click in a General or Lookup properties box in the Field Properties area of the table design window, the Hint box in the right side of the window will tell you if the selected property cannot be changed.

Renaming Linked or Imported Tables

Most objects will have their original file names when you import or link them to Access. After you've imported or linked such a file, however, you can give it a more descriptive name in your Access database window. For instance, you could rename an imported or linked dBASE table from *CredCard* to *Credit Cards (From dBASE)*.

To quickly rename an imported or linked table, right-click on its name in the database window, choose Rename from the shortcut menu, type a new name, and then press ↵.

Speeding Up Linked Tables

Although linked tables behave a lot like Access tables, they're not actually stored in your Access database. Each time you view linked data, Access must retrieve records from another file that may be on another computer in the network or in a SQL database. You might grow some gray hairs waiting for this to happen.

These guidelines can help speed up performance in a linked table on a network or SQL database:

- Avoid jumping to the last record of a large table unless you need to add new records.

- View only the data you absolutely need and don't scroll up and down unnecessarily.

- If you frequently add new records to a linked table, create a form that has the Data Entry property on the Data tab set to Yes. That way, Access won't bother to display any existing records from the table when you enter data (see Chapter 13). This *data entry* mode (also called *add* mode) can be much faster than opening the form in edit mode and jumping to the last record. (If you need to see all the records again, choose <u>R</u>ecords ➤ <u>R</u>emove Filter/Sort.)

N O T E

Here are three more ways to open a form or table in data entry mode. 1) Choose <u>R</u>ecords ➤ <u>D</u>ata Entry after opening a table or form. 2) Choose Open Form In Add Mode as the <u>C</u>ommand for a form you've added to a switchboard with the Switchboard Manager (see Chapters 3 and 21). 3) In a macro design window, use the OpenForm action to open a form, and set the action's Data Mode action argument to Add (see Chapter 20).

- Use queries and filters to limit the number of records that you view in a form or datasheet.

- Avoid using functions, especially domain-aggregate functions such as DSum( ), anywhere in your queries. These require Access to process *all* the data in the linked table. See Chapter 10 for more about these functions.

- When sharing external tables with other users on a network, avoid locking records longer than you need to. Hogging the locks will slow response time for others and make you unpopular in a hurry. See Chapter 18 for more about using Access on a network.

Using the Linked Table Manager

Access stores information about links to tables in your database. If you move the file that contains the linked table to another folder, Access won't be able to open the linked table. Fortunately, the Linked Table Manager can find the moved tables and fix things up quickly. Here's how to use it:

1. Open the database that you've linked the objects to.

2. Choose Tools ➤ Add-Ins ➤ Linked Table Manager to open the Linked Table Manager dialog box (see Figure 7.5). This dialog box shows the linked objects and the full path names of the associated source files.

3. To select the linked tables you want to update, click on the appropriate check boxes. If you select a table accidentally, click on its check box again to deselect (clear) the box. Or, click on the Select All or Deselect All buttons to check or clear all the check boxes in one step.

4. To force the Linked Table Manager to request the location for each table you checked in step 3, select (check) Always Prompt For New Location.

5. Click on OK.

6. Use the Select New Location Of ... dialog box that appears next, to find the folder that contains the moved source table, and then double-click on the file name that contains the linked table. Repeat this step as needed.

FIGURE 7.5

The Linked Table
Manager dialog box
for a database with
several linked files

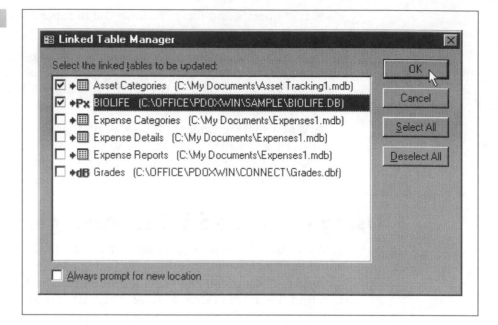

What the Linked Table Manager Cannot Do

The Linked Table Manager is great for finding *files* that have wandered off to a different folder or disk drive or have been renamed. However, if anyone has renamed the linked *table* or changed its password, Access won't be able to find the table and the Linked Table Manager won't be able to fix the problem. In these cases, you must delete the link and then relink the table with the correct table name and/or password.

Also, don't expect the Linked Table Manager to move the database or table files for you. For that job, you'll need to use Windows Explorer or My Computer. Or, go to any Access Open, File New Database, Link, Import, or Select New Location Of … dialog box; then, right-click on an empty area below the Look In list, choose Explore from the shortcut menu, and explore as you would with Windows Explorer.

T I P The Select New Location Of ... dialog box works like the Open, File New Database, Import, and Link dialog boxes you already know and love. See Chapters 1 and 5 for techniques you can use in these dialog boxes.

7. When Access tells you that the links were refreshed successfully, click on OK, and then click on Close in the Linked Table Manager dialog box.

Deleting the Link to a Linked Table

When you no longer need to use a linked table (or Access can't find it because someone has renamed it or changed its password), you can delete the link. To do this, open the database window that contains the linked table and click on the Tables tab. Then, click on the table whose link you want to delete, and press the Delete key. When asked if you're sure you want to delete the link, click on Yes.

Remember that deleting a link deletes the information used to access the linked table, but it has absolutely no effect on the table itself. You can relink the table at any time.

Importing or Linking Spreadsheets and Text Files

You can import or link any of these spreadsheet and text formats into Access tables:

- Microsoft Excel versions 2, 3, 4, and 5 and Excel 7 (also known as Excel for Windows 95 or Excel 95).

- Lotus 1-2-3 or 1-2-3 for Windows (.wk1, .wk3, and .wk4 files). Lotus .wk1 and .wk3 can be imported, but not linked; Lotus .wk4 files can be imported and linked.

- Delimited text (values are separated by commas, tabs, or other characters).

- Fixed-width text, including Microsoft Word Merge (each field value is a certain width).

When importing from a text file, you can create a new table, or append the data to an existing table. If your spreadsheet or text file contains field names in the first row, Access can use them as field names in the table.

Access looks at the first row of data and does its best to assign the appropriate data type for each field you import. For example, importing cells A1 through C10 from the spreadsheet at the top of Figure 7.6 creates the Access table at the bottom of the figure. Here we told Access to use the first row of the range (row 1) as field labels. Values in row 2 (the first row of "real" data) were then used to determine the data types for each field.

FIGURE 7.6

Importing a range of cells from an Excel spreadsheet into an Access table

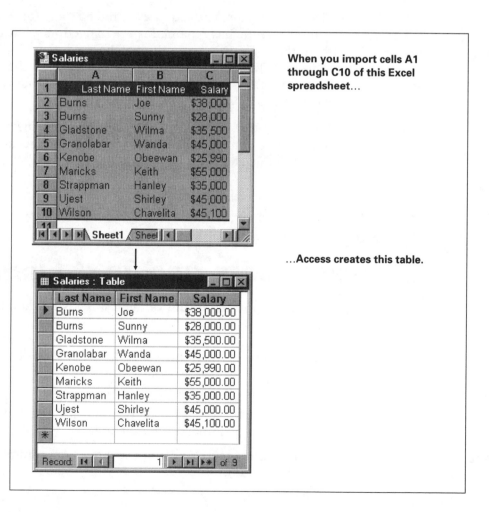

When you import cells A1 through C10 of this Excel spreadsheet...

...Access creates this table.

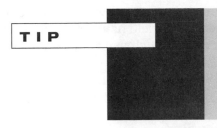

TIP You can change the field names and data types assigned to an imported table during the import procedure. Alternatively, you can create an empty table with the field names and data types you want, and then *append* an imported text file to the empty table.

In Figure 7.7, we imported a delimited text file, in which each field is separated by a comma and text fields are enclosed in quotes. Again we asked Access to use the first row as field labels. Access used the second row to determine each field's data type.

FIGURE 7.7

Importing from a delimited text file into an Access table

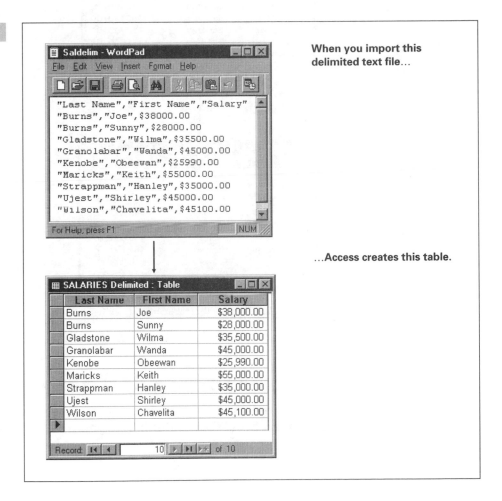

Figure 7.8 shows the results of importing a fixed-width text file into an Access table. This time, we told Access the field name to use for each field (it correctly figured out the other details, such as field position and data type).

FIGURE 7.8

Importing from a fixed-width text file into an Access table

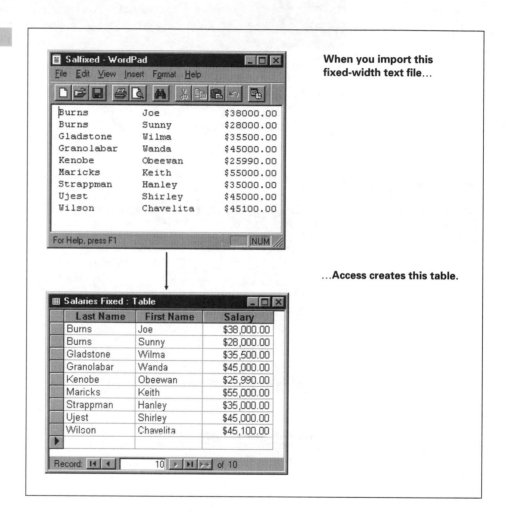

When you import this fixed-width text file...

...Access creates this table.

Importing or Linking Spreadsheets

Importing or linking a spreadsheet into Access is a snap, thanks to the Import Spreadsheet Wizard. But before you import or link, remember that the data in your spreadsheet must be arranged so that:

- Each value in a given field contains the same type of data;
- Each row contains the same fields;
- The first row in the spreadsheet contains either field names or the first actual data you want to import, or you've defined a named range for the data you want to import).

If the spreadsheet you intend to use doesn't fit this specification, you'll need to fix it before importing or linking it into Access.

To import or link a spreadsheet:

1. Start from the Access database window in which the table should appear and choose the Import or Link command.

2. From the Files Of Type drop-down list, choose the spreadsheet format you want to import. Your choices are Microsoft Excel (for importing or linking) and Lotus 1-2-3 (for importing only).

3. Locate the spreadsheet file you want to import or link, and then double-click on it in the list below Look In. The Wizard will take over.

4. If your worksheet contains a named range or multiple sheets, you'll see a dialog box similar to Figure 7.9 (the Import Spreadsheet Wizard and Link Spreadsheet Wizard dialog boxes are the same, except for their title bars). Choose whether to Show Worksheets or Show Named Ranges, click on the worksheet or named range you want to use, and then click on Next.

5. Figure 7.10 shows the next dialog box you'll see. If the first row of the range you're importing or linking contains labels that you want to use as field names for the table, select (check) First Row Contains Column Headings. If you don't check this box, Access will start importing or linking data with the first row of the range, and will assign the name "Field" followed by a sequential number as the field names (Field1, Field2, Field3, …). Click on Next to continue.

6. If you're importing, you'll see the dialog box shown in Figure 7.11. From here you can specify information about each field you're importing. To tell the Wizard which field you want to define, click

FIGURE 7.9

This Import Spread-sheet Wizard dialog box appears if your worksheet contains multiple sheets or named ranges. If you're linking an Excel worksheet, the Link Spreadsheet Wizard dialog box will be the same, except for its title bar.

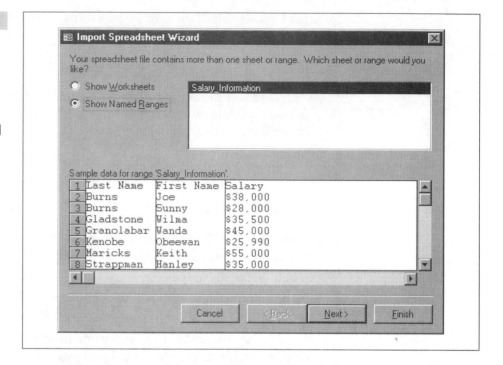

FIGURE 7.10

This dialog box lets you specify whether the first imported or linked row contains field names. In this example, we're importing the spreadsheet shown at the top of Figure 7.6. Again, the Link Spreadsheet Wizard dialog box is similar.

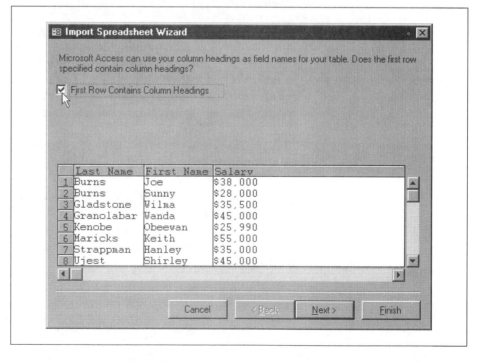

FIGURE 7.11

This dialog box lets you specify the field name, indexing, and data type for each imported field, and it lets you skip fields as needed.

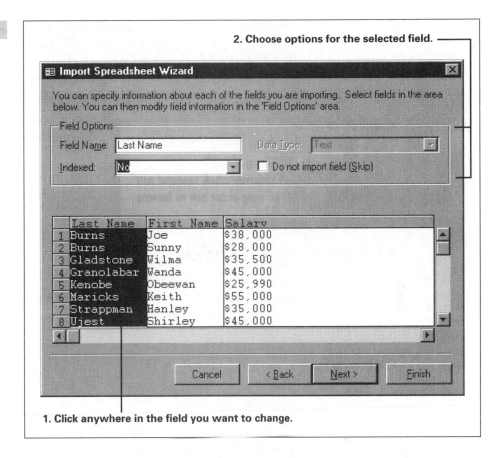

2. Choose options for the selected field.

1. Click anywhere in the field you want to change.

anywhere on the sample data for that field in the lower part of the dialog box. Then, fill in the Field Name box, specify whether the field is indexed by choosing No, Yes (Duplicates OK), or Yes (No Duplicates) from the Indexed drop-down list, and specify a data type by choosing an option from the Data Type drop-down list (if available). If you prefer to skip the field—that is, not to import it—select (check) Do Not Import Field (Skip). Repeat step 6 as needed, and then click on Next.

7. If you're importing, the next dialog box will let you specify how Access should assign the primary key. You can let Access add the primary key, choose your own primary key from a drop-down list of available field names, or omit the primary key. After making your selection, click on Next to continue.

8. The last dialog box lets you specify a table name. If you're importing, you also can choose whether to analyze the new table's structure with the Table Analyzer Wizard. (Chapter 16 describes the Table Analyzer Wizard.) Complete this dialog box and then click on Finish.

9. If you're asked for permission to overwrite an existing table, click on Yes to overwrite the table and continue with step 10, or click on No to return to step 8.

10. When Access tells you that it has finished importing or linking the table, click on OK. You'll see the new table name in the database window.

Importing or Linking Text Files

A *delimited* text file is one in which fields are separated by a special character such as a comma or tab, and each record ends with a carriage-return/linefeed combination. Typically, character data items are enclosed in quotation marks, as shown at the top of Figure 7.7.

A *fixed width* text file is one in which each field is a specified width, and each record ends with a carriage-return/linefeed combination (see the top of Figure 7.8).

Before importing or linking a text file, make sure it's arranged so that each value in a given field contains the same type of data and the same fields appear in every row. The first row can contain the field names you want Access to use when creating the table.

The procedure for importing or linking text files is controlled by a Wizard that's fast and painless to use. In fact, it takes much longer to read these steps than to do them:

1. Start from the Access database window in which the table should appear and choose the Import or Link command.

2. From the Files Of Type drop-down list, choose Text Files.

3. Locate the text file you want to import or link, and then double-click on it in the list below Look In. The Wizard will take over (see Figure 7.12).

FIGURE 7.12

The first Text Import Wizard dialog box lets you choose a format for importing your data. If you're linking the text file, the Link Text Wizard dialog box will look the same, except for its title bar.

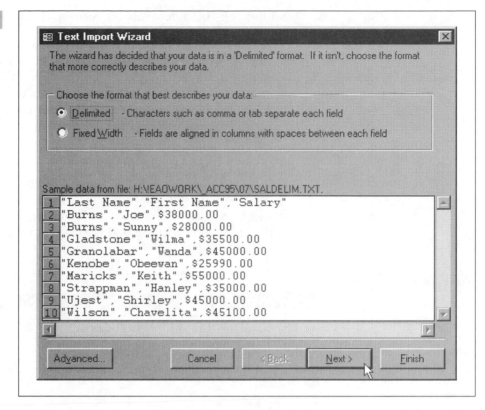

4. If Access didn't guess the correct format, choose the format that describes your data (either Delimited or Fixed Width), and then click on Next.

NOTE

The Advanced button in the Text Import Wizard and Link Text Wizard dialog boxes lets you define, save, load, and delete import specifications. You can use an import specification if you want more control over such things as the order of dates, date delimiters, time delimiters, and other details. In most cases, it's not necessary to use the Advanced button, because the Wizard defines the specification for you. There's more about using import specifications later in this chapter.

5. What happens next depends on your choice in step 4:

- If you chose <u>D</u>elimited, you'll see the dialog box shown in Figure 7.13. Choose the delimiter that separates your fields, specify whether the first row of text contains field names, and specify the character that encloses text within fields (the Text <u>Q</u>ualifier). As you make choices, the sample data in the dialog box will reflect your changes, so you can see immediately whether your choices make sense.

- If you chose <u>F</u>ixed, you'll see the dialog box shown in Figure 7.14. You might not need to change any of the settings, but if you do, the instructions in the dialog box explain how (it's easy!). As you specify the field breaks and field widths, the sample data in the dialog box will reflect your changes.

FIGURE 7.13

This Text Import Wizard dialog box lets you choose the delimiter and text qualifier (enclosing character for fields) for a delimited text file. You also can specify whether the first row of text contains field names. The Link Text Wizard dialog box is similar.

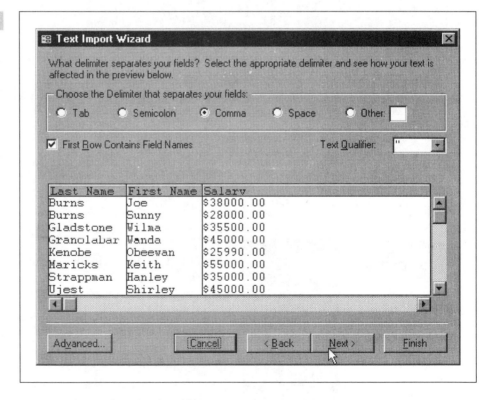

FIGURE 7.14

This Text Import Wizard dialog box lets you specify the position and width of each field in your fixed width file. The Link Text Wizard dialog box is similar.

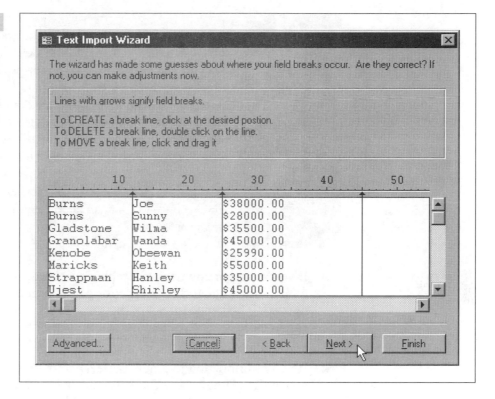

6. After completing the dialog box shown in Figure 7.13 or 7.14, click on <u>N</u>ext.

7. If you're linking a text file, skip to step 8. If you're importing a text file, the next dialog box lets you choose whether to store your data in a new table or an existing table:

   - **To save the data in a new table,** select In A Ne<u>w</u> Table, click on <u>N</u>ext, and continue with step 8.

   - **To add the imported data to the end of an existing table,** choose In An E<u>x</u>isting Table, use the drop-down list to select the existing table, and then click on <u>N</u>ext. Skip to step 10.

WARNING

When you add imported data to the end of an existing table, each field in the data file you're importing must have the same data type as the corresponding field in the destination table, each field must be in the same order, the data must not duplicate data in primary key fields, and the data must not violate any validation rules. If you're using the first row as field names, the field names in your data file must exactly match the names of your table fields. (Appropriate error messages appear if the data breaks any rules, and Access gives you a chance to continue importing data or to cancel the import procedure.)

8. If you're importing to a new table or linking, specify the field name, indexing, and data type for each field, and skip fields as needed. The procedures are the same ones given for step 6 of the earlier procedure "Importing or Linking Spreadsheets." Repeat this step as needed, and then click on Next.

9. If you're importing to a new table, specify how Access should assign the primary key. You can let Access add the primary key, choose your own primary key from a drop-down list of available field names, or omit the primary key. Click on Next to continue.

10. The last dialog box lets you specify a table name. If you're importing, you also can choose whether to analyze the table's structure with the Table Analyzer Wizard (see Chapter 16). Complete this dialog box and then click on Finish.

11. If you're asked for permission to overwrite an existing table, click on Yes to overwrite the table and continue with step 12, or click on No to return to step 10.

12. When Access tells you that it has finished importing or linking the table, click on OK. You'll see the new table name in the database window.

Using an Import or Link Specification

Often, you can ignore the Advanced button in the Text Import Wizard and Link Text Wizard dialog boxes, and just focus on the main steps given in the previous section. But suppose dates in your text file aren't in the standard month/day/year order used in the United States. Perhaps your data uses a period instead of a slash as a date separator. Or maybe the text file was created with an MS-DOS or OS/2 program instead of a Windows program.

In situations such as these, you must use an *import specification* to provide extra details about your file's format. To load a previously saved specification or to define a new one, click on the Advanced button in any Text Import Wizard or Link Text Wizard dialog box (see Figures 7.11–7.13). Figure 7.15 shows the Import Specification dialog box for a delimited text file, and Figure 7.16 shows one for a fixed width text file. As you'd expect, the Link Specification dialog boxes are the same, except for their title bars.

FIGURE 7.15

The Import Specification dialog box for a delimited text file. The Link Specification dialog box is similar.

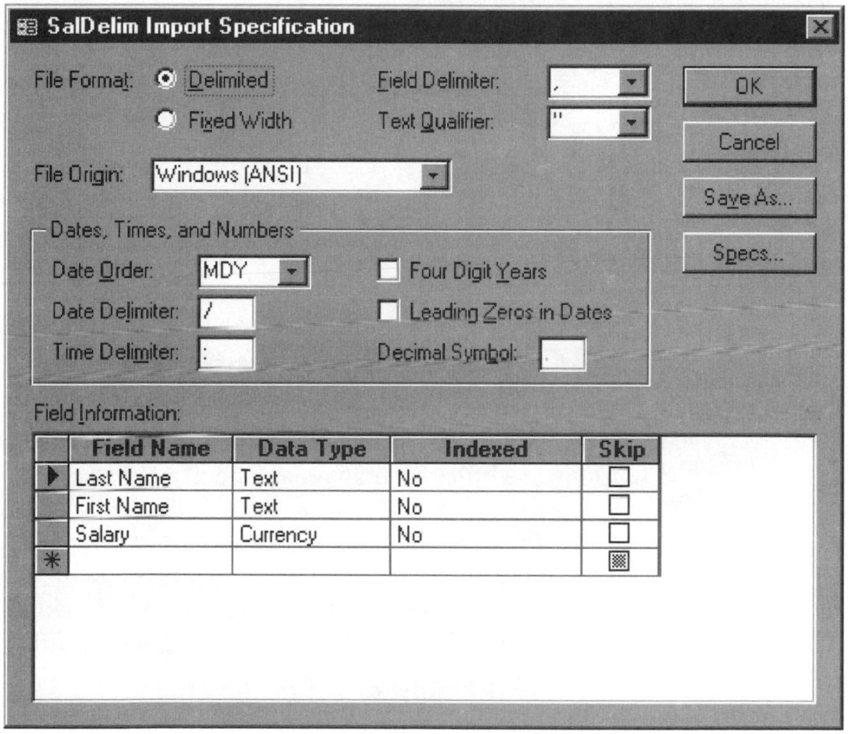

FIGURE 7.16

The Import
Specification dialog
box for a fixed width
text file. The Link
Specification dialog
box is similar.

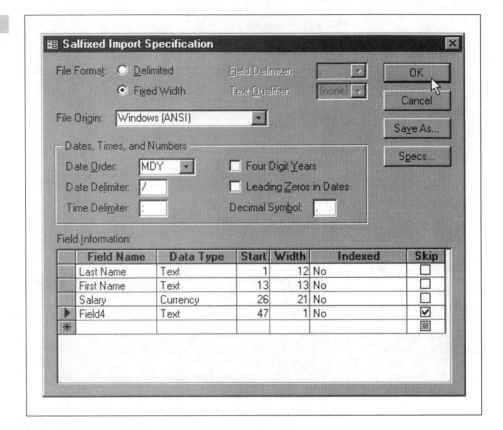

Filling in the Specification

At the top of the Import Specification or Link Specification dialog box,
you can specify the File Format (either Delimited or Fixed Width). For
delimited files, you also can specify:

Field Delimiter   If the text file uses a character other than a
comma (,) to separate fields, type the correct character, or open
the drop-down list and select one. The drop-down list includes
comma, semicolon, tab, and space options.

Text Qualifier   If the text file uses a delimiter other than double
quotation marks (") to surround text fields, type the correct character, or open the drop-down list and select a character. Select
{none} if your file doesn't use a text delimiter.

In the center portion of the dialog box, you can change these settings:

File Origin   Controls the way Access interprets extended characters (those with ASCII codes higher than 128). If the text file was created with a Windows program, choose Windows (ANSI) from the File Origin drop-down list. If the file was created with a DOS or OS/2 program, choose DOS or OS/2 (PC-8).

Date Order   If the text file has dates that aren't in the MDY (month, day, year) order commonly used in the United States, choose an option from the Date Order drop-down list. Foreign dates often appear in a different order, such as DMY (day, month, year) in France or YMD (year, month, day) in Sweden.

Date Delimiter   If the text file has dates that aren't separated by a slash (as in 11/9/53 for November 9, 1953), type the delimiter character in the Date Delimiter text box. Some countries outside the United States use different delimiters, such as the period in France (09.11.53) and the hyphen in Sweden (53-11-09).

Time Delimiter   If hours, minutes, and seconds are delimited by a character other than a colon (:), specify the correct character in the Time Delimiter text box.

Four Digit Years   If years in your text file include all four digits, as in 11/9/1953, select Four Digit Years.

Leading Zeros In Dates   If the dates in your text file include leading zeros, select Leading Zeros In Dates. (United States dates normally appear without leading zeros.)

Decimal Symbol   If a character other than a period (.) is used for the decimal point in numbers with fractions, specify the correct character in the Decimal Symbol text box.

In the Field Information area near the bottom of the dialog box, you can define the Field Name, Data Type, and Indexed options for each field much as you do in table design view. To skip a field during the import, check the appropriate box in the Skip column. If you're working with a fixed width file, you also can specify the Start and Width for each field (however, it's often easier to drag the vertical lines in the dialog box shown in Figure 7.14). If you do adjust the Start and Width values manually, make sure that no gaps exist between any two fields, and that no fields overlap.

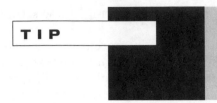

TIP   To calculate the Start value of a field, add the Start and Width values of the previous field. In Figure 7.16, for example, Field 1 starts at 1 and its width is 12. Thus, Field 2 must start at 13 (1 + 12).

Managing Import and Link Specifications

You can save your specifications to use later when importing or exporting similar text files, and you can retrieve and delete import specifications as needed. Just use these two buttons in the Import Specification or Link Specification dialog box:

> **Save As**   Lets you save an import/export specification. Click on Save As, type a descriptive name for your specification (or accept the suggested name), and then click on OK. Access will save your specifications and return you to the Import Specification dialog box.

> **Specs**   Lets you use or delete an existing import/export specification. Click on the Specs button, and then click on the specification you want to work with. Then, to use the selected specification for the current file, click on the Open button. To delete the specification, click on the Delete button, click on Yes, and then click on Cancel.

Continuing with the Import or Link

When you're done changing the import or link specifications, click on OK in the Import Specification or Link Specification dialog box. You'll return to the Wizard dialog box you were using when you clicked on the Advanced button.

Refining an Imported Table's Design

After importing a table, you can improve its design in several ways. To get started, open the table and switch to design view. Then, as necessary...

- **Change field names or add descriptions**. This is especially helpful if you didn't import field names along with the data.

- **Change data types**. Access does its best to guess the correct data type for each field based on the data you imported, and it gives you a chance to make adjustments. However, you can refine the initial choices as needed.

- **Set field properties** such as Field Size, Format, and so forth.

- **Set a primary key** to uniquely identify each record in the table and to improve performance.

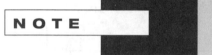

N O T E   See Chapter 6 for more information about changing and customizing tables.

Troubleshooting Import Problems

 If Access has problems importing records into your table, it will display a message similar to the one shown below. For each record that causes an error, Access adds a row to a table named *xxx* _ImportErrors (or *xxx* _ImportErrors1, *xxx* _ImportErrors2, …) in your database, where *xxx* is the name of the imported table. You can open that "ImportErrors" table from the database window to view the error descriptions.

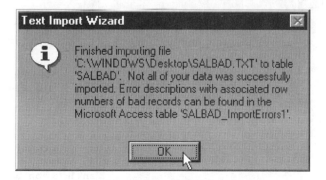

Figure 7.17 shows the ImportErrors table Access created when we tried to import the delimited text file shown at the top of the figure. Notice that

the third line contains a tilde (~) instead of a comma as the field delimiter, and the sixth line has an exclamation point (!) where the decimal point belongs. The SALBAD table at the bottom of the figure contains the records Access imported from the text file. Notice that the bad record in line 3 of the Salbad text file was imported into the table as a blank record, and the bad currency field in line 6 was imported as a blank field.

FIGURE 7.17

The delimited text file at the top of this figure caused the errors shown in the Import-Errors table. The valid records from the text file were stored in the SALBAD table.

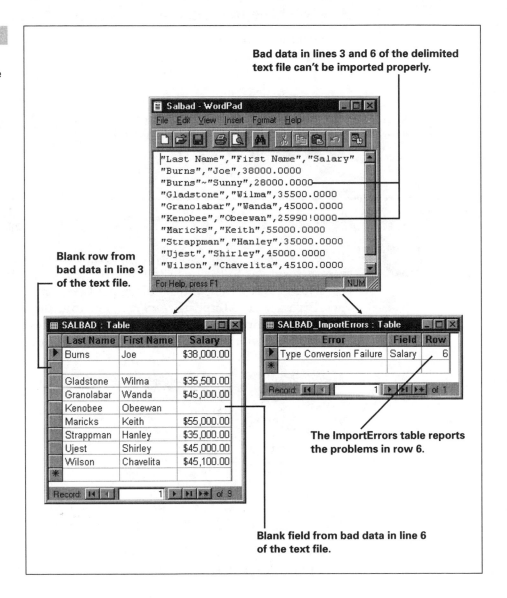

Bad data in lines 3 and 6 of the delimited text file can't be imported properly.

Blank row from bad data in line 3 of the text file.

The ImportErrors table reports the problems in row 6.

Blank field from bad data in line 6 of the text file.

TIP

When importing a text file that might have bad data, do not assign any primary key. The resulting table records will appear in the same order as they appear in the text file, and blank table records and fields will be easier to trace to the corresponding lines in the text file. After cleaning up any problems with the imported data, you can assign a primary key to the table.

Problems When Importing to New Tables

When importing records into a *new* table, Access may run into these problems:

- Access chose an erroneous data type for a field because the first row of data didn't properly reflect the type of data you were importing. This can happen if you forget to check the First Row Contains Field Names option, or if a field that contains mostly text values has a number in the first row.

- One or more rows in the file contain more fields than the first row.

- The data in the field doesn't match the data type Access chose for the field, or the data is blank. For example, a number may contain a bad character (as in the example of Figure 7.17), or a row may contain extraneous characters or summary information.

Problems When Importing to Existing Tables

When importing records to an *existing* table, Access may be tripped up if:

- The data in a numeric field is too large for the field size of a table field. For example, Access can't import a record if the table field has a Field Size property of Byte, but the data contains a value greater than 255.

- One or more records in the imported data contain duplicate values for a primary key field in the table, or for any field that has an Indexed property set to Yes (No Duplicates).

- One or more rows in the file contain more fields than the table contains.

- The data in a text file or spreadsheet field is the wrong type for the corresponding table field. For instance, the table field may be a Currency type, but the data contains a person's name.

TIP   Importing can take some time. But if the wait seems unreasonably long, it may be a sign that many errors are occurring. To cancel the import, press Ctrl+Break.

If Access reports errors or your imported table contains blank fields or records, open the ImportErrors table and try to figure out what went wrong. You may need to correct your data file, or you may need to change the structure of an existing table. After solving the problems, you can import the data again.

Be careful to avoid adding duplicate records when importing the data the next time. One way to prevent duplicate records is to copy your original data file and delete from the copy all records that made it successfully into the table. Make any necessary corrections to your data or table; then choose In An Existing Table when importing your data. Another way is to delete the table you imported the first time, and then import again; or, just let Access overwrite the first table you imported.

 ➤ For more information about the ImportErrors table, look up the *Import Errors Table* topic in the Access Help Index.

Exporting Data from Access

You can export data from your Access tables to any of the text file, spreadsheet, or database formats already discussed; this makes it easy to maintain your data in Access and use it in many other programs. You also can export Access database objects to other Access databases and to your electronic mail program.

N O T E Many database programs do not allow table and field names to contain spaces or have up to 64 characters (as Access does). When you export a table, Access automatically adjusts names that aren't allowed in another program.

You can export data from your Access database with any of these options (you'll learn more about them soon):

Save As/Export   (On the File menu and the database window's shortcut menu) Converts an Access database object to Microsoft Access, Microsoft Excel (5-7, 4, or 3), Text Files, Paradox (3, 4, or 5), Lotus 1-2-3 (WK1 or WK3), dBASE (III, IV, or 5), Microsoft FoxPro (2.0, 2.5, 2.6, or 3.0), Rich Text Format, Microsoft Word Merge, and ODBC Databases.

OfficeLinks   (On the Tools menu and the OfficeLinks drop-down toolbar button) You can save data to a file and immediately start the appropriate Microsoft program. These options include Merge It (with a Microsoft Word document), Publish It (as a Microsoft Word RTF file), and Analyze It (with Microsoft Excel).

Send   (On the File menu) Converts an Access database object to a Microsoft Excel, Rich Text Format, or MS-DOS Text file, and then sends the file to someone else via electronic mail.

Exporting Objects

The basic steps for exporting objects are remarkably similar to those for importing objects:

1. Start from the database window that contains the object you want to export. If you want to export the entire object, click on the object's name on the database window. If you want to export selected records from a table or query, open the table or run the query, and then select the records you want to export.

2. Choose File ➤ Save As/Export, or right-click on a gray area in the database window and choose Save As/Export.

3. In the next dialog box, choose To An External File Or Database, and then click on OK. The Save Table dialog box will appear.

4. In the Save As Type drop-down list, choose the export format for the data. For example, click on the drop-down list button next to Save As Type, and then scroll down to and click on Rich Text Format to copy the object to a Rich Text Format file.

5. Locate the folder that should contain your new file, and then type a file name in the File Name text box, or accept the suggested file name.

TIP The techniques for locating drives, folders, and files in the Save As dialog box are the same ones that work in the Open and File New Database dialog boxes (see Chapters 1 and 5, respectively).

6. If you chose Microsoft Excel 5-7, Text Files, or Rich Text Format, you also can choose one or more of these options:

Save Formatted   Select (check) this option (if it's available) to save the exported data with as much formatting as possible; deselect (clear) this option to omit formatting in the exported data.

AutoStart   Select (check) this option to immediately open the exported file for viewing in the appropriate program.

All or Selection   Choose All to save the entire file; or choose Selection to save records that you selected in step 1.

7. Click on the Export button. If the file name you chose already exists, you'll be asked if you want to replace the existing file; click on Yes to replace the file and continue with step 8, or click on No to leave the file alone and return to step 5.

8. Respond to any additional prompts and dialog boxes that appear.

Access will copy your Access object to the format you requested, and save the results in the file you chose in step 5. If you chose AutoStart in step 6, the file will open in the appropriate program (click on the program window's Close button or choose File ➤ Exit to return to the Access database window).

➤ For more help on exporting objects, go to the Access Help Contents, open the *Exporting Or Sharing Data And Objects With Other Applications* book, open the *Exporting Data* book, and then double-click on an appropriate topic. You also can look up topics and subtopics under *Exporting Data...* in the Access Help Index. The following sections show detailed procedures for exporting to different types of destination files.

Exporting to Text and Excel 5–7 Files

You can export Access tables, queries, forms, and reports to text files that are useful with word processing programs, and to Excel version 5–7 worksheets. Here's how:

1. Do steps 1–3 of the general "Exporting Objects" procedure, given in the previous section.

2. In the Save As Type drop-down list, choose one of these export formats for the data.

   - **To export Access data for use with text-based word processors** such as Windows Notepad or WordPerfect for DOS, choose Text Files.

   - **To export Access data as a delimited Microsoft Word for Windows mail merge data file**, choose Microsoft Word Merge.

   - **To export Access data as a formatted Rich Text Format file**, choose Rich Text Format. You can edit this type of file in Microsoft Word, WordPad, and other Windows word processors.

   - **To export Access data to an Excel version 5–7 worksheet,** choose Microsoft Excel 5–7.

3. Locate the folder that should contain your new file, and then type a file name in the File Name text box (if necessary).

4. If you wish, choose the Save Formatted, Autostart, All, or Selection options described in the general procedure for exporting objects.

5. Click on Export.

6. If you chose Text Files, and you *did not* choose Save Formatted, the Text Export Wizard will take over. The dialog boxes and

options are similar to those described for the Text Import Wizard. See "Importing or Linking Text Files" and Figures 7.11–7.15, earlier in this chapter.

Access will save the data file in the format you chose. The first row of the spreadsheet or text file will contain the field names from the table or query. If you selected Autostart in step 4, the exported file will open in the appropriate program, and you can view or change it as needed (click on the program window's Close button or choose File ➤ Exit to return to the Access database window).

Exporting to Spreadsheets, Paradox, FoxPro, or dBASE

Use the following procedure to export Access tables and queries to Microsoft Excel, Lotus 1-2-3, Paradox, FoxPro, or dBASE files. Later sections explain how to export to other database formats.

1. Do steps 1–3 of the general "Exporting Objects" procedure.

2. In the Save As Type drop-down list, choose one of the Microsoft Excel, Paradox, Lotus 1-2-3, dBASE, or Microsoft FoxPro export formats for the data.

3. Locate the folder that should contain your new file. If necessary, type a file name in the File Name text box.

4. Click on Export.

The resulting database or spreadsheet file will contain all the data from your table or query. For spreadsheets, the first row will contain the field names from the table or query.

Exporting to a SQL Database

To export an Access table or query to a SQL database:

1. Do steps 1–3 of the general "Exporting Objects" procedure.

2. In the Save As Type drop-down list, choose ODBC Databases.

3. In the Export dialog box that appears, specify a name for the table in the ODBC database, and then click on OK.

4. In the SQL Data Sources dialog box, double-click on the ODBC data source you want to export to. (If necessary, you can define a new data source for any installed ODBC driver by clicking on the New button and following the instructions that appear. After creating the new data source, you can double-click on it to continue.)

5. Enter whatever information your ODBC data source requires, clicking on OK as needed. As for importing ODBC data sources, you may need to enter a logon ID and password.

Access will connect to the ODBC data source and create the new table.

N O T E   When you export an Access table to an ODBC database, Access does not export the primary key and index information for the table. If you later link to your exported table without having modified its design in the ODBC database, Access will treat the table as read-only.

 ➤ For more about exporting tables to ODBC data sources, look up ODBC, *Exporting Access Data* in the Access Help Index.

Exporting to Another Access Database

Earlier in this chapter, you learned how to import or link objects from another Access database to the open database. You also can perform the inverse operation: copy a table, query, form, report, macro, or module from your open database to another existing Access database. Here are the steps to follow:

1. Do steps 1–3 of the general "Exporting Objects" procedure.

2. In the Save As Type drop-down list, choose Microsoft Access.

3. Locate the folder that contains the Access database you want to export to, and then click on the database name in the list below Save In.

4. Click on Export.

5. In the Export dialog box, specify the name for the object you're exporting, or accept the suggested name. If you're exporting a

table, choose whether to export the table's Definition And Data or its Definition Only. Then click on OK.

6. If the database you're exporting to already has an object with the name you specified in step 5, you'll be asked whether to replace the existing database object with the one you are exporting. Click on Yes if you want to replace the existing object with the one you're exporting; or, click on No if you don't want to replace the original object (you'll be returned to step 5).

Access will copy the object to the other database.

Using OfficeLinks

For some real razzle-dazzle, you can use OfficeLinks features to export Access data to a file and immediately start the appropriate Microsoft Office program. To use these features, choose the object or selection you want to export. Click on the drop-down arrow on the OfficeLinks toolbar button and then choose an option, or choose options from the Tools ➤ OfficeLinks menu. Here's an example of the OfficeLinks toolbar button after we clicked on its drop-down arrow:

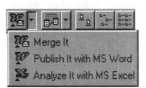

Table 7.2 briefly describes the OfficeLinks drop-down toolbar button options and the Tools ➤ OfficeLinks menu options you can use. The OfficeLinks toolbar button is available on the database window's toolbar and the print preview toolbar.

To use OfficeLinks:

1. Go to the Access database window, click on the tab for the type of data you want to export (Tables, Queries, Forms, or Reports), and then select the object you want to export. Or, open the table or run the query and select the rows you want to export. Or, open an object in print preview (choose File ➤ Print Preview).

2. Choose Tools ➤ OfficeLinks, and then choose the appropriate option. (The Merge It option is available for tables and queries only.)

TABLE 7.2: OfficeLinks Drop-down Toolbar Button Options and Tools ➤
OfficeLinks Options for Output to Other Microsoft Programs

OPTION NAME	PROGRAM NAME
Merge It	Microsoft Word for Windows (mail merge feature)
Analyze It With MS Excel	Microsoft Excel
Publish It With MS Word	Microsoft Word for Windows

3. Answer any prompts, if they appear.

Access will create the output file in the current folder and then open the file in the program you chose in step 2. When you're ready to return to Access, close the program by clicking on its Close button or choosing File ➤ Exit.

N O T E   What you see in Access isn't necessarily what you get in the program opened by OfficeLinks. *Examples:* Data on Access forms and reports that you export to Excel will appear in rows and columns. Data on forms that you export to Word is stored in Word tables. And graphics and OLE objects will be blank, because they can't be exported.

Mailing an Access Object

You can use the Send feature to export Access objects to Microsoft Excel (*.xls), Rich Text Format (*.rtf), and MS-DOS Text (.txt) format. Rather than creating an ordinary file (as the Export and OfficeLinks features do), Send embeds the data as an icon in an electronic mail (e-mail) message and then sends the message to your recipient list. To use Send:

1. In the Access database window, click on the tab for the type of object you want to send (Tables, Queries, Forms, Reports, or Modules), and then click on the object you want to send.

2. Choose File ➤ Send.

3. In the Send dialog box, select the export format you want to use. Click on OK.

4. If a Choose Profile dialog box appears, choose a profile, and then click on OK.

5. Your electronic mail program will take over. Respond to any prompts that appear, sign on (if necessary), and send the message as usual.

NOTE As for the OfficeLinks features, what you see in Access isn't necessarily what you get in your e-mail messages. *Examples:* Data on Access forms and reports that you mail in Excel format will appear in rows and columns on a spreadsheet. Data on forms that you mail in Rich Text Format is stored in tables. And graphics and OLE objects will be blank.

TIP In most electronic mail programs, you can preview and even change the object before sending it to the recipient. When the e-mail message appears, just double-click on the object's icon within the message. For example, if you're sending a Customers table in Microsoft Excel format, double-click on the Customers.xls icon in your message to open the object in Excel. After viewing the object, close the program (File ➤ Exit), save your changes if necessary, and send the e-mail message normally.

To retrieve the file, the recipient must sign on to electronic mail, open your mail message as usual, and double-click on the object's icon in the message file. This action will start the program that's associated with the file you sent and let the recipient read the file. For example, if the recipient double-clicks on a .xls file icon in the message, the file will open in Microsoft Excel.

NOTE   The File ➤ Send command is available only if your mail program is installed properly and it supports Messaging Application Programming Interface (MAPI). To use Access with an e-mail program that supports the Vendor Independent Mail (VIM) protocol, you must install and set up the dynamic-link library (named Mapivim.dll), which converts MAPI mail messages to the VIM protocol. You'll find information about installing and setting up VIM support in the Microsoft Office Resource Kit, available from Microsoft.

Importing and Exporting from Non-Supported Programs

If you want to import data from, or export data to, a program other than one that Access supports directly, you can use some intermediate format that Access *does* support.

For instance, most programs let you import and export data in delimited text format. Thus, you could export data to a delimited text file from one program and then import that delimited text file into the other program.

Many programs also can use files that are in another program's format, either directly or after converting the file with some help from you. For example, Quattro Pro can open Lotus 1-2-3 .wk3 format files directly, and Access can create such files. Therefore, to export Access data to Quattro Pro, use the Export feature to export the Access table to Lotus 1-2-3 WK3 format; then start Quattro Pro and open the exported .wk3 file normally. Similarly, both Microsoft Works and Microsoft Access can open and create dBASE files. So, to export Access data to a Works database, use the Export feature in Access to export the Access table to dBASE format; then start Microsoft Works and open the existing dBASE file. No sweat!

 ➤ For information on importing or exporting files in some other program, check that program's documentation. Be aware that delimited files often go by the name *ASCII delimited file*, *ASCII text file*, or simply *DOS text file*.

Where to Go from Here

If you took the hands-on lessons in Chapter 3, you already know the basic steps for adding, editing, and viewing data. In this case, you can skip Chapter 8 and move on to Chapter 9, where you'll learn how to sort, search, and print your data. But if you skipped those lessons, or you just want to know some extra tricks and tips for entering data more efficiently, continue with Chapter 8 now.

What's New in the Access Zoo?

Linking, importing, and exporting data features are easier to use and more powerful in Access for Windows 95 than in Access 2.0. New and revised features include:

- New and revised Wizards.
- Simplified dialog boxes.
- Links to text files and Excel worksheets.
- Subreports exported along with the main reports for .txt (Text), .rtf (Rich Text Format), or .xls (Excel) file formats.
- Revised OfficeLinks toolbar buttons.
- Easier-to-find menu options.

CHAPTER

8

Adding, Editing, and Viewing Data

IN Chapters 6 and 7 you learned how to open a database, create and open tables, and import or link to tables from other sources. In this chapter, you'll learn how to add, change, and delete data in tables. We'll also introduce forms in this chapter, but you'll learn much more about forms in Chapters 11 and 13.

Datasheet View and Form View

You can work with Access data using either *datasheet view* or *form view*:

Datasheet View   (Also called *table view*.) You can see many records on the screen, in a tabular format.

Form View   You can see one record at a time, in a format that resembles paper fill-in-the-blank forms.

Figure 8.1 shows table data in datasheet view, and the same data in form view.

Creating an Instant Form

Normally you'll be taken into datasheet view when you open a table. If you want to use form view, you must create a form or use an existing form. (Of course, you need to create the form only *once*, as long as you save it after you create it.) Chapters 11 and 13 cover forms in detail, but if you're itching to set up a quick-and-easy form right now, follow these steps:

1. In the database window, click on the Tables or Queries tab, and then click on the name of an existing table or query.

FIGURE 8.1

You can view several records at a time in datasheet view. You generally work with only one record at a time in form view.

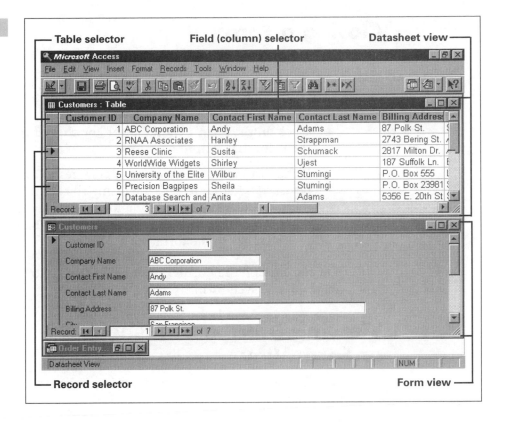

Table selector   Field (column) selector   Datasheet view

Record selector   Form view

2. Click on the drop-down arrow next on the New Object toolbar button (shown at left, and the second-to-last toolbar button). Then choose AutoForm from the list that appears. Or, choose Insert ➤ AutoForm from the database menu.

Access builds a simple form and displays it on your screen.

TIP

If you don't mind doing a few extra mouse clicks, you can get a nicer-looking instant form than the simple AutoForm feature produces. In step 2 above, choose New Form (instead of AutoForm) from the drop-down list on the New Object toolbar button. Then double-click on AutoForm: Columnar in the New Form dialog box that appears.

Closing a Form

To close the form when you're done using it:

1. Make sure the form is in the active window. (If in doubt, click on the form's title bar.)

2. Click on the form's Close button, or choose File ➤ Close from the menu bar, or press Ctrl+W.

3. If the form is new, or you made changes to an existing form, you'll be asked whether to save the form. To save the form, click on Yes; then, if you're prompted for a form name, type a form name (or accept the suggested name) and click on OK. If you don't want to save changes to the form, click on No.

You can click on the Forms object tab in the database window to view the names of all saved forms.

Viewing Data in Datasheet or Form View

You can view table data anytime, using either the datasheet view or the form you created:

Datasheet View To view data in datasheet view, click on the Tables or Queries tab on the database window. Then double-click on the table or query whose data you want to view. Or click on the table or query name and then click on the Open button on the database window. Or, right-click on the table or query name and choose Open.

Form View To view data in form view, click on the Forms tab on the database window, and then double-click on the form you want to open. Or click on the form name, and then click on the Open button on the database window. Or, right-click on the form name and choose Open.

NOTE You can open a table or a query in datasheet view, and you can create a form for a table or a query and then open that form. Any time you open a form, you're also opening the underlying table or query automatically.

WARNING Some types of queries change data or create tables rather than display data, so be careful about opening just any old query. You'll learn more about queries in Chapter 10.

Switching between Datasheet View and Form View

When you open a form, you can easily switch between views. To do so, click on the drop-down arrow next to the Form View toolbar button (the first toolbar button); then choose an option from the menu (Design View, Form View, or Datasheet View). Or, choose appropriate options from the View menu (Form Design, Form, or Datasheet).

The form view options *won't* appear if you open the table in datasheet view. So when you want maximum flexibility in switching between views, open the form rather than the table.

The Design View option is always available. How it acts depends on how you got to the current view:

- If you opened the current table in datasheet view, the Design View options will take you to the underlying table design (the table's structure).

- If you opened a form, the Design View option will take you to the form's underlying design (see Chapters 11 and 13).

Table 8.1 shows a summary of the Table View or Form View toolbar buttons you'll see from various views.

TABLE 8.1: Toolbar Buttons for Switching among Views

IF YOU'RE IN THIS VIEW...	THE VIEW BUTTON LOOKS LIKE THIS...
Form View or Datasheet View	
Form Design View	
Table Design View	

TIP

To quickly switch to the view shown on the Form View or Table View toolbar button, click on that button, without clicking on the button's drop-down arrow first.

Why Design View?

If you get confused, just remember that design view is for designing (creating and changing) *objects*—not for managing data. You cannot see or change data from design view. If you're in design view and want to return to your data, switch to datasheet view or form view.

Here's another way to look at it: If you open a table in datasheet view, and want to switch to form view, you can't use the toolbar button or <u>V</u>iew menus to do so, because Access won't know *which* form you want to open. So you'll need to open the appropriate form if you want all the flexibility that Access offers.

If You Get Lost...

If you get lost, you can close all the objects until you see only the database window, or you can quickly bring the database window to the forefront by pressing F11. From there, you can click on the tab for any type of object, click on the name of any object, and then click on the <u>N</u>ew, <u>O</u>pen (or <u>P</u>review or <u>R</u>un), or <u>D</u>esign buttons, as explained under "Working in the

Database Window" in Chapter 1. (Believe it or not, this procedure becomes second nature after you've done it a few times.)

Customizing the Datasheet View

Customizing datasheet view can be a quick and easy way to display and print an attractive list of data in a table. Figure 8.2 shows the original datasheet for a Products table, along with a customized version of that same datasheet. You can use a special Formatting (Datasheet) toolbar, menu commands, and right-clicking to change the appearance of datasheet view in a flash. The next few sections explain how.

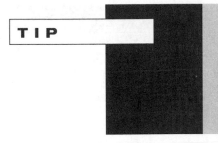

TIP

To print a tabular report that uses the same formatting shown in datasheet view, customize datasheet view, and select records if you wish (as explained in this chapter). Then choose File ➤ Print (Ctrl+P), fill in the Print dialog box, and click on OK. (To preview the records first, choose Print Preview instead of File ➤ Print.)

Using the Formatting Toolbar

The Formatting (Datasheet) toolbar, shown in Figure 8.3, makes it easy to change the appearance of text on the datasheet, to choose a color for the datasheet's background, foreground, and grid, and to control the appearance of gridlines.

To use this toolbar, you first must display it on the screen (of course). Here's how:

- In datasheet view, right-click on the current toolbar, and then select (check) Formatting (Datasheet).

- Or, if no toolbar is visible, choose View ➤ Toolbars. In the Toolbars dialog box, scroll down to and select (check) Formatting (Datasheet), and then click on Close.

FIGURE 8.2

A sample Products table in its original and customized datasheet views. We've removed the gridlines and changed the font to give the datasheet a custom look.

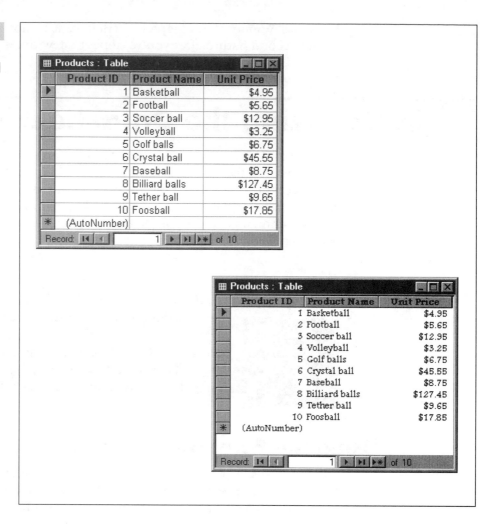

FIGURE 8.3

The Formatting (Datasheet) toolbar lets you customize datasheet view.

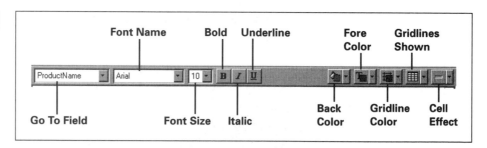

N O T E

When you want to hide the Formatting (Datasheet) toolbar again, repeat one of the steps above, except *deselect* (clear) the Formatting (Datasheet) option.

Once the Formatting toolbar is visible, you can use it in many ways:

- **To jump to a particular column in the currently selected record,** choose a column (field) name from the Go To Field drop-down list.

- **To change the font for all text in the datasheet view,** choose a font name from the Font Name drop-down list.

- **To change the font size for all text in the datasheet view,** choose a font size from the Font Size drop-down list.

- **To boldface all text in the datasheet view,** click on the Bold button. To turn off boldface, click on the Bold button again. Use this same technique with the Italic and Underline buttons to turn italics and underline on or off.

- **To change the datasheet's background color,** click on the drop-down arrow next to the Back Color button and then click on the color you want. Use this same technique with the Fore Color and Gridline Color buttons, respectively, to choose foreground (text) and gridline colors.

- **To change the appearance of gridlines (or to hide them),** click on the drop-down arrow next to the Gridlines Shown button, and then click on the picture that shows the type of gridlines you want. Use the same technique with the Cell Effect button to add a flat, raised, or sunken effect to the gridlines.

N O T E

When you choose a sunken or raised effect for gridlines, Access always places horizontal and vertical lines on the grid. When you choose a flat effect for gridlines, Access can apply horizontal gridlines only, vertical gridlines only, both types of gridlines, or no gridlines.

Changing the Datasheet Appearances in One Fell Swoop

Instead of using the Formatting (Datasheet) toolbar to tweak appearances one at a time, you can use the Format ➤ Cells and Format ➤ Font commands on the menu bar to set several appearances at once.

- To change the appearance of the gridlines or choose a background color, choose Format ➤ Cells.

- To change the font name, font style, size, color, and other font effects, choose Format ➤ Font.

- To change the default appearance of datasheets for all databases that you open, choose Tools ➤ Options, and then click on the Datasheet tab. See Chapter 15 for more about personalizing Access.

When the Cells Effects or Font dialog box appears, choose the settings you want. The sample area in the dialog box will reflect your current selections. When you're done, click on OK to accept the changes; or, click on Cancel (or press Esc) to discard them.

Selecting and Arranging the Datasheet Rows and Columns

While in datasheet view, you can rearrange the datasheet columns, adjust the height of rows, change the column widths, and even hide columns.

Selecting Datasheet Columns

If you want to resize, move, or hide more than one adjacent column at a time, you first must select the columns you want to work with. Here are some techniques to use:

- **To select one column,** click on the field selector at the top of the column.

- **To select multiple columns,** drag the mouse pointer through several field selectors. Or click on the field selector for the first column you want to select. Then, use the horizontal scroll bar if you need to, and Shift-click on the field selector for the last column you want to select.

- **To deselect selected columns,** click in the data area of any column.

NOTE   When you move the mouse pointer to a field selector, the pointer changes to a thick, black ↓ shape.

Here's an example of a datasheet with one column selected:

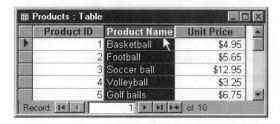

Arranging Datasheet Rows and Columns

You can use the following tricks to adjust the height and width of rows and columns, to move columns, and to hide and redisplay columns:

- **To change the height of all the rows,** drag the bottom edge of a row selector (shown at left) up or down. Or choose Format ➤ Row Height, or right-click on a row selector and choose Row Height; then, enter a height (in points) or select Standard Height to use Access's standard row height, and click on OK.

- **To change one column's width,** drag the vertical bar next to that column's field selector (shown at left) to the left or right. Or, to quickly get the best possible fit for the column, double-click on that vertical bar.

- **To change the width of one or several adjacent columns,** select the column(s) you want to resize. Next, choose Format ➤ Column Width; or, right-click on any data within the selection and choose Column Width. In the Column Width dialog box, enter a width (in number of characters) or select Standard Width and click on OK, or click on Best Fit. Alternatively, just drag the vertical bar next to a selected column's field selector to the left or right.

NOTE

When right-clicking on records after selecting multiple columns, be sure to right-click on *data* within the selection. Do not right-click on a field selector, or you'll turn off the selection in adjacent columns.

- **To move column(s)**, select the column(s) you want to move. Then click on one of the highlighted field selectors and drag the selection to the left or right.(The mouse pointer changes to the shape shown at left as you drag.)

- **To hide columns**, select the column(s) you want to hide. Next, choose Format ➤ Hide Columns; or, right-click on any data within the selection and choose Hide Columns.

- **To hide or redisplay any columns you wish,** choose Format ➤ Unhide Columns. Select (check) the column names you want to show, deselect (clear) the ones you want to hide, and then click on Close.

Freezing and Unfreezing Columns

When the table is wider than the screen, scrolling to the rightmost columns will force the leftmost columns off the edge of the window. Instead of scrolling back-and-forth to figure out which record the cursor is in at the moment, you can freeze one or more columns so they never scroll out of view.

In Figure 8.4, we froze the Company Name, Contact First Name, and Contact Last Name columns in the Customers table. This makes it easy to scroll to the Phone Number field without losing sight of the customers' names.

To freeze one or more columns:

1. Select the column or columns you want to freeze.

2. Choose Format ➤ Freeze Columns, or right-click on any data within the selection, and then choose Freeze Columns from the shortcut menu.

FIGURE 8.4

Customers data in datasheet view with the Company Name, Contact First Name, and Contact Last Name columns frozen, so they don't move out of view when we scroll over to the Phone Number field. Notice the heavy vertical line between the last frozen field (Contact Last Name) and the first unfrozen one (Phone Number).

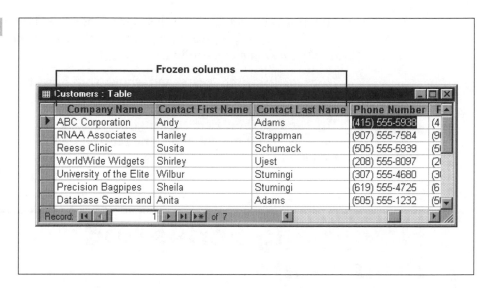

The selected columns move to the leftmost positions in the datasheet automatically, and remain visible as you scroll the datasheet columns to the right. A heavy vertical line separates the frozen columns from the unfrozen ones.

To unfreeze the columns, choose Format ➤ Unfreeze All Columns.

NOTE

If the horizontal scroll bar disappears after you freeze columns, you won't be able to view the unfrozen columns or scroll to them. To solve this problem, either unfreeze all the columns, or resize the frozen columns smaller. Then resize the datasheet window larger (if necessary) until the horizontal scroll bar reappears.

Saving or Canceling Your Datasheet Changes

If you've customized the datasheet view, you'll be asked if you want to save the layout changes when you close the table. To keep the customization settings for future sessions, click on Yes. To discard the settings, click on No.

You also can save your changes to the datasheet layout at any time. To do so, choose File ➤ Save, or press Ctrl+S, or click on the Save button on the Table Datasheet toolbar.

Now we'll switch gears and show you how to navigate forms and datasheets and how to enter data into your tables.

 ➤ You can find more details about customizing the appearance of datasheet view by searching for topics under *Datasheet View* in the Access Help Index.

Navigating Forms and Datasheets

You can use any of these techniques to *navigate* (move around in) a table. (Of course, you won't be able to scroll from record to record until you put some data in the table.)

- **To move through records**, use the navigation buttons at the bottom of the form or datasheet window. Or, choose Edit ➤ Go To and then choose the appropriate command from the pull-down menu. The Go To options are First, Last, Next, Previous, and New.

- **To scroll through records in datasheet view**, use the vertical scroll bar at the right edge of the window. As you drag the scroll box, the current record number and total records will appear next to the scroll bar, like this:

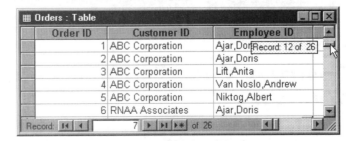

- **To scroll through columns in datasheet view**, use the horizontal scroll bar at the bottom edge of the window.

- **To scroll more fields into view in form view,** use the vertical scroll bar at the right edge of the window or the horizontal scroll bar at the bottom edge of the window.

N O T E As usual, scroll bars appear only if the current window is too small to hold all the information at once. (If the window is too small, however, scroll bars won't appear. Just resize the window larger as needed.)

- **To move from field to field and from record to record,** use the keys listed in Table 8.2.

- **To go to a particular record based on the contents of a field,** you can use Find (for example, you can look up *Doe* or *Granolabar* in the LastName field of the Customers table). See Chapter 9 for more details.

TABLE 8.2: Summary of Keyboard Techniques for Navigating a Table

KEY(S)	DESCRIPTION
F2	Switches between navigation and editing modes.
F5	Selects the record number box (see Figure 8.5). Type a new record number and press ↵ to go to that record.
↑, ↓	Moves to next or previous record (datasheet view), or next or previous field (form view).
Ctrl+↑, Ctrl+↓	Moves to first or last record in a table (highlight remains in current column or field).
←, →	Moves to next or previous character (editing mode), next or previous field (navigation mode).
Ctrl+←, Ctrl+→	Moves one word left or right in editing mode.
Tab, Shift+Tab	Moves to next or previous field.
↵	In datasheet view, moves to next field. In form view, ends a short line or paragraph or inserts a blank line, in a memo field or text field that has Enter Key Behavior property set to New Line In Field.

TABLE 8.2: Summary of Keyboard Techniques for Navigating a Table (continued)

KEY(S)	DESCRIPTION
Ctrl+↵	Ends a short line or paragraph or inserts a blank line, in a memo field or lengthy text field that has Enter Key Behavior set to Default.
PgUp, PgDn	In datasheet view, scrolls up or down one window full. In form view, scrolls to previous or next record. On a multipage form, scrolls to the previous or next page, or to the same page on the previous or next record.
Ctrl+PgUp, Ctrl+PgDn	In datasheet view, scrolls right or left one window full. In form view, scrolls to previous or next record.
Home, End	Moves to first or last field of record (navigation mode), or to start or end of text line (editing mode).
Ctrl+Home, Ctrl+End	Moves to first field of first record or last field of last record (navigation mode), or to start or end of text or memo field (editing mode).

For quick reminders about how to scroll through records, search Help for *Shortcut Keys, Datasheet And Form View Keys* or *Datasheet View, Navigating,* or *Form View, Navigating.*

Adding Data to a Table

Adding new data to a table is just a matter of going to a new, blank record and typing the contents of each field. After filling one field, you can press Tab or ↵ to move to the next field. Or, click on the next field you want to add data to—just as though you're filling in a Windows dialog box. Here are the steps:

1. If you haven't already done so, open the table in datasheet view or open a form in form view. Then, if the cursor is *not* already in a

blank record, use one of these techniques to go to a new, blank record:

- Click on the New Record toolbar button (shown at left).
- Choose <u>E</u>dit ➤ <u>G</u>o To ➤ Ne<u>w</u> from the menu bar.
- Click on the New Record button on the navigation bar near the bottom of the window (see Figure 8.5).

2. Type whatever you want to put into the current field (the field where the cursor is). Then press Tab or ↵ to move to the next field, or click on the next field you want to fill.

3. Repeat step 2 until you've finished entering data in the record.

FIGURE 8.5

Navigation buttons on the navigation bar

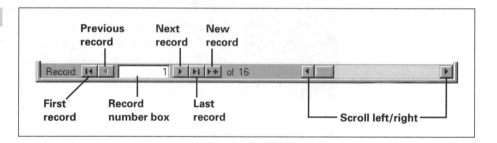

Tips for Adding Records

Here are some pointers for adding records to a table:

(AutoNumber)   If the table contains an AutoNumber field, that field will display just the word *(AutoNumber)*, or a portion of that word. Don't worry about it, and don't try to change it. Access will fill that field automatically when you enter data into some other field in the record.

Empty   To leave a field empty, don't type anything into that field. Just press Tab to move to the next field, or click on the field you want to fill next. (You cannot move to another record if you leave a Required field blank.)

Date/Time   You can press Ctrl+; to insert the current date. Or press Ctrl+Shift+; (that is, Ctrl+:) to insert the current time.

Ditto　If you want to repeat the field entry from the previous record into a new record, press the Ditto key (Ctrl+" or Ctrl+').

OLE/Memo Fields　Use the special techniques for filling in OLE object and memo fields, discussed later in this chapter.

After you fill in the last field of a record, you can press Tab or ↵ to go to the next blank record. If you don't want to add another record, close the table or form (or go to a previous record). Don't worry about accidentally creating a blank record.

> **N O T E**　As you type into a text or memo field, Access will correct certain mistyped words, such as *hte* (changed to *the*), *THey* (changed to *They*), and *sunday* (changed to *Sunday*) as soon as you move the cursor out of the word. This magic is the work of AutoCorrect, which you'll learn about in Chapter 9. There you'll also learn how to check spelling in text and memo fields.

Saving a Record

Access saves the entire record to disk when you move to another record—you need not do anything special to save each record. However, if a record can't be saved because it fails validity checks, you'll see an error message describing the problem. See "Troubleshooting Data Entry and Editing Problems" later in this chapter for help.

 ➤ For quick reminders on how to add records to a table, go to the Access Help Contents, open the *Working With Data* book, and peruse any of the related subtopics and books that interest you.

The Tiny Icons

While you're adding and editing table data, you'll see these icons at the left side of the datasheet or form window.

　Current record.

New, empty record.

 Record is being edited; current changes not saved yet.

How Do I Insert a Record?

You don't. This might seem odd, especially if you're a spreadsheet user. But there's no reason to insert a new record between existing records in Access, because you can sort the records in any order, at any time. So just continue to add new records to the bottom of the table, and then use techniques described in Chapter 9 to alphabetize or sort the records later.

Changing Data in a Table

Changing the data in a table is easy. Just move the cursor to the data you want to change, and then use standard Windows text-editing techniques to make your changes. It's important, however, to check the screen to see whether the field contents are selected before you make a change. Figure 8.6 shows the difference.

- If the current field contents *are* selected, anything you type will instantly *replace* the current field contents. To deselect before typing, press F2 or click where you want to make a change within the field.

- If the field contents are *not* selected, anything you type will be inserted at the cursor position. You can use the ← and → keys to position the cursor within the field.

TIP

If you accidentally replace all the contents of a field when you meant to insert text, you can use any undo technique to immediately fix the error. That is, press Esc, or click on the Undo toolbar button, or choose Edit ➤ Undo, or press Ctrl+Z.

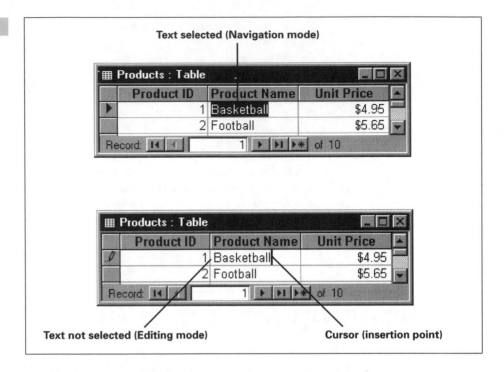

Navigation Mode vs. Editing Mode

Whether a field's contents are selected when you first get to that field depends on whether you're using *navigation mode* (keyboard) or *editing mode* (mouse) to move from field to field:

- If you enter a field using the keyboard (for example, by pressing →, ←, Tab, or Shift+Tab), that field's contents are selected instantly. This mode is called *navigation mode* because the arrow keys navigate you from one field to the next.

- If you move the cursor to a field by clicking, the cursor moves to the exact mouse pointer position, and text is *not* selected. This mode is called *editing mode* because the arrow keys position the cursor for editing the field's contents.

 To switch quickly between navigation and editing modes, press the F2 key any time.

Keys for Editing Table Data

Table 8.3 summarizes *keys* you can use to edit data in datasheet view and form view. Remember that you also can use the *mouse* to select text within a field: simply drag the mouse pointer through text to select that text within a field.

 ➤ If you ever need reminders on editing data, look up the topic *Fields, Editing Data Within*, and subtopics under *Data Entry* in the Access Help Index.

TABLE 8.3: Keys for Editing Data in a Table

KEY	DESCRIPTION
F2	Switches between navigation mode (where pressing arrow keys selects a field) and editing mode (where pressing arrow keys moves the cursor within a field).
Backspace	Deletes selection, or deletes character to left of cursor.
Delete	Deletes selection, or deletes character to right of cursor.
Insert	Toggles between insert and overwrite modes.
Ctrl+' or Ctrl+" (same as Ctrl+Shift+')	Copies data from field above.
Escape (Esc)	Undoes changes to field (first press), then remaining changes to record (second press).
Ctrl++ (plus sign)	Adds new record.
Ctrl+–	Deletes current record.
Ctrl+;	Inserts the current date.
Ctrl+:	Inserts the current time.
Shift+↵	Saves the current record, as long as data in that record passes all validity checks.
Ctrl+Alt+Spacebar	Inserts field's default value (if any).

Selecting Records and Fields

The row selector at the left of each record lets you select an entire record with a single mouse click:

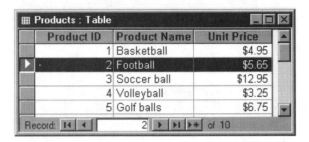

In datasheet view, you can select several adjoining records (see below) by dragging the mouse pointer through their record selectors. Or you can click on the record selector of one record, and then Shift-click on the selector of another record. Or, you can select all the records in the table by clicking on the table selector in the upper-left corner of the table (see Figure 8.1).

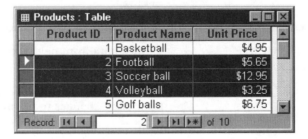

Table 8.4 summarizes ways to select and deselect data in a table. The sections that follow explain how to delete, copy, and move the selected data.

TABLE 8.4: Techniques for Selecting Data in a Table

TO SELECT...	DO THIS...
Part of field contents	Drag mouse pointer through a portion of the field, or use Shift+→, Shift+←, Shift+Home, or Shift+End.
Word to left or right	Press Shift+Ctrl+→, or Shift+Ctrl+←.
Full field contents	Move to the field with an arrow key, or press F2 to switch from cursor to selection, or click on the field name (the label portion, not the field contents) in form view.
Entire record	Click on the record indicator at the far left edge of the record or form, or choose Edit ➤ Select Record, or press Shift+Spacebar (navigation mode).
Multiple records	In datasheet view, drag the mouse pointer through appropriate record selectors, or extend the selection by Shift-clicking on the last record you want to select, or hold down the Shift key while clicking on adjacent record selectors, or extend the selection using Shift+↓ or Shift+↑.
Entire Column	In datasheet view, click on field selector at top of column, or press Ctrl+Spacebar in navigation mode.
Multiple columns	Drag mouse pointer through field selectors, or Shift-click on multiple field selectors, or press Ctrl+Spacebar to select column, then Shift+→ or Shift+← to extend selection.
Entire table (in datasheet view)	Choose Edit ➤ Select All Records, or press Ctrl+A or Ctrl+Shift+Spacebar, or click on table selector (see Figure 8.1).
Without using the mouse	Hold down the Shift key while moving the cursor with the arrow keys. Or press F8 to switch to "extend" mode (EXT appears in status bar), and then use the cursor-positioning keys or mouse to extend the selection area. Or press F8 repeatedly to select the word, field, record, and then entire table. To turn off extended selection, press Esc (EXT disappears from status bar).
Cancel selection	Press the F2 key, or click on any data.

Deleting Data

Deleting data is simply a matter of selecting the data you want to get rid of, and then pressing the Delete key.

Deleting Data within a Field

Here are two ways to delete data within a field:

- Place the cursor where you want to start deleting data, and then press the Delete or Backspace key as needed to delete one character at a time.

- Select the data within the field, and then press Delete or Backspace to delete all the selected text at once.

If you change your mind, and want to bring back the deletion, press Esc or click on the Undo toolbar button. Or, choose Edit ➤ Undo Delete from the menu bar or press Ctrl+Z.

Deleting Records

To delete entire records:

1. Select the records you want to delete using the record selector at the left of each record.

2. Press Delete (or choose Edit ➤ Delete).

WARNING   When you delete one or more records, there's no way to undo that deletion unless you re-enter those records from scratch. So think carefully before you proceed.

3. You'll be asked if you're sure about deleting the record(s). Click on Yes to delete the selected records, or click on No to avoid deleting the records.

If you want to delete the current record only, here's a shortcut. Make sure the cursor is in the record you want to delete, and then click on the Delete Record toolbar button (shown at left), or choose Edit ➤ Delete Record. Answer Yes or No, as appropriate, when asked to confirm the deletion.

Other Ways to Delete Records

There are still other ways to delete records. For example, you can delete all the records that meet some criterion, such as all types of Billiard Balls in the Products table. How can you do this? One way is to create a filter (Chapter 9) that isolates those records, select all those records (choose Edit ➤ Select All Records or press Ctrl+A), and then press Delete. Another way is to construct a Delete query (see Chapter 10).

Copying and Moving Data

You can use all the standard Windows cut-and-paste techniques to move and copy selected data within a table, as well as between Access and other programs. As in any Windows program, the general technique is to:

1. Select the data you want to move or copy.

   - **If you want to copy (duplicate)** the selected data, click on the Copy toolbar button, or choose Edit ➤ Copy, or press Ctrl+C.

   - **If you want to move** the selected data, click on the Cut toolbar button, or choose Edit ➤ Cut, or press Ctrl+X.

2. Move the cursor to where you want to put the data you copied or cut, and then click on the Paste toolbar button, or choose Edit ➤ Paste, or press Ctrl+V.

NOTE   To add records to the end of an Access table, choose Edit ➤ Paste Append in step 2.

Access will try to complete your request, though it may need more information, depending on where you cut or copied *from* and where you pasted *to*. Read any messages that appear on the screen, and respond accordingly.

When Cut-and-Paste Won't Work

Access might not be able to paste selected data into a table for several reasons:

- Access cannot paste incoming data that is incompatible with the current data type(s). For example, you can't paste letters into a Number or Currency field.

- Access cannot paste incoming data that duplicates data in a primary key field, or that duplicates data in an indexed field that doesn't allow duplicate entries.

- If the incoming data is too long for the field, data that doesn't fit will be truncated (chopped off). You can increase the amount of data that a field will hold by changing the field's Field Size property (see Chapter 6).

- If the incoming data fails a validation check that you've defined for the field, you can't paste the faulty data.

If Access can't complete a paste operation for any of these reasons, it will place problem data in a table named Paste Errors. You can open the Paste Errors table to view the data that wasn't pasted, and then perhaps paste data from that table into the original table on a field-by-field basis.

Using OLE to Store Pictures, Sounds, and Other Objects

You can put pictures, sounds, charts, videos, and other objects into a field in a table using OLE, pronounced *olay*. Of course, you can put such objects into a field only if you've defined that field's data type as OLE Object (see Chapter 6).

NOTE Do not confuse an *OLE object* (such as a chart, sound clip, or drawing) with an *Access database object* (such as a table, form, report, or macro). An OLE object is created in a program outside of Access. Once you've embedded or linked the OLE object into an Access table field, you usually can update the object without leaving Access.

Suppose you're creating a table to store information about employees and want to store a résumé in each record. Furthermore, you want to use WordPerfect, Microsoft Word, or Windows WordPad to create and edit those résumés. In that case, you must define the field that should contain the résumé as the OLE Object data type—*not* the Text or Memo data type.

Figure 8.7 shows the structure of a table named Star Search Models (*not* part of the sample databases discussed in other chapters) that we'll refer to as we work through some examples here. Notice that we've defined several fields as the OLE Object data type.

OLE has been around since the release of Windows 3.1. If you're already familiar with the concepts and jargon that go along with that technology, skip to "An Easy Way to Insert Objects" later in this chapter. But if you're new to OLE, you'll get a crash course next.

About OLE Servers and Clients

OLE lets you insert objects from one Windows program into another. In the OLE world, there are two main types of programs, *servers* and *clients*.

Server An OLE server is a program that can "serve up" objects for use in other programs. Examples of OLE servers include the Windows Paint, Sound Recorder, and WordPad applets that come with Windows, the Microsoft Graph program that comes with Access, and the other programs in Microsoft Office (including Word, Excel, and PowerPoint).

Client An OLE client is a program that can accept the services (that is, the objects) provided by programs such as those named above.

FIGURE 8.7

A sample table named
Star Search Models
with several fields
defined as the OLE
Object data type

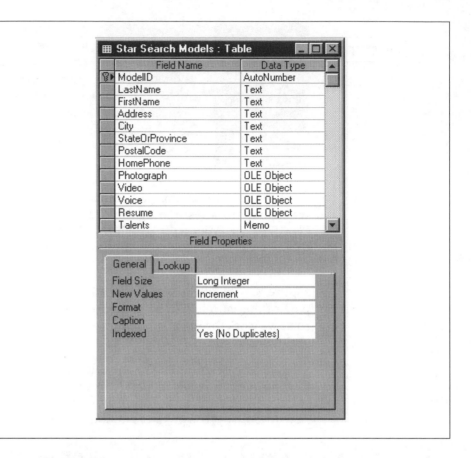

NOTE

Access can act as a client or a server. Thus, you can embed or link an Excel spreadsheet into an OLE Object field in Access (here, Access is a client). You also can embed or link an Access database into an Excel spreadsheet, by choosing Insert ➤ Object from the Excel menu bar (here, Access is a server and the database appears in the spreadsheet as a "package").

You rarely have to worry about whether a program is a server or not, because all you really care about is the object. Let's say you scan a photograph and store that photo in a file named HelenPhoto.bmp. All you have to do is tell Access to stick HelenPhoto.bmp into any OLE object field, and you're done.

About the Source Program

Another buzzword that tags along with OLE is *source program*. In OLE, the source program is the one that's used to create or edit the object. Suppose you use Microsoft Word to type a résumé, and save that résumé as a file named HelenResume.doc. In this case, HelenResume.doc is the OLE object, which you can put into your Access table, and Word is the *source program* for that object.

Similarly, if you have a sound file named HelenVoice.wav on your disk, its source program probably is Windows Sound Recorder, or some other sound-editing program.

Linking vs. Embedding

There are two ways to insert an OLE object into an Access table, *embedding* and *linking*. The difference, in a nutshell, is:

Embed   A separate copy of the object is put into your table. The copy in your table is completely independent of the original object.

Link   Access maintains a connection to the original source object, so if one copy changes, the other copy changes as well.

Imagine that you created a document with Word, and saved it with the file name HelenResume.doc. Then you inserted that document into an Access table. A week later, you fire up Word and change HelenResume.doc. If you originally *embedded* HelenResume.doc in your Access table, the copy in your Access table *will not* reflect the changes you made via Word. But if you *linked* HelenResume.doc into your Access table, the copy in your Access table *will* reflect those changes.

An Easy Way to Insert Objects

The easiest way to insert (link or embed) an object into your Access table is simply to "pull in" a completed copy of the object. By "completed copy," we mean an object such as a sound, picture, or other document that's already stored on disk. (You'll learn how to create OLE objects on the fly later in this chapter.) You need to know *where* that object is stored, and what its name is. For example, a recorded sound might be stored as c:\Mymedia\HelenVoice.wav.

If you know the name and location of the object you want to insert into your file, here's how to insert that object:

1. If you haven't already done so, start Access and open the appropriate database and table. (You can open the table in either datasheet view or form view, it doesn't matter which. Just *don't* use design view!)

2. Move to the record and OLE Object field where you want to put the object.

3. Right-click on the field and choose Insert Object, or choose Insert ➤ Object from the Access menu bar.

4. Click on the Create From File option button in the Insert Object dialog box that appears. The dialog box will look something like this:

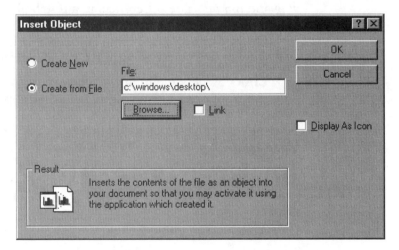

5. If you know the exact location and name of the object you want to insert (for example, c:\Mymedia\HelenVoice.wav), type that into the File text box. You also can use the Browse button to look around for the object.

6. After you've put the location and name of the object into the File text box, you can do any of the following:

   • **To establish a link** between the original object and the copy that's in your table, select (check) the Link check box.

- **To embed a copy** of the object in your table, leave the <u>L</u>ink check box cleared.
- **To display the object as an icon only**, select (check) the <u>D</u>isplay As Icon check box.
- **To display the full object** (such as a photo), leave the <u>D</u>isplay As Icon dialog box cleared.

7. Click on OK.

What the Object Looks Like

What you'll see once the object is in your table depends on several factors:

- In datasheet view, only a brief description of the object is visible, as shown below.

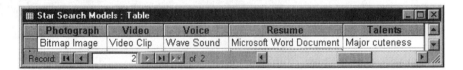

- In form view, the actual object appears if it's a picture, chart, or some other visual object (see Figure 8.8).
- If the object is a sound or another non-visual item, or you selected <u>D</u>isplay As Icon when you inserted the object, an icon representing the object appears on the form, as shown in Figure 8.8.

N O T E   We used techniques explained in Chapters 11 and 13 to create the form shown in Figure 8.8.

Activating and Editing OLE Objects

Some objects that you put into a table, such as photos or charts, are meant to be looked at (though you also might need to edit them sometime). Other objects, such as sounds and animation clips, are meant to be activated. You can activate or edit an object by double-clicking on it.

FIGURE 8.8

OLE objects from the Star Search Models table, shown in form view

What happens after you double-click depends on the type of object:

• If you double-click on a displayed object, you'll open the *source program* for that object. The object will appear either in a separate program window, or in a frame that allows in-place editing within the Access window. You can change that object if you wish. To return to Access, exit the source program by choosing its File ➤ Exit command or clicking on its Close button (if a separate window opened), or click outside the editing frame (if the object appears within the Access window). Respond to any prompts that appear on the screen.

• If you double-click on a sound, video, or similar object, Access will "play" the object.

TIP   You can right-click on an object to open an instant menu of commands relevant to that type of object.

Other Ways to Insert Objects

There are several more ways to insert objects. You can use cut-and-paste techniques to insert all or part of an existing object. Or, create an object right from your Access table. Or, use drag-and-drop to embed an object from the server program into an Access OLE object field. The next few sections describe all these tricks.

Using Cut-and-Paste to Insert (Part of) an Object

You can use the Windows Clipboard to cut and paste all of an object, or part of an object, into an Access table:

1. To make things simple, open your Access data in datasheet view or form view.

2. Start the object's source program. For example, to start Paint, click on the Start button on the Windows taskbar, and then choose Programs ➤ Accessories ➤ Paint.

3. In the source program, create or open the object you want to insert into your Access table. If you want to link the object, the object must be saved in a named file on disk.

4. To insert only part of the object, select that part using the program's techniques. For example, use the Select tool in Paint to select a portion of the picture.

5. Press Ctrl+C or choose Edit ➤ Copy from the source program's menu bar.

6. Click on the Microsoft Access button on the Windows taskbar.

7. Put the cursor in your Access table, in the appropriate field.

8. To *embed* the object, press Ctrl+V or choose Edit ➤ Paste from the Access menu bar. *Then skip the rest of the steps below (you're done)*.

9. To *link* the object or change its data type, choose <u>E</u>dit ➤ Paste <u>S</u>pecial from the Access menu bar. You'll see a Paste Special dialog box, similar to this one:

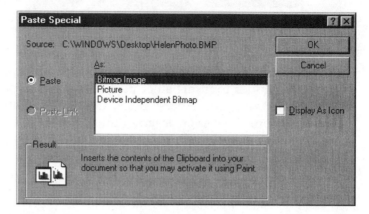

10. Choose options that reflect what you want to do. For example:

- From the option buttons, choose <u>P</u>aste to embed the object, or Paste <u>L</u>ink to link it.

- Choose a different paste format from the <u>A</u>s list. For example, choosing Picture embeds the object as a picture that cannot be modified or activated.

- Select (check) <u>D</u>isplay As Icon to display the object as an icon. The icon will appear, along with a Change <u>I</u>con button that lets you change the icon if you wish.

11. Click on OK.

The form in Figure 8.8 shows a Paint picture that we selected and pasted into our Access table. Remember that only a brief description of the object will appear in datasheet view. (We'll explain how to make the picture fit better into its container soon.)

Creating an Object Just Before You Insert It

To create an OLE object before you place it in an Access field:

1. Start in datasheet view or form view, with the cursor resting in the OLE object field that will contain the object.

2. Choose <u>I</u>nsert ➤ <u>O</u>bject from the Access menu bar, or right-click on the field and choose Insert Object.

3. In the Insert Object dialog box, choose Create <u>N</u>ew.

4. From the list of object types, double-click on the type of object you want to create.

5. In the source program, create the object.

6. When you're done, choose <u>F</u>ile ➤ E<u>x</u>it... from the source program's menu bar (if the program opened in a separate window), or click outside the OLE object field (if you're editing in-place).

7. If asked about updating the embedded object, click on <u>Y</u>es or OK.

That's it—you're done. You should be able to see the object in its field whenever you're in form view.

Using Drag-and-Drop and OLE 2

You've probably heard about OLE 2, the version of OLE that supports drag-and-drop and in-place editing. *Drag-and-drop* means that you can copy an object from any source to any destination just by dragging it across the screen. No need to go through any menus or the Windows Clipboard.

In-place editing means that when you double-click on an OLE object in (say) your Access table, you won't be taken to the object's source program. Rather, the tools and capabilities of the source program will "come to you."

N O T E   The Microsoft Office and Novell PerfectOffice suites are examples of Windows programs that support OLE 2. If you have Microsoft Word installed, try using it as the server as you follow the steps below.

It's easy to use drag-and-drop to embed an OLE object from a server document into your Access table:

1. Open your Access table or form as usual and scroll to the record that contains the OLE object field you want to update.

2. Start the OLE 2 server program, and then open or create the object you want to embed into your Access table.

3. Select the object using normal selection techniques for the server program.

4. Make sure you can see the server program and your Access table or form. To do this quickly, open the two program windows you want to work with (and close or minimize others to reduce clutter); then right-click on an empty part of the Windows taskbar and choose Tile Horizontally or Tile Vertically.

Drag and Drop from Access to Other Programs

In addition to dragging and dropping from some program into Access OLE object fields, you also can drag and drop selected data from Access to other programs. Not all programs support such shenanigans, but WordPad, Word, and Excel certainly do. Suppose you want to drag and drop some data from Access into a Word table or an Excel spreadsheet. Here's how you'd do that:

1. Select the rows in Access datasheet view.

2. Open a Microsoft Word for Windows 95 document or a Microsoft Excel for Windows 95 worksheet.

3. Make sure you can see the windows for both Access and the program you'll be dropping the data into. To do so, right-click on an empty part of the Windows taskbar and choose Tile Horizontally or Tile Vertically.

4. Move the mouse pointer just to the right of a row selector within the selected Access data. The mouse pointer changes to a hollow white arrow when it's positioned correctly.

5. Drag the selection to the Word document or Excel spreadsheet window, and then release the mouse button.

The selected data from Access will be copied to the Word document or Excel spreadsheet.

5. Do one of the following to drag-and-drop the selected object:

- **To *copy* the selected object** from the server program to the Access table field, hold down the Ctrl key while dragging the selection from the server program to the appropriate OLE Object field in your Access table or form.

- **To *move* the selected object** from the server program to the Access table field, drag the selection (without holding down the Ctrl key) from the server program to the appropriate OLE Object field in your Access table or form.

6. To conserve memory, close the server program.

About Bound and Unbound Objects

In this chapter, we've discussed techniques that are specific to putting a *bound OLE object* into a table field. By "bound" we mean that the object is "tied to" a specific table.

As you'll see in later chapters (and various Help windows), however, Access can store an *unbound OLE object*, which is an OLE object that's attached to a form or report, rather than to a table. You'll learn how to put an unbound OLE object on a form in Chapter 13.

 ➤ For more information about linking and embedding objects, look up *OLE Objects* and its subtopics in the Access Help Index.

Special Techniques for Memo Fields

If you need to type lots of text into a memo field, your best bet is to create a form for that table (see the "Talents" memo field back in Figure 8.8). Alternatively, you can press Shift+F2 to open a Zoom box. Either trick will give you more space to work in. As you'll soon discover, what happens when you press the ↵ key in a memo field can vary, but here's what's most common:

- **If you're typing in a memo field on a *form*,** pressing ↵ ends a short line, starts a new paragraph, or inserts a blank line in the text, as it does in most word processing programs.

- **If you're typing in a memo field on a *table datasheet*,** pressing ↵ leaves the field and moves onto the next field or record. If you're typing data in a *Zoom box*, pressing ↵ (or clicking on OK) closes the Zoom box. To insert a new line instead of leaving the field or closing the Zoom box, press Ctrl+↵ (instead of ↵) to end a short line or paragraph or to insert a blank line.

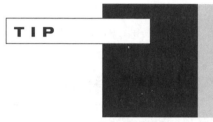

TIP

Try using the Zoom box (Shift+F2) any time you need to enter more text than will fit in the standard input area. The Zoom feature is available in property sheets, datasheet view, and grid cells in the design views for tables, queries, advanced filter/sort, and macros.

Controlling the Enter Key Behavior

It turns out that the behavior of the ↵ key within forms is governed by a property named Enter Key Behavior. To change this property, switch to the form's design view. Then, click on the control that has the property you want to change, open the property sheet (View ➤ Properties), click on the Other tab on the property sheet, and then click on the Enter Key Behavior box. Now change the property to either of these settings:

Default When selected, Access takes the action specified in the Move After Enter setting anytime you press ↵ in the field during data entry. For controls that display text fields, the Enter Key Behavior property usually is set to Default.

NOTE

To change the default Move After Enter setting, choose Tools ➤ Options from the menu bar, click on the Keyboard tab in the Options dialog box, and then choose one of the Move After Enter settings. Your options are Don't Move, Next Field (the default choice), or Next Record. Click on OK. See Chapter 15 for more about personalizing Access.

New Line In Field   When selected, Access inserts a new-line character anytime you press ⏎ in the field during data entry. For controls that display memo fields, the Enter Key Behavior property usually is set to New Line In Field.

See Chapter 13 for more about changing properties on forms.

Special Techniques for Sizing Photographs

Photographs are tricky little devils to put into tables or onto forms, because any distortion or clipping is so immediately obvious. Suppose you scan a 3 × 5 photo, and use the OLE techniques described earlier in this chapter to put a copy of that photo into a field in an Access table. In your form, you try various size modes—Clip, Stretch, and Zoom—as shown below. But nothing quite gives the fit you're looking for.

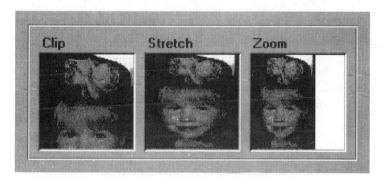

The problems are:

Clip   The photo is larger than its frame in this case, so Clip shows only the upper-left corner of the photo.

Stretch   The photo stretches (or shrinks) along both axes to fit within the frame, which distorts the picture.

Zoom   The photo stretches (or shrinks) along one axis to fit in the frame, which minimizes distortion but leaves a big chunk of white space within the frame.

The solution to the problem is straightforward—crop and size the photo *while you're scanning it,* so that it will fit nicely into its container. Let's take it from the top, so you can see how to measure the size of a container exactly.

TIP

Another solution to the problem of ill-fitting photos is to size the container on the form to fit the photos. Of course, all the photos you intend to display on the form must be the same size.

Step 1: Create the Table and Field

First, if you plan to put a photo in each record of a table, you'll need a field in the table's structure to hold the photo. That is, you need to give that field a data type of OLE Object. For example, the Photograph field of the Star Search Models table (see Figure 8.7) is an OLE Object field that can store photos. After creating the table structure, close and save it in the usual manner.

Step 2: Create the Form

Next, create a form that will display the photo and other data in the table. Use the techniques described in Chapters 11 and 13 to create the form and to size, position, and align its controls to your liking. The form in Figure 8.8, shown earlier, certainly will do the trick for displaying photos and other information. (If you just want to use a simple form, click on your table name in the database window, and then choose Insert ➤ AutoForm, as described earlier in this chapter.)

Step 3: Measure the Photo's Container

When you're happy with the general appearance of the form, open it in (or switch to) design view. Click on the control that will display the photo, open the property sheet (View ➤ Properties), and then click on the Format tab. Locate the Width and Height properties, and jot down those measurements (you'll need them in a moment). Figure 8.9 shows our Star Search form in design view. The control that displays the photo is

FIGURE 8.9

The control that will display the photo in our sample form measures .9514 inches wide, and 1.2431 inches tall.

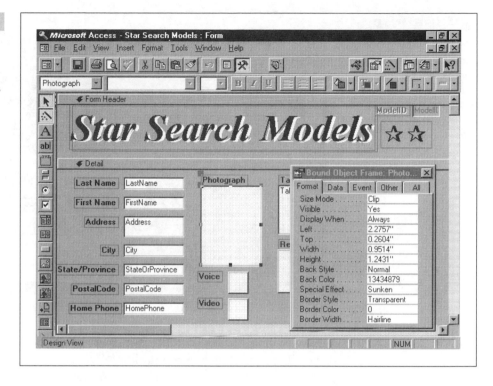

selected, and its property sheet is open. As you can see, the width of that control is .9514 inches, and its height is 1.2431 inches.

Step 4: Scan, Crop, and Size the Photo

Once you know the size of the container that will display the photo, you can scan the photo, and also crop and size it to its container. Remember, to do this while you're scanning, so you don't have to resize the photo after it has been stored on disk. Not surprisingly, most scanner software offers much more control and flexibility in this respect than a program such as Access, which is designed to do other things.

In Figure 8.10, we've scanned a photo using the scanning software (DeskScan II) that comes with the HP ScanJet IIc (other scanning programs offer similar capabilities). We've scaled the image to 28 percent (28%), and framed a portion measuring 0.95-inches wide by 1.25-inches tall—pretty close to the size of the container in our Access form.

FIGURE 8.10

While scanning this photo, we cropped the portion that we want to appear on the screen, and sized it to fit perfectly in its container.

Be sure to size and crop, to the same size as the container, any other photos you'll be putting into the table.

Step 5: Link or Embed the Picture

Save the scanned image. Then, return to your Access database, open your form, and put the picture in its container using the OLE techniques described earlier. If you sized the image carefully, it should fit perfectly into its frame without distortion, as shown earlier in Figure 8.8.

Troubleshooting Data Entry and Editing Problems

 ➤ Next we'll look at solutions for some common problems that you might encounter when entering and editing data.

Duplicate Key Message

If the new record you entered into the table duplicates the contents of the primary key field in some other record, you'll see this error message when you try to move to another record:

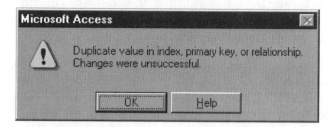

This message can be confusing because it doesn't appear until after you've filled in the record. Remember that it's referring to the field you defined as the primary key (or to an indexed field that doesn't allow duplicates) when you created the table's design.

To wiggle out of this jam, click on OK. Then do one of the following:

- **To correct the duplicate**, move the cursor to the field that defines the primary key, and enter a new, unique value in that field.

- **To avoid adding the record at all**, choose Edit ➤ Undo Current Field/Record, or press Esc, to erase the entire new record.

If you really *do* need to put duplicate entries into the field, get out of the jam as described above. Then return to the table's design view and either remove the "no duplicates" (or primary key property) from that field, or use two or more fields to define the primary key.

Can't Have Null Value in Index

If you see the message *Index Or Primary Key Can't Contain A Null Value* when you attempt to leave a record, it means you've left the primary key field (or an indexed field with the Required property) in the current record empty. Click on OK to return to the table. Then, fill in the field that requires a value. Or, to delete the entire new record, choose Edit ➤ Undo Current Field/Record or press Esc.

Value Isn't Appropriate for This Field Type

If you enter the wrong type of data into a field, you'll see a message that the data you entered doesn't fit the Data Type or FieldSize property setting for the field. For example, this message will appear if a field is defined as the Date/Time data type in the table design, and you try to type a name, address, or dollar amount into that field.

Once again, click on OK to clear the message, enter the correct type of data into the field, and then save the record again (by moving to some other record). Or, press Esc to have Access undo your changes to the record.

New Records Seem to Disappear

If records seem to disappear after you enter them, don't panic. Simply close the table, and open the table again. Remember that if the table has a primary key, Access maintains an ongoing sort order based on the field(s) that define the primary key. However, it doesn't re-sort the table until after you close it (waiting to re-sort the table makes data entry faster).

So even though new records are at the bottom of the table when you enter them, they'll be in their proper sort-order position the next time you open the table. You can scroll around to find those records to verify that they're in the table.

Data Fails Validation Rule

If you've assigned a validation rule or the Required property to a field (see Chapter 6), and the new data in the field fails the validation rule, you'll see this message (or whatever custom message you defined for the field):

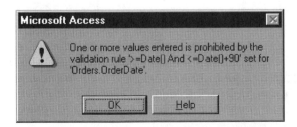

Click on OK to clear the message. You must change the field value so it passes the validity check, or delete the entire record, before you can move on to another field.

If the data is indeed valid, and it's your validity check that's at fault, make the field pass the currently assigned validity check or delete the record. Then return to the table's design view and fix the Validation Rule property for that field. If necessary, fix fields that violate the newly assigned validation rule.

Access Won't Let You Add or Change Any Data

Several factors can prevent you from adding or changing data.

- If you can't change any data in the table, the Allow Edits property may be set to No for your form.

- If you can't edit certain fields, the Enabled and Locked properties for that field on your form may be set to prevent editing. See Chapter 13 for more about forms and field properties.

- If you're sharing data on a network, you may be warned that a record you just changed has been changed by another user since you started editing it. You can then save the record and overwrite the changes the other user made (click on Save Record), copy your changes to the Clipboard and display the other user's changes in the field (click on Copy To Clipboard), or drop your changes (click on Drop Changes). If you chose Copy To Clipboard, you can then choose Edit ➤ Paste Append to add your record from the Clipboard to the table.

- If you're working on a secured system, the database administrator (the person in charge of keeping the database secure) can withhold the right to change, and even view, certain data. If you can't get at some data you need to change, ask your database administrator to extend your rights as necessary.

- If the current record contains an AutoNumber field that displays (AutoNumber), and you can't move the cursor to a new record, try entering data into any field in the current record (except the AutoNumber field). Once some data exists, the AutoNumber field will be updated and you can move the cursor to a new record.

Changing the Table Design from Datasheet View

Earlier we said that datasheet view is just for entering data, and table design view is just for changing the table's structure. Actually, that was a teeny tiny lie. The truth is that you can use datasheet view to:

- Change a field (column) name
- Insert a new text field or lookup field
- Delete a field
- Create a table from a blank datasheet

As you'd expect, the changes you make to the table's structure in datasheet view also will be reflected in design view, and vice versa. So, if you'd like to change your table's design without leaving datasheet view, read on. (Sorry, you can't change the structure of linked tables.)

WARNING

Changing field names and deleting fields can have important consequences for objects in your database that expect those fields to be available. So don't make design changes in datasheet view unless you're sure they won't adversely affect other objects. Also be aware that Access doesn't ask for permission to save the changes when you insert a column from datasheet view.

Renaming a Column

It's easy to change a column name while you're in datasheet view. To tell Access which column you want to rename, use one of these techniques.

- Double-click on the field selector at the top of the appropriate column. The column name will be selected, as shown below:

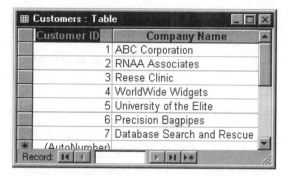

- Click on the field selector at the top of the column whose name you want to change. Then, right-click on the selection, and choose Rename Column. Again, the column name will be selected.

- Click anywhere in the column whose name you want to change, and then choose Format ➤ Rename Column. You guessed it, the column name will be selected.

With the column name selected, type a new name and then press ↵. Access will change the name in the field selector. If you switch to table design view, you'll see that the Field Name has changed there as well.

Inserting a Column

To insert a new column (field) to the left of any existing column in the datasheet, open the table in datasheet view, and then:

1. Click in the column that will become the new, blank column, and then choose Insert ➤ Column. Or, right-click on the field selector at the top of the appropriate column, and choose Insert Column. A new column will appear in the datasheet.

2. Rename the column as explained in "Renaming a Column," above.

The new field will have a Text data type and a field size property of 50. If you don't like these settings, switch to table design view and change them.

Inserting a Lookup Column

Chapter 6 gave you the full scoop on defining lookup fields from table design view. Here's how to insert a new lookup column (field) from datasheet view:

1. Click in the column that will become the new, blank column, and then choose Insert ➤ Lookup Column. Or, right-click on the field selector at the top of the appropriate column, and choose Insert Lookup Column. The Lookup Wizard will take over.

2. Respond to each Lookup Wizard dialog box (see Chapter 6), choosing options and clicking on the Next button as usual. When you've filled in the last dialog box, click on Finish to create the lookup column.

3. Rename the column (if necessary), as explained above in "Renaming a Column."

The new field's Data Type and field properties will be set automatically. Of course, you can switch to table design view and change the data type and field properties if you wish.

Deleting a Column

Deleting a column in datasheet view is easy, but be careful! When you delete a column, you're also deleting all the data in that column. What's more, you can't undo the column deletion. Here are the steps:

1. Do one of the following:

   - Right-click on the field selector at the top of the column you want to delete (the column will be selected), and choose Delete Column.

   - Click on any data in the column, and then choose Edit ➤ Delete Column.

2. You'll be asked if you want to permanently delete the selected field and data. If you're sure you want to delete the column, click on Yes. If you've changed your mind, click on No to leave the column alone.

If you chose Yes in step 2, the column will disappear from the datasheet (and from the list of fields in design view).

NOTE If you try to delete a field that's part of a relationship, an error message will tell you to delete its relationships in the Relationships window first. Click on OK to clear the error message, go to the Relationships window and delete the relationship (see Chapter 6), and then try deleting the field again.

Creating a Table from a Blank Datasheet

If you're more accustomed to using spreadsheets than databases, you might prefer to create tables from a blank datasheet, like this:

1. Open the database in which you want to create the new table.

2. Click on the Tables tab on the datasheet window, and then click on the New button.

3. In the New Table dialog box, click on Datasheet View and then click on OK (or double-click on Datasheet View).

4. Type data into each column and row of the datasheet, as needed.

5. Use the techniques described earlier under "Renaming a Column" to name the columns (initially, they'll be named Field1, Field2, Field3, ...).

6. To save your changes and name the table, click on the Save toolbar button, or choose File ➤ Save Layout.

7. When the Save As dialog box appears, type a table name (up to 64 characters), and then click on OK.

8. When asked if you want to define a primary key, click on either Yes to assign a primary key with a field name of ID, or No to save the table without a primary key.

Access will evaluate the data you've entered and automatically create appropriate field types and formats. To further customize the design of your new table, switch to design view and change the design as needed. When you're finished using the table, click on its Close button or press Ctrl+W.

 For more information about changing the table design from datasheet view, look up *Datasheet View* in the Access Help Index, and then choose either of these subtopics: *Adding Fields To Tables* or *Field Names*. For details about deleting fields, look up *Delete Fields In Datasheet View* in the Access Answer Wizard, then double-click on *Delete A Field*, and then click on *Delete A Field From A Table In Datasheet View*.

Where to Go from Here

In this chapter, you've learned the basics of customizing datasheet view, entering data, and changing the table structure from datasheet view. Continue with Chapter 9 now to learn how to sort (or alphabetize) your data, search for particular records, filter out unwanted records temporarily, and print your data.

What's New in the Access Zoo?

Several new features were added since Access 2.0 to help you enter data and work with datasheet view more easily. These new features let you:

- Customize the appearance of datasheet view by changing the text and background colors and the appearance of the datasheet grid.
- Drag and drop selected data from datasheet view into programs such as Microsoft Excel, Word, and WordPad.
- Change field names, add new fields (columns), delete fields, and create a new table from datasheet view.

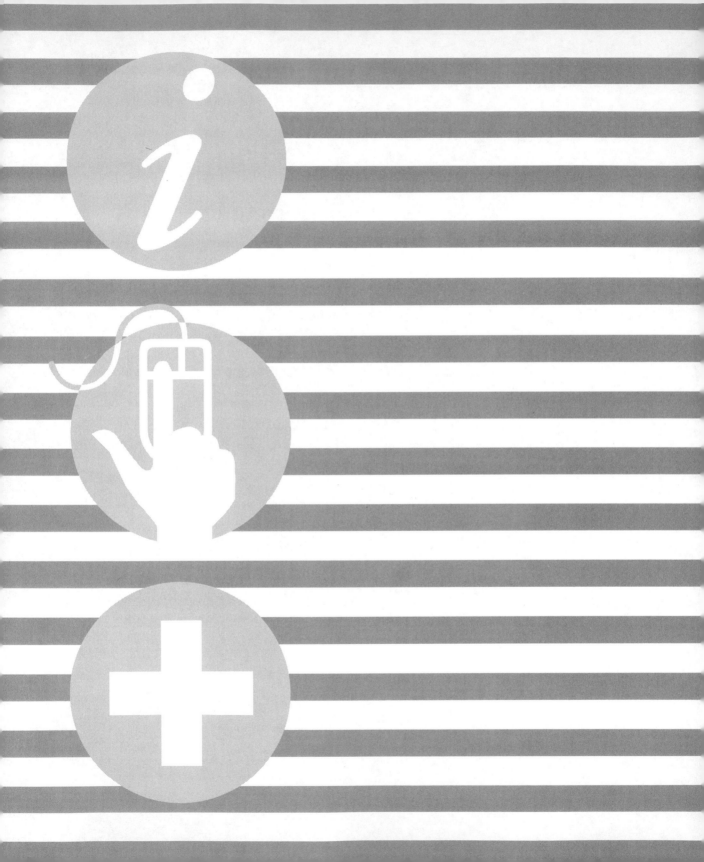

CHAPTER

9

Sorting, Searching, Filtering, and Printing

IN this chapter we'll look at ways to sort (alphabetize), search for, replace, filter, and print data. These operations are available in both datasheet view and form view, although you may prefer to experiment with them from datasheet view where the effects are most obvious.

Sorting (Alphabetizing) Your Data

Sorting data simply means to put it into some meaningful order. For example, we often sort lists and address books alphabetically to make it easy to find information. When you're working with paper, sorting is a tedious and boring process. But with Access, all it takes is a few mouse clicks.

Quick and Easy Sorting

Here's how to do a quick, simple sort based on any field in your table (except a Memo or OLE Object field):

1. If your table, query, or form isn't already open, open it in datasheet view or form view (as appropriate).

2. Click on the field on which you want to base the sort. For example, to put employee names into alphabetical order, click on the LastName column selector (in datasheet view) or the LastName field (in form view).

3. Do one of the following:

- **To sort records in ascending order** (smallest-to-largest or A to Z), click on the Sort Ascending toolbar button (shown at left), or choose <u>R</u>ecords ➤ <u>S</u>ort ➤ <u>A</u>scending. Or right-click on the column selector (in datasheet view) or the current field (in form view) and choose Sort Ascending from the shortcut menu.

- **To sort records in descending order** (largest-to-smallest or Z to A), click on the Sort Descending toolbar button (shown at left), or choose <u>R</u>ecords ➤ <u>S</u>ort ➤ <u>D</u>escending. Or right-click on the column selector (in datasheet view) or the current field (in form view), and choose Sort Descending from the shortcut menu.

In datasheet view, you can easily verify the results by reading down the column that you based the sort on (see Figure 9.1). The results of the sort won't be so apparent in form view, because you can see only one record at a time. But if you scroll through the records, you'll see that you're now scrolling though them in a sorted order. (If you're viewing a form, you can switch from form view to datasheet view to verify the sort.)

FIGURE 9.1

The original Employees table and the sorted Employees table, shown in datasheet view. We changed the sample data that Access provides.

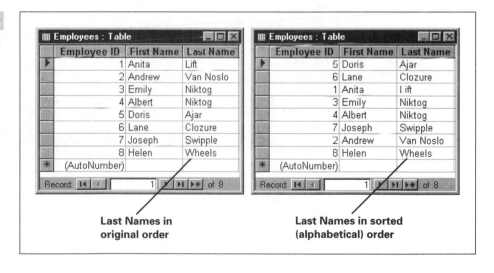

Last Names in original order

Last Names in sorted (alphabetical) order

Sorts-within-Sorts

Sometimes you may need to sort on two or more fields. For example, if there are many names in a table, you might want to sort on the LastName and the FirstName fields. That way, surnames will be in alphabetical order, and within each name, they'll be sorted by the person's first name, as shown in Figure 9.2.

It's easy to base a sort on two or more fields:

1. Open the table or query in datasheet view. Or, if you're currently viewing a form in form view, switch to datasheet view.

2. The fields you're sorting on must be in adjacent columns. If necessary, move the fields that you want to use to the leftmost column positions (see Chapter 8). Access will do the sort from left to right. Thus, to sort by surname and then by first name, arrange the

FIGURE 9.2

Sorting an Employees table on two fields and on a single field

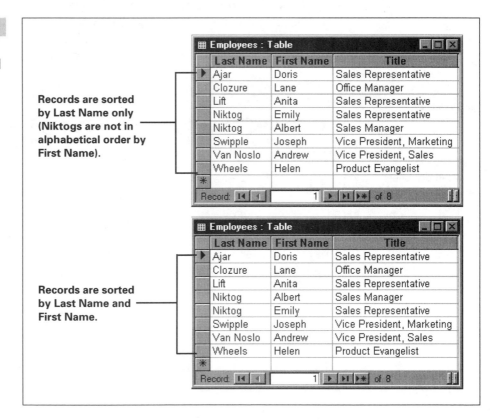

columns with the LastName column just to the left of the FirstName column.

3. Select the column(s) you want to base the sort on. To do so, click on the first column, and then Shift-click on additional column(s). In the example below, we moved the LastName and FirstName fields to the leftmost column positions, and then selected those fields for sorting:

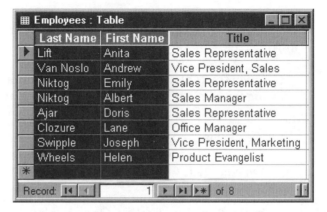

Last Name	First Name	Title
Lift	Anita	Sales Representative
Van Noslo	Andrew	Vice President, Sales
Niktog	Emily	Sales Representative
Niktog	Albert	Sales Manager
Ajar	Doris	Sales Representative
Clozure	Lane	Office Manager
Swipple	Joseph	Vice President, Marketing
Wheels	Helen	Product Evangelist

4. Click on the Sort Ascending or Sort Descending toolbar button (depending on the order you want) or use the equivalent menu options or shortcut menu options, given earlier.

Returning the Records to Their Original Order

When you're ready to return the records to their original, unsorted order, choose Records ➤ Remove Filter/Sort. Or right-click anywhere in the datasheet or form and choose Remove Filter/Sort.

N O T E   Any time you close the table after using the sort feature (described above) or the filter feature (described later in this chapter), Access will ask if you want to save changes to the design of your table. If you choose <u>Y</u>es, Access stores the current sort and filter in the table's Filter and Order By properties.

➤ To learn more about sorting, go to the Access Help Contents, open the *Finding And Sorting Data* book, open the *Sorting Data In Tables, Queries, And Forms* book, and then choose a sorting subtopic that interests you.

Finding Individual Records

Scrolling through records is fine for browsing. But when you're in a hurry, you'll probably want to use these search techniques to find specific data in your table:

1. Open the table, query, or form that contains the data you're looking for (if it isn't already open). You can use either datasheet view or form view—it doesn't matter which.

2. If you want to search only one specific field, click on that field. The Find feature can search fields that have any data type *except* Yes/No, OLE Object, or Lookup.

3. Click on the Find toolbar button (shown at left). Or choose Edit ➤ Find or press Ctrl+F. Or right-click on the column selector (in datasheet view) and choose Find from the shortcut menu. You'll see the Find In Field dialog box, shown below.

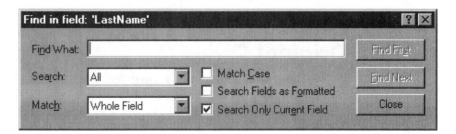

4. In the Find What text box, type the text you want to look for (for example, **Niktog**). To make the search more general, you can include the wildcard characters listed in Table 9.1.

5. Select or deselect the Match Case, Search Fields As Formatted, and Search Only Current Field options, choose a search direction (Up, Down, or All) from the Search drop-down list, and choose a match option (Whole Field, Any Part Of Field, or Start Of Field)

from the Match drop-down list as needed. *Note:* If you're searching in a lookup field, andthe Match box is set to Whole Field or Start Of Field, be sure to select (check) Search Fields; otherwise the search will fail.

N O T E

By default, the Find and Replace features do a "Fast Search" in which Access searches the current field and matches the whole field. To change the default setting, choose Tools ➤ Options, click on the Edit/Find tab in the Options dialog box, and then choose an option under Default Find/Replace Behavior. For more details, see Chapter 15 or click on the ? button in the Options dialog box and then click on the Edit/Find option you're curious about.

6. To start the search, click on the Find First button (to find the first occurrence of the text in the table) or the Find Next button (to find the next occurrence relative to the cursor position).

TABLE 9.1: Wildcard Characters You Can Use in the Find What Text Box

WILDCARD	STANDS FOR	EXAMPLE
?	Any single character	**Sm?th** matches *Smith, Smyth, Smath,* and so on.
*	Zero or more characters	**Sm*** matches *Smith, Smithereens, Sm'ores, Sm.*
#	Any numeric digit	**9## Oak St.** matches any addresses in the range of *900 Oak St.* to *999 Oak St.*
[ ]	Any characters in the brackets	**Sm[iy]th** matches *Smith* or *Smyth,* but not *Smath.*
–	Any characters within the range (must be within brackets)	**[N–Z]** matches any text starting with the letters N through Z, provided that you also select Match ➤ Start Of Field.

TABLE 9.1: Wildcard Characters You Can Use in the Find What Text Box (continued)

WILDCARD	STANDS FOR	EXAMPLE
!	Any character except (must be within brackets)	[!N–Z] matches any text that doesn't start with the letters N through Z, provided that you also select Match ➤ Start Of Field.
"" (two double-quotes)	Zero-length strings	"" matches zero-length strings, provided that you also select Match ➤ Whole Field.
Null *or* Is Null	An unformatted blank field.	**Null** matches empty fields, provided that you also select Match ➤ Whole Field and have not selected (checked) Search Fields As Formatted.

Access will find the first record (if any) that matches your request. If the dialog box is covering data that Access has found, drag the box out of the way.

Repeat steps 4–6 above (or click on Find Next) until you've found the record you want. If Access tells you it can't find the search item, click on OK to end the search. When you're done searching, click on Close or press Esc to close the dialog box.

TIP

After closing the Find dialog box, you can press Shift+F4 to find the next occurrence of text you last searched for.

 ➤ For more help on finding records, go to the Access Help Contents, open the *Finding And Sorting Data* book, open the *Finding Records Or Data* book, and then choose the subtopic you're interested in.

Fixing Typos Automatically

If you're not such a hot typist, you'll be happy to know that Access can check and correct your spelling automatically as you type, or anytime you wish. You'll learn next about the AutoCorrect and Spelling features, which can search out typing mistakes and render them harmless.

TIP The AutoCorrect and Spelling features in Access are almost identical to the ones you'll find in other Microsoft Office programs, including Word and Excel.

Correcting Mistakes As You Type

If you frequently find yourslef typng (oops, *yourself typing*) certain words incorrectly, or you often want to replace abbreviations (such as CEFG) with their longer forms (Close Enough For Government Work), the Auto-Correct feature can help you. You simply teach AutoCorrect the word or abbreviation it should replace, and then provide its replacement word or phrase. In the future, Access will substitute the typo or abbreviation with its replacement word or phrase. AutoCorrect also can correct capitalization errors that occur when you type TWo INitial CApitals (instead of just one) in a word, or you forget to capitalize names of days.

NOTE Adding new words to the list of automatic replacements has *no effect* on existing text.

Setting Up AutoCorrect Words and Settings

To teach AutoCorrect new words or to change the AutoCorrect settings, open any database object or go to the database window. Then...

1. Choose <u>T</u>ools ➤ AutoCorrect. Figure 9.3 shows a sample Auto-Correct dialog box, after we filled in the R<u>e</u>place and <u>W</u>ith boxes.

FIGURE 9.3

Use the AutoCorrect dialog box to customize the way Access replaces text automatically as you type into text or memo fields. Choose Tools ➤ AutoCorrect to get here.

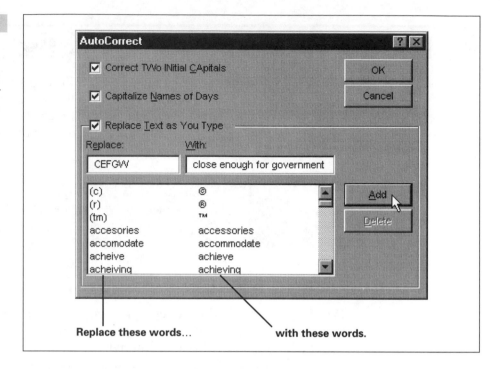

Replace these words... **with these words.**

(Notice that Access comes with an extensive list of commonly mistyped words that it can replace automatically.)

2. Use these techniques to turn AutoCorrect features on or off:

- **To replace two initial capital letters** with just one initial capital letter, select (check) Correct TWo INitial CApitals. Deselect this option to prevent automatic replacement when you type two initial capital letters.

- **To capitalize names of days** if you forget to do so, select (check) Capitalize Names Of Days. Deselect this option to prevent automatic capitalization when you type day names.

- **To replace words shown in the left column** of the AutoCorrect dialog box with words shown in the right column, select (check) Replace Text As You Type. Deselect this option to prevent automatic replacements as you type.

3. Use these techniques to add, change, and delete words in the replacement list:

- **To add a new word to the replacement list,** type the misspelling or abbreviation into the Replace text box. Then type the correction or expanded form of the word into the With text box. Click on Add to add the items to the list.

- **To change a word or its replacement,** scroll to and then click on the appropriate word in the list below the Replace and With text boxes (the words are listed in alphabetical order). The Replace and With boxes will show the item you selected. Change the Replace or With text as needed, and then click on the Add or Replace button (whichever is available) to update the list.

- **To delete a word and its replacement,** scroll to and click on the appropriate word in the list. Then click on the Delete button.

4. Repeat steps 2 and 3 as needed. When you're finished using the AutoCorrect dialog box, click on OK.

NOTE   You can add new words to the AutoCorrect list during a spell check. See "Checking Your Spelling" for details.

Using AutoCorrect During Data Entry

As you type new text or paste a word or abbreviation into a text or memo field, AutoCorrect will fix typos or expand abbreviations automatically. (AutoCorrect has no effect on existing text.) The automatic correction takes place when you type a space or punctuation mark in the field, or move the cursor to another field.

If you need to cancel an automatic replacement as you're typing, press Ctrl+Z (or choose Edit ➤ Undo AutoCorrect); the text will reappear as you typed it. To reinstate the automatic correction, press Ctrl+Z again (or choose Edit ➤ Undo).

 ➤ Need more information? Go to the Access Help Contents, open the *Working With Data* book, open the *Checking Spelling And Automatically*

Correcting Errors As You Type, and then explore the automatic correction subtopics as needed.

Checking Your Spelling

Access can check and correct the spelling in text or memo fields of a datasheet, or in selected text in a datasheet or form. Fields that don't have a Text or Memo data type are ignored during a spell check.

Here's how to start a spell check:

1. Do one of the following, depending on how much text you want to spell check:

   - **To check spelling in datasheet view,** select the records, columns, fields, or text within a field.
   - **To check spelling in form view,** select the field or text within the field you want to check.
   - **To check all text and memo fields in a table**, go to the database window, click on the Tables or Queries tab, and then click on the table or query you want to check. Or, open the table or query in datasheet view and select all the columns.

2. Click on the Spelling toolbar button (shown at left), or choose Tools ➤ Spelling, or press F7. Spell checking will start immediately.

3. Once spell checking begins, what you do next depends on what (if any) errors are found (see "Correcting or Ignoring a Word" below).

4. When the spell check is complete, click on OK to clear the completion message.

Correcting or Ignoring a Word

When the spell checker finds a word that isn't in its dictionary, it will highlight the word in your datasheet or form, suggest a correction if it can, and pause so you can decide what to do next. Figure 9.4 shows the Spelling dialog box after it tripped over the word *Foosball,* which isn't in its dictionary.

FIGURE 9.4

The Spelling dialog box after Access found a word that wasn't in its dictionary

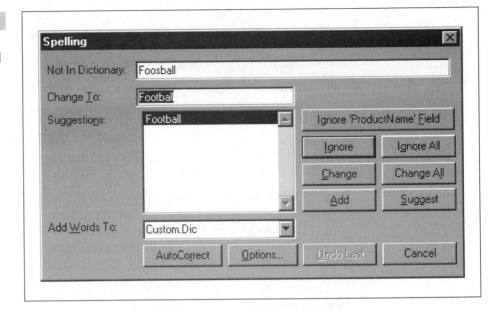

You can click on any of these buttons (if they're available) when the spell checker is waiting for you to make a correction:

Ignore 'xxx' Field   (where *xxx* is a field name). Click on this button to ignore the named field during the current spell check. Spell checking will continue.

Ignore or **Ignore All**   Click on Ignore to ignore the current occurrence of the word shown in the Not In Dictionary box. Click on Ignore All to ignore all occurrences of the word shown in the Not In Dictionary box. Spell checking will continue.

Suggest   Click on the Suggest button, or type a word into the Change To box and then click Suggest, to see alternatives to the word shown in the Change To box. To copy one of the suggested words into the Change To box, click on the word you want to copy in the list next to Suggestions. You can repeat these steps as needed.

Change or **Change All**   Lets you replace one occurrence (Change) or all occurrences (Change All) of the word shown in the Not In Dictionary box with the word shown in the Change To box. If necessary, use the Suggest button described above, or type a word into the Change To box, or click on a word in the Suggestions list to copy the word you want to use as the replacement word into the Change To box; then, click on the Change or Change All button, as appropriate. Spell checking will continue.

Add Lets you add the word shown in the Not In Dictionary box to the spelling dictionary that's shown in the Add Words To box. If necessary, choose a dictionary name from the Add Words To drop-down list before you click on the Add button. (Do not add words that truly are misspelled to your dictionary! See the sidebar titled "Maintaining Custom Dictionaries" for more details.)

AutoCorrect Adds the word shown in the Not In Dictionary box to the AutoCorrect dictionary, and assigns the word in the Change To box as the replacement word. This button saves you the trouble of manually adding words that you commonly mistype to the AutoCorrect dictionary (as explained earlier in this chapter).

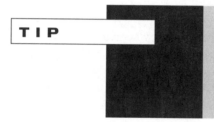

TIP

If you add a word to the AutoCorrect dictionary accidentally, complete the spell check (or cancel it). Then, choose Tools ➤ AutoCorrect, highlight the incorrect word in the replacement list, and click on the Delete button.

Options Takes you to the Spell Options dialog box (shown below). From here you can choose which language Dictionary to use, and choose whether to:

- **Always Suggest** alternate spellings, or suggest them only when you click on the Suggest button;

- Suggest words **From Main Dictionary Only,** or offer suggestions from both the main dictionary and the custom dictionary;

- Ignore **Words In UPPERCASE** (such as ASPCA), or include those words when spell checking;

- Ignore **Words With Numbers** (such as RNAA47), or include those words when spell checking.

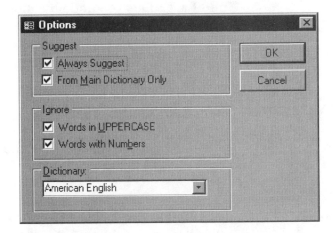

Maintaining Custom Dictionaries

You can create a custom dictionary anytime you're using the Spelling dialog box. This trick can be handy if you want to set up a new custom dictionary for storing special-purpose terms. To create a custom dictionary:

1. In the Spelling dialog box, erase any dictionary name that appears in the Add Words To combo box.

2. Type a valid dictionary name and press ↵ or choose an existing custom dictionary from the combo box's drop-down list. The default dictionary name is *custom.dic*, but you can use any name for your dictionary, as long as that name ends with a period and the letters *dic*. For example, *mywords.dic* and *medical terms.dic* are valid dictionary names.

3. If Access asks for permission to create the dictionary, click on Yes.

The custom dictionary is a plain text file that lists one word per line, in alphabetical order by word. Custom dictionaries are stored in the folder \Program Files\Common Files\Microsoft Shared\Proof on drive C (if you chose the default installation location). If you add a misspelled word to a custom dictionary by accident, you can use Windows Notepad or Windows WordPad (in text mode) to delete the incorrect words. Edit carefully!

After choosing options in the Spell Options dialog box, click on OK.

Undo Last   Lets you undo the most recent change the spell checker made. Click on this button as necessary to back out of changes one by one.

Cancel   Ends the spell check and returns you to the datasheet or form.

 ➤ For more details about spell checking, go to the Access Help Contents, open the *Working With Data* book, open the *Checking Spelling And Automatically Correcting Errors As You Type,* and then investigate the spelling subtopics.

Replacing Data in Multiple Records

In addition to letting you fix spelling errors in some or all text and memo fields, Access lets you instantly change the contents of a field throughout all (or some) of the records in your table. But before you even think of experimenting with this Replace feature, please make sure you understand the following warning.

WARNING

You can "undo" only the last individual change that Replace makes. To play it safe, make a copy of the table before you replace data. That way, if you make a major mistake, you can close the table, and then rename the unchanged original copy of the table to write over the version that has unwanted changes. See Chapter 1 for help on copying and renaming database objects.

To replace data in a table:

1. If you haven't already done so, open the table, query, or form that contains the data you want to change.

2. If you want to limit replacement to a single field, click on that field. The Replace feature can replace text in fields that have any data type *except* OLE Object, AutoNumber, and Lookup.

3. Choose Edit ➤ Replace or press Ctrl+H. You'll see the Replace In Field dialog box, shown below.

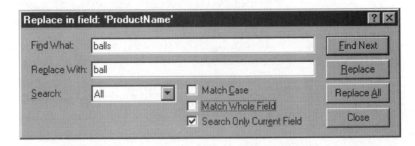

4. In the Find What text box, type the value you want to search for and change. You can use the wildcard characters listed in Table 9.1 if you wish.

5. In the Replace With text box, type the replacement text.

6. Select or deselect the Match Case, Match Whole Field, and Search Only Current Field options, and choose a search direction (Up, Down, or All) from the Search drop-down list as needed. Then do one of the following:

- **To make the change automatically** (so that Access won't ask you to verify each occurrence), click on the Replace All button.

- **To verify the changes in each record**, click on the Find Next button. (If necessary, drag the dialog box out of the way, so you can see what data Access is about to change.) Then, if you do want to change the current record, click on Replace. If you don't want to change the current record, click on Find Next. Repeat this step as needed.

7. If you chose Replace All in step 6, you'll have a chance to change your mind. Click on Yes to continue with step 9, or click on No to cancel the operation and return to step 4, 5, or 6.

8. When Access cannot find any more matches, it will display a message. Click on OK to clear the message.

9. When you're done replacing records, click on the Close button.

Here are some tips you might want to know about:

- **To globally replace large amounts of data** more quickly, or to perform calculations on data (for example, raising certain product prices by 10 percent), use an *Update query,* rather than Replace. See Chapter 10 for more about Update queries.

- **To change the default settings** for the Find and Replace features, choose Tools ➤ Options and click on the Edit/Find tab. Change the settings under Default Find/Replace Behavior as needed, and then click on OK. Chapter 15 explains more about personalizing Access.

A Search-and-Replace Example

Suppose that several people enter data into your table. Some of them spell names such as *Los Angeles* in full, while others use abbreviations such as *L.A.* This inconsistency might cause you problems down the road. Imagine that you want to send a form letter to all Los Angeles residents. If you isolate records that have Los Angeles in the City field, you'll miss all the ones that contain L.A. Why? Because computers aren't smart enough to know that Los Angeles and L.A. mean the same thing.

Anyway, the cure for your dilemma is to change all the *L.A.* entries in the City field to *Los Angeles* (or vice versa). To do that, click on the City field, choose Edit ➤ Replace, and then fill in the dialog box this way:

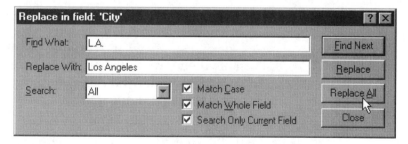

To start the replacement, click on the Replace All button and bingo—you're done! (Just answer any questions that appear on the screen.)

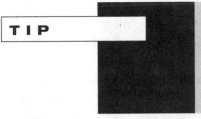

TIP To prevent the L.A. city names from creeping into your data in the future, you might want to add an AutoCorrect entry that changes "L.A." to "Los Angeles" automatically. See "Correcting Mistakes As You Type" earlier in this chapter.

 ➤ If you ever need reminders or help while replacing data, go to the Access Help Index, and look up *Replacing Values In Fields*.

Filtering Out Unwanted Records

You can use *filters* to temporarily isolate (or *select*) records you want to see, and to hide unwanted records. For example, you can focus on your California customers while hiding information about customers located in other states. There are several ways to create a filter:

- **Filter By Selection** and **Filter Excluding Selection** let you create a filter by selecting text or clicking in a field that contains the text you want to filter. See "Filtering by Selection or Exclusion" below.

- **Filter By Form** lets you create a filter by typing the values you're looking for into a fill-in-the-blanks form or datasheet. See "Filtering by Form" below.

- **Advanced Filter/Sort** lets you use a window that's similar to a query design window to create a filter. You can choose each field to search or sort by, and specify the sort order and values you're looking for. See "Using Advanced Filter/Sort" below.

NOTE You can filter fields that have any data type *except* Memo or OLE Object.

> Table 9.2 compares the three filtering methods briefly, and the following sections explain how to use each one. If you still need more information, go to the Access Help Index and explore the subtopics under *Filters*.

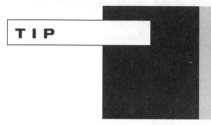

TIP   To switch between designing a Filter By Form and designing an Advanced Filter/Sort, open the Filter menu in the design window for either type of filter, and then choose Filter By Form or Advanced Filter/Sort as appropriate.

TABLE 9.2: Filtering Methods Compared

IF THIS IS WHAT YOU WANT TO DO...	FILTER BY (OR EXCLUDING) SELECTION	FILTER BY FORM	ADVANCED FILTER/SORT
Find records that meet one criterion *And* other criteria	Yes (if you specify the criteria one at a time)	Yes	Yes
Find records that meet one criterion *Or* other criteria	No	Yes	Yes
Find records that contain expressions as criteria	No	Yes	Yes
Find records and sort them in ascending or descending order at the same time	No	No	Yes

Filtering by Selection or Exclusion

Let's suppose you've found a record that contains some data you're looking for—perhaps an order for tether balls in the Order Details table. Now you want to find all the other orders for that product, or all the orders for products *except* tether balls. Access makes jobs like these ridiculously easy:

  1. Open the table, query, or form you want to filter (in datasheet view or form view).

2. Locate the record and field that contains an instance of the data you want Access to filter. For example, in the Order Details table, locate a record that displays the value *Tether ball* in the ProductID field.

3. Tell Access how much of the field to match, as follows:

- **To match the entire field**, select the entire field, or click in the field without selecting anything. *Example:* To match *Tether ball* (the entire field), click in a field that displays a value of *Tether ball*, as shown below.

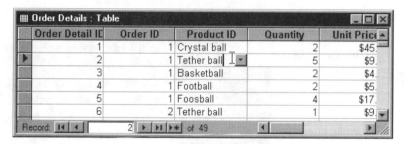

- **To match part of a field, starting with the first character** in the field, select text starting at the beginning of the field (see below). *Example:* To match fields that start with *Foo*, highlight *Foo* at the start of a field. Items such as *Football*, *Foosball*, and *Foot Powder* will match.

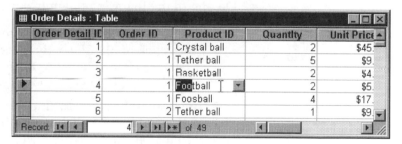

- **To match part of a field, after the first character** in the field, select text within the field. *Example:* To match fields that contain *ball* (preceded by a space), highlight the word *ball* and the space that appears before ball, as shown below. Items such as *Crystal ball* and *Tether ball* will match, but

Football and *Foosball* will not (because there's no space before *ball* in those item names).

> **N O T E**
>
> In the above example, Access will not match *Golf balls* when you apply the filter, because the pattern " ball" doesn't fall exactly at the end of the field. To isolate Golf balls along with Crystal ball and Tether ball, select " ball" in a record that contains *Golf balls* in the ProductID field. This forces Access to use a more general pattern that says "Find the word ball preceded by a space *anywhere* in the field," rather than the less general pattern "Find the word ball preceded by a space at the end of the field."

4. Do one of the following to apply your filter:

- **To show only records that have matching values in the field**, click on the Filter By Selection toolbar button (shown at left), or choose Records ➤ Filter ➤ Filter By Selection, or right-click on the field and choose Filter By Selection.

- **To show only records that *do not* have matching values in the field,** right-click on the field and choose Filter Excluding Selection. (Access will filter out records that contain null values in the field as well as records that contain values that match the current field or selection.)

The datasheet view or form view will instantly reflect your filtering choices. The navigation bar at the bottom of the datasheet or form window displays *(Filtered)*, and the status bar shows *FLTR*, to remind you that you're looking at a filtered view of data.

To filter the remaining records even more, simply repeat steps 2–4 as needed. You also can use the sorting techniques discussed earlier in this chapter to sort or alphabetize the records.

NOTE When you apply a filter, you're actually setting the Filter property for the table query or form. To view this property, switch to design view, and then choose View ➤ Properties or click on the Properties toolbar button. If you're viewing form design properties, click on the Data tab on the property sheet. If you're viewing query properties, click in the gray upper part of the query design window.

Removing or Reapplying a Filter

It's easy to remove a filter or reapply it at any time:

- **To remove (or reapply) the filter only,** click on the Remove Filter toolbar button (shown at left). This button is a toggle—you click on it to remove the filter (the button will appear pushed out), and you click on it again to reapply the filter (the button will appear pushed in). The ToolTip under the button will flip-flop between Remove Filter and Apply Filter, to reflect what action the button will take when you click on it.

- **To remove both the filtering and sorting,** right-click on any data field and choose Remove Filter/Sort. Or, choose Records ➤ Remove Filter/Sort.

TIP The steps given above for reapplying and removing a filter work for *all* types of filters—Filter By Selection, Filter Excluding Selection, and Advanced Filter/Sort. You also can remove filters and sorting by clearing the Filter and Order By properties, respectively, on the property sheet in table design, query design, or form design view.

Saving Your Filter with the Datasheet or Form

You can save the filter so that it will be remembered the next time you open your table, query, or form. The following steps work for *all* types of filters—Filter By Selection, Filter Excluding Selection, and Advanced Filter/Sort:

1. Return to the datasheet window or form window.

2. Click on the Save toolbar button, or press Ctrl+S, or choose File ➤ Save Layout or File ➤ Save; or, close the datasheet and click on Yes when asked if you want to save changes to the design.

NOTE   Access automatically saves filters applied to a form when you close the form. Therefore, you don't have to explicitly save a form to use the filter the next time you open the form. Simply click on the Apply Filter button (or its equivalent menu options and right-click shortcuts) to reapply the last filter you used.

The next time you open the datasheet or form, all the data will appear. To filter the data again, click on the Apply Filter button.

TIP   To create a form or report that automatically inherits the filter you've saved with a datasheet, open the data-sheet, apply the filter, and click on the Save toolbar button. Then click on the drop-down arrow next to the New Object toolbar button and choose the AutoForm, AutoReport, New Form, or New Report option.

Filtering by Form

If you prefer a fill-in-the-blank method for designing your filters, try the Filter By Form feature. Here's how to use it:

1. Open the table, query, or form you want to filter (in datasheet view or form view).

2. Click on the Filter By Form toolbar button (shown at left), or choose <u>R</u>ecords ➤ <u>F</u>ilter ➤ <u>F</u>ilter By Form. If you're in datasheet view, you'll see a blank, one-row datasheet, as shown in Figure 9.5. If you're in form view, you'll see a blank form instead (see Figure 9.6).

3. Click in the field you'll use to specify criteria that records must meet to be included in the filtered set of records.

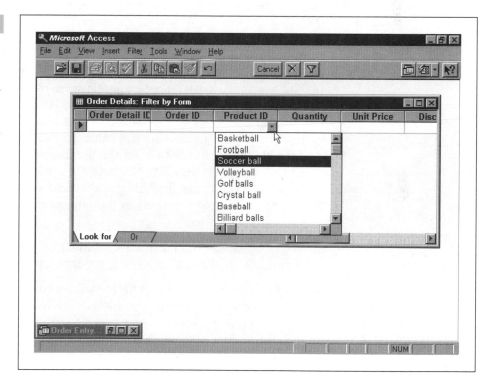

FIGURE 9.6

The Filter By Form window shown as a blank form, after we filled in some values and opened the list for the EmployeeID field. In this example, the bottom of the main form and subform includes Look For and Or tabs.

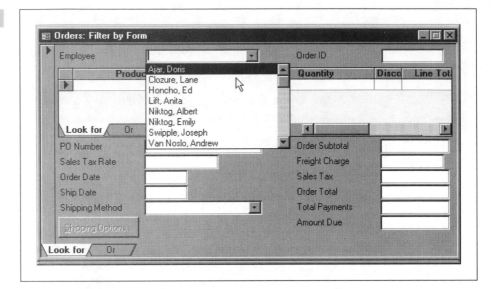

NOTE

A *criterion* is a set of limiting conditions, such as *tether ball* or *>47*, in a query or filter. One or more criteria are used to isolate a specific set of records.

4. Enter criteria by selecting the value you're searching for from the drop-down list in the field (if the list includes values) or by typing a value or expression into the field. In a moment, we'll give you some tips and tricks for filling in the fields. You'll learn more about entering expressions in the later section on "Using Advanced Filter/Sort."

5. To specify additional criteria that must be true in any given record that makes it through the filter, repeat steps 3 and 4 as needed.

6. If you want to specify alternative values that records can have in order to make it through the filter, click on an Or tab at the bottom of the window, and then specify criteria for that tab by repeating steps 3 and 4 as needed. You can continue setting up more Or criteria, and you can flip to a different tab by clicking on it.

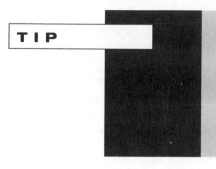

TIP

Think of additional values shown on the same tab as meaning "And." For example, to include orders in which the product ordered is *tether ball* and the quantity ordered is *5*, specify *tether ball* in the ProductID field, and *5* in the Quantity field. To also see orders for 2 of any item, click on the Or tab and type 2 in the Quantity field.

7. When you're ready to apply the filter, click on the Apply Filter toolbar button, or choose Filter ➤ Apply Filter/Sort from the menus.

Access will filter the records as you asked, and display them in the datasheet or form. As for Filter By Selection, you can remove the filter and save the filter from datasheet view or form view as needed.

A Filter By Form Example

Let's look at an example that will show how easy it is to use Filter By Form. Suppose you want to isolate records in the Order Details table in which customers ordered five (5) tether balls. You also want to see any order for basketballs, or any order for two (2) or more crystal balls. Here are the steps:

1. Open the Order Details table in datasheet or form view (we'll use datasheet view for our example).

2. Click on the Filter By Form toolbar button.

3. In the ProductID field, type **tether ball** (if you're using the sample data that Access provided, typing **t** is enough to display *tether ball* in the field).

NOTE

Filters usually are not sensitive to uppercase and lowercase letters, so *you* don't have to worry about them either. Thus, you can search for *tether ball*, or *Tether Ball,* or *TETHER BALL*, and so forth. Remember, however, that spaces *are* important, so a search within our sample data for *tetherball* will fail. (Filters on attached data *might* be case-sensitive. For example, SQL Server can be configured to be either case-sensitive or case-insensitive.)

4. In the Quantity field, type **5**. The Filter By Form window looks like this:

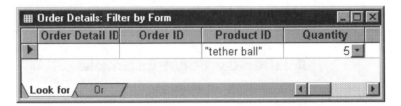

5. Click on the Or tab at the bottom of the Filter By Form window, click in the ProductID field, and then type **basketball** (or just **bask,** given our sample data), as shown below:

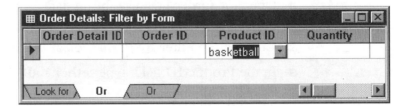

6. Click on the next Or tab at the bottom of the window, click in the ProductID field, type **crystal ball** (or just **c**), click in the Quantity field, and then type **>=2** (which means greater than or equal to 2). Here's what you'll see:

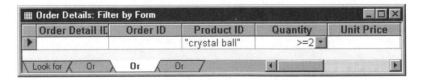

7. Click on the Apply Filter toolbar button to see the results.

8. As a finishing touch, select the ProductID and Quantity columns, and then click on the Sort Ascending toolbar button. This step sorts the results by ProductID and then by quantity within the same ProductID.

Figure 9.7 shows the Order Details datasheet after we did the eight steps above. As you see, we've isolated all basketball orders, crystal ball orders of two or more, and tether ball orders of five.

FIGURE 9.7

Filtered records in the Order Details table

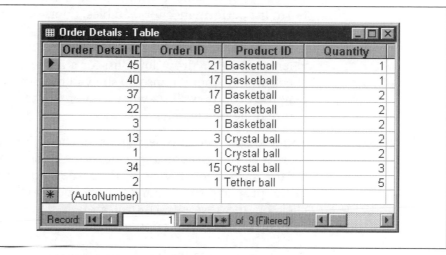

Order Detail ID	Order ID	Product ID	Quantity
45	21	Basketball	1
40	17	Basketball	1
37	17	Basketball	2
22	8	Basketball	2
3	1	Basketball	2
13	3	Crystal ball	2
1	1	Crystal ball	2
34	15	Crystal ball	3
2	1	Tether ball	5
(AutoNumber)			

Record: 1 of 9 (Filtered)

Tips and Tricks for Using the Filter By Form Window

These tips and tricks can help you use the Filter By Form window more efficiently:

- **To clear all fields in the Filter By Form window,** click on the Clear Grid toolbar button (shown at left), or choose Edit ➤ Clear Filter.

- **To delete an Or tab at the bottom of the Filter By Form window,** click on the tab you want to delete, and then choose Edit ➤ Delete Tab.

- **To get quick help with using the Look For or the Or tabs** on the Filter By Form window, click on the Help toolbar button or press Shift+F1, and then click on the tab you need help with.

Speeding Up Filter By Form Performance

Using Filter By Form will be fast on small tables, but it might be slow on very large ones. Fortunately, you can speed up overall performance for Filter By Form, or optimize performance on individual forms.

If lists seem to display slowly while you're creating a Filter By Form filter, you can change some settings to speed things up. To speed up Filter By Form list performance for *all* tables, queries, and forms, choose Tools ➤ Options, and then click on the Edit/Find tab. Check or clear options in the Show List Of Values In group, and enter a maximum list size to display when you open a drop-down list for a field value. The more options you check and the more items you show in lists, the slower your filter will display the drop-down lists when you create the filter. Click on OK when you're done making changes.

You also can speed up performance when displaying Filter By Form lists for text box controls on a specific form. To begin, open the design window for the form, choose View ➤ Properties, and then click on the Data tab in the property sheet. For each text box control you want to optimize, click on the text box control and then choose an appropriate Filter Lookup property. Your options are:

Database Default   Use the settings shown on the Tools ➤ Options ➤ Edit/Find tab.

Never   Never show available values in the drop-down list for this field; instead, show only *Is Null* and *Is Not Null* in the list.

Always   Always show available values in the drop-down list for the field.

Perhaps an example can help you decide when to turn off Filter Lookup for a field on a form. Suppose you work for a huge company, and you often use Filter By Form to select employees who have a particular last name. Because you rarely use the FirstName field's drop-down list when filtering by form, you can speed things up by setting the FirstName field's Filter Lookup property to Never. With this setting, an accidental click on the FirstName field's drop-down list won't bog you down while Access creates a long list of first names that you don't need to see anyway.

(Of course, you can always click in the FirstName field and type a first name value if you occasionally want to filter by first name.)

TIP

If you often use the same non-indexed field to filter your data, consider adding an index to that field, as explained in Chapter 6.

Using Advanced Filter/Sort

The Advanced Filter/Sort feature can be convenient to use if you need to create complex filters. With Advanced Filter/Sort, you can sort fields and specify selection criteria all at once, without having to switch from tab to tab (as with Filter By Form). To use it:

1. Open the table, query, or form you want to filter, in datasheet view or form view.

2. Choose Records ➤ Filter ➤ Advanced Filter/Sort. The filter design window, shown in Figure 9.8, will appear.

FIGURE 9.8

The Filter window for the Order Details table. The first step generally is to copy the field (or fields) you want to search from the field list into the QBE grid.

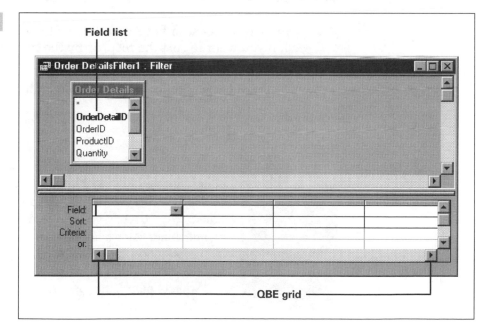

TIP

You can view and update the "advanced" filter that's behind a Filter By Selection, Filter Excluding Selection, or Filter By Form at any time. Just create one of these filters as explained earlier in the chapter, and then choose Records ➤ Filter ➤ Advanced Filter/Sort or Filter ➤ Advanced Filter/Sort (depending on which options are available on the menu bar).

3. From the list in the upper pane of the window, drag the name of a field you want to search or sort by into the QBE grid in the lower pane of the window. Or, double-click on a field to copy it to the next available Field cell in the QBE grid.

NOTE

QBE is short for *query-by-example*, so named because you *query* (ask for) certain records by presenting *examples* of what you want. (The search criterion you enter is the "example.") The QBE grid for a filter is similar to the QBE grid for a query (see Chapters 3 and 10).

4. If you wish, choose either Ascending or Descending from the Sort cell, if you want to sort the records by the field you specified in step 3.

5. Type the value you're looking for into the Criteria cell under the field name.

NOTE

Access may translate your criteria into syntax it understands by adding quotation marks or other punctuation marks to whatever you type into the Criteria cells. Usually you can enter criteria without the quotation marks or other punctuation marks, although it's perfectly fine to type them yourself. The examples in Table 9.3 show ways to enter equivalent criteria with and without punctuation marks.

6. You can repeat steps 3–5 to specify as many criteria as you wish. (We'll explain more about how to enter criteria under "Creating Complex Filters" later in this chapter.) Figure 9.9 shows the QBE grid after we copied the ProductID and Quantity fields to the QBE grid, typed **9** (the ProductID for a tether ball) into the Criteria cell below the ProductID field, and chose Ascending from the Sort cell below the Quantity field.

7. When you're ready to apply the filter, click on the Apply Filter/Sort toolbar button, or choose Filter ➤ Apply Filter/Sort.

Any records that do not meet the criteria you specified will just disappear from view. But don't worry—they're only hidden, not gone. The navigation bar shows *(Filtered)* and the status bar includes an *FLTR* indicator, to remind you that some records are hidden.

As for Filter By Form and Filter By Selection, you can remove the filter set up with Advanced Filter/Sort (click on the Remove Filter toolbar button), and you can save the filter with your datasheet or form (click on the Save toolbar button in datasheet or form view).

When you remove the filter, all the records in the table will be accessible again, and the *(Filtered)* and *FLTR* indicators will disappear. To reapply the filter, simply click on the Apply Filter toolbar button.

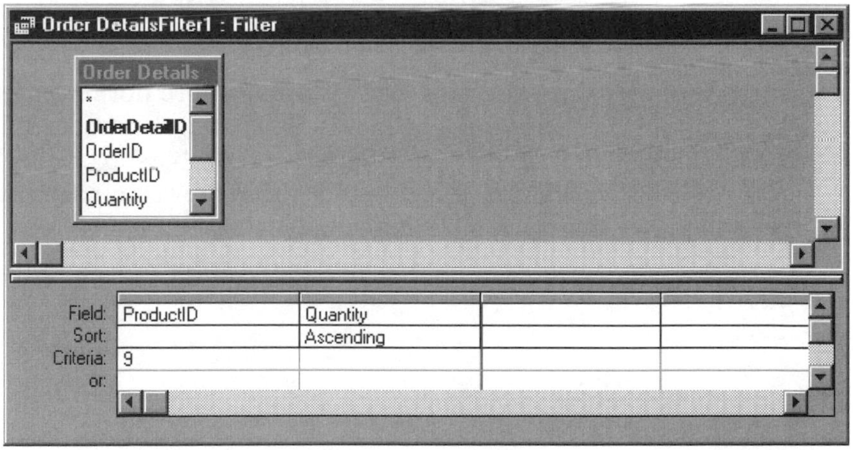

FIGURE 9.9

A completed Filter window that will select only tether ball records (ProductID 9), and sort the Quantity field in ascending (smallest-to-largest) order

Using Lookup Fields in Filters

Entering Criteria values for a lookup field can be trickier in an Advanced Filter/Sort than it is in the simpler filters discussed earlier. That's because, in those simpler filters, Access creates an internal lookup query that joins lookup fields to their related tables and plugs in appropriate criteria values. To see this for yourself, create a Filter By Selection, Filter Excluding Selection, or a Filter By Form filter that selects values in a lookup field (such as ProductID), and apply the filter. Then choose Records ➤ Filter ➤ Advanced Filter/Sort to see the internal query that Access created automatically.

With the Advanced Filter/Sort feature, only one table (the table you're creating the filter for) usually appears in the filter window. Because you don't have the convenience of displaying values from the internal lookup query, you must enter (into the QBE grid's Criteria cell) the value that's actually stored in the lookup field, *not* the value shown when you're viewing the lookup field in a datasheet or form. In Figure 9.9, for example, we wanted to isolate orders for *tether balls*. To do that, we had to type **9** (the ProductID of a tether ball)—not the word *tether ball*—into the Criteria cell below ProductID.

See Chapter 6 for more about lookup fields and Chapter 10 for more about automatic joins between tables.

Creating Complex Filters

When filtering your records, you're not limited to looking for one value in one field. The fact is, you can isolate records based on the contents of any combination of fields in the table. For example, you can select "all the orders that were placed within the last 60 days by companies in Bellevue, Washington or Jackson, Mississippi."

NOTE

You can set up the same criteria with either Filter By Form or Advanced Filter/Sort. The main difference between these filtering methods is that Advanced Filter/Sort lets you see all your criteria at once, whereas you must switch from tab to tab to see the Or conditions in a Filter By Form filter. Also, Filter By Form doesn't offer built-in sorting (but, after applying the Filter By Form filter, you can arrange columns you want to sort by from left-to-right, select them, and then click on the Sort Ascending or Sort Descending toolbar buttons).

Choosing Fields to Filter

When setting up an Advanced Filter/Sort, you first need to tell Access which fields to filter or sort, by copying field names from the field list into the QBE grid (see Figure 9.8). You've already learned two ways to copy field names, but here's the complete list of techniques for reference:

- **To quickly locate a field name** in the field list, click in the field list and type (as many times as needed) the first letter of the field name you want to see, or use the vertical scroll bar.

- **To copy a field name** into the QBE grid, double-click on the field name in the field list, or drag it from the field list to the first row (see Figure 9.9). Or, click in an empty Field cell in the QBE grid, and then type the first few letters in the field name. Or, click in the Field cell, click on the drop-down arrow button that appears, and then scroll to and click on the field you want to copy.

- **To copy several field names** to the QBE grid, Shift-click to select multiple adjacent field names in the field list, or Ctrl-click to select nonadjacent field names. Then drag any one of the selected field names into the QBE grid.

- **To copy all the field names** from the field list into the QBE grid, double-click on the title at the top of the field list, and then drag any selected field name down to the QBE grid.

Specifying Selection Criteria

The selection criteria tell Access what you're looking for. To specify criteria, you type an expression in the Criteria cell under a field name. The expression can be the exact thing you're looking for (such as **Smith** or **100** or **6/15/96**), or it can use comparison operators such as > (greater than), < (less than), and so forth. Here are some rules about typing an expression:

- In a number, currency, or autonumber field, don't include a currency sign or thousands separator. For instance, type **10000** to search for the value $10,000.

- In a date/time field, the left-to-right order of the month, date, and year ultimately must match the order defined on the Date tab of the Regional Settings Properties dialog box in Windows Control Panel. For instance, in the United States, you can enter **11/9/96** or **9 November 1996** or **9-Nov-96** or **Nov 9 96,** and Access will replace the entry automatically with #11/9/96#.

- In a text field, you can type the text you're looking for in either uppercase or lowercase letters. Put quotation marks around text that includes spaces, punctuation, or Access operators.

- In a memo field, you'll probably want to use the * wildcard to search for text embedded within the field. See "Finding Part of a Field" later in this chapter for examples.

- In a Yes/No field, enter −1, Yes, True, or On for Yes; or 0, No, False, or Off for No.

- Operators are optional. If you omit the operator, Access assumes you mean equals (=).

Using Operators and Wildcard Characters

When typing expressions in the QBE grid or the Filter By Form datasheet or form, you can use the operators and wildcards listed in Table 9.3 and the mathematical operators shown in Table 9.4.

You also can use the Date( ) function to search for records by date, relative to the current date. Table 9.5 shows some examples. Another function, DateAdd( ), is handy for specifying a range of dates based on some interval other than days.

TABLE 9.3: Operators and Wildcard Characters

OPERATOR	OPERATOR MEANING	EXAMPLE	EXAMPLE MEANING
Comparison Operators			
=	Equals	=smith *or* ="smith"	Equals *smith*
>	Greater than	>5000	Greater than *5,000*
<	Less than	<1/1/95 *or* <#1/1/95#	Less (earlier) than *January 1, 1995*
>=	Greater than or equal to	>=M *or* >="M"	Greater than or equal to the letter *M*
<=	Less than or equal to	<=12/31/95 *or* <=#12/31/95#	Less (earlier) than or equal to *December 31, 1995*
<>	Not equal to	<>CA *or* <>"CA"	Does not equal *CA*
Between	Between two values (inclusive)	Between 15 and 25	A number from 15 to 25
In	Within a set or list of values	In(NY, AZ, NJ) *or* In("NY", "AZ", "NJ")	New York, Arizona, or New Jersey
Is Null	Field is empty	Is Null	Records that have *no* value in this field
Is Not Null	Field is not empty	Is Not Null	Records that *do* have a value in this field
Like	Matches a pattern	Like MO-* *or* Like "MO-*"	Records that start with *MO-* followed by any other characters (see Wildcard Characters in this table)
Logical Operators			
And	Both are true	>=1 And <=10	Between 1 and 10
Or	One or the other is true	UT or AZ *or* "UT" or "AZ"	Either Utah or Arizona
Not	Not true	Not Like MO-??? *or* Not Like "MO-???"	Records that don't start with *Mo-* followed by exactly three characters.

TABLE 9.3: Operators and Wildcard Characters (continued)

OPERATOR	OPERATOR MEANING	EXAMPLE	EXAMPLE MEANING
Wildcard Characters			
?	Any single character	P?-100 *or* "P?-100"	Values that start with *P* followed by any single character, followed by -*100*
*	Any characters	(619)* *or* "(619)*"	Any text that starts with *(619)* e.g., phone or fax numbers
[*field name*]	Some other field in the QBE grid	<[UnitPrice]	Records where this field's value is less than the value in the UnitPrice field

TABLE 9.4: Mathematical Operators

OPERATOR	MEANING
+	Addition
−	Subtraction
*	Multiplication
/	Division
\	Integer division
^	Exponent
Mod	Remainder of division (modulo)
&	Join two text strings

TABLE 9.5: Sample Date() and DateAdd() Functions

EXAMPLE	EXAMPLE MATCHES
Date( )	The current date
<=Date( )	The current date and all dates before
>=Date( )	The current date and all dates after
<=Date( )-30	Dates earlier than or equal to 30 days ago
Between Date( ) And Date( )-30	Dates within the last 30 days
Between Date( ) And Date( )+30	Dates within the next 30 days
Between Date( )-60 And Date( )-30	Dates between 30 and 60 days ago
>DateAdd("m",1,Date( ))	Dates that are greater than 1 month ("m") from the current date
Between DateAdd ("m",-2,Date( )) And Date( )	Dates between two months ago and the current date
Between DateAdd("m",2,Date( )) And Date( )	Dates between the current date and two months from now
<DateAdd("yyyy",-1,Date())	Dates that are earlier than 1 year ("yyyy") ago

For more information on functions and how to use them, go to the Access Help Index, look up *References, Functions* or search for the function you're interested in.

Specifying "And/Or" Criteria

Sometimes you'll want to show only those records that meet all of your criteria. For instance, to locate records in the Customers table for Wilbur Stumingi in San Diego, structure your criteria to match only records that have Wilbur in the ContactFirstName field *and* Stumingi in the Contact-LastName field, *and* San Diego in the City field.

At other times you'll want to show records that match *any of* the search criteria. For example, you might want to show products that have a unit price of $4.95 or $12.95.

Table 9.6 summarizes the techniques you use in the QBE grid to specify "And" and "Or" relationships among criteria.

TABLE 9.6: Techniques for Specifying "And" and "Or" Relationships

TO SPECIFY THIS RELATIONSHIP...	IN...	DO THIS...
AND	Multiple fields	Place the criteria in the same row of the QBE grid.
AND	A single field	Use the **And** operator.
OR	Multiple fields	Place the criteria in separate rows of the QBE grid.
OR	A single field	Use the **Or** operator, or use the **In** operator, or *stack* the criteria in the QBE grid.

Arranging the QBE Grid

If you're creating a really complex filter with lots of fields, you may want to rearrange the QBE grid. Roughly the same techniques that work for customizing the datasheet view also work with the QBE grid. For example:

- **To select a QBE column**, click on the column selector at the top of the column. (The mouse pointer changes to a heavy black ↓ when it's positioned on a column selector.)

- **To select multiple columns**, drag the mouse pointer through several column selectors. Or click on the column selector for the first column you want to select, and then Shift-click on the column selector for the last column you want.

- **To select a criteria row**, click on the row selector at the left edge of the row. (The mouse pointer changes to a heavy black → when it's positioned on a row selector.)

- **To select multiple criteria rows**, drag the mouse though the row selectors of several rows. Or click on the row selector of the first row you want to select, and then Shift-click on the row selector of the last row you want.

- **To delete the selected rows or columns**, press the Delete key or choose Edit ➤ Delete Row or Edit ➤ Delete Column.

- **To insert as many blank rows or columns as you selected**, press the Insert key or choose Insert ➤ Row or Insert ➤ Column.

- **To move the selected rows or columns**, click on the row selector (for selected rows) or the column selector (for selected columns), inside the selected area. Then drag the selected rows or columns to a new position.

To adjust column widths in the QBE grid, drag or double-click on the right boundary of the column selector at the top of the column(s).

Sample Filters

The various operators, functions, and "And/Or" logic that Access provides allow you to create a practically endless variety of filters. Following are some examples of filters that are meaningful in the context of our sample database; they should give you some food for thought (and useful guidelines) for creating your own filters.

Finding Part of a Field

Wildcards are useful for finding information that's embedded within a field. The filter below will isolate records for customers on the street named Polk in the city of San Francisco.

Field:	BillingAddress	City	
Sort:			
Criteria:	Like "*polk*"	"San Francisco"	
or:			

Initially, we typed the criterion into the BillingAddress field as simply *polk*. Access added the "Like" and quotation marks automatically.

The City criterion, San Francisco, is on the same row as the BillingAddress field criterion. So, in order to pass through the filter, a record must have Polk somewhere within the BillingAddress field, and also have San Francisco in the City field.

Wildcard characters work with all data types except OLE Objects. Suppose you create a table of journal references, and the table structure includes a memo field named Abstract. To find all the records that have the phrase "vernal equinox" embedded somewhere in the Abstract field, set the field's filter criterion to *vernal equinox* or *Like "*vernal equinox*"*.

Wildcards are handy for isolating records with dates in a specific month. This criterion isolates records that have dates in March, 1995, stored in the Order Date field (assuming the standard mm/dd/yy notation for dates in the United States):

Field:	OrderDate	
Sort:		
Criteria:	Like "3/*/95"	
or:		

Finding Ranges of Values

You can use the various comparison operators to search for ranges of data values. For example, the filter below isolates customers whose last names begin with the letters A through M, and sorts the names alphabetically by last name.

Field:	ContactLastName	
Sort:	Ascending	
Criteria:	Between "A" And "N"	
or:		

Notice that we used N at the high end of the range. That's because any name (or word) beginning with the letter *m*, even mzzxxyxyx, is "less than" *n*. But anything that comes after the letter *n* (in the dictionary) is considered to be greater than "*n*". So, even a simple last name like *na* is excluded because *na* is greater than *n*.

Here's a filter that isolates and sorts (by PostalCode) customers located in the postal code range 92000 to 99999-0000:

Field:	PostalCode	
Sort:	Ascending	
Criteria:	Between "92000" And "999990000"	
or:		

N O T E

When entering criteria, be sure to specify only characters that are actually stored in the table. For example, the input masks for fields in Wizard-generated tables display punctuation characters (such as hyphens in a Zip code and parentheses in a phone number) in a datasheet or form, but they do not store those characters in the table. That's why we omitted the hyphen punctuation character in the Criteria cell shown above.

Here's a simple filter that isolates and sorts (by UnitPrice) records in the Products table that have a Unit Price value of $25.00 or less.

Field:	UnitPrice	
Sort:	Ascending	
Criteria:	<=25	
or:		

Filtering Dates

The filter below isolates records with dates from the first quarter of 1995 (January 1 through March 31, 1995). In this example, we didn't have to type the # symbols. Access adds them automatically when you type a date into the Criteria cell.

Field:	OrderDate	
Sort:		
Criteria:	Between #1/1/95# And #3/31/95#	
or:		

TIP You can use the Date( ) function in a filter to stand for the current date. See Table 9.5 earlier in this chapter.

Accepting Several Values from a Field

Suppose you want to isolate customers in the states of Alaska, California, and Wyoming. In this case, you want to accept records that have AK or CA or WY in the StateOrProvince field. There are three ways to set up the filter. Here's one:

Field:	StateOrProvince	
Sort:		
Criteria:	"ak" Or "ca" Or "wy"	
or:		

This "stacked" setup works just as well:

Field:	StateOrProvince	
Sort:		
Criteria:	"ak"	
or:	"ca"	
	"wy"	

And so does this version, which uses the "In" operator to list acceptable entries:

Field:	StateOrProvince	
Sort:		
Criteria:	In ("ak","ca","wy")	
or:		

No particular method is "better than" another. So use whichever method seems most natural or convenient. Remember, too, that Access isn't picky about uppercase and lowercase letters in the Criteria cells; therefore, it's fine to enter the abbreviation for Alaska as **AK** or **Ak** or **ak**, or even **aK**.

Saving a Filter as a Query

Earlier in this chapter, we showed you how to save a filter with the datasheet or form. Filters saved with the datasheet or form are available anytime you open the datasheet or form and apply the filter, and anytime you display a filtered datasheet or form and then create a new form or report from the filtered records.

You also can save a filter as a separate query object, which will be available anytime you need it. Here's how:

1. Return to the Advanced Filter/Sort filter design window. If you're viewing the datasheet or a form, choose Records ➤ Filter ➤ Advanced Filter/Sort. If you're in the Filter By Form window, choose Filter ➤ Advanced Filter/Sort.

2. Click on the Save toolbar button, or choose File ➤ Save As Query, or right-click in the upper pane of the window and choose Save As Query.

3. Type a name for the query and click on OK. As usual in Access, the name can be up to 64 characters, including blank spaces (see the sidebar titled "Object Naming Rules" in Chapter 6). Access will save the filter as a query.

When you want to reuse the query in the future:

1. Open the table to which you want to apply the filter. This must be the same table you used to create the filter originally.

2. Return to the filter window (see step 1 of the procedure for saving a filter as a query, just above).

3. Choose File ➤ Load From Query, or right-click in the upper pane of the window and choose Load From Query.

4. Double-click on the name of the filter you saved earlier. The filter will appear in the filter window. (The filter might look slightly different from the one you saved earlier, but it will work the same way.)

5. To apply the filter, click on the Apply Filter toolbar button.

Troubleshooting Filters

➤ Remember these points if your filtered results seem to have gone awry:

- If an Access operator (such as the word And) happens to occur within text that you're searching for (such as the company name *Dewey Cheathem And Howe*), place the entire text in quotation marks:

  `"Dewey Cheathem And Howe"`

  Otherwise, Access will misinterpret your text as

  `"Dewey Cheathem" And "Howe"`

- If you're searching for text that contains punctuation marks (that is, anything other than numbers or letters), put quotation marks around the text. You can use single quotation marks ('') or double quotation marks ("").

- Avoid confusing "And" and "Or" logic. This logic doesn't always work the way you'd think of it in English. For instance, to find customers in Mississippi and Washington, you must use an "Or" criterion, such as **"MS" Or "WA"**. If you use an "And" criterion instead, Access never finds a match. That's because Access can't answer Yes when it asks the question "Does this record have MS in the StateOrProvince field, and WA in the StateOrProvince field?"

- Remember that each Criteria row in the filter asks an entirely separate and independent question. If Access can answer "Yes" to any one of those questions, the record passes through the filter.

This last point is an important one, and the cause of much confusion among neophyte database users. For example, look at this filter, and see if you can figure out which Order Detail records will get through it.

Field:	ProductID	Quantity	
Sort:			
Criteria:	9	5	
or:		3	

At first you might say "It'll show all the orders for tether balls (ProductID 9) in which the Quantity ordered is 5 or 3." But that's not exactly correct. The filter will show all the tether balls in which the quantity ordered is 5, and all products (regardless of ProductID) for which the quantity ordered is 3. Why? Because there are two separate questions being asked of each record:

Question 1: Does this record have 9 in the ProductID field and 5 in the Quantity field?

Question 2: Does this record have 3 in the Quantity field?

Any record that can pass either question comes through the filter. The second question above places no filter criterion on the ProductID field.

If you want to select all the tether ball orders that have a quantity ordered of 5, and all the tether ball orders that have a quantity ordered of 3, you must set up two complete questions, like this:

Field:	ProductID	Quantity	
Sort:			
Criteria:	9	5	
or:	9	3	

This second filter asks these two questions:

Question 1: Does this record have 9 in the ProductID field and 5 in the Quantity field?

Question 2: Does this record have 9 in the ProductID field and 3 in the Quantity field?

Only records that have the 9/5 combination or the 9/3 combination will pass through the filter.

As with most things in Access, you can get help as you create your own advanced filters. Go to the Access Help Index, search for *Filters*, and explore any topics of interest. As you scroll through the *Filters* topics, you'll discover a *Troubleshooting Problems* subtopic that can help you diagnose and solve problems with filters.

Quick Prints

 If you're looking at a datasheet or form on the screen, and need a printed copy of that object, you can click on the Print toolbar button (shown at left) to print the data without being prompted for further information. Of course, there are fancier ways to print things, as the next few sections will explain.

Previewing Your Printout

To get a sneak preview of how the data on the screen will look when printed:

1. Start from datasheet view or form view, then...

 2. Click on the Print Preview toolbar button (at left) or choose File ➤ Print Preview. A full-page image of the datasheet or form will appear.

3. Do any of the following:

   - **To zoom into or out of a portion of the image,** click on the Zoom toolbar button, or click on the image itself. Figure 9.10 shows our sample Products table after zooming in on the data.

   - **To zoom so that you can see two pages at a time,** click on the Two Pages toolbar button. To return to one-page view, click on the One Page toolbar button.

   - **To zoom to any magnification** between 10 and 200 percent, click on the drop-down arrow next to the Zoom Control box on the toolbar, and then choose a magnification.

   - **To output the data to another Microsoft program,** click on the drop-down arrow next to the OfficeLinks toolbar button, and then choose Merge It, Publish It With MS Word, or Analyze It With MS Excel. (See Chapter 7.)

   - **To select options from a convenient shortcut menu,** right-click anywhere in the image and choose an option from the menu, shown below. *Zoom* offers the same magnification options shown in the Zoom Control box, *Pages* displays up to 20 "thumbnail" pages at a glance, *Save As/Export* exports

FIGURE 9.10

The Print Preview window for our sample Products table, after zooming in on the data

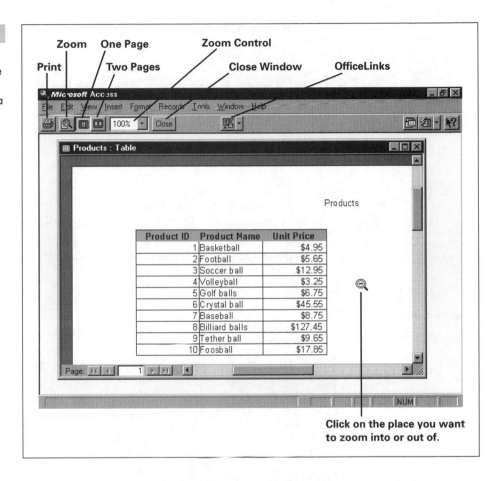

Click on the place you want to zoom into or out of.

data to another format (see Chapter 7), and *Send* sends the data as an e-mail message (see Chapter 7).

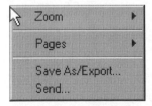

- **To immediately print** whatever is in the print preview window, click on the Print toolbar button. Or, choose File ➤ Print (or press Ctrl+P) and continue with step 3 of the procedure given in the next section.

- **To return to datasheet view or form view without printing,** click on the Close toolbar button.

Printing Your Form or Datasheet

To print the current form view or datasheet view data without previewing it first:

1. If you want to print selected records, select the record(s) you want to print.

2. If you want to use the default printing options and print immediately, click on the Print toolbar button (shown at left), and you're done. If you want more control over printing, choose File ➤ Print or press Ctrl+P. You'll see the Print dialog box, shown in Figure 9.11.

FIGURE 9.11

The Print dialog box

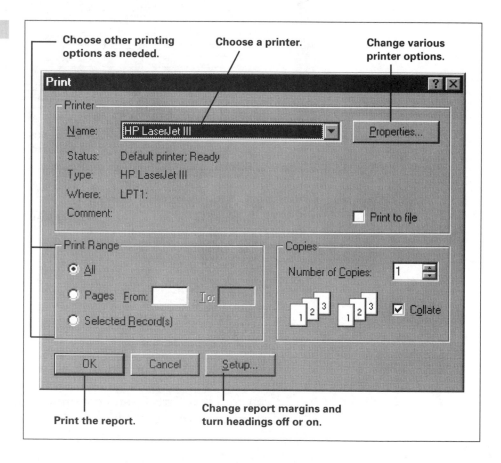

3. Choose options in the Print dialog box, as needed (more on these options in a moment).

4. When you're ready to start printing, click on OK.

 ➤ Most of the printing options are quite straightforward, but if you need more help, see "Changing the Page Setup" and "Changing Printer Properties" below, or click on the ? button in the upper-right corner of the dialog box and then click on the option you're curious about. You also can explore topics in the Access Help Index that start with the word *Printing*.

Changing the Page Setup

The Setup button in the Print dialog box takes you to the Page Setup dialog box (see Figure 9.12). From there you can choose margin settings for your printed output, and choose whether to print headings or whether to print the data only—without borders, gridlines, or layout graphics.

NOTE The options available depend on the type of object you're printing. For example, Figure 9.12 shows the Page Setup dialog box for a table that we opened in datasheet view. The Page Setup dialog box for a form or report also includes a Layout tab; on the Margins tab, the Print Data Only check box replaces the Print Headings check box shown in Figure 9.12.

You can reach a more powerful Page Setup dialog box than the one shown in Figure 9.12 by choosing File ➤ Page Setup from the menu bar. When you use the menu bar options, you can change the page margin and header settings (from the Margins tab), and you can change various printer settings and properties (from the Page tab). If you're printing a form or report, you'll also find a Layout tab, which lets you control such things as the distance between rows of data on a report.

Changing Printer Properties

If you want to change the properties for the currently selected printer, click on the Properties button in the Print dialog box. Or, if you choose File ➤ Page Setup, click on the Page tab, click the Use Specific Printer

FIGURE 9.12

The Page Setup dialog box appears when you click on the Setup button in the Print dialog box. A more powerful Page Setup dialog box opens when you choose File ➤ Page Setup from the menu bar.

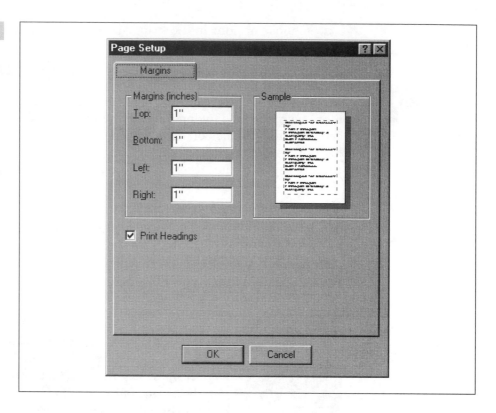

option, click on the Printer button, select a printer (if necessary), and then click on the Properties button.

Figure 9.13 shows the Paper tab of the Properties dialog box for an HP LaserJet III printer. Other types of printers will have different tabs and property settings.

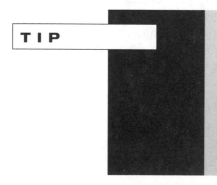

TIP

For even more control over your printer's properties, click on the Start button on the Windows taskbar, and choose Settings ➤ Printers (or use any equivalent techniques for opening the Printers window). Then right-click on the printer you want to customize and choose Properties. Changes that you make by starting from the Printers window affect printer properties for *all* Windows programs, not just Access.

FIGURE 9.13

The Properties dialog box for an HP LaserJet III printer

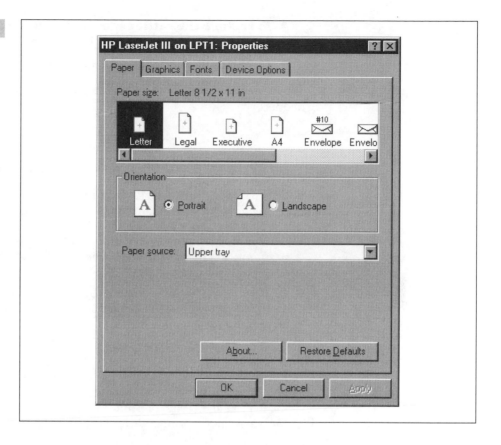

You use the Properties dialog box for a printer the same way you use properties dialog boxes for other objects in Windows:

1. Click on the tab for the property you want to change.

2. Set any options you want on the selected tab. If you're unsure about what to do, click on the ? button in the upper-right corner of the Properties dialog box, and then click on the option or button you need help with.

3. Repeat steps 1 and 2 as needed.

4. Click on any of the buttons described below:

   - **To display copyright information and the printer driver version number**, click on the About button in the Paper tab. Click on OK to close the About dialog box.

- **To restore the settings to their factory defaults,** click on the Restore Defaults button in any tab that offers it.
- **To apply the settings you've chosen so far,** click on Apply.

5. When you're done choosing printer Properties, click on OK as needed.

Making Your Print Settings Stick

At first glance, it's downright tricky trying to figure out which print settings will stick each time you print and which won't. These tips can help you:

- Changes made in the Print dialog box are always temporary; the next time you open the Print dialog box (File ➤ Print or Ctrl+P), the default settings reappear.

- Changes made from the Page Setup dialog box or printer Properties dialog box are stored with each form and report, and will take effect anytime you open the form or report and print. (This is true whether you get to those dialog boxes from the Print dialog box or the File ➤ Page Setup menu options.)

- Print settings are always returned to the defaults after you print and close a table, query, or module. That is, changes you make in the Print, Page Setup, or printer Properties dialog boxes are discarded after you print and close the table or query.

Printing Tips

Here are some tips that should come in handy whenever you're printing from datasheet or form view:

- If you customize datasheet view before printing, your printout will show the custom datasheet.

- The Print Preview window will reflect any changes that you make via the Page Setup dialog box (File ➤ Page Setup).

- If you've created a shortcut to an Access object on the Windows desktop or in a folder, you can quickly preview, print, or send the object via e-mail. First locate the shortcut, and right-click on it.

Then choose Pre_v_iew, _P_rint, or Se_n_d To ➤ Mail Recipient from the shortcut menu.

- In Windows 95, you can print by dragging the shortcut icon for your Access object to a printer icon. To locate your printer icons, open My Computer and double-click on the Printers folder; or, click on the Start button on the Windows taskbar, and choose _S_ettings ➤ _P_rinters. Or open Control Panel (Start ➤ _S_ettings ➤ _C_ontrol Panel) and double-click on the Printers folder.

See Chapter 1 for information about creating shortcuts from Access objects.

What's New in the Access Zoo?

The folks at Microsoft added many new features to Access for Windows 95. These include:

- AutoCorrect, which corrects typos and expands abbreviations as you type them into text or memo fields.

- Spell checker, which can replace mistyped words in text and memo fields and add replacement words to the AutoCorrect dictionary.

- Filter By Selection and Filter Excluding Selection, which instantly select data that matches (or does not match) the current field or selection in a datasheet or form.

- Filter By Form, which lets you type filter criteria into a "fill-in-the-blank" form. For many people, this feature is easier to use than Advanced Filter/Sort.

- Advanced Filter/Sort, which is the same as the filter feature from Access 2 (_R_ecords ➤ Edit _F_ilter/Sort).

- Ability to save filters with tables and forms. The next time you open the table or form, simply click on the Apply Filter toolbar button to filter the records. Any new reports or forms that you create from filtered records also inherit the filter.

- More powerful Print Preview, with options to preview multiple thumbnail pages and to zoom to magnifications between 10 and 200 percent.

Where to Go from Here

This chapter has presented a potpourri of procedures for sorting, searching, filtering, and printing data in datasheet view and form view. The next stop is to learn about queries, which let you ask questions about data and change data automatically. If you feel comfortable using the Advanced Filter/Sort features described in this chapter, queries will seem easy.

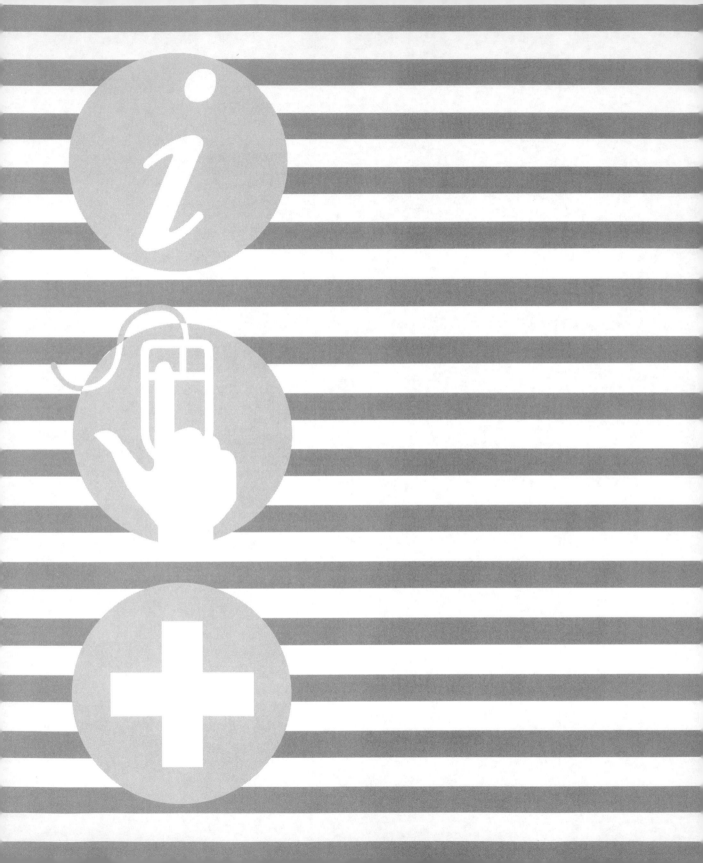

CHAPTER

10

Querying
Your Tables

QUERIES allow you to answer questions about your data, to extract specific information from tables, and to change selected data in various ways. In fact, the ability to perform queries is a key reason for using database management programs—rather than spreadsheets or word processing programs—to manage large amounts of related data. In this chapter, you'll learn how to use the Query Wizards and the graphical *query by example (QBE)* tools in Access to query your data with relative ease.

As you read through this chapter, keep in mind that many techniques for customizing datasheet view and creating filters apply to queries as well. So if you haven't worked through Chapter 9, you should do so before diving into queries. You also should understand basic table design concepts presented in Chapter 6 and know how to edit in datasheet view, as explained in Chapter 8.

What Queries Let You Do

Queries let you see what data you want, in the order you want it. They also allow you to perform calculations on your data; to create sources of data for forms, reports, charts, and other queries; to make global changes to tables; and to create new tables.

TIP

If the main reason you're creating a query is to use it as a source of records for a multi-table form or report, you may not need to set up a query at all. Often, the Form Wizard or Report Wizard offers a faster way to simultaneously design the form or report and create an SQL statement that defines the record source for you. Chapters 11 and 12 describe these versatile Wizards in more detail. Of course, if you have many records, a form or report will operate faster if it uses a saved query (rather than an SQL statement) as its record source.

When you run most types of queries or apply a filter, Access collects the data you ask for in a *dynaset*. Although the dynaset looks and acts like a table, it's actually a dynamic or "live" view of one or more tables. Therefore, changes that you make after running a query usually will affect the underlying tables in the database itself.

NOTE

A dynaset is an updatable type of *recordset,* which is any collection of records that you can treat as an object. Some types of queries—such as those that create crosstabs and other summaries—generate recordsets in which some or all fields are not updatable.

Types of Queries

You can create several types of queries, as summarized below:

Select Query   The most commonly used query type, a Select query lets you select records, create new calculated fields, and summarize your data. Select queries are similar to the filters discussed in Chapter 9.

However, unlike filters, Select queries also let you:

- Query more than one table.
- Create new calculated fields.
- Summarize and group your data.
- Choose which fields to show or hide.

Crosstab Query Groups data into categories and displays values in a spreadsheet-like format with summary totals. You can use Crosstab queries to compare values and see trends in your data, to view summary data such as monthly, quarterly, or yearly sales figures, and to answer questions such as *Who has ordered how many of what?* Crosstabs are especially useful as the basis for reports and charts.

Make Table Query Creates a new table from a dynaset. Use Make Table queries to create a backup copy of a table, save a history table of old records you'll be deleting from another table, select a subset of data to report on, or create a table for exporting to other applications.

Update Query Lets you make global changes to data in one or more tables. These queries offer a powerful, fast, and consistent way to change many records in one fell swoop. For example, you can use an Update query to increase the price of all tether ball items by 25 percent, or to empty out certain fields.

Append Query Adds records from one or more tables to the end of an existing table. Append queries are especially useful for adding old records to the end of a history table. You can then convert the Append query to a Delete query (described next) and delete the old records from the original table.

Delete Query Deletes a group of records from one or more tables. For instance, you can delete all customer records for people who haven't bought anything in five years or more. Or, after appending data to a history table, you can use a Delete query to remove the old records from the original table.

Pass-Through Query Strictly for SQL mavens, Pass-Through queries send commands directly to a SQL database server using the syntax required by that server. For information on this topic, search for *Queries, Pass-Through Queries* in the Access Help Index.

Data Definition Query   Also for SQL mavens, data definition queries use SQL language statements to create or change database objects in the current database. To learn about this topic, search for *Queries, Data-Definition Queries* in the Access Help Index.

Union Query   Another one for SQL mavens, Union queries use SQL language statements to combine corresponding fields from two or more tables or queries into one field. See *Queries, Union Queries* in the Access Help Index for details.

Access offers two ways to create queries: Query Wizards and the "from-scratch" methods. We'll look at the Query Wizards first.

Using Query Wizards

Query Wizards offer a quick and easy way to perform the special-purpose queries listed below.

Simple Query Wizard   Creates a Select query for one or more tables. The resulting query can do simple selection, or it can calculate sums, averages, counts, and other types of totals.

Crosstab Query Wizard   Creates a crosstab for a single table or query.

Find Duplicates Query Wizard   Finds duplicate records in a single table or query.

Find Unmatched Query Wizard   Finds records in one table that have no related records in another. For example, you can use this Wizard to create queries that find customers who haven't placed orders, or to find employees who haven't sold orders to any customers.

Often the Query Wizards will be able to set up the perfect query for your needs. But even if the query that the Wizard creates is only "almost good enough," using the Wizards can save you time in the initial query design. Remember, you can always switch to design view (discussed soon) and tweak the Wizard-generated query as needed.

To use the Query Wizards:

1. From any window in an open database, click on the drop-down arrow next to the New Object toolbar button (the second-to-last button on the toolbar) and then choose New Query. Or, from the database window, click on the Queries tab and then click on the New button, or choose Insert ➤ Query.

2. In the New Query dialog box, double-click on one of the options described above (Simple Query Wizard, Crosstab Query Wizard, Find Duplicates Query Wizard, or Find Unmatched Query Wizard.

3. Follow the Wizard's instructions and complete the dialog boxes that appear. (See Chapter 3 for information about basic techniques you can use with Access Wizards.)

In a flash, you'll have a new query that you can either use as is, or customize as needed.

Creating, Running, Saving, and Changing a Query

Now let's look at the basic steps for creating queries from scratch and for running, saving, and changing queries. Later in the chapter you'll learn how to refine the basics to set up any query you want.

Creating a Query from Scratch

The Query Wizards can create the specialized queries discussed in the previous section. If you'd like to create other types of queries, however, you'll need to start from scratch, without a Query Wizard. Here are the steps to follow:

1. From any window in an open database, click on the drop-down arrow next to the New Object toolbar button (second-to-last button on the toolbar) and then choose New Query. Or, from the database window, click on the Queries tab and then click on the New button, or choose Insert ➤ Query.

2. In the New Query dialog box, double-click on Design View. A *query design window* named Query1 : Select Query opens and the Show Table dialog box appears (see Figure 10.1).

FIGURE 10.1

The Select Query window and Show Table dialog box appear when you create a new query from scratch.

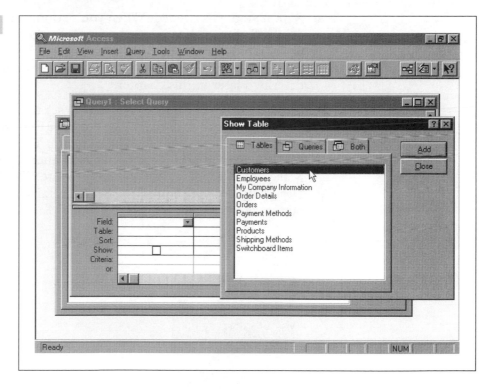

3. Use any of these techniques to add the tables you want to query:

   - **To choose which objects to list** in the Show Table dialog box, click on the Tables, Queries, or Both tabs at the top of the Show Table dialog box.

   - **To add an object to the query design window,** double-click on the object you want to add; or highlight the object and then click on the Add button.

   - **To add multiple adjacent objects to the query design window,** click on the first object you want to select; then Shift-click on the last object you want (or drag your mouse through the object names). Click on Add.

   - **To add multiple non-adjacent objects to the query design window,** click on the first object you want to select, then hold down the Ctrl key and click on each remaining object. Click on Add.

4. Repeat step 3 as needed. When you're done, click on Close. Join lines will appear automatically if you created relationships between tables (Chapter 6), or if Access can figure out the relationships on its own. You also can join the tables manually, as described later in this chapter.

5. To pick the type of query you want to set up, click on the drop-down list next to the Query Type toolbar button (shown below), or choose options from the Query menu. Your options are Select (the default and most commonly used query type), Crosstab, Make Table, Update, Append, and Delete. (See "About the Query Design Window's Toolbar" below for details about the toolbar buttons.)

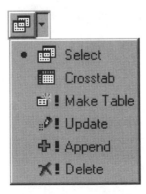

TIP   To convert one type of query to another, simply choose the appropriate type from the Query Type toolbar button or the Query menu.

6. In the tables area, double-click on fields that you want to display in the dynaset or use in selection criteria. Or drag the fields from the tables area to the QBE grid. Or select the fields from the drop-down list in the Field row of the QBE grid.

7. In the Criteria rows under the appropriate column in the QBE grid, specify any selection criteria that you want to use for isolating records in the dynaset. The techniques are similar to those for designing a filter (see Chapter 9).

8. Fill in other areas of the QBE grid as needed (see "Refining Your Query" later in the chapter).

9. If you wish, specify properties for the query itself, or for an individual field. See "Refining Your Query" below.

The example in Figure 10.2 shows a complex Select query that's based on several related tables. This query will:

- Select records in which the order was placed in February, 1995, and the quantity times the unit price ([Quantity]*[Order Details]![Unit Price]) is greater than $75.

- Display the ContactLastName and ContactFirstName fields from the Customers table (see the Field and Table rows in Figure 10.2), the OrderDate from the Orders table, the Quantity and UnitPrice from Order Details, a calculated field named $, and the Product-Name field from the Products table. In the dynaset, the $ field will have the column heading *Total Price* and will appear in Currency format (see the Field Properties sheet in the figure).

- Sort the results by ContactLastName and ContactFirstName (in ascending order) and OrderDate (in descending order) for multiple orders from the same customer.

N O T E   Because both the Order Details and the Products tables have a UnitPrice field, we had to explicitly tell Access to use the UnitPrice field in the *Order Details* table when multiplying the Quantity times the Unit Price in the query. To specify the table name and field name, use the format *[TableName]![FieldName]*, as in [Order Details]![UnitPrice].

Figure 10.3 shows the dynaset produced by this query.

Tips for Using the Query Design Window

Here are some tips and shortcuts for designing a query:

- **To clear all the items from the QBE grid,** choose Edit ➤ Clear Grid. Caution: You cannot undo Clear Grid.

FIGURE 10.2

A Select query to find orders for a specified date and dollar amount of items

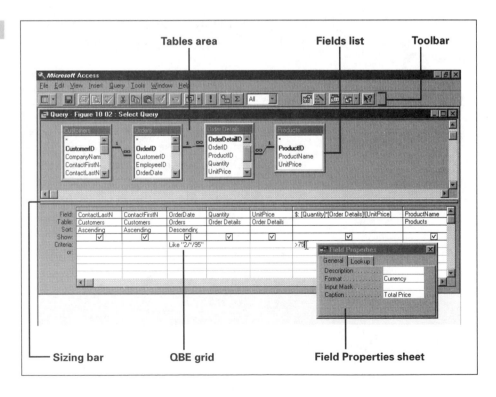

FIGURE 10.3

The dynaset produced by the query in Figure 10.2

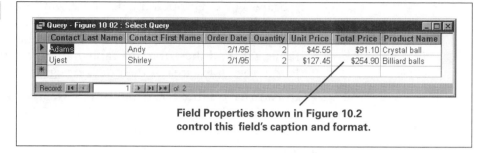

Field Properties shown in Figure 10.2
control this field's caption and format.

- **To expand the editing area for an input cell in the QBE grid,** click in the cell you want to expand and then press Shift+F2. Or right-click on the cell and choose Zoom. In the Zoom Box that appears, edit the text as needed and then click on OK to close the box.

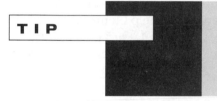

The Zoom Box is available anywhere an expanded input area might be handy, including property sheets, a table's design or datasheet view, the QBE grid, the filter window, and the macro window.

- **To see which table each field in the QBE grid is from or to hide that information,** choose View ➤ Table Names or right-click on the QBE grid and choose Table Names. When you select (check) the View ➤ Table Names option or the Table Names shortcut menu option, a Table row will appear in the QBE grid (see Figure 10.2). When you deselect the option, this row is hidden.

- **To change a field name in the QBE grid,** click to the left of the field name's first letter in the QBE grid, and then enter the new name followed by a colon. We used this technique to change the original name of an expression field to $ in Figure 10.2. The new field name will be used in the dynaset, unless you've specified a Caption in the Field Properties sheet (see Figures 10.2 and 10.3).

- **To add tables to the query design window,** click on the Show Table toolbar button (shown at left), or right-click on an empty place in the tables area and choose Show Table, or choose Query

➤ Show Table. Or open the database window (F11) and then choose Window ➤ Tile Vertically so that you can see the database and query design windows. Next, click on the database window's Tables tab, and then drag the table name from the database window to the tables area of the query design window.

- **To remove a table from the query design window,** click on the table and then press the Delete key. (This doesn't remove the table from the database, only from the query design window.)

- **When a query gets too complicated,** consider using two. Create, test, and save the first query. Then, with the first query open in the query design or datasheet window, click on the drop-down arrow next to the New Object toolbar button, choose New Query, and then double-click on Design View. Now design, test, and save your second query (which will be based on the first one). In the future, you can just run the second query to get the results you want.

 ➤ For help with designing queries, look up any of the subtopics under *Queries* in the Access Help Index. Or, go to the Help Contents, open the *Working With Queries* book, open the *Creating A Query* book, and explore subtopics there (a great jumping off point is the *Create A Query* subtopic).

Viewing the Dynaset

You can view the dynaset anytime:

- Click on the Query View toolbar button (shown at left), or choose View ➤ Datasheet.

TIP If you need to cancel a query while it's running, press Ctrl+Break. (This cancel procedure may not work for very large queries.)

The dynaset will appear in Datasheet view (see Figure 10.3). From here you can do any of the following:

- **Edit records in the dynaset.** Your changes will update the underlying tables.

- **Customize the dynaset's appearance.** Use the same techniques you use to customize a datasheet (see Chapter 8). You can save your layout changes when you save the query.

- **Sort the dynaset.** Use the same techniques you use to sort a table (see Chapter 9).

- **Filter the dynaset.** Use the same techniques you use to filter a table (see Chapter 9).

- **Preview and print the dynaset as for any other table.** To preview the data, click on the Print Preview toolbar button or choose File ➤ Print Preview. When you're ready to print the data, click on the Print toolbar button or choose File ➤ Print. Chapter 9 offers more details on printing.

- **Return to the query design window.** To do so, click on the Query View toolbar button (shown at left) or choose View ➤ Query Design. Your query will reappear in the query design window exactly as you left it.

Viewing the SQL Statement Behind a Query

If you're familiar with SQL (or you'd like to become better acquainted), you can view or edit your query in SQL view. To switch to SQL view, open the query in design or datasheet view. Then click on the drop-down arrow next to the Query View toolbar button and choose SQL View; or choose View ➤ SQL. View or change the SQL statement as needed, and then click on the Query View toolbar button to see the results in datasheet view.

WARNING   SQL (Structured Query Language) is used behind the scenes in queries and other Access objects. However, it's not for the faint of heart or the inexperienced database user. Be careful when changing SQL statements; if you make mistakes, your queries and other objects may not work properly. For more about SQL, look up *SQL Statements, Using In Queries* in the Access Help Index.

Running an Action Query

If you've designed an action query (Make Table, Update, Append, or Delete query), switching to datasheet view will let you see which records will be affected when you *run* the query. But no changes will be made to any tables, and no new tables will be created. Previewing in datasheet view gives you a chance to look before you leap.

When you're sure the dynaset shows exactly which records the action should act on, you can run the query this way:

1. Return to the query design window and click on the Run toolbar button (shown at left), or choose Query ➤ Run.

2. Respond to any prompts from the action query to confirm your changes. (There's more about action queries later in the chapter.)

TIP If the action query's confirmation messages annoy you, or you're not getting confirmation messages, choose Tools ➤ Options, and then click on the Edit/Find tab. Then, to make sure confirmation messages appear (the *safest* choice), check the Action Queries box under Confirm. To suppress those messages, clear the Action Queries box. Click on OK to close the Options dialog box.

The action query will do its job, and you'll be returned to the query design window.

NOTE Running a Select query or Crosstab query is the same as viewing the query's datasheet.

  ➤ For help with viewing and running action queries, look up subtopics under *Action Queries* in the Access Help Index.

Saving Your Query

To save a new or changed query, use any of these techniques:

- If you're in the query or datasheet window, click on the Save toolbar button (shown at left), or choose File ➤ Save, or press Ctrl+S.

- If you're done with the query for now, close the query design window or datasheet view (for example, choose File ➤ Close or press Ctrl+W). When asked if you want to save your changes, click on Yes.

If this is a new query, you'll be prompted for a query name. Type a standard Access name (up to 64 characters, including blank spaces) and then click on OK. Note that Access won't let you save the query with the same name as an existing table or query.

When you save a query, Access saves *only* the query design, not the resulting recordset. That way, the query will operate on whatever data is in your tables at the time you run the query.

Opening a Saved Query

To reopen a saved query:

1. Start in the database window and click on the Queries tab.

2. Do one of the following:

- **To view the query's dynaset or run an action query**, double-click on the query name, or highlight the query name and then click on Open.

- **To open the query's design window**, highlight the query name and then click on Design.

After opening the query, you can switch between datasheet view and design view by clicking on the Query View toolbar button.

About the Query Design Window's Toolbar

As you saw back in Figure 10.2, the query design window's toolbar holds many buttons. Proceeding from left to right on the toolbar, Table 10.1 briefly describes what each one does. (In Table 10.1, we've omitted the standard Copy, Cut, and Paste buttons, which appear on most Access toolbars, and the Print, Print Preview, Spelling, and Format Painter buttons, which are dimmed and unavailable.)

TABLE 10.1: The Query Window's Most Important Toolbar Buttons

BUTTON	BUTTON NAME	WHAT IT DOES
Design View / SQL SQL View / Datasheet View	Query View (Design View)	Switches to the query window, where you can design or change your query.
	Query View (SQL View)	Switches to SQL view, where you can use SQL statements to design or change your query.
	Query View (Datasheet View)	Switches to datasheet view, where you can view the dynaset. If you're designing an action query, use this button to preview which records the query will affect.
	Save	Saves your latest changes to the query.
	Undo	Undoes your most recent change to a criterion entry (when you are still in that field).
Select / Crosstab / Make Table / Update / Append / Delete	Query Type (Select)	Displays the QBE grid for a Select query.
	Query Type (Crosstab)	Displays the QBE grid for a Crosstab query.
	Query Type (Make Table)	Displays the QBE grid for a Make Table query.
	Query Type (Update)	Displays the QBE grid for an Update query.
	Query Type (Append)	Displays the QBE grid for an Append query.

TABLE 10.1: The Query Window's Most Important Toolbar Buttons (continued)

BUTTON	BUTTON NAME	WHAT IT DOES
	Query Type (Delete)	Displays the QBE grid for a Delete query.
	Run	Runs an action query. For Select and Crosstab queries, this button has the same effect as the Query View (Datasheet View) button.
	Show Table	Lets you add more tables to the tables area of the query window.
	Totals	Displays a Total row in the QBE grid. Use this row to specify how data will be grouped and summarized.
All	Top Values	Lets you choose whether to return a specified number of records, a percentage of records, or all values. Access uses the left-most sorted field to choose which top values to display. You can choose a setting from the Top Values button's drop-down list, or type a number (e.g., **25**) or a percentage (e.g., **47%**) into the Top Values combo box.
	Properties	Opens the property sheet, where you can change field or query properties.
	Build	Opens the Expression Builder, which makes it easier to enter complicated expressions.
	Database Window	Opens the database window.

TABLE 10.1: The Query Window's Most Important Toolbar Buttons (continued)

BUTTON	BUTTON NAME	WHAT IT DOES
AutoForm / AutoReport / New Table / New Query / New Form / New Report / New Macro / New Module	New Object (AutoForm)	Creates a new automatic form that's based on the current query.
	New Object (AutoReport)	Creates a new automatic report that's based on the current query.
	New Object (New Table)	Lets you create a new table. The table is not based on the current query.
	New Object (New Query)	Lets you create a new query that's based on the current query.
	New Object (New Form)	Lets you create a new form that's based on the current query.
	New Object (New Report)	Lets you create a new report that's based on the current query.
	New Object (New Macro)	Lets you create a new macro. The macro is not based on the current query.
	New Object (New Module)	Lets you create a new module. The module is not based on the current query.
(Help button)	Help	Lets you click in any area and open a context-sensitive Help window.

Refining Your Query

In the next few sections, we'll explain how to refine your queries.

Filling in the QBE Grid

Filling in the QBE grid is perhaps the trickiest part of designing a query. Figure 10.2 showed a typical Select query and its QBE grid. The rows that appear in the grid depend on the type of query you're designing. For example, no Sort row will appear in a Delete query.

Here are some techniques you can use to fill the rows in the QBE grid for a Select query. Later sections will provide more examples.

- **In the Field row,** enter the fields you want to work with. Use double-clicking or dragging to add fields from the fields list (see Chapter 9). Or, to tell Access to display all fields even if the table structure changes, use the asterisk (*) field name (see "Using the Asterisk in a QBE Grid" below). Or double-click on the table name to select all fields, and then drag any field to the Field row (all fields will come along for the ride). Or use the drop-down list in the Field row to select the field you want. You also can create new calculated fields in the Field row (see "Totals, Averages, and Other Calculations").

- **In the Sort row,** choose the sort order you want for each field. Your options are Ascending, Descending, or (Not Sorted). Like filters (Chapter 9), query fields are sorted in left-to-right order, so you may need to reposition columns in the grid.

Using the Asterisk in a QBE Grid

You can use the asterisk in a QBE grid to tell Access that you want all fields to appear in the dynaset. The resulting dynaset will *always* contain all the fields in the table, even if you add or delete fields in the table structure later.

To add the asterisk to a Field column in the QBE grid, double-click on the asterisk (*) at the top of the appropriate fields list, or drag the asterisk to the grid. The Field column will show the table name followed by a period and the asterisk, like this:

```
Customers.*
```

If you use the asterisk, you still can sort on, select, group by, calculate with, and do other operations with a specific field. To do so, add the appropriate field to the QBE grid. Then, to prevent that field from appearing twice in the dynaset, deselect the field's Show box. In the example below, we've used the asterisk to display all fields in the Products table, and have cleared the Show check box under the ProductName and UnitPrice fields. The resulting dynaset lists products for which the unit price is greater than $40, in alphabetical order by ProductName and without repeating any fields.

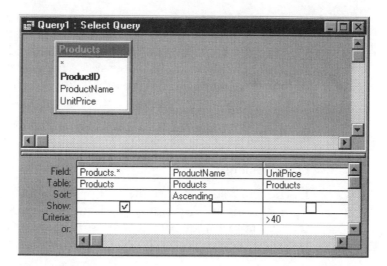

TIP

When you design Make Table, Delete, or Append queries, consider using the asterisk so that the query always operates on the current structure of the underlying table, and the operation includes all the fields.

Changing Field Properties

Field properties govern the appearance of fields in the dynaset. By default, fields added to the QBE grid will inherit properties of the underlying table. However, calculated fields, such as the field *$:[Quantity] * [Order Details]![UnitPrice]* shown in Figure 10.2, do not inherit properties. To assign or change field properties:

1. Click in the field you want to change. (Make sure its Show box is checked, or you won't be able to view or set field properties.)

2. If the Field Properties sheet isn't visible, click on the Properties toolbar button (shown at left). Or, right-click in the field and choose Properties. Or, choose <u>V</u>iew ➤ <u>P</u>roperties from the menus.

3. Click on the tab that contains the properties you want to change, and then change the properties as needed.

To change field properties in another field, simply click in that field and change the properties as needed. When you're done using the Field Properties sheet, click on the Properties button again or click on the Close button at the upper-right corner of the Field Properties sheet.

Shown below is the Field Properties sheet for the field that multiplies the quantity ordered field ([Quantity]) by the unit price field ([Order Details]![UnitPrice]) in Figure 10.2. Here we've changed the format to *Currency* and set the caption to *Total Price*. When Access displays the dynaset, this calculated field's numbers will appear as dollar amounts (for example, $35.00) and the column heading will be *Total Price* (see Figure 10.3).

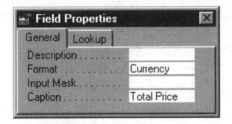

NOTE If you don't specify a field's Caption property, Access will use the field name that's assigned in the QBE grid as the column heading in the dynaset, unless the field has a caption in the underlying table.

 ➤ To find out what a property does, click in a property box on the property sheet and then press F1, or press Shift+F1 (or click on the Help toolbar button) and then click on the property you're interested in.

Changing Query Properties

You also can change properties of the entire query. The steps are the same as for changing field properties, except that in step 1 you click on an empty place in the *tables area* at the top of the query design window. The resulting Query Properties sheet looks like this for a Select query:

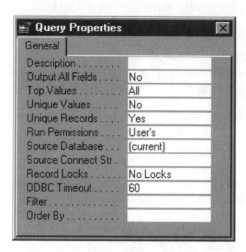

Viewing Unique Values

When you query a single table, Access normally shows all records that match what you're looking for. Sometimes, however, you'll want to eliminate duplicates by changing the Unique Values property in the Query Properties sheet from No to Yes.

Figure 10.4 illustrates this point. Here, in order to see which credit card numbers are represented in the Payments table, we've queried to show non-empty CardHoldersName fields only. Notice that all records, including duplicate values, appear on the left side of the figure. To get rid of those duplicates (see right side of the figure), we changed the query's Unique Values property to Yes.

Here are some tips for working with unique values:

- Make sure the QBE grid includes only the field or combination of fields you want to view unique values in. For instance, to see unique credit card numbers, include only the CreditCardNumber field. To see unique combinations of credit card name and credit card number (for example, to show customers who paid with more than one credit card), include both the CardHoldersName and CreditCardNumber fields.

- All property settings affect the current query design window. To see duplicate records again, change Unique Values back to No.

FIGURE 10.4

The Unique Values
query property
controls whether
duplicate records
appear in a
single-table query.

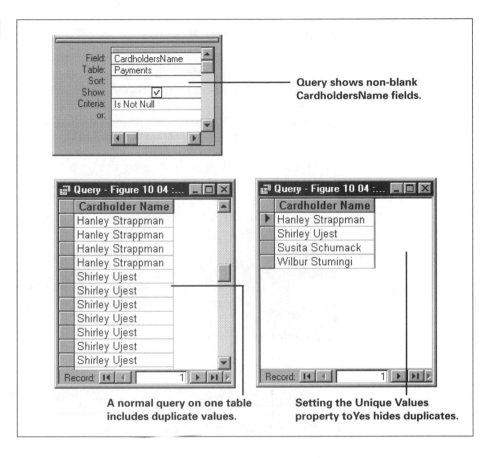

Query shows non-blank
CardholdersName fields.

A normal query on one table
includes duplicate values.

Setting the Unique Values
property to Yes hides duplicates.

- If you want to count duplicate values in your data, use a Totals query. See "Totals, Averages, and Other Calculations" below.

NOTE

When you query multiple related tables, Access normally returns the unique records (that is, the Unique Records property is Yes), but not the unique values. To see the duplicate records in a multi-table query, change the query's Unique Records and Unique Values properties to No. To see only the unique records and values in a multi-table query, change the Unique Values properties to Yes (the Unique Records property changes to No automatically).

Displaying Top Values

If you want Access to return only the top *n* records in the list, or the top *n* percent of the records, you can change the Top Values property in the Query Properties sheet or the Top Values combo box on the toolbar. Suppose you want to display the top 10 payments in the Payments table. The query shown in Figure 10.5 will return the first 10 records, plus any records in which all the fields match the values in the 10th record.

Note that the field used to display the Top *n* values must be the leftmost Sort field in the QBE grid, and that you must sort that field in Descending order if you want to see the topmost values. (To see the bottom *n* values, change the Sort order to Ascending.) Figure 10.6 shows the results of the query in Figure 10.5.

TIP

To return the highest or lowest values without displaying any duplicate records, set the Unique Values property in the Query Properties sheet to Yes.

FIGURE 10.5

A query for displaying the top 10 values

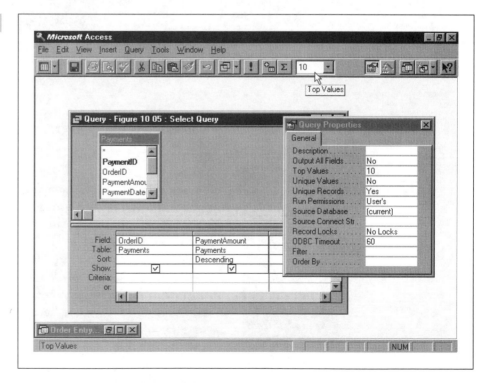

FIGURE 10.6

The results of showing top 10 values

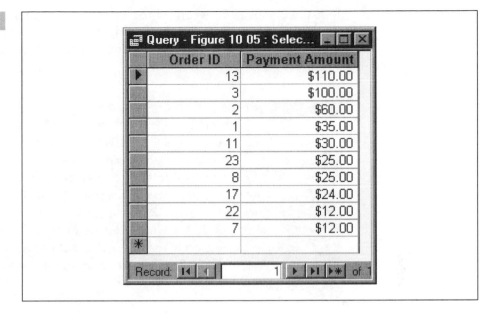

FIGURE 10.6

The results of showing top 10 values

Joining Tables

You can join tables to limit the records in your dynaset or to display data from several related tables at once. For example, if you join the Customers and Orders tables, the dynaset will show only those records that are related to one another (typically, this will be customers who have unfilled orders in the Orders table). Similarly, if you join the Employees and Orders tables, the dynaset will show only the employees associated with orders in the Orders table.

Access will join tables for you automatically when you add them to the query design window, if...

- You've established a relationship between those tables (see Chapter 6).

- Or the tables include fields that have the same name and the same (or compatible) data type. For example, because the Customers and Orders tables both have a numeric field named CustomerID, Access can join them automatically.

Join lines appear between joined tables in the query design window to show you what kind of relationship the tables have, which fields are joined, and whether the relationship enforces referential integrity (see Figure 10.2).

TIP

Sometimes you might not want Access to join tables automatically unless you've purposely set up relationships between those tables via the Relationships window (Tools ➤ Relationships). To prevent automatic joins based on a "best guess" about which tables and fields are related, choose Tools ➤ Options and click on the Tables/Queries tab in the Options dialog box. Then deselect (clear) the Enable AutoJoin check box and click on OK. See Chapter 15 for more about personalizing Access.

You can join tables in three ways—inner join (also called equi-join), outer join, or self join—as described in the following sections.

Inner Joins

In an *inner join*, records in the joined tables must have the same values for fields that are joined. This type of join answers questions such as "Which customers have placed new orders?" You saw an inner join in Figures 10.2 and 10.3. When Access joins tables automatically on the basis of field names and data types, it always creates an inner join.

Outer Joins

In an *outer join*, all records from one table are added to the dynaset even if there are no matching values in the joined field from the other table. Records from the second table are combined with those from the first table *only* if there are matches in the joined field. There are two types of outer joins: left outer joins and right outer joins.

Using the Employees and Orders example, a *left outer join* will show all employees and any orders they've sold (order information for some employees will be blank), as shown in Figure 10.7.

FIGURE 10.7

A left outer join of the Employees and Orders table, along with the resulting dynaset

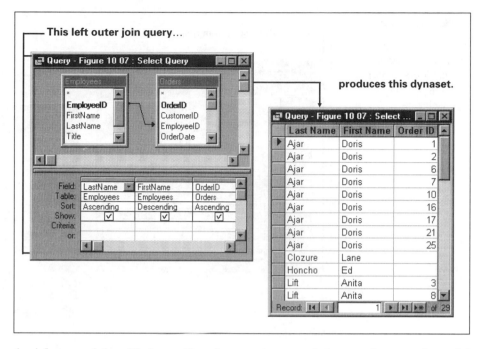

A *right outer join* will show all order numbers and the employees who sold them (employees who didn't sell orders won't appear in the dynaset), as shown in Figure 10.8.

Self Joins

In a *self join*, the table is joined to itself. The self join can be handy when one field within the table refers to another field within the same table. Consider, for example, the revised Employee table (named Employees With Supervisors) shown below.

Employee ID	First Name	Last Name	Title	SupervisorID	Wo
1	Anita	Lift	Sales Representative	4	(206)
2	Andrew	Van Noslo	Vice President, Sales	9	(206)
3	Emily	Niktog	Sales Representative	2	(206)
4	Albert	Niktog	Sales Manager	2	(206)
5	Doris	Ajar	Sales Representative	4	(206)
6	Lane	Clozure	Office Manager	9	(206)
7	Joseph	Swipple	Vice President, Marketing	9	(206)
8	Helen	Wheels	Product Evangelist	9	(206)
9	Ed	Honcho	President	9	(206)
(AutoNumber)				0	

Record: 7 of 9

FIGURE 10.8

A right outer join of the Employees and Orders table, along with the resulting dynaset

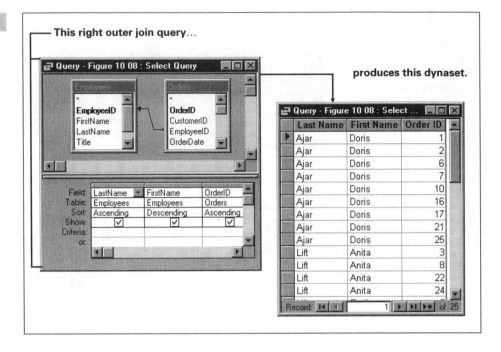

Figure 10.9 shows a query that produces a list of supervisors and the employees they manage. To clarify the meaning of each column in the dynaset, we assigned captions to each field. Looking at the dynaset, it's easy to see this company's pecking order: President Ed Honcho manages Lane Clozure, Joseph Swipple, Andrew Van Noslo, and Helen Wheels; Sales Manager Albert Niktog manages Doris Ajar and Anita Lift; Vice President (Sales) Andrew Van Noslo manages Albert Niktog and Emily Niktog.

To create a self join, add the same table to the query design window twice (Access will add an underscore followed by a number to the second table name, as in Employees With Supervisors_1). Then create an inner join between appropriate fields in the two tables (see the next section). In Figure 10.9, for example, we joined the EmployeeID field from the Employees With Supervisors table on the left to the SupervisorID field from the Employees With Supervisors_1 table on the right.

FIGURE 10.9

This self join on an Employee table shows supervisors and their subordinates. Although it isn't obvious from this example, the table on the left is named Employees With Supervisors; the self join table on the right is named Employees With Supervisors_1.

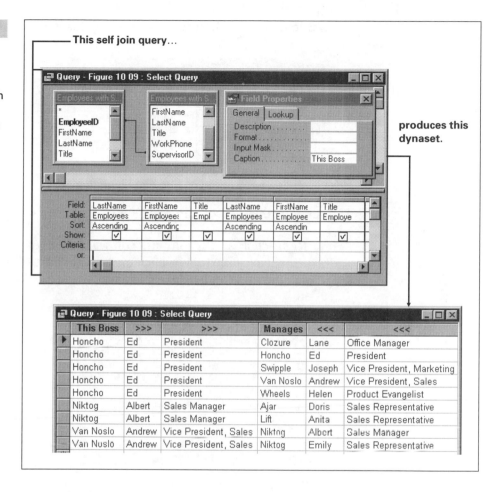

Defining an Inner Join

To define any type of join, you first define an inner join:

1. Start in the query design window and add any tables you want to join. If join lines appear automatically, you're done.

2. To join tables manually, drag the field name from one table onto a field name containing the same kind of data in another table. Usually you'll want to drag a primary key (which appears in bold).

3. Release the mouse button.

Inner join lines will connect the joined fields in each table, as shown here:

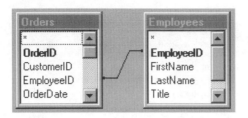

Changing the Join Type

To change the type of join between two tables:

1. Right-click on the join line you want to change and choose Join Properties. Or double-click on the thin part of the join line. You'll see the Join Properties dialog box:

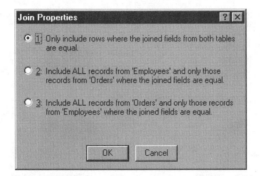

NOTE If your mouse isn't on the thin part of the join line, or the join line isn't bold when you double-click on it, the Query Properties sheet may appear instead of the Join Properties dialog box. If this happens, close the Query Properties sheet and try again.

2. In the Join Properties dialog box, choose the option you want. Option 1 produces an inner join. Option 2 creates a left outer join. Option 3 makes a right outer join.

3. Click on OK. Access will update the appearance of the join line to reflect your choice in step 2.

Figures 10.7 and 10.8 show left and right outer join lines, respectively.

TIP　　If you find yourself creating manual joins often, you can establish a permanent relationship between the tables. To do so, return to the database window, choose Tools ➤ Relationships, or click on the Relationships toolbar button; then define the type of join you want (see Chapter 6).

Deleting a Join

Deleting a join is easy:

1. Click on the thin part of the join line you want to delete, so that it appears bold.

2. Press the Delete key.

WARNING　　If the join line isn't bold when you press Delete, you may delete a table from the query design window. If that happens, you'll need to add the table (Query ➤ Show Table) and its fields again.

 ➤ For help with joining tables, look up *Joins* and its subtopics in the Access Help Index.

Showing an Entire Database Structure

As explained in Chapter 6, you can use the Relationships window to get "the big picture" of all the tables in your database and how they're related to one another. Here's a quick review of how to do this:

1. Return to the database window and choose Tools ➤ Relationships, or click on the Relationships toolbar button.

2. To show all the relationships, choose <u>R</u>elationships ➤ Show All or click on the Show All Relationships toolbar button.

3. If necessary, rearrange the tables on the screen so the join lines don't look like a pile of spaghetti (see Figure 10.10).

FIGURE 10.10

The Relationships window for the Order Entry database

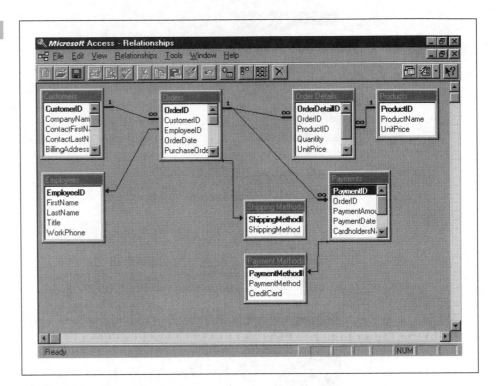

Creating AutoLookup Queries

Suppose a customer calls to place an order. Being a lazy typist, you don't want to re-enter customer information that's already in the Customers table. To save your typing fingers, you can create a special Select query called an *AutoLookup query*. Then, simply enter a valid CustomerID and Access will fill in the customer information automatically.

AutoLookup works in queries in which two tables have a one-to-many relationship and the join field on the "one" side of the relationship has a unique index. That is, the join field on the "one" side must either be a primary key or have its Indexed property set to Yes (No Duplicates).

N O T E

Do not confuse a lookup field (Chapter 6) with an autolookup query. A lookup field displays a list of values that makes it easier to enter data into one specific field. An autolookup query automatically fills in corresponding data on the "one" side of a one-to-many query when you enter new data in the join field on the "many" side. As Figure 10.11 shows, you can use a lookup field (for example, CustomerID) in an autolookup query.

In the classic example of Customers and Orders, the CustomerID field in the Customers table is a primary key on the "one" side of the relationship. The CustomerID field in the Orders table is on the "many" side of the relationship.

Here's the secret to designing an AutoLookup query:

- Put the join field from the "many" side of the query into the QBE grid. This field is the *autolookup* field. For example, add the CustomerID field from the Orders table (not the Customers table) to the grid.

N O T E

For AutoLookup to work, you must be able to update the autolookup field from the "many" side of the query. If you try to change a field that can't be updated, Access will display an explanatory message in the status bar.

Figure 10.11 shows an AutoLookup query in which CustomerID (from the Orders table) is the autolookup field for customer information. Figure 10.12 shows the dynaset after we chose RNAA Associates from the drop-down list for the CustomerID field in the empty row at the bottom of the datasheet. As soon as we selected a company name from the autolookup field, Access filled in the corresponding customer information automatically.

FIGURE 10.11

An AutoLookup query uses the join field from the "many" side of the relationship to look up and fill in information from the "one" side automatically.

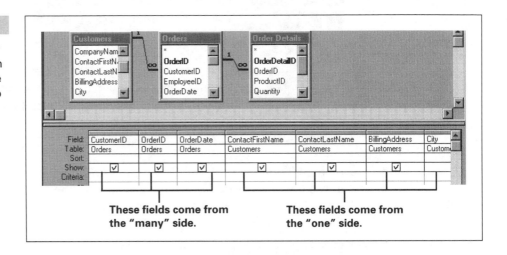

FIGURE 10.12

The dynaset created by the AutoLookup query in Figure 10.11. After we chose RNAA Associates from the CustomerID drop-down list, Access filled in the customer information automatically.

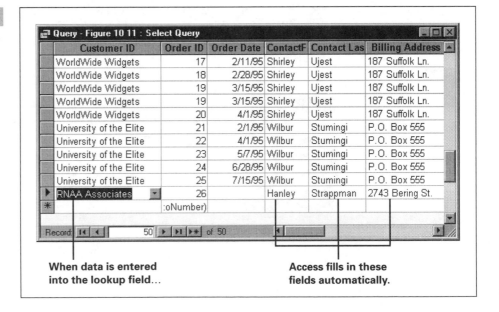

WARNING

When designing queries for data entry purposes, be sure to include required fields and validated fields, and be sure to check their Show boxes on the QBE grid. If the query doesn't include such fields, Access may display error messages about bad or missing data in those fields; unfortunately, the person entering the data won't be able to fix the problem because the fields aren't there. A Catch-22 situation if there ever was one!

Prompting for Selection Criteria

If you find yourself changing the criteria each time you run a Select query, consider using *parameters* instead of specific values in the criteria. A parameter acts as a sort of place holder that you can fill in when you run the query.

To define a parameter:

1. Create your query normally, but omit the criteria for now.

2. Click on the Criteria cell of the field you want to search. In place of the data you're searching for, type a parameter in square brackets. The parameter can't be the same as an existing field name (though it can include the field name), and is best worded as a question or a prompt that tells the user what to do. Repeat this step for each field that you want to define as a parameter.

3. Choose Query ➤ Parameters, or right-click on an empty place in the tables area of the query design window and choose Parameters. You'll see the Query Parameters dialog box (Figure 10.13 shows a completed example).

FIGURE 10.13

This query uses two parameters to prompt for criteria when you run the query.

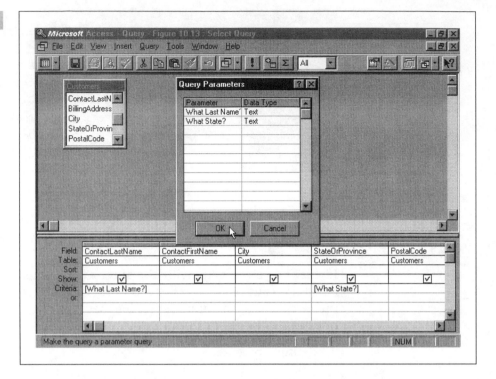

FIGURE 10.13

This query uses two parameters to prompt for criteria when you run the query.

4. In the Parameter column, type the first parameter you want Access to prompt for *exactly* as you typed it into the Criteria cell, but without the square brackets. (If the spellings don't match exactly, Access will prompt for both spellings when you run the query and you won't get the results you want.)

5. In the Data Type column, choose a data type for the parameter. This should match (or be compatible with) the data type of the field the parameter is in. (Access usually fills this in automatically when you tab to or click in the Data Type cell.)

6. Repeat steps 4 and 5 for each parameter. When you're done, click on OK.

T I P

As a shortcut, you often can skip steps 3–6 in the procedure above and not bother to define any parameters in the Query Parameters dialog box. When you run the query, it will display the prompts you entered in step 2, in order from the leftmost prompt to the rightmost prompt. However, you *should not* skip these steps if 1) You're using parameters in a Crosstab query or in a parameter query that a Crosstab query or chart is based on, or 2) You're creating a parameter for a field with the Yes/No data type or for fields that come from a table in an external database. For Crosstab queries, you also must set the ColumnHeadings property in the Query Properties sheet.

Figure 10.13 shows a query that uses parameters. Whenever you run this query, Access first displays this message:

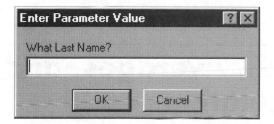

You can type any name you want, such as **Adams,** and click on OK. Next you'll see the message "What State?" This time, type a state name, such as **CA**, and click on OK. (Access always prompts for parameters in the order in which you list them in the Query Parameters dialog box. If you've left that dialog box blank, it prompts in order from leftmost parameter to rightmost parameter.) The resulting dynaset will show only California customers whose last name is Adams.

You also can use the parameter as part of a search criterion. For instance, you can replace the *[What Last Name?]* criterion in Figure 10.13 with:

```
Like [What Last Name?]&"*"
```

When you run the query, Access will show the same message. But your entry will be substituted with the more general "Like" expression. So if you enter **Adams**, Access will convert that to **Like Adams★** and display records that begin with the letters *adams* (Adams, Adamson, Adams and Lee, and so on).

N O T E

The & operator concatenates strings on either side of it. Thus, *Like "★"&[What Name?]&"★"* translates into *Like ★Adams★* if you enter *Adams* in the Enter Parameter Value dialog box. This example matches records such as McAdams, Adams, Adamson, and so on.

The bottom line is that you can use parameters anywhere you'd type normal text or a field name in a Criteria cell.

 ➤ As usual, help is available for setting up parameter queries. In the Access Help Index, a good place to start is the *Queries, Parameter* topic.

Using Totals, Averages, and Other Calculations

Access provides several ways to perform calculations on your data:

- You can perform calculations in Criteria cells, as discussed in Chapter 9.

- You can perform a calculation and display the results in a calculated field that isn't stored in the underlying tables. Back in Figure 10.2, for example, a calculated field named **$** multiplied the [Quantity] field times the [Order Details]![Unit Price] field. The results appear in the Total Price column of Figure 10.3.

- You can group records according to certain fields and display summary calculations for the grouped data. This lets you determine how many items were ordered on various dates, how many orders were placed by each customer, the dollar value of orders for each product, and so on.

You'll learn how to use calculated fields and data summaries in the following sections.

Using Calculated Fields

To create a calculated field, click in an empty Field cell in the QBE grid and type an expression that will do the calculation. When referring to other fields in the QBE grid, be sure to enclose their names in square brackets. If more than one table in your query has the same field name, you must specify both the table name and the field name, using the format *[TableName]![FieldName]*. For instance, to multiply the quantity field by the unit price field of the Order Details table, type **[Quantity]*[Order Details]![UnitPrice]** in an empty Field cell.

You can give the calculated field its own heading in the dynaset and use that heading as a field name in still other calculations. Just precede the calculation with the heading you want to use, followed by a colon, like this:

```
ExtPrice:[Quantity]*[Order Details]![UnitPrice]
```

Now you can use the *ExtPrice* calculated field in another calculated field. This example calculates the price with sales tax:

```
WithTax:[ExtPrice]*(1+[SalesTaxRate])
```

Here's the QBE grid for these calculations:

Field:	ProductName	SalesTaxRate	ExtPrice: [Quantity]*[Order Details]![UnitPrice]	WithTax: [ExtPrice]*(1+[SalesTaxRate])
Table:	Products	Orders		
Sort:	Ascending	Ascending		
Show:	☑	☑	☑	☑
Criteria:				

And here are the results:

Product Name	Sales Tax Rate	ExtPrice	WithTax
Baseball	6.00%	$8.75	$9.27
Baseball	7.25%	$17.50	$18.77
Basketball	0.00%	$4.95	$4.95
Basketball	5.00%	$9.90	$10.40
Basketball	6.00%	$9.90	$10.49
Basketball	7.25%	$9.90	$10.62
Basketball	7.25%	$4.95	$5.31
Billiard balls	0.00%	$127.45	$127.45
Billiard balls	0.00%	$254.90	$254.90
Billiard balls	5.25%	$127.45	$134.14
Crystal ball	0.00%	$45.55	$45.55
Crystal ball	0.00%	$45.55	$45.55
Crystal ball	0.00%	$45.55	$45.55
Crystal ball	0.00%	$45.55	$45.55
Crystal ball	0.00%	$136.65	$136.65

Record: 9 of 49

You can use the **&** operator to join text and fields into a single calculated field. When using this operator, be sure to enclose any text, including blank spaces, in quotation marks.

Let's look at some examples of calculated fields that use the **&** operator to display values from the Employee table's FirstName and LastName fields in a single column in the query result.

Assuming the FirstName is *Helen* and the LastName is *Wheels*, the calculated field shown below will display the result *Helen Wheels*:

```
[FirstName]&" "&[LastName]
```

To display the result as *Wheels, Helen* use this calculated field:

```
[LastName]&", "&[FirstName]
```

And if you're feeling in an expansive mood, you can use this calculated field:

```
"Hey "&[FirstName]&" "&[LastName]&"! How are ya?"
```

to display:

```
Hey Helen Wheels! How are ya?
```

The tips below will help you make the most of calculated fields:

- If you don't provide a name for a calculated field, Access will assign a meaningless name, such as *Expr1*, *Expr2*, *Expr3*, and so on. You can change these to more useful names as needed.

- If you misspell a field name within square brackets, Access will treat the field as a parameter when you run the query. You'll need to click on Cancel in the Enter Parameter Value dialog box and return to query design view to correct the faulty field name.

- You can change the properties of the calculated field to control the caption and format displayed in the dynaset. (Right-click on the field, choose Properties, and define the properties you want to use.)

- When typing lengthy calculations, use Zoom (press Shift+F2) to expand the input area as described earlier in the chapter.

- You can use Expression Builder (see Figure 10.14) to help you enter complicated calculations or criteria into a cell. To open Expression Builder, click in the cell you want to edit, and then click on the Build toolbar button (shown at left); or, right-click on the cell and choose Build. You can then type in and change the expression directly in the editing panel at the top of the dialog box. Or, to have Expression Builder enter field names, operators, and expressions for you, position the cursor in the editing panel, then click and double-click on items in the three lower panels of the dialog box or click on the operator buttons above the panels. (For more help with Expression Builder, click on the <u>H</u>elp button in the dialog box.) When you're ready to leave Expression Builder and save your expression, click on OK.

- You can't change the contents of a calculated field in a dynaset. But you *can* change other fields. The calculated field will be recalculated automatically.

 ➤ Access provides literally dozens of functions that are useful in calculated fields. Some of the most useful are discussed under "Creating Your Own Calculation Expressions" later in this chapter. To find out about any Access function, search for *Functions, Reference Topics* in the Access Help Index or look up a specific function name, such as *Avg Function*.

FIGURE 10.14

The Expression Builder

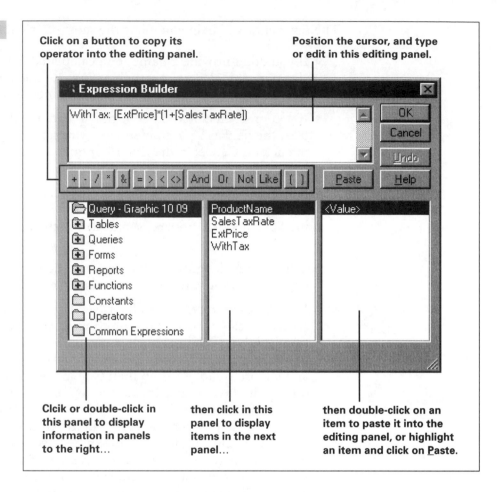

Click on a button to copy its operator into the editing panel.

Position the cursor, and type or edit in this editing panel.

Clcik or double-click in this panel to display information in panels to the right...

then click in this panel to display items in the next panel...

then double-click on an item to paste it into the editing panel, or highlight an item and click on Paste.

Summarizing Your Data

Suppose you want to know the number of customers in Los Angeles, or the average price of products purchased in February. For jobs like these, you need *summary calculations*. Summary calculations differ from calculated fields in that they compute some value, such as a sum or average, on *multiple records* within a table.

TIP

For a truly easy way to summarize your data, use the Simple Query Wizard, described earlier in this chapter.

To perform a summary calculation:

1. Create a simple Select query as usual. Drag any fields you want to group by, or perform calculations on, to the QBE grid. Do not include the asterisk (*) field name in QBE grid.

Σ

2. Click on the Totals toolbar button (shown at left). Or, choose View ➤ Totals. A new Total row will appear in the QBE grid, with *Group By* in each column.

3. Leave the Total row set to *Group By* for fields that you want to use for grouping (or categorizing, or subtotaling).

4. In the Total cell for the field you want to summarize, choose one of the summary options listed in Table 10.2.

TABLE 10.2: Summary Operators Used in Queries

SUMMARY OPERATOR	COMPUTES	WORKS WITH DATA TYPES
Avg	Average	AutoNumber, Currency, Date/Time, Number, Yes/No
Count	Number of non-blank values	All
First	Value in first record	All
Last	Value in last record	All
Max	Highest (largest) value	AutoNumber, Currency, Date/Time, Number, Text, Yes/No
Min	Lowest (smallest) value	AutoNumber, Currency, Date/Time, Number, Text, Yes/No
StdDev	Standard deviation	AutoNumber, Currency, Date/Time, Number, Yes/No
Sum	Total	AutoNumber, Currency, Date/Time, Number, Yes/No
Var	Variance	AutoNumber, Currency, Date/Time, Number, Yes/No

5. Add calculated fields, sorting specifications, and selection criteria as needed. Then...

- If you added selection criteria to columns that you don't want to group by, change the Total cell for those columns to *Where*.

- If you created calculated fields in columns that you don't want to group by, change the Total cell for those columns to *Expression*.

6. Click on the Query View toolbar button to see the results.

Remember these points as you design summary queries:

- Don't be concerned if Access changes your Totals queries slightly after you save, close, and reopen them. The queries will still work fine! For example, Access might change the summary operator in the Totals cell from *Avg* to *Expression*, and transform the Field cell from an entry such as this:

```
Avg: [Order Details]![UnitPrice]
```

to an aggregate function, such as this:

```
Avg: Avg([Order Details]![UnitPrice])
```

- You can't update the fields in the snapshot created by a Totals query.

N O T E

Unlike a Select query (which creates a *dynaset* that's usually updatable), a Totals query creates a *snapshot*. Although a snapshot looks the same as a dynaset on the screen, you cannot update any of the data in a snapshot.

- You can summarize as many fields as you wish, and you can include multiple copies of the same field in the QBE grid. Here's an example that displays the number of products and the average, minimum, and maximum price of products ordered in February:

Field:	OrderDate	Count: ProductName	Avg: [Order Details]![UnitPrice]	Min: [Order Details]![UnitPrice]	Max: [Order Details]![UnitPrice]
Table:	Orders	Products			
Total:	Group By	Count	Avg	Min	Max
Sort:					
Show:	✓	✓	✓	✓	✓
Criteria:	Like "2/*/95"				
or:					

	Order Date	Count	Avg	Min	Max
▶	2/1/95	9	$25.26	$4.95	$127.45
	2/11/95	4	$6.08	$4.95	$8.75
	2/18/95	2	$26.15	$6.75	$45.55
	2/25/95	1	$5.65	$5.65	$5.65
	2/28/95	1	$17.85	$17.85	$17.85

- To base calculations on all records in the table, do not use *Group By* in any column. For instance, to count the customers in the Customers table, put just the CustomerID field in the QBE grid and use the Count operator.

- To base calculations on groups of records (that is, to *subtotal* a group of records), use *Group By* in the Total cell for all fields that make up the group. This example counts the number of customers in each city and state/province:

Field:	City	StateOrProvince	CustomerID
Table:	Customers	Customers	Customers
Total:	Group By	Group By	Count
Sort:			
Show:	✓	✓	✓
Criteria:			

- You can sort on summarized fields to "rank" them. For instance, if you're calculating the average unit price for products sold each month, sort the UnitPrice field in descending order to rank products from highest average price to lowest, as shown in Figure 10.15. In Figure 10.15, we used the Format([OrderDate],"mmmm") function to extract the month name from the order date.

- You can specify search criteria for fields that you're grouping by, as you would in any query. This limits the display to the groups you chose in the Criteria cells of the Group By field or fields.

FIGURE 10.15

Average Price (descending) by month ordered. The function Format([OrderDate], "mmmm") extracts the month name from the order date.

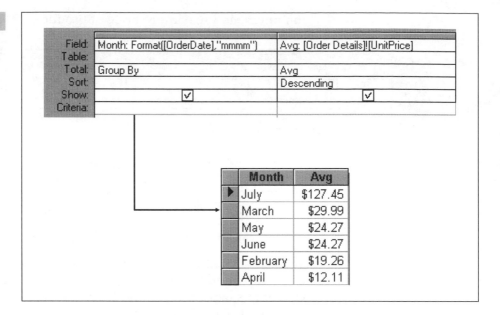

• To apply a search criterion *after* calculating the summary, enter that criterion in the field where you're doing the calculation. The example below calculates the average price of products sold in each month, and displays only those with an average price greater than $15, in descending order.

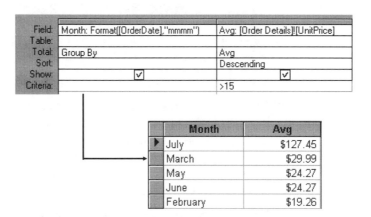

• To apply a search criterion *before* the calculation takes place, use the *Where* operator in the Total cell for the field you want to select first. You also must deselect the Show box for that field. The example below limits the average price calculations to products sold to customers outside the state of California. Compare the numbers shown below (which exclude the purchases by California customers) with the averages shown in Figure 10.15 (which include those purchases):

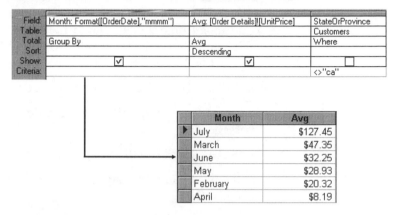

Field:	Month: Format([OrderDate],"mmmm")	Avg: [Order Details]![UnitPrice]	StateOrProvince
Table:			Customers
Total:	Group By	Avg	Where
Sort:		Descending	
Show:	☑	☑	☐
Criteria:			<>"ca"

Month	Avg
July	$127.45
March	$47.35
June	$32.25
May	$28.93
February	$20.32
April	$8.19

- Summary calculations normally exclude blank records, but they will include zero values in a numeric field. If you need to count all records, including blanks, use **Count(*)** in the column's field cell, as shown below:

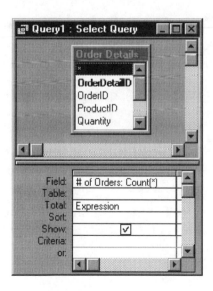

TIP

Assuming you don't mind including records that contain null values, the calculation Count(*) runs much faster than Count([*fieldname*]).

- You can summarize calculated fields. However, the expression in each calculated field must refer to "real" fields, not to other calculated fields. For example, if you've defined the calculated field

ExtPrice:[Quantity]*[UnitPrice]

and want to calculate the average sales tax, you can't use the expression

AvgSalesTax:[ExtPrice]*1.05

for the field you're averaging. Instead you must repeat the calculation, like this:

AvgSalesTax:[Quantity]*[UnitPrice]*1.05.

 ➤ For more help with calculating totals, look up *Totals In Queries* in the Access Help Index.

Creating Your Own Calculation Expressions

You can use Access functions to design your own summary expressions for analyzing data. To do this:

1. Activate totaling in the query design window by clicking on the Totals toolbar button.

2. Start in a blank column of the QBE grid. If you're using an *aggregate function* or *domain aggregate function* (described just below), choose *Expression* in the column's Total cell. For *formatting functions*, set the Total cell to *Group By*.

3. In the Field cell of the column, enter an expression that uses the function you want. Some of the most useful functions are listed in Table 10.3.

TABLE 10.3: Useful Access Functions

FUNCTIONS	WHAT THEY DO	EXAMPLE
Aggregate Functions		
Avg, Count, Max, Min, StDev, Sum, and Var	Perform statistical calculations on a group of records in the current table.	*Avg([Quantity]*[UnitPrice])* averages the quantity times the unit price for a group of records.
Domain Aggregate Functions		
DAvg, DCount, DMax, DMin, DStDev, DStDevP, DSum, DVar, and DVarP	Perform statistical calculations on all records in any table or query, overriding *Group By* expressions.	*DSum("[Quantity]*[UnitPrice]", "Order Details")* shows the total quantity times the unit price for all records in the Order Details table.
Formatting Functions		
CCur, CDbl, CInt, CLng, CSng, CStr, and CVar	Convert expressions from one format to another. You can use these functions instead of changing a field's properties.	*CCur(Avg([Quantity]*[UnitPrice]))* converts to currency format the average quantity times the unit price for a group of records.
Format	Formats a number, date, time, or string.	*Format([OrderDate], "mmmm")* displays the month portion of the OrderDate field.
Left	Returns the leftmost *n* characters in a string.	*Left([LastName],1)* displays the first letter of the LastName field.
Mid	Returns a string that's part of another string.	*Mid([PhoneNumber],1,3)* displays the area code portion of a phone number field. This example assumes three-character United States area codes in which the parentheses aren't stored in the table.
Right	Returns the rightmost *n* characters in a string.	*Right([Ship CSZ],5) displays the last five characters of a hypothetical Ship CSZ field (a combined City, State, and Zip Code field). This example assumes five-character United States zip codes.*

N O T E   You can use Zoom (Shift+F2) when entering lengthy functions into the Field cell. Always type expressions on a single line (even if they don't appear on one line in this book).

4. Fill in other rows and columns in the QBE grid as needed.

5. Run the query as usual.

You'll find that the following types of functions are especially useful for summarizing data:

Aggregate Functions   Calculate statistics on a group of records in the current table. *Examples:* Count, Avg, Sum, Min, Max, and Var.

Domain Aggregate Functions   Calculate statistics on an entire table or query, overriding any Group By expressions. *Examples:* DCount, DAvg, DSum, DMin, DMax, and DVar.

Formatting Functions   Return specified parts of the data, or format data in specific ways. *Examples:* Left, Right, Mid, and Format. These functions are useful with many types of calculated fields, not just summary calculations.

 For a complete list of Access functions, search for *Functions, Reference Topics* in the Access Help Index. You also can use the Access Help Index to look up individual functions by name.

Sample Summary Calculation Expressions

For practice, let's look at some sample summary calculations. The example in Figure 10.16 groups and sorts records by Month, and it calculates both the value of orders in each month and each month's contribution to the whole, expressed as a percentage.

In Figure 10.16, we used the calculation shown below to isolate the month number portion of the order date; then we sorted this column in ascending order and hid it from view (you can't see this calculation in Figure 10.16, because it has scrolled off the right edge of the screen). This trick puts the months in January, February, March, April, etc. order,

FIGURE 10.16

This example uses the Sum and DSum functions to calculate each month's contribution to total sales. It also uses the DatePart function to extract the month number from the OrderDate, so that we can present the results sorted chronologically by month rather than alphabetically by month name. See the text for details of each calculation in this QBE grid.

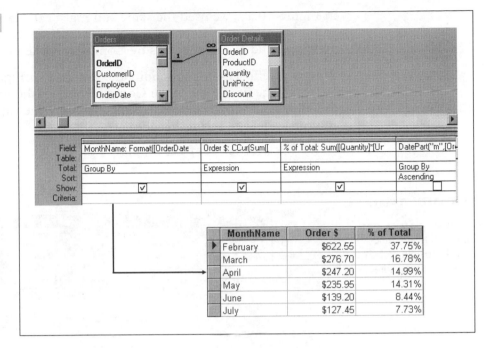

rather than displaying them in alphabetical order by month name (April, February, July, June, etc.).

```
DatePart("m",OrderDate)
```

The calculation in the first column shows the month name portion of the order date:

```
MonthName: Format([OrderDate],"mmmm")
```

We used this calculation in the second column of the QBE grid:

```
Order $:CCur(Sum([Quantity]*[UnitPrice]))
```

The calculation in the QBE grid's third column is:

```
% of Total:Sum([Quantity]*[UnitPrice])/
    DSum("[Quantity]*[UnitPrice]","Order Details")
```

We used the Field Properties sheet to format the *% Of Total* column as a percentage.

You can replace "mmmm" in the Format function to group by other time intervals. For example, "ww" groups by week of the year (1–54); "q" groups by quarter; "yyyy" groups by year; and "hh" groups by hour.

In Figure 10.17, we used the same summary calculations for the second and third columns. However, this time we added the Customers table to the query and grouped orders by CompanyName instead of month.

With little effort, you can modify the example in Figure 10.17 to group orders by the first letter of the CompanyName (though there isn't an especially good reason to do so). Simply replace the expression in the first column's Field cell with this one:

```
FirstLetter:Left([CompanyName],1)
```

FIGURE 10.17

This example uses the Sum and DSum functions to calculate each company's total sales.

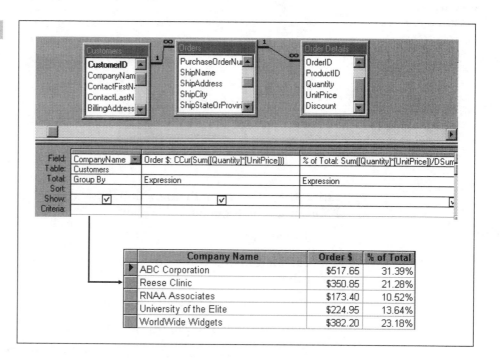

Creating Crosstab Queries

Crosstab queries let you cross-tabulate data in a row-by-column fashion. The example in Figure 10.18 answers the question "Who ordered how many of what?"

FIGURE 10.18

A Crosstab query
makes it easy to see
who ordered how
many of what.

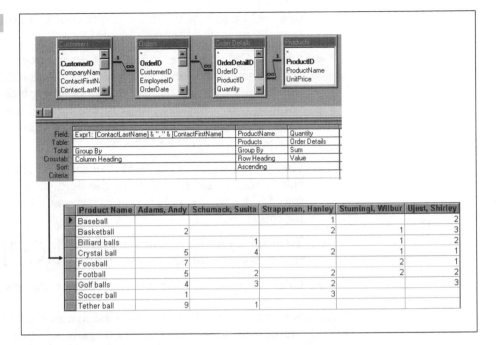

Product Name	Adams, Andy	Schumack, Susita	Strappman, Hanley	Stumingi, Wilbur	Ujest, Shirley
Baseball			1		2
Basketball	2		2	1	3
Billiard balls		1		1	2
Crystal ball	5	4	2	1	1
Foosball	7			2	1
Football	5	2	2	2	2
Golf balls	4	3	2		3
Soccer ball	1		3		
Tether ball	9	1			

TIP

To quickly create crosstabs of data in a single table, use the Crosstabs Query Wizard, described earlier in this chapter.

When designing a Crosstab query, you must decide which fields to use for row headings, column headings, and summary values, and how you want to summarize the values (for example, as sums or averages). Here are the steps to follow:

1. Starting in the query design window, choose the tables you want to use and put fields (including calculated fields) into the QBE grid. You can specify any search criteria and sorting you need.

2. Click on the drop-down arrow next to the Query Type toolbar button, and then choose Crosstab. Or, choose Query ➤ Crosstab.

3. Choose Row Heading in the Crosstab cell for the field you want to use for row headings. You can designate more than one field, but at least one field must have *Group By* in its Total cell. In place

of a Field name, you can use expressions to group values together (see the next step for an example).

4. Choose Column Heading in the Crosstab cell for the field you want to use for column headings. Only one field is allowed, and it must contain *Group By* in its Total cell. In place of a Field name, you can use expressions to group values together. Figure 10.18 shows the expression *Expr1: [ContactLastName]&", "& [ContactFirstName]* used this way.

5. Choose Value in the Crosstab cell for the field you want to summarize. Then, in the Total cell for the field, choose the type of summary you want (usually *Sum* or *Average*). Don't choose Group By for this field.

6. To group by additional fields without displaying them in the results, choose (Not Shown) in the Crosstab cell for those fields.

7. Click on the Query View toolbar button to view the results.

Access automatically determines crosstab column headings from the data in the table, and then sorts the headings in left-to-right order across the columns. You can change this behavior with these steps:

1. Create and run the query as described above. Print the results or jot down the column headings, and then return to the query design window.

2. Open the Query Properties sheet (right-click on an empty spot in the tables area and choose Properties or click on the Properties toolbar button).

3. In the Column Headings box, type the headings you want to use (spelled exactly as they appear in the output) in the order you want them. Separate each heading with a semicolon (;) or new line (Ctrl+↵). Or, enclose the headings in double-quotes and separate them with commas (see Figure 10.19). For example, type **January;February;March;**... or **"January","February","March"**,....

4. Run the query again to see the revised column headings.

The crosstab shown in Figure 10.19 has two row heading fields (Product-Name and StateOrProvince). The column headings are taken from the month portion of the order date. We changed the Query Properties to list only the months February, March, April, May, June, and July (there were no orders in the other months, so we omitted them).

The online Help can guide you through crosstab setup. Just look up any of the topics under *Crosstab Queries* in the Help Index for details. Or, for fast setup, use the Crosstab Wizard to create a Crosstab query, and then switch to the query design window and tweak the design as needed.

FIGURE 10.19

Crosstab queries to calculate number of orders by month for each product and state group. We used Query Properties to choose which months appeared and in which order.

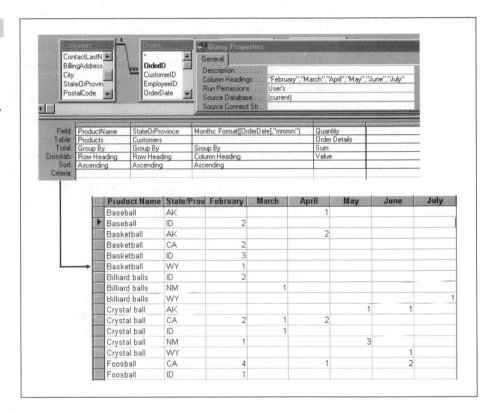

Creating Action Queries

Action queries differ from the queries discussed so far because they change or delete data in a table. The four types of action queries are:

Update Queries   Change data in a group of records.

Append Queries   Copy a group of records from one table to another.

Delete Queries   Delete records from a table.

Make Table Queries   Create a new table from a group of records in another table.

Action queries are very fast and can do a lot of damage if they aren't exactly right. So keep these datasaving tips in mind:

- **Always back up your database, or (at least) the tables you're going to change.** To copy a table, go to the database window, click on the Tables tab, and then click on the table you want to copy. Choose Edit ➤ Copy (Ctrl+C), choose Edit ➤ Paste (Ctrl+V), type a new name for the table, and then click on OK.

- **For extra safety,** you can design and test a Select query. Then, when you're sure it will act on the proper records, convert it to an action query. To convert from one type of query to another, click on the drop-down arrow next to the Query Type toolbar button, and then choose the appropriate option from the list, or choose equivalent options from the Query menu. (The steps in the sections below take a slightly more streamlined, yet still safe, approach to designing and running action queries.)

- **In the database window,** double-clicking on an action query (or highlighting the query and clicking on Open) *runs* the query. To warn you that this will happen, an exclamation point and descriptive icon appear beside the query name in the database window (see example below).

⠿ ! Query - Increase Price By 15%

 ➤ To get help with action queries, go to the Access Help Index and double-click on the topic *Action Queries, Creating*; then click on the button next to the appropriate "What do you want to do?" topic. Or, go to the Help Contents, open the *Working With Queries* book, open the *Creating Action Queries, Crosstab Queries, And Parameter Queries* book, open the *Action Query* book, and then choose a subtopic from the list.

Update Queries

Update queries let you change all records or groups of records very quickly. To create an Update query:

1. In the query design window, click on the drop-down arrow next to the Query Type toolbar button, and then choose Update. Or, choose Query ➤ Update from the menus. The Query Type button changes, as shown at left.

2. Add the tables, include fields you want to update and fields you want to use for selection criteria, and set criteria to select the records you want to update, just as for a Select query.

3. In the Update To cell for each field you want to change, type a new value for the field, or type an expression that will calculate a new value. If you want to empty out a field, type **Null** in the Update To cell for that field.

4. To see which records will be updated before you update them, click on the Query View toolbar button (shown at left), or choose View ➤ Datasheet. Adjust the query criteria and preview the results until you select the records you want to update.

5. To run the Update query, return to the query design window and click on the Run toolbar button (shown at left), or choose Query ➤ Run.

6. When prompted with the number of rows that will be updated, click on Yes if you want to proceed, or click on No to cancel the operation.

N O T E You can't use an Update query to update totals queries, calculated fields, or locked tables.

The left side of Figure 10.20 shows a Select query and the products it will find. The right side shows the Select query after we converted it to an Update query that raises prices for those items by 15 percent. After running the Update query, we converted it back to a Select query (by clicking on the drop-down arrow next to the Query Type button and choosing Select)

FIGURE 10.20

A Select query to search for records with a current price less than $20, along with the Update query that raises prices of those products by 15 percent

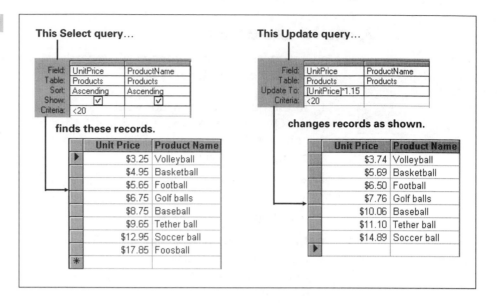

and displayed the revised records shown at the bottom right. Some items no longer appear because their prices are now $20 or more.

Understanding Cascaded Updates

Recall from Chapter 6 that you can use the Relationships window to define one-to-many relationships between tables, to enforce referential integrity between such tables, and to cascade updates to related fields automatically. If you do this, Access will carry over updates to the related field from the "one" side of the relationship to the related field on the "many" side, even if your Update query doesn't include tables on the "many" side.

Suppose we set up a one-to-many relationship and enforced referential integrity between Suppliers (a table that's not in our sample Order Entry database) and Products. Further suppose we selected Cascade Update Related Records on the "one" side of each relationship. Therefore, if we use an Update query to change the SupplierID for a record in Suppliers, Access automatically updates the corresponding SupplierID in the Products table.

If you've defined Cascade Update Records for related tables, you don't need to create an Update query when you simply want a change to the primary key on the "one" side to carry over to related records on the "many" side. Instead, go to form view or datasheet view for the table on the "one" side and change the data in the appropriate primary key field. Access will update the related field in the "many" side table automatically.

NOTE   Values in AutoNumber fields can't be changed by editing in a table or form, or by running an update query. In the sample Order Entry database, all the IDs—including CustomerID, EmployeeID, OrderID, and ProductID—on the "one" side are defined as primary keys with the AutoNumber data type.

Append Queries

An *Append query* copies some or all records from one table (the *source table*) to the bottom of another table (the *target table*). This is handy when you use separate tables with similar structures to manage data.

For example, you might use a Products table to store current products and an OldProducts table to store discontinued products. Or you might store current, unfilled orders in an Orders table and filled orders in a *history table* named OrdHist.

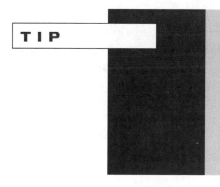

TIP   To quickly create a new table that has the same structure as an existing table, click on the Tables tab on the database window, click on the table that has the structure you want to copy, choose Edit ➤ Copy (Ctrl+C), and then choose Edit ➤ Paste (Ctrl+V). When the Paste Table As dialog box appears, type a new table name (for example, OldProducts), choose Structure Only, and click on OK.

The example below will append records for shipped orders to the bottom of another table that has the same structure.

Field:	ShipDate	Orders.*
Table:	Orders	Orders
Sort:	Ascending	
Append To:		OrdHist.*
Criteria:	Is Not Null	

To create an Append query:

1. In the query design window, click on the drop-down arrow next to the Query View toolbar button, and then choose Append. Or, choose Query ➤ Append from the menus. (After you complete step 3, the Query Type button changes, as shown at left.) You'll see this dialog box:

2. If the table is in the same database, skip to step 3. If the table you want to append to is in a different database, click on Another Database, press Tab, and specify the drive, folder, and name of that database (for example, **c:\My Documents\Mydata**).

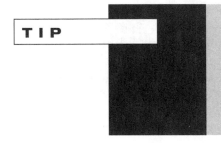

TIP
To look for the target database, right-click on the Start button, choose Explore or Find, and then use standard Windows techniques to locate the database. When you find what you're looking for, close Explorer or Find, and then type the appropriate location into the File Name text box below Another Database.

3. From the Table Name drop-down list, choose the target table, and then click on OK.

4. In the query design window, add tables, include fields you want to copy and fields being used for selection criteria, and set criteria to select the records you want to append, just as for a Select query.

5. If the field names in the source table match those in the target table, Access will fill in the appropriate Append To cells for the

target table automatically. You can change this if necessary. If you're using the asterisk to copy all fields from the source table, delete field names from the Append To cells of columns that contain selection criteria.

6. To preview your changes, click on the Query View toolbar button (or choose <u>V</u>iew ➤ Data<u>s</u>heet). Adjust the query and preview the results until you select the records you want to append.

7. To run the Append query, return to the query design window, and then click on the Run toolbar button or choose Query ➤ <u>R</u>un.

8. When prompted with the number of records that will be appended, click on <u>Y</u>es if you want to proceed, or click on <u>N</u>o to cancel the operation.

If an error message dialog box appears, respond to its prompts (there's a <u>H</u>elp button if you need it), as discussed later in "Troubleshooting Action Queries."

Here are some important points about Append queries:

- When designing an Append query, you work with the source table. Records are *copied* (not moved) from the source table to the target table.

- The two tables must have similar structures and field names, but they needn't have identical structures.

- If the source table has more fields than the target table, extra fields are ignored.

- If the source table has fewer fields than the target table, fields with matching names are updated, and any additional fields are left blank.

- Access will copy *only* those fields that are included in the source table's QBE grid to the target table.

- If the two tables have identical structures, you can use the asterisk instead of field names in both the Field cell and the Append To cell. If the QBE grid also includes fields with selection criteria, leave the Append To cell for those fields blank.

- If the target table has a primary key, the results will appear in sorted order (by primary key) rather than with all the new records at the bottom.

- To have Access assign new AutoNumber values to records as they come into the target table, *exclude* the AutoNumber field (if any) from the source table's QBE grid.

- To retain AutoNumber values from the source table in the target table, *include* the AutoNumber field in the source table's QBE grid. *Warning:* If the AutoNumber field is a primary key in the target table, the incoming records must not contain values that generate key violations.

- If you need to append only a few records to a table, you may prefer to use Paste Append (see Chapter 8).

- Chapter 7 explains how to append records to a non-Access database.

Delete Queries

Delete queries let you delete a group of records that meet specific search criteria in one fell swoop. This query, for example, will delete shipped Orders from the Orders table:

Field:	ShipDate	Orders.*
Table:	Orders	Orders
Delete:	Where	From
Criteria:	Is Not Null	

The procedures for setting up a Delete query depend on whether you're deleting records from one table only (or from multiple tables involved in a one-to-one relationship), or from multiple tables that are involved in a one-to-many relationship.

WARNING You can't undo Delete queries! So be sure to preview the records that will be deleted before you run the query.

Deleting Records from One Table

Let's take the simplest case first: deleting records from a single table or from multiple tables in a one-to-one relationship. Here are the steps to follow:

1. In the query design window, click on the drop-down arrow next to the Query View toolbar button, and then choose Delete. Or, choose Query ➤ Delete from the menus. The Query Type button changes, as shown at left.

2. Add the tables, include fields you'll be using to select specific records, and set criteria to select the records you want to delete, just as for a Select query.

3. If you're querying multiple tables, double-click on the asterisk (*) for each table you want to delete records from.

4. To preview your changes, click on the Query View toolbar button (or choose View ➤ Datasheet). Adjust the query and preview the results until you select the records you want to delete.

5. To run the Delete query, return to the query design window, and then click on the Run toolbar button or choose Query ➤ Run.

6. If you're prompted with the number of rows that will be deleted, click on Yes if you want to proceed, or click on No to cancel the operation.

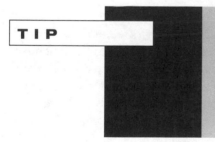

TIP

After running an Append query to append records from a "current" table to a "history" table, you can click on the drop-down arrow next to the Query Type toolbar button and choose Delete to convert the Append query into a Delete query. Then click on the Run toolbar button to delete the old records from the "current" table.

Understanding Cascaded Deletes

If you've defined referential integrity between tables involved in a one-to-many relationship and you've also selected Cascade Delete Related Records, Access will delete records on the "many" side of the relationship for you automatically, even if you haven't included the "many" side table in the query.

Considering the sample Order Entry database, there's a one-to-many relationship between Customers and Orders, and between Orders and Order Details. The tables on the "one" side of the relationship have cascaded deletes selected. Therefore, if we create a single-table Delete query to delete a particular Orders record, Access will delete the requested Orders record and its corresponding Order Details records automatically.

Likewise, if we create a single-table Delete query to delete a particular Customers record, Access will delete that customer, along with any corresponding Orders and Order Details records for that customer—deleting, in effect, records in three related tables (which may or may not be what you want).

If you've defined Cascade Delete Related Records between related tables, you don't have to set up a Delete query when you want a deletion on the "one" side of the relationship to carry over to the "many" side. Simply go to form view or datasheet view for the table on the "one" side and delete the appropriate record or records. Access will delete the related records in the "many" side tables automatically!

WARNING

The technique described above creates a delete cascade that will delete records in *all* related tables that have Cascade Delete Related Records selected in Relationships. Before you delete a record that in turn might delete records in other related table(s), make sure you know how the relationships between your tables are set up, and which tables will be affected. See Chapter 6 for information about creating relationships between tables.

Deleting Records from Multiple "One-to-Many" Tables

If you haven't set up cascaded deletes and want to delete records from multiple tables that are involved in a one-to-many relationship, you need to run two Delcte queries, like this:

1. In the query design window, click on the drop-down arrow next to the Query Type toolbar button, and then choose Delete. Or, choose Query ➤ Delete.

2. Add the tables you want to use in the query.

3. From the table on the "one" side of the relationship (for example, Products), drag the field or fields you want to use for selection criteria and define the criteria as usual.

4. In the table (or tables) on the "many" side of the relationship (for example, Orders), double-click on the asterisk (*).

5. Preview the query and run it as usual. This takes care of deleting records on the "many" side of the relationship.

6. Return to the query design window and delete from the window any tables from the "many" side (for example, Order Details).

7. Preview the resulting query on the "one" side table and run it again.

Make Table Queries

A *Make Table* query creates an entirely new table from the results of a query. Use Make Table queries to:

- Work with a "frozen" copy of your data (perhaps for printing reports or charting).

- Create an editable copy of the recordset that results from a summary, crosstab, or unique values query.

- Export data to nonrelational applications such as spreadsheets, word processors, and other programs that can't combine data from multiple tables.

To create a Make Table query:

1. In the query design window, click on the drop-down arrow next to the Query View toolbar button, and then choose Make Table. Or, choose Query ➤ Make Table from the menus. (After you complete step 3, the Query Type button changes, as shown at left.) You'll see a dialog box that's similar to the one shown earlier for Append queries.

2. If the table you want to create is in the same database, skip to step 3. If the table is in a different database, choose Another Database, press Tab, and specify the folder location and name of that database (for example, **c:\My Documents\Mydata**).

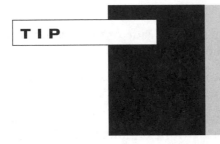

TIP As for Append queries, you can right-click on the Start button, choose Explore or Find, and then use standard Windows techniques to locate the target database. When you find what you're looking for, close Explorer or Find, and then type the appropriate location into the File Name box below Another Database.

3. In the Table Name drop-down list, type in or choose the table you want to make, and then click on OK. If you choose the name of an existing table, Access will *overwrite* that table.

4. In the query design window, add tables and fields, and set criteria to select the records and fields for the new table, just as for a Select query.

5. To preview your changes, click on the Query View toolbar button. Adjust the query and preview the results until you select the records you want to include in the new table.

6. To run the Make Table query, return to the query design window and click on the Run toolbar button.

7. If you chose an existing table in step 3, you'll be asked if you want to continue. Click on Yes if you want to delete the old table and continue, or No to return to the query design window without

deleting the table. (If necessary, you can click on the drop-down arrow next to the Query Type toolbar button, choose Make Table again, and specify a different table.)

8. When prompted with the number of rows that will be copied, click on <u>Y</u>es to proceed, or <u>N</u>o to abandon the operation.

Troubleshooting Action Queries

Action queries must obey the same rules that apply when you're entering or editing data from the keyboard. If the action query is about to break a rule, you'll see a dialog box like this one:

At this point, the query hasn't really been executed (even though the message implies otherwise). If this message appears, click on <u>N</u>o. Then return to the query or the original data, fix any problems, and rerun the query. The most common causes of problems are:

- An Append query or Update query is trying to enter data that isn't appropriate for the data type of the field. For Append queries, make sure the data types in the target table match the data types of the source table. For Update queries, make sure the update value is the correct data type for the field.

- An Append query or Update query is trying to add records that will cause key violations in a table that has a primary key. Remember, the primary key must have a unique value, and it can't contain null values. In an Append query, the "lost" records that violate the key won't be added to the target table (though, of course, they'll remain in the source table). In an Update query, no changes are made to records that will violate the key.

- Another user has locked records that your action query is trying to change. Your best bet is to cancel the query and wait until no one is using the table(s) involved in your query. Then try again.

- An action query is about to violate a referential integrity relationship between two tables. For instance, a Delete query can't delete records from the "one" side of a one-to-many relationship if the table on the "many" side contains related records. (It can, however, delete those records if the relationship allows cascaded deletes, as discussed in Chapter 6 and earlier in this chapter.)

What's New in the Access Zoo?

Most features of queries are the same in Access for Windows 95 as they were in Access 2.0. However, a few things are new:

- The Simple Query Wizard lets you retrieve data from one or more tables, display selected fields, group information by date, and perform summary calculations on fields.

- You can specify the type of query you want to create by choosing options from the Query View toolbar button or the Query menu.

- You can filter and sort the datasheet after running a Select query.

- You can display top values (for example, the top 20 records or the top 10 percent of records) by using the Top Values combo box on the query design window's toolbar.

- The Options dialog box (Tools ➤ Options) settings give you more control over query behavior. For example, from the Tables/Queries tab in the Options dialog box, you can prevent automatic join lines between tables that have fields of the same name and data type but do not have relationships defined in the Relationships window. From the Edit/Find tab, you can control whether action queries prompt you to confirm your changes.

Where to Go from Here

In this chapter, you've learned how to create many types of queries to ask questions about and perform calculations on your data, to update data, to delete data, and to add data from one table to another. In the next chapter, you'll learn how to generate forms instantly, with Form Wizards. As you'll discover, forms can display data from tables or queries.

Creating Forms
with Form Wizards

A form offers an alternative way to view and work with data in your tables. Unlike the datasheet view, which always displays data in rows and columns, a form can display data in just about any format. Perhaps the most common use of a form is to create a "fill-in-the-blanks" view of your data that resembles a paper form your company already uses.

Form Wizards make it easy to create great-looking data entry forms in about two seconds flat. You just pick the style you want, click your mouse a few times, and voilà, a form appears. You can use any Wizard-created form, except a chart or PivotTable (described later in this chapter), to enter data into tables. This chapter explains how to use Form Wizards to create several types of predesigned forms. These designs (with a few tweaks here and there) probably can handle most of your data entry needs.

TIP You can save lots of time by using Form Wizards to set up forms, even if you plan to extensively customize those forms later. Chapter 3 explains how to work with Wizards and gives you hands-on practice with them.

Just in case you're wondering whether Access has more form design tools to offer, the answer is a resounding *Yes!* If you need a more elaborate form than the Form Wizards can create, Chapter 13 explains how to design and customize forms and reports.

 If you need extra help with designing a new form, double-click on the *Working With Forms* book in the Access Help Contents, and then double-click on books and topics that interest you.

What Kinds of Forms Can the Form Wizards Create?

The Form Wizards can create several types of forms showing fields from one or more tables and/or queries. To help you decide which type of Wizard-designed form might be best for your own data, we'll show some representative examples. Then we'll explain how to create forms with Wizards, save those forms, and use them effectively.

Columnar Forms

In a columnar form, each field appears on a separate line with a label to its left; only one record is shown on each screen. The Wizard fills the first column with as many fields as will fit on a single screen, then it fills the next column with as many fields as will fit, and so forth. Figure 11.1 shows a sample columnar form for the Customers table.

Customers	
Customer ID	
Company Name	ABC Corporation
Contact First Na	Andy
Contact Last Na	Adams
Billing Address	87 Polk St. Suite 5
City	San Francisco
State/Province	CA
Postal Code	94117-
Country	USA
Contact Title	Owner
Phone Number	(415) 555-5938
Fax Number	(415) 555-5939

Record: 1 of 7

TIP

You can customize the styles available in Form Wizards. To get started, open any form in design view, and choose Format ➤ AutoFormat, or click on the AutoFormat button on the Form Design toolbar. In the AutoFormat dialog box, click on the format you want to customize, and then click on the Customize button. See Chapter 13 for more details.

Tabular Forms

Figure 11.2 shows a tabular form for the Products table. As you can see, tabular forms display fields in a horizontal row, with field labels at the top of the form. Each new row represents a new record.

Tabular forms are best when you want to display just a few relatively narrow fields, and you want to see several records at once. To avoid spending

FIGURE 11.2

A tabular form for the Products table, in the Clouds style. The tabular layout is best when you have just a few narrow fields to display and you want to see several records on a single screen.

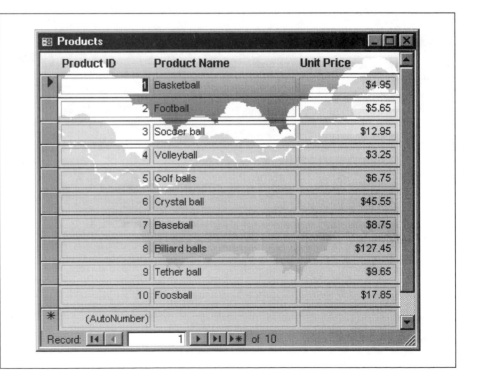

most of your time scrolling back and forth in a tabular form, add just a few fields to the form.

Datasheet Forms

A datasheet form initially displays data in datasheet view, much as it appears when you open a table or run a query, or when you use the Form View toolbar button to switch to datasheet view in any form. This type of form is often used as the basis for subforms, described in a moment. Figure 11.3 shows a datasheet form for the Employees table.

You can switch a datasheet form to form view by choosing View ➤ Form, or by clicking on the drop-down arrow next to the Form View toolbar button and then choosing form view. In form view, the fields appear in a tabular layout, but only one record is visible on each page of the form. Figure 11.4 shows the Employees form after we switched from datasheet view to form view; this example uses the International style.

FIGURE 11.3

A datasheet form for the Employees table, in datasheet view

FIGURE 11.4

The datasheet form, shown in for view. To resize the window to fit snugly, we chose Window ➤ Size To Fit Form.

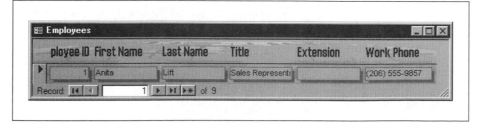

N O T E   The Form Wizards take their best guess when trying to fit labels and fields on your form. After creating the form, you may need to switch to design view and refine the design. In Figure 11.4, for example, the Employee ID label is cut off because the font is too large. To fix this problem, switch to design view and widen the label control or choose a smaller font for the labels.

Hierarchical Forms

Sometimes you'll want to work with related tables in your forms. For example, you might want to design an order form that includes customer and order information, along with details about the products ordered. A hierarchical form showing data from tables that have a one-to-many relationship is perfect for jobs like this.

The Form Wizards can create hierarchical forms in two basic flavors: a main form and subforms, or a main form and linked forms. (A *subform* is a separate form that's embedded in a main form.)

Figure 11.5 shows a main form with subforms, and it displays information from four tables: Customers, Orders, Order Details, and Products. The main form shows fields from the Customers table, arranged in columnar layout. The subforms for the Orders table and the Order Details and Products tables appear in datasheet layout.

N O T E   The main form and subform often go by the names *main/subform, form/subform,* or *master-detail form.*

Linked forms, such as those shown in Figures 11.6 and 11.7, also present multi-table data hierarchically. But instead of showing all the fields from the main table scrunched on the same page used for subforms, the main table's fields appear on a separate form. You can then click on the command button near the top of the form to show records that are synchronized with the record on the first form. The linked form can be a main form or a main form with a subform (see Figure 11.7).

FIGURE 11.5

This hierarchical main form shows fields from the Customers table, and its two datasheet subforms show fields from the Orders, Order Details, and Products tables. This example uses the Colorful2 style.

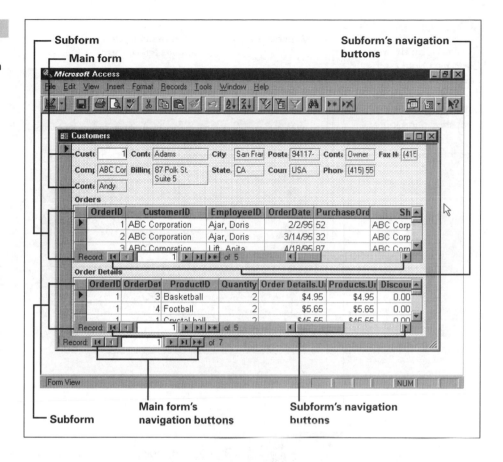

To produce the forms shown in Figures 11.5–11.7, we ran the Form Wizard and selected all fields from the Customers, Orders, and Order Details tables, and just the Unit Price field from the Products table. While viewing the Order Details subform, we dragged the Unit Price field for the Products table next to the unit price field for the Order Details table; this arrangement lets us see the unit price from the Products table while we enter the actual selling price into the unit price field of the Order Details table. We also dragged the OrderID field in the Order Details subform to the left of the OrderDetailID field.

FIGURE 11.6

A linked form showing Customers data on the main form. Clicking on the Orders command button displays the form shown in Figure 11.7. This example uses the Flax style.

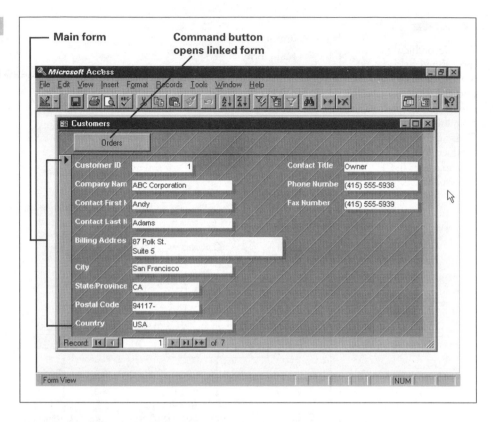

TIP

If you've already created forms that include the necessary linking fields, you can quickly combine them into a main form with a subform. To do so, open the main form in design view, press F11 to bring the database window to the front, click on the Forms tab on the database window, and choose Window ➤ Tile Vertically. Then drag the subform from the database window to an appropriate spot on the main form's design window, and respond to any prompts that appear. See Chapter 13 for more details.

FIGURE 11.7

The linked form and subform appear when we click on the Orders button shown in Figure 11.6. This form shows Orders, Order Details, and Products information for the customer whose name appears in Figure 11.6. To return to the main form, close the linked form.

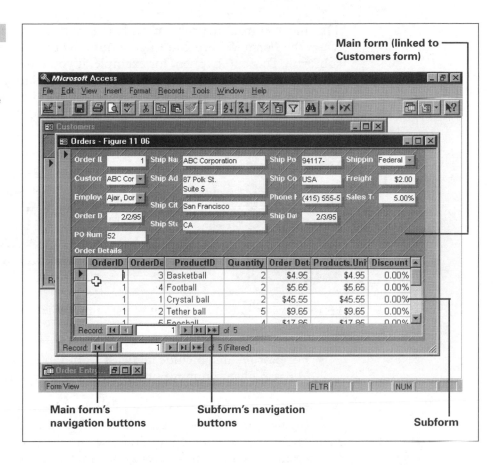

Making Hierarchical Forms Work Properly

To work properly, the main form and subform must be linked by a common field in a *one-to-many relationship* (or, less often, a one-to-one relationship). That is...

- The table or query on the "one" side—for example, Customers—supplies data for the main form.

- The table or query on the "many" side—for example, Orders—supplies data for the subform.

- The forms are linked by a primary key field on the "one" side and a normal field (called the *foreign* key) on the "many" side. In the Customers and Orders example, CustomerID is the primary key field on the "one" side, and a foreign key on the "many" side.

The most common problem with creating hierarchical forms occurs when the Form Wizard can't figure out how to link your main form and subform. This can happen, for example, if you haven't explicitly set up a relationship between the tables, either via the Relationships window or a multi-table query. As you'll see shortly, the Form Wizard will let you know when this problem exists, and it will give you a chance to set up relationships.

NOTE   Chapter 6 explains how to use the Relationships window to define relationships between tables in your database. Chapter 10 explains how to use queries to define relationships, select specific data, and perform calculations on data. Chapter 13 explains how to set properties that link main forms and subforms.

Here's how to get the most out of using the Form Wizards to create hierarchical forms:

- For best results, include all fields from tables on the "many" side. You can always remove unwanted fields or rearrange them later.

In some cases involving multiple related tables that have lookup fields, Access might not connect the related tables and fields properly, and it might not tell you that it couldn't. For example, when we included all the Order Entry database fields from our sample Customers, Orders, Order Details, and Products tables on a form, the drop-down list for the ProductID field in the Order Details subform was empty and the lookup values displayed incorrectly.

To work around this glitch, we opened the problem subform (Order Details Subform) in Form Design view, opened the property sheet (View ➤ Properties), and clicked on the problem OrderDetails.ProductID control. Then we changed its Row Source property to *Products*, its Column Count property to 2, and its Column Widths property to 0";1" and saved the subform. See Chapter 6 for information about lookup fields, and Chapter 13 for details about working with properties.

- Avoid renaming subforms or linked forms, because doing so can make it impossible for Access to find and open those forms. If you do rename the forms, you'll need to open each main form and subform in design view, choose <u>V</u>iew ➤ <u>P</u>roperties (if the property sheet isn't visible), and click on the All tab on the property sheet. Then, fix every reference to the old form name in the Name and Source Object properties, and in all Event Procedures (you can edit any event procedure, and then use the <u>E</u>dit ➤ <u>R</u>eplace command to globally change references in the current module). Be sure to fix these properties for the entire form, and for any command buttons and subforms on the form.

 ➤ For more details about creating hierarchical forms, look up *Subforms, Creating* in the Access Help Index. Chapter 13 explains how to alter properties and select controls. See Parts Four and Five for more about events and the Visual Basic program code that's used in Event Procedures.

Charts

Charts convert the numbers in your data to useful graphs, so that you can better understand the meaning of those numbers. The chart in Figure 11.8 shows the contribution of each customer's orders to the company's total sales. We used a Select query as the data source for the sample

A pie chart showing the contribution of each customer's orders to total sales. We tweaked the appearance of this chart after the Chart Wizard created it.

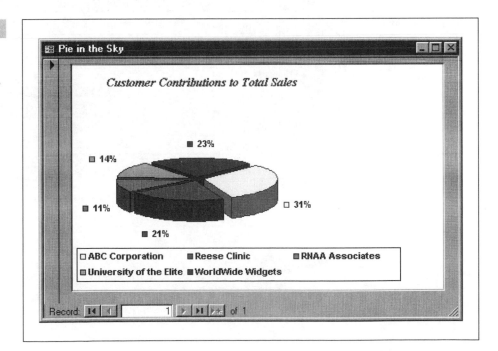

chart (see Figure 10.17 in Chapter 10). Chapter 14 explains how to create charts.

PivotTables

A PivotTable lets you summarize large amounts of data, much as a Crosstab query does (see Chapter 10). But a PivotTable is more flexible than a Crosstab query, because it lets you interactively switch the row labels, column labels, and summary calculations as needed. In Figure 11.9, you see a PivotTable that's based on the query shown below. Chapter 14 explains how to create and use PivotTables.

FIGURE 11.9

This PivotTable shows the number of each product sold, by state. After opening this form in Access, we clicked on the Edit PivotTable button (not shown) to launch Microsoft Excel and customize the PivotTable as needed.

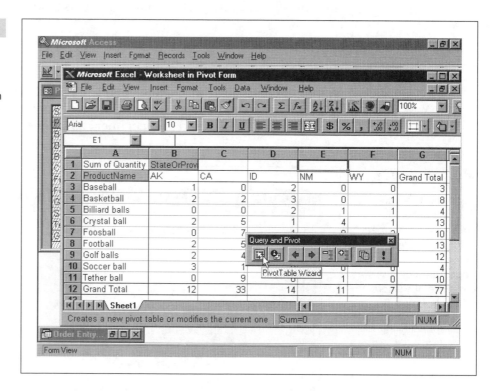

NOTE

You must have Microsoft Excel installed to create and use PivotTables.

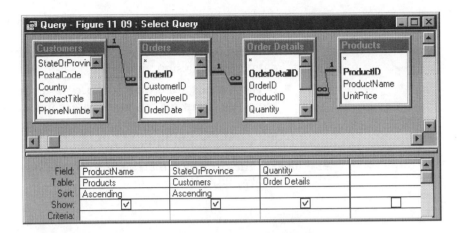

Using Wizards to Create a Form

Now that you've seen the many types of forms the Form Wizards can create, why not try the Wizards? The steps are easy:

1. Start from any of these places:

- **To base your form on a specific table,** start from the database window, click on the Tables tab, and highlight the table name. Or open the table in datasheet view. If the table has a filter and sort order associated with it, the new form will inherit the filter and sort order automatically (see Chapter 9).

NOTE

You also can start your form from table design view. If you do, however, the form can be displayed in design view only, and you'll get an error message that your table is exclusively locked (click on OK to clear the message). To view the form in form view, pull down the <u>W</u>indow menu and switch to the table design window. Then close the table design window (Ctrl+W), switch back to the form design window, and click on the Form View toolbar button.

- **To base your form on a specific query (or saved filter),** start from the database window, click on the Queries tab, and highlight the query name. Or open the query in datasheet or design view.

- **If you're not sure which table or query you want to base the form on,** start anywhere in Access (of course, a database must be open), or click on the Forms tab in the database window.

2. Click on the drop-down arrow next to the New Object toolbar button. You'll see this menu:

3. Choose one of these options:

AutoForm   Creates a one-column form using the template named in the Form Template box on the Forms/Reports tab of the Options dialog box (Tools ➤ Options ➤ Forms/Reports; see Chapter 15). Typically, this template is named "Normal," and it resembles the Standard style shown in Figure 11.1. After choosing this option, skip to step 11—you're done! Using the AutoForm option makes sense only if you selected a table or query in step 1.

New Form   Opens the New Form dialog box, shown here:

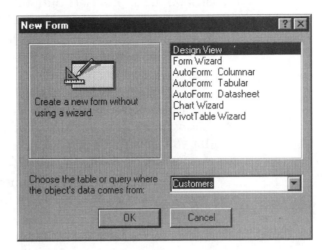

TIP

To open the New Form dialog box in fewer steps, click on the Forms tab in step 1, and then click on the New button in the database window. Or, start from any tab on the database window, and choose Insert ➤ Form. To create an AutoForm quickly, highlight a table or query name on the Tables or Queries tab in the database window, and then choose Insert ➤ AutoForm.

4. In the drop-down list near the bottom of the New Form dialog box, choose the table or query you want to base the form on. (This may be filled in for you already.)

NOTE

You must select a table or query before choosing any of the AutoForm Wizards or the Chart Wizard in step 5. If you plan to use the Form Wizard or PivotTable Wizard in step 5, you'll have another chance to choose tables and queries.

5. In the list near the top of the New Form dialog box, click on one of the options described below, and then click on OK; or just double-click on the appropriate option. When you click on an option, the area in the left side of the dialog box will show an example and describe the form the selected option will create. Your options are:

Form Wizard   Opens the Form Wizard. From here, you can select which tables, queries, and fields to include on the form, create subforms or linked forms (if appropriate), choose a style for the form, and specify a title and name for your form(s). Figures 11.1–11.7 showed examples of forms that we created with the Form Wizard.

AutoForm: Columnar   Without asking any more questions, creates a columnar form from all the fields in the selected table or query (see Figure 11.1).

AutoForm: Tabular   Without asking any more questions, creates a tabular form (see Figure 11.2).

AutoForm: Datasheet   Without asking any more questions, creates a datasheet form (see Figures 11.3 and 11.4).

NOTE   When you choose AutoForm: Columnar, AutoForm: Tabular, or AutoForm: Datasheet, Access places fields in the order they're defined in the table design or query, puts the name of the table or query on the form's title bar, and uses the default style. The default style is the style you (or someone else) chose most recently. If necessary, the Wizard will create a main form and subforms, even if you don't ask it to. After choosing an AutoForm option, skip to step 11 and then save your form.

Chart Wizard   Creates a form that displays a free-standing chart of your table or query data (see Figure 11.8 and Chapter 14).

PivotTable Wizard   Creates a form that can display a Microsoft Excel PivotTable (see Figure 11.9 and Chapter 14).

6. Assuming you chose Form Wizard in step 5, you'll see the first Form Wizard dialog box, shown in Figure 11.10. Use any of the techniques described below to add as many fields from as many tables or queries as you need, and then click on Next.

- **To select a table or query**, click on the drop-down arrow button below Tables/Queries, and then choose the table or query to use.

- **To add one field to the form**, click in the Selected Fields list where the new field should appear (optional). Then double-click on the field in the Available Fields list, or click on the field in the Available Fields list and then click on the > button. The field you select will move to the Selected Fields list and will appear on the form in the order shown.

- **To copy all the Available Fields to the Selected Fields list**, click in the Selected Fields list where the new fields should appear (optional); then click on the >> button.

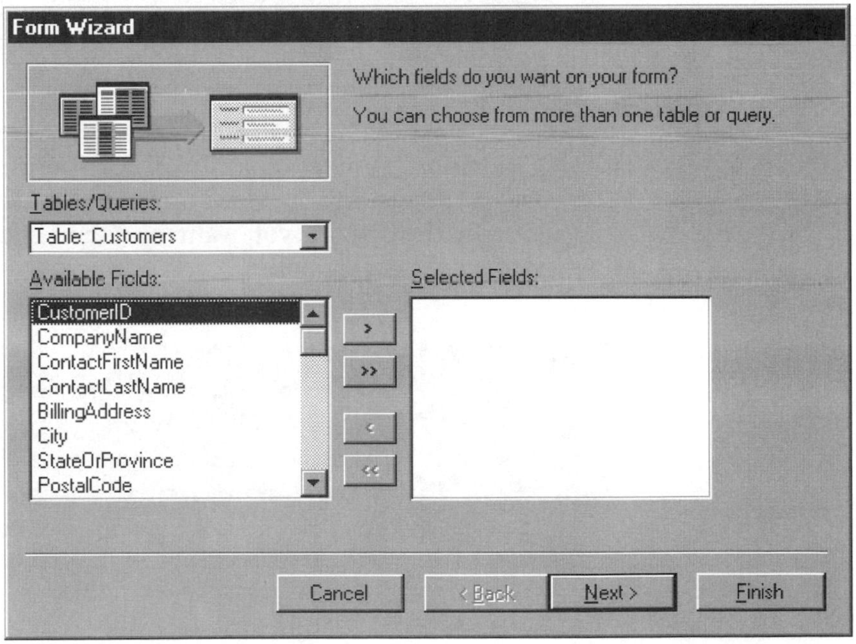

FIGURE 11.10

Use this Form Wizard dialog box to specify which fields should appear on your form. You can select fields from as many tables and queries as you wish. Access will use your selections to decide how to lay out the form.

- **To remove a field from the Selected Fields list,** double-click on that field, or click on the field and then click on the < button.

- **To remove all fields from the Selected Fields list,** click on the << button. The fields will reappear in the Available Fields list.

7. If you chose fields from multiple tables, but haven't defined relationships between the tables yet, the Wizard will display the dialog box shown below. Click on OK if you want to exit the Wizard and define relationships (see Chapter 6); or click on Cancel to return to step 6 and remove some fields from your form.

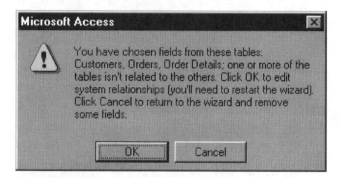

8. In the next dialog box or two, you'll be asked to choose a layout of Columnar, Tabular, Datasheet, Form With Subform(s), or Linked Forms, depending on which tables and fields you selected in step 6. Choose the options you want, and then click on Next to continue to the next dialog box.

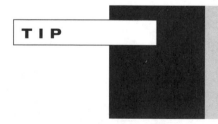

TIP

As you make choices in the dialog boxes described in steps 8 and 9, the Wizard will give you detailed instructions and show previews of your form as it takes shape. Just watch the screen carefully and you shouldn't have any trouble figuring out what to do.

9. When asked to choose a style, click on one of the available styles and then click on Next. For maximum readability, choose the

Standard style. (As Chapter 13 explains, you can customize the styles and create new ones of your own. Later in this chapter, we'll show you how to change a form's style instantly.)

10. In the last Form Wizard dialog box (see Figure 11.11), accept or change the suggested title(s), choose the option that lets you view or enter information (because this option usually is most convenient), and then click on Finish.

WARNING

The title you select in step 10 is used for the form name, the form's Caption property (which displays text on the form's title bar), the command button's Caption property (which displays text on the command button of a main form that has a linked form), and in Visual Basic code that Access creates behind the form. If the form already exists in the database, you'll have a chance to overwrite the existing form, or choose a different title.

FIGURE 11.11

The last Form Wizard dialog box asks what title you want for the form, what you want to do next, and whether you want to display Help on working with the form. It's often easiest to accept the default settings and click on Finish. This example shows a final dialog box for a form with linked subforms; the final dialog box for a simple form without subforms is similar.

Form Wizard

What title do you want for each linked form?

First form: Customers
Second form: Orders
Subform: Order Details Subform

That's all the information the wizard needs to create your linked forms.

Do you want to open the main form or modify the design of the forms?

⦿ Open the main form to view or enter information.
○ Modify the design of the forms.

☐ Display Help on working with the forms?

Cancel | < Back | Next > | Finish

11. Access will create your form and display it in form view.

12. If you wish, resize the form or maximize it. As long as the form is *not* maximized, you can choose Window ➤ Size To Fit Form to get a nice snug fit of the form window around the form's fields.

After your form appears in form view, you can...

- Use your form to edit existing records or add new ones (see "Opening and Using a Form").

- Edit or add records in datasheet view. To switch to datasheet view, choose View ➤ Datasheet, or click on the drop-down arrow button next to the Form View toolbar button and choose Datasheet View.

How the Wizards Build Your Form

The Form Wizards perform much sorcery as they construct your forms from nothing more than your answers to a few questions. For their most important conjuring jobs, the Wizards make sure data from multiple tables is synchronized properly, and they size and place fields and buttons on the form so that everything fits on the screen.

If the form is based on fields from multiple tables and/or queries, the Wizard creates an SQL statement behind the form that specifies which tables, queries, and fields to use and sets up the necessary table relationships. All this happens automatically, so you don't have to worry about it, and you rarely need to set up multi-table queries just to display fields from several tables at once.

When sizing each control, the Wizard lays out all the necessary fields, regardless of the current page/form size. If the resulting form is too big for the screen, it calculates the ratio of the total size of the too-big form to the desired page/form size; then it shrinks every control by that ratio to create a form of the maximum allowable size. Because the Wizard uses a simple ratio method for sizing controls on forms—rather than trying millions of combinations to arrive at something that's esthetically pleasing—you may need to switch to design view and tweak the size, position, or font for controls that appear squashed. Chapter 13 explains how to do all that.

- Change the form's design in design view, as explained in Chapter 13. To switch to design view, click on the Form View toolbar button, or choose <u>V</u>iew ➤ Form <u>D</u>esign, or click on the drop-down arrow button next to the Form View button and choose Design View. Typically, you'll just need to rearrange or widen the fields and labels. You had a chance to rearrange and resize fields in the Chapter 3 hands-on lessons.

- Print or print preview the form (see Chapters 3 and 9).

- Sort or filter the records, or search for records that meet specific criteria (see Chapters 3 and 9).

- Save and close the form (see "Saving a Form" later in this chapter).

Saving a Form

If the Wizard didn't save your form automatically, you should save the form if you want to use it later. Here's how:

1. To save and close the form, choose <u>F</u>ile ➤ <u>C</u>lose, or press Ctrl+W, or click on the Close button at the upper-right corner of the form; then click on <u>Y</u>es. Or, if you just want to save your latest changes, press Ctrl+S, or choose <u>F</u>ile ➤ <u>S</u>ave, or click on the Save toolbar button (shown at left).

2. The first time you save a form that hasn't been saved before, you'll be prompted to enter a name for it. Type a name (up to 64 characters, including blanks), and then click on OK.

Opening and Using a Form

If you've closed a form, you can reopen it with these steps:

1. Start in the database window and click on the Forms tab.

2. Do one of the following:

- **To open the form in form view** (with data displayed), double-click on the form name you want to open, or click on it and then click on the <u>O</u>pen button.

- **To open the form in design view** (where you can change the form's design), click on the form name and then click on <u>D</u>esign.

Assuming you've opened the form in form view, you can use any technique discussed in Chapter 8 to edit data and add or delete records. Table 11.1 summarizes what you can do.

TABLE 11.1:   Navigating and Editing in Forms

TO DO THIS...	PRESS, CLICK, OR CHOOSE THIS	TOOLBAR BUTTON
Switch from editing mode to navigation mode (cursor moves from field to field)	F2, or Tab, or Shift+Tab, or click on the field name	
Switch from navigation mode to editing mode (cursor moves within a field)	F2 or click in a field	
Navigate in Editing Mode		
End of field (multi-line field)	Ctrl+End	
End of line	End	
One character to left	←	
One character to right	→	
One word to left	Ctrl+←	
One word to right	Ctrl+→	
Start of field (multi-line field)	Ctrl+Home	
Start of line	Home	

TABLE 11.1: Navigating and Editing in Forms (continued)

TO DO THIS...	PRESS, CLICK, OR CHOOSE THIS	TOOLBAR BUTTON
Edit in a Field		
Delete character to left of cursor	Backspace	
Delete character to right of cursor	Delete	
Delete selected text	Select text, then press Delete or Backspace	
Delete to end of word	Ctrl+Delete	
Delete to start of word	Ctrl+Backspace	
Insert default value for a field	Ctrl+Alt+Spacebar	
Insert new line	Ctrl+↵	
Insert system date	Ctrl+;	
Insert system time	Ctrl+: (same as Ctrl+Shift+;)	
Insert value from same field in previous record (ditto)	Ctrl+' or Ctrl+" (same as Ctrl+Shift+')	
Navigate in Navigation Mode		
Current field (of the next record)	Ctrl+Page Down	
Current field (of the previous record)	Ctrl+Page Up	
Cycle forward or backward through header, detail section, and footer of form	F6 (forward) or Shift+F6 (backward)	
Down one page or to next record if you're at end of a record	Page Down	
First field (of the first record)	Ctrl+Home	
First record	First Record navigation button or Edit ➤ Go To ➤ First	◄❘
Last field (current record)	End	
Last field (last record)	Ctrl+End	

TABLE 11.1: Navigating and Editing in Forms (continued)

TO DO THIS...	PRESS, CLICK, OR CHOOSE THIS	TOOLBAR BUTTON
Last record	Last Record navigation button or Edit ➤ Go To ➤ Last	▶❙
Next field (current record)	Tab, or →, or ↵	
Next record	Next Record navigation button or Edit ➤ Go To ➤ Next	▶
Previous field (current record)	Shift+Tab or ←	
Previous record	Previous Record navigation button or Edit ➤ Go To ➤ Previous	◀
Specific record	F5 then type record number and press ↵	1
Up one page or to previous record if you're at end of a record	Page Up	

Copy, Cut, and Paste Clipboard Contents

TO DO THIS...	PRESS, CLICK, OR CHOOSE THIS	TOOLBAR BUTTON
Copy selected text to Clipboard	Ctrl+C or Copy button, or Edit ➤ Copy	📋
Cut selected text to Clipboard	Ctrl+X or Cut button, or Edit ➤ Cut	✂
Paste selected text from Clipboard	Position cursor; then press Ctrl+V or click on Paste button, or Edit ➤ Paste	📋

Add, Delete, Select, and Save Records

TO DO THIS...	PRESS, CLICK, OR CHOOSE THIS	TOOLBAR BUTTON
Add new record (shows all existing records; navigation buttons work normally)	Ctrl++ (plus sign), or New button or New navigation button, or Edit ➤ Go To ➤ New	▶＊ ▶＊
Add new record in Data Entry mode (hides all existing records)	Records ➤ Data Entry. To resume normal editing, choose Records ➤ Remove Filter/Sort or right-click form and choose Remove Filter/Sort.	

TABLE 11.1: Navigating and Editing in Forms (continued)

TO DO THIS...	PRESS, CLICK, OR CHOOSE THIS	TOOLBAR BUTTON
Delete current record	Ctrl+– (minus sign), or select current record and press Delete or click Delete Record button	
Save changes to current record	Shift+↵	
Select all records	Ctrl+A or Edit ➤ Select All Records	
Select current record	Click on Record Selector bar at left edge of form, or Edit ➤ Select Record	
Undo all changes to current field or record	Esc, Ctrl+Z, or Undo button, or Edit ➤ Undo repeatedly	
Undo most recent change	Esc, or Ctrl+Z, or Undo button, or Edit ➤ Undo once	

Miscellaneous Operations

Datasheet view	Form View button's drop-down arrow, then Datasheet View; or View ➤ Datasheet	
Design view	Form View button's drop-down arrow, then Design View; or View ➤ Form Design	
Filter (apply)	Apply Filter button, or Records ➤ Apply Filter/Sort, or right-click on form and choose Apply Filter/Sort	
Filter By Form (create/edit)	Filter By Form button, or Records ➤ Filter ➤ Filter By Form, or right-click on form and choose Filter By Form	
Filter Excluding Selection (create/edit)	Right-click on form and choose Filter Excluding Selection	
Filter By Selection (create/edit)	Filter By Selection button, or Records ➤ Filter ➤ Filter By Selection, or right-click on form and choose Filter By Selection	

TABLE 11.1: Navigating and Editing in Forms (continued)

TO DO THIS...	PRESS, CLICK, OR CHOOSE THIS	TOOLBAR BUTTON
Filter (create/edit advanced)	Records ➤ Filter ➤ Advanced Filter/Sort	
Filter (remove)	Remove Filter button or Records ➤ Remove Filter/Sort, or right-click on form and choose Remove Filter/Sort	▽
Find a record	Ctrl+F, or Find button, or Edit ➤ Find	🏵
Form view	Form View button's drop-down arrow, then Form View, or View ➤ Form	
Print preview records	Print Preview button or File ➤ Print Preview	🔍
Print records	Print button, Ctrl+P, or File ➤ Print	🖨
Replace text in a record	Ctrl+H or Edit ➤ Replace	
Sort records (A–Z, 0–9 order)	Sort Ascending button or Records ➤ Sort ➤ Ascending, or right-click on form and choose Sort Ascending	A↓Z
Sort records (Z–A, 9–0 order)	Sort Descending button or Records ➤ Sort ➤ Descending, or right-click on form and choose Sort Descending.	Z↓A

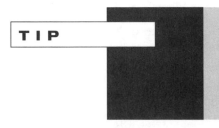

TIP

Copying offers a quick way to create a new form that's based on an existing form. To copy a form, click on the Forms tab in the database window, highlight the form to copy, and press Ctrl+C. Next, press Ctrl+V, type a name for the new form, and click on OK.

Getting Around in Hierarchical Forms

Once you've created a main/subform (see Figures 11.5 and 11.7), using it is similar to using normal forms (see Table 11.1). However, there are some crucial differences, which are described in Table 11.2.

If you created a linked form, click on the command button at the top of the main form, and then use the main form and subform as described in Table 11.2. When you're finished using the linked form, click on its Close button or press Ctrl+W.

TABLE 11.2: Special Techniques for Using Main/Subforms

TO DO THIS...	PRESS OR CHOOSE THIS...
Using Navigation Mode	
Exit subform or move to next field if not in subform	Ctrl+Tab or click in main form
Exit subform or move to previous field if not in sub-form	Ctrl+Shift+Tab or click in main form
Move cursor from main form to subform	End or click in subform
Move cursor from record to record in main form	Click on main form's navigation buttons, or click in main form and choose appropriate options from Edit ➤ Go To menus
Move cursor from record to record in subform	Click on subform's navigation buttons, or click in subform and choose appropriate options from Edit ➤ Go To menus
Move cursor to first editable field in main form	Ctrl+Shift+Home or click in first editable field in main form
Toggle between subform datasheet view and subform form view	Click in subform, and then choose View ➤ Subform Datasheet

TABLE 11.2: Special Techniques for Using Main/Subforms (continued)

TO DO THIS...	PRESS OR CHOOSE THIS...
Adding, Deleting, or Changing Records	
Add record to main form	Position cursor in main form, and then click on New toolbar button or choose Edit ➤ Go To ➤ New
Add record to subform	Position cursor in subform, and then click on New toolbar button or choose Edit ➤ Go To ➤ New
Change data in main form	Position cursor in appropriate field of *main form* and edit as usual
Change data in subform	Position cursor in appropriate field of *subform* and edit as usual
Delete record in main form	Click on record selector in *main form*, press Delete, and then click on Yes
Delete record in subform	Click on row selector in *subform*, press Delete, and then click on Yes

Additional points to remember about main/subforms are:

- Be especially careful to notice where the cursor is when you add or delete records in main/subforms. See Table 11.2 for details.

- You can adjust the row height, column width, and position of columns on the subform just as you do in a table's datasheet view (see Chapter 8). For example, you can drag the rows or columns, just as you would any grid in datasheet view. Access will save your changes automatically.

- You can set a filter for records in the main form or the subform(s).

- If you add a record to a subform and then change your mind while the cursor is still in the record, click on the Undo toolbar button (shown at left) or press Esc.

Changing the Style for a Form

Suppose you used the Form Wizards to create a form that has the Flax or International style, and now you decide that the Standard style would look better. You needn't re-create the form to change its style. Just follow these steps:

1. Open the form in design view. If you're starting from the database window, click on the Forms tab, click on the form you want to change, and then click on the Design button. Or, if the form is currently open in form view, click on the Form View toolbar button (shown at left) or choose View ➤ Form Design.

2. Choose Format ➤ AutoFormat, or click on the AutoFormat button (shown at left) on the Form Design toolbar. You'll see the AutoFormat dialog box, shown in Figure 11.12.

3. In the AutoFormat dialog box, click on the format you want to use. The sample form in the dialog box will reflect your current choice.

4. Click on OK to reformat the form, and respond to any prompts that appear.

FIGURE 11.12

Use the AutoFormat dialog box to instantly change the style for your form, or to customize an existing style. Switch to form design view and choose Format ➤ AutoFormat to open this dialog box.

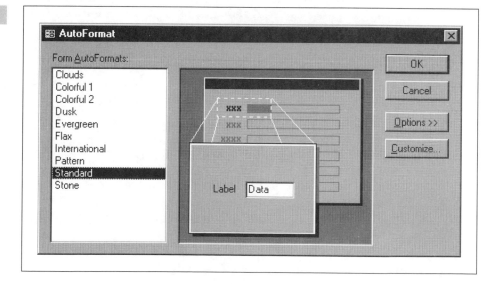

5. Save your changes (Ctrl+S) and click on the Form View toolbar button, or choose <u>V</u>iew ➤ <u>F</u>orm, to switch back to form view.

 ➤ See Chapter 13 for more about designing forms, using the AutoFormat feature, and creating custom styles. Or, look up *AutoFormat and its subtopics in the Access Help Index.*

Where to Go from Here

This chapter introduced the many types of instant forms you can create with Form Wizards. From here, you can continue with Chapter 12 to learn about designing instant reports with Report Wizards, or skip to Chapter 13 to learn about designing new forms and reports from scratch and customizing existing forms and reports.

What's New in the Access Zoo?

Although Access 2.0 also offered Form Wizards, the Form Wizards in Access for Windows 95 are more powerful and easier to use. Here are some highlights:

- The Form Wizard lets you choose fields from multiple tables or queries and automatically figures out how to link the tables if you've already defined relationships between them. You don't have to create a multi-table query first.

- The Form Wizards can create a main form with up to two subforms, or a main form and a linked form with subform.

- Forms automatically inherit filters from their source tables or queries.

- The AutoFormat feature lets you change the entire look of any form with a few mouse clicks.

CHAPTER

12

Creating Reports
with Report Wizards

FOR most of us, printing the data stored in tables or the information gathered from queries is an essential part of using a database. Access Report Wizards provide easy-to-use, yet powerful tools for creating reports in several predefined formats. Even if you plan to customize the designs later (as we did in many examples shown in this chapter), you'll save time if you use the Report Wizards to set up reports.

NOTE Chapter 3 explains how to work with Wizards and gives you hands-on practice with Report Wizards. Chapter 9 covers printing. In Chapter 13, you'll learn how to design forms and reports from scratch and how to customize existing designs.

 If you need more help with designing a new report, open the *Working With Reports* book in the Access Help Contents and explore subtopics in the *Basics* and other books. Or, double-click on *Reports, Creating* in the Help Index and explore the subtopics that appear.

What Kinds of Reports Can the Wizards Create?

The Report Wizards can create several types of reports showing fields from one or more tables and/or queries. To help you decide which type of Wizard-designed report might be best for your own data, we'll show some examples. Then we'll explain how to create, save, and use Wizard-generated reports.

Columnar (Vertical) Reports

In a columnar or vertical report, each field appears on a separate line with a label to its left. Figure 12.1 shows a sample columnar report for the Products table.

Products

Product ID	1
Product Name	Basketball
Unit Price	$4.95
Product ID	2
Product Name	Football
Unit Price	$5.65
Product ID	3
Product Name	Soccer ball
Unit Price	$12.95
Product ID	4
Product Name	Volleyball
Unit Price	$3.25
Product ID	5
Product Name	Golf balls
Unit Price	$6.75
Product ID	6
Product Name	Crystal ball
Unit Price	$45.55
Product ID	7
Product Name	Baseball
Unit Price	$8.75
Product ID	8
Product Name	Billiard balls
Unit Price	$127.45

Tuesday, September 05, 1995   Page 1 of 2

Tabular Reports

Figure 12.2 shows a tabular report for the Products table. As you can see, tabular reports display fields in a horizontal row, with field labels at the top of the report. Each new row represents a new record.

FIGURE 12.2

A tabular report for the Products table, in the Bold style. The tabular layout is best when you have just a few narrow fields to display and you want to see many records on a single page.

Products

Product ID	Product Name	Unit Price
1	Basketball	$4.95
2	Football	$5.65
3	Soccer ball	$12.95
4	Volleyball	$3.25
5	Golf balls	$6.75
6	Crystal ball	$45.55
7	Baseball	$8.75
8	Billiard balls	$127.45
9	Tether ball	$9.65
10	Foosball	$17.85

Tuesday, September 05, 1995

Groups, Totals, and Summary Reports

Groups/totals reports such as the one shown in Figure 12.3 organize your data into groups that appear in tabular format. At your request, the Wizard will calculate sum, average, minimum, and maximum values for numeric and currency fields in each group, and display sums as percentages of totals.

Sometimes the Report Wizard Needs Your Help

The Report Wizard does its best to format your reports correctly. But sometimes you'll need to add your own formatting refinements in report design view, especially for reports that present summary calculations and are based on queries that also involve calculations. Fortunately, making such refinements takes only a few minutes and is much faster than building a complicated report from scratch.

For example, after the Report Wizard created the first version of the report shown in Figure 12.3, the Quantity column heading was a bit too narrow, and formats for the Sum, Avg, Min, Max, and grand total calculations weren't quite right. To fix these problems, we switched to report design view, opened the property sheet (View ➤ Properties), and clicked on the property sheet's Format tab. Then we did the following:

- Widened the bold Quantity label near the top of the report design.
- Selected all the controls that present summary calculations and changed their Text Align property to Right.
- Selected controls that display summary calculations and grand totals for money amounts and changed their Format property to Currency.
- Selected the control that displays average quantity (Avg in the Quantity column) and changed its Format property to Fixed.
- Opened the Sorting And Grouping dialog box (View ➤ Sorting And Grouping), selected OrderDate in the Field/Expression column, and changed the Keep Together group property to Whole Group.

We also made similar changes to the first version of the report shown in Figure 12.5. See Chapter 13 for more about changing report formats.

FIGURE 12.3

A Casual style groups/totals report that's grouped by Order Date and subtotaled on numeric and currency fields. This report is in "Outline1" form. We tailored the appearance of this report after the Report Wizard created it.

Orders by Date

Order Date   2/1/95

Product Name	Quantity	Unit Price	Discount	$ Before Tax
Basketball	1	$4.95	0.00%	$4.95
Basketball	2	$4.95	0.00%	$9.90
Billiard balls	2	$127.45	0.00%	$254.90
Crystal ball	2	$45.55	0.00%	$91.10
Foosball	4	$17.85	0.00%	$71.40
Football	1	$5.65	0.00%	$5.65
Football	2	$5.65	0.00%	$11.30
Football	1	$5.65	0.00%	$5.65
Tether ball	5	$9.65	0.00%	$48.25

Summary for 'Order Date' = 2/1/95 (9 detail records)

Sum	20			$503.10
Avg	2.22	$25.26	0.00%	$55.90
Min	1	$4.95	0.00%	$4.95
Max	5	$127.45	0.00%	$254.90
Percent	25.97%			30.57%

Order Date   2/11/95

Product Name	Quantity	Unit Price	Discount	$ Before Tax
Baseball	2	$8.75	0.00%	$17.50
Basketball	1	$4.95	0.00%	$4.95
Basketball	2	$4.95	0.00%	$9.90
Football	1	$5.65	0.00%	$5.65

Summary for 'Order Date' = 2/11/95 (4 detail records)

Sum	6			$38.00
Avg	1.50	$6.08	0.00%	$9.50
Min	1	$4.95	0.00%	$4.95
Max	2	$8.75	0.00%	$17.50
Percent	7.79%			2.31%

Monday, October 09, 1995   Page 1 of 7

The group/totals report shown in Figure 12.3 is based on the query shown in Figure 12.4. The calculation in the last column of the query is as follows:

```
$ Before Tax:CCur([Quantity]*
   [Order Details].[UnitPrice]*(1-[Discount]))
```

Summary reports are just like group/totals reports—except that they omit the detail records between each group. Figure 12.5 shows a report that's almost the same as Figure 12.3, only designed as a summary report (we omitted the Product Name field in Figure 12.5). This report is based on the query shown in Figure 12.4.

FIGURE 12.4

This multiple-table query supplies data for the report in Figure 12.3, showing orders placed in 1995. See Chapter 10 for more about creating queries like this one.

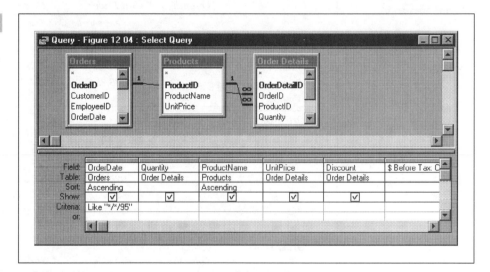

Charts

Charts convert the numbers in your data to meaningful graphs. The chart in Figure 12.6 shows the contribution of each customer's orders to the company's total sales. We used a Select query as the data source for the sample chart (see Figure 10.17 in Chapter 10).

Charting is basically the same, whether you display the chart on a form or a report. So once you know how to create a form-based chart, you also know how to create a report-based chart. Chapter 14 explains how to create charts.

FIGURE 12.5

A summary report looks like a group/totals report, but without the detail records between each group. For variety, we've shown this report in the Corporate style, in "Outline2" format. We tailored the appearance of this report after the Report Wizard created it.

Orders by Date (Summary)

Order Date		2/1/95		
	Quantity	Unit Price	Discount	$ Before Tax

Summary for 'OrderDate' = 2/1/95 (9 detail records)

Sum	20			$503.10
Avg	2.22	$25.26	0.00%	$55.90
Min	1	$4.95	0.00%	$4.95
Max	5	$127.45	0.00%	$254.90
Percent	25.97%			30.57%

Order Date		2/11/95		
	Quantity	Unit Price	Discount	$ Before Tax

Summary for 'OrderDate' = 2/11/95 (4 detail records)

Sum	6			$38.00
Avg	1.50	$6.08	0.00%	$9.50
Min	1	$4.95	0.00%	$4.95
Max	2	$8.75	0.00%	$17.50
Percent	7.79%			2.31%

Order Date		2/18/95		
	Quantity	Unit Price	Discount	$ Before Tax

Summary for 'OrderDate' = 2/18/95 (2 detail records)

Sum	2			$52.29
Avg	1.00	$26.15	0.05%	$26.15
Min	1	$6.75	0.00%	$6.74
Max	1	$45.55	0.10%	$45.55
Percent	2.60%			3.18%

Order Date		2/25/95		
	Quantity	Unit Price	Discount	$ Before Tax

Summary for 'OrderDate' = 2/25/95 (1 detail record)

Sum	2			$11.30
Avg	2.00	$5.65	0.00%	$11.30
Min	2	$5.65	0.00%	$11.30
Max	2	$5.65	0.00%	$11.30
Percent	2.60%			0.69%

Monday, October 09, 1995   *Page 1 of 5*

FIGURE 12.6

A pie chart showing the contribution of each customer's orders to total sales. We tailored the appearance of this chart after the Wizard created it.

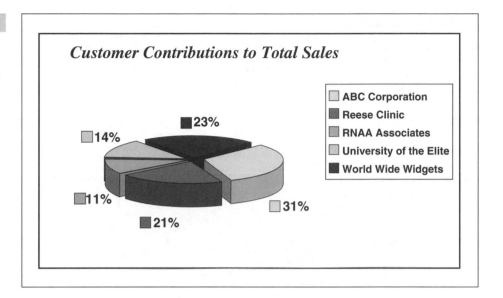

TIP

If you've already saved a chart as a form, you can quickly convert it to a report. To do so, click on the Forms tab in the database window, right-click on the chart you want to save as a report, choose Save As Report, type a name for the new report, and then click on OK. The newly saved report will appear when you click on the Reports tab in the database window.

Mailing Labels

You can design mailing labels that will print on standard Avery mailing label stock. Figure 12.7 shows some garden-variety mailing labels formatted for Avery 5196 (3.5″ diskette) labels. See "Creating Mailing Labels," later in this chapter to find out how to produce mailing labels from your Access data.

Mailing labels sorted in postal code, last name, and first name order. This example is formatted for Avery 5196 (3.5″ diskette) labels. We used a Format function to display the postal codes with hyphens in them (for example, 92575-4747).

Wilbur Stumingi
University of the Elite
P.O. Box 555
Lander, Wy 82520-
USA

Shirley Ujest
WorldWide Widgets
187 Suffolk Ln.
Boise, ID 83720-
USA

Susita Schumack
Reese Clinic
2817 Milton Dr.
Albuquerque, NM 87110-
USA

Anita Adams
Database Search and Rescue
5356 E. 20th St.
Santa Fe, NM 87110-3857
USA

Sheila Stumingi
Precision Bagpipes
P.O. Box 23981
San Diego, CA 92575-4747
USA

Andy Adams
ABC Corporation
87 Polk St.
Suite 5
San Francisco, CA 94117-
USA

Hanley Strappman
RNAA Associates
2743 Bering St.
Anchorage, AK 99508-
USA

Using Wizards to Create a Report

The procedures for creating a report with Wizards depend on the type of report you choose, but these are the basic steps:

1. Start from any of these places:

   - **To base your report on a specific table,** start from the database window, click on the Tables tab, and highlight the table name. Or open the table in datasheet view. If the table has a filter and sort order associated with it, the new report will inherit the filter and sort order automatically (see Chapter 9 and "Removing a Filter and Sort Order," later in this chapter for more details).

N O T E You also can start from table design view. If you do, however, the report can be displayed in design view only, and you'll get an error message that your table is exclusively locked (click on OK to clear the message). To view the report in print preview, pull down the Window menu and switch to the table design window. Then close the table design window (Ctrl+W), switch back to the report design window, and click on the Report View toolbar button.

- **To base your report on a specific query (or saved filter),** start from the database window, click on the Queries tab, and highlight the query name. Or open the query in datasheet or design view.

- **If you're not sure which table or query you want to base the report on,** start anywhere in Access (of course, a database must be open), or click on the Reports tab in the database window.

2. Click on the drop-down arrow next to the New Object toolbar button. You'll see this menu:

3. Choose one of these options:

AutoReport Creates a one-column report using the template named in the Report Template box on the Forms/Reports tab of the Options dialog box (Tools ➤ Options ➤

Forms/Reports; see Chapter 15). Typically, this template is named "Normal," and it is completely plain. After choosing this option, skip to step 11—you're done! Using the AutoReport option makes sense only if you selected a table or query in step 1.

New Report Opens the New Report dialog box, shown here:

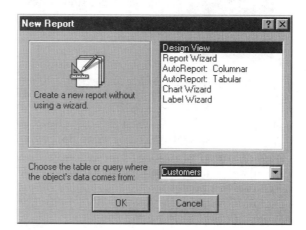

TIP

To open the New Report dialog box in fewer steps, click on the Reports tab in step 1, and then click on the New button in the database window. Or, start from any tab on the database window, and choose Insert ➤ Report. To create an AutoReport quickly, highlight a table or query name on the Tables or Queries tab in the database window, and then choose Insert ➤ AutoReport.

4. In the drop-down list near the bottom of the New Report dialog box, choose the table or query you want to base the report on. (This may be filled in for you already.)

NOTE You must select a table or query before choosing any of the AutoReport Wizards, the Chart Wizard, or the Label Wizard in step 5. If you plan to use the Report Wizard in step 5, you'll have another chance to choose tables and queries.

5. In the list near the top of the New Report dialog box, click on one of the following options, and then click on OK (or just double-click on the appropriate option). When you click on an option, the area in the left side of the dialog box will show an example and describe the report the selected option will create. Your options are:

Report Wizard   Opens the Report Wizard. From here, you can select which tables, queries, and fields to include on the report, choose how to group, total, and summarize your report, choose a style for the report, and specify a title and name for your report.

AutoReport: Columnar   Without asking any more questions, creates a columnar report from all the fields in the selected table or query (see Figure 12.1).

AutoReport: Tabular   Without asking any more questions, creates a tabular report (see Figure 12.2).

NOTE When you choose AutoReport: Columnar or AutoReport: Tabular, Access places fields in the order they're defined in the table design or query, puts the name of the table or query on the report's title and title bar, and uses the default style. The default style is the style you (or someone else) chose most recently when using the Report Wizard. After choosing an AutoReport option, skip to step 11 and then save your report.

Chart Wizard   Creates a report that displays a free-standing chart of your table or query data (see Figure 12.6 and Chapter 14).

Label Wizard Creates mailing labels from your table or query (see Figure 12.7 and "Creating Mailing Labels," later in this chapter).

6. Assuming you chose Report Wizard in step 5, you'll see the first Report Wizard dialog box, shown in Figure 12.8. Use any of the following techniques to add as many fields from as many tables or queries as you need, and then click on Next.

- **To select a table or query**, click on the drop-down arrow button below Tables/Queries, and then choose the table or query to use.

- **To add one field to the report**, click in the Selected Fields list where the new field should appear (optional). Then double-click on the field in the Available Fields list, or click on the field in the Available Fields list and then click on the > button. The field you select will move to the Selected Fields list and will appear on the report in the order shown.

FIGURE 12.8

Use this Report Wizard dialog box to specify which fields should appear on your report. You can select fields from as many tables and queries as you wish. Access will use your selections to decide how to lay out the report.

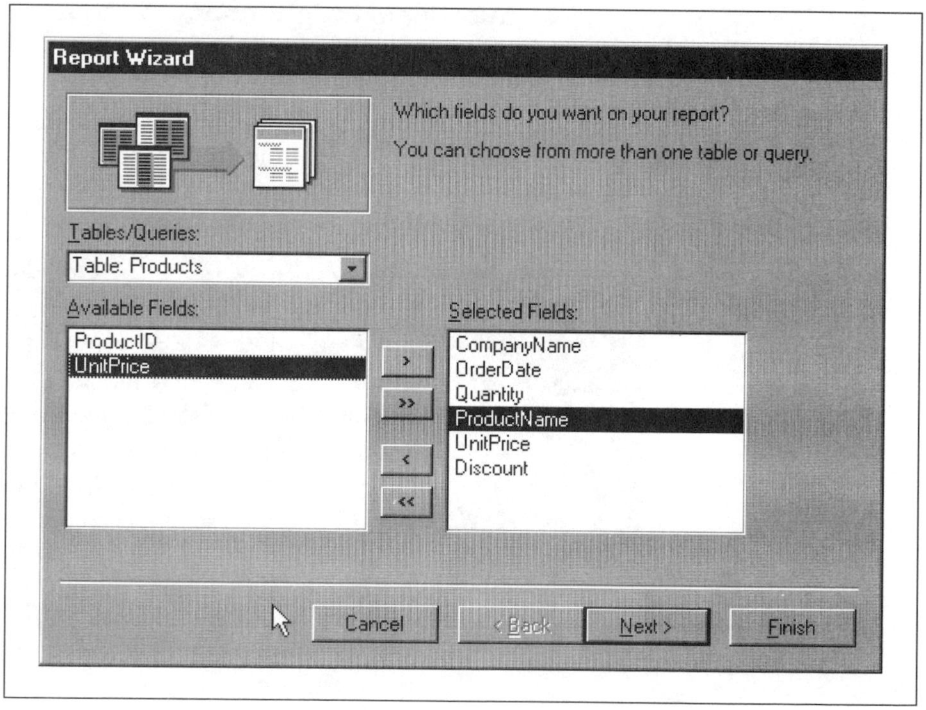

- **To copy all the <u>A</u>vailable Fields to the <u>S</u>elected Fields list,** click in the <u>S</u>elected Fields list where the new fields should appear (optional); then click on the >> button.

- **To remove a field from the <u>S</u>elected Fields list,** double-click on that field, or click on the field and then click on the < button.

- **To remove all fields from the <u>S</u>elected Fields list,** click on the << button. The fields will reappear in the <u>A</u>vailable Fields list.

7. If you chose fields from multiple tables, but haven't defined relationships between the tables yet, the Wizard will display the dialog box shown below. Click on OK if you want to exit the Wizard and define relationships (see Chapter 6); or click on Cancel to return to step 6 and remove some fields from your report.

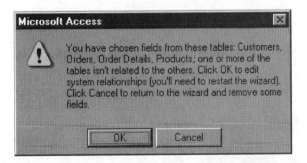

8. In the next few dialog boxes, you'll have a chance to customize your report. Your options will depend on which tables and fields you selected in step 6 and whether you choose to group your data. Pick the options you want in each dialog box, and then click on <u>N</u>ext to continue to the next dialog box. Here's a summary of the dialog boxes you'll see:

> **How to view your data**   The dialog box shown in Figure 12.9 appears if the report can be grouped in various ways. Choose the grouping option you want to use, and then click on <u>N</u>ext.

Use this Report Wizard dialog box to choose how to view a report that can be grouped in more than one way. This dialog box appears only if it's needed.

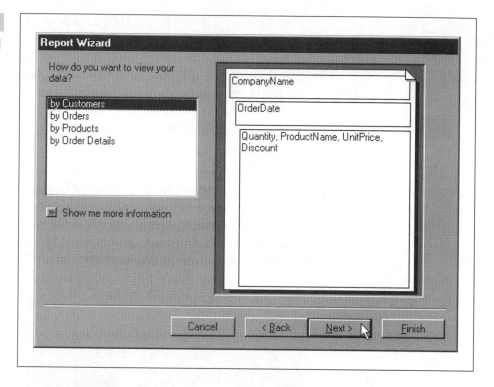

TIP

As you make choices in the dialog boxes described in steps 8 and 9, the Report Wizard will give you detailed instructions and show previews of your report as it takes shape. Just watch the screen carefully and you shouldn't have any trouble figuring out what to do.

Grouping levels and grouping options The dialog box shown in Figure 12.10 appears if your report can be grouped by additional levels. To choose a grouping field, double-click on it; or click on the field name and then click on the > button. To move it up a level, click on the ↑ button in the dialog box; to move it down a level, click on the ↓ button. To remove the bottom-most grouping field, click on the < button (repeat as needed). If you want to control the grouping interval for your additional fields, click on the Grouping Options button in the dialog box,

This Report Wizard dialog box lets you choose additional grouping fields and pick grouping intervals for those fields. This dialog box appears only if it's needed.

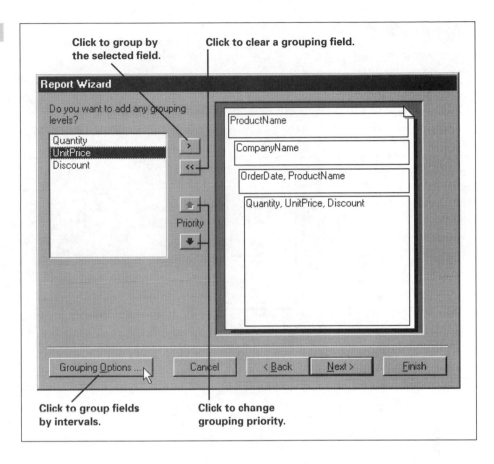

Click to group by the selected field.

Click to clear a grouping field.

Click to group fields by intervals.

Click to change grouping priority.

choose the interval you want from the appropriate Grouping Intervals drop-down lists, and then click on OK. Click on Next to continue.

Sort order for detail records and summary options
The dialog box shown in Figure 12.11 appears if your report is grouped. From here, you can sort detail records by up to four fields, in ascending or descending order. To control various groups/totals and summary options, click on the Summary Options button (if it's available); then, select the options you want to use (see Figure 12.12) and click on OK. Click on Next to continue.

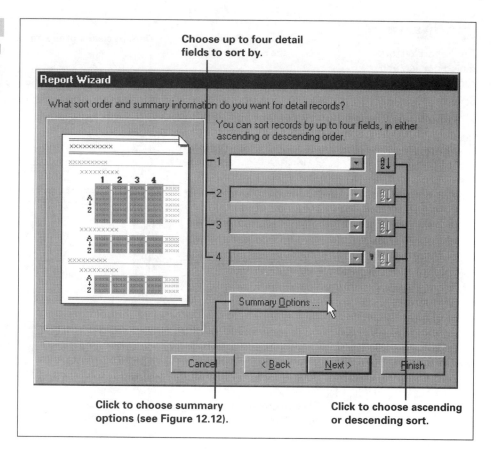

Choose up to four detail fields to sort by.

Click to choose summary options (see Figure 12.12).

Click to choose ascending or descending sort.

Report layout The appearance of this dialog box depends on whether your report is grouped. If it's grouped, it will resemble Figure 12.13; if it isn't grouped, it will resemble Figure 12.14.

9. When asked to choose a style, click on one of the available styles and then click on Next. (As Chapter 13 explains, you can customize the styles and create new ones of your own. Later in this chapter we'll show you how to change a report's style instantly.)

10. In the last Report Wizard dialog box (see Figure 12.15), accept the suggested title or change it if you wish, make sure you've selected Preview The Report (because this option usually is most convenient), and then click on Finish.

FIGURE 12.12

Clicking on the Summary Options button in the dialog box shown in Figure 12.11 takes you to this Summary Options dialog box. From here, you can choose which summary values to calculate, whether to show value details, and whether to calculate the "percent of total" for summed fields.

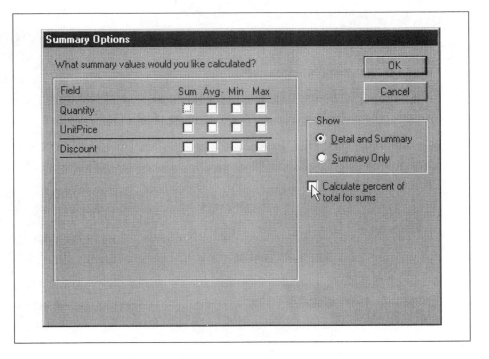

FIGURE 12.13

Use this dialog box to choose a layout for a grouped report.

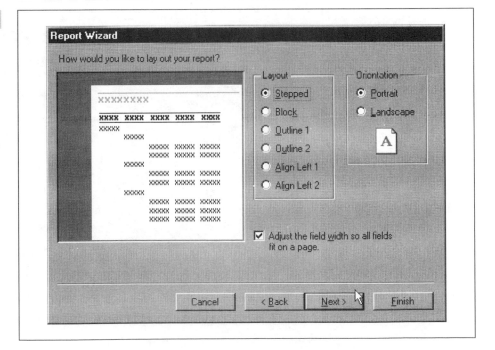

FIGURE 12.14

Use this dialog box to choose a layout for a report that isn't grouped. The term "Vertical" in the Layout group of this dialog box means the same as "Columnar."

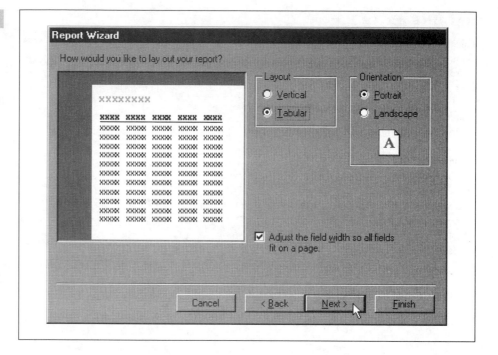

FIGURE 12.15

The last Report Wizard dialog box asks what title you want for the report, what you want to do next, and whether you want to display Help on working with the report. It's often easiest to accept the default settings and click on Finish.

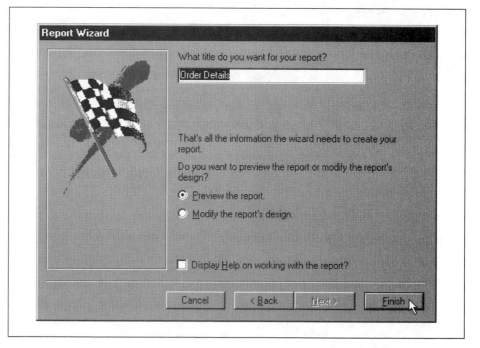

WARNING

The title you select in step 10 is used for the report name, the report's Caption property (which displays text on the report's title bar), and the report's title. If the report already exists in the database, you'll have a chance to overwrite the existing report or choose a different title.

11. Access will create your report and display it in the print preview window.

Figure 12.16 shows a sample report in the print preview window. Anytime your report appears in this window, you can...

- **Print the report.** To print without opening the Print dialog box, click on the Print toolbar button (see Figure 12.16). To print from the Print dialog box, press Ctrl+P or choose File ➤ Print, choose your printing options, and then click on OK (see Chapter 9 for more about printing).

- **Zoom out or in on the report.** Click on the Zoom toolbar button or click the magnifying glass mouse pointer on a spot in the report. You also can use the toolbar's Two Pages button and Zoom Control drop-down list, or right-click and choose Zoom or Pages options as needed (see Chapter 9).

- **Send the report to a Microsoft Word file** and open it in Word. Click on the drop-down arrow next to the OfficeLinks toolbar button, and then choose Publish It With MS Word.

- **Send the report to a Microsoft Excel spreadsheet** and open it in Excel. Click on the drop-down arrow next to the OfficeLinks toolbar button, and then choose Analyze It With MS Excel.

- **Send the report to your network mail program.** Choose File ➤ Send, select the format you want for the message file, and click on OK. When prompted, sign on to your mail system; then send the message as you would any network mail.

FIGURE 12.16

A sample report shown in the print preview window

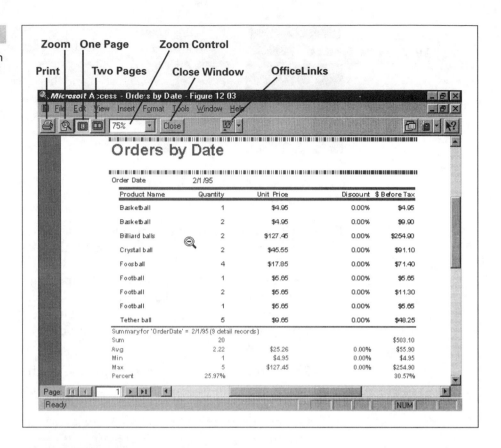

NOTE

Graphics and some complex formatting may not transfer to Microsoft Word or Microsoft Excel.

- **Close the print preview window and go to design view**, where you can change the report's design. Click on the Close toolbar button or press Ctrl+W. Often, you'll just need to rearrange or widen the fields and labels as described in Chapter 13.

- **Save and close the report** (see "Saving a Report" later in this chapter).

How the Wizards Build Your Report

The Report Wizards go through the same steps that the Form Wizards do as they conjure up your automatic reports. That is, they make sure data from multiple tables is synchronized properly, and they size and place fields on the report so that everything fits on the page.

If the report is based on fields from multiple tables and/or queries, the Wizard creates an SQL statement behind the report that specifies which tables, queries, and fields to use and sets up the necessary table relationships. Because the Wizard can do all this automatically, you'll rarely need to set up multi-table queries just to display fields from several tables at once.

When sizing each control, the Wizard lays out all the necessary fields, regardless of the current page size. If the resulting report is too big for the page, it calculates the ratio of the total size of the too-big report to the desired page size; then it shrinks every control by that ratio to create a report of the maximum allowable size. Because the Wizard uses a simple ratio method for sizing controls on reports, you may need to switch to design view and tweak the size, position, or font for controls that appear squashed.

TIP

You can use the File ➤ Save As/Export commands described in Chapter 7 to create a Microsoft Word mail merge document from a table or query. Chapter 7 also explains how to save reports as text files, Excel files, and Rich Text Format files.

 ➤ For more help with designing a new report with Wizards, look up *Wizards, ReportWizard* in the Access Help Index.

Creating Mailing Labels

You can design mailing labels that will print on standard Avery mailing label stock. Figure 12.7, earlier in this chapter, shows some standard mailing labels.

Preparing for Dot-Matrix or Tractor-Fed Labels

If you want to print labels on a dot-matrix or tractor-feed printer, you may need to adjust the page size before you start the Mailing Label Wizard. To do this, click on the Start button on the Windows taskbar, and then choose Settings ➤ Printers. Right-click on the icon for your dot matrix printer and choose Set As Default. Right-click on the dot matrix printer icon again, choose Properties, and then click on the Paper tab. Set the Paper Size to Custom, and specify the unit of measurement and the appropriate width and length. Click on OK, and then return to Access.

To learn more about creating labels for dot-matrix or tractor-feed printers, search for *Wizards, Label Wizard* in the Access Help Index, and then double-click on the topic *Create Mailing And Other Types Of Labels For A Dot-Matrix Printer*.

To create mailing labels using Report Wizards:

1. Start from the database window or from the datasheet view of a table or query as explained earlier.

2. Click on the drop-down arrow next to the New Object toolbar button, and choose New Report.

3. In the New Report dialog box, click on Label Wizard. Next, use the drop-down list at the bottom of the dialog box to select the table or query you want to base the report on (if it's not selected for you already). Click on OK.

4. In the dialog box shown in Figure 12.17, choose a label size, unit of measure, and label type as needed. If necessary, click on the Customize button in the dialog box, create a custom label size, and then click on Close. Or, select (check) Show Custom Label Sizes and select a custom label. Click on Next to continue.

5. When asked what font and color you want, choose font name, font size, font weight, and text color options. You also can select or deselect italics or underlining. Click on Next to continue.

FIGURE 12.17

This Label Wizard dialog box lets you choose a standard label size or a custom size. Click on the Customize button in this dialog box if you want to add or duplicate custom label sizes, delete an existing custom label size, or edit a label size. Select (check) or deselect (clear) Show Custom Label Sizes to toggle between showing built-in and custom label sizes.

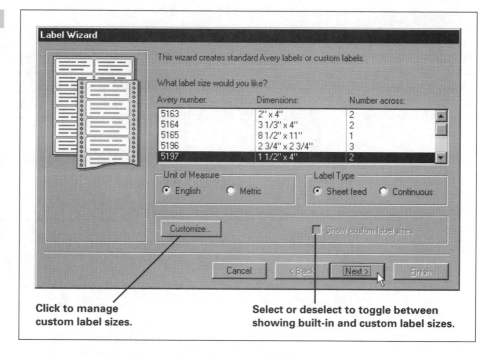

Click to manage custom label sizes.

Select or deselect to toggle between showing built-in and custom label sizes.

6. In the dialog box shown in Figure 12.18, choose the fields you want on the label. To add a field, position the cursor in the Proto-type Label box, and then double-click on a field in the Available Fields list. You also can type text or press ↵ at the cursor position. To delete fields or text from the Prototype Label box, select the text with your mouse and press the Delete key. Click on Next to continue.

NOTE

If the mailing label isn't large enough to hold all the lines and fields you specified, Access will explain the problem and let you know that some fields will be lost. You can return to previous Label Wizard screens (by clicking on the Back button as needed) and adjust your selections.

FIGURE 12.18

Use this dialog box to design your mailing labels. The Prototype Label box will reflect your latest changes, as shown in this example.

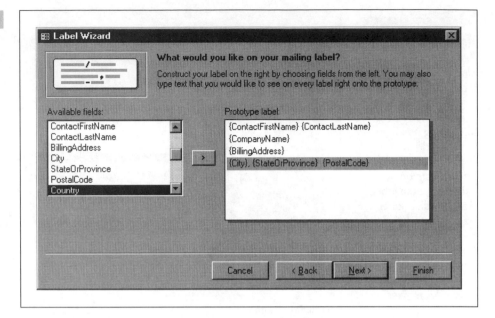

7. When asked which fields you want to sort on, select the fields in the order in which you want them sorted. For example, to sort customer labels for bulk mailing by zip/postal code, and then by last and first name within zip/postal code, double-click on Postal-Code, then double-click on ContactLastName, and then double-click on ContactFirstName. Click on Next to continue.

8. In the final dialog box, specify a name for your report or accept the selected name. The name must be unique, because the Label Wizard won't let you overwrite an existing mailing label report. Choose other options as needed (though the defaults usually are just fine), and then click on Finish.

WARNING   The title you select in step 8 is used for the report name, and the report's Caption property (which displays text on the report's title bar).

Access will create the mailing label report and display it on the screen.

N O T E If there isn't enough horizontal space to display the entire label format, Access will let you know. You can go to design view and tweak the report design as needed (see Chapter 13). Or, choose File ➤ Page Setup, click on the Layout tab, and then reduce the number of columns or the size of the columns.

Formatting Postal Codes and Phone Numbers

If you use the Access Wizards to create fields such as postal codes and phone numbers, the *input masks* cause values in those fields to be stored as text, without punctuation characters. The same input masks cause the appropriate punctuation marks to appear for those fields in forms and datasheets. For example, Access uses this input mask for PostalCode fields:

```
00000\-9999
```

And this input mask for PhoneNumber fields:

```
!\(999") "000\-0000
```

Although most reports created by the Wizards do take advantage of these input masks, the mailing labels don't. For example, a postal code might appear as either five numbers (85711) or nine numbers (857114747). A phone number might appear as 6195551234. To report those values in more readable formats, such as 85711-4747 for a postal code and (619)555-1234, you'll need to use the Format function in your reports.

For example, in design view for the mailing labels shown in Figure 12.7, we changed simple references to the postal code from [PostalCode] to:

```
Format ([PostalCode],"!@@@@@-@@@@")
```

To format a phone number field, such as [PhoneNumber], you could use this Format function:

```
Format ([PhoneNumber],"!(@@@) @@@-@@@@")
```

See Chapter 10 and look up *Format Function* in the Access Help index for more about formatting text (string) values.

Saving a Report

If the Wizard didn't save your report automatically, you should save the report if you want to use it later. Here's how:

1. To save and close the report, return to design view by clicking on the Close button on the print preview toolbar. Then, choose File ➤ Close or press Ctrl+W, and click on Yes. Or, if you just want to save your latest changes, press Ctrl+S, or choose File ➤ Save, or click on the Save toolbar button (shown at left).

2. The first time you save a report that hasn't been saved before, you'll be prompted to enter a name for it. Type a name (up to 64 characters, including blanks), and then click on OK.

Opening a Report

If you've closed a report, you can reopen it with these steps:

1. Start in the database window and click on the Reports tab.

2. Do one of the following:

   - **To open the report in print preview** (with data displayed), double-click on the report name you want to open, or click on it and then click on the Preview button.

   - **To open the report in design view** (where you can change the report's design), click on the report name and then click on the Design button.

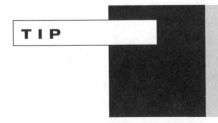

TIP

Copying offers a quick way to create a new report that's based on an existing report. To copy a report, click on the Reports tab in the database window, highlight the report to copy, and press Ctrl+C. Next, press Ctrl+V, type a name for the new report, and click on OK.

Removing a Filter and Sort Order

If your report is based on a table or query that you've filtered or sorted in datasheet view, the report will inherit the filter and sort order automatically and will be filtered or sorted anytime you preview or print it. You can remove the filter or sort from the report, by following these steps:

1. Open the report in design view.

2. Choose <u>V</u>iew ➤ <u>P</u>roperties if the property sheet isn't open. Click on the Data tab on the property sheet.

3. Choose <u>E</u>dit ➤ Select <u>R</u>eport to make sure you've selected the entire report.

4. Double-click on the Filter On property in the property sheet to change that property from Yes to No. If necessary, double-click on the Order On property to change it from Yes to No.

5. Save the report design (Ctrl+S).

The next time you preview or print the report, the records will not be filtered or sorted. If you later want to use the report with the filter and/or sorting, repeat the five steps above, except change the Filter On and/or Order On property from No to Yes in step 4.

Changing the Style for a Report

Just as you can change the overall style for forms, you also can change report's style without re-creating the report from scratch. It's easy:

1. Open the report in design view. If you're starting from the database window, click on the Reports tab, click on the report you want to change, and then click on the <u>D</u>esign button. Or, if you've switched to print preview from design view, click on the Close toolbar button (shown at left) or choose <u>V</u>iew ➤ Report <u>D</u>esign.

2. Choose F<u>o</u>rmat ➤ <u>A</u>utoFormat, or click on the AutoFormat button (shown at left) on the Report Design toolbar. You'll see the AutoFormat dialog box, shown in Figure 12.19.

FIGURE 12.19

Use the AutoFormat
dialog box to instantly
change the style for
your report or to
customize an existing
style. Switch to report
design view and
choose Format ➤
AutoFormat to open
this dialog box.

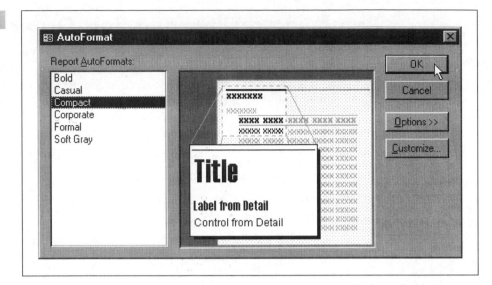

3. In the AutoFormat dialog box, choose the format you want to use, and then click on OK.

4. Save your changes (Ctrl+S) and click on the Report View toolbar button, or choose View ➤ Print Preview, to switch back to the print preview window.

Where to Go from Here

This chapter introduced the many types of instant reports you can create with the Report Wizards. From here, you can continue with Chapter 13 to learn how to design new reports and forms from scratch and how to customize existing reports and forms.

What's New in the Access Zoo?

The Report Wizards in Access for Windows 95 are more powerful and easier to use than the ones in Access 2.0. Here are some highlights:

- The Report Wizard lets you choose fields from multiple tables or queries and automatically figures out how to link the tables if you've already defined relationships between them. You don't have to create a multi-table query first.

- The Report Wizard lets you group and summarize your reports in a variety of ways. For example, you can group reports on up to four fields. You also can display sum, average, minimum, and maximum values for numeric and currency fields, display details and summaries or just summary information, and show percentages of totals for fields that you've summed.

- Reports automatically inherit filters and sort order from their source tables or queries.

- The AutoFormat feature lets you change the entire look of any report with a few mouse clicks.

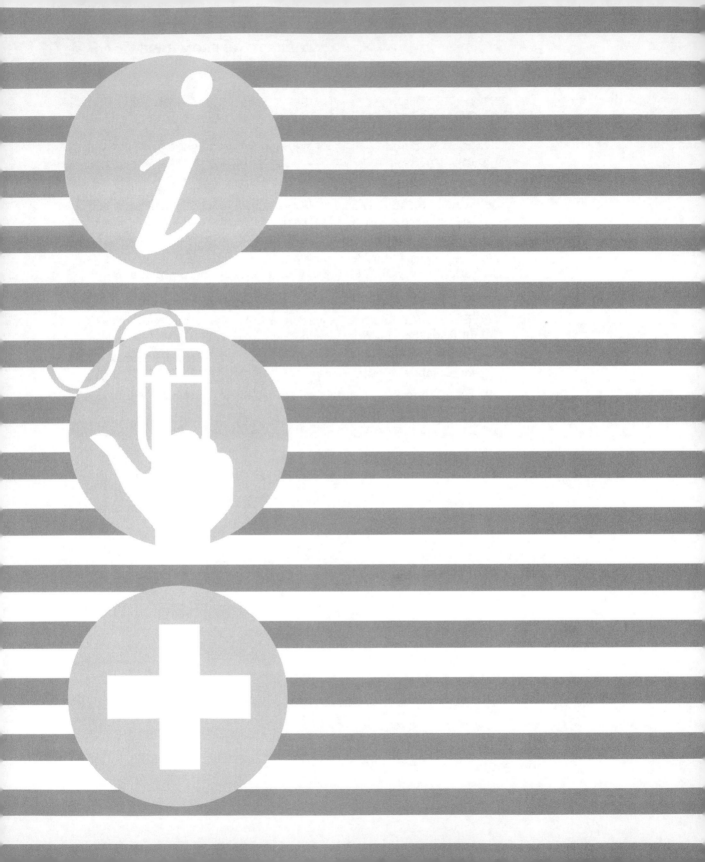

CHAPTER

13

Creating Custom Forms and Reports

ACCESS has some truly awesome tools for creating high-powered, good-looking forms and reports. If you've ever used a Windows drawing or painting package, you probably won't have any trouble learning to use the design tools. (If you've never used one of those programs, the mouse skills involved may take a little practice, but the overall process is still fairly simple.)

As you read this chapter, remember that you can customize the basic designs created by Form Wizards and Report Wizards (see Chapters 11 and 12), or you can create your own designs from scratch. If you're new to form and report design, you'll definitely want to start with a Wizard-created design so you can experiment with the design tools right away.

TIP

If you're planning to experiment extensively with Access form and report design tools, set up a new table—perhaps named All Field Types—that has one field for each data type that Access offers, and enter some records into it. Then use the Form Wizards and Report Wizards described in Chapters 11 and 12 to create a form or report that's based on fields in your "All Field Types" table.

Switching to Design View

To change the appearance of an existing form or report, you must switch to design view using any of these techniques:

- **To change a form or report that's not open,** go to the database window and click on the Forms or Reports tab (as appropriate) in the database window. Click on the name of the form or report you want to change and then click on the <u>D</u>esign button in the database window; or, right-click on the form or report name and choose Design.

- **To change a form or report that's open** on your screen, click on the Form View button (at left, top) on the Form Design toolbar or choose <u>V</u>iew ➤ Form <u>D</u>esign if you're editing a form, or the Close Window (Close) button (at left, bottom) on the Print Preview toolbar or choose <u>V</u>iew ➤ Report <u>D</u>esign if you're editing a report. Note that if you opened the report in print preview, clicking on the Close Window button will close the report; you'll need to open it as described above.

TIP The lessons in Chapter 3 gave you some hands-on practice with changing a form in form design view.

Remember that the tools for changing your form or report design are available in design view *only*. Therefore, except where the instructions specifically say to start from another view, be sure you're in design view before using any procedures described below.

TIP When working with forms and reports, it's a good idea to hide the taskbar temporarily. To do this, right-click on an empty area on the taskbar, choose <u>P</u>roperties, and select (check) Always On <u>T</u>op and A<u>u</u>to Hide. Then click on OK. See the sidebar titled "Maximizing Your On-Screen Real Estate" in Chapter 1 for more details.

Previewing and Saving Your Changes

As you work in design view, you'll want to preview your handiwork from time to time. To do that, click on the Form View toolbar button (if you're designing a form) or the Report View button (if you're designing a report). Those buttons are the first ones on the Form Design and Report Design toolbars.

You also can preview your form or report by choosing options on the View menu:

- To preview a form in form view, choose View ➤ Form.
- To preview a form in datasheet view, choose View ➤ Datasheet.
- To preview a report in print preview, choose View ➤ Print Preview.
- To preview a report in layout preview (which presents just enough sample data to show you what the report will look like), choose View ➤ Layout Preview. You also can switch to Layout Preview by clicking on the drop-down arrow on the Report View toolbar button and then choosing Layout Preview.

When you're ready to make more changes, go back to design view, as described in the previous section.

It's also a good idea to save your changes whenever you're happy with them. Simply click on the Save toolbar button (shown at left), or press Ctrl+S.

Creating a Form or Report from Scratch

Here's how to create an entirely new form or report, without using the Wizards.

1. Start from the database window, and use one of these techniques:

   - Click on the Forms or Reports tab in the database window and then click on the <u>N</u>ew button in the database window.
   - Click on the Tables or Queries tab, click on the table or query you want to attach to your form or report, and then click on the drop-down arrow next to the New Object toolbar button. Now, choose either New Form or New Report, as appropriate.

2. The New Form or New Report dialog box will open (see Figure 13.1 for an example of the New Form dialog box). To attach the form or report to a table or query, choose one from the drop-down list in the dialog box. You don't need to choose a table or query if you're creating an unbound form, such as a dialog box or a switchboard (see Chapter 21).

3. Click on the Design View option in the dialog box, and then click on OK (or double-click on Design View).

FIGURE 13.1

The New Form dialog box. The New Report dialog box is similar.

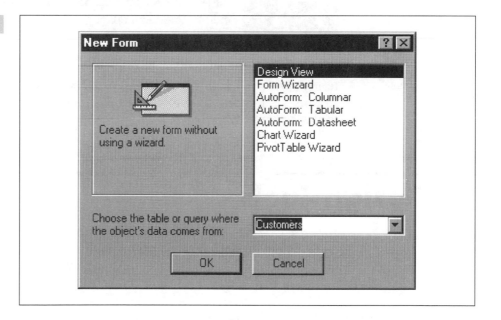

NOTE

If the datasheet for the table or query has a filter or sort associated with it, the new form or report will inherit the filter and sort order automatically. Chapter 9 explains how to add and apply filters and sorting in forms. "Removing a Filter and Sort Order" in Chapter 12 explains how to deactivate or activate the filter and sort for a report.

You'll be taken to a blank form or report window in design view. Think of this window as an empty canvas, on which you're free to create anything you want. Of course, you do need to understand the available tools and techniques before you start creating anything. That's what the rest of this chapter is all about.

TIP

To undo a mistake you've made in design view, press Ctrl+Z, or click on the Undo toolbar button, or choose Edit ➤ Undo immediately.

 ➤ For online details about the design process, go to the Access Help Contents, open the *Working With Forms*, or *Working With Controls On Forms Or Reports*, or *Working With Reports* book; then open additional books and topics as needed.

Design Tools

Figures 13.2 and 13.3 show an empty form and report, respectively, in design view. In both figures, we've maximized the design window to increase the available work space. Let's take a quick look at the design tools shown in the figures.

Choosing a Style for Your Design

Initially your form or report design will have a standard look, which works well for most people. However, Access comes with several predefined

FIGURE 13.2

An empty form
(maximized) in
design view

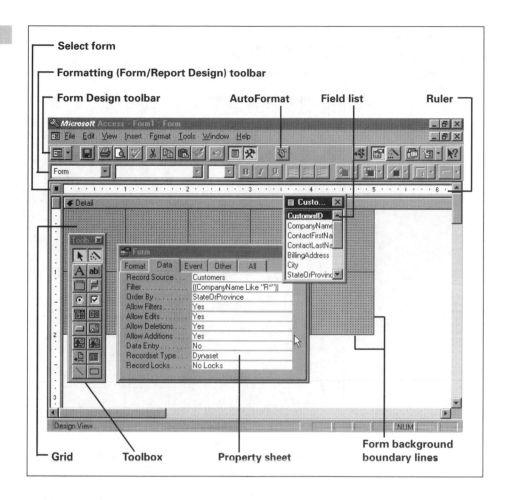

styles you can use to change the appearance of a form design's background and the font, color, and border of controls on a form or report.
As you'll learn later, you also can create custom styles of your own.

NOTE   *Control* is Access lingo for any graphical object on a
form or report that displays data, performs some action,
or makes the form or report easier to read.

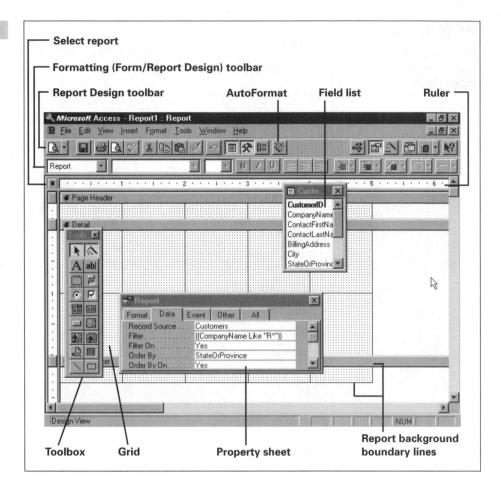

To choose a style for your design:

1. If you want your changes to apply to certain controls only, select those controls first (see "Selecting Controls, Sections, Forms, and Reports" later in this chapter). If you don't select controls first, Access will apply the new style to the entire design.

2. Choose Format ➤ AutoFormat, or click on the AutoFormat button (shown at left) on the Form Design or Report Design toolbar. The AutoFormat dialog box will open (see Figure 13.4).

3. In the Form AutoFormats or Report AutoFormats list, click on the style you want to use. The sample picture will change accordingly.

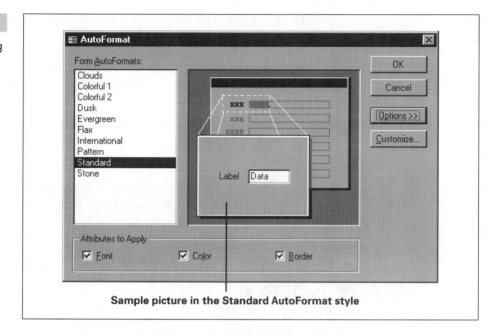

Sample picture in the Standard AutoFormat style

4. The new style usually affects the design's background and the Font, Color, and Border of controls. To change this behavior, click on the Options button. Then select (check) the styles you want to apply, or deselect (clear) styles you want to leave unchanged (see Figure 13.4). Again, the sample picture will reflect your changes.

5. Click on OK.

Access will apply the new style to the background of a form, to existing or selected controls, and to new controls. (Of course, you can change the style anytime you want a different look by repeating steps 1–5 above.)

If your design contains a control whose appearance isn't defined for the AutoFormat style you chose, an Update AutoFormat dialog box similar to this one will appear:

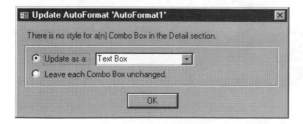

Choose one of these options, and then click on OK:

- **To update the current control with the style for another type of control** in the AutoFormat style, click on the drop-down arrow next to Update As A and then choose the control that has the style you want to use.

- **To leave the current control's appearance unchanged,** choose Leave Each *xxx* Unchanged (where *xxx* is the type of control that doesn't have a predefined style).

 For more about creating your own AutoFormat styles, see "Customizing AutoFormat Styles," later in this chapter. Or, look up *AutoFormat* and its subtopics in the Access Help Index.

The Field List, Design View Toolbars, and Toolbox

The field list, design toolbars, and toolbox (see Figures 13.2 and 13.3) are optional tools that you'll learn more about later in this chapter. Here's a crash course on what they do:

Design View Toolbars   The design view toolbars—Form Design or Report Design, Toolbox, and Formatting (Form/Report Design)—offer a treasure trove of menu shortcuts, formatting features, and design tools. You'll probably want to keep all these toolbars handy as you work.

Field List   Lists all the fields in the underlying table or query. To place a field, simply drag it from the field list to your design.

Toolbox   Provides tools for adding controls to your design.

TIP

The Formatting (Form/Report Design) toolbar lets you choose color, special effects, borders, and line thickness for a control. Many buttons on this toolbar work the same way as those on the Formatting (Datasheet) toolbar, described in "Customizing the Datasheet View" in Chapter 8.

For now, just knowing how to hide and display those tools (and the property sheet) is sufficient.

- **To display or hide the design toolbars**, right-click on any visible toolbar or the toolbox, and then choose the toolbar you want to display or hide. If no toolbars are visible, choose <u>V</u>iew ➤ Tool<u>b</u>ars, select (check) or deselect (clear) the toolbars you want to show or hide, respectively, and then click on the Close button in the Toolbars dialog box.

- **To display or hide the toolbox,** choose <u>V</u>iew ➤ <u>T</u>oolbox or click on the Toolbox button (shown at left) on the Form Design or Report Design toolbar.

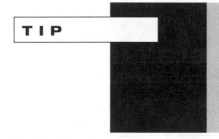

TIP   If you've hidden the toolbox and the toolbars, you can redisplay them without opening the Toolbars dialog box. First, choose <u>V</u>iew ➤ Toolbox. Next, right-click on the toolbox and choose Form Design or Report Design. Then right-click on the toolbox again and choose Formatting (Form/Report Design).

- **To display or hide the field list**, choose <u>V</u>iew ➤ Field <u>L</u>ist. Or, click on the Field List button (shown at left) on the Form Design or Report Design toolbar.

You can size and move the tools using these techniques:

- **To change a toolbar or toolbox to a floating palette of buttons**, double-click on an empty area within the tool. Or drag an *empty* area within the tool away from the edge of the screen, and release the mouse button.

- **To move a floating toolbar or toolbox**, drag its title bar.

- **To size a floating toolbar or toolbox**, drag any border.

- **To display a floating toolbar or toolbox as a single row or column** of buttons, double-click on an *empty* (non-button) area within the tool. Or drag the tool to an edge of the screen and, when the outline expands to the length of the edge you've dragged

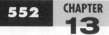

to, release the mouse button. (Sorry, you can't display the Formatting (Form/Report Design) toolbar in a single column at the left or right edge of the screen.)

> For details about working with toolbars, see "Using the Toolbars" in Chapter 1. To find out what a toolbar or toolbox button is for, point to it with your mouse and then look at the ToolTip below the mouse pointer and the status bar at the bottom of the screen. For online Help with toolbars, search for *Toolbars, Positioning* and *Toolbars, Showing And Hiding* in the Access Help Index.

The Property Sheet

You can use the *property sheet* (shown below) to view or change the properties of a selected control or controls, or of the entire report or form. The properties that appear on the property sheet depend on what part of the design you've selected.

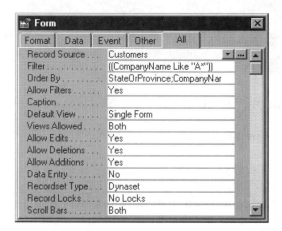

Like many tools in design view, the property sheet can be *toggled* on or off, displayed or hidden. To display or hide the property sheet, use any method below:

- Click on the Properties button (shown at left) on the Form Design or Report Design toolbar.
- Choose <u>V</u>iew ➤ <u>P</u>roperties from the menu bar.
- Right-click on any object and choose Properties.

TIP If the property sheet isn't visible, you can open it by double-clicking on an empty place on the design or by double-clicking on any control.

Changing a Property

To change a property:

1. Select the object or objects you want to change. (See "Selecting Controls, Sections, Forms, and Reports" later in this chapter.)

2. Open the property sheet as described above (View ➤ Properties).

3. Click on the tab for the type of properties you want to change. (Properties that don't make sense for all selected objects won't appear on the property sheet.) From left to right, the property tabs are:

> **Format** Lets you specify appearance properties. Format properties are changed automatically when you move or resize a control, and when you use the Formatting (Form/Report Design) toolbar buttons to customize a control.

> **Data** Lets you specify the source of the data, and the data's display format. On forms, Data properties control such things as default values, and allowable values. On reports, Data properties also control whether a text box shows a running sum.

> **Event** Lets you control what happens when certain events occur. For example, an On Click event property defines what happens when you click on a command button in form view. You'll learn more about event properties in Part Four of this book.

> **Other** This is a catch-all category for things such as the name of a control when it's used in expressions, macros, and procedures; the text that appears on the status bar when you select the control in form view; how the ↵ key behaves during data entry (see Chapter 8); whether the AutoCorrect feature is enabled (see Chapter 9); the custom shortcut menu that appears when you right-click on a form or control; and the ControlTip text that pops up when you point to the control in form view.

All Displays all available properties for the control. When you're not sure which tab contains the property you're looking for, click on the All tab.

4. Click in the text box next to the property you want to change. A drop-down list button and/or Build button (...) may appear.

TIP

When you select multiple controls and then change properties, your changes will affect all the selected controls. Thus, you can change the background color or font for an entire group of objects in one fell swoop. For another way to copy properties from one object to another, see "Copying Properties to Other Controls," later in this chapter.

5. Do one of the following:

- Type the property value you want. If you're entering lots of text into the box, you can press Shift+F2 (Zoom) to expand the box.

- Click on the drop-down button if one is provided, and choose the property from the list.

- Click on the Build button (...) if one is provided, and build an expression with help from a "builder" dialog box.

- Double-click in the text box to choose the next available property from the drop-down list. Double-clicking is especially handy for quickly flipping Yes/No values.

TIP

Take some time to explore the properties of controls on a form or report that you generate with a Wizard. To avoid becoming overwhelmed by the sheer number of properties available, look at the properties on the Format, Data, Event, and Other properties tabs separately, rather than trying to wade through all properties on the All tab.

➤ To learn more about what a property does, click in the appropriate property text box and look at the status bar at the bottom of the screen for a brief description. If you still need more details about the property, press F1.

The Ruler

The ruler is most helpful when you're sizing or moving objects by dragging. As you drag, a shadow on the ruler indicates the object's size and location. To hide or display the ruler:

- Choose View ➤ Ruler.

The Grid

You can use the grid to align objects on the design. To hide or display the grid:

- Choose View ➤ Grid.

NOTE   If you've turned on the grid, but can't see the grid dots, set the grid density to 24 or less (as described in a moment).

Snapping to the Grid

As you move and size objects on the screen, they'll usually snap (align) to points on the grid, making it easier for you to keep objects aligned. This will happen even if the grid isn't visible at the moment. To turn grid snap off:

- Choose Format ➤ Snap To Grid to activate or deactivate grid snap.
- Or, to disable grid snap temporarily, hold down the Ctrl key while moving or sizing an object.

Changing the Grid Density

The grid dots are visible only when the grid density is set to 24 or fewer dots per inch (and when Grid on the View menu is selected). To change the grid density:

1. Open the property sheet (View ➤ Properties) and click on the Format tab.

2. Select the form or report. To do so, choose Edit ➤ Select Form (if you're designing a form), or choose Edit ➤ Select Report (if you're designing a report). The property sheet shows properties for the form or report as a whole.

3. Scroll down to the Grid X and Grid Y properties, and set each to 24 or smaller. (The default setting is 24 for both properties.)

4. If you wish, close the property sheet.

Sizing Controls and Aligning Them to the Grid

To tidy up your design, you can size all the controls on the design and you can align them to the current grid. Here's how:

1. To select all the controls, choose Edit ➤ Select All (or press Ctrl+A).

2. Do either (or both) of the following:

   - **To size all the controls** so they touch the nearest grid-points, choose Format ➤ Size ➤ To Grid.
   - **To align all controls to the grid**, choose Format ➤ Align ➤ To Grid.

All the controls will size or align to their nearest grid mark. You can make additional changes using techniques described later under "Moving Controls" and "Resizing Controls."

Changing the Size of the Form or Report

If the grid is on, the form or report background shows cross-hair lines at 1-inch intervals. It also shows grid dots (if the grid density is 24 or less). Most important, the background shows the actual boundaries of the form or report (see Figures 13.2 and 13.3). If the form or report is too large or too small, you can change the size anytime you wish:

- **To change the width,** drag the right boundary line of the background to the left or right.

- **To change the height,** drag the bottom boundary line of the background up or down.

- **To change both the width and the height,** drag the lower-right boundary line diagonally.

Sizing the Background to Prevent Spillover Pages

If you want all your data to fit across a single page in a printed report, the background width *plus* the report margins must be less than (or equal to) the paper width.

To adjust the margins, choose File ➤ Page Setup from the design window's menu bar. Click on the Margins tab, use the Margins options in the dialog box to set margin widths (see Figure 13.5), and then click on OK.

N O T E

If you try to change the margins to some small number, and Access increases the width you specify, it's not a malfunction. Access is adjusting your entry to compensate for the printer's *dead zone*. The dead zone is the area at the outer edge of the page where the small wheels that pull the paper through the printer are located. The printer can't print in the dead zone.

FIGURE 13.5

The Page Setup dialog box

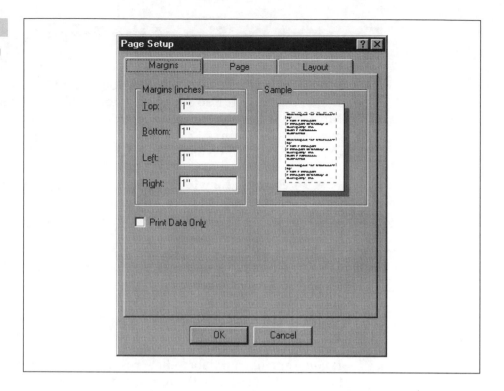

Designer Skills

Becoming an Access designer is a three-step process. First you must learn what tools are available in design view, then you must learn how to use them, and finally you must play with them until you can create any form or report your imagination can conjure up. The rest of this chapter should help you achieve the first two steps; the last step you'll have to do on your own.

Adding Bound Controls (Fields)

When you want to show data from the underlying table or query in your form or report, you should add a *bound control* to your design. The most commonly used bound controls are text boxes. (Bound controls are created automatically when you use a Form Wizard or Report Wizard.)

N O T E   *Unbound* controls can include results of calculations and objects such as informational text, graphics, lines, and boxes that aren't connected to underlying data. Some Wizards also add unbound controls to the designs they create.

To add a bound control to your design:

1. Display the field list if it's not visible (choose <u>V</u>iew ➤ Field <u>L</u>ist).

2. Use any of these techniques:

- **To add one field to the form or report,** drag the field from the field list to the place where it should appear in the design.

- **To copy all fields to your form or report at once,** double-click on the title bar in the field list, and then drag the selected fields to the design.

- **To copy several fields,** use standard Windows techniques (for example, Shift-click or Ctrl-click) to select multiple fields in the field list and then drag the selected fields to the design.

Access will create a text box, list box, check box, combo box, or bound OLE object control, depending on the data type and the Display Control property defined for the field in the underlying table design or query design. (The Display Control property is on the Lookup tab of the table design view property sheet; see Chapter 6.)

The control will include a label that displays either the field's name or whatever text you assigned to the field's Caption property in table design view. If you want to change the label text, click inside the label until the insertion point appears, and then edit the text (or select the label text and type new text to replace it).

Of course, you also can use other tools in the toolbox to create a bound control, but it's not as easy as dragging fields from the field list.

About Inherited Properties

The bound controls will inherit all the Lookup properties from the underlying table fields, along with these General properties: Format, Input Mask, Caption, Default Value, Validation Rule, Validation Text, and Decimal Places.

Even though the Default Value, Validation Rule, and Validation Text properties are inherited, you won't see their settings on the Data tab of a new control's property sheet. You can add a Validation Rule, Validation Text, and Default Value property to the control on the form if you wish. If you do so, Access uses the form's Validation Rule and Validation Text *in addition* to the underlying table's validation rule for the associated field. The Default Value property assigned on the form will override the table's Default Value property.

Selecting Controls, Sections, Forms, and Reports

Before you can change, move, or delete objects in the design, you must select them. The first step is to click on the Select Objects toolbox button (shown at left), so that it appears "pushed in." Then use any of these techniques:

- **To select one control,** click on the control. Sizing and move handles will appear, as shown in Figure 13.6.

- **To select adjacent controls,** start at any point outside a control and drag a rectangle over the controls you want to select.

FIGURE 13.6

A selected control. This example shows the parts of a text box, which is a *compound control* that has both a label and a field.

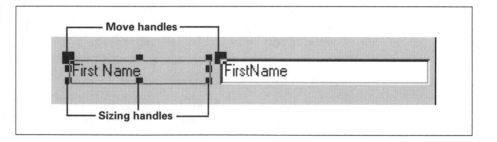

TIP

To control how precise you must be when dragging the selection rectangle over adjacent controls, choose <u>T</u>ools ➤ <u>O</u>ptions and then click on the Forms/Reports tab in the Options dialog box. Next choose either <u>P</u>artially Enclosed (lets you drag the rectangle through only part of a control or group of controls) or F<u>u</u>lly Enclosed (requires you to drag the rectangle completely around the control or group of controls). Click on OK to save your changes.

- **To select nonadjacent controls,** parts of compound controls (such as a field and its label), or overlapping controls, hold down the Shift key and click on each control you want to select. This standard Windows technique is called *Shift-clicking*.

- **To use the ruler to select controls,** move the mouse pointer to the horizontal or vertical ruler. (The pointer changes to a ↓ or →, respectively.) Then click on the line that goes through all the controls you want to select. Or drag the mouse along the ruler until shading encloses the controls you want to select, and then release the mouse button.

- **To select a section in a form or report,** click on the gray bar that shows the section name. (You'll learn more about sections shortly.)

- **To select all controls on a form or report,** choose <u>E</u>dit ➤ Select <u>A</u>ll or press Ctrl+A.

- **To select the entire form or report,** choose <u>E</u>dit ➤ Select For<u>m</u> or <u>E</u>dit ➤ Select <u>R</u>eport. Or, if the rulers are visible, click on the box where the rulers intersect (below the <u>F</u>ile menu). Or, click on the Select Objects drop-down list (shown at left) on the Formatting (Form/Report Design) toolbar, and then choose Form or Report from the top of the list.

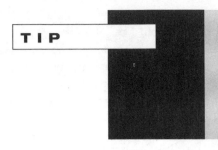

TIP If the property sheet "blanks out" suddenly when you click on a control that's already selected, you can restore the property display in either of two ways: press ↵ if you want to keep any changes you've typed into the control; or press Escape if you don't mind discarding any changes you've typed in.

Here's how to deselect controls:

- **To deselect all selected controls,** click in an empty area of the design.

- **To deselect certain controls in a group of selected controls,** Shift-click on the controls you want to deselect.

Working with Selected Controls

Once you've selected a control (or a group of controls), you can delete, move, resize, or align your selection and change spacing between selected controls.

Deleting Controls

To delete controls:

- Select the controls you want to delete and press Delete. If you change your mind, immediately choose Edit ➤ Undo, or press Ctrl+Z, or click on the Undo button on the Form Design or Report Design toolbar.

To delete just the label portion of a compound control, click on the label and press Delete.

TIP To hide the label temporarily without deleting it, change the label's Visible property to No on the Format tab of the property sheet.

Moving Controls

You can position controls anywhere on the design. Select the control or controls you want to move, and then...

- **To move entire selected controls,** pass the mouse pointer over the controls until the pointer changes to an open hand, and then drag the selection to a new position. (To move controls to a different *section* of the report or form, make sure all selected controls are in the same section, and then drag them to the new location.)

- **To move part of a selected compound control,** pass the mouse pointer over the *move handle* in the upper-left corner of the control until it changes to an upward-pointing hand, and then drag the control to a new position.

T I P   You can hold down the Shift key while dragging to move the control vertically or horizontally only.

- **To move a selected control by a very small amount,** press Ctrl+→, Ctrl+←, Ctrl+↑, or Ctrl+↓. The control will move in the direction of the arrow key you pressed while holding down the Ctrl key.

Resizing Controls

If a control is too large or too small, you can resize it in various ways. As always, you begin by selecting the control or controls you want to change.

- **To resize selected controls,** move the mouse pointer to a sizing handle (the pointer changes to a two-headed arrow), drag the sizing handle until the controls are the proper size, and then release the mouse button. If you've selected multiple controls, all controls will be resized by the same amount.

- **To size selected controls so that their data will fit the contents,** choose Format ➤ Size ➤ To Fit.

- **To size selected controls to the nearest grid mark,** choose Format ➤ Size ➤ To Grid.

- **To resize a label control to fit snugly around the label text,** double-click on one of the label's sizing handles.

- **To make selected controls the same size,** choose Format ➤ Size, and then pick To Tallest, To Shortest, To Widest, or To Narrowest. Access will resize all selected controls according to the option you chose (for example, all selected controls will be as tall as the tallest control in the selection).

- **To size selected controls by a very small amount,** press Shift+→, Shift+←, Shift+↑, or Shift+↓.

Aligning Controls

Your forms and reports will look much nicer if text and data are neatly aligned. Here's how to align controls:

1. Select the controls you want to line up.

2. Choose Format ➤ Align from the menus, or right-click on a selected control and choose Align.

3. Choose Left, Right, Top, Bottom, or To Grid, as appropriate. For example, if you choose Format ➤ Align ➤ Left, all selected controls will align with the leftmost control in the selection.

NOTE

If selected controls are overlapping when you align them, Access will place the controls in a staggered arrangement, which probably isn't what you want. It's best to make sure the controls don't overlap *before* you try to align them.

Adjusting the Horizontal and Vertical Spacing

You can further fine-tune your design by adjusting the horizontal and vertical spacing between two or more selected controls:

1. Select the controls you want to adjust. If you want to space the controls an equal distance apart, select three or more controls.

2. To adjust horizontal spacing between selected controls, choose Format ➤ Horizontal Spacing. To adjust vertical spacing, choose Format ➤ Vertical Spacing.

3. Choose one of these spacing options:

Make Equal   Makes the horizontal or vertical distance between three or more selected controls equal. Access will space the selected controls evenly within the space that's available between the highest (or leftmost) and the lowest (or rightmost) selected control.

Increase   Increases the horizontal or vertical space between selected controls by one grid point.

Decrease   Decreases the horizontal or vertical space between selected controls by one grid point.

Duplicating Controls

The Duplicate feature offers a quick and easy way to create an evenly spaced and aligned copy of one or more selected controls. Simply select the control(s) you want to duplicate, and choose Edit ➤ Duplicate (or right-click on the selection and choose Duplicate). You can then resize or move the copied control, or change its properties, as desired.

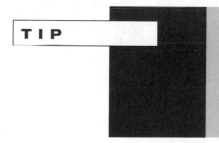

TIP

To create multiple copies of one or more controls with the same relative spacing and position for each copy, duplicate the control(s) once, adjust the spacing and position as needed (without making any other changes), and then make as many duplicates of the still-selected controls as you need.

Changing the Font, Color, Border, Appearance, and More

The Formatting (Form/Report Design) toolbar (see Figure 13.7) provides many great ways to beautify a control. You can change the text font and alignment; add foreground, background, and border colors; add special effects such as a raised, sunken, or etched border; and choose border width.

Follow these steps to work with this toolbar:

1. If the toolbar isn't visible, right-click on any toolbar that is visible and choose Formatting (Form/Report Design). If no toolbar is visible, choose View ➤ Toolbars, select (check) Formatting (Form/Report Design), and then click on Close.

2. Select the control or controls you want to customize.

3. In the Formatting (Form/Report Design) toolbar, click on a button or click on the drop-down arrow next to a button and then choose an option to apply the effect you want. (In the Back Color and Border Color drop-down palettes, clicking on the Transparent button makes the selected control transparent, so that the color shown in the control is the same as the color of the control, section, or form behind it.) As usual, you can find out what a button is for by moving the mouse pointer to the button and waiting a moment for a ToolTip to appear.

TIP

After pulling down the Back Color, Fore Color, Border Color, Border Width, or Special Effect palettes on the toolbar, you can drag them off the toolbar to leave them open as you work. To return any palette to the toolbar, click on the drop-down arrow for its toolbar button, or click on the palette's Close button.

NOTE

Instead of using the toolbar, you can select the control(s) and change format properties in the property sheet; but that's doing it the hard way (unless the property sheet offers additional features that aren't available on the toolbar). For example, you can select from 16 million different colors by using the property sheet, instead of only the 56 different colors shown in the color palettes.

FIGURE 13.7

Use the Formatting (Form/Report Design) to choose fonts, text alignment, colors, borders, and special effects for a control. In this example, we've clicked on the drop-down arrow next to the Border Color button.

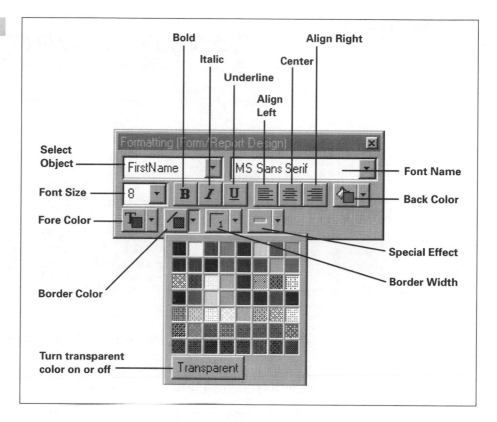

Controlling the Tab Order

The *tab order* controls the order in which the cursor moves through fields on a form when you press the Tab and Shift+Tab keys. After you've re-arranged fields in a form, the current tab order may seem jumbled when you use the form in form view. To fix the tab order, follow these steps:

1. In form design view, choose View ➤ Tab Order. You'll see a Tab Order dialog box similar to the example shown in Figure 13.8.

2. In the Section group, select the section you want to redefine (for example, choose Detail).

3. To have Access quickly set the tab order from left to right and top to bottom, click on the Auto Order button.

FIGURE 13.8

The Tab Order
dialog box

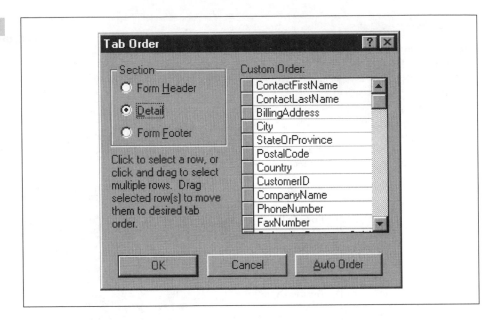

4. To assign the tab order manually, click on or drag through the row
   selector(s) for the rows you want to reposition. Then move the
   mouse pointer to one of the selected row selectors and drag the
   row or rows to a new position in the Custom Order list.

5. Repeat steps 3 and 4 as needed, and then click on OK.

In form view, pressing Tab will now move the cursor forward in the new
tab order. Pressing Shift+Tab will move the cursor backward in the
new tab order.

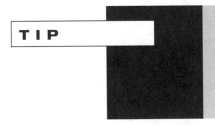

TIP

To prevent the cursor from landing on a control when
you press Tab or Shift+Tab in form view, return to form
design view and set the Tab Stop property for that
control to No. You'll find this property on the Other tab
of the property sheet.

Copying Properties to Other Controls

Suppose you've formatted a control just the way you want it, and now want other controls to have the same look. Making this happen is quick and easy:

1. Select the control that has the formatting you want to copy to another control.

2. Do one of the following:

- **To copy the format to one other control**, *click* on the Format Painter button (shown at left) on the Form Design or Report Design toolbar.

- **To copy the format to several other controls**, *double-click* on the Format Painter button.

3. Click on the control that should have the new format.

4. If you double-clicked on the Format Painter button in step 2, continue clicking on other controls that should have the new format. When you're done copying the format, press Esc or click on the Format Painter button again.

The format painter will copy any formatting properties that you can set via the Formatting (Form/Report Design) Toolbar, and almost every property that you can set via the Format tab on the property sheet. Pretty nifty!

Adding Help, Menus, and Prompts to Controls

By now, you've probably taken advantage of status bar prompts, shortcut menus, and ToolTips to help you figure out what to do next or to do something more quickly. Guess what? You can add these conveniences to any control on your form, just by updating properties on the Other tab of the property sheet.

NOTE

When you drag names from the field list to your design, Access automatically fills in the Status Bar Text property with any text that appears in the Description column for that field in table design view. If the Description is blank, the Status Bar Text also will be blank.

To set up custom help text and shortcut menus that will appear in form view, select the control you want to customize (in form design view), open the property sheet (View ➤ Properties), and then click on the property sheet's Other tab. Now assign values to any of these properties. Figure 13.9 shows a completed example:

Status Bar Text Displays a message on the status bar when the cursor lands in the control.

Shortcut Menu Bar Displays a custom shortcut menu when you right-click on the control. Chapter 24 explains how to create custom shortcut menus.

FIGURE 13.9

A memo field to which we've assigned Status Bar Text, Shortcut Menu Bar, and ControlTip Text properties.

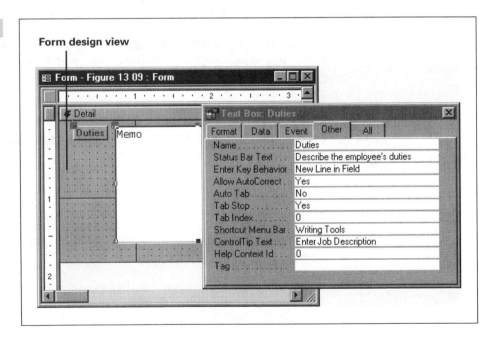

ControlTip Text   Displays a pop-up message when you point to the control with the mouse. ControlTips are similar to the ToolTips that appear when you point to toolbar buttons.

Help Context ID   Displays information from a custom Help file that's named in the Help File property (the Help File property appears on the Other tab when you select the entire form). The custom Help will appear if you move the focus to (click on) the control in form view and then press F1. You can create a custom Help file using Microsoft's Windows Help Compiler and a rich-text format text editor, such as Microsoft Word for Windows or the Windows WordPad. Many third-party companies also offer Help authoring tools.

N O T E   The Windows Help Compiler and the *Help Compiler Guide* come with the Microsoft Access Developer's Toolkit, Microsoft Visual Basic, Microsoft Visual C++, and the Microsoft Software Development Kit (SDK). Please contact Microsoft for more information about these tools.

Figure 13.10 shows the form from Figure 13.9, after we switched to form view, clicked in the field, and let the mouse pointer rest in the field for a moment. Right-clicking on the field would display a menu of options from our Writing Tools shortcut menu (not shown).

 For more about any of these "helpful" properties, open the property sheet (<u>V</u>iew ➤ <u>P</u>roperties), click on the Other tab, click in the appropriate property box, and then press F1.

Customizing AutoFormat Styles

You can customize existing AutoFormat styles, add new styles, and delete unwanted styles in a flash. Any new styles you add will be available to the Form Wizards and Report Wizards, and in the AutoFormat dialog box shown back in Figure 13.4.

FIGURE 13.10

The field from Figure 13.9, in form view. Notice the status bar text at the bottom of the screen and the ControlTip text near the mouse pointer.

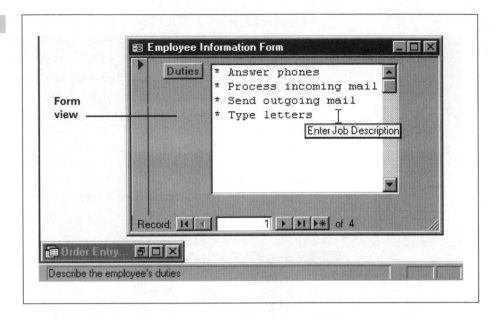

To add, change, or delete the AutoFormat styles:

1. If you want to create a new style or update an existing style with formatting from the current form or report, customize the font, color, and border controls in each section as needed. You also can set background colors for each section and choose a Picture for the form background. (For more about displaying background pictures, see "Adding a Background Picture" later in this chapter.)

2. Go to the AutoFormat dialog box (see Figure 13.4). To do so, click on the AutoFormat button on the Form Design or Report Design toolbar, or choose Format ➤ AutoFormat.

3. If you want to update or delete an existing AutoFormat, click on that format in the Form AutoFormats or Report AutoFormats list.

4. Click on the Customize button in the dialog box. You'll see a Customize AutoFormat dialog box similar to this one:

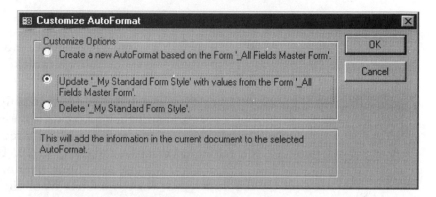

5. Choose one of the three options shown, using these guidelines:

- **To create a new AutoFormat style** based on formats in your current form or report, choose the first option.

- **To update the selected AutoFormat** with formats from your current form or report, choose the second option.

- **To delete the selected AutoFormat,** choose the third option.

6. Click on OK, and then click on Close.

Specifying the Record Source on the Fly

If you've accidentally chosen the wrong source for data in your report or form, or you wish to change it, here's what to do:

1. Open the property sheet (View ➤ Properties), and click on the Data tab.

2. Select the entire form or report (Edit ➤ Select Form or Edit ➤ Select Report).

3. Click on the Record Source property box on the property sheet's Data tab. A drop-down list button and a Build (...) button will appear.

4. Do one of the following:

- Type the table name or query name of the record source into the property box, or choose a table or query from the drop-down list.

- If you'd like to build a query on the fly, click on the Build (...) button, and click on Yes if a message appears. Define a query that selects and displays the records you want, using techniques discussed in Chapter 10. Test and save the query if you wish. When you're done defining the query, choose File ➤ Close (or press Ctrl+W, or click on the Close button in the SQL Statement dialog box) and answer Yes if prompted to save your changes. Press ↵ to move the cursor to the next property box. An SQL statement will appear in the Record Source property box; this SQL code is just an equivalent way to express the query.

5. Preview the report or switch to form view.

 ➤ If you see **#Name?** or **#Error?** in a control, that control has become undefined as a result of your efforts in step 4. Return to design view, delete the incorrect or extraneous control(s), and drag the appropriate field(s) from the field list to your design. Or, open the property sheet in design view (View ➤ Properties), select the control you want to change, click on the Control Source box on the property sheet's Data tab, and type in or select the appropriate field or expression.

For more information about troubleshooting #Name? and #Error? problems, look up *Troubleshooting Forms* in the Access Help Index or Answer Wizard, double-click on *Troubleshoot Forms*, and then click on the button next to *I Need Help Troubleshooting Problems With Controls On My Form*.

Sections, Headers, and Footers

All reports and forms are divided into the sections described below, to help you control what appears where on the finished form or report. We'll show some examples in a moment.

Form Sections

Forms are divided into as many as five sections:

Form Header   Always visible at the top of a form; printed only on the first page.

Page Header   Printed at the top of each page when you print forms (never visible in form view).

Detail   Generally used to show fields (data) from an underlying table or query.

Page Footer   Printed at the bottom of printed forms only. Never visible in form view.

Form Footer   Always visible on the bottom of the form window; printed only on the last page.

Figure 13.11 shows the design view for a completed form, with a form header and footer, page header and footer, and detail section. Figure 13.12 shows the same form in form view. Remember that page headers and footers appear only on printed copies of the form and in print preview, so you'll never see them in form view. In Figure 13.13, you see the same form in print preview, with its page header clearly visible (to see the *Confidential! Secret!...* page footer in print preview, click on the form to make it fit on the page, or use the vertical scroll bar to scroll to the bottom of the form).

Report Sections

Reports can have sections similar to those in forms. But reports also can have grouping sections, which allow you to break data into separate

FIGURE 13.11

A sample form in design view, illustrating the various sections.

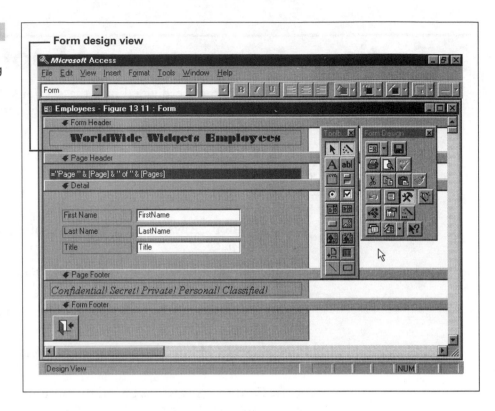

groups. Each group can have its own header and footer. Here's a summary of the sections:

Report Header   Printed once, at the beginning of the report (*Example:* a cover page).

Page Header   Printed at the top of each page.

Group Header   Printed at the top of each group.

Detail   Printed once for each record in the underlying table or query.

Group Footer   Printed at the bottom of each group (often used to place subtotals at the end of each printed group).

Page Footer   Printed at the bottom of each page.

Report Footer   Printed once at the end of the report. Often used to display grand totals at the end of a report that includes subtotals.

FIGURE 13.12

The design shown in
Figure 13.11 looks like
this in form view.

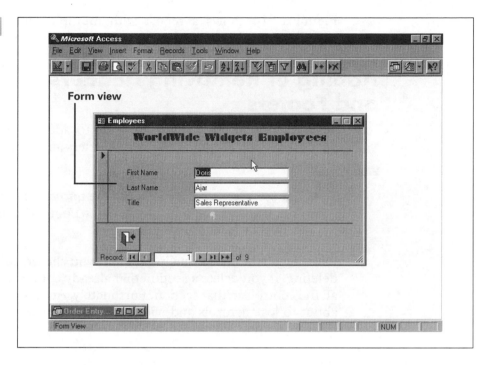

FIGURE 13.13

In print preview (and
in printed copies of the
form), the design
shown in Figure 13.11
looks like this.
Although it's cut off on
this figure, the
*Confidential! Secret!
Private! Personal!
Classified!* page footer
also will appear at the
bottom of each page
in print preview and
on the printed copies.

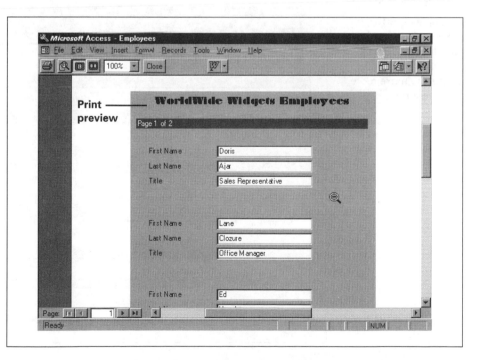

Figure 13.14 shows a report with multiple sections in design view, and Figure 13.15 shows the printed report.

Adding or Removing Headers and Footers

The View menu provides commands to add and remove report page headers and footers, and form page headers and footers. Adding a header or footer section is easy:

- Choose View, and then choose the *unchecked command* for the section you want to add (Page Header/Footer, Form Header/Footer, or Report Header/Footer).

Deleting a section is equally easy, but you should think carefully before deleting. If you delete a section that already contains controls, you'll lose all the controls in that section. Fortunately, Access will warn you if you're about to lose controls and will give you a chance to change your mind. (This operation has no "undo.")

FIGURE 13.14

A sample report showing sections of a report design. In this example, we hid the toolbars to make more of the report visible.

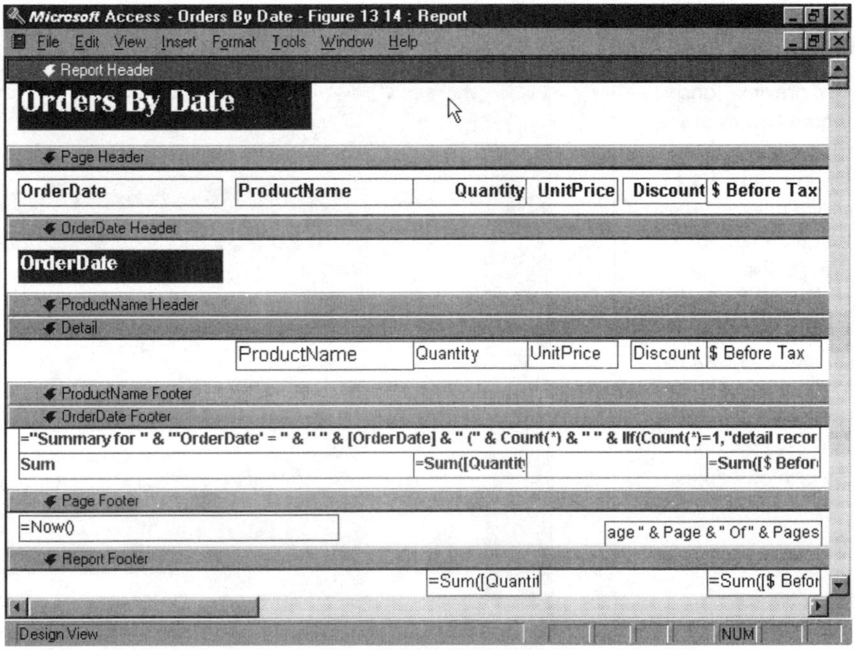

FIGURE 13.15

The report produced by the design in Figure 13.14. This report is sorted and grouped on the OrderDate and ProductName fields (although, the ProductName group header and footer are empty). The report header, page header, group header, detail, group footer, and page footer sections are labeled.

Group footer   **Page header**

    Group header   **Report header**

Orders By Date

OrderDate	ProductName	Quantity	UnitPrice	Discount	$ Before Tax
2/1/95					
	Basketball	1	$4.95	0.00%	$4.95
	Basketball	2	$4.95	0.00%	$9.90
	Billiard balls	2	$127.45	0.00%	$254.90
	Crystal ball	2	$45.55	0.00%	$91.10
	Foosball	4	$17.85	0.00%	$71.40
	Football	1	$5.65	0.00%	$5.65
	Football	1	$5.65	0.00%	$5.65
	Football	2	$5.65	0.00%	$11.30
	Tether ball	5	$9.65	0.00%	$48.25

Summary for 'OrderDate' = 2/1/95 (9 detail records)
Sum   20 $503.10

2/11/95					
	Baseball	2	$8.75	0.00%	$17.50
	Basketball	1	$4.95	0.00%	$4.95
	Basketball	2	$4.95	0.00%	$9.90
	Football	1	$5.65	0.00%	$5.65

Summary for 'OrderDate' = 2/11/95 (4 detail records)
Sum   6 $38.00

2/18/95					
	Crystal ball	1	$45.55	0.00%	$45.55
	Golf balls	1	$6.75	0.10%	$6.74

Summary for 'OrderDate' = 2/18/95 (2 detail records)
Sum   2 $52.29

Wednesday, September 06, 1995   Page 1 Of 5

Page footer   **Detail**

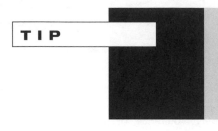

> **TIP**
>
> It's a good idea to save your design (File ➤ Save or Ctrl+S) before you delete a section. That way, if you accidentally delete the wrong section, you can close your design without saving it (File ➤ Close ➤ No), and then reopen the previous copy in design view.

To delete a section:

- Choose <u>V</u>iew, and then choose the *checked command* for the section you want to delete. If Access asks for confirmation, click on <u>Y</u>es only if you're sure you want to delete all the controls in that section.

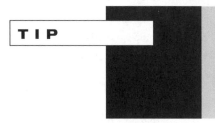

> **TIP**
>
> You can move controls to another section of the form or report before deleting the section (see "Moving Controls" above for details). You also can resize a section, as explained later in this chapter under "Sizing a Section."

Grouping Data in Reports

You can group data in reports (but not in forms) by creating Sorting And Grouping sections. These sections are handy for sorting data and printing subtotals, as shown earlier in Figure 13.15.

Sorting And Grouping sections differ from the other sections described above in that:

- You can use Sorting And Grouping sections only in reports (not forms).

- You don't use the <u>V</u>iew menu to add or remove sorting and grouping headers or footers.

- A Sorting And Grouping header or footer is often based on some field from the underlying table or query, or some expression that involves a field.

The Easy Way to Create Groups/Subtotals

The easiest way to create a report with sorting and grouping sections is to start from the database window and use the Report Wizards to create the report (see Chapter 12). When the Wizard is done, your report design will include the sorting and grouping sections and controls needed to print subtotals, grand totals, and percentage totals. You can then switch to design view and tweak the report groupings to perfection.

Grouping without a Wizard

If you prefer to set up sorting and grouping sections without any help from a Wizard, follow these steps:

1. In report design view, click on the Sorting And Grouping button (shown at left) on the Report Design toolbar, or choose <u>V</u>iew ➤ Sorting And Grouping from the menus. You'll see the Sorting And Grouping dialog box. A completed example is shown in Figure 13.16.

FIGURE 13.16

The report from Figure 13.15, shown in design view, with the Sorting And Grouping dialog box open on the screen

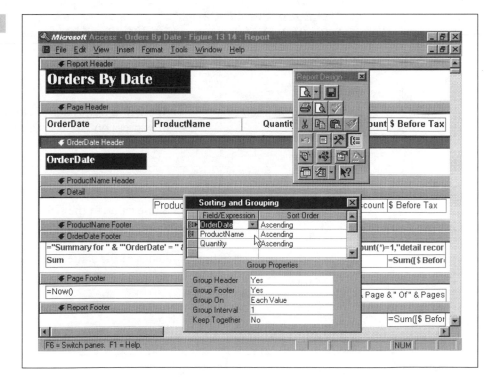

2. Use the drop-down list under Field/Expression to select the field to group by, or type a custom expression of your own.

3. To arrange groups from largest-to-smallest order (for example, from Z to A, or from December to January), change the Sort Order from Ascending to Descending.

4. Change these properties in the lower pane of the dialog box, as needed:

> **Group Header**   To create a header section for the group, change the Group Header property from No to Yes.
>
> **Group Footer**   To create a footer section for the group, change the Group Footer property from No to Yes.
>
> **Group On**   To choose how you want to form the groups, select options from the Group On drop-down list. The available options depend on the type of field you're grouping on, as summarized in Table 13.1.

TABLE 13.1: Group On Properties for Various Field Types

CHOOSE THIS GROUP ON PROPERTY	TO GROUP RECORDS ON
Text Fields	
Each Value	Same value in the field or expression
Prefix Characters	Same first n number of characters in the field or expression (set n with the Group Interval property)
Date/Time Fields	
Each Value	Same value in the field or expression
Year	Dates in the same calendar year
Qtr	Dates in the same calendar quarter
Month	Dates in the same month
Week	Dates in the same week
Day	Dates on the same day

TABLE 13.1: Group On Properties for Various Field Types (continued)

CHOOSE THIS GROUP ON PROPERTY	TO GROUP RECORDS ON
Hour	Dates in the same hour
Minute	Dates in the same minute
AutoNumber, Currency, or Number Fields	
Each Value	Same value in the field or expression
Interval	Values that fall in the interval you specify in the Group Interval property

Group Interval   To change the interval or number of characters to group on, type a number into the Group Interval box. For instance, to group records by the first three letters of a customer's last name, change Group On to Prefix Characters and set the Group Interval to 3.

Keep Together   To prevent a group that's less than a page in length from being split across two pages, change this property from No to Whole Group (keep the entire group together) or With First Detail (keep just the group header and first detail record together).

5. If you wish, add any of the following to the header or footer section: fields from the field list, calculated controls (for subtotals and totals), horizontal lines, rectangles, and page breaks. See "Creating Calculated Controls" and "Adding Page Breaks" later in this chapter for more about those topics.

Creating More than One Group

You can add more than one level of grouping, if you wish. For instance, you might want to group orders first by OrderDate and then by ProductName within OrderDate, and then by Quantity within ProductName, as shown in Figure 13.16.

To add another level, open the Sorting And Grouping dialog box. Click in the Field/Expression column where you want the new group to appear in the grouping hierarchy. If you need to open up a new row in the dialog box, click on the row selector where the blank row should appear, and then press Insert. Now fill in the Field/Expression, Sort Order, and Group Properties as described above.

Deleting, Moving, or Changing a Group Header/Footer

You can hide, delete, or move a grouping section, and you can change the field or expression used for grouping, as follows:

- **To hide a group header or footer section (but keep the grouping),** click in the appropriate row in the Sorting And Grouping dialog box. Then change the row's Group Header or Group Footer property (as appropriate) to No. Records will still be grouped and sorted as before, but the selected group header or footer for this section won't be printed.

- **To delete a grouping section**, click on the appropriate row selector in the Sorting And Grouping window, press the Delete key, and click on <u>Y</u>es when asked for confirmation. Records will no longer be grouped or sorted by the field or expression, and any group headers and footers for this section will disappear from the report.

- **To move a grouping section,** click on the appropriate row selector in the Sorting And Grouping window and then drag the selected row up or down to a new position in the grouping hierarchy. Access will rearrange the group header and footer sections in the report design immediately.

- **To change the field or expression used for grouping,** click in the appropriate Field/Expression box in the Sorting And Grouping dialog box. Then select another field name from the Field/Expression drop-down list or type in a different expression. To change the field displayed in the group header or footer section, delete the old field from the appropriate section in the report design and then drag a new one from the field list. Or select the control and change its Control Source data property.

Hiding Duplicate Data in a Report

The sample report in Figure 13.15 and the corresponding report design in Figure 13.16 illustrate how the Sorting And Grouping feature can hide duplicate data. In those examples, we placed the OrderDate control in the

OrderDate Header section (*not* in the Detail section). That way, the order date information appears only when the order date changes, not on every detail line.

There's another way to hide duplicate data in a report, one that doesn't require the Sorting And Grouping feature. Here are the steps:

1. Base the report on a query or table datasheet that's sorted by the field you want to group on, or create the query on the fly, as discussed earlier in "Specifying the Record Source on the Fly."

2. Put the bound control for the group header in the detail section of the report. In Figure 13.17, for example, we put CompanyName in the detail section and used it as a sort field.

3. Open the property sheet (View ➤ Properties), click on the control whose duplicate values you want to hide, and change the Hide Duplicates property on the Format tab to Yes. You also might want to change the Can Shrink property to Yes (to eliminate blank lines during printing) and the Can Grow property to Yes (to allow text such as the company name to expand as needed). Here's a sample property sheet with these properties set:

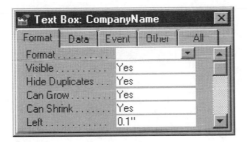

Sizing a Section

Keep in mind that blank space in a form or report design *always* shows up as blank space in the final form or report. Suppose you leave a blank, 2"-high page footer section at the bottom of a report design. Later, when you print the report, every page will have two extra inches of blank space at the bottom!

FIGURE 13.17

A report that's sorted by CompanyName, OrderDate, and OrderID and suppresses duplicate values in all three fields. We used the Report Wizard to create an ungrouped Tabular report on the Customers and Orders tables, and then changed the report's Record Source on the fly to sort each field in Ascending order.

Orders by Customer

Company Name	Order Date	Order ID
ABC Corporation	2/1/95	1
	3/14/95	2
	4/18/95	3
	5/21/95	4
	6/25/95	5
Reese Clinic	2/18/95	11
	2/25/95	12
	3/26/95	13
	4/15/95	14
	5/1/95	15
RNAA Associates	2/1/95	6
	4/1/95	7
	4/9/95	8
	5/11/95	9
	6/12/95	10
University of the Elite	2/1/95	21
	4/1/95	22
	5/7/95	23
	6/28/95	24

Monday, September 11, 1995   Page 1 Of 2

To fix the problem, change the height of the section as follows:

- Move the mouse pointer to the divider at the bottom of the section. When the pointer changes to a cross-hair (shown below), drag the divider up or down; then release the mouse button.

A section can't be made smaller than the space required by the controls within that section. If you can't make a section as narrow as you'd like, first size and/or move the controls in the section so that they take up less height. Then resize the section again.

Summarizing Your Data by Hiding a Section

Suppose you've set up a report with detail lines, subtotals, and totals. Now you want to show *only* those subtotals and totals, without the detail lines. This type of report is called a *summary report* because it summarizes your data without providing unwanted details. That is, summary reports let you focus on the forest (your bottom line), while conserving the trees (paper).

In Chapter 12, you learned how to use the Report Wizards, which can produce summary reports quite easily. But you also can set up summary reports (or hide any section in a form or report) without using a Wizard. The secret is simply to hide or delete information in the appropriate section, using either of these methods:

- Click on the band at the top of the section you want to hide. (For example, click on the Detail band to hide detail lines in a summary report.) Now open the property sheet (<u>V</u>iew ➤ <u>P</u>roperties), click on the Format tab, and change the section's Visible property to No. This method leaves all the controls in the section, but doesn't show the contents of the section in the finished form or report. If you change your mind about hiding the information in the section, just click on the section's band again, open the property sheet, click on the Format tab, and change the section's Visible property back to Yes.

- Delete all controls from the section; then size the section so that it has no height at all. Of course, this method is more drastic than the one above, and it doesn't allow you to redisplay the section later.

Adding Your Own Controls

You've already learned how to add controls to a report or form by dragging field names from the field list. But bound controls are only the tip of the object iceberg. In the sections that follow, you'll learn how to use the *toolbox* to create more than a dozen different types of controls.

Using the Toolbox

The toolbox (shown in Figure 13.18 and briefly described in Table 13.2) provides all the tools you'll need to create your own controls.

FIGURE 13.18

The Toolbox provides all the buttons you need to design controls of your own

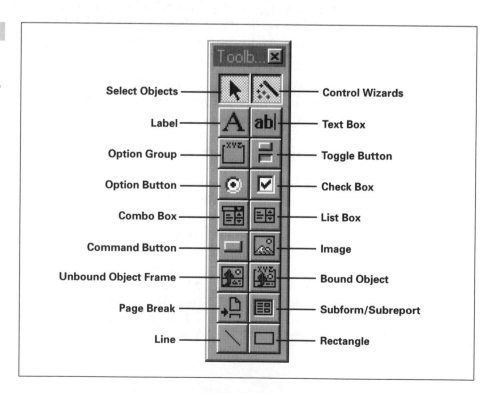

TABLE 13.2: The Toolbox Buttons Shown in Figure 13.18

BUTTON NAME	WHAT IT DOES
Select Objects	Lets you select controls in the design window.
Label	Creates a control that displays descriptive text (e.g., title, caption, instructions).
Option Group*	Creates a control that frames a set of check boxes, option buttons, or toggle buttons. In form view, only one option in the group can be selected at a time.
Option Button	Creates a control that you can select or clear. (Sometimes called a radio button.)
Combo Box*	Creates a control that's like a list box and text box combined. In form view, you can either type the text into the combo box or select an item from the drop-down list.
Command Button*	Creates a control that opens a linked form, runs a macro, calls a Visual Basic function, or runs a Visual Basic procedure.
Unbound Object Frame*	Creates a control that displays a picture, graph, or OLE object that isn't stored in the underlying table or query.
Page Break	Creates a control that starts a new page in a report or form, or a new screen in a multi-screen form.
Line	Creates a control that appears as a straight line. Used for decoration.
Control Wizards	Turns the Control Wizards on or off. In this chapter, we assume that the Control Wizards button is selected (pushed in), so that Wizards are available to help you create option boxes, combo boxes, list boxes, charts, and command buttons.
Text Box	Creates a control that gives you a place to enter or view text in a form or report. Also used to display calculation results.
Toggle Button	Creates a control that acts as an on/off button. Toggle buttons can display text or a picture.
Check Box	Creates a control that you can select (check) or clear.

TABLE 13.2: The Toolbox Buttons Shown in Figure 13.18 (continued)

BUTTON NAME	WHAT IT DOES
List Box*	Creates a control that gives you a list of choices.
Image	Creates a control that displays a picture. Image controls display faster and offer more image formats than Unbound Object controls, and they're recommended when you don't need to edit the object directly from the form or report.
Bound Object Frame	Creates a control that displays an OLE object (such as a picture) that is stored in the underlying table or query. (It's easiest to create bound controls by dragging fields from the field list.)
Subform/ Subreport	Inserts a form or report within the form or report you're designing now.
Rectangle	Creates a control that appears as a rectangle or square. Used for decoration.

* A Wizard will take you through the setup steps if the Control Wizards button is selected.

The Chart button, which creates a control that displays a chart, doesn't appear in the toolbox initially. Chapter 14 explains how to add this button and produce charts.

To create custom controls (such as the Calendar control provided with Access), choose Insert ➤ Custom Control.

Figure 13.19 shows a hodge-podge form, in form view, with all the controls that Access offers (except a chart). Figure 13.20 shows the same form in design view. Of course you'll probably never create a form as weird as this one, but it does illustrate the possibilities.

Here's how to open the toolbox if it isn't visible:

- Click on the Form Design or Report Design toolbar's Toolbox button (shown at left), or choose View ➤ Toolbox.

FIGURE 13.19

A hodge-podge form in form view. This form includes every type of Access control, except a chart.

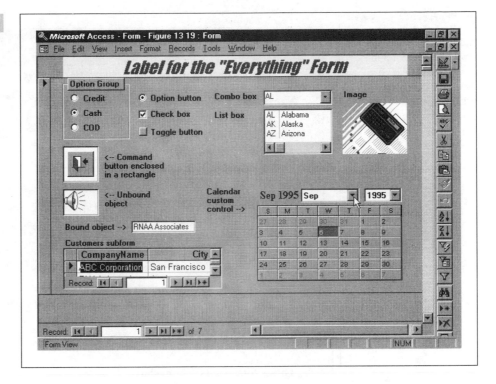

Once you've opened the toolbox, using it is easy. The Select Objects and Control Wizards buttons are *toggle buttons* that you can click on to activate or deactivate. The steps for using the other buttons appear below:

1. Click on the toolbox button you want to use. (If you want this button to remain selected until you choose another one, double-click on the toolbox button.)

2. Click where you want the upper-left corner of the control to appear, or drag an outline to define the size and location of the control you're creating.

3. Respond to any prompts that appear (as described in the following sections).

4. Click on the Select Objects toolbox button (if it's not selected already). Then select the control and adjust its size, position, colors, borders, lines, and other properties as needed.

FIGURE 13.20

The hodge-podge form from Figure 13.19 in design view. We've hidden the toolbar, grid, and ruler so you can see the controls more easily.

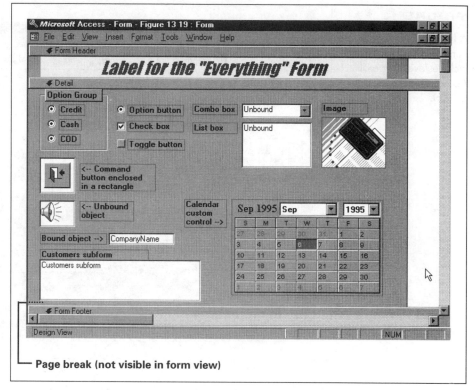

Page break (not visible in form view)

 ➤ To quickly learn how to use one of the toolbox buttons, click on the button you're interested in and press F1. Or, click on the Help button on the Form Design or Report Design toolbar, and then click on the toolbox button you want to know more about.

Changing Default Properties for Toolbox Tools

If you find yourself repeatedly changing the same old properties for a certain type of control, you can alter that control's *default* properties.

For the Current Form or Report Only...

There are two main ways to change the default properties for newly created controls in the current form or report.

Here's one method:

1. Open the property sheet (<u>V</u>iew ➤ <u>P</u>roperties), and click on the All tab (or the tab for whichever group of properties you want to change).

2. Click on the toolbox button for the object whose default properties you want to change. The title bar of the property sheet will reflect the name of the control you selected in step 1.

3. Change the properties as needed.

Here's the other method:

1. Set the properties for the controls that should serve as the model for other controls of the same type. For example, draw a rectangle and assign it properties that should be used for other rectangles in the design.

2. Select the control or controls that have the properties you want to copy.

3. Choose F<u>o</u>rmat ➤ Set <u>C</u>ontrol Defaults.

New controls placed in the design will have the new default properties you set.

T I P

To copy the properties from one control to other controls on your design, use the Format Painter. See "Copying Properties to Other Controls," earlier in this chapter.

For Future Form and Report Designs...

Access also offers two ways to use your customized controls and other characteristics of the current design as defaults for *new* forms or reports.

The first way is to use your customized form or report design as a *template* for future designs. Access uses form and report templates to set up the initial appearance of a design:

- Any time you create a new design without a Wizard.

- Any time you use the AutoForm Wizard (Insert ➤ AutoForm or the equivalent New Object toolbar button) or AutoReport Wizard (Insert ➤ AutoReport or the equivalent New Object toolbar button) to create a new design.

To specify your current form or report as a template:

1. Set the default controls for the form or report design, as described in the previous section, and then save the form or report (Ctrl+S).

2. Choose Tools ➤ Options and click on the Forms/Reports tab in the Options dialog box.

3. Change the Form Template or Report Template option from Normal (the default template that comes with Access) to the name of the customized form or report you want to use for setting default characteristics in new designs.

4. Click on OK.

Access will use the template named in the Forms/Reports tab of the Options dialog box for new designs that you create without Wizards and for new designs created with the AutoForm and AutoReport Wizards.

NOTE   The Form Template and Report Template settings apply to any database you open or create. If the specified template isn't in the currently open database, Access will use the Normal template instead. To use your templates in other databases, import or export the templates as needed (see Chapter 7).

The second method is to create a new AutoFormat style or update an existing AutoFormat style with properties from the current design. You can then use the new or updated style to restyle the current form or report design or to set the initial appearance for any new ones you create. See "Customizing AutoFormat Styles" and "Choosing a Style for Your Design" earlier in this chapter.

Adding Labels

Labels display descriptive information such as titles, captions, or instructions on your form or report. The text in a label stays the same from record to record.

 To create a label, click on the Label toolbox button (shown at left), click where the upper-left corner of the label should appear or drag an outline to define the label's location and size, and then type the text for the label. Text will wrap automatically within the label. If you want to force text to a new line as you're typing, press Ctrl+↵. Press ↵ when you're finished typing the label text.

To customize the label, select the label, and then use the property sheet, or the Formatting (Form/Report Design) toolbar (see Figure 13.7), to change the text appearance, colors, borders, and so forth.

Adding Text Boxes

 Text boxes provide a place for you to enter or view text. To create a text box, click on the Text Box tool (shown at left). Then click where the upper-left corner of the text box should appear, or drag an outline to define the text box location and size. A field label and unbound text box will appear in your design.

TIP If you want your design to include a field from the underlying table or query, it's easiest to drag that field name from the field list.

- **To change the contents of the text box,** open the property sheet (View ➤ Properties), select the text box *control* (not the label), and then change the Control Source data property to a field name or expression.

- **To change the label text,** click in the label and edit the text normally. Or change the label's Caption property on the property sheet's Format tab.

- **To hide the label,** select the label and then change the Visible property on the property sheet's Format tab to No.

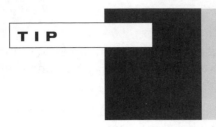

T I P

To prevent Access from creating labels when you add text boxes to the current form or report design, click on the Text Box tool in the toolbox, and then change the Auto Label property on the property sheet's Format tab to No.

Adding Option Groups

An option group (shown below) contains a set of related buttons or check boxes from which you can select one button or check box in form view (option groups are rarely used on reports). This control is especially useful when only one in a small list of options is valid and you don't need to let the user type in a value.

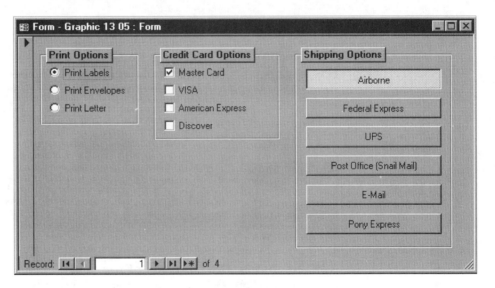

The selected option can be "remembered" so that the form can later decide what to do next (for example, print labels). Or the selection can be stored in a table field (for instance, the options could store *1* in the PaymentMethod field if you choose *Master Card* in form view).

To create an option group:

1. Make sure the Control Wizards toolbox button (shown at left) is selected (pushed in).

2. Click on the Option Group toolbox button (shown at left), and then click in the design or drag an outline where the control should appear. The Option Group Wizard will take over.

3. When prompted, type the labels you want for each option, pressing Tab or ↓ after each entry. Each label must be unique. When you're done typing labels, click on <u>N</u>ext (or press ↵) to continue.

4. You can choose whether to assign an option as the default selection in new records that you create. When prompted, either choose No, I Don't Want A Default or select an option from the drop-down list next to Yes, The Default Choice Is. Click on <u>N</u>ext to continue.

5. You'll be asked to assign a numeric value to each option. Usually you can accept the suggested values and click on <u>N</u>ext. Each value must be unique. These values can either be stored in a table field or used in a macro or Visual Basic code to make decisions about what to do next (for example, a value of 1 can mean "pay via Master Card").

6. When asked what you want Access to do when you select a value in your option group in form view, choose either of the options described just below, and then click on <u>N</u>ext.

    Save The Value For Later Use   Uses the value to make decisions in a macro or other procedure. The value is saved only as long as the form is open in form view.

    Store The Value In This Field   Stores the value in the table field you choose from the drop-down list.

7. When asked what style and type of buttons you want for the group, choose the options you want. The example in the Option Group Wizard dialog box will reflect your current choices. When you're done, click on <u>N</u>ext.

NOTE It's customary in Windows programs to use the default style, Option Buttons, for buttons within an option group. This style makes it clear that only one option button in the group can be selected at a time. However, you also can display the option group buttons as check boxes (only one button can be checked at a time) or toggle buttons (only one button can be pushed in at a time).

8. When asked what label you want for the group, type a label and then click on Finish.

The option group and its label will appear on the design. You can select the option group or its label and change their appearance with the usual techniques. If you'd like to change how an option group behaves, open the property sheet (View ➤ Properties), click on the Data tab, and then do any of the following:

- **To control which field is updated** when you make a selection in form view, click on the frame around the option group and change the field name listed in the Control Source property. To simply have Access remember the selected value (updating no fields), delete the field name in the Control Source property.

- **To change the option group's default selection**, click on the frame around the option group and change the Default Value property.

- **To change the value assigned to a selection**, click on the appropriate option button, check box button, or toggle button in the group; then change the Option Value property. Make sure all the values assigned to buttons in your option group are unique.

NOTE Chapter 20 discusses how to create macros, and Chapter 25 introduces Visual Basic programming. In Chapter 22, you'll learn about using check boxes to make decisions.

Adding Toggle Buttons, Option Buttons, and Check Boxes

Toggle buttons, option buttons, and check boxes are simply different spots on the same leopard. That is, each control provides a button or check box that you can either select or deselect in form view.

Remember from the previous section that option groups are used to select just one item in a related group of items. By contrast, the individual controls discussed in this section typically are used to set any number of independent fields to Yes or No. For example, you can use a check box named Tax Exempt to indicate the tax exempt status of an order, another named Paid to indicate whether an order is paid, and still another named Filled to indicate whether an order has been filled. Most Windows programs use check boxes for these purposes; but Access also lets you use option buttons or toggle buttons.

N O T E   You can use the Toggle Button, Option Button, or Check Box tools in the toolbox to add more options to an existing option group. Access automatically assigns an Option Value data property to new controls that you add, but you should check the value to make sure it's what you want.

To create one of these controls, click on the appropriate tool in the toolbox, and then click in the design or drag an outline where the control should appear. The Toggle Button, Option Button, and Check Box tools are shown here:

You can change the Data properties for the button or check box as described above for option group buttons.

Adding Combo Boxes and List Boxes

Combo boxes and list boxes (shown below) let you choose a field's value from a list.

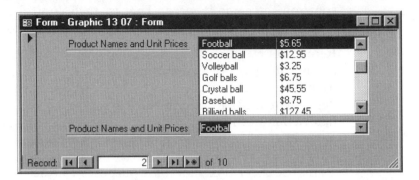

Combo boxes (above, at bottom), combine a text box with a drop-down list. The list stays hidden in form view until you click on the drop-down button next to it. You can either type a value into the text box or select it from the list. In list boxes (above, at top), the list is always visible, and the selected option is highlighted.

To create a combo box or list box:

1. Make sure the Control Wizards toolbox button (shown at left) is selected (pushed in).

2. Click on the Combo Box button (left, top) or List Box button (left, bottom) in the toolbox, as appropriate, and then click in the design or drag an outline where the control should appear. The Combo Box Wizard or List Box Wizard will take over.

3. When asked how you want your box to get its values, choose one of these options, and then click on Next:

> **I Want The Box To Look Up The Values In A Table Or Query**   Access displays the list from a table or query you select.
>
> **I Will Type In The Values That I Want**   Access displays the list from values that you type.

Find A Record On My Form Based On The Value I Selected In My Box   Access displays the values from fields that are in the form's underlying table or query records.

4. Do one of the following, depending on your choice in step 3:

- **If you chose to look up the values in a table or query**, select the table or query and click on <u>N</u>ext. Then select the fields you want to see in the combo box or list box and click on <u>N</u>ext. Continue with step 5.

- **If you chose to type in the values**, type the number of columns to display and press Tab. Now type in values for each column and row (pressing Tab to advance to the next column or row). When you're finished entering values, click on <u>N</u>ext. When prompted, choose the column in your combo box or list box that contains the value you want to either remember or store in the table, and then click on <u>N</u>ext. Skip to step 6.

- **If you chose to display values from fields on the form**, choose the fields on your form that contain the values you want to see in the combo box or list box, and then click on <u>N</u>ext (these fields will become columns in your combo box or list box). Continue with step 5.

5. Adjust each column in your combo box or list box as instructed on the screen. If you chose to display values from fields on your form, you can select (check) Hide Key Column (Recommended) to hide the primary key field in the combo box or list box; or deselect (clear) this check box to show the primary key field. You also can rearrange columns as you would in datasheet view (see Chapter 8). Click on <u>N</u>ext.

6. If asked what you want Access to do when you select a value in your combo box or list box in form view, choose either of these options, and then click on <u>N</u>ext:

   Remember The Value For Later Use   Uses the value to make decisions in a macro or other procedure. The value is saved only as long as the form remains open in form view.

   Store That Value In This Field   Stores the value in the table field you select from the drop-down list.

7. When asked what label you want for the combo box or list box, type a label (if you wish) and click on Finish.

The combo box or list box (and its label) will appear. If you'd like to change the properties of a combo box or list box, open the property sheet (View ➤ Properties), and click on the box portion of the control (not the label). Then customize the properties as explained next.

TIP You can easily change a combo box to a list box, and vice versa, as explained later in the section "Presto Change Type."

The most important properties on the *Data* tab of the property sheet for a combo box or list box are:

Control Source Specifies which field is updated when you select an item in the box. To simply have Access remember the selected value, delete the field name in the Control Source property box.

Row Source Type Specifies where the row data comes from (table or query, list of values, or list of field names).

Row Source Tells Access how to get data for each row. If you've selected Table/Query as the Row Source Type and have no idea about how to enter SQL statements for the Row Source, don't despair. Simply click in the Row Source box, and then click on the Build (...) button that appears. Now design (or modify) a query that will select and display the row data you want. When you're done, choose File ➤ Close ➤ Yes, or press Ctrl+W and then click on Yes.

Bound Column Specifies which column number supplies data for the Control Source.

Limit To List Specifies whether to let the user enter values that aren't shown in the combo box drop-down list.

Default Value Specifies the default value assigned to the Control Source when you create a new record in form view.

The most important properties on the *Format* tab are:

Column Count   Specifies the number of columns to display in a combo box or list box.

Column Heads   Specifies whether column headings appear in a combo box or list box.

Column Widths   Specifies the width of each column shown in the box. Column widths are listed in column order from left to right and separated with a semicolon (;). Set the column width to 0 if you don't want to display the column.

List Rows   Specifies the number of rows to show in a combo box's drop-down list.

List Width   Specifies the width of the drop-down list in a combo box. For example, type **2** for a 2″-wide drop-down list. Or type **Auto** to make the drop-down list as wide as the text box.

Adding the Current Date and Time

It's easy to display the current date and time anywhere on a form or report. To do so:

1. Choose Insert ➤ Date And Time.

2. Fill in the Date And Time dialog box that appears (see below).

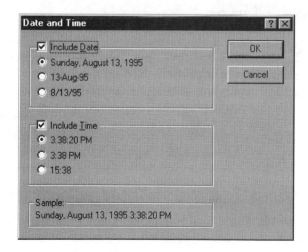

3. Click on OK. A new text box will appear in the form header or report header (if one is visible), or in the detail section. It looks something like this:

```
=Format(Date(),"Long Date") & " " &
```

4. Drag the new text box to wherever it should appear in your design.

5. Switch to form view or print preview to see the results.

Presto Change Type

Access offers a time-saving *morphing* feature that lets you instantly convert one type of control into any other compatible type. For example, you can convert a list box to a combo box, or change a check box to a toggle button with just a couple of mouse clicks. Here's how:

1. Select the control you want to convert to another type.

2. Choose Format ➤ Change To, or right-click on the control and choose Change To.

3. Choose any control type that's available in the menu that appears.

4. Change the control's properties as needed.

Adding Lines

 You can draw a line anywhere within a section on a form or report design. Click on the Line toolbox button (shown at left); then click in the design or drag an outline where the line should appear. To create a perfectly vertical or horizontal line, hold down the Shift key while you drag.

After creating a line, you can select it and move or resize it as needed. You also can use the Formatting (Form/Report Design) toolbar to change the line's color, thickness, or special effects.

Drawing Frames Around Controls

 The rectangle tool is especially nice for drawing neat frames around any control. To use it, click on the Rectangle toolbox button (shown at left), and then click in the design or drag an outline where the rectangle should appear.

If the frame contains a background color, the frame may cover the controls behind it. That's easy to fix. Select the frame, and then choose For-mat ➤ Send To Back. If you'd like to add a background color or other special effect to the frame, select the rectangle, and choose the effects you want from the buttons and colors in the Formatting (Form/Report De-sign) toolbar. Raised, sunken, and etched effects and colored backgrounds look especially nice.

Adding Page Breaks

 You can add a page break to force a new page on a printed form or report. To do so, click on the Page Break toolbox button (shown at left), and then click in the design where you want the page to break. (If you no longer want the page to break, select the page break control and press Delete. You also can drag the page break to a new place on the design.)

Here are some points to remember about page breaks:

- To avoid splitting data across pages, place the page break above or below other controls (not in the middle of a control).

- In a form, the page break will appear in the printed copy only, not on the screen. (The next section explains how to break forms into multiple screens.)

- To print page breaks before or after a section in the printed form or report, click in the section where you want the page break, open the property sheet (View ➤ Properties), click on the Format tab, and then change the Force New Page property from None to Before Section, After Section, or Before & After.

Creating a Multi-Screen Form

If you want to create a form in which each page is the same size, and each window shows only one page at a time, follow these steps:

1. Design your form normally.

2. Add a page break wherever you want the form to break, with each page break equidistant from the previous one. For example, if each detail area should be two inches high, put the first page

break at 2″, the next one at 4″, and so on. You can use the vertical ruler's guidelines to help you adjust the page break position; or, open the property sheet (View ➤ Properties), click on the Format tab, and set the Top property for each page break to the measurement you want (Access will move the page break automatically when you change the Top property).

3. Size the Form Footer so that the top of the form footer section is at a multiple of the screen size you've chosen. Continuing with our 2″ screen example, if you've placed page breaks at 2″ and 4″ and the last field is at 5.25″, place the form footer at the 6″ mark on the ruler.

4. Select the form (Edit ➤ Select Form), open the property sheet (View ➤ Properties), and then click on the Format tab. Now, set Default View to Single Form; set Auto Resize to Yes; and set Auto Center to Yes.

5. Save and close the form.

To see the results, go to the database window and open the form. If the form is maximized, click on the window's Restore button. Then choose Window ➤ Size To Fit Form.

Now, to view each screen of your form, press the Page Up and Page Down keys or click above or below the scroll box in the vertical scroll bar. Pressing Page Up at the top of the form will take you to the previous record; pressing Page Down at the bottom of the form will take you to the next record.

Adding Page Numbers to a Printed Form or Report

Access makes it easy to add page numbers to a printed form or report. Here's how:

1. Choose Insert ➤ Page Number. You'll see the Page Numbers dialog box, shown below.

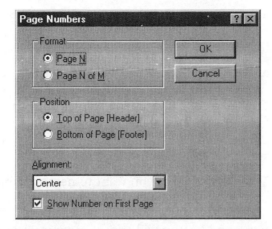

2. Select the format, position, and alignment, and choose whether to show the page number on the first page.

3. Click on OK.

A text box control similar to the one shown below will appear at the top or bottom of the page (depending on your choice in step 2).

="Page " & [Page

Adding Command Buttons

Command buttons perform some action when you click on them in form view. For instance, you can add buttons that navigate through records, save or print records, open and close forms, print reports, run other programs, and so on. To create a command button:

1. Make sure the Control Wizards toolbox button (shown at left) is selected (pushed in).

2. Click on the Command Button toolbox button (shown at left); then click in the design or drag an outline where the button should appear. The Command Button Wizard will take over.

3. When asked what the button should do, click on an action category (for example, Record Navigation) in the Categories list, and then click on an action (for example, Go To Next Record) in the Actions list. Click on Next to continue. If prompted for details

about the action you chose, complete the dialog box, and then click on Next.

4. When asked what the button should look like, either choose Text and enter the text that should appear on the button, or choose Picture and then select a picture. (To see all available pictures, select the Show All Pictures check box. To select a custom bitmap picture or icon from your hard drive, click on the Browse button, and then double-click on the file you want to use.) Click on Next to continue.

5. When asked what you want to name the button, type a meaningful name and then click on Finish.

The command button will appear in your design. To test the button's action, switch to form view and click on the button.

TIP

On command buttons that show pictures instead of text, it's a good idea to set the Status Bar Text and ControlTip Text properties on the Other tab of the command button's property sheet. Initially, the ControlTip Text will be set to the name of the action you chose. See "Adding Help, Menus, and Prompts to Controls" earlier in the chapter for details.

Adding Pictures, Sounds, and Other Objects

Your forms and reports can include pictures, sounds, and other objects. These can be standalone *unbound* objects, such as a company logo. Or they can be *bound* objects, stored in the underlying table or query.

Adding an Unbound Picture or Object

Unbound objects stay the same from record to record. Use them to display such things as a company logo on a report or form header or to attach a sound file, containing instructions, to the form header.

To create an unbound object:

1. Click on the Unbound Object Frame toolbox button (shown at left), and then click in the design or drag an outline where the control should appear. Or click in the section where you want to insert the object and choose Insert ➤ Object. You'll see an Insert Object dialog box similar to the one shown in Figure 13.21.

2. If you want to display the object as an icon, select (check) Display As Icon.

3. Do one of the following:

- **To create the object from scratch,** choose Create New, select an object type from the Object Type list, and then click on OK. Create the object in its source program, and then exit the program as appropriate. (For most programs, you can choose File ➤ Exit & Return, or click on the program window's Close button, or press Alt+F4. Click on Yes if asked whether you want to update the object.)

- **To create the object from an existing file,** choose Create From File. The Insert Object dialog box will change to include a Browse button and a Link check box. Type the file name in the File text box, or use the Browse button to locate the file. If you want to link the object so that it changes

FIGURE 13.21

The Insert Object
dialog box

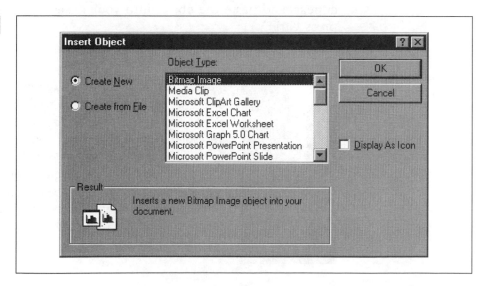

whenever the original file changes, select (check) <u>L</u>ink. If you want to display the object as an icon, select (check) <u>D</u>isplay As Icon. Click on OK.

4. The object will appear in design view. If you want to be able to edit a picture or play a sound in form view, open the property sheet (<u>V</u>iew ➤ <u>P</u>roperties), click on the Data tab, and change the object's Enabled property to Yes.

> **TIP**
>
> Your form may scroll faster from record to record if you put the unbound object in the form header or footer section (*not* in the detail section).

If you want to edit the object while you're in design view, you can double-click on the object; or right-click on the object and choose ...Object ➤ <u>E</u>dit from the shortcut menu that appears. Or select the object and choose <u>E</u>dit ➤ ...<u>O</u>bject ➤ <u>E</u>dit from the design view menus.

Here's an even quicker way to put an unbound OLE object into your design. Open the program you used to create the object (or use the program to create a new object). Select the object using the program's usual tools, and then copy the data to the Windows Clipboard (choose <u>E</u>dit ➤ <u>C</u>opy or press Ctrl+C). Close the program if you wish, and switch back to your form or report design. Now click in the section where the object should appear, and paste the object into your design (choose <u>E</u>dit ➤ <u>P</u>aste or press Ctrl+V).

> **TIP**
>
> If the source program you're copying from supports OLE 2, try the drag-and-drop method. Right-click on an empty part of the Windows taskbar and choose Tile <u>V</u>ertically so you can see both the Access window and the window that contains the object you want to copy. Then Ctrl-drag the selected object from the source program to your form or report design. The programs in the Microsoft Office and Novell PerfectOffice suites support OLE 2, and so does the WordPad word processor (which comes with Windows 95).

Adding a Picture or Image

You also can use an Image control to display unbound pictures and logos on your forms or reports. Image controls are faster than unbound object controls, and are recommended if you don't need to change the picture after adding it to the design. To add an image to your design:

1. Click on the Image toolbox button (shown at left), and then click in the design or drag an outline where the control should appear. Or click in the section where you want to insert the object and choose Insert ➤ Picture. You'll see an Insert Picture dialog box similar to the one shown in Figure 13.22.

2. Locate and double-click on the picture you want to insert.

The image will appear on your design.

FIGURE 13.22

The Insert Picture dialog box after we clicked on the Preview button in the dialog box

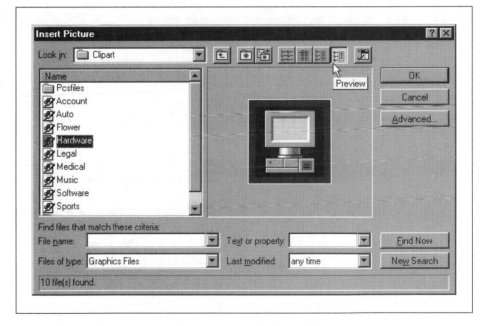

TIP

If you want to display a different picture in an Image control, right-click on the control, choose Properties, click on the Format tab in the property sheet, and then click in the Picture property box. Next, click on the Build (...) button, and then locate and double-click on a file name in the Insert Picture dialog box.

Adding a Background Picture

Suppose you'd like to add a background to your form or report, such as a picture of clouds, or a scanned image of a preprinted form or photograph. It's easy to do if you follow these steps:

1. Select the entire form or report (choose Edit ➤ Select Form or Edit ➤ Select Report).

2. Open the property sheet (View ➤ Properties) and click on the Format tab.

3. Scroll down to and click in the box for the Picture property, and then click on the Build (...) button that appears.

4. When the Insert Picture dialog box appears (see Figure 13.22), locate and double-click on the picture you want to use for the background design.

5. If you wish, change the Picture Size Mode, Picture Alignment, and Picture Tiling properties as needed.

The picture you selected will appear as a background for the form or report design. To see the full effect of your new background, switch to form view or print preview. Later in this chapter, we'll give you some pointers on sizing pictures and setting up Access forms that look like the preprinted paper forms you may be using now.

To remove the picture background, repeat steps 1 and 2 above, scroll down to and click in the Picture property box, select and delete the file name text, and then press ↵. When prompted, click on Yes to delete the picture from the background.

Using Non-Bitmap Pictures

Pictures come in many formats—bitmap (.bmp), Windows Metafile Format (.wmf), and Tagged Image File Format (.tif)—to name just a few. If you use the Image tool to place a graphic on a form or report, Access usually can display that image perfectly, because the Image tool can interpret many different picture formats.

However, if you use the Unbound Object Frame tool to put a non-bitmap image into a form or report design (or you store the image in an OLE Object table field), you may get an object package, rather than the original artwork, when you try to view that image.

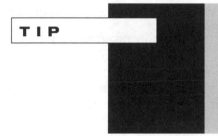

T I P   Use the Image tool or Picture property to place an image if you won't need to change the image later. Use the Unbound Object Frame tool if you will need to change the image. The Image tool and Picture property offer the widest variety of displayable image formats to choose from.

For example, suppose you use the Unbound Object Frame tool in form design view to place a Windows Metafile object in the Form Header of a form. Instead of seeing the picture that was contained in the object you placed, you'll see a package icon that looks like this in form design view (its appearance in form view is similar):

Acwiz.wmf

N O T E   In design view or datasheet view, you can double-click on the package to view its contents, if an association exists between the package type and a program on your computer.

If you prefer to see the actual picture (rather than the object package icon) on your form or report, you'll need to convert the image to a bitmap (.bmp) file or to some other graphics format that Access can display. To make that conversion, you can use a graphics conversion program, such as Hijaak for Windows (published by Inset Systems, tel. (203) 740-2400).

Once you've converted the object to a bitmap file, you can insert it via the Unbound Object Frame tool (or the Picture property or Image tool), as explained earlier in this chapter.

After placing the picture, open the property sheet (View ➤ Properties), click on the Format tab, and then experiment with the Size Mode or Picture Size Mode property settings—Clip, Stretch, and Zoom—to see which option offers the best fit. See "Controlling the Size of Pictures," later in this chapter for more details on customizing the picture size.

If you don't have a fancy graphics conversion program, try this trick to convert the graphic to a .bmp file:

1. Place the graphic into a word processing program (such as Word-Perfect for Windows) using that program's tools.

2. Select the object in the word processing document (usually by clicking on it), and copy it to the Windows Clipboard (press Ctrl+C).

3. Exit your word processing program (if you wish).

4. Open Paint. Paste the graphic into Paint (press Ctrl+V) and save the file as usual. Voilà! You've saved the graphic as a bitmap file.

Here are some other things you can do after copying a graphic to the Clipboard in your word processing program:

- Switch back to your Access form or report design. Click in the section where the image should appear, and then paste the image (press Ctrl+V or choose Edit ➤ Paste). Again, the image will appear as a picture in your form or report (though it will be embedded as a word processing document, rather than a Paint picture). Double-clicking on the image in design view will take you back to the word processing program.

- Store the picture in a table, as a bound OLE object. Open the table in datasheet view or form view, click in the appropriate record and OLE Object field, and press Ctrl+V or choose Edit ➤ Paste to store the embedded picture.

Coloring the Picture Background

In some cases, the picture background will be white (or some other color). Setting the Back Color to Transparent won't help that if the white background color is actually a part of the bitmap image. If you want the background color of the bitmap to match the background color of your form or report, you'll need to use the Windows Paint applet or some other graphics program to change the bitmap image's background color.

If the image is mostly white background, you'll need to crop the image. Use Paint, or a better graphics program if you have one. In Paint, select the area you want to crop, and choose Edit ➤ Copy To to copy just the selected area to a file. For more information on Microsoft Paint, start Paint (Start ➤ Programs ➤ Accessories ➤ Paint) and choose Help ➤ Help Topics or press F1.

Adding an OLE Object Field

Bound object controls are used to display a picture, chart, or any OLE object that's stored in the underlying table or query. Unlike unbound objects, bound objects will change from record to record. In form view, you can change the bound object by double-clicking on it (see Chapter 8 for more information on entering data into OLE objects fields).

The easiest way to add an OLE object to your report or form is to drag it from the field list to your design. The field must be defined in the table as an OLE Object data type. (You also can use the Bound Object Frame tool to create the object, but it's not as easy.)

When you first add an OLE object to a form or report design, Access displays it actual size, clipping it to fit within the object frame if necessary.

Adding a Custom Control

Access comes with one custom control—a Calendar Control—that makes it easy to fill in a date field. Some custom controls also come with the Microsoft Access Developer's Toolkit and are documented there, and others are available from third-party companies or in other Microsoft products such as Visual Basic 4.0.

To insert a custom control into your design:

1. Click in the section where the new control should appear.

2. Choose Insert ➤ Custom Control, select a control from the Select A Custom Control list, and click on OK.

3. Complete any prompts that appear.

Here are some tips for using the Calendar Control that comes with Access:

- **To "connect" the calendar control to a date/time field,** select the calendar control in design view, open its property sheet (View ➤ Properties), click on the Data tab, and then set the Control Source property to the name of your date/time field.

- **To customize the appearance of the calendar control,** right-click on it and choose Calendar Control Object ➤ Properties, or double-click on the calendar control. Then, change the properties as needed and click on OK.

The example below shows part of a form after we added a date/time field (Order Date) and connected it to a calendar control. To set the value in the date/time field, we chose a month and year from the calendar, and then clicked on the date we wanted to use (February 1, 1995 in this example). Finally, we clicked in the date/time field to update its value with the date that's selected in the calendar.

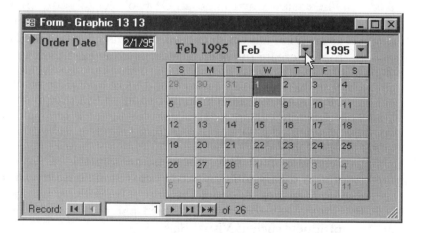

➤ For more information about custom controls, look up *Custom Controls* and its subtopics in the Access Help Index.

Controlling the Size of Pictures

If you're not happy with the way Access sizes a picture or custom control, you can change the control's Size Mode (or Picture Size Mode) property:

1. Open the property sheet (<u>V</u>iew ➤ <u>P</u>roperties), and then click on the Format tab.

2. Select the object you want to change, or select the entire form (<u>E</u>dit ➤ Select Fo<u>r</u>m) or report (<u>E</u>dit ➤ Select <u>R</u>eport) if you want to change the background picture.

3. Choose one of these options from the Size Mode or Picture Size Mode property's drop-down list:

   Clip   Displays the object at actual size. If the object is larger than the control frame, Access will clip the image at the borders. Clip is the fastest display method.

   Stretch   Sizes the object to fill the control. Stretch may change the object's original proportions, especially in circles and photos (bar charts and line charts should look just fine).

   Zoom   Sizes the object's height or width to fill the frame without distortion, then shows the entire object without clipping.

TIP

Remember that if you're working with a picture stored in a table field, the size mode affects the display of every picture in the table. For example, you *can't* assign the Clip size mode to one record, and the Zoom size mode to another. This is why it's so important to size and crop equally all the photos you'll be putting into a table.

The example below shows the same picture with different Size Mode properties assigned.

Changing the Front-to-Back Order of Controls

You can create some interesting effects by changing the front-to-back order of controls. That's how we added the drop-shadow gray rectangle around the computer example above and the squares below. We also used the technique to place the white box first in front of the black one and then behind it in the example shown below.

To change the front-to-back order of controls:

1. Select the control or controls you want to move in front of or behind another control.

2. Choose Format ➤ Bring To Front or Format ➤ Send To Back, as appropriate.

To use this feature to uncover objects hidden by a newly drawn rectangle, select the rectangle and choose Format ➤ Send To Back.

Creating Calculated Controls

A *calculated control* uses an expression as its control source. Calculated controls let you display values calculated from data in one or more fields, or from other controls. For example, you can calculate the extended price of an item by multiplying the value in the quantity field by the value in the unit price field, like this:

```
=[Quantity]*[UnitPrice]
```

Access doesn't store the result of a calculated control in a table; instead, it recomputes the value each time the record is displayed. (In form view, calculated controls are read-only.)

To create a calculated control:

1. Create a control of any type that has a Control Source property on the Data tab of the property sheet. Typically, you'll use text boxes for this purpose, but combo boxes, list boxes, unbound and bound object frames, toggle buttons, option buttons, and check boxes also work.

2. With the control selected, use one of these methods to enter the expression:

   - Type an equal sign (=), followed by the calculation expression, directly into the box. *Example:* In a text box, type **=[Quantity]*[UnitPrice]** to multiply the value in the Quantity field by the value in the UnitPrice field.

   - In the Control Source data property box, type the expression (preceded by an equal sign).

   - In the Control Source data property box, click on the Build (...) button to open the Expression Builder. Expression Builder handles the messy details of Access expression syntax while you focus on what you want to do. Choose items in the dialog box by clicking and double-clicking on entries in the three panels near the bottom of the dialog box and clicking on operator buttons above the panels. As you do this, Expression Builder automatically puts in the square brackets, dots, exclamation points, and other details required. When you're done using Expression Builder, click on OK.

The top panel in Figure 13.23 shows a finished expression in Expression Builder. Here are the steps we followed in the Expression Builder dialog box to create that expression:

1. In the bottom-left panel, we double-clicked on the *Functions* folder (which is marked with a plus sign), and then clicked on *Built-In Functions.*

FIGURE 13.23

A completed
expression in
Expression Builder

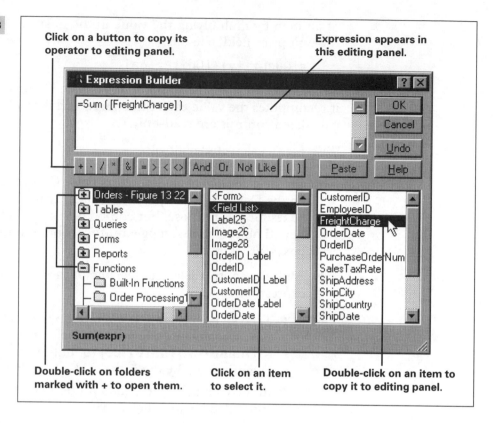

2. In the bottom-center panel, we clicked on *<All>*.

3. In the bottom-right panel, we scrolled down to the *Sum* function and double-clicked on it to copy the function **Sum (<expr>)** to the editing panel at the top.

4. In the top panel, we clicked on *<expr>* to select it.

5. In the bottom-left panel, we clicked on *Orders Freight - Figure 13 22* (the name of the form we were designing).

6. In the bottom-center panel, we clicked on *<Field List>*.

7. In the bottom-right panel, we double-clicked on *FreightCharge* to copy that field name to the editing panel.

8. We clicked on OK to close the Expression Builder dialog box and copy the expression into the Control Source property box. (If you don't type the initial = sign in the expression, Access will add it automatically when you click in another property box.)

9. We pressed ↵ to complete the entry and move the cursor down to the next property box.

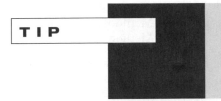

TIP

Instead of double-clicking on an item in the bottom-right panel, you can highlight the item and then click on the <u>P</u>aste button in the dialog box. Either way, Access will copy the item into the editing panel.

Keep the following points in mind as you enter calculated controls:

- For check boxes, option buttons, and option groups, you must change the Control Source data property. You can't simply type the expression into the control.

- Chapters 9 and 10 show examples of calculation expressions for filters and queries. To use those examples in a control, simply precede the example with an equal sign. Table 13.3 offers a few more examples.

- The Expression Builder provides the easiest way to enter functions, and to reference fields in tables, queries, forms, and reports. You also can use it to display page numbers and dates.

- You can use the Format property on the Format tab of the property sheet (or the Format function) to display calculated expressions in any format you wish.

 ➤ For more information about entering expressions into calculated controls, search for *Expressions* subtopics in the Access Help Index, or click on the <u>H</u>elp button in Expression Builder.

Adding a Subform or Subreport

A subform or subreport is simply a form within a form or a report within a report. Figures 13.24 and 13.25 show a main form with a subform and a main report with a subreport, respectively.

In Chapters 11 and 12, you learned how the Form Wizards and Report Wizards can create main/subforms and main/subreports for you automatically. The same concepts described in those chapters also apply when you're creating a main/subform or main/subreport without a Wizard.

TABLE 13.3: Sample Expressions for Calculated Controls

EXPRESSION	SAMPLE RESULT
=[ShippingMethodID] & ": " & [ShippingMethod]	*1: Federal Express* if ShippingMethodID is 1 and ShippingMethod is FederalExpress.
=[Quantity]*[UnitPrice]	*350* if Quantity value is 10 and UnitPrice value is 35.
=[Products Subform].Form! [UnitPrice] * 1.15	*46* if UnitPrice on a subform named Products Subform is 40.
="Page " & [Page] & " of " & [Pages]	*Page 3 of 5* on page 3 of a 5-page printed report or form.
=Now( )	System date and time.
=DatePart("yyyy",Now( ))	1995 (year portion of system date and time).
=UCase([LastName] & ", " & [FirstName])	*STRAPPMAN, HANLEY* if LastName is *Strappman* (or *strappman* or *STRAPPMAN*) and FirstName is *Hanley* (or *hanley* or *HANLEY*)

Here are the essential facts you need to know:

- Generally you use a subform or subreport when there's a one-to-many relationship between the data in the main form or report and the data in the subform or subreport. The main form or report is on the "one" side of the relationship, and the subform or subreport is on the "many" side. *Example:* A main form based on the Orders table and a subform based on the Order Details table will show each order and its related order details.

- You must create and save the subform or subreport before you can use it in a main form or report.

- Each main form or report can contain more than one subform or subreport, and you can have up to two nested subforms/subreports

FIGURE 13.24

A main Orders form with an Order Details subform in form view

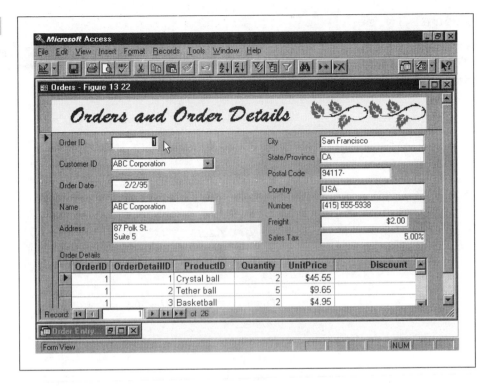

in a main form or report. (A nested subform/subreport is one that contains a subform/subreport of its own.)

- To display the subform as a datasheet, change the subform's Default View property on the Format tab to Datasheet. It's usually best to display a subform as a datasheet.

- In the main form or report, you can use expressions to refer to values in the subform or subreport. See "Creating Calculated Controls" above.

- Chapter 11 explains how to navigate through main forms and their subforms.

...Without a Wizard

To add a subform/subreport to a main form or report, without using Wizards:

1. Open your main form or report in design view, and then press F11.

Orders and Order Details

Order Date	Order ID		
2/1/95	1		
Product Name	**Quantity**	**Unit Price**	**Extended Price**
Basketball	2	$4.95	$9.90
Crystal ball	2	$45.55	$91.10
Foosball	4	$17.85	$71.40
Football	2	$5.65	$11.30
Tether ball	5	$9.65	$48.25
☞ Totals	15		$231.95

Order Date	Order ID		
3/14/95	2		
Product Name	**Quantity**	**Unit Price**	**Extended Price**
Crystal ball	1	$45.55	$45.55
Football	1	$5.65	$5.65
Golf balls	2	$6.75	$13.50
Soccer ball	1	$12.95	$12.95
Tether ball	1	$9.65	$9.65
☞ Totals	6		$87.30

Page 1 of 9

2. Choose Window ➤ Tile Vertically so that you can see both the database window and the form or report design.

3. Click on the Reports or Forms tab in the database window, as appropriate. (For example, click on the Forms tab if you're designing a main form.)

4. Drag the icon for the form or report you want to insert from the database window to your design. Usually, you'll want to put the subform/subreport into the detail section of your design.

5. To check or fix the subform/subreport link to the main form or report, open the property sheet (<u>V</u>iew ➤ <u>P</u>roperties), click on the Data tab, and then click on the Subform/Subreport's border (not the label).

- The **Source Object** property should show the subform or subreport name.
- The **Link Child Fields** property should refer to the linking field (or fields) in the subform or subreport.
- The **Link Master Fields** property should refer to the linking field (or fields) in the main form or report.

...With a Wizard

You also can use the Subform/Subreport Wizard to add the subform or subreport. This often is the easiest way to combine a subform or subreport with the main form or report. Here's how:

1. Start in the design view for the main form or report, and make sure the Control Wizards toolbox button is selected (pushed in).

 2. Click on the Subform/Subreport toolbox button (shown at left), and then click in the design or drag an outline where the subform or subreport should appear. The Subform/Subreport Wizard will take over.

3. When asked how you want to create your subform or subreport, do one of the following:

- **To create a subform or subreport from existing tables and queries** and specify how to link them, choose Table/Query and then click on <u>N</u>ext. In the next dialog box, choose fields from as many tables and queries as you wish, and then click on <u>N</u>ext.
- **To create the subform or subreport from an existing report or form,** choose Forms (or Reports), choose the appropriate form or report from the drop-down list, and then click on <u>N</u>ext.

TIP

As a shortcut, you can press F11 (if necessary) and choose Window ➤ Tile Vertically to show the form or report design and the database window side by side. Then click on the Tables or Queries tab in the database window, and drag the table or query to the place on the design where you want the subform or subreport to appear. Continue with step 4 below.

4. When asked whether you want to choose fields from a list or to define which fields link your main form or report to the subform or report, fill in the dialog box according to the instructions shown, and then click on Next.

5. When asked what name you want for your subform or subreport, type a name (or used the suggested name), and then click on Finish.

6. If necessary, use the Data tab on the property sheet to check or fix the link between the main form/subform or main report/subreport, as described in step 5 of the earlier procedure for creating subforms and subreports without Wizards.

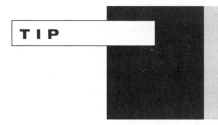

TIP

You might want to select the subform or subreport in the main form or main report and then change its Format properties. For example, change the Can Grow and Can Shrink properties to Yes and change the Border Style property to Transparent.

Showing Fields from Another Table or Query

It's usually easiest to produce a form or report if the underlying query or table includes all the fields you want to display. However, you can still show data from other tables or queries even if they're not part of the underlying data. Here are some techniques to use:

- Add a subform or subreport, as described just above.

- In forms, base the form on a query that uses dynamic lookup (AutoLookup). See Chapter 10 for an AutoLookup query example.

- In forms and reports, create a combo box or list box as explained earlier in "Adding Combo Boxes and List Boxes." (If the field you place on a design is defined as a lookup field in the underlying table, a combo box or list box will appear automatically.)

- Use the DLookup function to display the value of a field that's not in the record source for your form or report. For details on this technique, look up *DLookup Function* in the Access Help Index. Note that using Dlookup usually isn't as efficient as creating a query that contains the records you want to use and then basing your form or report on the query.

Putting a Pre-Printed Form on the Screen

If data to be entered into your tables will come from a preprinted form, such as a magazine subscription card, you can simplify the transcription process by scanning the printed form and using it as the background for your Access form, so that the two will look exactly alike.

The whole trick to putting a pre-printed form on your screen is to first scan the pre-printed form to get an electronic bitmap image of it. Next, use that bitmap image as the background picture for the form. Finally, align controls from the underlying table or query with prompts on the pre-printed forms. The following sections explain each step in detail.

NOTE

See "Special Techniques for Sizing Photographs" in Chapter 8 for tips on sizing and storing photographs in OLE Object fields.

Step 1: Scan the Pre-Printed Form

You can scan the pre-printed form into a file. If you don't have a scanner, contact a local print shop, desktop publishing, or electronic pre-press service bureau to see if they can scan the form for you. Be sure to size and crop the form to ensure that it will fit nicely on the screen. Figure 13.26 shows an example in which we've scanned a subscription form from a magazine, using the scanning software that came with an HP ScanJet IIc scanner.

Save the scanned image to a bitmap file with a name that will be easy to remember later. We named ours *MSJ.bmp*. (Be sure to remember which folder contains the file, so you'll know where to look for it later.)

FIGURE 13.26

A sample subscription form scanned and cropped in the scanning software for the HP ScanJet IIc scanner

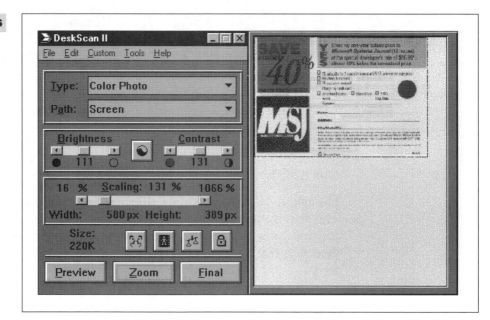

Step 2: Create the Table

Next, if you haven't already done so, create a table that will store data from the form. When creating the table, include at least one field per "blank" on the fill-in-the-blank form. Figure 13.27 shows the table we created to hold data from a preprinted subscription form. After creating the table structure, close and save the table normally.

FIGURE 13.27

The structure of a sample table named MSJ, to hold data from a subscription form. This table structure reflects the structure of the original scanned form.

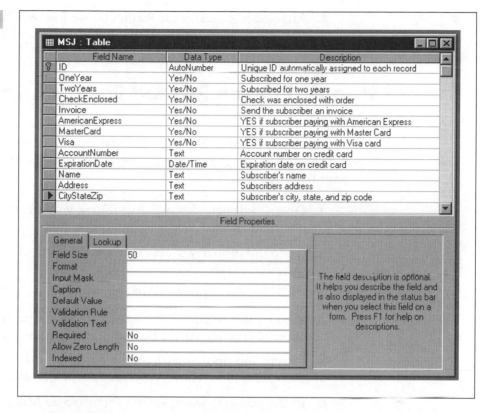

	Field Name	Data Type	Description
⚷	ID	AutoNumber	Unique ID automatically assigned to each record
	OneYear	Yes/No	Subscribed for one year
	TwoYears	Yes/No	Subscribed for two years
	CheckEnclosed	Yes/No	Check was enclosed with order
	Invoice	Yes/No	Send the subscriber an invoice
	AmericanExpress	Yes/No	YES if subscriber paying with American Express
	MasterCard	Yes/No	YES if subscriber paying with Master Card
	Visa	Yes/No	YES if subscriber paying with Visa card
	AccountNumber	Text	Account number on credit card
	ExpirationDate	Date/Time	Expiration date on credit card
	Name	Text	Subscriber's name
	Address	Text	Subscribers address
▶	CityStateZip	Text	Subscriber's city, state, and zip code

Field Properties

General	Lookup
Field Size	50
Format	
Input Mask	
Caption	
Default Value	
Validation Rule	
Validation Text	
Required	No
Allow Zero Length	No
Indexed	No

The field description is optional. It helps you describe the field and is also displayed in the status bar when you select this field on a form. Press F1 for help on descriptions.

TIP

If you plan to query the data from the forms, or use the data to create form letters and other reports, be sure to break the name and address data into several fields (see Chapter 6).

Step 3: Create a Simple Form

Next, create an instant form as the starting point for your custom form. Here's how:

1. In the Access database window, click on the name of the table that will hold the data (MSJ in our example).

2. Click on the drop-down button next to the New Object toolbar button and then choose AutoForm, or choose Insert ➤ AutoForm.

3. After Access creates the form, choose File ➤ Close ➤ Yes and save the form in the usual manner. (We named our form *MSJ Form*.)

Step 4: Put the Printed Form on the Screen

Next, put the scanned image of the printed form onto the AutoForm you created. You can use the form's various Picture properties to do so. Here are the steps to follow:

1. Open, in design view, the AutoForm you created earlier (for example, MSJ Form).

2. Open the property sheet (View ➤ Properties), and then click on the Format tab.

3. To select the entire form, choose Edit ➤ Select Form.

4. Scroll down to and click on the Picture property in the property sheet, then click on the Build (...) button for that property.

5. Locate and double-click on the name of your scanned image. In our example we chose MSJ.bmp as the picture.

6. In the property sheet, set the Picture Size Mode, Picture Type, Picture Alignment, and Picture Tiling properties as shown below:

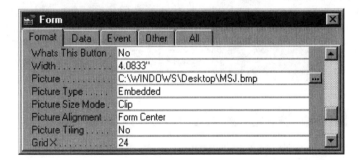

The original controls are still on your form, covering the background picture. To make the controls easier to see, choose Edit ➤ Select All from the menu bar to select all the controls, and then use the Back Color button on the Formatting (Form/Report Design) toolbar to make the control backgrounds opaque white or some other color that's easy to see. Figure 13.28 shows an example.

FIGURE 13.28

The scanned image on a form, in design view. Controls from the underlying table float above the background image, though in no particular order yet.

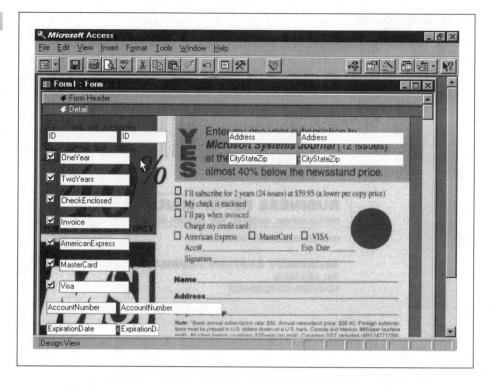

Step 5: Size and Position the Controls

The last step is to drag each control into position, and delete the labels. Figure 13.29 shows an example in which we've positioned controls and removed their labels (except for the OneYear label). Then we switched to form view, and typed some sample data.

Printing a Report from the Form

If you want to print reports similar to the forms you use for data entry, follow these steps:

1. Open the form in form view or form design view. Or, go to the database window, click on the Forms tab, and then click on the form you want to print.

2. If you want to view the report before printing it, choose File ➤ Print Preview and preview to your heart's content.

FIGURE 13.29

Our sample MSJ Form with data for one record typed in. We need only delete the OneYear label on the form to make it look just like the pre-printed form we scanned in originally.

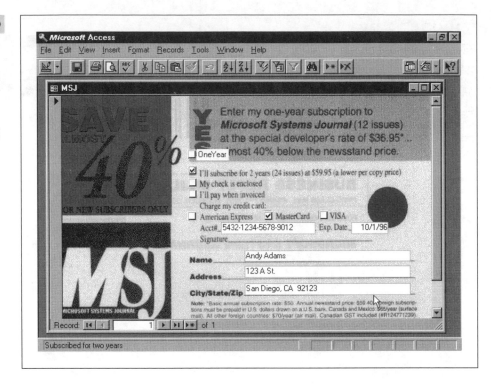

3. When you're ready to print the form, choose File ➤ Print, select any options you need from the Print dialog box, and then click on OK. Access will print the form image, along with the data from the table.

If you're printing on pre-printed blank forms, rather than on blank paper, you may want to hide the image on the report background by printing the data only. To do this, go to the Print dialog box (step 3 above), click on the Setup button, select (check) Print Data Only, and then click on OK. Choose other options in the Print dialog box as needed, and then click on OK again.

Saving the Form as a Report

You also can save the form as a report. To do so, return to the database window, click on the Forms tab, and then right-click on the form you want to save as a report. From the shortcut menu, choose Save As Report, type a name for the report (for example MSJ Report), and then click on

OK. You can then print the report or change the design as you would any normal report.

One Page per Form, Please

It's easy to ensure that each report is printed on a new page, with these steps:

1. Open the form or report in design view.

2. Click on the band across the top of the Detail section.

3. Open the property sheet (View ➤ Properties), and then click on the Format tab.

4. Change the Force New Page property to After Section.

5. Close and save the form or report (File ➤ Close ➤ Yes).

Then print the report normally, as convenient.

Form Letters, Mailing Labels, Etc.

Even though you're using a pre-printed form to store and retrieve data, those data are stored in a plain old Access table. So feel free to design reports for form letters, envelopes, mailing labels, a customer directory—whatever—from that table. Or, if you have Microsoft Word for Windows 95 (either separately or as part of the Microsoft Office suite), you can export data to Word:

1. In the database window, highlight the name of the table or query that will supply the data in the database window (MSJ in our example).

2. Click on the drop-down list next to the OfficeLinks toolbar button, and then click on the Merge It button (or choose Tools ➤ Office-Links ➤ Merge It from the menus). This activates the Microsoft Word Mail Merge Wizard.

3. When asked what you want the Wizard to do, choose either Link Your Data To An Existing Microsoft Word Document or Create A New Document And Then Link The Data To It.

4. Click on OK.

5. If you chose to link to an existing Word document, select the document in the dialog box that appears and click on Open.

6. Microsoft Word will start automatically and will display either an existing Word document or a new blank document, depending on your choice in step 3.

7. From here, you can insert merge fields from the table into your Word document (using the Insert Merge Field toolbar button), edit the document text, and use any other features offered in Word.

8. When you're ready to merge the Word document with the data in your Access table, click on the Mail Merge Helper toolbar button or choose Tools ➤ Mail Merge, and then click on Merge. Fill in the dialog box that appears and click on Merge once more.

9. When you're done using Word, choose File ➤ Exit. When asked whether to save your documents, save (at least) your mail merge main document. You'll be returned to Access.

After saving your mail merge main document in Word, you can return to Word at any time, open that document, and perform the merge again (starting with step 8 above). Any changes you've made to your Access data will be reflected in the merged output.

 ➤ For help on using mail merge, search for *Mail Merge* in Word's Help Index. Chapters 4 and 7 of this book also provide information about using other Microsoft Office programs with your Access data.

First Aid for Designing Forms and Reports

Designing perfect forms and reports usually involves some trial and error. This section describes some common problems and how to solve them.

 ➤ **Grid dots are invisible**   Turn on the grid (View ➤ Grid). If the dots are still invisible, select the report or form (choose Edit ➤ Select Form or Edit ➤ Select Report, or click on the square where the vertical and horizontal rulers intersect), open the property sheet (<u>V</u>iew ➤ <u>P</u>roperties), click on the Format tab, and change the Grid X and Grid Y properties to 24 or less.

The property sheet blanks out unexpectedly when you click on a control that's already selected   Press ↵ if you want to keep any changes that you've typed into the control, or press Esc if you don't mind losing the changes you've typed.

You can't size the form/report background properly   Some control or line probably is in the way. Try turning off the grid lines, setting the form or report background to white, and maximizing the window so you can see all the controls more easily. Move or resize controls as needed (be sure to look for controls at the edges of the report or form). Resize the background again.

The margins are too large   Choose <u>F</u>ile ➤ Page Set<u>u</u>p, reduce the settings on the Margins tab, and click on OK.

You need to put more on each page   Reduce the margins, increase the background dimensions, resize controls smaller, and move controls closer together to make room.

Blank pages appear in printed reports   This will happen if the width of the report plus the left and right margins exceed the width of the page. Try some combination of the following: Reduce the margins in page setup (<u>F</u>ile ➤ Page Set<u>u</u>p), resize controls smaller and move them closer together, and reduce the report background width.

You don't want detail records in a subtotals/totals report   Open the property sheet, click on the Format tab, click in the report's Detail section, and change the Visible property to No.

Report shows duplicate values   Use the Sorting And Grouping feature, or select the control that shouldn't show duplicate values, open the property sheet, click on the Format tab, and change the Hide Duplicates property to Yes. See "Hiding Duplicate Data in a Report," earlier in this chapter.

Form or report shows duplicate records   Base the form on a query whose Unique Values property is set to Yes (see Chapter 10). Or create a "unique values" query for the Record Source on the fly as described earlier in "Specifying the Record Source on the Fly."

Your records aren't sorted the way you want them Base the form or report on a table or query that's sorted the way you want it. Or create a query for the Record Source on the fly as described earlier in "Specifying the Record Source on the Fly." Or, if you're designing a report, use the Sorting And Grouping features described earlier under "Grouping Data in Reports."

Your form or report is using the wrong table or query Specify a new Record Source as described under "Specifying the Record Source on the Fly."

#Name? appears in a field in form view, print preview, or the printed report You've probably changed the Record Source for your form or report, and now some controls are invalid. Either delete the bad controls, or change their Control Source data property to a field or expression that reflects the current record source. This problem also can occur if the Control Source is misspelled, or the field in the underlying table or query no longer exists.

#Num! appears in a field in form view, print preview, or the printed report This message appears in a control that contains a calculation expression in which the divisor evaluates to zero (computers hate it when you try to divide by zero). For instance, #Num! will appear if [GrandTotal_Qty] in this expression evaluates to zero:

```
=[Total_Qty]/[GrandTotal_Qty]
```

To solve the problem, test for a zero divisor. For instance, change the simple expression above to the more robust expression shown here:

```
=IIf([GrandTotal_Qty]>0,[Total_Qty]/
   [GrandTotal_Qty],0)
```

The above IIF function translates to: "If the grand total quantity is greater than zero, display the total quantity divided by the grand total quantity. Otherwise, display zero."

#Error appears in a field in form view, print preview, or the printed report You've probably entered an incorrect expression into a calculated field, or you're using a circular reference to a control (for example, in a control named MyCalc, you've entered an expression such as *=[Num1]*[Num2]+[MyCalc]*). Switch to design view and correct the expression.

You want to create or print a report from a form This is easy. Right-click on the form in the database window and choose Save As Report. Then type a new name for the report and click on OK. If you just want to print the form as a report, open the form in design view or form view, and then choose File ➤ Print Preview.

You want to create a form from a report This isn't so easy. Your best bet is to create the form from scratch or to use a Form Wizard that produces a form similar to the original report. You also can select controls from various sections of the report design, copy them to the Windows Clipboard, and then paste them into the form design.

 ➤ For more troubleshooting advice, look up *Troubleshooting Forms* and *Troubleshooting Reports* in the Access Help Index.

Where to Go from Here

In this chapter, you've learned just about anything anyone could ever need to know about creating and customizing forms and reports. If you'd like to learn how to create charts and PivotTables, continue with Chapter 14 now. Or, if charts and PivotTables aren't your top priority, go ahead and explore topics in Part Three or Part Four.

What's New in the Access Zoo?

There's a ton of new features for designing forms and reports in Access for Windows 95, including these:

- The form and report Wizards are new and improved.

- Filters are inherited automatically from the underlying table or query.

- The AutoFormat feature lets you change the look of a form or report with just a few mouse clicks. You also can design your own custom AutoFormat styles, and update existing styles.

- You can display a background picture by selecting the entire form or report design and changing the Picture property on the Format tab of the property sheet. Background pictures display very quickly.

- Add fast-scrolling static pictures to your designs with the Image tool or by choosing Insert ➤ Picture in design view.

- The Formatting (Form/Report Design) toolbar puts many handy formatting features at your mouse tips (oops, fingertips). Try out the special effects on this toolbar's Special Effect button.

- Copy formats from one control to another, via the Format Painter. Or, select a control and choose Format ➤ Set Control Defaults to save the control's properties as the new default for new controls of the same type.

- Instantly change one selected control to another control type with the Format ➤ Change To command.

- Create custom screen tips that appear when the mouse pointer touches a control in form view, and set up shortcut menus that appear when you right-click on a control in form view. To do so, select the control and set the ControlTip Text and Shortcut Menu Bar properties on the property sheet's Other tab.

- Adding page numbers and the current date/time is a snap with the new Insert ➤ Page Number and Insert ➤ Date And Time commands.

- Drag and drop OLE objects, tables, or queries to your design as needed.

- Try out the new Calendar custom control (Insert ➤ Custom Control), which lets you fill in date/time fields by clicking on a date on the calendar.

- Enjoy faster performance in several areas, including combo boxes and print preview.

CHAPTER

14

Creating Charts and PivotTables

ACCESS offers many ways to analyze and summarize your data graphically with line charts, pie charts, bar charts, and other types of business charts. Charts can display numerical data in a compact, visual format that's easy to understand. They also can uncover trends and relationships that might otherwise go unnoticed.

PivotTables offer another way to summarize data. But instead of showing your data as a picture (the way charts do), PivotTables present the data in a tabular layout that you can change (pivot) dynamically.

In this chapter, we'll first show you how to create charts in forms and reports. Then we'll show you how to set up PivotTables. In no time, you'll be able to set up dazzling business charts and information-packed Pivot-Tables with just a few mouse clicks.

 There's plenty of online help to supplement the basic techniques presented in this chapter. For details on charting, look up *Charts* (or *Graphs*) and then explore the related subtopics in the Access Help index. You also can use the extensive online help that's available from the <u>H</u>elp menu in Microsoft Graph.

For help with PivotTables, look up the *PivotTables* subtopics in both the Microsoft Access and the Microsoft Excel Help indexes.

N O T E   Before reading this chapter, you should know how to create, save, and use expressions in queries (Chapters 9 and 10), and you should know how to create forms and reports (Chapters 11–13).

Charting Your Data

Charting takes a bit of trial and error to bring out the best in your data. But it will be easier if you know some basic charting terminology.

There are two general categories of charts: 2-D (two-dimensional) and 3-D (three-dimensional). To help you get your bearings, Figure 14.1 shows a typical 2-D column chart, and Figure 14.2 shows a sample 3-D column chart of the same data (though we've formatted the data labels differently and removed the legend). Both figures are labeled to indicate the chart's many body parts. As you'll discover later in the chapter, you can use Microsoft Graph to customize any of the labeled areas to your heart's content.

FIGURE 14.1

A typical 2-D column chart, labeled with the names of areas you can customize

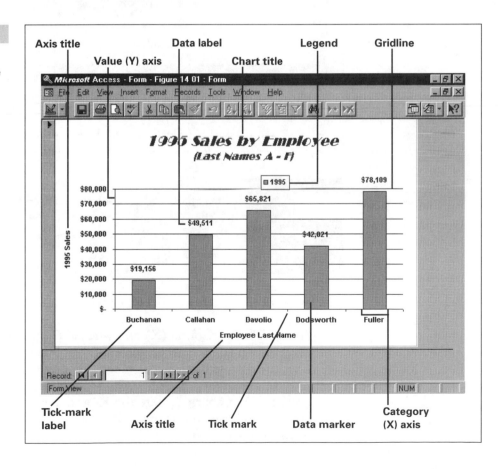

FIGURE 14.2

A typical 3-D chart, labeled with the additional parts that won't appear on a 2-D chart

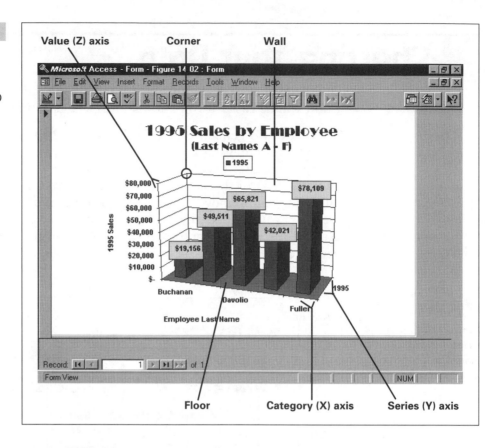

FIGURE 14.2

A typical 3-D chart, labeled with the additional parts that won't appear on a 2-D chart

NOTE

Throughout this chapter, we've used data from the Northwind sample database that comes with Access. Chapter 1 of this book explains how to open this database.

The most important elements of a chart are described below:

Axes The horizontal (X) and vertical (Y) lines that establish the range of values plotted on the chart. Normally, the X-axis categorizes the data and the Y-axis measures the values. This is true for most charts, except pie charts and doughnuts (which have no axes) and bar charts (where the X- and Y-axes are reversed). 3-D charts also have an imaginary Z-axis (or *value* axis) projecting outward from the chart.

Series A group of related data points from a single field that you plot, usually against the vertical axis. In charts, a data series appears as a line or a set of bars, columns, or other markers (depending on the chart type). You can plot several series in a chart.

Titles Text that appears at the top of the chart and along the axes.

Gridlines Lines that extend across the tick marks on an axis across the area you're plotting.

Tick marks Small marks along an axis that divide it into segments of equal length. These make the chart easier to read and indicate the scale.

Labels These appear at each tick mark to identify values on the axis. You also can label each data value.

Scale The scale defines the range of values on the axes and the increments used to divide the axes by tick marks.

Slice In a pie chart, each slice represents a single charted value (glance ahead to Figure 14.4).

Choosing the Data You Want to Chart

The main trick to charting your data is to decide exactly *which* data to chart. Once you've done that, the Chart Wizard will lead you through the steps necessary to describe *how* to chart that data.

If all the fields to be charted are in a single table, you can just base the chart on that table. However, if you want to chart fields from two or more separate tables, or you want to chart the results of calculations on table fields, you'll need to create a query to join those tables or perform those calculations, and then base the chart on that query.

When designing the query, be sure to include the following fields in the QBE grid:

- **Include at least one field for categorizing the data.** Typically the category fields will appear on the chart's horizontal (X) axis. For instance, if you're charting sales by product category, include the CategoryName field. If you're charting salesperson performance, put EmployeeID or LastName in the QBE grid. You can include more than one category field, if necessary. Thus, to chart sales by product category *and* by month, you'd include the CategoryName field and a date/time field (such as OrderDate) in the QBE grid.

● **Include the field, or a calculated field, that you want to total, average, or count.** Typically, this field will appear on the chart's vertical axis. This field should be a numeric or currency value (such as extended price or quantity sold) that Access can total, average, or count and plot on the chart, or another type of field that Access can count. You can chart more than one field.

N O T E

Charts can be based on a table, Select query, Crosstab query, or Totals query. You can chart up to six fields of any data type *except* Memo or OLE Object (in fact, the Chart Wizard won't even show Memo and OLE Object fields in dialog boxes that let you choose fields).

When you've finished creating the query, you should save it (File ➤ Save) and close it (if you wish). Remember that only the design will be saved. So, as the data changes in the table in the future, any charts that you've based on that query will change automatically to reflect the latest data in the table. (There are two ways to prevent this updating, if necessary. See "Freezing the Data in Your Chart" later in this chapter.)

Figure 14.3 shows an example in which we've joined several tables from the Northwind database in a query (note the join lines). Here we've included only two fields in the QBE grid:

CategoryName   We want to chart total orders by product category, so we've included this column in the QBE grid.

ExtendedPrice   The second column contains an expression named ExtendedPrice, which calculates the numeric values (Quantity times UnitPrice) to be summed and charted.

Figure 14.4 shows a pie chart that's based on the query shown in Figure 14.3. Each pie slice shows total sales within one product category.

Now suppose you want to chart total sales by employees, and you want to break sales down by the order date. You could start with a QBE grid similar to the one shown in Figure 14.5.

FIGURE 14.3

The QBE grid in this query includes two fields, CategoryName and ExtendedPrice (a calculated field).

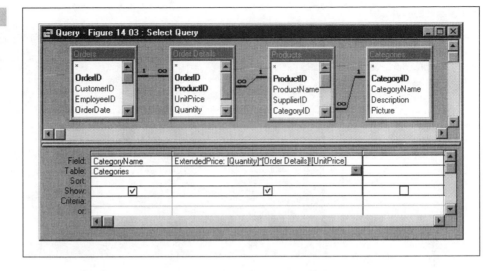

FIGURE 14.4

A pie chart based on the query shown in Figure 14.3. Each slice of the pie represents the total sales in one product category. We used Microsoft Graph 5.0, described later, to customize this chart.

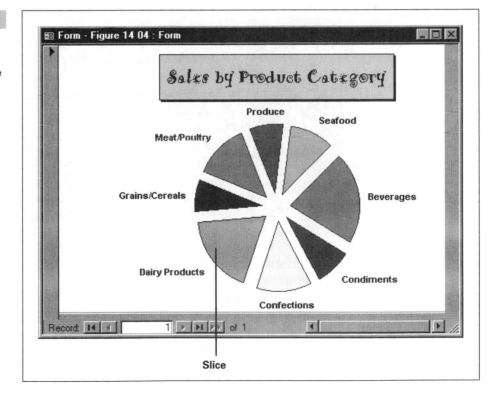

FIGURE 14.5

The QBE grid contains the columns for the LastName, OrderDate, and the Sales (extended price). It also limits the selected employees to those whose last names start with the letters A through F.

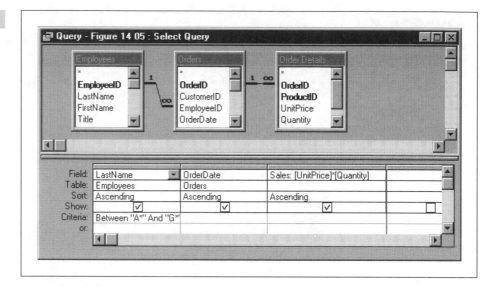

TIP

When the query or table being charted includes a date/time field such as OrderDate, the Chart Wizard will let you group the date/time data. Therefore, you often don't need to group the data in the query. However, if your chart will contain too much data along the X-axis or in pie slices, and the Chart Wizard doesn't offer any way to group that data, it's best to specify criteria in your query. In Figure 14.5, for example, we used criteria in the query to limit employee names shown on the X-axis to last names that start with letters in the first part of the alphabet.

The sample chart back in Figure 14.1 shows one possible chart type and format for this data. In that example, the Y-axis shows total sales amounts (labeled in the axis as 1995 Sales). The X-axis shows employee Last-Names (labeled as Employee Last Name). Each column (data marker) represents the total sales for a particular employee and for the year 1995. The legend explains which year each column represents (1995 in this case).

To create the example in Figure 14.2, we used the same query as for Figure 14.1, but this time we displayed it in a 3-D column chart. Notice how this chart shows the employee's LastName on the X-axis and the year (from the OrderDate field) on the Y-axis; it uses a third Z-axis for the values.

For both charts, we responded to questions from the Chart Wizard in the same way. That is, we chose to chart the OrderDate, LastName, and Sales fields; we grouped the OrderDate values by year and limited the values to dates in 1995; and we summed the Sales field. When the Chart Wizard asked what type of chart we wanted, we chose a 2-D column chart for Figure 14.1 and a 3-D column chart for Figure 14.2. The Chart Wizard figured out how to arrange the data on the chart automatically. Later, we used Microsoft Graph to customize each chart further.

Notice that in both Figures 14.1 and 14.2, we're charting just the extended price ([Quantity]*[UnitPrice]). To include discounts, shipping charges, and/or sales tax in the chart, we'd need to create the appropriate expressions and totaling queries (see Chapter 10 for examples).

About Freestanding and Embedded Charts

Once you've decided which fields to include on the chart, and you've created and saved the appropriate query, you must decide *how* you want to display the chart. You can display charts either as *freestanding charts* or as *embedded charts*.

Freestanding Charts

Freestanding charts (see Figures 14.1, 14.2, and 14.4 above) are forms or reports that display only a chart. Like the proverbial cheese, the freestanding chart is meant to stand alone by showing overall results. For example, you can use a freestanding chart to sum total sales by category, to count customers in each state, or to show average sales by employee by month or year. Although it's still considered an "embedded" object, a freestanding chart isn't used as part of a larger report or form. To create a freestanding chart, you start from the database window, rather than from form or report design view. See "Creating a Freestanding Chart" for more details.

Embedded Charts

Embedded charts are part of a larger form or report. Embedded charts can be linked to the underlying table or query, so they change to reflect values that relate to the currently displayed record (see Figures 14.7 and 14.8). Or they can be unlinked, so they do not change as you scroll from record to record (see Figure 14.6).

To embed a chart within a form or report, you start from the form design window or report design window, and use the Chart toolbox button or the Insert ➤ Chart command. When creating an embedded chart, you can embed the chart in either of two ways:

- As an *unlinked chart*, that doesn't change from record to record.

- As a *linked* chart that does change from record to record.

Use an *unlinked* embedded chart when you want to display multiple copies of the same chart. For instance, Figure 14.6 shows two forms, each for a different product category and each showing a copy of the same chart of 1995 sales in all product categories.

Use a *linked* embedded chart when you want the chart to change from record to record. For instance, by linking a chart of 1995 sales figures to a form that shows data from a Categories table, you can display sales results for just the category whose data you're viewing at the moment, as shown in Figure 14.7.

FIGURE 14.6

An unlinked embedded chart is the same in each record, or each printed report. Here the chart displays 1995 sales for every product category. As usual, we've customized the chart for dramatic effect.

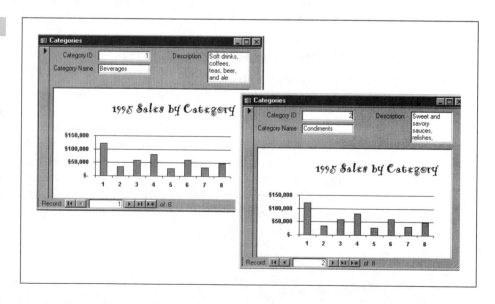

FIGURE 14.7

A chart that's linked to
the CategoryID field of
the Categories table
shows the 1995 sales
for one category at a
time (Beverages, in this
example).

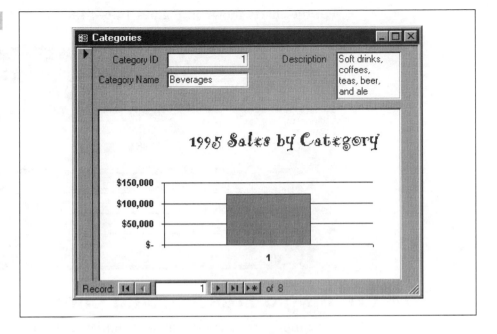

When you scroll to another record, the same chart shows the sales performance of *that* category only, as shown in Figure 14.8.

FIGURE 14.8

Scrolling to another
record shows the same
chart, but only for the
Condiments category.

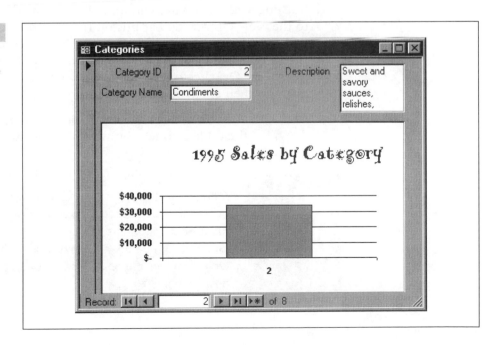

For the charts shown in Figures 14.6–14.8, we used this query:

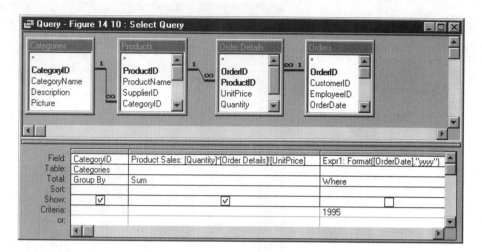

Creating a Freestanding Chart

Assuming you've already created and saved the query (or table) you want to base the chart on, you can follow these steps to create a freestanding chart.

1. Starting at the database window, click on the drop-down list next to the New Object toolbar button (second-to-last on the toolbar), and then choose either New Form or New Report. Or, choose Insert ➤ Form or Insert ➤ Report from the database window's menu bar. Or, click on the database window's Forms or Reports tab, and then click on the New button.

2. In the New Form or New Report dialog box, select from the drop-down list the table or query on which you want to base the form.

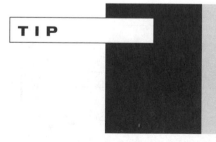

TIP

As a shortcut to steps 1 and 2 above, you can start from the database window, click on the Tables or Queries tab, and highlight the table or query you want to chart. Or start from an open table or query. Then use the New Object toolbar button or Insert menu options, as described in step 1.

3. Click on the Chart Wizard option in the list, and then click on OK; or double-click on Chart Wizard.

4. When asked which fields contain the data you want for your chart, choose up to six fields, and then click on Next to continue.

5. When asked what type of chart you'd like, click on the button that represents the appropriate chart type. The Chart Wizard dialog box will describe the selected type in more detail (see Figure 14.9). Click on Next to continue.

6. When asked how you want to lay out the data in your chart, follow the guidelines below to place fields on the chart and to summarize and group number and date/time fields as needed. As you make changes, the sample chart will reflect your current selections (see Figure 14.10). Click on Next when you're ready to continue.

   • **To put data on the chart**, drag and drop field buttons onto the appropriate places in the sample chart.

   • **To summarize number data on the chart**, double-click on a number field in the chart. A Summarize dialog box will open (see Figure 14.11). Click on a Summarize option and then click on OK.

FIGURE 14.9

Use this Chart Wizard dialog box to choose a chart type.

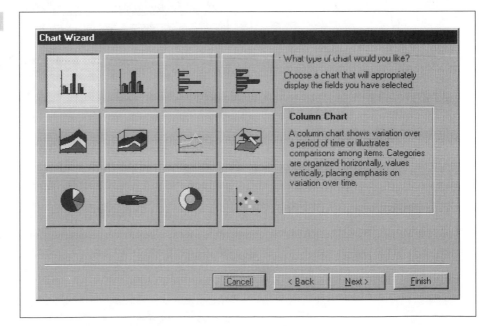

FIGURE 14.10

Use this Chart Wizard
dialog box to place
fields on the chart axes
and to group or
summarize date/time
and number fields.

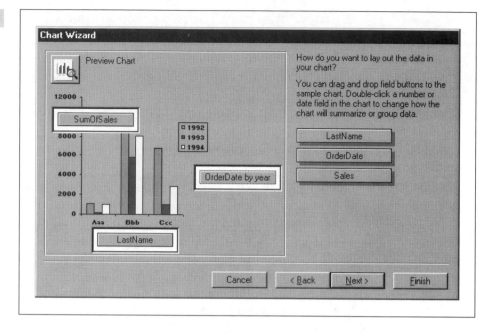

FIGURE 14.11

Use the Summarize
dialog box to choose
how you want to
summarize numeric
data.

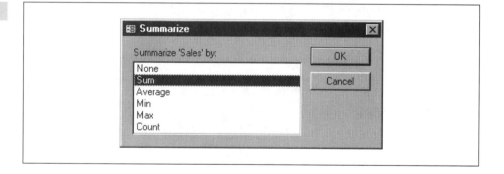

- **To group date/time data and limit it to a range,** double-click on a date/time field in the chart. A Group dialog box will open (see Figure 14.12). Choose how you want to group the date/time field (by Year, Quarter, Month, Week, Day, Hour, or Minute). If you want to chart a limited range of date/time values, select (check) the Use Data Between option, and fill in the starting and ending values you want to include. Click on OK when you're done choosing options.

FIGURE 14.12

Use the Group dialog box to choose how to group a date/time field and to specify the range of dates to include in the chart.

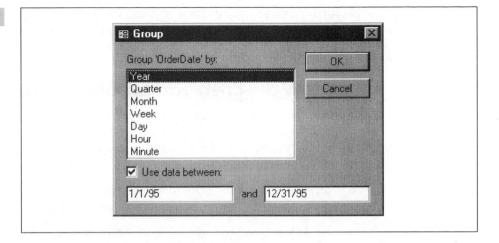

- **To remove fields from the chart**, drag the appropriate button off the chart. The word *Series*, *Data*, or *Axis* will appear in the empty spot.

- **To preview the chart in Microsoft Graph**, click on the Preview Chart button near the upper-left corner of the dialog box. When you're done previewing, click on the Close button in the Sample Preview dialog box that appears.

7. When the last Chart Wizard dialog box appears, specify a title for your chart, choose whether to display a legend, and select other options as needed. Then click on Finish and wait for the Wizard to do its job.

The finished chart will appear in form view, print preview, or design view, depending on your choice in step 7.

Using the Freestanding Chart

Remember that any freestanding chart you create will be stored in a form or report. So when the chart is open in form view or print preview, you can switch back to design view as usual. When you're in form view or print preview, you can print the chart with File ➤ Print (or Ctrl+P). We'll explain how to customize the chart in design view later in this chapter.

You can close and save the chart with the usual File ➤ Close ➤ Yes commands. To reopen the chart, click on the Forms or Reports tab in the database window, and then double-click on the name of the appropriate form or report. The chart will show current data (unless you based it on a "frozen" table or converted it to an image, as described later in this chapter).

Creating an Embedded Chart

To create an embedded chart of either type, follow this basic procedure:

1. (Optional) Add the Chart button to the form design or report design toolbox, as explained shortly. You need to do this only once.

2. Create and save the form or report you'll be placing the chart in. Be sure to leave enough room for the chart.

3. If you need to base the chart on a query, create a query for the chart.

4. Open, in design view, the form or report you created in step 2 and use the Chart button in the toolbox or the Insert ➤ Chart command on the menus to create and embed the chart.

Now let's look at each step more closely.

Adding the Chart Tool to the Toolbox

There are two ways to create embedded charts:

- Use the Insert ➤ Chart command on the form design or report design menus.

- Use the Chart button in the toolbox.

Although the Insert ➤ Chart command always appears on the design view menus, the Chart toolbox button isn't available initially. This button is easy enough to add:

1. Open any form or report in design view. For instance, click on the Forms tab in the database window, click on any form name, and then click on the Design button.

2. Make sure the toolbox is visible (View ➤ Toolbox).

3. For maximum flexibility, display the toolbox as a floating palette (see Figure 14.13). If the toolbox is docked at an edge of the design window, you can change the toolbox to a palette by moving

the mouse pointer to an empty place near one of the toolbox buttons, and then double-clicking on that empty spot.

4. Right-click on the toolbox and choose Customize from the shortcut menu.

5. In the Customize Toolbars dialog box that appears, click on Toolbox in the Categories list (see Figure 14.13).

6. Move your mouse pointer to the Chart button in the Buttons area (see Figure 14.13), and then drag that button on top of any button in the toolbox or to an empty spot in the toolbox.

7. If you wish, reposition the Chart button within the toolbox by dragging it to a new spot. (If you decide to remove the Chart button, simply drag it off the toolbox.)

8. When you're finished customizing the toolbox, click on the Close button in the Customize Toolbars dialog box.

FIGURE 14.13

The form design window after we changed the toolbox to a floating palette, right-clicked on the Toolbox, chose Customize, and then clicked on Toolbox in the Categories list. We're currently pointing to the Chart button in the Buttons area, and need only drag the Chart button to the toolbox to install the Chart button there.

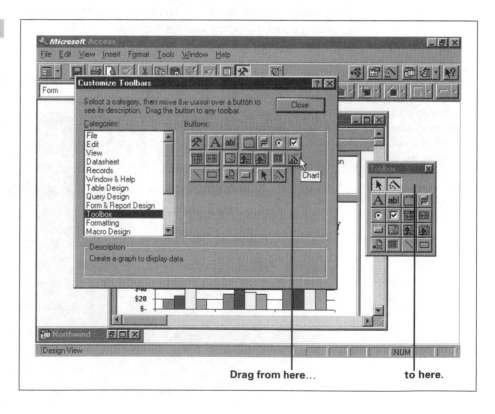

Drag from here...   to here.

The Chart button will be available in the toolbox anytime you design a form or report.

> For more information about creating and customizing toolbars (and the toolbox), see Chapter 23. Or, look up *Toolbar Buttons, Adding* in the Access Help Index, and then double-click on one of the subtopics that appears.

Creating the Report or Form

You can use standard techniques to create the form or report that will contain the chart, based on whatever table (or query) you wish. Just be sure to leave enough room for the chart that you'll be embedding later.

Figure 14.14 shows a sample form, in form view, that's based on the Employees table in the Northwind sample database. This form includes the EmployeeID, HireDate, FirstName, LastName, and Photo fields from the table. We've left empty space in the form for the embedded chart.

When you've finished designing the initial form or report, you should save it; then close or minimize the form or report to get it out of the way while you create the query for your chart.

FIGURE 14.14

A sample form, in form view, based on the Employees table in the Northwind database that comes with Access. We've left empty space for the chart we'll be embedding later.

The EmployeeID field uniquely identifies each employee.

Creating the Query for the Embedded Chart

When creating a query for an embedded chart, you can follow the guidelines described earlier under "Choosing the Data You Want to Chart." However, if you want the chart to change on a record-by-record basis, you also must include the field that links the chart to the report or form, since this field will tell the chart *which* data to display.

For instance, when creating a chart of total sales to embed on the form shown in Figure 14.14, you must include the field that links the data from that query to the Employees table. In this example, the EmployeeID field in the Orders table identifies which employee sold each order. Therefore, the underlying query must include that EmployeeID field, as shown in Figure 14.15.

If you don't want the chart to change on a record-by-record basis, you won't need to provide a linking field. But you still must set up a query if the chart will plot the results of calculations on table fields or if the chart is based on fields that come from more than one table.

FIGURE 14.15

When creating a linked chart that changes on a record-by-record basis, you must include the field that links the chart to the report or form.

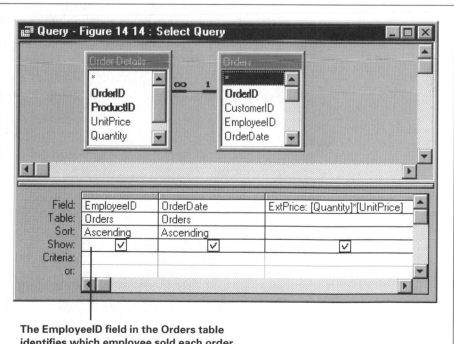

The EmployeeID field in the Orders table
identifies which employee sold each order.

Once you've created the query for the chart, you can close and save it (File ➤ Close ➤ Yes).

Embedding the Chart

Now that you've created a report or form to hold the chart, and a query upon which to base the chart, you can embed a chart into the report or form. The steps for creating an embedded chart are nearly identical to those for setting up a freestanding chart. The main differences are that you use the Chart toolbox button or the Insert ➤ Chart command to get started, and you must decide whether to link the chart to the form or report. Here are the steps:

1. Open the form or report you want to embed the chart into, in design view. If you plan to use the Chart toolbox button and the toolbox is hidden, choose View ➤ Toolbox or click on the Toolbox toolbar button to display it.

2. Click on the Chart toolbox button (shown at left). Or, choose Insert ➤ Chart from the menu bar.

3. On the form or report design, click on the place where the upper-left corner of the chart should appear, or drag to define the size of the chart. The Chart Wizard will take over.

4. When asked where you want your chart to get its data, select Tables, Queries, or Both from the bottom of the dialog box. Then highlight the table or query that contains the data and click on Next, or just double-click on the table or query you want to use.

5. When asked which fields contain the data you want for the chart, double-click on those fields (or click on the >> button to copy all the available fields). You can choose up to six fields. Click on Next to continue.

6. When asked what type of chart you would like, click on the chart type you want to use, and then click on Next.

7. When asked how you want to lay out the data in your chart, follow the guidelines given in step 6 of "Creating a Freestanding Chart" earlier in this chapter to place fields on the chart and to summarize and group number and date/time fields as needed. As you make changes, the sample chart will reflect your current selections (see Figure 14.10). To produce the finished example shown in Figure 14.17, we chose not to show the EmployeeID, to show

the OrderDate along the X-axis, to group orders by month, and to limit the chart to OrderDates between 1/1/95 and 12/31/95. Click on <u>N</u>ext when you're ready to continue.

8. The next Chart Wizard dialog box, shown in Figure 14.16, lets you choose whether the chart should change from record to record. Do one of the following, and then click on the <u>N</u>ext button to continue.

- **To link the chart and the form** so that the chart changes from record to record, choose the appropriate linking fields from the Form Fields and Chart Fields drop-down lists, or accept the suggested field names if they're correct. You can link up to three different fields.

- **To have the chart stay the same from record to record,** delete the field names or choose <No Field> from the top of the drop-down lists.

9. When the last Chart Wizard dialog box appears, specify a title for your chart, choose whether to display a legend, and select other options as needed. Then click on <u>F</u>inish and let the Wizard to do its job.

FIGURE 14.16

This Chart Wizard dialog box lets you choose whether the chart should change from record to record. To produce the example shown later in Figure 14.17, we chose EmployeeID for the linking fields, as suggested by the Chart Wizard.

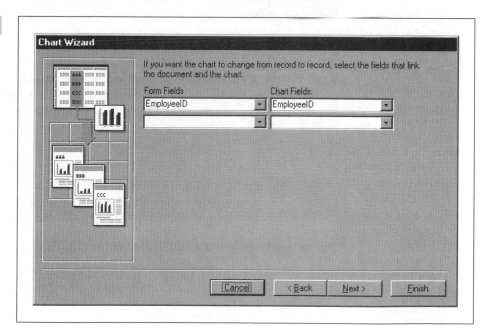

An embedded object frame with a sample chart appears on the form or report. You can size and move that frame, or change its properties, using the standard techniques. You also can customize the chart as discussed shortly. To view the finished chart, switch to form view if you're working with a form, or to print preview if you're working with a report.

Figure 14.17 shows (in form view) the finished Employee Summary form after we embedded a chart that's linked to the form's EmployeeID field.

T I P

If you created a freestanding chart, and later decide to convert it to a chart that's embedded in a form or report, you don't have to start again from scratch. Instead, select the entire form or report in design view (Edit ➤ Select Form or Edit ➤ Select Report), and change the Record Source property on the Data tab of the property sheet to the name of the chart's underlying table or query. Then use the field list to add new controls to the form or report. If necessary, change the chart control's Link Child Fields and Link Master Fields properties so the chart will change as you scroll from record to record (see the next section).

Changing the Linking Fields

After creating an embedded chart, you may want to change the linking fields. This might be necessary, for example, if you chose the wrong linking fields while creating the chart, or you decide to link a previously un-linked chart to your form or report. To change the linking fields:

1. Switch to design view, and select the control that displays the chart (click on it once, so it has sizing handles).

2. Open the property sheet if it isn't already open (choose View ➤ Properties or click on the Properties toolbar button).

3. Click on the Data tab in the property sheet.

4. Change the Link Child Fields property to the appropriate linking field(s) in the chart's underlying table or query (for example, EmployeeID).

FIGURE 14.17

The finished Employee Summary form (in form view) after embedding a column chart that's linked to the form's EmployeeID field. This chart is based on the query shown in Figure 14.15. As usual, we customized the chart with Microsoft Graph 5.0.

5. Change the Link Master Fields to the appropriate linking field(s) in the main form or report (for example, EmployeeID).

In the example below, the chart's Link Child Fields and Link Master Fields properties are each set to EmployeeID.

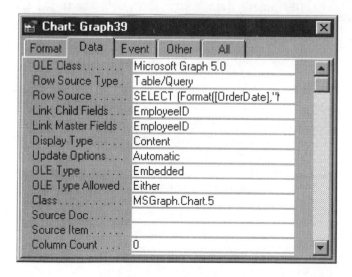

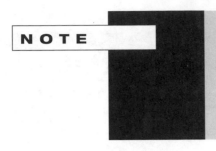

N O T E   The field names listed in the Link Master Fields and Link Child Fields do not have to be the same. For example, if the employee identifier field is named EmployeeID in one table, and SalesPerson in the other table, that's OK. However, both fields must have the same kind of data and the same (or compatible) data type and size.

Changing the Chart's Query on the Fly

Let's suppose that after creating a freestanding or embedded chart, you realize that it doesn't present exactly the set of data you want. Perhaps you'd like to limit the data to a different time interval. Or maybe you'd rather present average values or plot the number of records instead of charting sums. There are two ways to do this:

- Delete the freestanding form from the database window. Or, in form design or report design view, delete the embedded chart. Then, if necessary, change and save the query used to isolate the data. Finally, recreate the chart from scratch. This approach is rather drastic, but it might be quicker if you haven't spent any time changing the chart's appearance (as described shortly).

- Go to form design or report design view and customize the chart's data source using on-the-fly techniques discussed below. With these techniques, you change the underlying query that isolates the chart's data, rather than deleting the chart. On-the-fly changes are preferable if you've already spent some time customizing your chart, or you want to make a few quick changes without leaving design view.

It's easy to create another form or report that contains a chart similar to one you've already designed. Just use normal copy and paste techniques in the database window to copy the original form or report, as discussed in Chapter 1. Or, open the form or report in design view, form view, or print preview; then, choose **F**ile ➤ Save **A**s, type a new name, and click on OK. Finally, open the copied form or report in design view and use the on-the-fly techniques described in this chapter to customize the chart.

If you opt for the on-the-fly method, here are the steps to follow:

1. Starting in form design or report design view, click on the chart control to select it.

2. Open the property sheet if it's not already open (<u>V</u>iew ➤ <u>P</u>roperties) and click on the Data tab in the property sheet.

3. Click in the Row Source property box, and then click on the Build (…) button that appears. You'll be taken to a SQL Statement : Query Builder window like the one shown in Figure 14.18.

4. Modify the query using the standard techniques discussed in Chapter 10. In Figure 14.19, for example, we changed the sample query to calculate average sales instead of total sales and to limit the charted data to records in the first quarter of 1995.

FIGURE 14.18

The SQL Statement : Query Builder window appears after you select the chart control, open the property sheet, and click on the Build (…) button in the Row Source data property box.

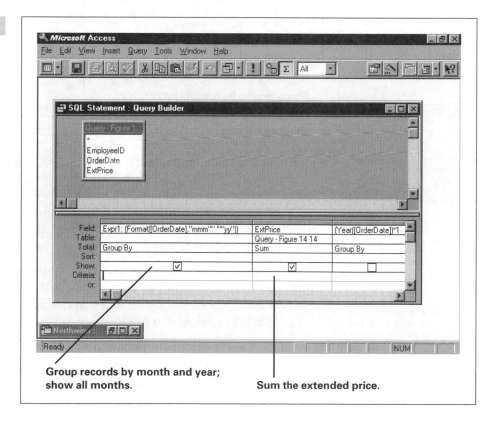

Group records by month and year; show all months.

Sum the extended price.

FIGURE 14.19

In this example, we revised the query from Figure 14.18 to show average sales and to limit data to records in the first quarter of 1995.

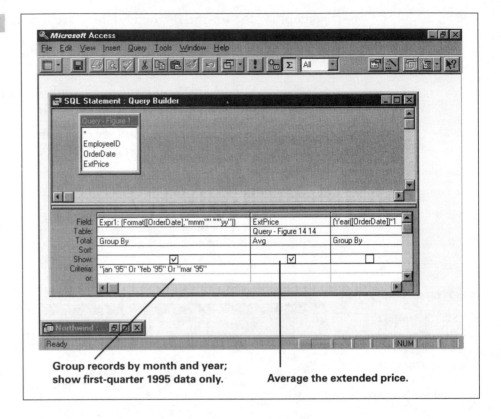

Group records by month and year; show first-quarter 1995 data only.

Average the extended price.

5. To preview the query results, click on the Query View or Run toolbar button, or choose <u>V</u>iew ➤ Data<u>s</u>heet or <u>Q</u>uery ➤ <u>R</u>un. If necessary, return to the query design window (by clicking on the Query View toolbar button or choosing <u>V</u>iew ➤ Query <u>D</u>esign) and make any necessary changes. Repeat this step until the query returns the data you want.

6. When you're done changing the query, click on the query design window's Close button, or choose <u>F</u>ile ➤ <u>C</u>lose, or press Ctrl+W. When asked about saving changes to the SQL statement, click on <u>Y</u>es. You'll be returned to the form design or report design window.

7. Switch to form view or report print preview to see the effects of your on-the-fly changes.

Customizing a Chart

Your chart may need some final tweaking after you finish creating it. To customize the chart, change its properties in design view, or use the design techniques described in Chapter 13, or refine it in Microsoft Graph 5.0 as described in the sections that follow.

Changing the Chart's Size, Position, and Properties

You can make some changes to the size and appearance of the chart right in the report or form design window. Open the form or report that contains the chart (in design view); then click on the chart or its frame. Once the frame is selected, you can do any of the following:

- Change its background (fill) color, border color, and general appearance using the Formatting (Form/Report Design) toolbar. If that toolbar isn't visible, right-click on any visible toolbar or the toolbox and choose Formatting (Form/Report Design); or, choose View ➤ Toolbars, select (check) Formatting (Form/Report Design), and then click on the Close button.

- Move and size the frame using the standard techniques for moving and sizing controls. (However, to change the size of the chart itself, you'll need to use Microsoft Graph, as described in the next section.)

- Change other frame properties using the property sheet. (If the property sheet isn't visible, click on the Properties toolbar button or choose View ➤ Properties.)

Using Microsoft Graph to Customize the Chart

To make changes directly to the chart, you use Microsoft Graph. Getting started is easy:

- Open the form or report that contains the chart (in design view), and then double-click on the chart.

You'll be taken to Microsoft Graph, and your screen will resemble Figure 14.20. (Microsoft Graph 5.0 is a Windows 3.1-style program. As such, it doesn't support long file names, and it uses the Windows 3.*x*-style dialog boxes and online Help.)

> **TIP**
>
> To have the chart shown in Microsoft Graph reflect your actual data, switch to form view or print preview at least once after creating the chart and before changing it.

Microsoft Graph has its own menu bar, three toolbars, and an extensive Help system. Its desktop contains two windows: a Datasheet window (not used with charts based on data from Access tables) and a Chart window.

FIGURE 14.20

Double-clicking on a chart in design view takes you to Microsoft Graph, where you can customize the chart.

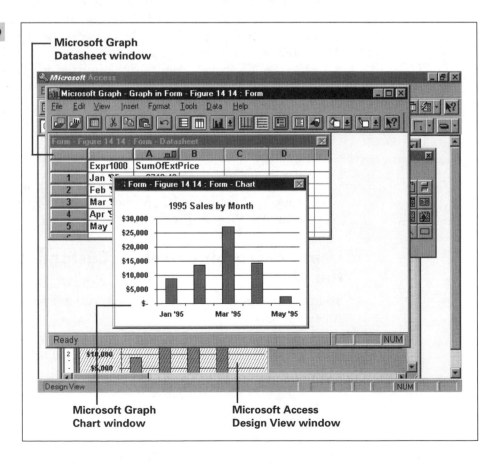

Microsoft Graph
Datasheet window

Microsoft Graph
Chart window

Microsoft Access
Design View window

To customize the chart, first make sure the Chart window is in front (click on it if necessary). To tailor an area of the chart, you can choose options from the menu bar, or double-click on an area, or right-click on an area and choose options from the shortcut menu. For example, double-clicking on a data axis on a bar chart opens the Format Axis dialog box shown in Figure 14.21. From here you can click on the appropriate tab in the dialog box and then change the patterns, scale, font, number format, or alignment of data on the axis. (Click on the Help button if you need more information about the dialog box.) When you're done making changes, click on OK.

The best way to learn how to customize a chart is simply to experiment until you get the look you want. Each time you make a change, the Chart window will reflect your latest tweak. If you make a mistake and discover it immediately, you can choose Edit ➤ Undo... or press Ctrl+Z (or click on the Undo button on the Standard toolbar) to restore the chart to its most recent appearance.

The following guidelines will help you experiment more efficiently:

- **To view the Microsoft Access and Microsoft Graph program windows at the same time,** resize the Microsoft Graph and Access windows smaller than full-screen (if the windows are currently maximized, you'll need to click on the Restore button

FIGURE 14.21

You can double-click on an axis and use the Format Axis dialog box to change the patterns, scale, font, number format, or alignment of data on the axis.

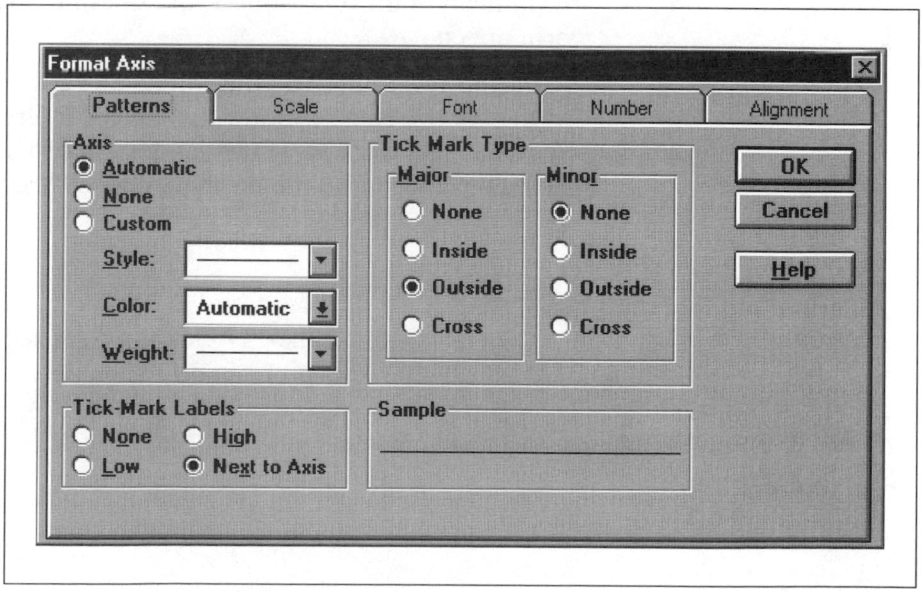

before resizing them). You also might want to minimize any programs *other than* Access and Graph. Now right-click on an empty area on the Windows taskbar, and then choose either Tile Vertically or Tile Horizontally. In Access, the chart will be marked with diagonal hash marks as a reminder that Microsoft Graph is active (see Figure 14.20). Displaying both windows at once makes it easier to see immediately what effect changes made in Graph will have on your form or report design in Access.

- **If no data appears on a chart that's linked to your form or report,** you're probably looking at a record that does not satisfy the query underlying the chart. Close Microsoft Graph (choose File ➤ Exit & Return To... or click on Graph's Close button). Then switch to form view or report print preview and scroll to a record that does display a chart. Now return to design view and double-click on the chart again.

- **To customize a particular area of the chart,** right-click on that area and choose an option from the shortcut menu. Or double-click on the area you want to change.

- **To change the chart's magnification in the Microsoft Graph window,** choose View ➤ Zoom from the Microsoft Graph menus, select the magnification you want, and then click on OK. It's often handy to reduce the magnification so that you can see and work with the entire chart at once. Be aware that changing the magnification in Microsoft Graph doesn't resize the chart on your form or report.

- **To resize the chart in your form or report design,** drag the borders of the chart window in Microsoft Graph to reflect the chart size you want in your final design. (To see the chart at full magnification before resizing, choose View ➤ Zoom ➤ 100% ➤ OK.)

TIP

To fit the chart's frame to the resized chart, return to form design or report design view and choose Format ➤ Size ➤ To Fit from the menus.

- **To display or hide the Microsoft Graph toolbars,** choose View ➤ Toolbars, select or deselect the appropriate toolbars, and click on OK. (Or right-click on any visible toolbar and click on the name of the toolbar that you want to show or hide.)

- **To find out what a Microsoft Graph toolbar button is for,** move the mouse pointer to that button and wait for the ToolTip and status bar message to appear. (If no ToolTip appears, choose View ➤ Toolbars ➤ Show ToolTips ➤ OK.) For additional help with a toolbar button, click on the Help button in the Standard toolbar (it's labeled with a large question mark); then click on the toolbar button you're curious about.

- **To change the chart type,** choose Format ➤ Chart Type or right-click on the chart and choose Chart Type from the shortcut menu; then select an option in the Chart Type dialog box that appears. For greater control over the chart type, click on the Options button in the Chart Type dialog box. You also can select a chart type from the Chart Type drop-down button on the Standard toolbar.

- **To associate the data series with the horizontal rows shown in the Microsoft Graph Datasheet window,** choose Data ➤ Series In Rows, or click on the By Row button on the Standard toolbar.

- **To associate the data series with the vertical columns shown in the Microsoft Graph Datasheet window,** choose Data ➤ Series In Columns, or click on the By Column button on the Standard toolbar.

- **To change the color of a data series,** double-click on the data series you want to change, click on a color sample, and then click on OK. Or click on the data series and then choose a color from the Color drop-down button on the Standard toolbar.

- **To delete the chart's titles, data labels, legend, axes, gridlines, or other anatomical parts,** select the object you want to delete, and then press Delete (or right-click on the object and choose Clear).

- **To insert titles, data labels, legend, axes, gridlines, or other anatomical parts,** choose appropriate options from the Insert menu (or right-click on the chart and choose an Insert... option).

- **To customize any area of the chart**, double-click on it, or right-click on it and choose the Format... option. You also can select certain objects (such as titles or axes) and click on appropriate buttons in the Formatting toolbar.

- **To customize the spacing between tick labels,** double-click on the axis to open the Format Axis dialog box (see Figure 14.21). If the tick labels are too crowded or too far apart, click on the Scale tab. Then, if the axis displays numbers, increase or decrease the Major Unit for scaling. For instance, if you double the major unit number, only half as many tick marks will appear on the axis. If the axis displays text, you can increase or decrease the number of categories between tick-mark labels and tick marks. You may need to adjust other options in the Scale dialog box to get the effect you want.

- **To change the alignment and orientation of tick labels,** double-click on the axis, click on the Alignment tab, and choose the text alignment and orientation options you want.

- **To add arrows, shapes, and text annotations to your chart,** click on an appropriate button in the Drawing toolbar, then drag in the chart area to define the size of the object. If you're not sure how to use a Drawing toolbar button after selecting it, look at the status bar of the Microsoft Graph window for a hint.

When you're done making changes, choose File ➤ Exit & Return To... or click on the Microsoft Graph window's Close button. Remember that if you changed the chart's size in Microsoft Graph, you can return to Access (design view), select the chart control, and choose Format ➤ Size ➤ To Fit. This will resize the frame for a better fit.

Building a Better Chart

Even after you've mastered the mechanics of creating charts, you still may need to experiment further in order to produce charts that are easy to understand. The tips offered below should help to make your experiments more efficient.

- **Pick the chart type that most clearly represents your data.** For example, line charts are good for illustrating trends. When you want to show how each element contributes to a total, try an area chart or stacked bar chart. If your goal is to compare values, column charts and bar charts are good choices. Pie charts are ideal for showing the relative contributions of different parts to the whole.

- **Experiment until you find the best chart type for your data.** This is easy: In Microsoft Graph, choose F<u>o</u>rmat ➤ <u>C</u>hart Type and change the chart type.

- **Avoid cluttering your charts with unnecessary data or labels** that obscure the message you're trying to convey. For example, if you want to focus on first-quarter sales (January through March), there's no need to show sales for April through December. If necessary, use a query to filter out unwanted data.

- **Make important information stand out in your charts.** For example, explode the most important slice or slices in a pie chart, use bright colors or more noticeable patterns for key data items, or annotate important data points with Microsoft Graph's drawing tools. See the pie charts in Figure 14.22 for an example.

- **Beware of 3-D charts.** They give a more dramatic appearance, but can sometimes obscure important data points. 2-D charts often provide the clearest view of your data, as shown at the bottom of Figure 14.23. Sometimes, however, you can get a clearer view in a 3-D chart by changing its 3-D viewing angles in Microsoft Graph. To rotate a 3-D chart, choose F<u>o</u>rmat ➤ <u>3</u>-D View or right-click on it and choose 3-D View, then use the buttons in the Format 3-D View dialog box to adjust the elevation, rotation, and perspective (click on the <u>H</u>elp button in the Format 3-D View dialog box for details). Or, click on the edge of a wall of the chart, click on one of the sizing handles, and then drag as needed to rotate the chart and change its perspective.

- **Use a consistent scale** to show charts that contain related data. This will make the data easier to compare.

 ➤ For more help while you're using Microsoft Graph, click on the <u>H</u>elp button that appears in various dialog boxes, or press F1, or choose options from the <u>H</u>elp menu.

The annotation, percentage labels, and exploded pie slice in the sample chart at the bottom call attention to important details that may be less obvious in the chart at the top.

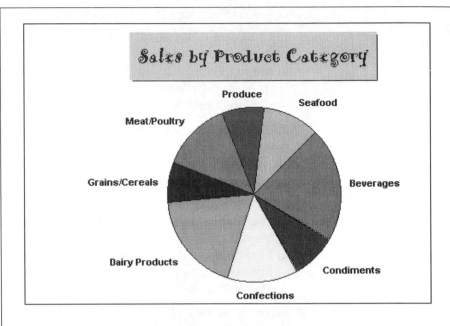

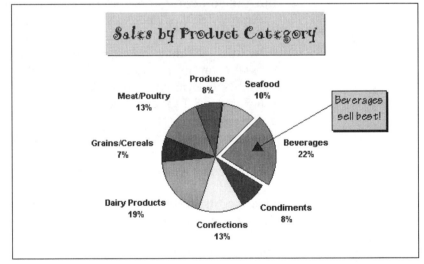

FIGURE 14.23

The 3-D chart in the sample chart at the top may look more dramatic, but the 2-D in the chart at the bottom presents the data more clearly.

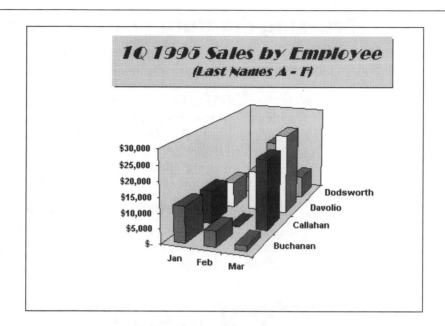

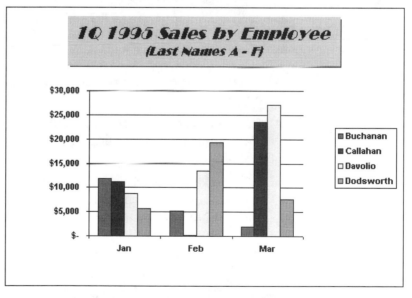

Freezing the Data in Your Chart

Recall that charts based on a query will always show up-to-date information. If you prefer, you can freeze the chart so that it shows data at a particular point in time and never changes. One way is to convert the chart to an image, as described just below. Another is to separate the chart from its underlying table or query by creating and running a Make Table query that places selected data in a separate table that never changes. Then you can base your chart on the frozen table, instead of the live data. (See Chapter 10 for more about Make Table queries.)

Changing the Chart to an Image

Normally your chart will display up-to-date information from the underlying table or query. If you prefer to freeze that chart's data so it never changes again, you can convert it to an image.

NOTE Only freestanding charts can be converted to images. Once you change the chart to an image, there's no way to undo that change, so use this technique with care!

1. Open the form or report that contains the freestanding chart, in design view.

2. Click on the chart to select it, and then choose Format ➤ Change To ➤ Image. Or right-click on the chart and choose Change To ➤ Image.

3. When asked to confirm the change, click on Yes if you're sure you want to freeze the chart into an image that cannot be changed. Or click on No to leave the chart alone.

TIP If you're sure the charted data will never change, convert the chart to an image to make your form or report open more quickly.

Charting Data from Other Programs

So far, we've focused on charts that display data from Microsoft Access tables and queries. However, your reports and forms also can chart data from other programs. Suppose your employee information is stored in an Access table, but your company's sales performance data is in a Microsoft Excel spreadsheet that's maintained by the Accounting department. You can use the embedding techniques described in the next section to send a memo (custom addressed to each employee) that graphically illustrates the company's sales performance.

Embedding Charts from Other Programs

Follow these steps to create a chart that uses data from another source, such as Microsoft Excel, Lotus 1-2-3, or data that you type directly into Microsoft Graph's Datasheet window.

1. Open your form or report in design view.

2. Click on the Unbound Object Frame toolbox tool (shown at left).

3. On the form or report design, click on the place where the upper-left corner of the chart should appear, or click and drag to define the chart's size. The Insert Object dialog box appears, listing all the OLE programs on your computer.

4. In the Insert Object dialog box, click on Microsoft Graph 5.0 Chart, and then click on OK.

As Figure 14.24 shows, Microsoft Graph opens with some "canned" sample data in the Datasheet window and a sample chart for that data in the Chart window. You can click in the Datasheet window and change the existing data as needed. The results will be reflected instantly in the Chart window.

If you prefer to clear the existing data and type in data or import data from another program, click on the Select All button (shown in Figure 14.24), and then press the Delete key. Now click in the cell where you want to start typing or importing data and use the guidelines below to put data into Microsoft Graph's Datasheet window:

- **To enter data into a cell,** select the cell you want to edit by clicking on it or using the arrow and Tab keys to reach the desired cell,

FIGURE 14.24

Microsoft Graph opens with some sample data and a sample chart. The sample data is for reference only—it's not stored in any Access table. In this example, we clicked on the Datasheet window to bring its data to the front.

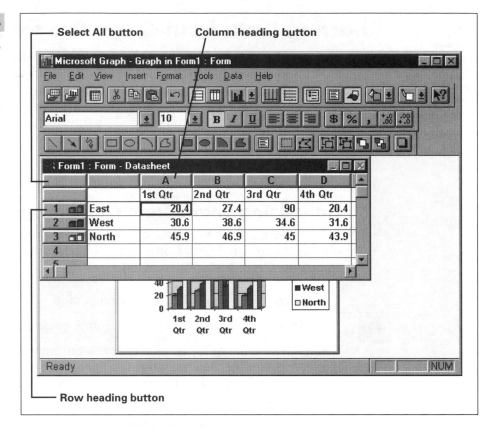

and then begin typing. Anything you type replaces the existing contents of the cell.

- **To import a text or spreadsheet file,** click where you want the first cell to appear. Choose Edit ➤ Import Data, select the type of file you want to import from the List Files of Type drop-down list, and then double-click on the file you want to import. Respond to any additional prompts that appear. For example, if you're importing a text file, a Text Import Wizard will ask you to provide more information about the file's format.

- **To import data from a Microsoft Excel chart,** choose Edit ➤ Import Chart, select the type of chart you want to import from the List Files of Type drop-down list, and then double-click on the chart you want to import. Respond to any additional prompts that appear.

Text files generally have extensions of .prn, .csv, or .txt; spreadsheet files have .wk* and .xl* extensions; Microsoft Excel charts have .xlc or .xls extensions.

- **To import data that you've copied to the Clipboard,** choose Edit ➤ Paste or press Ctrl+V.

After importing or typing in your data, you can click on the Chart window to view and customize your chart as desired. When you're finished, choose File ➤ Exit & Return To… or click on the Microsoft Graph window's Close button. The chart will appear in your Access form or report. If necessary, resize the chart in the design window, or return to Microsoft Graph and resize the Chart window.

You also can *link* charts developed in other programs that support OLE to unbound object frames in forms and reports, and to OLE Object fields in tables. Please see Chapters 8 and 13 for more information on using OLE to link and embed objects.

Creating PivotTables

PivotTables are powerful tools for gleaning management information from large amounts of data. Although they're similar to Crosstab queries (described in Chapter 10), PivotTables are much more powerful because they let you switch row and column headings dynamically and they let you filter data on the fly, so you can focus on just the information you need to know at the moment.

N O T E

PivotTables aren't really native Microsoft Access objects at all. They're embedded Microsoft Excel objects that you create and modify by starting from an Access form. Of course, you must have Microsoft Excel installed in order to use PivotTables and the PivotTable Wizard that creates them.

Figure 14.25 shows a sample PivotTable after we created it within an Access form (using the PivotTable Wizard) and then clicked on the form's Edit PivotTable button. This PivotTable answers the question: What were the 1995 total sales (by month) for Produce sold to all companies by all employees?

FIGURE 14.25

A PivotTable created from a query on the Northwind sample database that comes with Access

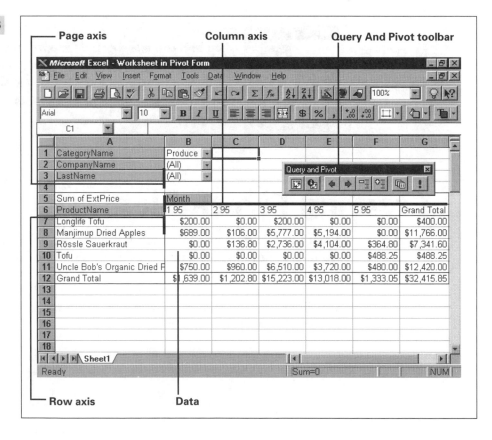

With just a few simple selections from the drop-down lists in the pages axis, this one PivotTable can answer many more questions:

- What were the 1995 total sales (by month) for Produce sold by the employee named Fuller to all customers?

- What were the 1995 total sales (by month) for Produce sold by the employee named Fuller to the company named La corne d'abondance?

- What were the 1995 total sales (by month) for all products sold by all employees to the company named La corne d'abondance?

- What were the 1995 total sales (by month) for all products sold by all employees to all customers?

You get the idea!

Now suppose you want to focus on employee sales performance rather than product sales performance. No sweat. Just drag the shaded Last-Name and ProductName controls to new positions on the PivotTable (see Figure 14.26), and the answers become clear instantly.

To summarize the sales by employee and product, move the Product-Name control to the row axis (just below the LastName control), and the PivotTable will change once more (see Figure 14.27). As you can see, the possibilities for rearranging the PivotTable are practically endless and easily explored.

Understanding PivotTable Buzzwords and Procedures

Before you create your first PivotTable, take a moment to understand the PivotTable buzzwords listed below. The labels on Figures 14.25–14.27 show how each of these terms relates to areas on the sample PivotTables.

Row The field or fields that contain values to use for row labels on the PivotTable's row axis. In Figure 14.25, the row field is Pro-ductName; in Figure 14.26, the row field is LastName; and in Figure 14.27, the row fields are LastName and ProductName.

Column The field or fields that contain values to use for column labels on the PivotTable's column axis. In Figures 14.25–14.27, the column field is Month.

FIGURE 14.26

The PivotTable from Figure 14.25, after dragging the ProductName control to the page axis and the LastName control to the row axis

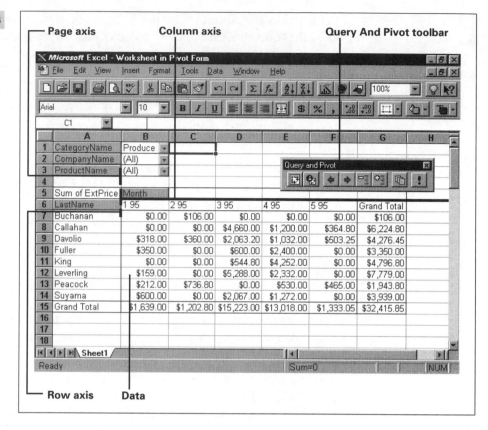

Data   The field or fields that contain values to summarize in the body of the table. In Figures 14.25–14.27, the data field is ExtPrice (extended price), and we've used the Sum function to summarize that field.

Page   The field or fields that contain values to use for labels on the PivotTable's page axis. You can use these fields to filter data in the PivotTable. In Figure 14.25, the page fields allow filtering on CategoryName, CompanyName, and LastName. This filter lets us limit summarized values to sales in a specific category (e.g., Produce), or to a certain company (e.g., La corne d'abondance), or by a particular employee (e.g., Fuller). In Figure 14.26, the page fields are CategoryName, CompanyName, and ProductName; and in Figure 14.27, the page fields are CategoryName and CompanyName.

FIGURE 14.27

The PivotTable from Figure 14.26, after moving the ProductName control from the page axis to the row axis

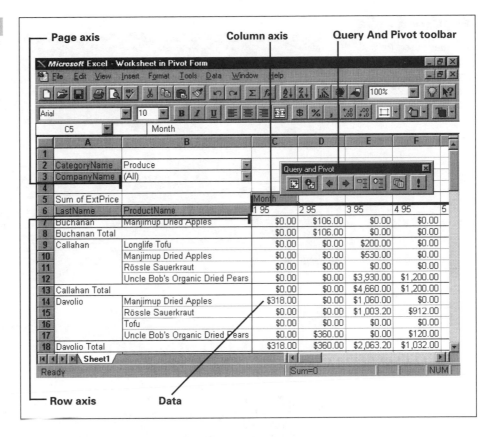

Creating a PivotTable requires just a few main steps:

1. If necessary, create and save a query for the PivotTable's underlying data (see Chapter 10). Figure 14.28 shows the query we used to produce the PivotTables shown in Figures 14.25–14.27. We used the following calculations for the ExtPrice (Extended Price), Month, and OrderDate fields, which are partially hidden in the Figure 14.28 QBE grid:

   - **ExtPrice:** [Quantity]*[Orders]![UnitPrice]
   - **Month:** Format ([OrderDate],"m yy")
   - **OrderDate:** Between #1/1/95# And #12/31/95#

FIGURE 14.28

The query used to produce the data for the PivotTables shown in Figures 14.25–14.27

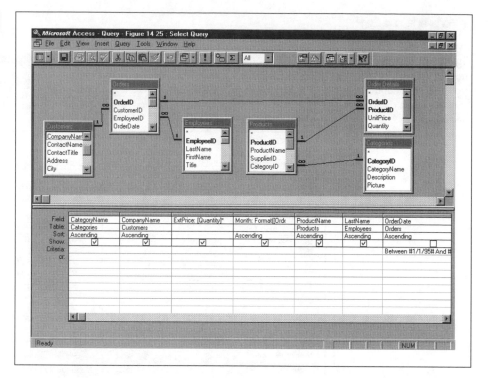

NOTE

Because the PivotTable Wizard lets you choose fields from multiple tables, you might not need to create a query. However, you *will* need a query if you want to display calculation results (e.g., extended price, which multiplies quantity times unit price) or you want to limit the results to certain records (e.g., orders placed in 1995).

2. Use the PivotTable Wizard to create a form that contains an embedded PivotTable. See "Creating a PivotTable with the Pivot-Table Wizard" below for details.

3. Open your form in form view, edit the PivotTable in Microsoft Excel as needed, and print the PivotTable if you wish. When you're finished editing, return to Access. All this is explained in "Editing a PivotTable" later in this chapter.

Creating a PivotTable with the PivotTable Wizard

Creating a PivotTable is easy, thanks to the PivotTable Wizard. Here's the easiest way to do the job:

1. Start at the database window and click on the Tables tab (to create the PivotTable from a table) or the Queries tab (to create the PivotTable from a query).

2. Click on the name of the table or query that contains the data for your PivotTable.

3. Choose Insert ➤ Form; or, click on the drop-down arrow next to the New Object toolbar button, and then choose New Form.

4. In the New Form dialog box, double-click on PivotTable Wizard.

5. Read the first PivotTable Wizard dialog box and then click on Next.

6. When asked which fields you would like to include in your Pivot-Table, select the table or query that contains the fields, and then select the fields to include. You can choose multiple fields and tables as needed (see Figure 14.29). Click on Next to continue.

FIGURE 14.29

Use this PivotTable Wizard dialog box to choose tables and fields for your PivotTable.

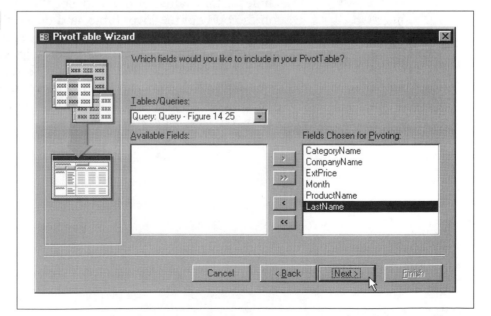

7. The next PivotTable Wizard dialog box (see Figure 14.30) lets you place the row, column, data, and page fields and customize the appearance and summary statistics for each field as needed. Follow the instructions in the dialog box and the guidelines below to set up your PivotTable. Then click on Next.

- **To show items in the field as row labels**, drag the appropriate field name(s) to the ROW area.

- **To show items in the field as column labels**, drag the appropriate field name(s) to the COLUMN area.

- **To summarize values in the body of the table**, drag the appropriate field name(s) to the DATA area.

- **To show fields that you want to use for filtering**, drag the appropriate field name(s) to the PAGE area.

- **To delete a field that you've placed on the PivotTable,** drag it off the white part of the PivotTable. Or double-click on the field's button within the PivotTable and then click on Delete.

- **To customize the field,** double-click on its button in the PivotTable. You'll see a PivotTable Field dialog box (there's an example below). This dialog box lets you assign a new name (label) to the field, choose different summary statistics, hide certain values of the field, specify the format of numbers in the body of the PivotTable, and delete the field from the PivotTable (the options available will depend on which field button you double-clicked on). For help with any option or button in the PivotTable Field dialog box, click on the ? button in the dialog box, and then click on the option or button you're curious about. After choosing options, click on OK to return to the PivotTable Wizard.

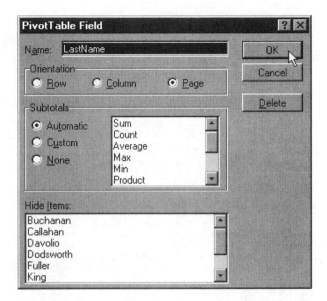

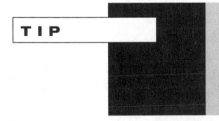

TIP

Don't worry if you fail to select the ideal field positions and appearance options in the PivotTable Wizard dialog box shown in Figure 14.30. You'll have a chance to change your mind later, when you edit the PivotTable in Microsoft Excel.

8. In the last PivotTable Wizard dialog box, type a name for the PivotTable (if you wish). For best results, leave the other options unchanged, as shown in Figure 14.31. Then click on Finish.

9. When the PivotTable form appears on your screen, save the form. To do so, click on the Save toolbar button, or choose File ➤ Save, or press Ctrl+S. Type a valid form name (up to 64 characters, including blank spaces), and then click on OK.

Figure 14.32 shows a PivotTable embedded in an Access form, in form view. Notice that the form doesn't show all the data in the PivotTable, and it doesn't offer any scroll bars. To see what's really in the PivotTable, you'll need to edit it, as explained next.

FIGURE 14.30

Use this PivotTable Wizard dialog box to place row, column, data, and page fields on the PivotTable and to customize the appearance of labels and data for those fields.

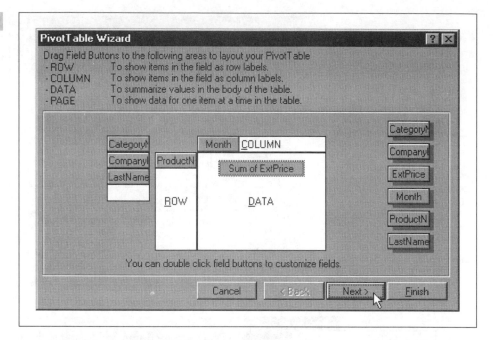

FIGURE 14.31

The last PivotTable Wizard dialog box lets you choose whether to show grand totals for columns and rows, whether to save data with the table layout, and whether to autoformat the table. It's best to stick with the default settings.

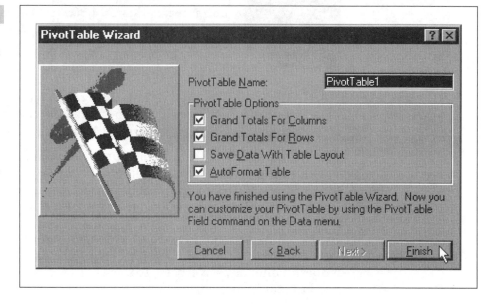

FIGURE 14.32

A PivotTable form in the Access form view window, after we created it with the PivotTable Wizard and saved the form

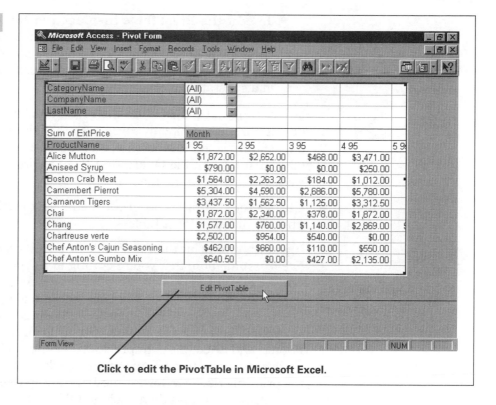

Click to edit the PivotTable in Microsoft Excel.

Editing a PivotTable

To view the details in a PivotTable or change the PivotTable in some way, you must edit the PivotTable in Microsoft Excel. As weird as it might seem, you must *start* the editing procedure from Access—not from Excel. Fear not, it's easy:

1. Open the form that contains your PivotTable in form view, if it isn't open already. That is, click on the Forms tab in the database window, and then double-click on the name of your PivotTable form.

2. Open the PivotTable in Microsoft Excel, using one of these techniques:

    • **To open the table in a separate Excel window**, click on the Edit PivotTable button below the PivotTable, or double-click on the embedded PivotTable.

- **To edit the PivotTable in-place (within the Microsoft Access window),** right-click on the PivotTable, and then choose Worksheet Object ➤ Edit. You probably won't use in-place editing very often because it's less flexible than editing in a separate Excel window.

3. You cannot make changes to the PivotTable unless the underlying data is current (or already saved with the table). To refresh the data and make it current, click on the Refresh Data button (shown at left) on the Query And Pivot toolbar, or choose Data ➤ Refresh Data from the menus.

4. Change the PivotTable as needed. The next section offers some tips for changing PivotTables.

5. If you want to print the PivotTable in Excel, try this shortcut (we'll assume here that you're editing in a separate Excel window). Choose File ➤ Page Setup from the Microsoft Excel menu bar. From the Page tab in the Page Setup dialog box, choose an Orientation (Portrait or Landscape), Scaling, and other options, as needed. You also can choose options from the Margins, Header/Footer, and Sheet tabs. To preview the report, click on the Print Preview button. To print the report, click on the Print button in the print preview window or the Page Setup dialog box, fill in the Print dialog box, and then click on OK.

6. When you're finished viewing, changing, and printing your Pivot-Table, return to Access, using one of these techniques:

   - **If you're editing in a separate Microsoft Excel window,** choose File ➤ Exit from the Microsoft Excel menu bar, or press Alt+F4, or click on the Excel window's Close button.

   - **If you're editing in-place within the Microsoft Access window,** click outside the PivotTable (for example, on an empty area of the form, below the hash marks that appear at the bottom of the PivotTable).

7. If you're done working with the form, close it (Ctrl+W). Any changes you made to the PivotTable in Microsoft Excel are saved automatically.

Customizing Your PivotTable in Microsoft Excel

There are many ways to customize a PivotTable once you've opened it in Microsoft Excel, and experimentation really is the best teacher when it comes to making PivotTables do what you want. These pointers should get you up and running quickly:

- **To pivot or reorder a field**, drag its shaded control button to a new page axis, row axis, column axis, or body position on the worksheet. We used this technique to rearrange the data in Figures 14.25–14.27. Watch the status bar for tips about how to drag and drop a control once you've started to drag it.

- **To return to the PivotTable Field dialog box** (shown earlier), double-click on a field control in the page, column, or row axis. Or, click on a field control or on a value in the area you want to customize; then click on the PivotTable Field button (shown at left) in the Query And Pivot toolbar, or choose <u>D</u>ata ➤ PivotTable F<u>i</u>eld. From here you can change the field label, summarization method, number formats, and other attributes as needed.

But My PivotTable Data Isn't Up to Date!

If you chose the default options in the last PivotTable Wizard dialog box, the underlying data that the PivotTable uses *is not* saved with the PivotTable or form. This is a safety measure to make sure you see the latest data any time you view the PivotTable. To see the most current data, you must open the PivotTable in Microsoft Excel and then refresh the data (<u>D</u>ata ➤ <u>Re</u>-fresh Data) each time you work with the PivotTable.

If you won't have access to the underlying Access table data and still want to edit the PivotTable later on, you'll need to save a copy of the data with the PivotTable. To do this, select (check) Save <u>D</u>ata With Table Layout in the last PivotTable Wizard dialog box, either when you first create the PivotTable in Access or after you open it in Excel and start the PivotTable Wizard again (choose <u>D</u>ata ➤ <u>P</u>ivotTable). Be aware that your Pivot-Table won't reflect changes to the original underlying data, unless you re-fresh the data again.

- **To return to the PivotTable Wizard dialog box**, click on the PivotTable Wizard button (shown at left) in the Query And Pivot toolbar, or choose <u>D</u>ata ➤ <u>P</u>ivotTable. See step 7 under "Creating a PivotTable with the PivotTable Wizard" and Figure 14.30 earlier in this chapter for details about using this dialog box.

- **To quickly discover other ways to customize the PivotTable**, right-click on the place you want to customize and then choose an option from the shortcut menu.

 ➤ For more information about customizing PivotTables in Microsoft Excel, look up *PivotTables* and its subtopics in the Excel Help Index.

Creating a Chart from a PivotTable

With just a few more keystrokes, you can create a chart from a PivotTable. Here's how:

1. Open the PivotTable in Microsoft Excel, as explained earlier in this chapter. Then customize the PivotTable fields as needed.

2. Select the PivotTable cells, *including* the column fields and row fields you want to chart, but *excluding* grand totals or page fields. To select cells, drag your mouse through them.

3. Choose <u>I</u>nsert ➤ <u>C</u>hart and then choose either <u>O</u>n This Sheet (to create the chart on the current sheet), or <u>A</u>s New Sheet (to view your chart on a new sheet).

4. Follow the instructions in the Chart Wizard dialog boxes.

5. View the chart (and print it if you wish). The chart always reflects your current selections in the page axis of the PivotTable. For example, if you select a category from the CategoryName page, the chart will show data for that category only.

6. When you're finished viewing your chart, exit Microsoft Excel (Alt+F4).

 ➤ For more details about charting PivotTables, look up *PivotTables, Plotting PivotTable Data* in the Microsoft Excel Help Index.

Troubleshooting PivotTable Problems

➤ PivotTables are quite easy to use, but if you're having the troubles listed below, you might not agree. Fortunately, the fixes for most PivotTable troubles are straightforward:

Data field is using the Count function rather than Sum to summarize a numeric field   Your numeric data may contain blank values. To fix the problem, open the PivotTable in Microsoft Excel, and click on the cell that says "Count Of" followed by the field name. Next, click on the PivotTable Field button in the Query And Pivot toolbar (or choose Data ➤ PivotTable Field), and then double-click on the Sum option in the PivotTable Field dialog box.

Data in the PivotTable is cut off and you can't see any scroll bars   You're probably viewing the form in Microsoft Access form view. Starting in Access form view, click on the Edit PivotTable button or double-click on the PivotTable. The PivotTable will open in Microsoft Excel and the scroll bars will appear.

Excel won't let you change your PivotTable   You've probably forgotten to refresh the data. Click on the Refresh Data button on the Query And Pivot toolbar, or choose Data ➤ Refresh Data.

Numbers aren't formatted properly (or at all) in the PivotTable   By default, numbers aren't formatted. To format numbers, click on a cell in the unformatted data, and then click on the PivotTable Field button in the Query And Pivot toolbar or choose Data ➤ PivotTable Field. Next, click on the Number button in the PivotTable Field dialog box, fill in the Format Cells dialog box that appears, and then click on OK twice.

Query And Pivot toolbar is missing in Excel   From the Microsoft Excel menu bar, choose View ➤ Toolbars, select (check) Query And Pivot, and then click on OK.

Starting from Microsoft Excel, you can't find the Pivot-Table   You can't get to the Access PivotTable from Excel. Start in *Microsoft Access* form view, and then click on the Edit Pivot-Table button or double-click on the PivotTable. The PivotTable will open in Excel and you can view and customize it as needed.

➤ For more information about troubleshooting problems with PivotTables, look up *PivotTables, Troubleshooting* in the Excel Help Index or the Access Help Index.

Where to Go from Here

In this chapter, you've learned how to summarize data with charts and PivotTables. If you've been following this book in sequence, you now know all the basics for working with Microsoft Access. But don't stop here! The next chapter explains how to personalize Access to your own working style.

What's New in the Access Zoo?

Truly useful management information is now just a few mouse clicks away. Although Access 2.0 offered Graph Wizards and Chart Wizards that worked reasonably well, the new Chart Wizard in Access for Windows 95 is much easier to use. Two other charting changes are:

- Graphs are now referred to as *charts*.

- The Chart toolbox button isn't installed automatically when you install Microsoft Access. You can add the button to the toolbox in form design view or report design view, as explained in this chapter (or just use the Insert ➤ Chart commands to create charts in form design or report design view).

The all-new PivotTable Wizard makes it easy to create Excel PivotTables from your Access data. PivotTables are powerful tools for summarizing data interactively in Excel's easy-to-understand tabular format. You can use Microsoft Excel's charting features to chart the PivotTable data.

PART THREE

Database Tuning
and Administration

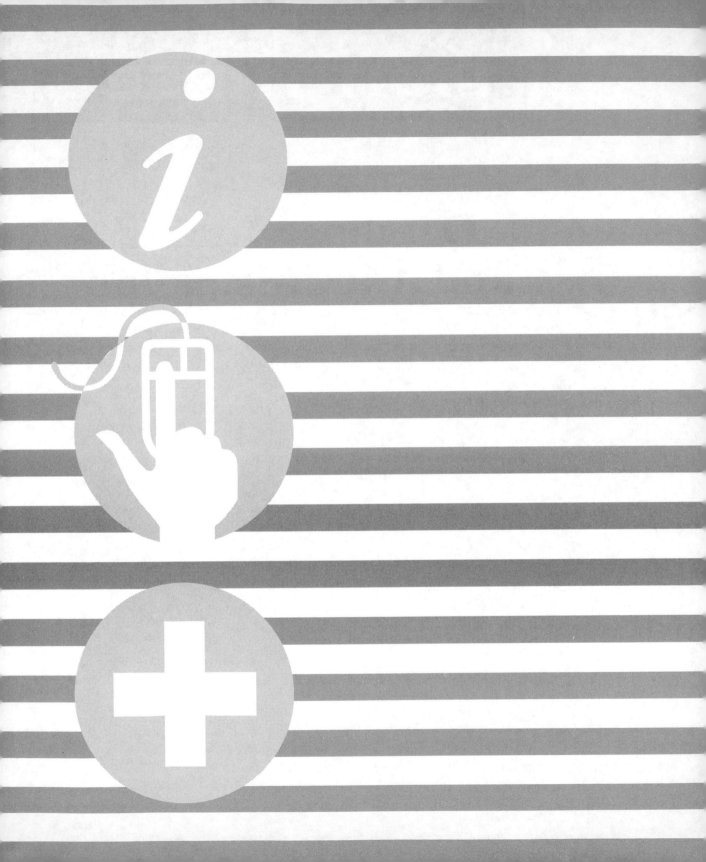

CHAPTER

15

Personalizing Access

YOU can tailor your Access work environment to your own requirements and working style. If you're happy with the way Access is working now, there's no need to change the default settings and you should feel free to skip this chapter. But if you'd like to learn how to tweak things a bit, read on.

Note that other chapters in this book explain how to customize the features described in Table 15.1, so we won't repeat those discussions here.

Personalizing Your Work Environment

You can personalize many aspects of your Access work environment by following the general steps below:

1. Open a database (if one isn't open already) and choose Tools ➤ Options. You'll see the Options dialog box, shown in Figure 15.1.

2. Click on a tab to select a category. (For your convenience, we've arranged the following sections in alphabetical order according to the category of options that each tab controls.)

3. Change options, as described in the sections that follow. Depending on the option you're setting, you can type a value, select a value from a drop-down list, select an option button, or select (check) or deselect (clear) a check box. Selecting a check box activates the associated option (that is, it says "Yes, I want this option"); deselecting the check box deactivates the option (that is, it says "No, I don't want this option").

4. When you're finished making changes, click on OK.

TABLE 15.1: Other Places to Learn about Customizing Access

TO CUSTOMIZE THIS...	USE THESE OPTIONS...	AND SEE THIS CHAPTER OR HELP INDEX TOPIC
Custom Controls	Tools ➤ Custom Controls	Look up *Custom Controls* subtopics in the Access Help Index.
Menus	Tools ➤ Add-Ins ➤ Menu Builder	24
Security	Tools ➤ Security ➤...	18
Toolbars	View ➤ Toolbars	23
Switchboards	Tools ➤ Add-Ins ➤ Switchboard Manager	21

FIGURE 15.1

Choosing Tools ➤ Options takes you to the Options dialog box, where you can change numerous default settings in Access.

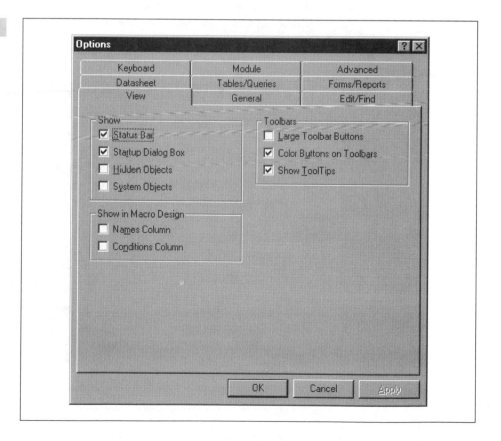

➤ For more about the options discussed in the following sections, choose Tools ➤ Options, and click on the appropriate category tab. Next, click on the ? button at the upper-right corner of the Options dialog box, and then click on the option you're interested in; or, right-click on the option name and choose What's This?; or click in a text box or combo box and press Shift+F1. You also can look up topics under *Default Settings* in the Access Help Index.

Changing Advanced Options

The Advanced options (see Figure 15.2) control how Access handles data in a multiuser environment and how it handles OLE and DDE operations.

The OLE/DDE options are as follows:

DDE Operations   Select or clear options to choose whether to Ignore DDE Requests from other programs and whether to Enable DDE Refresh at the interval given by the OLE/DDE Timeout (Sec) setting (see below).

Options		? X
Datasheet	Tables/Queries	Forms/Reports
View	General	Edit/Find
Keyboard	Module	Advanced

Default Record Locking
- ⦿ No Locks
- ◯ All Records
- ◯ Edited Records

Default Open Mode
- ⦿ Shared
- ◯ Exclusive

DDE Operations
- ☐ Ignore DDE Requests
- ☑ Enable DDE Refresh

Number of Update Retries: `2`

ODBC Refresh Interval [sec]: `1500`

Refresh Interval [sec]: `60`

OLE/DDE Timeout [sec]: `30`   Update Retry Interval [msec]: `250`

OLE/DDE Timeout (Sec)   Specify the interval, in seconds (from 0 to 300), that Access will wait before retrying a failed OLE or DDE operation.

 ➤ See Chapter 18 and the online Help for details about these multiuser options on the Advanced tab: Default Record Locking, Default Open Mode, Number Of Update Retries, ODBC Refresh Interval (Sec), Refresh Interval (Sec), and Update Retry Interval (Msec).

Changing Datasheet Options

The Datasheet options, shown in Figure 15.3, let you change the default appearance of the datasheet view when you first open a table or query. Most options are self-explanatory, so we won't trouble you with reading through the details about them. However, you might want to know about

FIGURE 15.3

The Datasheet options in the Options dialog box

Options		?	X

View	General	Edit/Find
Keyboard	Module	Advanced
Datasheet	Tables/Queries	Forms/Reports

Default Colors
Font: Black
Background: White
Gridlines: Silver

Default Font
Font:
Arial
Weight: Size:
Normal   10
☐ Italic   ☐ Underline

Default Gridlines Showing
☑ Horizontal
☑ Vertical

Default Column Width: 1"

Default Cell Effect
⊙ Flat
○ Raised
○ Sunken

☑ Show Animations

the Sho_w Animations option, which lets you enable or disable the animated insertion and deletion of records and columns in datasheets.

You can override the Default Colors, Default Gridlines Showing, Default Font, Default Column Width, and Default Cell Effect settings in datasheet view. To do so, choose the _F_ont, Ce_l_ls, and _C_olumn Width options on the F_o_rmat menu, or use the Formatting (Datasheet) toolbar, as explained in Chapter 8.

Changing Edit/Find Options

Use the Edit/Find options, shown in Figure 15.4, to choose the default method for doing a Find or Replace operation; to control whether to confirm various types of changes; and to control the size of value lists when you use filter by form.

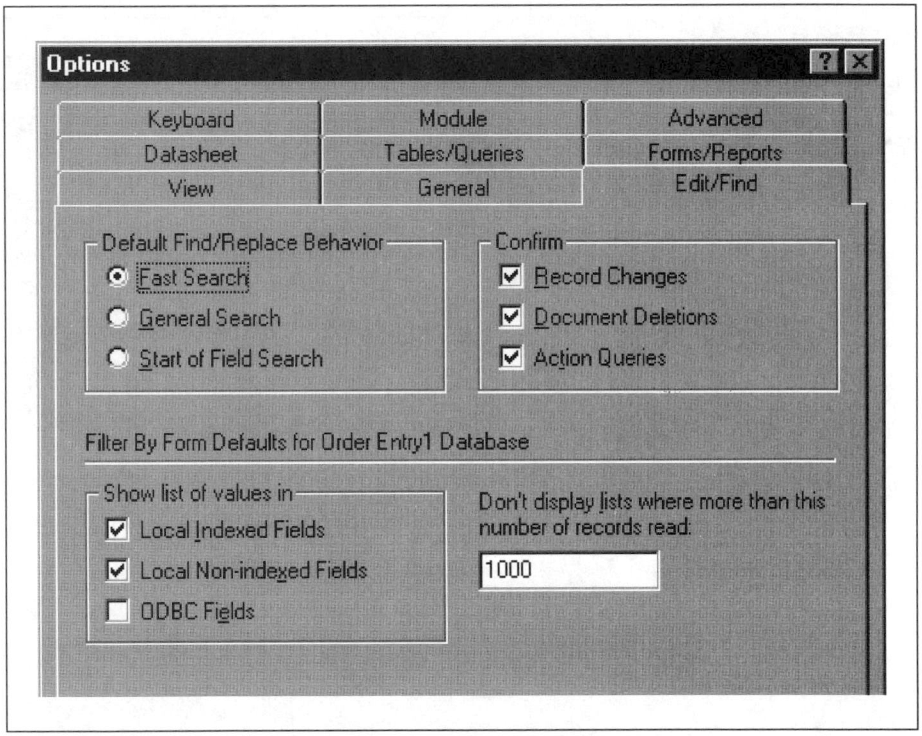

FIGURE 15.4

The Edit/Find options in the Options dialog box

The Default Find/Replace options are listed below. You can override these settings in the Find In Field (Edit ➤ Find) or Replace In Field (Edit ➤ Replace) dialog boxes, as explained in Chapter 9:

Fast Search   Searches the current field and matches the whole field.

General Search   Searches the current field and matches any part of the field.

Start Of Field Search   Searches the current field and matches the beginning character or characters in the field.

The check box options below *Confirm* let you control whether Access displays a confirmation message when you change a record (Record Changes), delete a database object (Document Deletions), or run an action query (Action Queries). It's a good idea to leave these options checked.

The options below *Filter By Form Defaults For Database* control which fields supply values when you use the Filter By Form feature (see Chapter 9), and how many rows to display in a filter by form list. These options affect the current database only, and you can set different defaults for other databases. You can override the options for a given filter by form operation, as explained in Chapter 9. To speed up filter by form operations, limit the Filter By Form Defaults settings to local indexed fields and reduce the number of records read.

Changing Forms/Reports Options

Use the Forms/Reports options, shown in Figure 15.5, to control the default templates used for form and report designs and to define the selection behavior when you drag the mouse pointer to select controls in form and report design view.

The Forms/Reports options are:

Selection Behavior   Choose Partially Enclosed to have Access select controls that are even partially contained within the frame. Choose Fully Enclosed to have Access select only controls that are completely contained within the frame you draw while dragging the pointer.

Form Template   The default is Normal, a built-in, general-purpose template that Access uses to create an AutoForm or blank

FIGURE 15.5

The Forms/Reports options in the Options dialog box

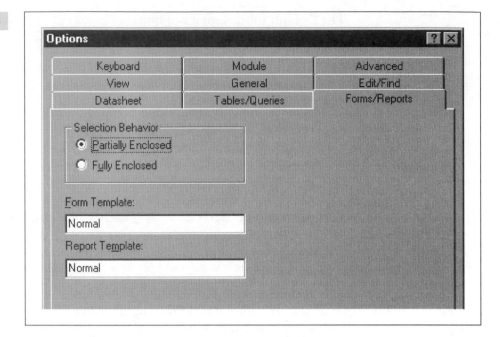

form. You can specify any existing form in the database as the form template, if you wish. If you specify a form that doesn't exist in the database, Access will use the built-in Normal form template.

Report Template As with forms, the default report template is Normal, but you can specify any existing report in the database as the report template. Access uses this template to create an AutoReport or blank report. If you specify a report that doesn't exist in the database, Access will use the built-in Normal report template.

NOTE Form and report templates define whether to include a form or report header and footer, whether to include a page header and footer, the dimensions of each section, and the default properties for each control. A template does not create controls on a new form or report.

When designing a form or report, you can override the default settings in many ways. For example, you can change the default properties for new controls that you add to a form or report in design view, and you can use AutoFormat styles to format all or part of a design. See Chapter 13 for complete details about designing forms and reports.

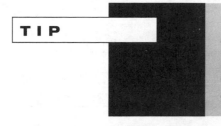

TIP

If you'd like to use custom control settings for all new forms or reports that you design, customize the properties for each control to your liking. Then save the design and define it as a template in the Form Template or Report Template option setting described above.

Changing General Options

The General options (see Figure 15.6) let you change these default settings:

Print Margins   Use the Print Margins options to assign default Left Margin, Right Margin, Top Margin, and Bottom Margin settings for new reports and forms (the settings have no effect on existing forms and reports). Initially all the margins are one (1) inch wide.

To change the margin settings in an existing form or report, open the form or report in design view, choose File ➤ Page Setup, click on the Margins tab, change the Top, Bottom, Left, and Right settings as needed, and then click on OK (see Chapter 9).

Default Database Folder   Specify the folder in which Access will store or search for databases. The default is the dot (.) which stands for the default Access working directory, a folder named My Documents. (If you rename the My Documents folder in Windows 95 later, Windows 95 will adjust the appropriate registry settings to point to the renamed folder automatically.)

New Database Sort Order   Choose the language used for alphabetic sorting of new databases. Options include General (for English), Traditional Spanish, Dutch, and several other languages. To change the sort method for an existing database, make the change here (in the New Database Sort Order text box), and then compact the existing database as discussed in Chapter 17.

FIGURE 15.6

The General options in the Options dialog box

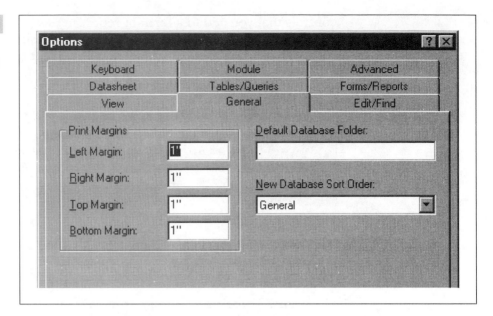

Changing Keyboard Options

The Keyboard options, shown in Figure 15.7, let you control how the ↵ key, arrow keys, Tab key, and insertion point behave when you use the keyboard to move within or between fields in a form or datasheet.

Move After Enter Determines what happens when you press ↵ in a field. Your options are Don't Move (↵ has no effect), Next Field (↵ moves the cursor to the next field), or Next Record (↵ moves the cursor to the first field in the next record).

Arrow Key Behavior Choose Next Field if you want the cursor to move to another field when you press ← or →, or choose Next Character if you want the cursor to move within the field when you press those keys. If Next Field is selected, you can press F2 and then ← or → to move the cursor within a field.

Behavior Entering Field Determines what happens when the cursor lands in a field. Your options are Select Entire Field, Go To Start Of Field, or Go To End Of Field.

Cursor Stops At First/Last Field Determines what happens in a datasheet when you press the ← key in the first field of a row or the → key in the last field of a row. Select (check) this option to

FIGURE 15.7

The Keyboard options in the Options dialog box

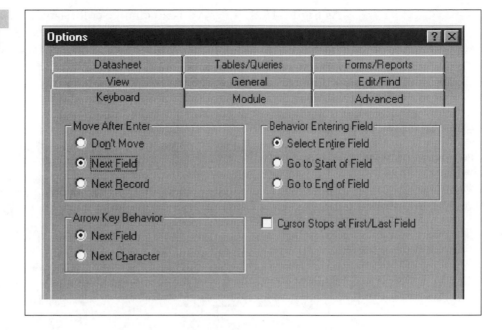

have the cursor stay in the current field, or deselect (clear) it to move the cursor to the previous or next record.

When designing a form, you can control the behavior of the ↵ key in text boxes (that is, Text and Memo fields). To do this, open the form in design view, open the property sheet, and click on the Other tab on the property sheet. Next, select the text box control, and then change the Enter Key Behavior property either to Default (so that it uses the Move After Enter setting discussed above) or to New Line In Field (so that pressing ↵ moves the cursor to a new line in the field). To simplify entry of multiple text lines in a Memo field, the control's Enter Key Behavior is initially set to New Line In Field. If you choose Default instead, you typically must press Ctrl+↵ to enter a new line in the Memo field's text box.

Changing Module Options

The Module Design options, shown in Figure 15.8, determine the default characteristics of the module design window used for creating Visual Basic procedures and functions (see Chapter 25).

As Figure 15.8 shows, you can change colors and font used for your code, various coding options, how code is displayed in the Module window (Code View), and some settings that apply to the Current Database Only. For more about using and customizing the Module window, see Chapter 25 and the online Help for the Module tab.

FIGURE 15.8

The Module options in the Options dialog box

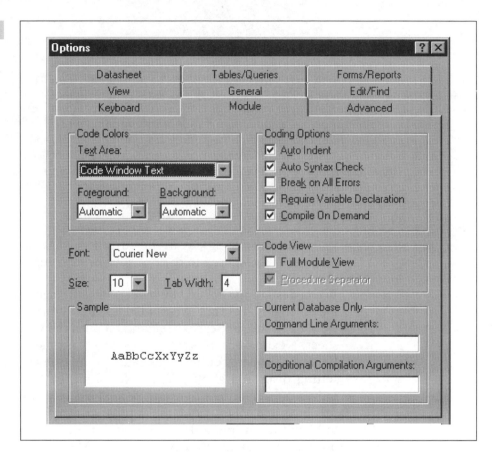

Changing Tables/Queries Options

Use the Tables/Queries options (see Figure 15.9) to choose defaults for new table fields and indexes, and to control default behavior in the query design window.

FIGURE 15.9

The Tables/Queries options in the Options dialog box

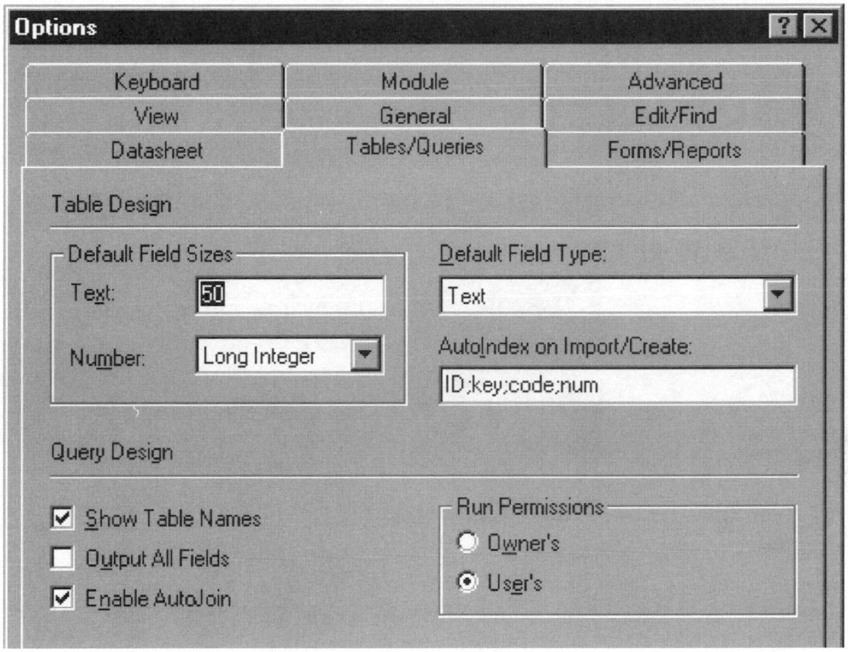

The Table Design options are:

Default Field Sizes   Lets you specify the default field size for newly created text and number fields in table design view. Specify a Text field size from 0 to 255; choose a default Number field size from the Number drop-down list.

Default Field Type   Lets you choose the default field type for newly created fields in table design view.

AutoIndex On Import/Create   Lets you specify field names that are indexed automatically when you first create them in table design view or when you import them from an external file. The Indexed property on the General tab of the table design window will display Yes (Duplicates OK) for automatically indexed fields.

In the AutoIndex On Import/Create text box, enter the beginning characters or ending characters that the automatically indexed field names should contain, and separate each field name (or partial field name) with a semicolon (;). *Example:* the AutoIndex On Import/Create setting shown in Figure 15.9 will cause Access to automatically index field names such as ID, MyID, KeyField, Code1, and AutoNum.

WARNING   Each table can have up to 32 indexes. You're likely to bump up against that 32-index limit rather quickly if you include many field names in the AutoIndex On Import/Create option, or if many fields that you create or import include the field names listed in the AutoIndex On Import/Create text box.

The Query Design options are:

Show Table Names   Lets you display or hide table names in the QBE grid. To override this setting, choose View ➤ Table Names in the query design window.

Output All Fields   When selected, all fields in a query's underlying tables or queries appear when the query is run; when deselected only the fields added to the QBE grid appear. To override this setting, change the query's Output All Fields property.

Enable AutoJoin   Lets you choose whether to create automatic inner joins between two tables that you add to the query design window. Access can create an inner join for tables if those tables are already joined in the Relationships window, or the tables contain fields that have the same field name and the same or compatible data type in each table. Even if you disable automatic joins, you can create them manually in the query design window.

Run Permissions   Choose Owner's to run new queries with the owner's permissions, or choose User's to run new queries with the current user's permissions. These permissions are important on secured databases. To view or change a query's owner, choose Tools ➤ Security ➤ User And Group Permissions from the menus, and then click on the Change Owner tab. To override the query's default run permissions, open the query in design view and change its Run Permissions property.

➤ See Chapter 6 for details about designing tables, Chapter 7 for more information about importing tables, Chapter 10 for more about queries, and Chapter 18 for tips on networking and security.

Changing View Options

Use the View options, shown in Figure 15.10, to control the appearance of the database window, toolbars, and macro design windows, and to choose whether the status bar and startup dialog box appear.

Status Bar   Lets you display or hide the status bar. (Your life will be easier if you leave the status bar visible, so you can see the helpful hints Access displays there.)

Startup Dialog Box   Controls whether the startup dialog box appears when you start Access. When this option is selected, Access displays the initial dialog box that lets you choose which database to open; when deselected, you're taken directly to the Access main menu, which has only the File, Tools, and Help menus.

FIGURE 15.10

The View options in the Options dialog box

Options	? ✕

Keyboard	Module	Advanced
Datasheet	Tables/Queries	Forms/Reports
View	General	Edit/Find

Show
- ☑ Status Bar
- ☑ Startup Dialog Box
- ☐ Hidden Objects
- ☐ System Objects

Toolbars
- ☐ Large Toolbar Buttons
- ☑ Color Buttons on Toolbars
- ☑ Show ToolTips

Show in Macro Design
- ☐ Names Column
- ☐ Conditions Column

N O T E If you turn off the startup dialog box, you must open a database (File ➤ Open Database) or create a database (File ➤ New Database) before you can choose Tools ➤ Options again.

Hidden Objects   Controls whether to display or hide objects in the database window if they have a property of Hidden. When you choose to display hidden objects, their icons will be dimmed in the database window. To hide an object, go to the database window, locate the object you want to hide, right-click on the object's name, select (check) the Hidden property near the bottom of the dialog box, and then click on OK.

System Objects   Controls whether to display or hide the names of internal system objects that Access creates, or system objects that you create. These system objects start with the letters Msys or Usys. If you select (check) the System Objects option, Access will show system objects along with other table names in the database window, though their icons will be dimmed. (It's best to leave these objects hidden to avoid confusion.)

W A R N I N G Don't mess around with any of the system objects that Access creates if you aren't absolutely sure of what you're doing. The results can be disastrous.

Names Column   Controls whether to display or hide the Macro Name column in the macro design window. To override this setting, choose View ➤ Macro Names from the macro design menus.

Conditions Column   Controls whether to display or hide the Condition column. To override this setting, choose View ➤ Conditions from the macro design menus.

Large Toolbar Buttons   Controls whether to display toolbar buttons in a large, easy-to-read format, or to display them at their normal small size. Large buttons are most useful on screens with video resolution higher than 640 by 480 pixels. When viewing large toolbar buttons on a VGA screen, double-click on an empty area of the toolbar to display the buttons in a floating palette that you can drag to a convenient spot.

T I P

To change your screen's video resolution on the fly (if your screen supports adjustable resolutions and you're using Windows 95), minimize Access and other programs you're running, so you can see the Windows 95 desktop. Then right-click on any blank area on the Windows desktop, choose Properties, click on the Settings tab in the Display Properties dialog box, drag the slider control below the Desktop Area option, and then click on OK. When prompted, click on OK and then click on Yes to accept the changes.

Color Buttons On Toolbars   Lets you display toolbar buttons in color or black-and-white.

Show ToolTips   Lets you display or hide the ToolTips on buttons and combo boxes. ToolTips appear when the mouse pointer rests on the button or combo box. ToolTips are a great help, so we suggest that you leave this option selected. (Note that this option has no effect on ControlTips that you add to your own forms and their controls; see Chapter 13.)

Personalizing a Database

There are several ways to personalize a database:

- Set *startup options* that take effect when you open the database. See the next section.

- Set *database properties* that document your database and make it easier to find the database later. See "Changing the Database Properties" in Chapter 5.

- Set *object properties* for objects that appear in the database window. See "Changing Properties of an Entire Table or Object" in Chapter 6.

Changing Startup Options

The Startup options let you control options that take effect when you open a particular database. You can use the Startup dialog box instead of, or in addition to, an AutoExec macro. The AutoExec macro will run after the Startup dialog box options take effect. (See Chapters 20 and 28 for more about macros.)

To set the Startup options:

1. Open the database for which you want to set startup options.

2. Choose Tools ➤ Startup; or, right-click on any gray area on the database window and choose Startup. You'll see the Startup dialog box, shown in Figure 15.11.

3. Change any of the options described just below.

4. Click on OK to accept the new settings and close the Startup dialog box.

5. If necessary, close the database and open it again.

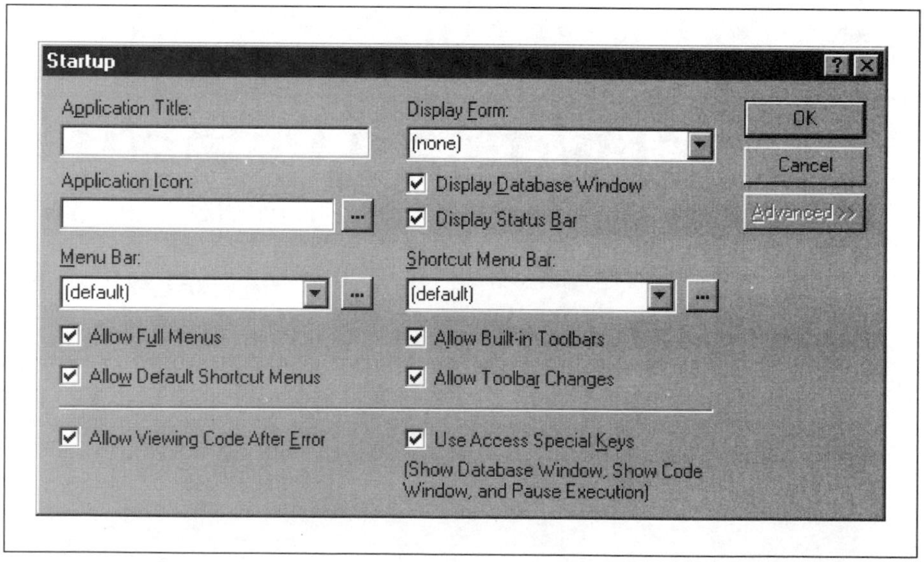

FIGURE 15.11

The Startup dialog box, after we clicked on the Advanced button

TIP

To bypass the Startup settings and use the default options shown in Figure 15.11, hold down the Shift key while opening the database.

The Startup dialog box options are described below. Note that some options take effect as soon as you close the Startup dialog box; however, others don't take effect until the next time the database is opened (these "delayed" options are marked with an asterisk below).

Application Title Lets you display your own application title in the Access title bar. Type the title you want to display. To use the default application title of *Microsoft Access,* leave the Application Title text box empty.

Application Icon Lets you replace the standard Access "key" icon with an application icon of your own choosing. The icon appears in the Access title bar and on the application's taskbar button. To specify an icon, type its name into the Application Icon text box; or, click on the Build (...) button next to the Application Icon option, locate the icon (*.ico) or bitmap (*.bmp) file you want to display, and then double-click on its file name. (On Windows NT, you can use icon files only, not bitmap files.) If you'll be distributing your application, it's best to put the icon or bitmap file in the same folder as your application. To use the default icon for Access, leave the Application Icon text box empty.

Menu Bar ★ Lets you choose a global menu bar to display when you open the current database. Choose an existing menu bar from the drop-down list next to the Menu Bar option, or choose (Default) to use the Access default menu bar. If you want to create a new menu bar on the fly, click on the Build (...) button next to the Menu Bar text box and build your menu bar as described in Chapter 24.

Allow Full Menus ★ Lets you choose whether a full set, or a restricted set, of menus appears on the Access built-in menu bars. Select (check) this option to display a full set of built-in menus; deselect (clear) this option to display a restricted set of built-in menus that doesn't allow design changes to database objects.

Allow Default Shortcut Menus ★ Lets you choose whether the Access default shortcut menus are available. Select (check) this option to display shortcut menus when you right-click on a toolbar or other object; deselect (clear) this option to prevent shortcut menus from appearing when you right-click.

Allow Viewing Code After Error ★   Lets you control whether to enable the Ctrl+Break key and allow code viewing in the Module window after a run-time error occurs in the application. (When you're finished developing your application, you may want to deselect this option to prevent users from viewing your code.)

Display Form ★   Lets you choose which form to display when the database is opened. To avoid displaying any form, choose (None) from the Display Form drop-down list. The applications you create with the Database Wizard specify a form named *Switchboard* as the Display Form.

Display Database Window ★   Lets you choose whether to display or hide the database window when you open the database. It's often handy to hide the database window if your database displays a form at startup. (Even if the database window doesn't appear at startup, you usually can display it anytime by pressing F11.)

Display Status Bar ★   Lets you choose whether the status bar appears at the bottom of the Access window (usually it's best to leave this option checked, so you can see the status bar). To turn off the status bar for all Access databases, choose Tools ➤ Options, click on the View tab, and deselect (clear) Status Bar. The status bar won't appear in the current database if you've turned off the status bar for the current database, all databases, or both.

Shortcut Menu Bar ★   Lets you choose a shortcut menu bar to display when you right-click on a form or report in form view or print preview. Choose an existing shortcut menu bar from the drop-down list next to the Menu Bar option, or choose (Default) to use the Access default shortcut menu bar. If you want to create a new shortcut menu bar on the fly, click on the Build (...) button next to the Shortcut Menu Bar text box (see Chapter 24).

Allow Built-In Toolbars ★   Lets you choose whether to allow users to display the Access built-in toolbars. This setting will not affect custom toolbars that you add. Normally you'll want to leave the toolbars available, unless you're developing an application that has its own custom toolbars and you don't want Access toolbars to appear.

Allow Toolbar Changes ★   Lets you choose whether to allow users to change the built-in toolbars and custom toolbars. Select (check) this option to allow changes to the toolbars. Deselect (clear) this option to disable the View ➤ Toolbars command and the right mouse button on toolbars.

Use Access Special Keys ★   Lets you choose whether to enable or disable these special keys: F11 or Alt+F1 (displays the database window), Ctrl+G (displays the debug window), Ctrl+F11 (toggles between the custom menu bar and the built-in menu bar), Ctrl+Break (stops code from running and displays the current module in the Module window).

 ➤ For details about any option in the Startup dialog box, right-click on the option name and click on What's This?, or click in an option's text box and then press Shift+F1. For information about important things to consider when you alter settings in the Startup dialog box, double-click on *Startup Dialog Box* in the Access Help Index, then double-click on the *Considerations When Setting Options In The Startup Dialog Box* topic.

Installing Wizards, Builders, and Menu Add-Ins

Access Wizards, builders, and menu add-ins are contained in special library databases. You can use the Add-In Manager to install or uninstall existing libraries, and to add new library databases.

NOTE   Library databases have the file extension .mda; otherwise, they are similar to standard database (.mdb). Several libraries come with Access and are installed automatically by the Setup program (see Appendix A); however, these libraries do not appear in the Add-In Manager dialog box. You also can create your own libraries or purchase them from third-party suppliers.

To get started with the Add-In Manager, follow these steps:

1. Choose Tools ➤ Add-Ins ➤ Add-In Manager. The Add-in Manager dialog box, shown in Figure 15.12, will appear. Installed libraries are marked with an ×.

2. Do one of the following:

   - **To add an add-in to the list**, click on the Add New button, locate and click on the add-in's file name in the File Open dialog box, and then click on OK (or double-click on the file name). This procedure copies the library to the Access installation folder (usually \MSOffice\Access) and installs it in the Available Add-Ins list.

   - **To install an available add-in**, click on the add-in name in the Available Add-Ins list, and then click on the Install button.

   - **To uninstall a currently available add-in**, click on the add-in name in the Available Add-Ins list, and then click on the Uninstall button. When the library is uninstalled, it's available on disk but won't be loaded into memory and can't be used. You can conserve memory and reduce the time it takes to load Access by uninstalling libraries that you aren't using.

FIGURE 15.12

The Add-In Manager dialog box with one add-in installed (this add-in is courtesy of Ken Getz at KNG Consulting).

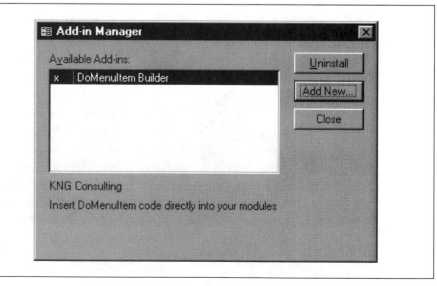

- **To quickly install or uninstall an add-in,** double-click on the add-in name in the A<u>v</u>ailable Add-Ins list (double-clicking will toggle the × on or off).

3. When you're done using the Add-In Manager, click on Close. You'll be returned to the database window.

| WARNING | Don't just experiment with installing and uninstalling add-ins. If you do, you might lose Wizards and options on the <u>T</u>ools ➤ Add-<u>I</u>ns menus. To restore lost add-ins, reinstall Access and any third-party add-ins. |

 ➤ You can learn more about the Add-In Manager by searching for *Add-In Manager* in the Access Answer Wizard. For details about creating and installing library databases, see Chapter 16 "Creating Wizards, Builders, and Add-Ins" in the Access manual titled *Building Applications with Microsoft Access for Windows 95.*

Customizing the Add-Ins

In previous versions of Access, you could customize Wizards by using the Add-In Manager. This feature is no longer available (and often isn't needed), because many Wizards allow customization when you use them.

 ➤ If you need to customize the Table Wizard, you can learn how to do so in the Access Developer's Toolkit. For more information on the Access Developers Toolkit, look up *Developer's Toolkit, Contents Of* in the Access Help Index.

Other Ways to Personalize Access

This chapter has discussed many ways to personalize Access. But there are more! You also can personalize the appearance and behavior of Access by changing options in Windows Control Panel, by specifying startup options on the command line that starts Access, and by customizing the registry file. The following sections briefly discuss these techniques.

Using Control Panel to Customize Access

Like most Windows programs, Access inherits many of its settings from options that you set in Windows Control Panel. To get started with Control Panel, click on the Start button on the taskbar, and choose Settings ➤ Control Panel (or double-click on the My Computer icon on your desktop, and then double-click on the Control Panel folder). When the Control Panel window opens, double-click on the icon for the settings you want to change (see Table 15.2). Remember that your changes in Control Panel will affect most other Windows programs.

TABLE 15.2: Useful Control Panel Settings for Customizing Access and Other Windows Programs

ICON	SETTINGS OPTION	WHAT IT DOES
32bit ODBC	32bit ODBC	Lets you add, delete, or configure data sources and install new 32-bit ODBC drivers on your computer. A data source includes the data source name, description, server, network address, network library, and other information used to identify and locate data on a network (see Chapter 18).
Display	Display	Lets you choose the colors used for various parts of the screen and change the appearance of your Windows desktop.
Fonts	Fonts	Lets you add and remove fonts and set TrueType options.
Network	Network	Lets you manage your network configuration, choose a primary network logon, enable or disable file and printer sharing, identify your computer to the network, and choose how to allow access to shared resources on your computer (see Chapter 18).

TABLE 15.2: Useful Control Panel Settings for Customizing Access and Other Windows Programs (continued)

ICON	SETTINGS OPTION	WHAT IT DOES
Passwords	Passwords	For networked computers, this option lets you change your Windows password and the password for other password-protected devices, allow remote administration of your computer, and choose personal preferences for users of your computer (see Chapter 18).
Printers	Printers	Lets you install and remove printers, change printing settings, and select the printer you want to use as the default printer.
Regional Settings	Regional Settings	Lets you specify international settings, including units of measurement, list separators, and formats for dates, times, currency, and numbers.
System	System	Lets you manage hardware devices on your computer, maintain hardware configuration profiles, and optimize various Windows settings for better performance. (Windows usually is optimized for better performance automatically.)

 ➤ For more information about the options listed in Table 15.2, see your Windows documentation, or use the Help ➤ Help Topics menus in Control Panel. You also can click on any Control Panel icon and look at the status bar to find out what it does, and you can right-click on options in the various Control Panel dialog boxes and choose What's This?.

Using Command-Line Options When Starting Access

You can use *startup options* to open a database automatically, run a macro, supply a user account name or password, and more, simply by specifying options on the command line that starts Microsoft Access. There are two ways to specify startup options, and we'll explain both methods shortly:

- **On the Start ➤ Programs Menus**   Access always starts with any options you've specified in the Start ➤ Programs menus. Typically, only one Microsoft Access entry appears on these menus.

- **In a Shortcut**   Access starts with any options you've specified in the shortcut. You can set up as many shortcuts as you need (see Chapter 1), and you can place those shortcuts in a folder or directly on your Windows desktop.

A standard Access startup command, without any command-line options, usually looks like this:

```
c:\msoffice\access\msaccess.exe
```

To specify command-line options, begin with the startup command shown above, then type a space, and then type additional options as needed (with each option separated by a space). The example below starts Access and opens the Order Entry1 database in the folder named My Documents on drive C (of course you must enter all the text on one line):

```
c:\msoffice\access\msaccess.exe
   "c:\My Documents\Order Entry1"
```

 **WARNING**

If the path to your database contains spaces, be sure to enclose the path in double quotation marks, as shown in the example above. If the path doesn't include spaces, you can omit the double quotation marks.

This example starts Access and opens the Order Entry1 database in runtime mode:

```
c:\msoffice\access\msaccess.exe
   "c:\My Documents\Order Entry1" /runtime
```

 ➤ Table 15.3 shows the most commonly used Access command-line options. For a complete list and more information, search for *Command Line Options* in the Access Answer Wizard, and then double-click on *Startup Command-Line Options* under *Tell Me About*.

TABLE 15.3: Commonly Used Access Command-Line Options

OPTION *	EFFECT
database	** Opens the specified *database*.
source database /Compact *target database*	** Compacts the *source database* to the name specified as the *target database*, and then closes Access. Omit the *target database* name if you want to compact the database to the *source database* name.
database /Excl	Opens the specified database for exclusive access. Omit the /Excl option to open the database for shared access in a multiuser environment.
/Nostartup	Starts Access without displaying the startup dialog box. Same as choosing <u>T</u>ools ➤ <u>O</u>ptions, and deselecting Startup Dialog Box on the View tab of the Options dialog box.
/Profile *user profile*	Starts Access using the options in the specified *user profile* instead of the standard Windows Registry settings created when you installed Microsoft Access. The /Profile option replaces the /ini option used in previous versions of Access to specify an initialization file. See the Microsoft Access Developer's Toolkit for tools and information about creating user profiles.
/Pwd *password*	Starts Access using the specified *password* (see Chapter 18).
/Repair *database*	Repairs the specified *database*, and then closes Access (see Chapter 17).
database /RO	Opens the specified database for read-only access.
database /Runtime	Starts Access in run-time mode and opens the specified *database*. In run-time mode, users cannot access the database window or open database objects in Design view. This option is useful for running turnkey applications, such as those the Database Wizard creates.
/User *user name*	Starts Access using the specified *user name* (see Chapter 18).

TABLE 15.3: Commonly Used Access Command-Line Options (continued)

OPTION *	EFFECT
/Wrkgrp *workgroup information file*	** Starts Access using the specified *workgroup information file* (see Chapter 18).
/X *macro*	Starts Access and runs the specified *macro*. You also can run a macro when you open a database by using an AutoExec macro (see Chapters 20 and 28).

* To specify a forward slash (/) or semicolon (;) on the command line, type the character twice. For example, to specify the password ;eao/rnaa47 on the command line, type ;;eao//rnaa47 following the /Pwd command-line option.

** Specify a path name if necessary. If the path name contains any spaces, enclose the entire path name in double quotation marks. See the example in the chapter.

Specifying Startup Options on the Start Menu

If you always want Access to use the same startup options, you can modify the Microsoft Access entry on the Start ➤ Programs menus:

1. Right-click on the Start button on the Windows taskbar, and choose Explore. The Exploring - Start Menu window will open.

2. In the right pane of the window, double-click on the Programs folder, and then double-click on folders as needed until you locate the Microsoft Access shortcut icon.

3. Right-click on the Microsoft Access shortcut icon and choose Properties. Or, click on the icon and press Alt+⤶.

4. In the Microsoft Access Properties dialog box, click on the Shortcut tab.

5. Press the End key to move the insertion point to the right of the Access startup command in the Target text box.

6. Type a space and enter the command-line settings you want to use.

7. If you wish, set the Start In, Shortcut Key, and Run options in the dialog box. (To learn more about any of these options, right-click on an option name and choose What's This?.)

8. Click on OK to return to the Exploring window.

9. Close the Exploring window.

The next time you use the Start ➤ Programs menus to start Access, your command-line options will take effect.

Specifying Startup Options in a Shortcut

Chapter 1 explained how to create shortcuts. Assuming you've already set up a shortcut for Microsoft Access, here's how to modify it to include startup options:

1. Locate the shortcut in a folder or on your desktop.

2. Right-click on the Microsoft Access shortcut icon and choose Properties, or click on the icon and press Alt+↵.

3. Fill in the Microsoft Access Properties dialog box, as explained in steps 4–7 of the previous section.

4. Click on OK to accept the changes.

The next time you double-click on an Access shortcut icon, Access will start with the command-line options you chose.

About the Registry File

When Access starts up, it reads various settings from the Windows *registry file*. (In Access 2.0, startup settings were stored in the initialization file, named \windows\msacc20.ini.) Many of these settings are defined when you install Access, and some are updated when you use certain Access utility options, such as the Workgroup Administrator discussed in Chapter 18. You'll rarely need to update the registry file manually, but if you do so, *be very careful*—and back up the registry first! Incorrect updates to the registry can prevent Access and other Windows programs from working correctly.

If you do need to update the registry, you must use the Registry Editor to make the changes. To get started, click on the Start button on the

Windows taskbar, choose <u>R</u>un, type **regedit**, and press ↵. Your changes will take effect the next time you start Access.

➤ To learn more about changing the registry, search for *Registry* in the Access Answer Wizard, and then explore subtopics as needed.

Where to Go from Here

In this chapter you've learned many ways to personalize Access to your own working style. The next chapter presents ways to analyze your databases and speed up their performance.

What's New in the Access Zoo?

The options for customizing Access for Windows 95 are organized differently than those in Access 2.0, and there are more of them. Here are some reminders to help upgraders figure out where to look for the most important options:

- **To begin customizing Access,** open the database you want to customize, or open any database if you want to change overall settings.

- **To customize startup options for all Access databases,** choose <u>T</u>ools ➤ <u>O</u>ptions. Then click on the tab for the category of options you want to work with (View, General, Edit/Find, Datasheet, Tables/Queries, Forms/Reports, Keyboard, Module, or Advanced), and change the options as needed. Click on OK when you're done.

- **To customize startup options for the current database,** choose <u>T</u>ools ➤ Startu<u>p</u>, and change the options as needed. Click on OK when you're done.

- **To install or uninstall add-ins, builders, and Wizards,** choose <u>T</u>ools ➤ Add-<u>I</u>ns ➤ <u>A</u>dd-In Manager. Note that you no longer can use the Add-In Manager to customize an add-in (and it's usually unnecessary to do so).

- **To control how Access starts,** supply command-line options to the Microsoft Access option on the Start menus or any Microsoft Access shortcut icon.

CHAPTER

16

Speeding Up
Your Database

IF you're dreaming of a database that screams along at the speed of a Formula 1 Ferrari, but you're getting performance that's more like the plod, plod, plod of a desert tortoise, this chapter may be just what you're looking for. Here you'll find tips for tweaking that tired database engine so that it races swiftly along the information superhighway.

As you read this chapter, keep in mind that you can't make a Ferrari out of a Volkswagen Bug, or a Pentium out of an 80386. But you can squeeze the best possible performance out of the computer hardware you do have. If you're still hungry for speed after trying the suggestions in this chapter, you can always throw money at the problem and invest in faster, more expensive hardware.

N O T E   For more tips on optimizing performance in a network environment, see Chapter 18.

So Where Do I Start?

For your convenience, I've divided this chapter into the five performance areas listed below:

- General Performance
- The Performance Analyzer
- Tables
- Queries
- Forms, Reports, and Printing

Start with the suggestions in the General Performance category, and then work your way to the other categories if you notice sluggishness in those areas. Within each section below, we've arranged the tips in the general order that you should try them. So, start at the top of each list of suggestions and work your way down to the bottom.

N O T E

The optimal settings in the categories that follow can vary with the type of computer hardware you're using to run Access. For best results, tweak one setting at a time, and monitor the performance after each change.

> You can find out more about optimizing Access performance by searching for *performance* in Help.

Speeding Up General Performance

There are two basic ways to speed up general performance. First, you can make changes to general Windows 95 settings; these may speed up many Windows applications, not just Access. Second, you can make changes through Access; these will speed up Access, but should have no effect on other Windows applications.

Tweaking Hardware and Windows 95 Settings

For best overall performance in Access and Windows, you should maximize the amount of memory and disk available, as discussed below:

- **Increase the memory (RAM) on your computer.** Access requires at least 12MB of RAM, but the more RAM you buy and install, the better the performance. Don't use any of your RAM for a RAM disk.

- **Optimize Windows 95.** Windows 95 can report any system optimization problems to you. You should check this report in the System Properties dialog box and take any action recommended. You should also check a couple of settings available to you from this dialog box. To see the system performance report and check these settings, follow these steps:

  1. Open the Control Panel by selecting the Settings option on the Start menu, then selecting the Control Panel item.

  2. Double-click on the System icon.

  3. In the System Properties dialog box, click on the Performance tab, and read the report within the Performance Status frame.

  4. Click on the File System button and select the typical role for your machine using the drop-down list box on the Hard Drive tab in the File System Properties dialog box. Set read-ahead optimization to Full using the slider control. Click on OK .

  5. Click on the Graphics button in the System Properties dialog box. Make sure the slider control for Hardware Acceleration in the Advanced Graphics Settings dialog box is set to Full, unless you are having problems with your display. In that case, you may wish to back off this setting a notch or two. The on-screen help will guide you in deciding where to leave this setting. Click on OK.

  6. Click on OK in the System Properties dialog box to accept the settings. If you are prompted to restart Windows 95, click on Yes to do so.

- **Optimize memory usage.** In most cases, letting Windows 95 manage memory for you is the best idea. However, in two situations you may need to set your own virtual memory parameters. If you have only a little space on your default Windows 95 drive or if a different hard disk drive has a faster access time, you should tell Windows 95 to use a different drive for virtual memory. Follow these steps:

  1. Open the Control Panel by selecting the Settings option on the Start menu, then selecting the Control Panel item.

  2. Double-click on the System icon.

3. In the System Properties dialog box, click on the Performance tab, then click on the Virtual Memory button. The dialog box will appear as shown in Figure 16.1.

4. Select the Let Me Specify My Own Virtual Memory Settings option button. Then select the faster or less full drive using the Hard Disk drop-down list box. If you have a choice, choose the fastest drive with at least 15MB of free space. Set a swap file size with a minimum size that, when added to the amount of system RAM, totals 25MB.

5. Click on the OK button, then close the System Properties dialog box by clicking on its OK button.

6. When you are prompted to restart Windows, click on Yes to do so. Restarting Windows makes the change in your swap file take effect.

FIGURE 16.1

The Virtual Memory dialog box

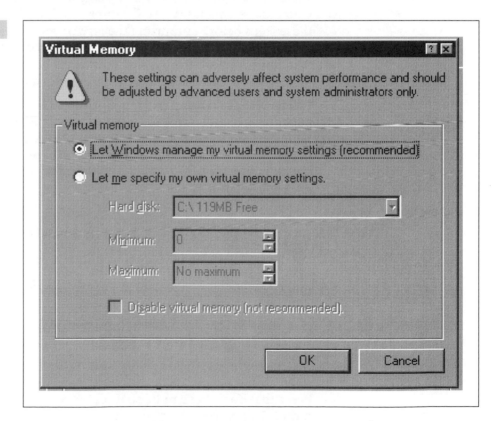

- **Close unneeded applications and TSRs.** You can make more memory available by closing applications and terminate-and-stay-resident (TSR) programs that you aren't using. Using DOS-based TSR programs can slow system performance because of shifts from protected mode into real mode to allow the TSR to run. To prevent TSR programs from running automatically when you start up your computer, delete the appropriate lines in auto-exec.bat or convert them to comments by preceding the lines with a REM command, for example:

```
Rem DOSKEY
```

- **Defragment your hard disk and compact your databases.** To speed disk performance and maximize the amount of free space available, you should periodically delete unnecessary files from your hard disk, defragment your hard disk with a "defrag" utility such as the Windows 95 Disk Defragmenter, and then compact your Access databases (see Chapter 17). You should also take these steps before optimizing the size of your Windows swap file, as discussed next. If you are using the Microsoft Plus! Pack for Windows 95, have the System Agent run ScanDisk and Disk Defragmenter nightly to keep your disk performance top notch.

- **Peel off that wallpaper.** If you have a full-screen (Tile) wallpaper bitmap on your Windows desktop, open Windows Control Panel and double-click on the Desktop icon. Now replace the wallpaper with a solid color or pattern bitmap, or no bitmap at all. Depending on your video display, this can free up between 256K and about 750K of RAM.

Tweaking General Access Settings

You can do the following in Access to improve performance:

- **Open single-user databases exclusively.** When opening databases that won't be shared with other users, select the Exclusive check box in the Open dialog box whenever possible. This will tell Access not to spend time tracking multiuser record locking.

- **Store single-user databases and Access on the local hard disk.** Response will be faster if you install Access, and all databases that don't have to be shared, on your local hard disk drive, rather than on a network server.

- **Use indexes wisely.** Indexes can speed access to data, but they also can slow down record updating (see Chapter 6). For best results with indexes, you should:

  - Create only as many indexes as necessary.
  - Create indexes on fields that you frequently sort by.
  - Create indexes on fields that you frequently search by.
  - In a multiple-field index, include only the fields that are absolutely necessary. You should only consider a multi-field index when you search or sort on a combination of fields. For example, if you frequently search for customers with a particular last name in a particular Zip Code, then a multi-field index on these two fields will help performance.

- **Put only tables on the server for multiuser databases.** Keep all other objects on the local machine's drive. You can use the Database Splitter Wizard to separate the tables for storage on the server.

- **Experiment with record locking strategies.** You want a strategy that minimizes editing conflicts but allows appropriate access to the database. You must strike a balance between the performance penalties of multiple concurrent access and the inconvenience penalties of restrictive record locking.

- **Adjust parameters to avoid locking conflicts.** Experiment with the values of Refresh Interval, Update Retry Interval, Number of Update Retries, and ODBC Refresh Interval. To find these settings, open the Tools menu, select Options, and click on the Advanced tab.

N O T E   For more information on record-locking strategies, see Chapter 18.

Using the Performance Analyzer

A new feature in Access 95 is the Performance Analyzer. This tool examines your database objects and reports ways to improve their performance. The Performance Analyzer provides Suggestions, Recommendations, and Ideas. The analyzer itself can perform Suggestion and Recommendation optimizations for you. Idea optimizations require that you work with Access's features yourself to perform the optimization.

NOTE The Performance Analyzer can examine database objects only. It cannot provide information about how to speed up Access itself or the underlying operating system.

To show you what the Performance Analyzer can do, we've used it to analyze a database created to hold names, addresses, and similar information for a nonprofit corporation. Figure 16.2 shows the results. As you can tell, the Performance Analyzer has provided several tips for improving the speed even of this relatively simple database.

To use the Performance Analyzer, follow these steps:

1. Open the database you want to analyze.

TIP Put a reasonable amount of data in your tables before running the Performance Analyzer. The query analysis step in particular takes into account the actual amount of data in each table.

2. From the Tools menu, select Analyze, then select Performance from the cascading menu.

FIGURE 16.2

Using the Performance
Analyzer on a simple
database

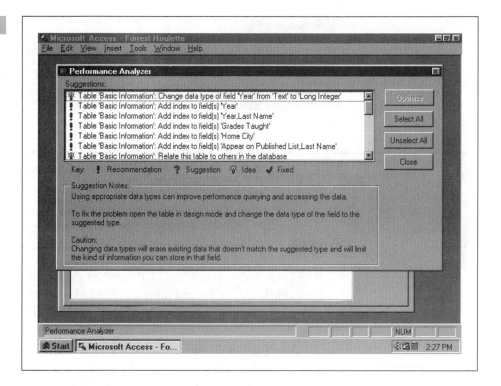

3. In the Performance Analyzer dialog box, select the type of object to optimize from the Object Type drop-down list box. Select the named objects of that type in the Object Name list box.

4. Repeat step 3 until you have selected all the objects you want to optimize.

5. Click on the OK button. The Performance Analyzer displays dialog boxes that tell you which objects it is analyzing. It then displays a list of Suggestions, Recommendations, and Ideas.

6. To implement a Suggestion or Recommendation, select it in the Suggestions list box and click on the Optimize button. Or to implement an Idea, open the appropriate table, query, form, report, macro, or module and make the change recommended.

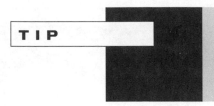

TIP You can select All in the Object Type list to see a list of all database objects. You can use the Select All and Unselect All buttons to speed the process of selecting items.

Speeding Up Tables

If you follow these techniques, you can design tables that operate in the most efficient manner possible. Access even provides help for improving tables in the form of the Table Analyzer Wizard.

- **Avoid redundant data.** Repeated data makes table access inefficient. Use the Table Analyzer Wizard to avoid common problems with tables. Select Analyze ➤ Tables from the Tools menu and follow the directions provided by the Wizard.

- **Select appropriate data types for your fields.** Choosing text where number would be better, for example, can increase the size of your tables and make join operations less efficient.

- **Build indexes for fields that will be searched, joined, or have criteria set.** Creating the indexes makes queries faster on the table.

Speeding Up Queries

Microsoft Access uses a special data-access technology known as "Rushmore" to optimize queries automatically whenever possible. You can help Access do the job more efficiently by following the guidelines below. (See Chapter 10 for more about queries.)

- **Use and display only the fields you need.** Include only the fields you need in a query, and clear the Show box in fields used as selection criteria if you don't need to display those fields in the query result.

- **Use sorting wisely.** Sorting can slow things down, especially when you sort on nonindexed fields.

- **Use Make Table queries for static data.** If you frequently need to base reports or analyses on data that doesn't change often, it's more efficient to run Make Table queries to create tables of selected (or calculated) data. Then, you can view or report on the new tables without running a query each time. If your data does change, you can run the Make Table queries again to re-create the static tables. Note that this technique does involve trade-offs: First, it uses extra disk space to hold the static tables. And second, if you forget to run the Make Table query after data changes, you won't get up-to-date information.

- **Use queries only when necessary.** Response will be faster if you base forms, reports, and other queries on tables (such as those created by Make Table queries), rather than a query. Queries will, of course, be necessary if you need to pull information from several different tables that change often, or if you need to sort the data on a form or report.

- **Create queries that can be optimized.** For faster performance, avoid using restrictive query criteria (AND, OR, and NOT) on calculated and nonindexed columns. You can also speed up queries by using the Between...And, In, and = (equal) operators on indexed columns.

- **Avoid using domain aggregate functions.** Domain aggregate functions, such as DLookup, can slow down processing because these functions must look up data in tables that aren't included in the query. If you need to include data from another table, it's best to add the table to the query or to create a subquery. (To learn about subqueries, search for *subqueries* in Help.)

- **Use fixed column headings in Crosstab queries.** Response will be quicker if you use fixed column headings in Crosstab queries whenever possible. To specify fixed column headings, go to query design view, choose <u>V</u>iew ➤ <u>P</u>roperties, click on an empty part of the tables area, and type the headings into the Column Headings property box (separated by commas), like this:

```
"Qtr1","Qtr2","Qtr3","Qtr4"
```

➤ For more information about optimizing queries, search for *optimizing queries* or *Rushmore technology* in Help.

Speeding Up Forms, Reports, and Printing

The following tips can speed up your forms, reports, and printing. (See Chapters 11–14 for more about designing forms and reports and creating graphs.)

- **Use Data Entry mode to add records to large tables.** When adding new records in forms or datasheets that have many existing records, choose <u>R</u>ecords ➤ <u>D</u>ata Entry to hide existing records while you add new ones. This is faster than moving to the blank record that follows the last record. To view all the records again, choose <u>R</u>ecords ➤ <u>R</u>emove Filter/Sort.

- **Use pictures instead of OLE objects.** If you don't need to update OLE Paintbrush objects, Graphs, and other embedded objects, convert them to pictures. To do this, go to form or report design view, right-click on the object, and choose …<u>O</u>bject ➤ <u>C</u>onvert. In the Convert dialog box, select Picture in the list box and click on OK.

- **Be stingy with bitmaps and other graphics on forms.** Bitmap and other graphic objects (such as lines, bordered fields, and opaque fields) can slow the form's opening and printing time. And color bitmaps will be slower than black-and-white bitmaps. Of course, the very things that make forms more attractive and fun to use also slow down their performance. So you'll need to decide whether the trade-off of speed for aesthetics is worthwhile.

- **Close forms when you're not using them.** This will free up memory.

- **Avoid sorting and grouping on expressions.** Reports will be faster if you avoid unnecessary sorting and grouping on calculated expressions.

- **Avoid overlapping controls on forms and reports.** These take more time to display.

- **Use imported tables, rather than attached tables.** If your forms include list boxes or combo boxes based on unchanging tables in another database, import those tables rather than attaching them to your database (Chapter 7). Imported tables will take up more disk space than attached tables, but processing will be faster.

- **Use fast printing techniques.** For faster printing of reports and forms, try these tips:

  - If you plan to print a form or report with a laser printer, open the form or report in design view, and choose Edit ➤ Select Form or Edit ➤ Select Report. Open the property sheet (View ➤ Properties), select Other Properties from the drop-down list, and set Fast Laser Printing to Yes.

NOTE   If you have an older laser printer, or need to print overlapping graphic items correctly, you'll need to leave Fast Laser Printing set to No.

  - Print in Portrait orientation where possible. Landscape printing can be slower, especially when printing many horizontal lines on non-laser printers.

Where to Go from Here

Improving the performance of your database applications makes users happy. They receive zippy response when they are working with the data. Once you have created a high-performance database application, however, you have to make it available to users. To do so, you have to know how to administer a database, which is the topic of the next chapter.

What's New in the Access Zoo?

We've just taken a look at many of the features that can improve the performance of Access for Windows 95. The features added in this version include:

- The Performance Analyzer, which helps you find possibilities for improving the speed of accessing your database.
- Windows 95's new methods for optimizing memory usage.

CHAPTER

17

Administering
Your Database

THIS chapter covers the mundane, yet essential, housekeeping tasks that fall into the category of *database administration*. Topics include how to back up, compact, convert, encrypt, decrypt, repair, replicate, and document the structure of your databases.

Many database administration tasks are optional, and you should feel free to pick and choose those that interest you most. However, the following section, "Backing Up a Database," is a *must* for anyone using Access on a single-user computer and for database administrators.

N O T E

The *database administrator* is the person who is responsible for maintaining the integrity and security of a database on a multi-user network (for example, making backups, compacting and repairing databases, protecting data from prying eyes). Database administration tasks are discussed in this chapter and in Chapter 18.

Backing Up a Database

Backing up your database is the cheapest and most effective way to ensure your data against disasters. For example, if your database structure becomes damaged due to an unexpected power loss, or your hard disk fails due to old age, flood, fire, or other catastrophe, your data can become unreadable and be irretrievably lost. This would be particularly disastrous with an Access database, since *every* object you create within a database is stored in one large database file! Up-to-date backups can save time, money, even your job—and they're easy to do. For maximum protection, store backups offsite, in a disaster-proof container.

NOTE   It is sometimes possible to *repair* a damaged database, as you'll learn later in the section "Repairing a Database." However, there's still no substitute for the protection that backups provide.

Exactly where you store your backups, and how often you make them, is up to you. If the database is small enough, you can back it up to a floppy. Or, you can use a file compression program to create a compressed copy of the database, and back that up to a floppy. For larger databases, you'll need to back up to a tape drive or perhaps a hard drive with removable disks.

You may also want to keep a second backup copy of the database on your local hard disk. That way, if you make a change to the original database that somehow corrupts the original, you can quickly copy the local backup to the original file name, without bothering with external drives or tape devices.

Backing up a database is basically a matter of copying two crucial files to the backup device:

- **The database file**   This file stores all your data and database objects and usually has the extension .mdb.

- **The system.mdw workgroup database file**   The Setup program creates system.mdw in the \access folder automatically. This file contains important information about each user's toolbar and option settings. It also stores workgroup security information. (A *workgroup* is a group of users who share data and the same system database file.)

WARNING   If the system.mdw file is lost or damaged, you won't be able to start Access. If you can't restore this file from a backup copy, you'll need to reinstall Access (see Appendix A) and set up any toolbars, option settings, and security again.

To create a database backup, follow the steps below:

1. Close any open database by choosing File ➤ Close Database.

2. If other users on the network share data in the database, make sure all other users also close the database, so there are no open copies on the system. (Database administrators: You may prefer to make backups in the wee hours of the morning, so that network users don't have to spend time twiddling their thumbs while you churn out database backups.)

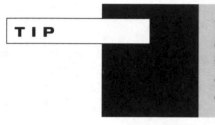

TIP

You can also back up individual database objects by creating a database and then importing the objects from the original database to the copy (see Chapter 7). The advantage of this approach is that users do not have to close the database first.

3. Switch to whatever program you use to make backups. This can be the Windows Explorer, the Copy command available in the MS-DOS window, the Windows 95 Backup program, a tape drive system, or some other backup utility.

4. Copy the .mdb file to the backup destination of your choosing.

5. Copy the workgroup file to the backup destination. If you haven't set up a custom workgroup, this will be the system.mdw file from your Access directory. See Chapter 18 for information about setting up a custom workgroup file.

Restoring a Database from Backups

To restore the database from a backup copy, use your backup software to copy the .mdb file from your backup device to the appropriate database file in the database folder. If the file system.mdw was lost or damaged, copy that file from the backup device to the \access folder.

WARNING   If the backup database and the original database have the same names, you'll be *replacing* the original file. If you want to keep the original file for some reason, rename the file before restoring the backup copy to your hard disk.

 ➤ For more information about making backups, search for *backup* and *system.mdw* in Help. Also consult the documentation that comes with your backup program.

Compacting a Database

As you add and delete records, macros, tables, and other objects in your database, the hard disk space formerly occupied by deleted objects can become fragmented into many small pieces that can't be used efficiently. This fragmentation, in turn, can slow down system performance to a sluggish pace and waste valuable disk space. The solution is to *compact* your databases periodically. Compacting reorganizes the space occupied by an Access database and can recover wasted space so that your system can perform better.

Before compacting a database, consider the following points:

- Because Access must copy the entire database during compacting, it will need as much available disk space as the database itself requires. You can check the size of the database, and the available disk space, with the Windows File Manager.

- To compact a database, you must have Modify Design permission for all tables in the database. Permissions are discussed in Chapter 18.

- The database must be *closed* when you compact it. You must check to make certain no one on your network is using the database before you attempt to compact it. If anyone has it open, the operation will fail.

- When you compact that table's database, if you've deleted records from the end of a table that has an AutoNumber field, Access will reset the next counter number to one more than the last un-deleted counter number.

To compact the database:

1. If the database you want to compact is open, choose File ➤ Close to close it. (Any users on the network must also close that database.)

2. Choose Tools ➤ Database Utilities ➤ Compact Database.

3. In the Database To Compact From dialog box, choose the drive, folder, and file name of the database that you want to compact, then select the Compact button.

4. In the Compact Database Into dialog box, select the database to compact in the list box, or type in a valid file name for the compacted database in the File Name text box. Next choose Save. Or, if you want to compact into the same database, double-click on the database name in the list box. If you use the same name in steps 3 and 4, Access will ask for permission to replace the original with the copy. (Choose Yes if you want to replace the existing file, or No if you want to specify a different name.)

Access will compact the database, displaying a progress message along the status bar as it does so.

NOTE To maintain optimum performance in your database, you must either compact it using its original name or rename it with its original name after compacting.

Compacting Other Areas of Your Hard Disk

As mentioned, a fragmented database can slow down Access performance. Likewise, a badly fragmented hard disk, or one that is low on free space, can slow down *all* the applications on your computer, including both Windows 95 and Access. In addition to compacting your databases, as described here, you should also defragment your hard disk periodically and make sure that your hard disk has plenty of free space available.

To perform this task, you can use the Disk Defragmenter provided with Windows 95 (select Start ➤ Programs ➤ Accessories ➤ System Tools ➤ Disk Defragmenter) or a defragmenter provided by another vendor. Most such tools work the same way. Select the drive you want to defragment, click on OK, then take a coffee break while the defragmenter does its work.

If you have the Microsoft Plus! Pack for Windows 95, you can use the System Agent to schedule the Disk Defragmenter to run on a periodic basis. We suggest scheduling it to run nightly to keep your disk working at top speed.

WARNING

You cannot use Disk Defragmenter to defragment a network disk, a CD, or a disk compressed with a compression program not supported by Windows 95.

 ➤ For more information about compacting databases, search for *compacting databases* in Help. For more about the Disk Defragmenter, search for *defragmenter* in Windows Help.

Converting from Other Access Formats

If you've upgraded to Access 95, you can use Access 95 to work with databases created under Access 1.*x* and Access 2.0, without going through any special conversion. However, before you can change the *structure* of any tables, modify the design of any objects, or add or remove database objects in an old database, you *must* convert that database to Access 95 format.

WARNING

You may not want to convert a database to Access 95 format. You may need to share such databases with users who have not upgraded or cannot upgrade to Windows 95 and Access 95. If you convert, such users will not be able to access the data. In addition, you should not convert databases accessed by applications created using Visual Basic 3.0 or 2.0 unless they are recompiled. Such applications need to be recompiled using Visual Basic 4.0 before they can be converted. The structure of the Data Access Objects has changed slightly in Access 95 and Visual Basic 4.0.

To convert a database:

1. If the database you want to convert is open, choose File ➤ Close to close it. (Any users on the network must also close that database.)

2. Use the Explorer to make a backup copy of the database. Make certain that all linked tables are still located in the folder that the database refers to.

3. Choose Tools ➤ Database Utilities ➤ Convert Database. If you are converting a secured database, you must have Open/Run, Open Exclusive, Modify Design, Administer, and Read Design permissions.

4. In the Database To Convert From dialog box, choose the drive, folder, and file name of the database that you want to convert, then select the Convert button.

5. In the Convert Database Into dialog box, select the database to convert in the list box, or type in a valid file name for the converted database in the File Name text box. Next choose Save. If you use the same name in steps 4 and 5, Access will ask for permission to replace the original with the converted copy. (Choose Yes if you want to replace the existing file, or No if you want to specify a different name.)

When you click on the Save button, Access converts the database, displaying information about the progress of the conversion on the status bar.

TIP

Access 1.x objects that contain a backquote character (') in their names will not convert. You must rename such objects using the version of Access in which they were created before you can convert them.

When Access converts a database, it constructs a special table called the ConvertErrors table. This table contains information about any validation rules that would not convert to Access 95. The ConvertErrors table contains fields describing the error, naming the field where it occurred, naming the table where it occurred, naming the table property containing the problem, and naming the value that would not convert. You can use this information to rewrite validation rules as necessary so that your database can function as it did before the conversion. In general, you will find yourself having to update user-defined functions; domain aggregate functions; totals functions; references to fields; and references to forms, queries, and tables.

Encrypting and Decrypting Your Database

You can *encrypt* a database to ensure that the database can be opened and viewed only in Access. Though encryption doesn't prevent another Access user from tampering with the database, it does prevent anyone from using another application (such as a word processor or utility) to inspect data in the database. Encryption is recommended if you plan to send a copy of a database to another Access user or to an off-site storage location.

TIP

You can use encryption/decryption in conjunction with the Access security features discussed in Chapter 18 and any security that your network software provides.

Decrypting reverses the encryption process. While you *can* open an encrypted database without decrypting it first, the database will be 10 to 15 percent slower in its encrypted state. Therefore, if you receive a copy of an encrypted database from another Access user, you probably should decrypt it before you start using it.

The following points apply to database encryption and decryption:

- Access automatically determines whether the database is encrypted. If the database isn't encrypted, Access encrypts it. If the database is already encrypted, Access decrypts it.

- The hard disk must have enough space available to store both the original database and the temporary copy that Access creates during encryption/decryption.

- The database must be closed when you encrypt or decrypt it. If anyone has it open, the operation will fail.

To encrypt or decrypt a database:

1. If the database you want to encrypt or decrypt is currently open, choose File ➤ Close. In a multiuser environment, all other users must also close the database. You must have Modify Design permission to encrypt or decrypt a secure database if user-level security is in force.

2. Choose Tools ➤ Security ➤ Encrypt/Decrypt Database.

3. In the Encrypt/Decrypt Database dialog box, choose the name of the database you want to encrypt or decrypt, then choose OK.

4. In the Encrypt Database As (or Decrypt Database As) dialog box, type in a valid file name for the encrypted (or decrypted) database and choose Save. Or, if you want to encrypt/decrypt into the same database, double-click on the database name in the list box. If you use the same name in steps 3 and 4, Access will ask for permission to replace the original with the copy. (Choose Yes if you want to replace the existing file, or No if you want to specify a different name.)

 ➤ For more information about encrypting and decrypting databases, search for *encryption* or *decryption* in Help.

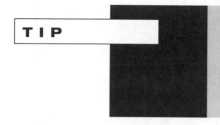

T I P   Just as they will not convert, Access 1.x objects that contain a backquote character (') in their names will not encrypt. You must rename such objects, using the version of Access in which they were created, before you can encrypt them.

Repairing a Damaged Database

Before turning off your computer, you should always exit Access properly, by choosing File ➤ Exit. Proper shutdown ensures that all your database objects are saved to disk and prevents damage to your database.

If a power outage or some other mishap occurs, some data might not be saved, and your open database could be damaged. In most cases, Access can detect the damage automatically, whenever you try to open, compact, encrypt, or decrypt the damaged database, and it will ask for permission to repair it. Simply choose OK when asked if you want to begin the repair process.

 Occasionally, however, Access might be unable to detect the problem, and the database may behave strangely. In such a case, you can use the Repair Database command to fix the corrupted database. Here's how:

1. Close any open databases using File ➤ Close. As usual, any users on the network must also close the database.

2. Use the Explorer to make a backup copy of the database.

3. Choose Tools ➤ Database Utilities ➤ Repair Database.

4. Choose the drive, folder, and name of the database you want to repair, then choose Repair.

Once the repair is done, choose OK to clear the message that appears. You should now be able to open the database with the usual File ➤ Open Database commands.

If you were editing data when Access shut down unexpectedly, your last change may be lost after you repair the database. Return to the form or datasheet you were working with and, if necessary, re-enter your changes.

Also check any other objects you were working on when the system shut down, and redo any changes that didn't make it into the database.

When Repair Doesn't Solve the Problem...

Sometimes hard-disk errors will prevent Access from repairing the database properly, or they may prevent Access from running at all. For these types of problems, you'll first need to run a hard-disk repair utility (such as ScanDisk, which comes with Windows 95). Then try running Access and repairing the database again. If Access won't run at all, you'll need to reinstall it with the Setup program, as explained in Appendix A. If you can't repair the database satisfactorily, you must restore it from a backup copy.

 ➤ You can find online information about repairing databases by searching for *repairing databases* in Help. To learn about ScanDisk, search Windows 95 Help for *ScanDisk*.

Viewing Information About Your Database

Once you have created a database of objects, you may want to review the attributes of those objects from time to time. Access provides you two means of examining the properties associated with objects in a database. First, you can click on any object in the Database window and then select Properties from the View menu. This action opens a Properties dialog box like the one shown in Figure 17.1. This dialog box tells you what the object is, when it was created, when it was last modified, who owns it, and whether it has the hidden or replicated attributes. You can enter further documentation into the Description text box if you desire to do so. In this way, you can store a description of each object in the database.

You can also view information about the database in general, as well as storing additional information which documents the database and helps you to locate it. To view this information, select File ➤ Database Properties. The properties dialog box shown in Figure 17.2 appears. The General tab displays the attributes of the database file. The Contents tab provides

FIGURE 17.1

The Properties dialog box for a table appears when you choose View ➤ Properties.

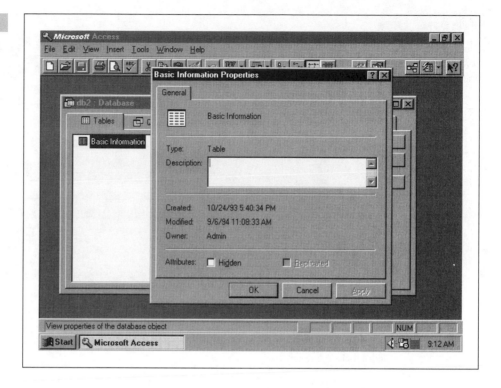

a list of all the objects in the database. The Statistics tab provides some summary information about how the database has been used.

The most useful tabs, however, are the Summary and Custom tabs. The Summary tab allows you to record information about who created the database and who owns it. You can also enter a description on this tab, as well as keywords to aid in searching for the file. The Custom tab allows you to define special properties for the database that help in searching for the file if you cannot remember its file name. Use the Name drop-down combination box to enter a name for the property. Select a type from the Type drop-down list box. Then enter a value for the property in the Value text box. To add to the list of custom properties for the database select the Add button. You can use the Summary and Custom tabs to record a lot of information that documents your database. You can also search for a database file using the summary information and custom properties called up by choosing the Advanced button in any file dialog box.

FIGURE 17.2

The Properties dialog box for an entire database

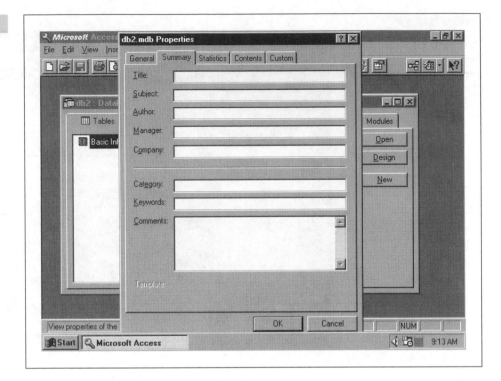

Documenting Your Database

When developing applications or sharing your database with other users, it's often helpful to include documentation about the various design elements in the database objects. For instance, you can preview or print a report of the properties, code, and permissions associated with controls on a form or report. Access makes it easy to produce database documentation for a single object, or for several objects at once.

To document an object or a set of objects, follow these steps:

1. Choose Tools ➤ Analyze ➤ Documentor. You'll see a Print Definition dialog box, as in Figure 17.3.

FIGURE 17.3

The Print Definition dialog box lets you choose which information to include in the object definition report.

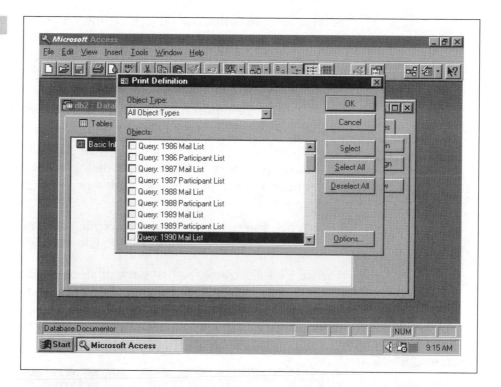

TIP

The Documentor does not usually install when you install Access. You may have to install it using the Add/Remove Programs icon in the Control Panel.

2. Select the type of objects you want to document in the Object Type drop-down list box. (Choose All Object Types to document the entire database.) Select the specific objects you want to document in the Objects list box. Use the Select and Select All buttons to simplify this process.

3. If you'd like to select which properties are documented for a form or report, click on the Options button; then select any properties you want using the option buttons presented in the Print Table Definitions dialog box and click on OK.

4. Choose OK to generate the object definition.

After a few moments, the Object Definition report will appear on your screen, in a print preview window. You can now do any of the following:

- To view the report, scroll through or zoom out or in as you would in any print preview window.

- To print the report, click on the Print toolbar button or choose File ➤ Print.

- To save the report as a table or as an external file, choose File ➤ Save As/Export. In the Save As dialog box, select the correct option button for saving as a table or as an external file, and choose OK.

- When you're done viewing the report, click on the Close Window toolbar button, or choose File ➤ Close.

Figure 17.4 illustrates the first page of an object definition report for the Calls table in a contact management database generated using the Database Wizard.

FIGURE 17.4

An object definition report's first page, in this case for the Calls table in a Contact management database

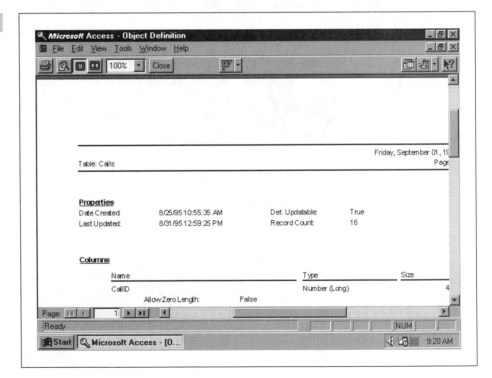

WARNING The object definitions can take some time to generate, so be patient. Grab a cup of coffee or turn on your favorite television soap opera or talk show to pass the time.

Replicating Your Database

These days almost everyone takes work with them on the road. What do you do when you want to take a copy of your database with you to work on? How do you manage changes you make while you are working away from the master copy? Access 95 allows you to replicate your database. When it is replicated, the database contains special tables and properties that enable Access to distinguish between the *design master*, the copy that determines the overall structure of the database, and a copy. Changes in design take place only within the design master and tools are available that allow you to synchronize all of the copies of the data.

Replicas can be managed either through Access or the Windows 95 Briefcase. You always have a choice of which you prefer to use to create and synchronize your replicas. Before creating a replica, you need to take three steps. First, remove the database password using Tools ➤ Security ➤ Unset Database Password. Second, be certain the Briefcase is installed. (If it is not, use the Add/Remove Programs icon in Control Panel to install it.) Third, make certain that Briefcase Replication was installed with Access. (If not, visit the Control Panel again.)

NOTE If Briefcase Replication is not installed, Access will present a dialog box informing you of this fact when you try to create a replica the first time.

Then follow these steps:

1. Open the Explorer and drag the database to the Briefcase. When you drop the database file on the Briefcase, Access automatically converts it for replication.

2. To create a replica using Access, make sure all users of the database on a network have closed the database.

3. Select Tools ➤ Replication ➤ Create Replica.

4. When the dialog box appears, choose Yes to close the database.

5. Choose either Yes or No in the next dialog box to make a backup of the database.

6. Use the file dialog box presented to select a location for the replica, and click on OK.

WARNING Converting to a replicable database is a one-way process. The only way to make it nonreplicable is to create a new database and import the data from one of the replicas.

You can make as many replicas of your design master as you wish. In fact, you can even make replicas from a replica. The total group of replicas you make is known as the *replica set* for the database. You add to the replica set by creating a new replica as described above. You remove replicas from the replica set by deleting the database file for the replica you want to remove. Only members of a replica set and their design master can synchronize their data.

How do you synchronize all of the changes made in your replica with the design master or with other replicas? The process is easy. Just follow these steps:

1. Open the Briefcase and select the database file.

2. From the Briefcase menu, select Update Selection. (You could also select Update All.)

The Briefcase then automatically merges the changes with the copy of the database, either design master or replica, available on your desktop computer. If you would rather manage synchronization from Access, follow these steps instead:

1. Open the database to synchronize.

2. Select Tools ➤ Replication ➤ Synchronize Now.

3. Select either the design master or another replica using the file dialog box, and then choose OK.

4. When prompted to close the database, click on Yes.

If members of a replica set develop synchronization conflicts, Access prompts you to resolve them when you open the replica that has the conflicts. Selecting Resolve in this dialog box causes Access to lead you step by step through the process of conflict resolution. You are offered the chance to copy fields or delete the conflicting record in order to resolve conflicts.

You may encounter a situation in which you feel that a replica has been updated so significantly that you would rather have it as the design master. You can convert any member of a replica set into a design master using this procedure:

1. Open the replica that will become the new design master.

2. Select Tools ➤ Replication ➤ Synchronize Now.

3. Select the current design master using the file dialog box and check the Make "Filename" the Design Master check box. (Access fills in "Filename" with the name of the file you opened in step 1.)

4. Choose OK to create the new design master.

You might also encounter a situation in which a well-meaning user has deleted the design master. In this case, choose the replica you want to use to replace the design master. Preferably this replica would be the most recently synchronized copy. Then synchronize this replica with as many others as you feel necessary to build an accurate master copy of the data. Finally, open the replica that will replace the design master and choose Tools ➤ Replication ➤ Recover Design Master. Click on the Yes button when Access prompts you to confirm that you have synchronized this replica with all others.

Where to Go from Here

You have just learned quite a bit about administering a database, in either a single-user or a multiuser environment. In discussing administration, we have covered topics that imply that your database resides on a network. The next chapter deals more fully with the issues of networking and security, and follows up on the issues dealt with briefly here.

What's New in the Access Zoo?

You've just taken a look at many of the features that make Access for Windows 95 so much easier for database administrators. These features include:

- The ability to replicate a database so that multiple users can work with copies of the data.

- The ability to convert Access 1.x and 2.0 databases to the Access for Windows 95 format.

- New assistance with documenting your databases.

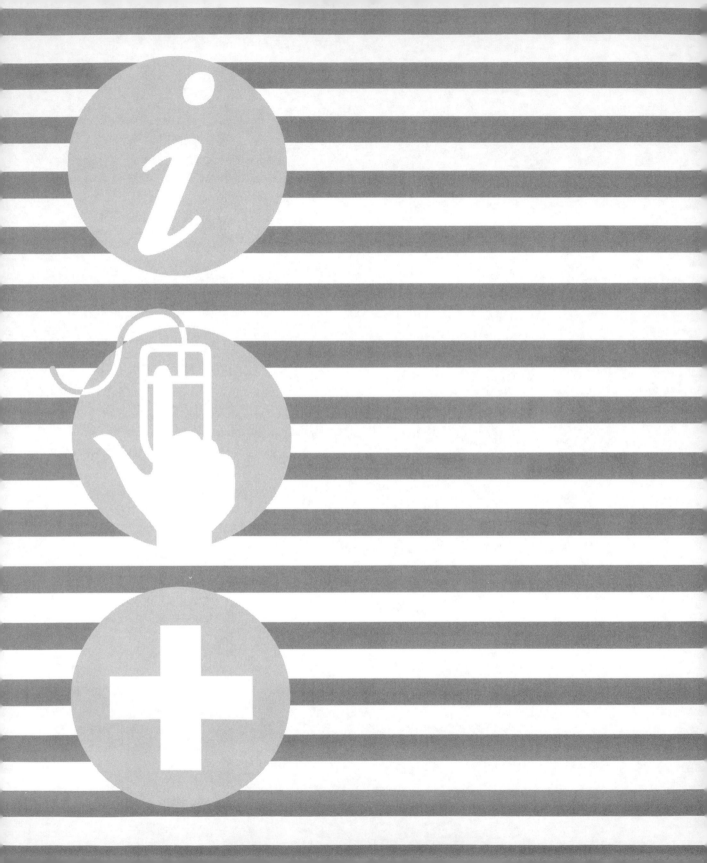

CHAPTER

18

Networking and Security

THIS chapter covers two issues that will be of interest to anyone responsible for an Access installation on a network. The first is the one on most network administrators' minds: how to get peak performance from Access on a network. The second topic is setting up a security scheme to prevent unauthorized users from accidentally or deliberately harming objects within your Access applications.

Two Ways to Allow Users to Share Data

In many organizations, it's important to give multiple users simultaneous access to the same data. Access is designed to support multiuser databases "out of the box," but there are some factors to consider carefully. The first is where to store the application itself. There are two ways you can set up your database to allow multiple users to share data and other objects, as discussed in the sections that follow.

Option 1: Put the Entire Database on the Server

One way to give multiple users access to a database is simply to put the entire database (that is, the entire Access .mdb file) on the server, as shown in Figure 18.1. With this approach, there's no difference between a single-user database and a multiuser one; you just transfer the database to a shared drive and tell your users where to find it.

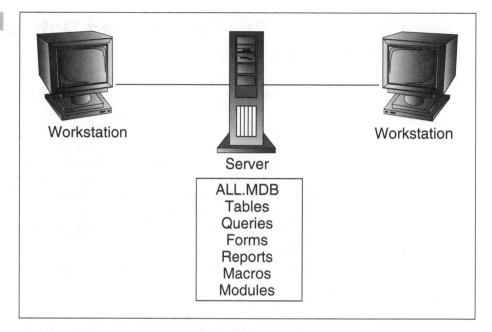

FIGURE 18.1

If you put the entire Access .mdb file on the server, all users will share all objects.

The one advantage to this approach is that all users share all the same objects. Thus, a change to any object, including a form, report, or macro, is instantly accessible to all users. Data changes—such as adding, editing, or deleting records from a table—are also immediately visible.

NOTE

You must be extremely careful when changing the design of any object in a shared database. If two users are doing design work in the same database simultaneously, the database may become corrupted if one saves changes to an object the other has already modified. For safety, let no more than one user at a time modify objects, and always keep a backup of any networked database. Make sure everyone logs off before you back up the database so you know it's in a consistent state.

Option 2: Put Only Shared Data on the Server

The downside to putting the entire database on the server is that you end up with a lot of network traffic. Virtually every object that each user opens needs to come across the network. This includes forms and reports, which are normally static in an application in use, as well as the changeable tables. As an alternative, you can put just the shared tables on the server, in a "data" database. Then set up a database that contains all objects *except* those shared tables, and put a copy of that "application" database on each workstation, as in the example shown in Figure 18.2. You can then use the File ➤ Get External Data ➤ Link Tables… menu item to link the tables in the "data" database to those in the "application" database so that all users can see the shared data.

 ➤ For more information on linked tables, see Chapter 7.

This approach has both an upside and a downside:

- It reduces network traffic because only shared table data is transmitted across the network. Forms, reports, and other objects are read from each user's local hard drive.

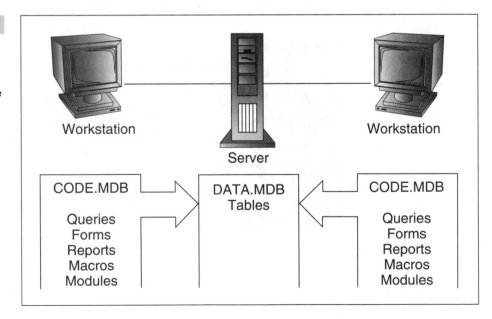

FIGURE 18.2

Splitting a database between a "data" database and an "application" database

Workstation   Workstation

Server

CODE.MDB	DATA.MDB Tables	CODE.MDB
Queries Forms Reports Macros Modules		Queries Forms Reports Macros Modules

- The network administrator can more easily back up just the tables in the database, because the tables are stored independently of the other objects.

- If a user changes some other object (such as a form, report, or macro), that change affects only his or her workstation. Other users never see that change.

(The last item in the list can be either a curse or a blessing, depending on whether the user improves or destroys the modified object.)

N O T E

To prevent users from changing objects, you'll need to use Access security features to protect your database objects (see "Securing Your Database," later in this chapter).

Separating the Tables

Putting just the shared tables on the network is easier than ever in Access 95, thanks to its new Database Splitter Wizard. Here we'll take you through an example using our Order Entry database generated using the Database Wizard.

To create the database of shared tables, you need to do the following (you'll already need to know how to use the Windows Explorer, or the MS-DOS prompt, to copy files and create directories):

1. Make a backup copy of the entire Order Entry database, and give this copy a new name. (In the case of this example, the original database is named Order Entry1.mdb. We made a copy called OrderEntryBackup.mdb. Long file names *are* useful.) This copy will provide you a safety net in case you later decide that you didn't really want to split the database after all.

2. Open the database that you want to split. Hold down the Shift key when you open the database so the Switchboard form won't open.

3. Select <u>T</u>ools ➤ Add-<u>i</u>ns ➤ <u>D</u>atabase Splitter. This action starts the Database Splitter Wizard, shown here.

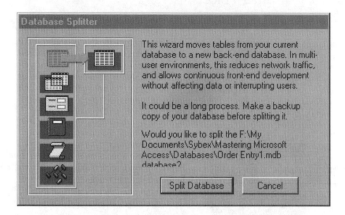

4. Read the information on the Wizard screen, then click on the Split Database button.

5. In the Create Back-end Database dialog box, enter a name for your back-end database in the File <u>n</u>ame text box. Make sure that its directory is the correct directory on the network drive. Then click on the Split button.

WARNING   Be sure to close all open objects (Tables, Queries, Forms, and Reports) before splitting your database. Otherwise, the Database Splitter will not be able to properly export and reattach the tables.

6. When you see a dialog box announcing that the database was successfully split, click on the OK button. You now have two versions of the database, the back-end version containing just the tables, and the original version containing all the rest of the objects and links to the tables in the back-end version.

7. Close the open version of the database.

At this point, the server holds a copy of the database tables (in their own .mdb file) that you want the users to share. By checking the Contents tab of the File ➤ Database Properties dialog box you can see that this "back-end" database contains only the tables from the original database, as shown in Figure 18.3.

The original Order Entry1.mdb file contains all of the other database objects, plus links to the tables in the Order Entry1_be.mdb database. The names of linked tables are now marked with an icon in the local database, as shown in Figure 18.4.

Now you can put a copy of the local database on every user's workstation. When the user opens the local copy of the database, Access will automatically link to the shared tables on the server and handle any conflicts that arise when two or more users try to edit the same data. (See "Editing on a Network" later in this chapter.)

FIGURE 18.3

Order Entry1_be.mdb contains only the tables from the original database.

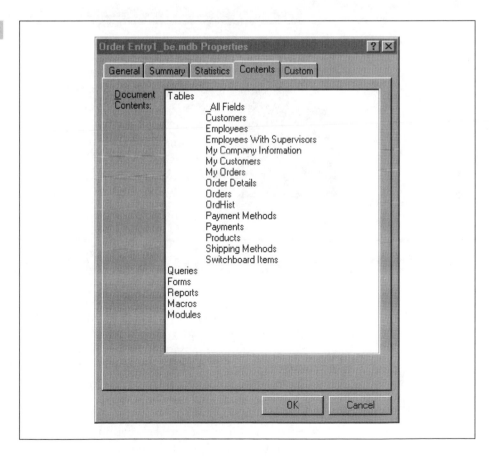

FIGURE 18.4

The Order Entry1.mdb database, after splitting, showing the tables linked to Order Entry1_be.mdb.

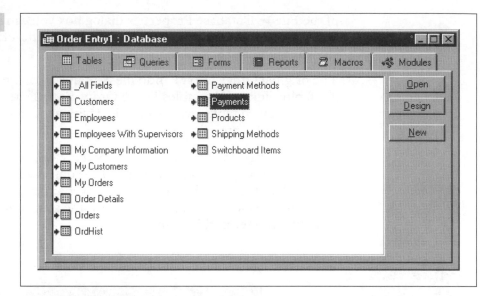

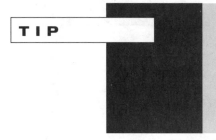

TIP

If you ever need to change the links to the tables, select Tools ➤ Add-ins ➤ Linked Table Manager. Check the Always prompt for new location check box in the Linked Table Manager dialog box, and you will have the opportunity to edit the link information using a standard file dialog box.

Preventing Exclusive Access

When users will be sharing data in an Access database, you need to make sure that no single user opens the database in Exclusive mode. Otherwise, no other users can open that database. Access for Windows 95 has changed its default behavior to support shared access more directly than previous versions. The default values for most settings support shared access. To make certain that use of Exclusive mode is discouraged or prevented, you can take these three steps:

- Instruct all users to make certain the Exclusive check box is cleared in the Open Database dialog box (after choosing File ➤

Open Database) before opening the database. (This check box is cleared by default. This approach assumes, of course, that all users will be conscientious about not choosing to open a database in Exclusive mode.)

- Choose Tools ➤ Options from the Access menu bar, select the Advanced tab, and make sure the Default Open Mode option is set to Shared, its default value. This setting automatically clears the Exclusive check box when the user first gets to the Open Database dialog box.

- Set up a security system (discussed later in this chapter) that denies the Open Exclusive permissions to selected users. This is the strictest control, since it doesn't even let users open the database exclusively.

Of course, you'll need to grant yourself and other administrative users the right to open the database in Exclusive mode, so that you can perform operations that require exclusive use, such as backing up, compacting, and repairing the database.

 ➤ For more information on compacting and repairing, see Chapter 17.

Creating Upgradeable Custom Applications

Separating the tables from the other database objects is also a good strategy if you plan to market a custom application that you've created, or if you need to maintain a database that you've already distributed on a network to multiple users.

You can put all the tables for an application in one database, and then put all the other objects in a separate database. Use the Database Splitter Wizard, as in the example above, to split all the tables in the separate database.

Be sure to distribute both databases to first-time buyers or users. When you release an upgraded version of your product, send the upgraders only the database (.mdb) file that contains the objects, not the database containing tables. That way, you don't have to worry about users overwriting their existing data when they install your upgraded version. Instead, they'll just link the new "front-end" database to their existing tables.

WARNING

It's best to avoid changing the structure of tables after the initial release of your application. Otherwise, you'll need to ship the revised tables, *and* you'll need to provide a convenient way for users to put their data into your newly structured tables. This can be a nuisance for both you and the upgraders.

Editing Data on a Network

Access uses a simple, common-sense strategy for handling conflicts that occur when two or more users edit the same data. The way Access handles such conflicts depends on the Record Locks property of the form your users are using to do the edits, as shown in Figure 18.5.

NOTE

We'll discuss conflict handling in datasheets a little later, since most often you'll have your network users working via forms.

If the Record Locks property is set to Edited Record, when one user is editing a record (so that the pencil symbol appears in that record's selector), and another user tries to edit that same record, the second user sees an international "No" symbol, indicating that the record is locked by another user.

FIGURE 18.5

Choices for the Record
Locks property

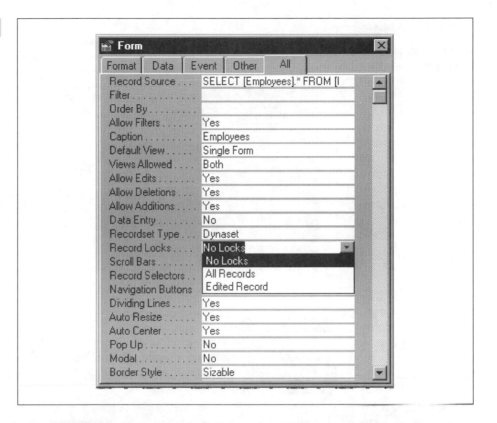

FIGURE 18.5

Choices for the Record
Locks property

TIP

Access may take up to 60 seconds to display the "No"
symbol when another user is editing a record. You can
change this on the Advanced tab of the Tools ➤ Options
dialog box. Set the Refresh Interval to the maximum
number of seconds you want Access to wait before
updating a record's locking status.

When the first user saves the changes, the No symbol disappears, Access
updates the view of the record on both machines, and the second user can
then view and change that same record. Figure 18.6 shows the situation
where one user has "locked out" another user by editing a record.

FIGURE 18.6

With Edited Record Locking, only one user can edit a record at a time. Other users are "locked out" of the record.

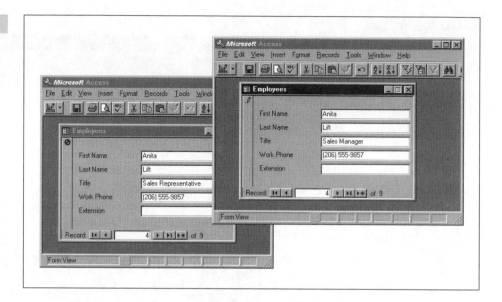

NOTE

Access saves the changes to a record whenever you move the cursor to another record, or choose Records ➤ Save Record, or press Shift+↵.

If Record Locks is set to No Locks, both users will be allowed to edit the record. However, when the second user tries to save the changes after the first user has done so, Access offers the second user the chance to overwrite the first user's changes, copy the record to the Clipboard for pasting into the table later, or discard the changes, with the dialog box shown in Figure 18.7.

If you get this dialog box on your screen, it means you have tried to modify a record that another user has already changed. You have three choices to deal with this situation:

- Choose Save Record to have your changes overwrite whatever the other user saved, without inspecting the records.

- Choose Drop Changes to leave the other user's record alone, and discard any changes you have made.

FIGURE 18.7

With No Locks, you'll get a Write Conflict warning when you try to change data that someone else has edited.

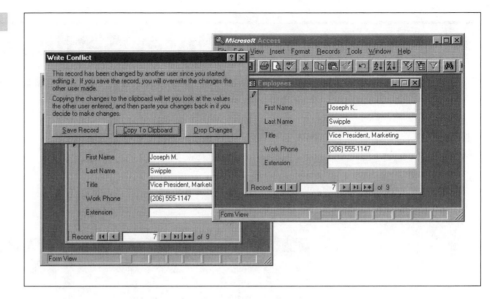

- Choose <u>C</u>opy to Clipboard to leave the other user's record alone, but place your own changes on the Windows Clipboard. When you do this, your form will be updated to show the other user's changes. If you decide you'd rather keep your version, simply click on the form's record selector to select the whole record, and choose <u>E</u>dit ➤ <u>P</u>aste or press Ctrl+V to return your changes to the form. Then save your record again.

Refreshing Network Data

Access automatically refreshes each user's screen at regular intervals, to help ensure that each user is seeing current data. However, you can force Access to refresh your data at any time by choosing <u>R</u>ecords ➤ Refre<u>s</u>h.

When Access refreshes the current form or datasheet, it updates changes and indicates deleted records. However, it does not reorder records, show new records, or update a dynaset to show or hide records that no longer meet the underlying query's selection criteria. To force Access to refresh a dynaset completely, press Requery (Shift+F9).

Tweaking Multiuser Settings

It's impossible to define a single network strategy that works perfectly for all situations. You may need to experiment with some of the default settings to get maximum performance, and minimal conflicts, on your own network. Here's how:

1. Choose Tools ➤ Options from the Access menu bar.

2. Click on the Advanced tab to view the multiuser and ODBC settings, as below.

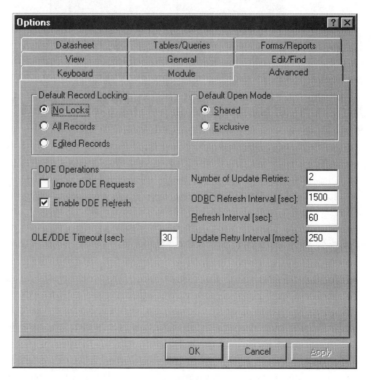

3. Use Table 18.1 (and the built-in help) to choose new settings.

4. Choose OK when you're done.

TABLE 18.1: Multiuser Options and Settings

OPTION	SETTING	RESULT
Default Record Locking	No Locks (default)	Records are not locked during edits.
	All Records	All records underlying a particular object (e.g., a form) are locked when that object is open.
	Edited Records	Only the record being edited is locked.
Default Open Mode	Shared	Database is open for shared use by default.
	Exclusive (default)	Database is open for exclusive use by default.
Refresh Interval	1 to 32,766 seconds (default = 60)	Updates your screen at the specified interval.
Update Retry Interval (see the section "Minimizing Conflicts")	0 to 1000 milliseconds (default = 250)	Waits for the specified time before trying again to save a locked record.
Number of Update Retries	0 to 10 (default = 2)	Number of times Access will automatically try to save a change to a record that another user has locked.
ODBC Refresh Interval	1 to 3600 seconds	Updates your screen at the specified interval when you're accessing a database using ODBC.
Ignore DDE Requests	Default is No (unchecked)	Determines whether Access responds to DDE requests from other applications.
Enable DDE Refresh	Default is Yes (checked)	Determines whether DDE links are refreshed whenever the screen is updated.
OLE/DDE Timeout	0 to 300 seconds (default = 30)	Determines how long Access waits for an OLE or DDE operation to complete.

Record Locking Strategies

The Record Locks property applies only to forms. The Default Record Locking setting in the Advanced options tab applies to datasheet views of Tables and Queries and to dynasets opened in Basic. The same rules for resolving write conflicts apply in all cases. If you encounter a record-locking conflict in a Visual Basic procedure, Access generates a custom error which you can trap and respond to.

 For more information on dealing with errors in your Visual Basic code, see Chapter 25, or look in the Access help index under *errors, trapping*.

Now that you know the various record locking settings, how do you choose between them? It depends on how your users use the data, and how much training you can give them. Let's look at the pros and cons of each strategy.

No Locks Strategy

As we explained above, when you use the No Locks strategy (sometimes called *optimistic locking*), records are not locked while being edited. Two users can edit the record at the same time. When you try to save your changes to a record that somebody else has also changed, you'll be given the option to overwrite the other user's changes, copy your version of the record to the Clipboard, or discard your changes, as discussed above.

While the No Locks strategy offers the most flexibility, it also creates two potentially unpleasant situations:

- After you make changes to a record, another user can easily overwrite those changes.

- Another user can lock a record that you're editing. You won't be able to save your changes until the other user unlocks the record.

An alternative to the No Locks strategy is to automatically lock whatever record is being edited.

Edited Record Strategy

When you choose the Edited Record locking strategy (sometimes called *pessimistic locking*), any record that's currently being edited by one user is locked and unavailable to all other users. No two people can edit the same record at the same time. The upside and downside to this approach are:

- On the upside, Access automatically ensures that no two users edit the same record at the same time. And you can be sure that once you start editing a record, you'll be able to save your changes.

- On the downside, other users may start getting irritated if you keep a particular record locked for too long. Even worse, a record lock in Access nearly always affects more than one record, since Access locks records in 2048-byte *pages*. This means that users can be locked out of records that no one else is editing, as shown in Figure 18.8.

N O T E   When you're attached to a SQL database via ODBC, the rules of the SQL database govern locking. Access always acts as if you've selected the No Locks (optimistic locking) strategy.

The solution to the problem, of course, is to practice good network citizenship and make sure that you always save a record immediately after you've made your changes. That way, other users will have instant access to the modified record.

FIGURE 18.8

A record locked by editing another record

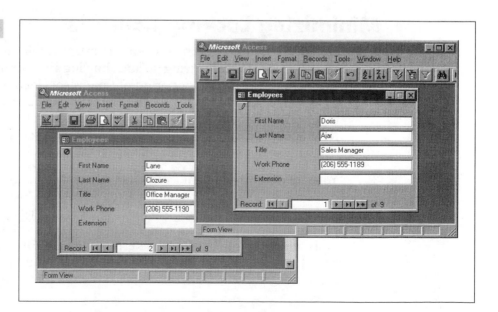

All Records Strategy

The most restrictive locking option is All Records, where once a user opens a form or datasheet, that user has a lock on all its records. No other users can change any records in the table as long as that person is using the table. Use this method only if you're absolutely sure that you want only one person at a time to be able to make changes to a table. The need for this is generally limited to administrative table changes that have to be completed without interference from other users.

Choosing a Locking Strategy

Which locking strategy should you use? This depends on your data and your application, of course. But for almost all networked Access applications, we've found that the benefits of the No Locks strategy far outweigh its disadvantages. Although you'll have to train your users to deal with the occasional write conflict errors that may occur, the gain in performance more than balances this.

In addition, in most workplaces you can use the natural workflow to reduce or eliminate record-locking conflicts. If Joe is responsible for customers whose last names start with A through M and Mary is responsible for those from N through Z, they won't even be trying to edit the same records at the same time.

Minimizing Locking Conflicts

When Access encounters a locking conflict, it will make several tries to save the record before giving up and showing an error message to the user. Access waits for whatever period of time is specified in the Update Retry Interval multiuser setting, and then tries to save the record again. It repeats this process as many times as you've specified in the Number of Update Retries setting. If it can't resolve the conflict after that number of tries, then it displays a locking conflict error message.

You can minimize update conflicts and error messages by tweaking those two settings. For example, if users frequently get locking error messages, and you think it's because too many people are trying to save data at the same moment, then *increase* both settings. Access will wait longer, and try more times, before showing the error message. Of course, if there really are a lot of locking conflicts, this will make your application appear to be more sluggish, as it makes multiple futile retries to save the data.

On the other hand, if you want Access to display a locking error message as soon as a conflict occurs, set the Number of Update Retries option to zero.

Securing Your Database

Access is designed to allow you to implement security on your database objects as you need it. By default, security is completely invisible to both the designers and the users of an Access database. As your needs require it, you can secure individual objects so that, for example, most users can't modify a particular form. If you are extremely concerned about security, you can use Access to remove all but a few ways to retrieve data from your tables. In networked applications, a well-designed security system can help make the application more maintainable by eliminating many sources of potential disaster.

Security Concepts

To understand Access security, you'll need to grasp four basic security concepts: *users* and *groups* have *permissions* on *objects*.

- An Access *user* represents a single person who uses an Access application. Users are distinguished by their user name, password, and a unique secret identifier called the Personal Identifier (PID). To use a secured Access application, a user has to type in her user name and password to be able to get to any objects.

- An Access *group* is a collection of users. You can use groups to represent parts of your organization, such as Development and Accounting, or simply security levels, such as High and Low. Often you'll find that assigning users to groups, and permissions directly to those groups, makes a security system more maintainable.

- An Access *permission* is the right to perform a single operation on an object. For example, a user can be granted read data permission on a table, allowing that user to retrieve data from that table. Both users and groups can be assigned permissions.

- An Access security *object* is any one of the main database container objects (table, query, form, report, macro, or module) or a database itself.

WARNING Because both users and groups can have permissions, you may have to check several places to determine a user's actual permissions. The user's actual permissions are the *least restrictive* combination of the user's own permissions (called explicit permissions) and the permissions of all groups the user belongs to (called implicit permissions). So if Mary has no permission to open the Accounting form, but she's a member of the Supervisors group that does have permission to open that form, she will be able to open the form.

Permissions Granted

Access includes a rich set of permissions that you can assign to groups and individuals on an object-by-object basis. You can grant any of the permissions listed in Table 18.2 to any group, or to any individual user in a group.

Access Logins

Every single time you start Access, you must supply a valid user name and password. Surprised? Think you've got a special copy of Access that doesn't require this? That's because Access does its best to be helpful. When you launch Access, it automatically tries to log you on as a user named Admin with a blank password. If this works—and unless you've activated your security system by assigning a password to the Admin user—then Access suppresses the login dialog box completely.

To be able to log in as any other user, you'll need to assign a password to the Admin user, as discussed below. The next time you start Access, you'll see this login dialog box:

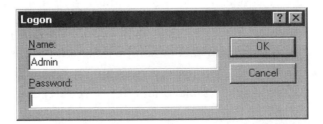

TABLE 18.2: Permissions You Can Assign to Individual Users and Groups of Users

PERMISSION	PERMITS USER TO...	CAN BE APPLIED TO...
Open/Run	Open a database, form, report, or run a macro	Databases, forms, reports, macros
Open Exclusive	Open a database with exclusive access	Databases
Read Design	Look at an object in design view	All object types
Modify Design	View, change, and delete objects	All object types
Administer	Full access, including the right to assign permissions to users	All objects, and the security system
Read Data	View, but not alter, data	Tables and queries
Update Data	View and change data, but not insert or delete	Tables and queries
Insert Data	View and add data, but not modify or delete	Tables and queries
Delete Data	View and delete data, but not add or modify	Tables and queries

If for some reason you decide to deactivate security, you can suppress the login dialog box by changing the Admin user's password back to a blank.

Workgroup Files

Access security information is stored in a workgroup file, which is named system.mdw by default. Access includes a tool to create new workgroup files, called the Workgroup Administrator. To create a new Workgroup file, follow these steps:

1. Locate the Workgroup Administrator (wrkgadm.exe) item in Explorer, and open it, as shown below.

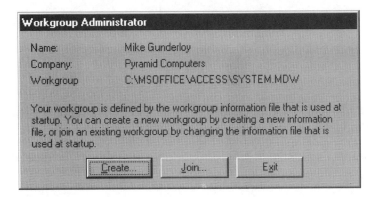

2. Click on Create….

3. Supply a name, organization, and unique Workgroup ID (WID). The WID is used by Access to make sure that your workgroup is unique. Store this information in a safe place—you'll need it if you ever need to re-create your original workgroup.

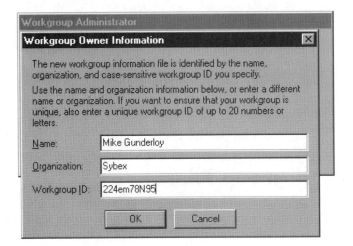

4. Supply a path and file name for the new Workgroup file. You should use the .mdw extension for this file.

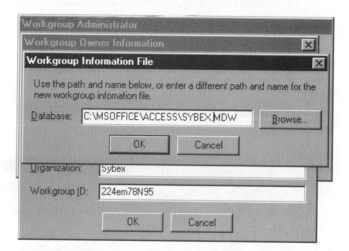

5. Click on OK three times to create the new workgroup, confirm its information, and return to the main Workgroup Administrator screen.

6. Click on Exit to close the Workgroup Administrator.

WARNING

The original workgroup file created when you install Access is *not secure.* This is because Access creates it for you using the user name and organization name you used for the Access install, and a blank WID. Anyone who can get to your computer and use Help ➤ About in any Office application can recover this information and so re-create your original workgroup file. Armed with this file, they can break any security scheme you design.

 ➤ To learn more about workgroups and the workgroup information file, search Help for this topic: *Workgroup information file.*

You can also use Workgroup Administrator to switch from one workgroup file to another. You'll need to do this if you have secured databases from two different sources. To switch workgroups, follow these steps:

1. Locate the Workgroup Administrator (wrkgadm.exe) item in Explorer and open it.

2. Click on the Join... button.

3. Either type in the name of the workgroup you want to join, or use the Browse... button to locate the file on your drive.

4. Click on the OK button twice to join the new workgroup and confirm the information message.

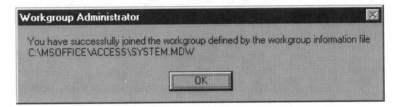

5. Click on Exit to close the Workgroup Administrator.

Built-in User and Groups

Every Access workgroup comes with the built-in user and groups listed in Table 18.3 and Table 18.4. This user and these groups are created by Access to provide you with a bare bones security system.

The most important thing to realize about the built-in user and groups is that most of them are not secure and cannot be made secure. The Admin user and the Users group are identical in every single workgroup file ever created. If you assign permissions to Admin or Users, you are in effect making those permissions available to any Access user.

TABLE 18.3: Default Access User

USER	MEMBER OF	COMMENTS
Admin	Admins, Users	Default logon user

TABLE 18.4: Default Access Groups

GROUP	CONTAINS	COMMENTS
Admins	Admin	Any member has full permissions on all objects, regardless of security.
Users	Admin	Members by default have permissions on all objects.

Since the Admin user has full permissions on all objects by default, and everyone is logged on as the Admin user unless they've made their security active, this system ensures that we can swap databases with one another without worrying about security.

Ownership: the Super Permission

Another important security concept is the idea of *ownership*. Whoever creates an object in the first place, or imports it from another database, is the initial owner of the object. The owner can give ownership to another user or group, or any member of the Admins group can reassign the ownership of any object.

TIP

Assigning object ownership to a group such as Developers makes it easier for multiple developers to work with objects in a secured database.

The owner of an object always has Administer permission on that object, even if someone else tries to take it away—and in some cases, even if the interface erroneously reports that they don't have this permission. What this means is that an object's owner can do anything with that object, no matter what anyone else tries to limit him or her to.

Working with Users and Groups

The first decision you need to make when implementing a security system is what users and groups you'll need. You'll need to keep at least one user—usually yourself—in the Admins group, since only members of the Admins group can create new users and perform other security tasks. Other users should be grouped by the tasks they need to perform, so that you can assign permissions to groups. Schematically, a security scheme for a small database might look like the one in Figure 18.9.

To work with users and groups, select Tools ➤ Security ➤ User and Group Accounts... from the Access menu. This will open the User and Group Accounts dialog box. From this dialog box, you can create and delete users and groups, assign users to groups, and change your own password.

The Users Tab

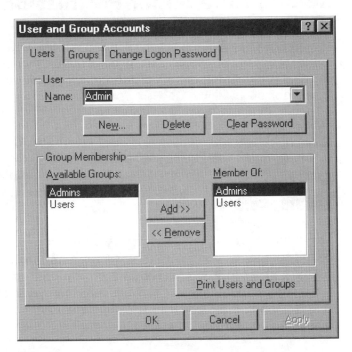

The Users tab has a combo box at the top where you can select any user in the system. The Group Membership section shows which groups this user is a member of.

FIGURE 18.9

Plan for security in an
Access database

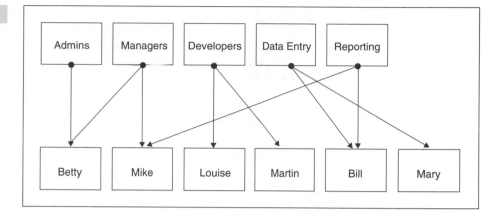

- To create a new user, click on the New... button. In the dialog
  box that appears, supply a unique name and Personal ID (PID)
  for the user. Click on the OK button to create the user. Access
  uses the PID to uniquely identify the user you've just created.

TIP

> The PID is *not* a password. New users are already
> created without a password. To assign a password to a
> user, close Access, reopen it, log on as the new user,
> and use the User and Group Accounts dialog box to set
> that user's password.

- To delete a user, select the user in the combo box and click on the
  Delete button, then click on the Yes button to confirm the delete.
  You can't delete any of the built-in users.

- To clear the password of a user who has forgotten his or her password, click on the Clear Password button.

- To add a user to a group, select the group in the left list box and
  click on the Add>> button.

- To remove a user from a group, select the group in the right-hand
  list box and click on the <<Remove button.

NOTE   You can't remove any user from the Users group, and you can't remove the last member from the Admins group.

The Groups Tab

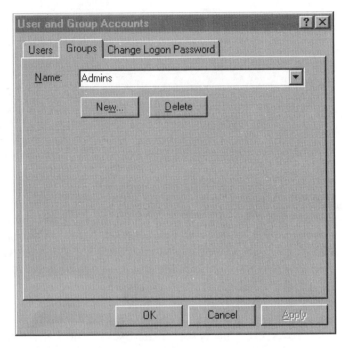

The Groups tab has a single combo box that shows you all of the existing groups in your database.

- To create a new group, click on the New... button, supply a name and Personal ID (PID) for the new group, and click on the OK button. Access uses the PID to make this new group unique.

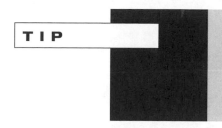

TIP

You should store all of the PIDs you use for both users and groups, along with the WID for your workgroup file. If your workgroup file is ever lost or corrupted, you can use this information to re-create the information it contains.

- To delete a group, select the group in the combo box, click on the <u>D</u>elete button, and click on the <u>Y</u>es button to confirm the deletion.

The Change Logon Password Tab

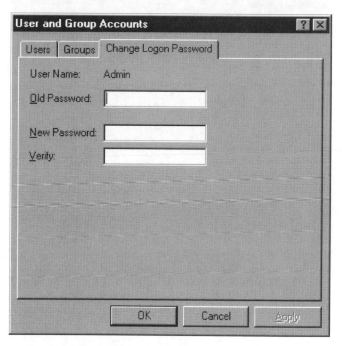

To change your password, enter your current password and then enter the new password, typing it the same way twice. This will allow Access to check and make sure you didn't accidentally mistype the new password.

Viewing Ownership and Permissions

To modify object permissions and ownership, select <u>T</u>ools ➤ Security ➤ User and Group <u>P</u>ermissions... from the Access menus.

The Permissions Tab

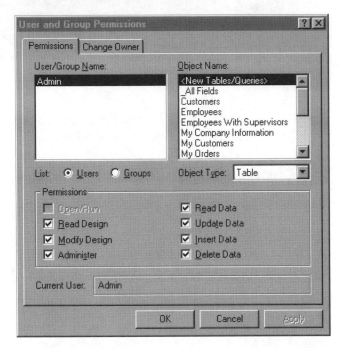

- To view a user's permissions on any object, first choose the Users radio button. Then click on the user whose permission you want to check in the list box. Select the type of the object from the combo box. Select the object in the object list box. The Permissions area will show the current explicit permissions for this user.

- To view a group's permissions on any object, first choose the Groups radio button. Then click on the group whose permission you want to check in the list box. Select the type of the object from the combo box. Select the object in the object list box. The Permissions area will show the current permissions for this group.

- To change permissions on an object, first choose the user or group you want to change permissions for, as above. Select the type of object from the combo box. Select one or more objects in the list box. Click in the Permissions check boxes to select or de-select the various permissions. When the correct set of permissions is showing, click on the Apply button to make the changes.

The Change Owner Tab

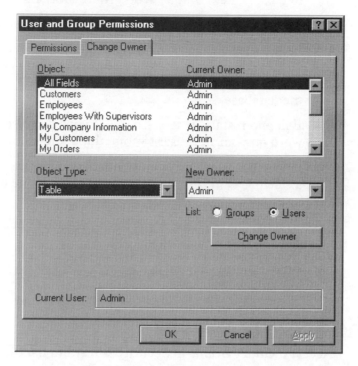

- To view the current owner of an object, select the Object Type in the left combo box. Select one or more objects. The New Owner combo box will show you the current owner of these objects. (If you select objects owned by more than one user or group, the box will remain blank.)

- To change ownership, select the Object Type in the left combo box. Select one or more objects. Select the New Owner from the combo box and click on Change Owner.

Securing Your Database

As you've seen so far, Access security can be a complex business. The interactions of users, groups, owners, objects, and permissions require careful study. However, there are some simple steps that will help you any time you need to secure a database. Following these steps rigorously will help ensure that your security system is without holes.

1. If you haven't done so already, use the Workgroup Administrator to create a new, unique Workgroup. Store the WID in a safe place.

2. Start Access, and create a new user for yourself to use. Add this user to the Admins group.

3. Change the Admin user password to any non-blank string. Store this password in a safe place, in case you later decide to desecure the database.

4. Exit and restart Access. Log in as your new user. Change the password on your new user to something known only to you.

5. Create any other users and groups you require. Store the PIDs in a safe place, in case you ever need to re-create one of these users or groups.

6. Run the Access Security Wizard (described below) to remove permissions from the database.

7. Assign permissions to those users and groups you want to be able to work with objects.

The Security Wizard

Access includes a built-in Security Wizard to handle some of the tedium of securing a database. The Security Wizard makes a new copy of your database owned by the user who runs the Wizard, makes sure all objects in that database are owned by that user as well, and removes all permissions for the Admin user and the Users group from these objects. It also encrypts your database, for protection from prying eyes armed with hex editors.

To use the Security Wizard, choose Tools ➤ Security ➤ User Level Security Wizard... from the menus. The Wizard starts by asking you which objects to secure, as shown in Figure 18.10. Most often, you will want to secure all objects in your database.

When you proceed from this dialog box, Access will prompt you for a file name for your new secured database. The Wizard will then create this new

FIGURE 18.10

When you launch the
Security Wizard, you
can choose exactly
which objects in your
database to secure.

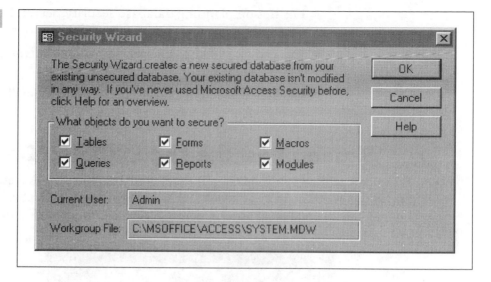

database and make secured copies of your objects in it. The process ends
with the congratulatory message shown here.

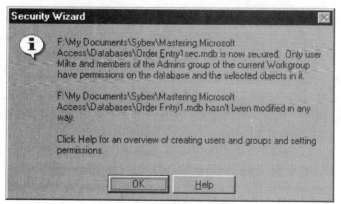

 ➤ Here are some additional sources of information about security:

- From the Access menu bar, choose <u>H</u>elp ➤ <u>C</u>ontents ➤ *Using Mi-crosoft Access* ➤ *Securing a Database*, and click on the topic you're interested in. You can then choose <u>O</u>ptions ➤ Print Topic from the Help window's button bar to print the topic as needed.

- For tips on planning database security, search for *security* in Help, choose <u>D</u>isplay, and then double-click on *Secure a Database*.

- You can also refer to Chapter 14 in the *Building Applications* manual that comes with your Access program.

- Clicking on Help from the Security Wizard will provide you with an overview of using Access security.

Skating Past the Logon Dialog Box

Once you've activated the logon procedure for Access (which you do by setting up a password for the Admin user), you'll always be faced with this dialog box as soon as you start Access:

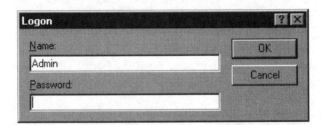

If you get tired of filling out the dialog box, you can put your user name and (optionally) your password into your startup command. That way, Access will fill in the dialog box automatically, and take you right past it.

To set up a custom startup command, you can use any combination of these three custom startup switches:

<database name>   If you want to create a shortcut to open a particular database when you start Access, follow the startup command with a blank space and the location and name of the database you want to open.

/User *<user name>*   To supply a user name at startup, follow the startup command with a space, followed by /User, followed by a space and your user name.

/Pwd *<password >*   To supply your password at startup, follow the startup command with a space, followed by /Pwd, followed by another space and your password.

You can set up a custom startup command by using Windows Explorer. The procedure we'll explain here doesn't change the way your original copy of Access works at all. Rather, it creates a new icon on your Windows desktop and associates it with your selected settings. Here are the exact steps:

1. Launch the Windows Explorer, make sure it doesn't fill the whole screen, and navigate to the folder containing the msaccess.exe program (usually this will be the c:\msoffice\access folder).

2. Holding down the *right* mouse button, drag this program out of Explorer and drop it on any blank area of your Windows desktop. Select Create Shortcut(s) Here from the context menu that appears when you drop the program.

3. Right-click on the icon you just created. Select Properties from the menu, and click on the Shortcut tab in the Properties dialog box.

4. Enter the command line switches in the Target text box and choose OK.

Let's suppose that you've been assigned the user name *Gondola*, and the password *omnipotent*. Furthermore, you want to have this shortcut automatically open the database named ContactManagement1.mdb on the c:\contact folder. In that case, you'd want to change the startup command in the Command Line text box to:

```
C:\MSOFFICE\ACCESS\MSACCESS.EXE c:\contact\
ContactManagement1.mdb /User Gondola /Pwd omnipotent
```

The one risk here, of course, is that anyone who has access to your computer, and a little knowledge of shortcuts, can look up your password in about two seconds flat. If that's a risk you cannot afford to take, then you can leave the password out of the startup command (in my example, remove */Pwd omnipotent*). In that case, you'll have to provide the password each time you start Access.

 ➤ For more information on custom Access startup commands, search Access's Help for *switches for starting Access*.

Password Security

As you've seen above, the full Access security model can be quite complex to implement and maintain. If you're interested only in protecting your own database from prying eyes, there's a new Database Password feature that provides you with a simpler way to lock up your data. This feature isn't really suitable for networked, multiuser applications, since it doesn't let you distinguish among individual users. But it can be an easy way to add some security to single-user databases.

To set a password on your database:

1. Open the database, being sure to check the Exclusive box on the File Open dialog box, and choose Tools ➤ Security ➤ Set Database Password....

2. Choose a password, and type it into both the Password and Verify boxes (typing it twice is a precaution to prevent you from making an accidental mistake the first time).

3. Click on the OK button.

When you attempt to open this database in the future, you'll see the dialog box below. Enter the same password you chose in Step 2 above to get into the database.

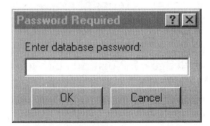

> **WARNING**
>
> If you ever forget your database password, all of your data will be lost forever. There's nothing anyone, including Microsoft, can do to bypass this password once it has been set. Be sure to pick something you'll remember, and to record the password in a safe place.

Where to Go from Here

In this chapter, we've introduced two of the most complex issues in Access: multiuser record locking and security. Now that you've learned about all the basic pieces you need to write useful Access databases, we're going to turn our attention to the things that distinguish a finished application from just another database. Part Four shows you how to add polish to your project with macros, toolbars, menus, and other tools to make your users' lives easier.

What's New in the Access Zoo?

Access for Windows 95 has improved its network capabilities and security in several ways. Here's a list of what's new:

- Record locking problems in multiuser applications have been minimized by changes within the Jet Engine.

- Multiple users can enter data at the same time without blocking each other out, as they did in previous versions of Access.

- The Security Wizard is built into Access instead of being a separate add-in.

- The Security dialog boxes have been rearranged and simplified.

- The new Database Password feature provides an alternative to full Access security for single-user databases.

PART FOUR

Building a Custom Application

Creating a
Custom Application

THIS chapter starts Part Four of this book, where we'll look at how to turn a database into an *application* (or *app*, for short). This chapter is also a transition for you, the reader, because you'll be going from the role of computer *user* to application *developer*. We'll explain what that's all about as we go along in this chapter.

What Is an Application?

An application is a database that's been automated, using menus, dialog boxes, and other familiar components of the Windows interface. The goal is to create a product that anyone—even people who know nothing about Microsoft Access—can use.

When you use the Database Wizard to design a database, the Wizard creates a simple application with forms, reports, and perhaps one or more switchboards. You can create much more elaborate applications than those that the Database Wizard creates by creating every database object from scratch. Or you can create all the database objects—tables, queries, forms, and reports—using the Database Wizard. Then you can create your own switchboards and dialog boxes to tie those objects together in a smooth, easy-to-use application.

Who's Who in Application Development

Before we begin our foray into applications development, you'll need to understand the terms *developer* and *user*:

Developer The person who creates the application—most likely yourself, since you're the one reading this book.

User The person, or people, who will be using the completed application. This person might be a computer neophyte.

This chapter marks your initiation into the ranks of application developers. As a developer, your mission is to *create* applications that people with little or no computer experience or training can use.

How Much Programming Is Involved?

Historically, only people with advanced training and experience in computer programming were able to build custom programs (applications). But with Access, you can create very sophisticated custom applications with little or no programming. Why? Because the tables, queries, forms, and reports that you create using techniques from the preceding chapters make up at least 90 percent of the overall application.

The other 10 percent of the application will consist of *macros* and/or *Visual Basic procedures* that determine how the application behaves as the user interacts with the program. We'll talk about macros and procedures in upcoming chapters. First you need to understand *events*, which are the triggers that launch your custom macros and procedures into action.

What Are Events?

The custom applications that you create with Microsoft Access are *event-driven*. In English that means that the application normally just sits there on the screen waiting for the user (the person using the mouse/keyboard) to do something. When the user does indeed do something, that triggers an *event* which the program then responds to.

Virtually every activity that occurs on the screen is an event. Here are some examples:

- Moving or clicking the mouse
- Pressing and releasing a key
- Moving the cursor to a control
- Changing the contents of a control

- Opening or closing a form
- Printing a report

For example, when you're using a form or switchboard, and you click on a command button, your action generates a "button click" event. The application *responds* to the event by carrying out whatever *action* the command button tells the program to do. The action is defined, by you, in the form of a macro or by Visual Basic code.

Microsoft Access can detect many kinds of events. And you can assign a custom action to any one of these events. Before we talk about how to create actions, let's talk about how you go about finding the events to which you want to assign custom actions.

Finding Event Properties

You assign an action to an event by assigning a macro or procedure name to an *event property*. Every form, report, and control has its own set of events. To see the events, you need to open the form or report in design view, and open the property sheet. Here are the exact steps:

1. With Access running, a database open, and the database window open on the screen, click on the name of the form or report whose events you want to explore.

2. Click on the Design button to open that object in design view. Then...

   - If you want to see events for the form as a whole, choose Edit ➤ Select Form, or click in the square in the upper-left corner where the rulers meet.

   - If you want to see events for the report as a whole, choose Edit ➤ Select Report, or click in the square in the upper-left corner where the rulers meet.

   - If you want to see events for a particular control, click on the specific control.

3. Open the property sheet (click on the Properties button or choose View ➤ Properties.)

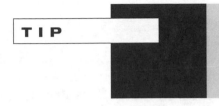

TIP   If you want to look at the events for a specific control, you can just right-click on the control and choose Properties from the shortcut menu. Then click on the Events tab.

4. Click on the Events tab.

The property sheet will show you all the events that you can assign actions to. The exact events that become available depend on which object is selected at the moment. For example, if you chose Edit ➤ Select Form under Step 2, the properties sheet would show event properties for the entire form, as in Figure 19.1.

If you click on a specific control before (or after) opening the property sheet, you'll see events for that particular control only. For example, Figure 19.2 shows the event properties for the currently selected combo box, named EmployeeID in this example.

FIGURE 19.1

Event properties for an entire form

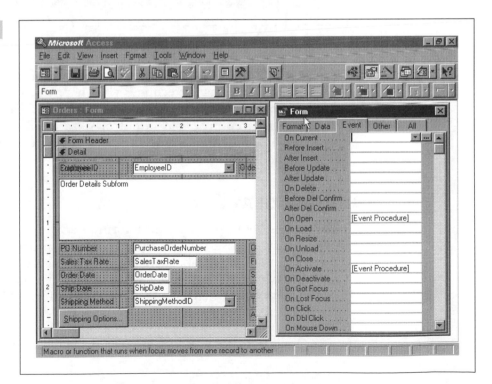

FIGURE 19.2

Event properties for a
single control on a form

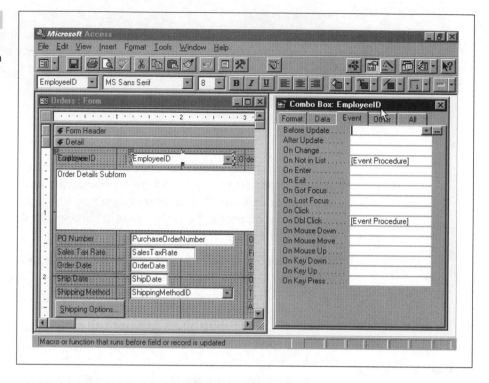

In Figures 19.1 and 19.2, you can see that some of the events have [Event Procedure] listed as the property. "Behind" that event procedure is the Visual Basic code that determines what happens when the event occurs. A little later in this chapter I'll show you how to create a control, and the action for that control using Control Wizards. But first, here's a quick overview of some of the many different types of events to which you can assign actions.

Sample Form Events

To see the event properties for a form as a whole, you open the form in design view, choose Edit ➤ Select Form, then open the property sheet and select the Events tab, as we did back in Figure 19.1. There are many events to which you can assign actions, but let's start by focusing on the events that occur when the user first opens a form. Here they are, in the order that they occur:

Open ➤ Load ➤ Resize ➤ Activate ➤ Current

You can assign an action to any one of these events using the On Open, On Load, On Resize, On Activate, and On Current properties. But why so many different events for the simple act of opening a form? Because having lots of events to assign actions to gives you great freedom in customizing how your custom application will behave when the user opens the form. For example, you can assign an action to the On Open property, and that action will play out first. You can assign a different action to the On Load event, and that action will play out second. You can assign custom actions to as many, or as few, event properties as you wish.

TIP As always, you can get more information about an event by clicking on the event name in the property sheet, and then pressing the Help key F1.

When the user closes a form, three events occur:

Unload ➤ Deactivate ➤ Close

To assign actions to these events, you use the On Unload, On Deactivate, and On Close event properties for the form.

To illustrate just how specific you can be when assigning actions to events, let's suppose you want some special action to occur when the user switches from one open form to another. The On Open and On Close events wouldn't do you any good in this case. However, the Activate and Deactivate events do occur when switching from one open form to another, like this:

Deactivate (first form) ➤ Activate (second form)

Sample Control Events

Every control on a form has its own set of event properties to which you can assign actions. The exact event properties that are available to you depend on the type of control you're working with at the moment. For example, the event properties for a text box are different from the event properties for a combo box.

But virtually all controls have some simple events that occur when the user enters the control (by clicking on or tabbing to it). Those events properties are:

Enter ➤ GotFocus

To assign actions to these events, you first need to select a specific control (still in design view), open the property sheet, and click on the Events tab, just as we did back in Figure 19.2.

When the user exits a control, these two events occur:

Exit ➤ LostFocus

Keep in mind that the events we've discussed here are just a few examples of the dozens of events that you can assign actions to. You'll see many, many more examples as we progress through this, and forthcoming, chapters. To get you started in creating your own controls, and assigning actions to the events that those controls generate, we'll turn our attention now to the *Control Wizards*, the easiest way to create custom controls and actions.

Creating a Control and Action in One Step

The easiest way to create a control, and to assign a custom action to it, is via the Control Wizards, available in the forms design screen. Here are the basic steps for creating a control and action, using the Control Wizards:

1. Open, in design view, the form to which you want to add a control.

2. Make sure the toolbox is open (if not, click on the Toolbox toolbar button or choose View ➤ Toolbox.)

3. Make sure the Control Wizards button in the toolbox is pushed in, as shown below.

4. Click on the type of control you want to create. (The Command Button tool is a good one to cut your teeth on, because it's easy to create and the Wizard offers many options.)

TIP   Remember, if you forget what type of control the various buttons in the toolbox create, you can just point to a button and wait for the ToolTip to appear.

5. Click, in the form, at about where you want to put the control you're about to create.

6. If the control you are creating is supported by the Control Wizards, you'll see the first Wizard screen. Just follow the Wizard's instructions and make your selections as you would with any Wizard.

When you've finished, you'll see the control on your form, already selected with sizing handles in case you want to move or resize the control.

To test the new control, switch to form view. In form view, use the control as you normally would. For example, if you created a command button, just click on the command button. When you do, the action you chose while completing the Wizard will be played out.

Note that when you add a control to a form, you changed the form. When you try to close the form, you'll be asked if you want to save the change. Choose Yes if you're happy with your new control, and want to save it.

An Example of Using Control Wizards

Let's take a look at a specific example of using the Control Wizards to create a fairly simple control. Suppose that you used the Database Wizard to create the Order Entry database. You open up the My Company Information form (Figure 19.3), and decide that perhaps you'd like to add a command button to that form that will allow the user to close the form without clicking on the built-in Close button.

First, we need to close the form (click on its Close button), and get to the database window. From there, reopen the form, but in design view this time. In this example, we would click on the Forms tab, click on My Company Information as the name of the form to modify, and then click on the Design button. You're taken to the forms design window.

The toolbox needs to be open. So if it isn't, click on the Toolbox button or choose View ➤ Toolbox. Then make sure the Control Wizards button in the toolbox is pushed in, as in Figure 19.4.

Now we can use the scroll bars surrounding the form to get down to the lower-right corner of the form, where we want to place the command button. Then we click on the Command Button tool in the toolbox, and then click down near the lower-right corner of the form to indicate where we want the button to appear.

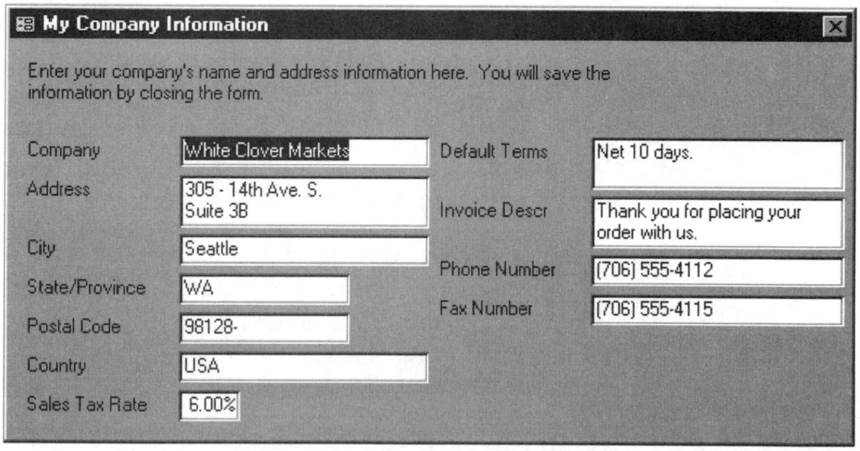

FIGURE 19.3

We'll use the Control Wizards to add a Close button to this form.

FIGURE 19.4

The My Company
Information form in
design view, with the
toolbox open and
Control Wizards
button pushed in

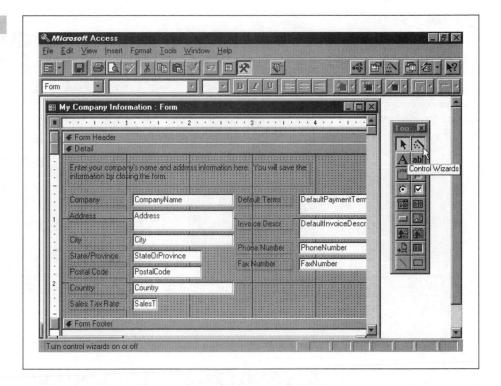

For a moment, we see an outline indicating where the button will appear. Then the Command Button Wizard kicks in automatically. The first Wizard window asks what we want this button to do. In this case, we choose Form Operations under Categories, and Close Form under Actions (since I want this button to close the form), as in Figure 19.5.

After making a selection we click on the Next> button, and the second Wizard window asks how we want the button to look. It suggests using the Exit picture, which is a door with an arrow pointing the way out. But in this example, we decide we'd rather have the button just show the word Close (with the C underlined). So we click on the Text option button, and type **&Close** in the text box, as in Figure 19.6.

The first window in the Command Button Wizard asks what you want the button to do, and provides many options grouped into several categories.

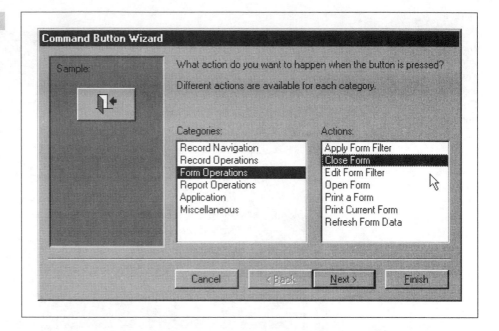

Here we've opted to put the word <u>C</u>lose, rather than a picture, on the command button we're creating. An ampersand in front of a letter means "underline the next letter."

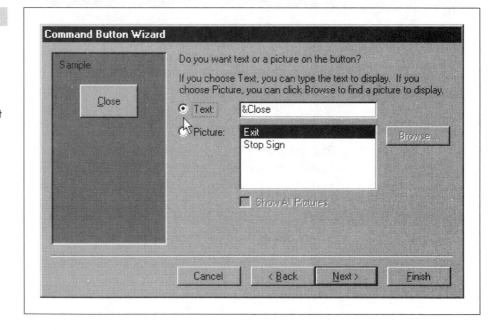

TIP

To underline a letter in a button's text, just put an ampersand in front of the letter you want underlined. As you'll see later in the book, the same technique applies to many controls, such as underlining hotkeys in your own custom menus. If you want to include an ampersand in the text on the button, just type two ampersands together, like this: &&.

We then hit the Next> button, and come to the last Wizard window, which asks what we want to name this button. The wizard will come up with a generic name, like Command23, but we can use a more descriptive one. In Figure 19.7 we've opted to name this button CloseCompanyInfo.

Finally, we choose Finish from the last Wizard window, and the Wizard disappears. Now we can see the new command button on the form. You can size and move this new button using the standard techniques. In Figure 19.8 you can see that we've moved the new command button close to the lower-right corner of the form.

FIGURE 19.7

Here we've opted to name the button CloseCompanyInfo.

Command Button Wizard

Sample:

Close

What do you want to name the button?

A meaningful name will help you to refer to the button later.

CloseCompanyInfo

That's all the information the wizard needs to create your command button.

☐ Display Help on customizing the button.

Cancel   < Back   Next >   Finish

FIGURE 19.8

The new <u>C</u>lose command button down near the lower-right corner of the form

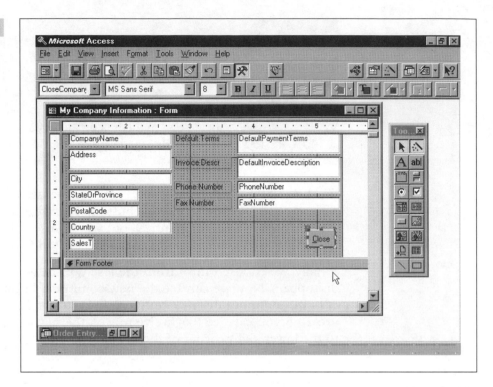

Now we can save the change and close the form. We can't use the new Close button to do that though, because the controls you create work only in form view, not design view. So to close and save this form you can choose <u>F</u>ile ➤ <u>C</u>lose from the menu bar, or click on the form's Close button. When asked if you want to save the changes to the design of the form, choose <u>Y</u>es. You'll be returned to the database window.

Testing the New Control

To test the new control, you first need to open the form in form view (not design view). So in this example, we could just double-click on My Company Information in the database window. The form appears looking pretty much the same as it did back in Figure 19.3, except that now we can also see the new custom Close button, as in Figure 19.9.

To test the new command button, just click on it. The form should close, which is all that we wanted this particular button to do.

FIGURE 19.9

The My Company Information form in form view, with the new Close button visible

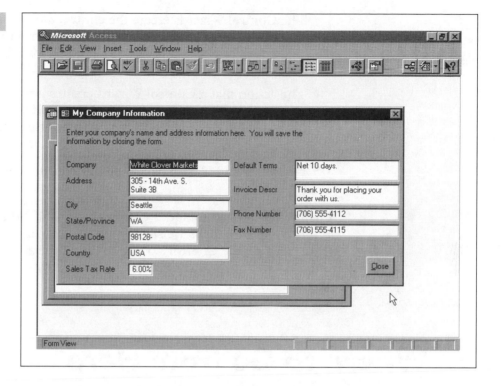

More Wizard-Created Controls

The command button to close a form is just one example of a control that you can create using Control Wizards. The Option Group, Combo Box, List Box, Command Button, Subform/Subreport tools in the toolbox also offer Wizards to make creating those types of controls a bit easier. Your best bet is to simply experiment, by creating a few different controls and seeing what happens. Here are a few points to keep in mind as you do so:

- Remember that you can only create controls in design view.

- The Control Wizards will appear *only* if the Control Wizard button in the toolbox is pushed in before you start creating the control.

- If you change your mind mid-stream, you can cancel the Wizard.

- If you create a control and then change your mind and want to get rid of it, just click on the control (in design view) and press Delete.

- The Control Wizards create the control *and* assign certain properties to it. To change the properties of a control that a Wizard has created, right-click on the control and choose Properties from the shortcut menu that appears.

- The action that a Control Wizard creates is written in Visual Basic, a topic we'll introduce in Chapter 25. If you want to take a peek at the code that the Wizard created, right-click on the control and choose Build Event from the shortcut menu that appears.

- Remember: to test the new control, you must be in form view, not design view.

Whenever you need to add a custom command button, combo box, or option group on a form, we suggest you first try using a Control Wizard. If you can't get the Control Wizard to create the action that you want the control to perform, your next best bet is to create a macro—the topic of our next chapter.

Where to Go from Here

There's lots to know about creating custom Access applications. Here are some pointers for finding specific topics of interest:

- To try some custom applications to see what they're like, see Appendix B and Appendix C.

- To learn about using macros to define custom actions, see Chapter 20.

- To learn about creating custom switchboards and dialog boxes for an application, see Chapters 21 and 22.

- To learn about creating custom menus and toolbars, see Chapters 22 and 23.

What's New in Access Zoo?

For those of you familiar with earlier versions of Access, here what's new in application development:

- **Database Wizard** It's not necessary to create a custom application completely from scratch. The Database Wizard, which we discussed earlier in the book, can whip together all the tables for your custom application and add some sample data to experiment with. You can use the forms and reports that Wizard creates, or replace them with custom forms and reports of your own.

- **Startup command** To specify your application's startup form, title-bar text, icon, menu, and toolbar, just select Tools ➤ Startup from Access's menu bar.

- **Database Splitter Wizard** If you'll be delivering your application to other people and want to make it easy to update forms and reports without changing their existing data, you can use the Database Splitter Wizard to separate the tables from the other objects. To run the Wizard, choose Tools ➤ Add-ins ➤ Database Splitter.

- **Macro to Visual Basic for Applications Converter** After you've gained some experience with Visual Basic, you'll probably find that Visual Basic code is easier to maintain and debug than macros. To convert your macros to Visual Basic, select the macro that you want to convert in the Database window, choose File ➤ Save As/Export ➤ Save As Visual Basic Module. Or to convert all the macros used in a particular form or report, open that form or report in design view, choose Tools ➤ Macros ➤ Convert Macros To Visual Basic.

- **Better Menu Builder** You can now create custom shortcut menu bars by using the Menu Builder. See Chapter 23 or search the Answer Wizard or help index for *shortcut menus*.

CHAPTER

20

Using Macros to Create Custom Actions

THE Control Wizards we discussed in Chapter 19 are the easiest way to create a control and a custom action for that control. But as you develop more sophisticated applications, you'll probably want to define custom actions that are more complex than the actions the Control Wizards offer.

When you can't get a Control Wizard to create the exact action you want to perform, you can use either of these two alternative techniques to define a custom action:

- Create a macro
- Or, write a Visual Basic procedure

Visual Basic requires that you type long strings of commands very, very accurately. Macros, however, let you define actions using the simpler point-and-click approach. So, unless you happen to be a Visual Basic whiz already, you'll probably find that macros are by far the quickest and easiest way to define a custom action in your application. In this chapter, we'll focus on macros.

How to Create a Macro

The "mechanics" of creating a macro are fairly straightforward:

1. In the database window, click on the Macros tab.

2. Click on the <u>N</u>ew button. You're taken to a *macro sheet* that's tentatively named Macro1, as in Figure 20.1.

FIGURE 20.1

A new, blank macro
sheet

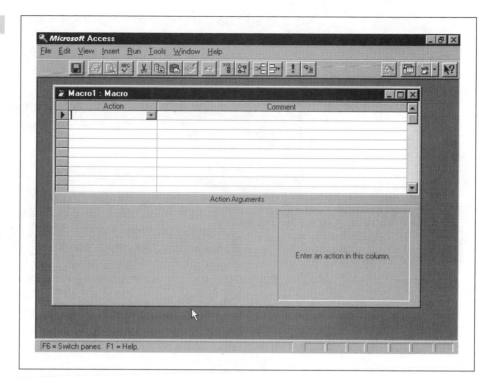

3. Click on the drop-down list button in the Action column. You'll
   see a partial list of possible actions, as below. (You can use the
   scroll bar, the ↓ key, or type a letter to scroll down the list.)

4. Choose whichever action best describes what you want the macro
   to do. For example, below we chose OpenReport (an action that
   will cause the macro to open up a report in this database). Notice

that in addition to the word OpenReport appearing in the action column, the lower portion of the window shows some *action arguments* to be filled in. And the hint box tells us what the selected action will do.

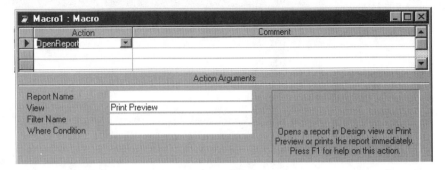

5. Next you need to "fill in the blanks" for this action under Action Arguments. For example, below we clicked next to Report Name, and can now use the drop-down list to choose *which* report we want the macro to open. Note too that the hint box is now giving us information that's specific to the Report Name argument that we're filling in.

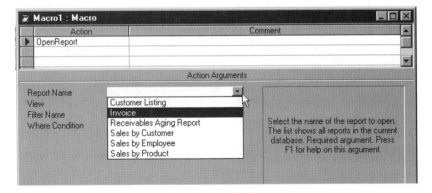

6. You need to fill in each *required argument* for your action. You can leave *optional arguments* blank, if you wish. To determine whether an argument is required or optional, click on the argument and read the hint box to the right.

7. Optionally, you can now click just to the right of the action you chose, and type in a plain-English description of what that action does, for future reference when you are exploring your macros

later down the road. Note the comment next to our OpenReport action below.

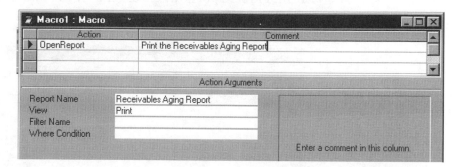

8. Now you can click on the cell just under the action you defined, and repeat steps 3-8 to define additional actions for this macro. When the macro is executed, it will perform every action in your macro, starting with the first and ending with the last. In Figure 20.2 we've added several actions and comments to our sample macro.

9. When you've finished with your macro, just close it and give it a name (choose File ➤ Close or click the × button in the upper-right corner of the macro sheet window). You can choose Yes to save your changes, and enter a new, more descriptive name for your macro.

FIGURE 20.2

A macro with several actions defined

The name you assigned to the macro appears in the database window whenever the Macros tab is active. For example, we named our macro PrintThreeReports when closing it. So now that name appears in the database window as you can see below.

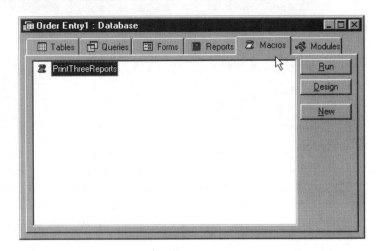

Determining When a Macro Plays

After you've created a macro, your next step is to determine *when* the macro will perform its actions. For example, you might want the macro to play:

- as soon as the user clicks on a particular command button on a form,
- or, right after the user changes the data in some control,
- or as soon as the user opens a particular form or report.

As we'll discuss later, you can also have the macro play when the user first opens the database (see "Creating a Macro to Run at Startup" later in this chapter). Or you can assign the macro to an option in a custom toolbar (Chapter 23) or menu (Chapter 24) that you've created. Your options for *when* the macro is triggered are virtually limitless. For now, let's just take a look at how you'd assign a macro to a report, form, or a particular control on a form:

1. In design view, open the form or report that you want to have trigger the macro.

   - If you want the form or report as a whole (i.e., open/close the form, open/close the report) to trigger the macro, choose Edit ➤ Select Form or Edit ➤ Select Report.

   - If you want a particular control in a form to trigger a macro, select that control by clicking on it once. (If you haven't created the control yet, you can do so right on the spot using the toolbox.)

   - You can even have a particular section of a form or report trigger the macro. Just click on the section bar in the design view (i.e., Detail in the reports design view).

2. Open the property sheet, and click on the Event tab. All the possible events for the selected form, report, control, or section will appear, as in the example below.

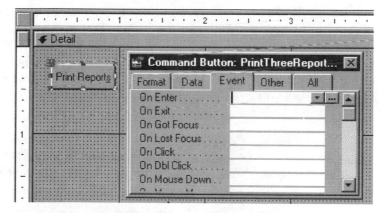

3. Click on the property that you want to have trigger the macro. For example, if you're assigning the macro to a command button, and want the macro to run when the user clicks on that button, click on the On Click property.

4. Choose the name of the macro you want to execute from the drop-down list that appears. For example, below we're assigning the

PrintThreeReports macro to the On Click property of a button we created earlier.

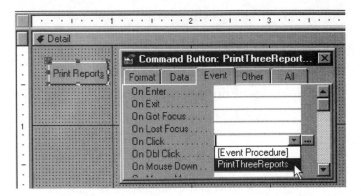

And now you're done. It's a good idea to save and close the form at this point, before you test the macro. Just choose File ➤ Close and choose Yes when asked about saving your changes.

Running the Macro

To run the macro, you need to play the role of the user by triggering whatever event activates the macro. For example, if you assigned the macro to the On Click property of a command button, you need to open the form (in form view) that holds the button, then click on that button, just as the user would. If you assigned the macro to the On Open property of a form, all you need to do is open the appropriate form.

TIP

You can run a macro simply by clicking on its name in the database window, and then clicking on the Run button. This is fine for testing a macro. But when creating a custom application, you want the user to have easier access to the macro.

All That in a Nutshell

Whether you're an absolute beginner or are accustomed to creating macros in other products, creating Access macros will probably take some getting used to. To summarize the procedure we presented in the step-by-step instructions, the basic procedure for creating a macro and assigning it to an event goes like this:

- In the database window, click on the Macros tab, and click on <u>N</u>ew.

- Use the Action column to choose an action. Then fill in the required arguments for that action. You can create several actions within a single macro.

N O T E   Remember that unlike some other products such as Word or Excel, Access does not include a macro recorder to automate the process of defining macro actions.

- Close and save the macro, giving it a name that will be easy to remember later.

- Open, in design view, the form or report that you want to "trigger" the macro.

- Select the control that will trigger the macro (or, choose <u>E</u>dit ➤ Select Fo<u>r</u>m or Edit ➤ Select <u>R</u>eport if you want a form or report event to trigger the macro).

- Open the property sheet, and click on the Event tab.

- Click on the specific event that you want to have trigger the macro, and then choose the macro name from the drop-down list that appears.

- Close and save the form.

Once you've done all that, the macro will play every time you trigger the event to which you assigned the macro. The macro will not run (ever) in design view. You must open the form in form view, or print the report, as a user would, in order to make the macro play its actions.

Summary of Macro Actions

Once you understand the mechanics of creating a macro and attaching it to some event, there's still the mind-boggling stage of "What can, and *can't,* I do using a macro?" There's no easy way to answer that—there are just too many possibilities, either way. But to give you an overview of the possibilities, we offer the following summary of every macro action. These actions are available when you click on the drop-down list in the Action column of the macro sheet:

AddMenu   Adds a menu to a custom menu bar (see Chapter 24).

ApplyFilter   Applies a filter, query, or SQL WHERE clause to a table, form, or report. Often used to filter records in the table underlying the form that launched the macro. You can use the ShowAllRecords action to clear the filter.

Beep   Just sounds a beep.

CancelEvent   Cancels the event that caused the macro to execute. For example, if a BeforeUpdate event calls a macro, that macro can test data and then execute a CancelEvent to prevent the form from accepting the new data.

Close   Closes the specified window. Typically used to close a form.

CopyObject   Copies the specified object to a different Access database, or to the same database but with a different name.

DeleteObject   Deletes the specified object, or the currently selected object in the database window if you don't specify an object.

DoMenuItem   Tells the macro to select and execute a command from an Access menu bar.

Echo   Hides, or shows, on the screen the results of each macro action as the macro is running.

FindNext   Repeats the previous FindRecord action to locate the next record that matches the same criterion.

FindRecord   Locates a record meeting the specified criterion in the current table (the table underlying the form that launched the macro).

GoToControl   Moves the focus (cursor) to the specified field or control on a form.

GoToPage   Moves the focus to the specified page in a multi-page form.

GoToRecord   Moves the focus to a new record, in relation to the current record (e.g. Next, Previous, First, Last, New.)

Hourglass   Changes the mouse pointer to a "wait" hourglass (so the user knows to wait for the macro to finish its job.)

Maximize   Expands the active (current) window to full-screen size.

Minimize   Shrinks the active (current) window to an icon.

MoveSize   Moves and/or sizes the active window to the position and measurement you specify in inches (or centimeters if you've defined that as your unit of measure in the Windows Control Panel).

MsgBox   Displays a message on the screen.

OpenForm   Opens the specified form and moves the focus to that form.

OpenModule   Opens, in design view, the specified Visual Basic module.

OpenQuery   Opens a Select, Crosstab, or Action query. If you use this to run an Action query, the screen will display the usual warning messages, unless you precede this action with a SetWarnings action.

OpenReport   Prints the specified report, or opens it in print preview or design view. You can apply a filter condition with this action.

OpenTable   Opens the specified table in datasheet, design, or print preview view.

OutputTo   Exports data in the specified object to Microsoft Excel (.xls), rich text (.rtf), or text (.txt) format.

PrintOut   Prints the specified datasheet, form, report, or module.

Quit   Exits Microsoft Access.

Rename   Renames the specified or selected object.

RepaintObject   Performs any pending screen updates or calculations.

Requery   Forces the query underlying a specific control to be re-executed. If the specified control has no underlying query, this action will recalculate the control.

Restore   Restores a minimized or maximized window to its previous size.

RunApp   Starts another Windows or DOS program. That application then runs in the foreground, and the macro continues processing in the background.

RunCode   Runs the specified Visual Basic Function procedure. (To run a Sub procedure, create a function procedure that calls the Sub, and have the macro run that function.)

RunMacro   Runs a different macro. After that macro has finished its job, execution resumes in the original macro starting with the action under the RunMacro action.

RunSQL   Runs the specified SQL statement.

Save   Saves the specified object, or the active object if no other object is specified.

SelectObject   Selects the specified object. That is, this action mimics the act of clicking on an object to select it.

SendKeys   Sends keystrokes to Access or another active program.

SendObject   Includes the specified database object in an e-mail message.

SetMenuItem   Sets the appearance of a command (e.g., "grayed" or "checked" in a custom menu. See Chapter 24).

SetValue   Sets a value for a control, field, or property. Often used to "auto-fill" fields on a form based on some existing data.

SetWarnings   Hides, or displays, all warning boxes such as those that appear when you run an action query.

ShowAllRecords   Removes an applied filter from the table, query, or form so that no records are hidden.

ShowToolBar   Shows or hides a built-in or custom toolbar (see Chapter 23).

StopAllMacros   Stops all running macros, turns Echo back on (if it was off), and reinstates warning messages.

StopMacro   Stops execution of the currently running macro.

TransferDatabase   Imports, exports, or links data in another database.

TransferSpreadsheet   Imports, exports, or links data from the specified spreadsheet.

TransferText   Imports, exports, or links data from a text file, and can also be used to export data to a Microsoft Word for Windows mail merge data file.

Keep in mind that you can get much more information about each action right on your screen. Just select the action and take a look at the hint box. If you need more information after reading the hint box, just press Help (F1).

Executing a Macro Action "If..."

You can make any action, or series of actions, in a macro be conditional on some expressions. For example, suppose you want to create a macro that adds 7.75 percent sales tax to a total sale, but only *if* the sale is made in the state of California. That is, if the State field on the current form contains CA, then you want the macro to fill in another field, named SalesTaxRate, with .0775 and use that value in calculating the sales tax and total sale. To illustrate what we mean, Figure 20.3 shows a sample form with the appropriate fields, named State, Subtotal, SalesTaxRate, SalesTax, and TotalSale.

FIGURE 20.3

A sample form
containing fields
named State, Subtotal,
SalesTax, and Total

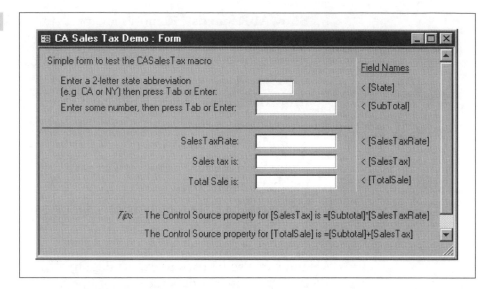

NOTE

Remember that in order to name a field on a form, you
need to open the form in design view. Then click on the
field you want to name, open the property sheet, and
click on the All tab. Then fill in the Name property with
whatever name you want to give that field. While
you're at it, you can use the Format property to assign a
format, such as Currency or Percent, to fields that will
contain numbers.

The last two fields on the form are calculated fields. The ControlSource
property for the SalesTax field contains the expression

   =[SalesTaxRate]*[SubTotal]

The Control Source property for the TotalSale field contains the
expression

   =[SubTotal]+[SalesTax]

After you've created and saved the form, you can create the macro in the
normal manner. But if you want to use conditions in the macro, you need

to open the Conditions column in the macro sheet. Just create (using New) or open (using Design) any macro sheet. Then click on the Conditions button in the toolbar, or choose View ➤ Conditions from the menu bar. A new column titled Condition appears to the left of the existing columns, as in Figure 20.4.

The condition you type in must be an expression that evaluates to either True or False, usually in the format *something* = *something*. For example the expression

[State]="CA"

evaluates to True only if the field named State contains exactly the letters CA. If the field named state contains anything but CA (or is empty) the expression [State]="CA" returns false.

FIGURE 20.4

The Conditions column now visible in the macro sheet

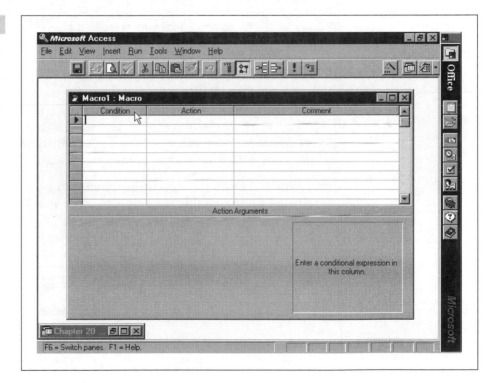

N O T E As with other text comparisons in Access, macro conditions are not case-sensitive. So "ca" or "Ca" or "cA" would all match "CA" in this case.

It's important to understand that the condition you specify affects only the action immediately to the right of the condition. If the expression proves True, the action is performed. If the expression proves False, then the action is completely ignored. Either way, execution then resumes at the next action in the macro.

T I P You can repeat the condition in a row by typing three periods (...) into the condition cell immediately beneath the cell that contains the condition. The ... characters mean "apply the condition above to this action."

So let's create the CASalesTax macro now. For starters, we'll have the macro set the SalesTaxRate field to zero. Then, the next action will check to see if the State field contains CA. If that's true, that action will put 0.775 into the SalesTaxRate field. The next actions will use the Repaint-Object command to recalculate the calculated controls SalesTax and TotalSale. Figure 20.5 shows the completed macro.

Since you can't see the action arguments for all three macro actions, we've listed them in Table 20.1, in the order in which they appear in the

TABLE 20.1: Condition, Action, and Action Arguments for Each Row in the CASalesTax Macro

CONDITION	ACTION	ACTION ARGUMENTS
	SetValue	Item: [SalesTaxRate]
		Expression: 0
[State]="CA"	SetValue	Item:[SalesTaxRate]
		Expression: 0.0775
	RepaintObject	

FIGURE 20.5

The CAStateTax macro

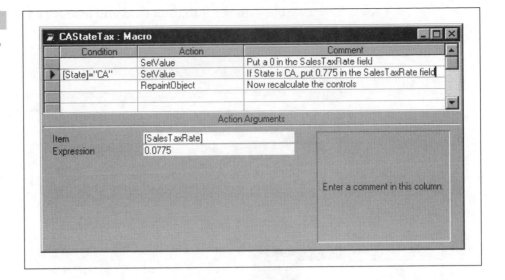

macro. (Leaving empty the action arguments for the RepaintObject action causes the entire object, the form in this example, to be recalculated):

After creating the macro, you close and save it with whatever name you wish. In this example we've named the macro CASalesTax.

Finally, you need to decide *when* this macro is called into action. In this case, there are two situations where we need the macro to recalculate the sales tax, after the user changes the value in the State field, as well as after the user changes the value in the Subtotal field.

So we open the form in design view, click on the State field, open the property sheet, click on the Event tab, and then assign the CASalesTax macro to the AfterUpdate property for that field, as below:

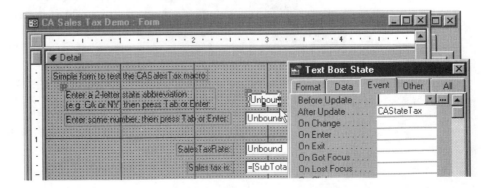

Then we click on the SubTotal field and also set its AfterUpdate property to the CASalesTax macro, as below.

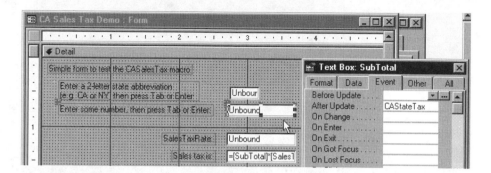

> ### TIP
>
> You can use Ctrl-click to select several controls, and then assign a macro to the same event on both controls at the same time.

Once those steps are complete we can save the form, and then open it in form view. Then, whenever we enter (or change) values in either the State or Subtotal fields (and press Tab or Enter to complete the entry), the SalesTaxRate, SalesTax, and TotalSale fields recalculate automatically. In the example shown in Figure 20.6 we entered CA in the State field, and 100 in the Subtotal field. As you can see, the three fields beneath show the correct sales tax rate, sales tax amount, and total sale.

> ### NOTE
>
> The AfterUpdate event is triggered only when you change the contents of a field and then move to another field.

Incidentally, the field names and *Tips* that you see in Figure 20.6 are just there for your own personal reference. They are just labels that have no effect on how the form functions. In "real life," there would be no need to show that information to the user of your application.

FIGURE 20.6

After typing CA in the State field, and 100 in the subtotal field, the macro and calculated controls automatically display the correct sales tax rate, sales tax amount, and total sale.

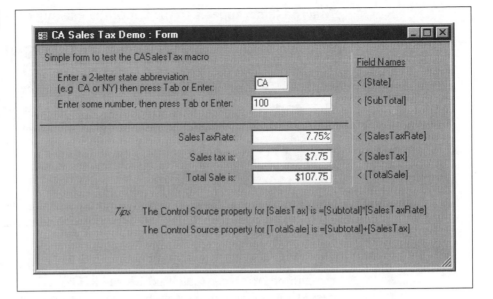

Creating Macro Groups

A macro sheet can actually contain several macros, each with its own macro name. Grouping several macros into a sheet can keep the list of macro names in the database window from becoming too lengthy and unwieldy. A good way to organize your macros is to put all the macros that go with a given form (or report) into a single macro sheet. That way, you can easily find all the macros that go with a particular form.

We often name our macro sheets for the form that triggers the macros in that sheet. For example, if we have a form named Customers, we might create a macro sheet named CustomerFormMacros that contains all the macros used by that form.

Creating a group of macros is a simple process. Just create or open a macro sheet in the usual manner. Then click on the Macro Names button in the toolbar. Or choose View ➤ Macro Names. A new column, titled

Macro Name, appears to the left of the existing columns, as below.

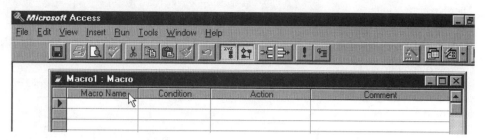

When adding a macro to the macro sheet, you need to type the macro name into the leftmost column. Then type in the first condition (if any), action, and comment in the usual manner. You can add as many actions to the macro as you wish.

Figure 20.7 shows an example with a macro sheet that contains five macros named AddNew, CalcTax, CloseAll, CloseForm, and PrintForm. Access stops running a macro when there are no more actions in the group, or when it hits the name of another macro. We've added a blank line between each macro for readability.

FIGURE 20.7

A macro sheet containing five macros named AddNew, CalcTax, CloseAll, CloseForm, and PrintForm

Macro Name	Condition	Action	Comment
			Macro group for a single form
AddNew		GoToRecord	Go to new record
CalcTax		SetValue	Put a 0 in the SalesTaxRate field
	[State]="CA"	SetValue	If State is CA, put 0.775 in the SalesTa
		RepaintObject	Now recalculate the controls
CloseAll		Close	Close the form, save automatically
		Quit	Save anything else that's open, and qu
CloseForm		Close	Close the form
PrintForm		DoMenuItem	Select the current record
		PrintOut	Print the currently selected record

Action Arguments

Close and save the macro sheet in the usual manner. In this example, let's say we decide to name the entire macro sheet MyGroup. Then you can assign macros to events using the standard technique. That is to open the form or report in design view; that will trigger a macro in the group. Click on the control that will trigger the macro (or choose Edit ➤ Select Form or Edit ➤ Select Report). Open the property sheet, and click on the drop-down list button for the event that you want to assign a macro to. The drop-down list now shows the names of all macros within all macro groups in the format

> *macrogroupname.macroname*

For example, below we're about to assign a macro to the On Click property of a control on a form. Notice that the drop-down list includes the names of all the macros within the macro group named MyGroup. To choose a specific macro to assign to this event, we just need to click on the macro's name. The property sheet will show the macro group name and macro name in the *macrogroupname.macroname* format, (e.g., My-Group.PrintForm).

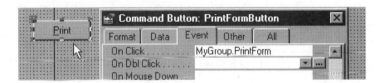

Editing Macros

To edit an existing macro, you just need to reopen the macro sheet. There are two ways to do so:

- If you're at the database window, just click on the Macros tab, click on the name of the macro (or macro group) you want to edit, and click on the Design button.

- If you're in a form's (or report's) design view, and want to edit a macro that you've already assigned to an event, just open the property sheet, click on the Event tab, then click on the ... button next to the name of the macro that you want to edit.

When you use the latter method to open a macro group, you'll be taken to the macro group in general, not the specific macro that you assigned to the event. But once you're in the macro sheet, you can easily scroll to the macro that you want to edit.

Changing, Deleting, and Rearranging Macros

Once you're in the macro sheet, you can move, delete, and insert rows using techniques that are virtually identical to the techniques you use in a datasheet:

1. Select a row by clicking on the row selector at the left edge of the row. Or select several rows by dragging the mouse pointer through row selectors or by using Shift+Click.

2. Once you've selected one or more rows you can do any of the following:

   - To delete the selected row(s), press Delete, or right-click on the selection and choose Delete Row, or choose Edit ➤ Delete Row from the menus.

   - To insert a row, press the Insert (Ins) key, or right-click on the selection and choose Insert Row, or choose Insert ➤ Row from the menu bar.

   - To move the selected row(s), click on the row selector again, hold down the mouse button, and drag the selection to its new position.

TIP

Arrange macros in a macro group in alphabetical order by name. That way, when you open the macro group you can easily find the specific macro you're looking for within that group.

- To copy the selection, press Ctrl+C or click on the Copy button, or right-click on the selection and choose Copy, or choose Edit ➤ Copy from the menu bar. The selection is copied to the Windows Clipboard. You can then use Edit ➤ Paste (Ctrl+V) to paste the copy into the same, or another, macro sheet.

- To undo any of the above changes, press Ctrl+Z or click on the Undo button or choose Edit ➤ Undo.

Keep in mind that any changes you make to the macro are *not* saved until you save the entire macro. If you close the macro without saving it, be sure to choose Yes when asked about saving your changes.

Referring to Controls from Macros

One of the most common uses of macros is to use the SetValue action to fill in a field on a form. For example, we used the SetValue action in an earlier example in this chapter to fill in a field named SalesTaxRate.

When you start doing this sort of thing with multiple forms, there are a couple of very important points to keep in mind:

- When referring to a control on some form *other than the form that launched the macro*, you must use the full-identifier syntax (i.e., [Forms]![*formname*]![*controlname*]) to refer to the control.

- Both forms must be open.

This can be one of the most confusing aspects of using macros, because if your macro opens a new form, you might think of that form as the "current form." But from Access's perspective, the form that *launched* the macro is "the current form," even if that form does not have the focus at the moment. Let's look at a simple example which illustrates this.

Let's say you have a form named FormA. The form contains a text box control named [OriginalText], as illustrated below.

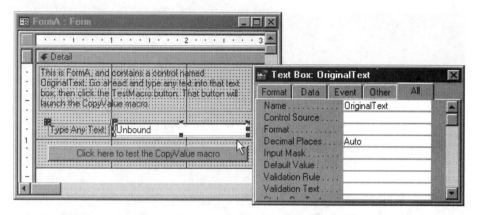

You also have a second form, named FormB, that contains a control named CopiedText, as shown below.

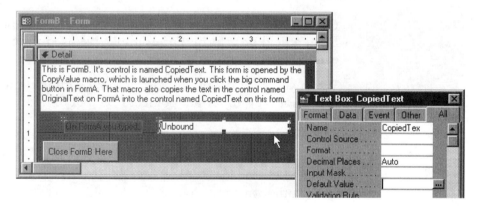

Let's say you want to create a macro that you'll launch from FormA. When you launch that macro, you want it to 1) open FormB and 2) take whatever text is in the [OriginalText] control on FormA and copy that text into the [CopiedText] control on Form B.

Figure 20.8 shows the appropriate macro (which we'll refer to as the CopyValue macro from here on out). Currently the cursor is in the SetValue action's cell so you can see the action arguments for that action. Table 20.2 shows the action arguments for both actions (where we omit an action argument, we have left the argument blank in the macro sheet as well).

FIGURE 20.8

The CopyValue macro showing the action arguments for the SetValue action

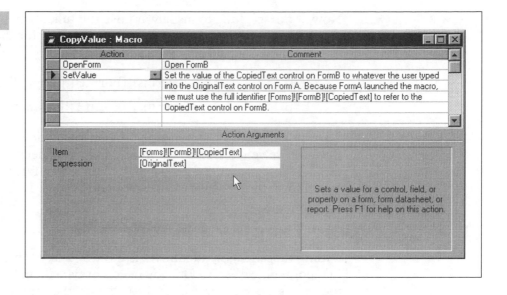

TABLE 20.2: Action Arguments for the CopyValue Macro Shown in Figure 20.8

ACTION	ACTION ARGUMENTS
OpenForm	Form Name: FormB
	View: Form
	Data Mode: Edit
	Window Mode: Normal
SetValue	Item: [Forms]![FormB]![CopiedText]
	Expression: [OriginalText]

Notice that we must refer to the [CopiedText] control using the full formal [Forms]![*formname*]![*controlname*], even though the OpenForm action has already opened FormB and FormB has the focus. We need to do so because FormA, not FormB, is the one the *launched* the macro. We can refer to the [OriginalText] control without all the formality, because [OriginalText] is the form that launched the macro.

Now, it doesn't hurt to just always use the full, formal syntax. For example, we could have used these action arguments for the SetValue action, and the macro would still work just fine.

Item:	[Forms]![FormB]![CopiedText]
Expression:	[Forms]![FormA]![OriginalText]

Though a bit more cumbersome, this approach does have one advantage. Because we've referred to forms and controls specifically, we don't need to waste brain cells trying to keep track of which form opened the macro, which form has the focus at the moment, and so forth.

Typing Lengthy Identifiers

Typing those lengthy identifiers is a bit of a task, and they can be prone to typographical errors. But you need not type them by hand. You can use the expression builder instead. Just click on the action argument you want to enter, then click on the build (…) button that appears next to the control. For example, in Figure 20.9 we clicked on the Item argument for the

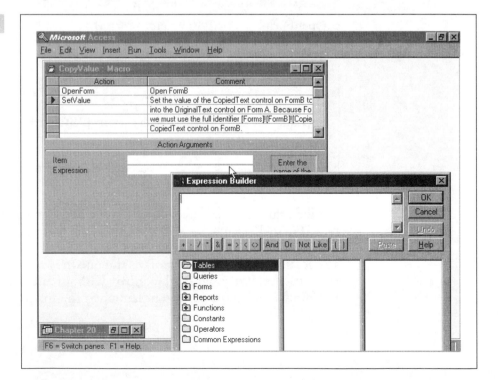

SetValue action, and then clicked on the Build button. Notice the Expression Builder.

Now we can specify a control simply by working our way down to it. In this case, we would double-click on Forms (since the control is on a form), then double-click on All Forms. Then we would double-click on FormB (since that's the one that contains the control we want to fill), and then double-click on CopiedText, the name of the control we want to fill. The top box in the Expression Builder now shows the proper expression for referring to the control (see Figure 20.10). When we click on the OK button, that control is copied into the Item: action argument.

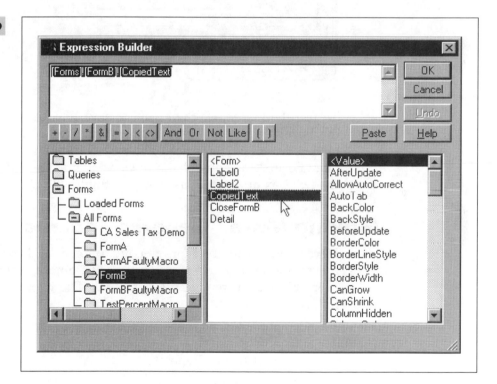

Assigning CopyValue to an Event

Anyway, getting back to the macro shown in Figure 20.9, let's assume we save it with the name CopyValue, and close it. Now we want that macro to play when the user clicks on the big command button on FormA.

So we need to open, in design view, FormA, click on the command button, open the property sheet, and click on the Event tab. Then we can click on the On Click property for that control and assign the CopyValue macro to that event as shown below.

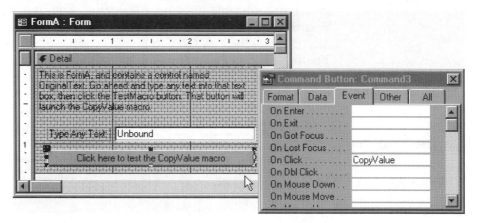

To test the macro, we then need to save FormA and close it (and close the FormB and CopyValue macros if they're open). Then open FormA, type in some text, and click on the big command button. The macro will open FormB and copy whatever we typed into the text box on FormA into the text box on FormB, as shown in Figure 20.11.

Making More "Generic" Macros

Here's another method for referring to forms and controls from within a macro. Rather than referring to a specific object, you can refer to "whatever object is current at the moment." The expressions you use are as follows:

> [Screen].[ActiveForm]
>
> [Screen].[ActiveReport]
>
> [Screen].[ActiveControl]
>
> [Screen].[ActiveDatasheet]

Let's take a look at another fairly simple example, using the [Screen].[ActiveControl] expression. First, let's say we have a form with three controls named FederalRate, StateRate, and CountyRate. Each of these controls'

FIGURE 20.11

We typed a value into FormA and then clicked on the big command button. That button launched the CopyValue macro which opened FormB and copied the text from FormA into the text box on FormB.

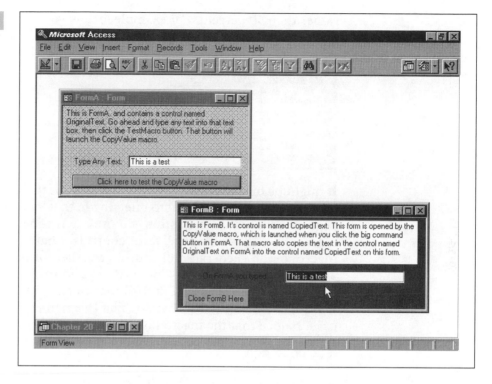

Format property is set to Percent. (Below you can see the Format property for the FederalRate control.)

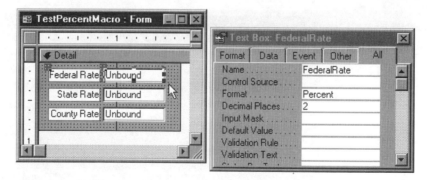

One of the problems with using the Percent format is that if the user types in a whole number, such as 30, the Percent format assumes 300 percent rather than 30 percent. For example, below you can see the results of typing in the values 30, 15, and 5 into this form in form view.

It might be nice to create a macro that says "If the user types in a number that's greater than or equal to one, divide that value by 100 to put it into percent format." To make things more interesting, we'll create a generic macro that will work with all three controls. That is, rather than create one macro for the [FederalRate] control, another for the [StateRate] control, and a third macro for the [CountyRate] control, we'll create a macro that refers to [Screen].[ActiveControl] that works with all three controls. Figure 20.12 shows such a macro, which I've named ConvertPercent in this case. Notice that the macro just has one condition and one action.

The condition,

> [Screen].[ActiveControl] >= 1

FIGURE 20.12

The ConvertPercent macro uses [Screen].[ActiveControl] to refer to whatever control launched the macro.

Macro Name	Condition	Action	Comment
ConvertPercent	[Screen].[ActiveControl]>=1	SetValue	Divide the content of the current
			control by 100 if the content is
			greater than or equal to 1.

Action Arguments

Item	[Screen].[ActiveControl]
Expression	[Screen].[ActiveControl]/100

Enter a comment in this column.

makes sure that the action is executed only if the content of the control is greater than, or equal to, one. The SetValue action arguments:

Item: [Screen].[ActiveControl]

Expression: [Screen].[ActiveControl]/100

take whatever number is currently in the value, and replace it with that same value divided by 100.

Next we close and save the macro. Then we need to open, in design view, the TestPercentMacro form, and set the BeforeUpdate event property of each control to the macro name, ConvertPercent in this example. Below you can see we've set the AfterUpdate event for the FederalRate control to the macro name. We'd just need to do the same for the StateRate and CountyRate controls before closing this form.

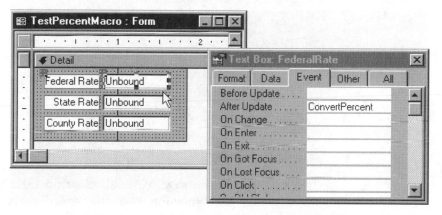

To actually test the macro, we need to go to form view. Nothing happens immediately because the AfterUpdate event occurs only *after* we type a new value into the control and move onto another control. In form view, let's say we again type 30 in the Federal Rate control, 15 into the State Rate control, and 5 into the County Rate control. The macro kicks in after each entry, giving the much better result shown below.

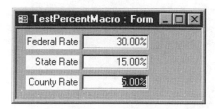

Dealing with Macro Errors

Everyone makes mistakes. Especially when creating macros. As you know, when you run a macro, Access executes the first action in the macro. Then the second action (if any), the third, and so on until it runs out of Action cells. If, however, Access has a problem executing one of the actions in your macro, it stops the macro and displays an *error message* that gives you some clue as to what's wrong. For example, while executing a macro you might come up with the (somewhat obscure) message below when Access hits a glitch.

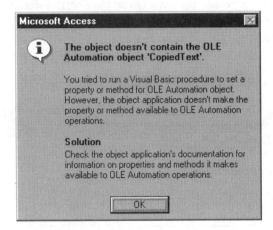

After reading the message, you can click on OK. You'll see the Action Failed dialog box showing you the specific action that caused the error, as in the example shown below. This box provides the following information:

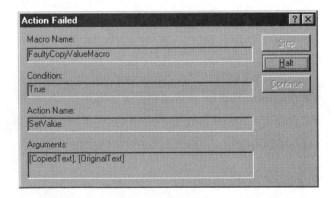

- **Macro Name**   The name of the macro that contains the faulty action.

- **Condition**   What the expression in the Condition column for the faulty line evaluated to (always True if the action has no condition.)

- **Action Name**   The specific action within this macro that caused the error.

- **Arguments**   The arguments you assigned to this action.

To get rid of the error message box, you need to click on the Halt button. If you then want to edit the offending macro, just open the macro's macro sheet in the usual manner (that is, click on the Macros tab in the database window, click on the name of the macro you want to edit, then click on the Design button). Once you get to the appropriate macro, and get to the offending action, you're pretty much on your own in trying to figure out why the action didn't work. You may want to check the hint box for clues. Or press F1 for more detailed information about the action, so you can determine the cause and come up with a solution.

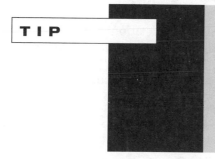

TIP

A common cause of macro errors is using faulty identifiers. For example, your macro might refer to a field named [ZipCode] that's not on the form that launched the macro. And therefore you need to add the [Forms]![*formname*]! Prefix. Or perhaps your macro is referring to a control on a form that is no longer open when Access tries to execute the action.

Single-Stepping through a Macro

When you run a macro, Access whizzes through all the actions in no time at all. If a particular macro is giving you a hard time, it might be worth a try to slow the macro way down, and watch the results of each action as Access performs them. To do this, you need to run the macro in *single-step* mode. To run a macro in single-step mode:

1. Open the macro's macro sheet (get to the database window, click on the Macros tab, click on the name of the macro you want to run in single-step mode, and then click on the Design button).

2. Click the Single Step button on the toolbar, or choose Run ➤ Single-Step from the menu bar.

3. Close and save the macro normally.

4. Run the macro normally by causing whatever event triggers the macro.

This time when you run the macro, Access will display the Macro Single Step window, shown below, just before it executes each action.

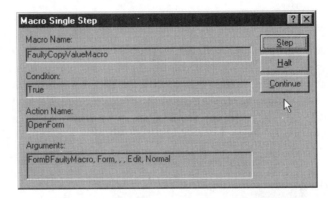

After observing the details of the action that's about to be played, you can use the command buttons to decide what you want to do next:

Step Executes the action whose details are currently displayed in the Macro Single Step dialog box.

Halt Stops the macro and closes the Macro Single Step dialog box.

Continue Turns off the Single Step mode and runs the rest of the macro normally.

Creating a Macro to Run at Startup

As you may know, you can use the Tools ➤ Startup commands on Access's main menu to specify how you want your application to look when the user first opens the database. (Those menu commands are available whenever the database window is displayed.) In addition, you can also have a macro perform tasks automatically when the user first opens your database. All you need to do is create a normal macro, and name it AutoExec.

The AutoExec macro runs *after* the options you defined in the Startup dialog box have been put into effect. So you want to make sure to take that into consideration when creating your AutoExec macro. For example, if you've cleared the Display Database Window option in the Startup dialog, there's no reason to have your AutoExec macro hide the database window, since it will already be hidden.

You can bypass the startup options and the AutoExec macro by holding down the Shift key as your database is opening. It's important for you, as an application developer, to keep this technique in mind because sometimes you might want to open your database from the user's perspective.

TIP

You can also press the F11 key to make the database window appear on the screen, unless you've turned off the Access Special Keys option under Tools, Startup or used the /runtime switch when launching Access.

At other times, you might want to go straight to the database window and standard toolbars so you can make changes to your application. To achieve the latter, just keep that Shift key depressed from the time you choose File ➤ Open Database until the database window appears on the screen.

Learning by Example

In this chapter, we've covered the "mechanics" of creating macros and assigning them to events. You'll see many practical "real world" examples of macros in the chapters that follow. Exploring macros in other peoples' applications is also a good way to round out your knowledge of macros. For example, the sample Northwind database that comes with your Access programs, as well as some of the applications on the CD that comes with this book, contain several examples of macros.

To view the macros in an application, just open the database normally, and get to the database window. In the database window, click on the Macros tab. Then click on any macro name and click on <u>D</u>esign to explore the macro's contents.

In some applications, you might be surprised to see very few macros, or even no macros at all. There are three reasons why even a very sophisticated Access application might have very few macros associated with it:

- The Control Wizards create Visual Basic code, not macros, to automate the controls you create.

- Many Access developers prefer Visual Basic code to macros, because they are already familiar with Visual Basic.

- Many application developers will use the built-in macro converter to convert their macros to Visual Basic code, and then delete the original macro.

Converting Macros to Visual Basic

Once you've created some macros and have them working properly, it's easy to convert them to Visual Basic code. To convert all the macros in a given form or report to code, first open the form or report in design view. Then choose <u>T</u>ools ➤ <u>M</u>acros ➤ <u>C</u>onvert Form's Macros to Visual Basic (or <u>C</u>onvert Report's Macros to Visual Basic if you're working with a report.)

If a particular set of macros isn't associated with a specific form (such as an AutoExec macro), you use a different technique to convert the macro. In design view, open the macro you want to convert. Then choose <u>F</u>ile ➤ Save <u>A</u>s/Export ➤ Save As Visual Basic <u>M</u>odule ➤ OK. When conversion is complete, you can find the Visual Basic version of the macro in the Modules tab of the database window.

Where to Go from Here

From here you can focus on different aspects of creating a custom application. Or you might want to see what Visual Basic is all about:

- To learn about creating custom switchboards and dialog boxes for your application, see Chapters 21 and 22.

- If you're interested in learning how to create custom toolbars and menus for your application, see Chapters 23 and 24.

- To learn about Visual Basic, that "other way" to create custom actions, see Chapter 25.

What's New in Access Zoo?

For those of you familiar with earlier versions of Access, here's what's new in the macros department:

- **Save action**: You can use the new Save action to have a macro save either a specific named object, or the active object if none is specified. You can also save the active object with a new name. For more information, search the Help index or Answer Wizard for *save action*.

- **Custom shortcut (right-click) menus**: You can create your own custom shortcut menus to assign to a form or individual controls on a form. For instant info, search the Answer Wizard or Help index for *shortcut menus*. For general information on custom menus, see Chapter 24. To see a custom shortcut menu in action, try right-clicking on any field in the Address Book form in Fulfill 95 (see Appendix C).

- **SetMenuItem action**: You can also use the SetMenuItem action in a macro to make a menu item appear dimmed or selected. Search the Answer Wizard or Help index for *SetMenuItem*. See Chapter 24 for general information about custom menus.

CHAPTER

21

Creating Custom Switchboards

A *switchboard* is a fancy term for a form that lets the user easily get from one place to another in your application. When you use the Access Database Wizard to create a database application, the Wizard creates a switchboard automatically. In this chapter we're going to look at techniques for customizing the switchboard that the Wizard creates. We'll also look at techniques for creating your own completely custom switchboards with whatever appearance you like.

Changing a Wizard-Created Switchboard

As you know, when you use a Database Wizard to create a database, the Wizard automatically creates a switchboard for that database. For example, when you use the Order Entry Wizard to create a database, that Wizard creates the switchboard shown in Figure 21.1.

The switchboard appears automatically when you first open the database. If you happen to be at the database window rather than the switchboard, you can just click on the Forms tab, click on the Switchboard form name, then click on the Open button to open the switchboard.

Changing Wizard-Created Switchboard Options

If you look at all the options on the Order Entry switchboard, you'll see that one option actually lets you change the switchboard itself (the fourth option down in this example). When you choose that option, you're taken to the Switchboard Manager dialog box, which will look something like Figure 21.2 (depending on the database you're using at the moment).

FIGURE 21.1

The switchboard as created by the Order Entry Database Wizard

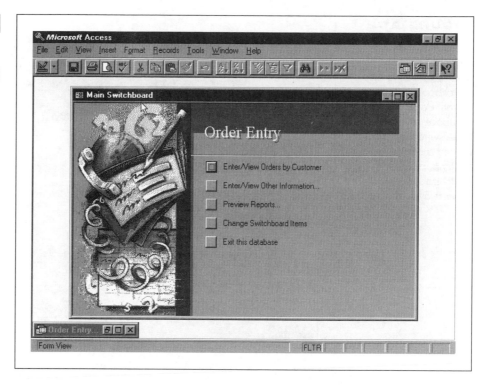

The command buttons on the Switchboard Manager are pretty self-explanatory. But just to summarize:

- **Close**   Click on Close *after* you've finished exploring/modifying switchboards.

- **New**   Creates a new, blank switchboard with whatever name you specify. To add options to that newly-created switchboard, click on its name and then click on the Edit button. You'll be taken to the Edit Switchboard Page dialog box described in the next section.

- **Edit**   To change an existing switchboard, click on its name and then click on the Edit button. You'll be taken to the Edit Switchboard Page dialog box described in the next section.

- **Delete**   To delete a switchboard, click on its name then click on the Delete button.

- **Make Default**   Makes the currently selected switchboard the *default* switchboard (the one that appears automatically when the user first opens the database.)

The Switchboard Manager lets you make changes to any switchboard in the current database. The database contains three switchboards named Main Switchboard, Forms Switchboard, and Reports Switchboard.

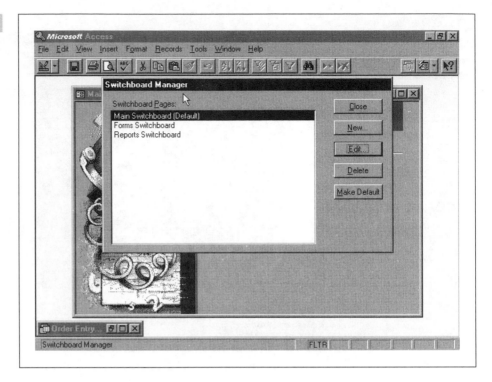

Defining and Changing Switchboard Items

When you choose the Edit button from the Switchboard Manager, you're taken to the Edit Switchboard Page. If you are working with a new switchboard, the list under Items On This Switchboard is blank. But you can use the New button to create new items. If you chose to Edit an existing switchboard, the items on that switchboard are listed under Items On This Switchboard, as in Figure 21.3.

The command buttons in the Edit Switchboard Page dialog box are also pretty self-explanatory. To summarize:

- **Close**   Choose this button when you've finished making changes, to return to the Switchboard Manager dialog box.

- **New**   Add a new item to this switchboard.

- **Edit**   Change the currently selected switchboard item.

FIGURE 21.3

The Edit Switchboard Page dialog box lets you add, change, and delete individual options on the currently selected switchboard.

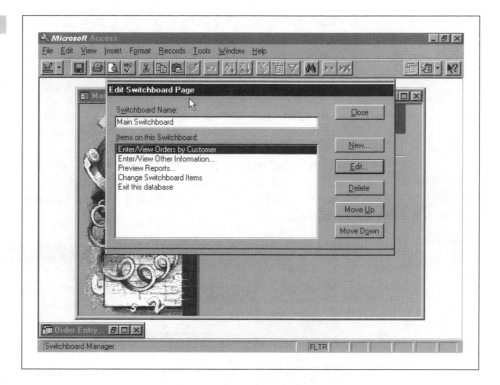

- **Delete**   Delete the currently selected switchboard item.

- **Move Up**   Move the currently selected switchboard item up in the list.

- **Move Down**   Move the currently selected switchboard item down in the list.

When you Edit a switchboard item, you're taken to the small Edit Switchboard Item dialog box, as in the example shown below.

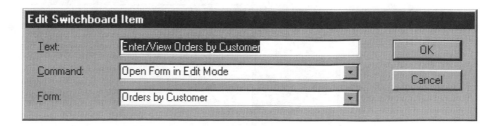

This dialog box is where you define how the item looks on the switchboard, and what happens when the user selects that item. In the example shown, the Text that actually appears on the switchboard is *Enter/View Orders By Customer*. To change that text just click anywhere in the text and make your changes using standard editing techniques.

The Command box describes what will happen when the user selects the item. In the example, when the user chooses *Enter/View Orders by Customer* the action that occurs is *Open Form In Edit Mode*. But you can change that action, if you wish, simply by choosing a new option from the Command drop-down list. As you can see below, you have quite a few options available to you for defining what happens when the user chooses the item.

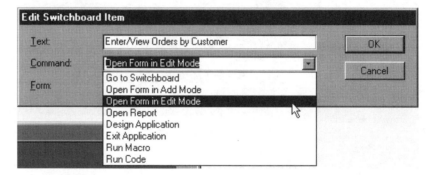

The last option in the Edit Switchboard Item dialog box lets you choose a specific object for the Command to act upon. For example, when the Command is Open Form in Edit Mode, the last option is titled Forms:, and you can select a specific form for the item to open, as below.

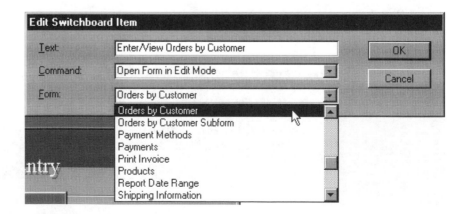

If, on the other hand, the Command box contained the action Open Report, the last option would be titled Report. And you could choose a specific report for the command to open.

After making changes to a Wizard-created switchboard, you need to get back to form view to see and test the effects of those changes. Select OK and Close, as appropriate, to work your way back to the database window. If you really want to see how things will look to a person opening the database for the first time, you can close, then reopen the database. To do so, you can just choose File ➤ Close from the Access menu bar. Then just click on File again and select the name of the database you just closed.

Changing Wizard-Selected Art

When you use a Database Wizard to create a database, you're also given the option of adding a picture to the database's switchboards. You can change that picture after the fact, if you wish, using any bitmap image on your hard disk. You can use an existing clip art image, a bitmap image you created yourself, or an image you digitized using a scanner.

To change the picture on a Wizard-created switchboard, follow these steps:

1. If the database isn't open yet, open it in the usual manner with Access's File ➤ Open Database menu commands.

2. If the switchboard is currently open, click on the Close (✕) button in the upper-right corner to close it. Get to the database window (if it's hidden or minimized, just press the F11 key).

3. In the database window, click on the Forms tab.

4. Click on the Switchboard form name, then click on the Design button.

5. Click on the picture that you want to change.

6. If the property sheet isn't open, open it now (click on the Properties toolbar button or choose View ➤ Properties).

7. In the property sheet, click on the All tab and scroll to the top of the sheet. You should see the control name Picture, as in Figure 21.4.

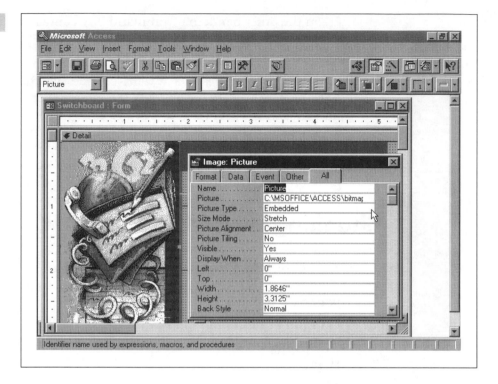

8. The second property in the property sheet is titled Picture, and shows the location and name of the picture that's currently displayed in the switchboard. Click on that property , then click on the Build (...) button that appears. The Insert Picture dialog box appears as in Figure 21.5 (though initially, your Insert Picture dialog box might show the contents of some folder other than the one named Dbwiz).

9. Browse to the folder and file that contains the picture that you want to display in your switchboard, then choose OK.

10. The picture you chose will replace the one that's currently in your switchboard, and will be stretched to fit the picture's container. You can use the Size Mode property to change the picture's sizing mode to Clip or Zoom, to see which mode works best.

11. To save the switchboard with the new picture and size mode, choose File ➤ Close and choose Yes when asked if you want to save your changes.

FIGURE 21.5

The Insert Picture dialog box will let you select a new picture to display in your Wizard-created switchboard.

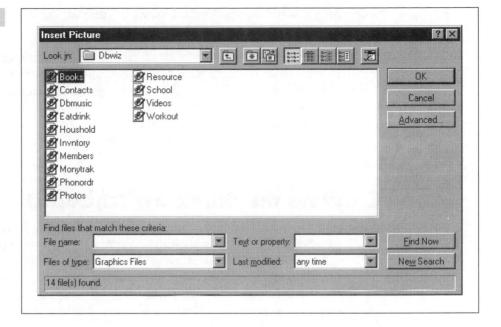

To see the results of the change, reopen the switchboard in form view. Or, if you want to be sure to view the switchboard from the user's perspective, close the entire database (File ➤ Close). Then reopen the entire database by clicking on the File menu, then the name of the database you just closed.

Note that the picture you chose will appear on all the database's switchboards. The reason is that the Database Wizards actually create only one switchboard per database. When you're *using* that database, it might appear as though you're going from one switchboard to another from time to time. But in fact, your database is just changing the title of, and items on, that one switchboard.

Creating a Switchboard from Scratch

As you know, the Database Wizards aren't the only way to create a database application. You can create all your tables, queries, forms, reports, and macros from scratch. Likewise, you can create custom switchboards for your application, completely from scratch.

To create a custom switchboard, first create a blank form that isn't bound to any table. To make it look like a switchboard rather than a bound form, you can hide the navigation buttons, record selectors, and other doo-dads that normally appear on bound forms. Then, you can add controls—such as command buttons—and macros to make the controls on the switchboard do whatever you want them to do. We'll take it step-by-step, starting in the next section.

Creating the Blank Switchboard Form

The basic idea behind a switchboard is to create a form that makes it easy for the user of your application to navigate from one form to another, or to print reports, or whatever. So typically you'd create tables, queries, forms, and reports for your application before you'd start in on the custom switchboards. Then, within that same database, you'd follow these steps to create a new, blank switchboard form:

1. In the database window, click on the Forms tab.

2. Click on the New button, then choose Design View from the New Form dialog box that appears. Leave the Choose A Table Or Query… option blank, and click on the OK button.

3. A new empty form opens in design view. The first thing you'll want to do is to set some properties for it. So if the property sheet isn't open, click on the Properties toolbar button, or choose View ➤ Properties from the menu bar.

4. You want to be sure the entire form is selected as the current object (because you're about to set form properties), so choose Edit ➤ Select Form from the menu bar, or click in the box where the rulers meet.

5. In the property sheet, click on the Format tab, and then set the first few Format properties as indicated below and shown in Figure 21.6. (Properties below that are marked with an asterisk are suggestions only. You might want to experiment with those properties when creating your own switchboards.)

FIGURE 21.6

Suggested Form properties for a custom switchboard

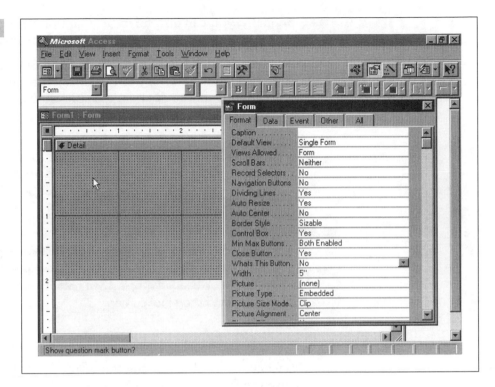

Default View:	Single Form
Views Allowed:	Form
Scroll Bars:	Neither*
Record Selectors:	No
Navigation Buttons:	No
Auto Resize:	Yes*
Auto Center:	Yes

TIP

Remember that you can get more information about a property right on your screen. Just click on the property you're interested in and press Help (F1).

6. Optionally, you can also fill in the Caption property with whatever text you want to appear in the title bar of the custom form.

7. If you want to color the form, click on the Detail band within the form. Then choose a color from Back Color button on the Formatting toolbar. If that toolbar isn't visible choose <u>V</u>iew ➤ Tool<u>b</u>ars, click on Formatting (Form/Report Design), then choose Close.

8. At this point, you may want to size and shape the form to approximately the size you want the switchboard to be. Drag the lower-right corner of the shaded area within the form design window to about the size you want to make the switchboard.

To size the gray area, move the mouse pointer to its lower-right corner until the mouse pointer turns into a four-headed arrow. Then hold down the mouse button and drag that corner.

9. You can save and name the form now. Choose <u>F</u>ile ➤ <u>C</u>lose, choose <u>Y</u>es when asked about saving the form, enter the name you want to give the form (e.g., Main Switchboard), and choose OK.

The Switchboard form is listed in the database window, in the Forms tab, just like all your other forms. And you can treat it as you would any other form:

- To see and use the form from the user's perspective, click on the form name and then click on the <u>O</u>pen button. (At this point, our sample form is completely blank.)

- To make changes to the form, open it in design view (click on the form name in the database window, then click on the <u>D</u>esign button).

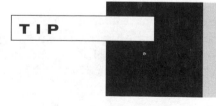

Once the form is open you can easily switch between form view and design view by clicking on the ... View button in the toolbar, or by choosing either <u>F</u>orm or Form <u>D</u>esign from the <u>V</u>iew menu in the menu bar.

Adding Controls to Your Custom Switchboard

Currently our switchboard is empty. We need to add some *controls* to allow the user to choose actions. As with all types of forms, you create controls using the toolbox in form design view. You can create any control you wish. But chances are you'll want to create mostly command buttons.

As you may recall from earlier chapters, you can use Control Wizards to create a control and action in one fell swoop. When creating controls on a switchboard, the decision on whether to use, or not to use, the Control Wizards centers around three factors:

- If the control will perform a single action, such as opening a form, and that form already exists, then you can use the Control Wizard.

- If the control will open a form (or report) that you have *not* yet created, you can create the control *without* using the Control Wizard. Later, after you've created the form or report that the control will act upon, you can go back to the switchboard and assign an action to the control.

- If the control will perform two or more actions, then you'll need to define the control's action using a macro (or Visual Basic code). You can create the control without the Control Wizard. Then later create the macro, and assign that macro to the control on the switchboard.

The last alternative is perhaps the most common when creating switchboard controls because typically you want the control to perform two actions: 1) open some other form or report and then 2) close the switchboard itself. So let's work through an example using that last approach.

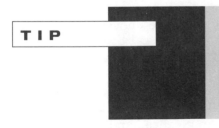

TIP

Here's a quick way to create a command button and assign a macro to it. First create the macro. And then just drag and drop the macro name onto the form (in design view). You'll get a command button whose On Click property launches the dropped macro!

Let's say we want to create a command button on our switchboard to open a form named AddressBook, and then close the switchboard. For this example, we'll also assume that we previously created the form named AddressBook, and it exists in the current database. Here's how you would proceed:

1. Open, in design view, the switchboard.

2. If the toolbox isn't already open, click on the Toolbox toolbar button, or choose <u>V</u>iew ➤ <u>T</u>oolbox.

3. We don't want to use the Control Wizard in this example. So we make sure the Control Wizard button in the toolbox is *not* pushed in, as below.

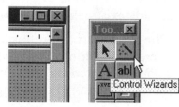

4. Next, we click on the Command Button button in the toolbox, then click at about where we want the button to appear in the switchboard. In Figure 21.7 you can see we've created a button which is (tentatively) captioned Command0.

5. Though it's not absolutely necessary to do so, we could close the Main Switchboard form now, just to get it out of the way, by choosing <u>F</u>ile ➤ <u>C</u>lose, and choosing <u>Y</u>es when asked to save changes.

Creating a Macro for the New Control

Next we need to create a macro that will open the Address Book form, and close the Main Switchboard form. Here's how we proceed with that:

1. In the database window, click on the Macros tab.

2. Click on the <u>N</u>ew button. A new blank macro sheet opens.

3. We'll probably want to put all the macros for the Main Switchboard into this macro sheet. So go ahead and open the Macro

FIGURE 21.7

Here we've created a command button without using the Control Wizard. The button has the generic name Command0.

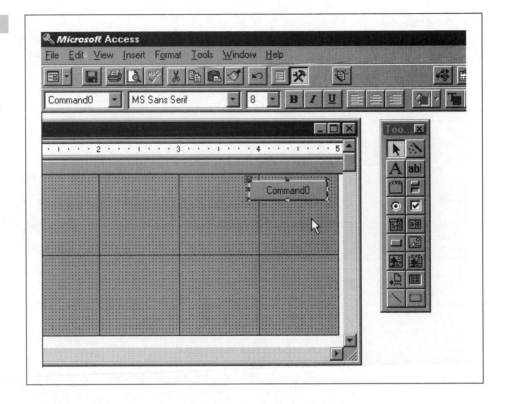

Name column (click on the Macro Names toolbar button). Or choose View ➤ Macro Names from the menu bar.

4. In the Macro Name column, type a name for this macro such as OpenAddressBook.

5. In the Action column to the right, choose the OpenForm action.

6. In the Action Arguments, specify the name of the form you want to open (AddressBook in this example). Figure 21.8 shows how the macro sheet would look at this point.

7. We also want to create a second action to close the Main Switchboard. So in the next Action column down, we choose the Close action. Then we fill in the action arguments as in Figure 21.9.

8. Now we can close the macro sheet and give it a name. In this example we would choose File ➤ Close, choose Yes when asked about saving the form, give it a name such as MainSwitchboard-Macros, and then choose OK.

FIGURE 21.8

The first action for the OpenAddressBook macro defined in the macro sheet

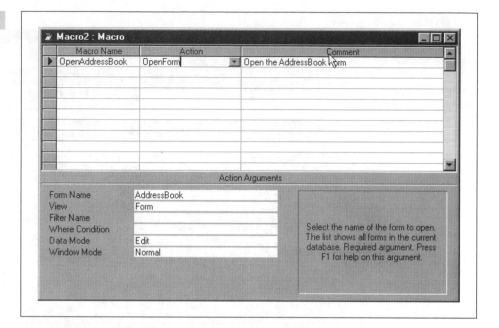

FIGURE 21.8

The first action for the OpenAddressBook macro defined in the macro sheet

FIGURE 21.9

The second action in the OpenAddressBook macro will close the Main Switchboard form.

Finally we need to assign that new macro to the On Click property of the button we created on the switchboard. While we're at it, we can change the caption on the button. Here are the steps:

1. In the database window, click on the Forms tab.

2. Click on Main Switchboard, and click on the Design button.

3. Click on the button to which we want to assign the macro (the button titled Command0 in this example).

4. Open the property sheet, and click on the Event tab.

5. Choose the On Click property, and choose the name of the macro you want this button to launch. In this example we want to choose the MainSwitchboardMacros.OpenAddressBook macro as in Figure 21.10

6. While we're here, we can also change the caption on the command button. Click on the Format tab in the property sheet.

FIGURE 21.10

Assigning the Main-SwitchboardMacros.OpenAddressBook macro to the On Click property of a button on the Main switchboard.

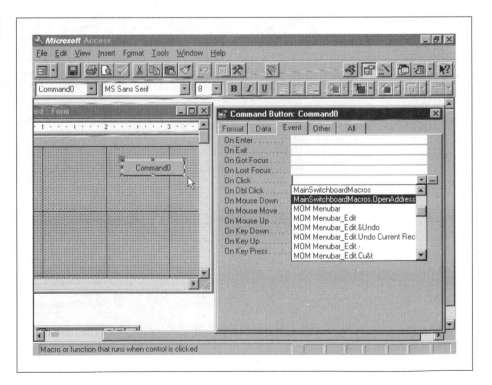

Then type in a caption such as &Address Book (which will appear as Address Book on the button), as in the example shown below.

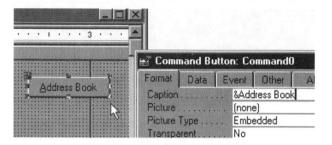

7. Now you can close and save the Main Switchboard form.

To test your new control and action, open the Main Switchboard in form view. Then click on the Address Book button. The macro will open the AddressBook form, and close the Switchboard, as in Figure 21.11

FIGURE 21.11

Clicking the Address Book button in the Main Switchboard opens this form and closes the switchboard.

➤ We realize we haven't mentioned anything about the AddressBook form prior to this chapter. But our goal here is to show you how to make a switchboard button open one form, and close its own form. In Chapter 28 and in Appendix C, we'll talk more about the AddressBook form, and the Fulfill application.

Making AddressBook Return to the Main Switchboard

In this particular application, clicking on the Address Book button in the Main Switchboard sends the user to a form named AddressBook. It stands to reason that, when the user closes the AddressBook form, she'd expect to be returned to the Main Switchboard.

We *could* make a button on the AddressBook form that closes the AddressBook, then opens the Main Switchboard again. But there's just one problem with that. Suppose the user closes the AddressBook form by clicking on the × button in the form's window, or by choosing File ➤ Close from the menu bar. Neither of those tasks would trigger the action to open the Main Switchboard. So here's what we need to do:

- Create a Close button that, when clicked, closes the AddressBook form.

- Then, go to the property sheet for the AddressBook form as a whole, and create an action that opens the Main Switchboard form. If we attach that action to the On Close property of the AddressBook form, it doesn't matter how the user exits the form—he or she will still be returned to the main switchboard.

We'll create the Close button on the AddressBook form first. Since we want this button to do one simple act, we can use the Control Wizard to define the control and action in one fell swoop. Here are the steps we would follow (since we've already created the AddressBook on our end):

1. Open, in design view, the AddressBook form.

2. Open the toolbox if it isn't already open (click on the Toolbox toolbar button or choose View ➤ Toolbox.)

3. Make sure the Control Wizard button in the toolbox is pushed in, because we can use its help in this case.

4. Click on the Command Button tool in the toolbox, then click at about where you want the close button to appear on the form (the lower-right corner in this example).

5. When the Command Button Wizard appears, we chose Form Operations and Close Form, as shown in Figure 21.12.

6. We choose Next> from the Command Button Wizard and the next screen asks about the appearance of the button. In this example we chose to have the button show the text &Close, as shown in Figure 21.13 (once again, the & symbol is used to specify the underlined hotkey).

7. Clicking Next> takes me to the Wizard window to name the button. This is the name used within Access, *not* the text caption that appears on the button. We could name the button anything we want. In this example we named the button CloseAddressBook-Form, and then clicked on the Finish button.

FIGURE 21.12

The new button we're adding to the Address Book form will close the form.

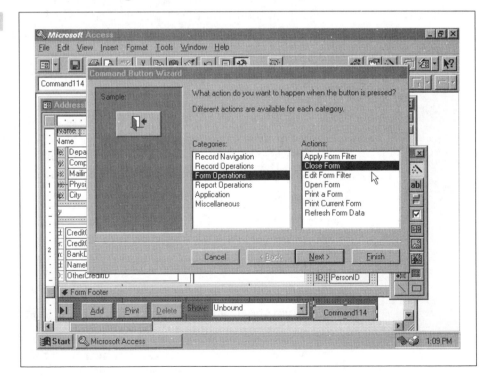

FIGURE 21.13

The Close button on the AddressBook form will be captioned Close.

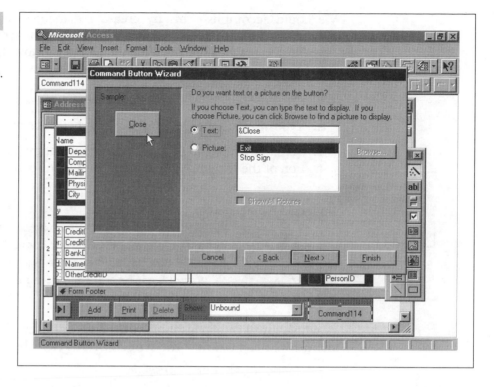

When the Command Button Wizard is done we're returned to our form, and can see the new button there. We can use the standard techniques for moving and sizing controls to put the button exactly where we want. In the figure below we've opted to put that button near the lower-right corner of the form.

Now we still need to make the closing of the AddressBook form automatically reopen the Main Switchboard form. Keep in mind that the user will probably have several means of closing that form—not just our new Close button. So we need to find a way of saying, "No matter how the user closes this form, open the Main Switchboard form again."

We could accomplish this by creating a macro that opens the Main Switchboard form. But let's try a slightly different approach here, just to "get our feet wet" in the world of Visual Basic. How do we write a Visual Basic procedure to open a form? Let's ask the Answer Wizard:

1. Choose <u>H</u>elp ➤ Answer <u>W</u>izard from Access's menu bar.

2. Type **open a form** as your request, then click on the Search <u>b</u>utton.

3. Scroll down to the Programming and Language Reference portion of the list, and double-click on OpenForm Method.

TIP   An *action* generally refers to macros, whereas a *method* generally refers to Visual Basic code. We chose Open-Form Method in step 3 because we want to check out the Visual Basic approach to doing this.

A whole lot of information about the OpenForm Method appears. But mainly we need to know the syntax. In this case the syntax is

```
DoCmd.OpenForm formname
```

followed by a bunch of optional arguments enclosed in square brackets. When we click on the Example option, we see that the name of the form to open needs to be enclosed in quotation marks. To make life easy, we can just copy the example shown from the help screen right into out property sheet. To do that we just drag the cursor through the part we want to copy, as in Figure 21.14, and then press Ctrl+C to copy that selection to the Windows Clipboard.

Now we can close the help screens until we get back to the AddressBook form, which is still in design view. Now here's how we make the act of closing this form automatically open the Main Switchboard form:

1. With the AddressBook form on the screen in design view, we choose <u>E</u>dit ➤ Select Fo<u>r</u>m because we want to work with the form properties as a whole (not properties of individual controls).

2. We open the property sheet, and click on the Event tab.

FIGURE 21.14

An example of using Visual Basic to open a form. We've selected the part we want to copy to our form.

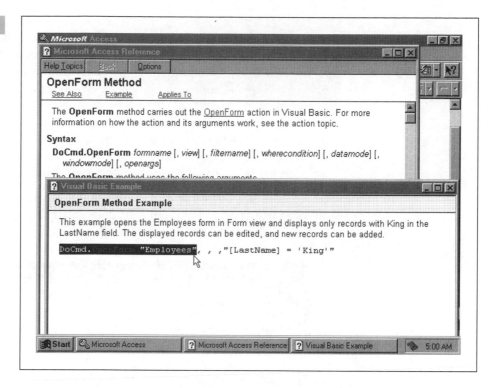

3. We click on the On Close property and a Build (...) button appears. Clicking on the Build button presents us with these options:

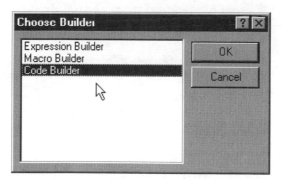

4. We're going to try our hand at some Visual Basic code here. So we click on Code Builder, then click on OK.

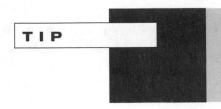

T I P

Remember, you can use either Visual Basic or macros to define many actions. Here we've used Visual Basic just because it's quick and easy to do so in this example. Chapter 25 introduces Visual Basic.

5. A new window pops up which already contains a couple of lines of Visual Basic Code, `Private Sub Form_Close` and `End Sub`. Any code we want to add must go between those two lines.

6. To add our copied line of code, we just need to put the cursor between the two existing lines of code, and then press Ctrl+V. Initially, the pasted text looks like this.

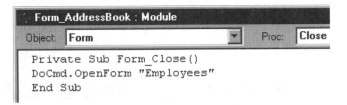

7. We want our code to open the form named Main Switchboard, not the form named Employees. So we need to change the form name in the code, as below. (You can also press Home to move the cursor to the start of the line, then press Tab to indent the line. It's sort of standard practice to indent the lines between the Private Sub and End Sub commands.)

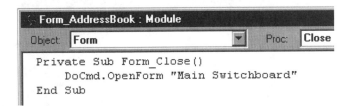

8. To see if we made any gross errors in our Visual Basic command, we can quickly *compile* the code. Just click on the Compile Loaded Modules button in the toolbar. If you did everything correctly, you won't see any error messages.

9. Now we can close the module window (the one that contains the Visual Basic code) by clicking on the Close (×) button in the upper-right corner of the module window, or by choosing File ➤ Close from the menu bar.

10. The property sheet now shows [Event Procedure] next to the On Close property, indicating that we've assigned a Visual Basic procedure to this event.

11. Now we can close and save the AddressBook form.

To test the effects of all this, we can now open, in form view, the Main Switchboard form. When we click on the Address Book button in that switchboard, the Address Book form should open, and the Main Switchboard form should disappear. When we close the AddressBook form, that form should disappear, and the Main Switchboard form should reopen.

Filling Out the Switchboard

We can continue work with the Main Switchboard form, adding whatever controls we think will be useful later down the road. We can also use the Label and Rectangle tools in the Toolbox to add some labels and boxes. The Back Color, Border Color, Border Width, and Special Effects buttons on the Formatting (Form/Report Design) toolbar can help make these embellishments even fancier.

TIP

If you create a rectangle around a group of buttons, and the rectangle ends up *covering* the buttons, don't panic. Just select (click on) the rectangle and choose Format ➤ Send to Back from the form design screen's menu bar.

The Main Switchboard example we're showing you in this chapter was actually the starting point for a "real" application, named Fulfill 95, that's on the CD-ROM that came with this book. And, as you'll see when you try that application, we've done quite a few embellishments on the Main Switchboard.

For example, we added a dark gray rectangle behind the command buttons, and a label (Focus On) to the upper-right corner of that rectangle. We also added a large white rectangle as a placeholder for Fulfill's logo, which we'll create and add later. Figure 21.15 shows the Main Switchboard, in form view at this stage of Fulfill's development.

When you explore the Fulfill application (which is included on the CD that comes with this book), you'll no doubt find that its main switchboard and other forms have evolved from what's shown here. We're not trying to confuse you. It's just that we had more time to work on the CD than we have had for the rest of the book. So we used that extra time to really beef up Fulfill with neat tricks.

 ➤ You can start exploring Fulfill at any time simply by copying it from the CD, and opening it up in Access for Windows 95. Appendices B and C near the back of this book will help you with all of that. Chapter 28 discusses ways of exploring Fulfill (and other custom Access applications) so you can start learning "by example" how all the pieces are put together in an Access custom database application.

FIGURE 21.15

The sample Fulfill application's Main Switchboard, in form view, under construction

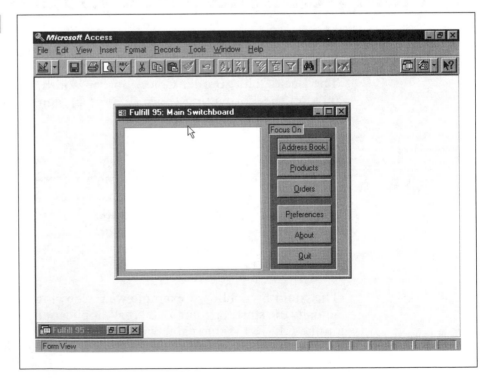

Making a Switchboard Appear at Startup

If you create a custom switchboard for your application, and want it to appear automatically when the user first opens your database, just set the Display Form option in Startup to the name of your switchboard. Here are the exact steps to follow:

1. Close any open forms to get to the database window.

2. Choose Tools ➤ Startup from the menu bar.

3. From the drop-down list box next to Display Form, choose the name of your main switchboard as I've done in Figure 21.16.

4. Choose OK.

FIGURE 21.16

Here we've defined the form named Main Switchboard as the first to appear when the database first opens.

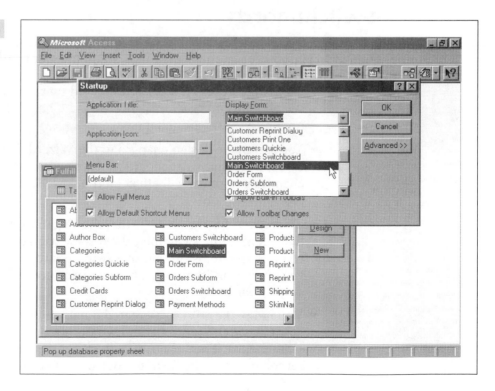

You can leave all the other settings in the Startup dialog box at their current settings until you're farther along in the development process. (More on those options in Chapter 28.) The next time you open the database, your custom switchboard will appear on the screen automatically.

Wizard-Created vs. Custom Switchboards

If you've read this entire chapter, you may be confused by the vast differences between Wizard-created switchboards and totally custom switchboards. Let's take a moment here to review the primary differences so you don't leave this chapter feeling confused on this topic.

Summary: Wizard-Created Switchboards

When you use a Database Wizard to create a database application, it is important to keep in mind the following points about the switchboard(s):

- To change items on a Wizard-created switchboard, open the switchboard in *form view*, and use the Change Switchboard Items option to make your changes.

- You can make design changes to the Wizard-created switchboard by opening that switchboard in design view. However, any changes you make will affect all the switchboards in that database application.

- The reason for the above is that the Database Wizard really only creates one switchboard per database application. It just changes the items on that one switchboard, automatically, when you choose an item that takes you to a (seemingly) different switchboard.

- You can make a Wizard-created database open with a different, custom switchboard of your own design. Just create your custom switchboard. Then choose Tools ➤ Startup ➤ Display Form and set the name of the form to your new custom switchboard.

Summary: Custom Switchboards

When you don't use a Database Wizard to create a database, keep the following points in mind:

- Initially, your database application will have no switchboards at all.

- You create a switchboard by creating a new form that's not bound to any table or query.

- To ensure that the switchboard form doesn't look like a data-entry form, turn off the form's record selectors, navigation buttons, scroll bars, datasheet view, and so forth by selecting the entire form in form view, and making appropriate changes to the property sheet.

- You need to add your own controls (i.e., command buttons) to a custom switchboard, using the toolbox in form design view.

- To make a switchboard appear automatically at startup, choose Tools ➤ Startup and set the Display Form option to the name of your switchboard.

Where to Go from Here

Next we'll look at ways of creating custom dialog boxes from scratch. As you'll see, the basic starting point is the same as for creating a custom switchboard. You create a form that's not bound to any table or query. Then you add appropriate controls and actions using the toolbox in the form design view.

If you prefer, you can explore other topics related to building custom applications:

- If you'd like to see the Fulfill 95 application's final custom switchboards, see Appendix C.

- If you'd like to take a look at some custom switchboards in other sample applications, see Chapter 28 for some tips.

- If you're interested in learning how to create custom toolbars and menus for your application, see Chapters 23 and 24.

- To learn about Visual Basic, that "other way" to create custom actions, see Chapter 25.

What's New in Access Zoo?

The ability to create an entire application using Database Wizards is, of course, entirely new in Access for Windows 95. Other related new features include:

- **Startup command**: To specify your application's startup form, title-bar text, icon, menu, and toolbar, just select Tools ➤ Startup from Access's menu bar.

- **Better Menu Builder**: You can now create custom shortcut menu bars by using the Menu Builder. See Chapter 24 or search the Answer Wizard or Help index for *shortcut menus*.

C H A P T E R

22

Creating Custom
Dialog Boxes

AS a Windows user, you've probably seen hundreds of dialog boxes. A dialog box is a window that pops up on the screen to give you information, or to ask questions about what you want to do next. You make your selections from the box, and then choose OK to proceed. Or, in some cases, you can choose a Cancel button to back out of the dialog box gracefully without making any selections.

You can create your own custom dialog boxes in your Access applications. The procedure is much like that for creating a switchboard: You start off with a blank, unbound form. Then you add some controls, and develop some macros or Visual Basic code to specify what happens when the user selects a control. You can also add some finishing touches, such as OK and Cancel buttons, and a special border. In this chapter, we'll look at all the factors involved by creating a sample dialog box for a sample database.

Our Goal

Before we begin our journey into creating a custom dialog box, let's define our goal. Suppose we have a database with a simple name and address table in it. We've also created a form for entering and editing data in that table, as shown in Figure 22.1.

Let's say, too, that we've also created four reports for this database already. You can see their names in the database window in Figure 22.2.

Now let's say our goal is to be able to hide the database window from the user of this application. In order to print a report, we want the user to just be able to click on the Print button at the bottom of the form. When he or she does so, a dialog box will pop up, to allow the user to choose one or more reports to print or preview. Figure 22.3 shows how we'll want that dialog box to look to the user.

FIGURE 22.1

A sample form in a
simple database

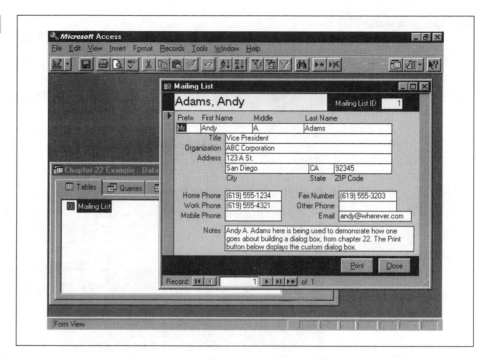

FIGURE 22.2

Reports defined for the
simple database

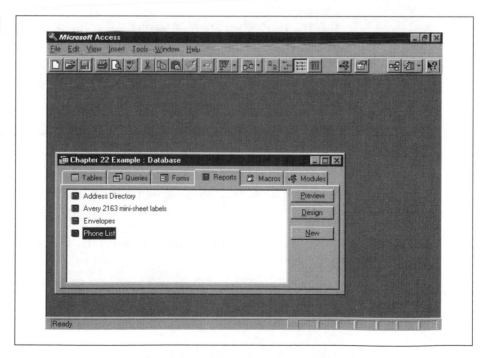

FIGURE 22.3

A custom dialog box appears when the user clicks on the Print button near the bottom of the form.

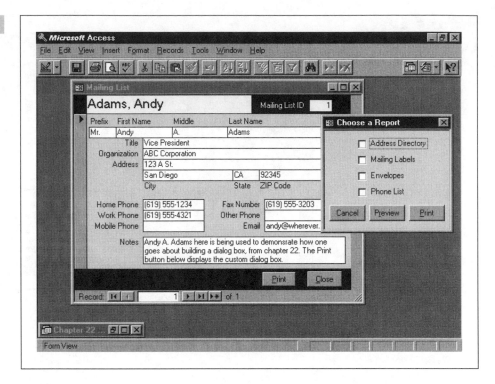

For the rest of this chapter, we'll look at the exact steps required to create such a dialog box. Remember, in this example we're assuming the table, form, and four reports have already been created. Our job here is simply to create the dialog box.

Step 1: Create the Dialog Box

Creating a blank dialog box is pretty much the same as creating a new, blank switchboard. Here are the steps to get started:

1. In the database window, click on the Forms tab, then click on New.

2. Choose Design View and leave the "Choose the table or query..." option blank.

3. Choose OK.

4. Open the property sheet (click on the Properties button in the toolbar, or choose <u>V</u>iew ➤ <u>P</u>roperties), and click on the Format tab in the property sheet.

5. Set the first few properties in the property sheet to the values shown in Figure 22.4.

FIGURE 22.4

An unbound form with Format properties set to make the form look like a dialog box

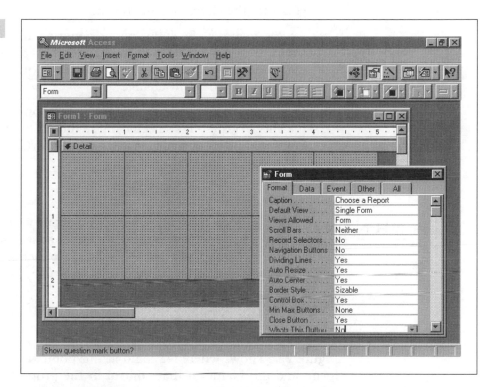

N O T E

Remember that the Caption property is the title that will appear in the title bar of your custom dialog box. So be sure to enter a caption that's suitable for the dialog box you're creating.

Adding the Check Box Controls

Now that we have a blank form to work on, we need to add the controls that the user will select from. You can use any of the controls that the toolbox offers. In this example, we'll use check boxes and command buttons. Here are the steps for adding one check box:

1. If the toolbox isn't open, open it (click on the Toolbox toolbar button, or choose <u>V</u>iew ➤ <u>T</u>oolbox).

2. Click on the Check Box tool then click in the form at about where you want the check box to appear.

3. Access creates a check box with a generic name and caption (most likely Check0). You can change the caption to something more descriptive, such as *Address Directory* (just click within the caption and type your change).

4. Open the property sheet, if it isn't already open, and click right on the check box (so it's selected). Use the All tab to give the check box a more descriptive name (e.g., *DirectoryChosen*) and, optionally, set its default value to No.

WARNING

Be careful when assigning names to controls that you don't inadvertently assign the name to the control's label. Always click right on the control you want to name before typing a control name into the property sheet. The top of the property sheet always shows the type, and current name of, the currently selected control.

Figure 22.5 shows where we stand at this point. The check box is on the form, and the Name of that control in the property sheet is *DirectoryChosen*. The label (caption) for the control (on the form itself) is *Address Directory*.

Next we would follow those same steps to create three more check boxes, one for each possible report. Figure 22.6 shows all four check boxes in place. Table 22.1 lists the caption for each check box, and the name we assigned to each check box. (You can't see the name of each check box because the property sheet shows properties for only one control at a time.)

FIGURE 22.5

This is the first check box control in our dialog box. Its caption is *Address Directory*, its name is *DirectoryChosen*.

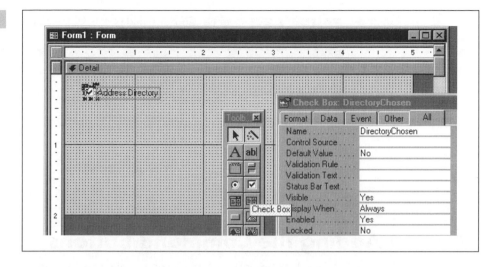

FIGURE 22.6

Four check box controls added to our dialog box

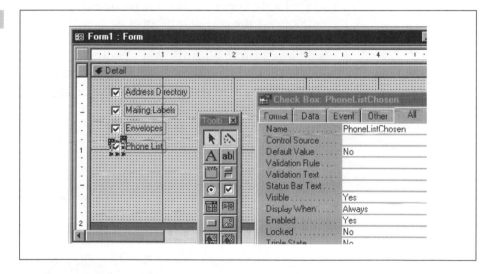

TIP

Check boxes can be difficult to align and space evenly. Try using Edit ➤ Select All to select all the controls, then use Format ➤ Size ➤ To Grid, Format ➤ Align ➤ To Grid and Format ➤ Vertical Spacing to get things in the ballpark. Then you can use other options under Format ➤ Align, as appropriate, to get things tidied up.

TABLE 22.1: Labels (Captions) and Names of the Four Check Boxes Shown in Figure 22.6.

CAPTION	NAME
Address Directory	DirectoryChosen
Mailing Labels	LabelsChosen
Envelopes	EnvelopesChosen
Phone List	PhoneListChosen

Adding the Command Buttons

After the check boxes are in place, we need to add the command buttons. You probably know the routine by now, but let's go through the steps to create one of the command buttons:

1. The Control Wizards won't really help here, because we haven't yet created the macros that will respond to the user's dialog box selections. So turn off the Control Wizards by clicking the button "out" as below.

2. Click on the Command Button tool, then click in the form at about where you want the command button to appear. A button with a generic name, such as Command0 appears.

3. Make sure the command button is selected, then use the All tab in the property sheet to give the button a name and caption.

In Figure 22.7 we've created a command button, named it CancelButton, and assigned the caption *Cancel*.

FIGURE 22.7

A command button captioned *Cancel* added to our custom dialog box

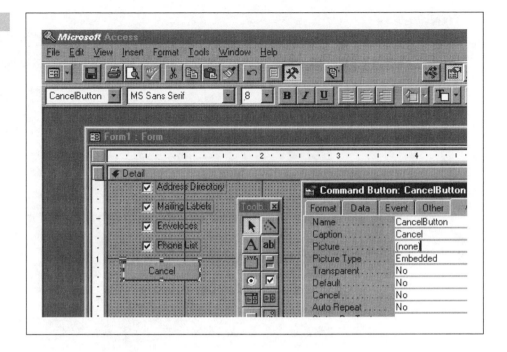

We would then repeat steps 1–3 to create two additional command buttons, captioned P&review (which shows up as Preview on the button face) and &Print (which shows up as Print). You can then use dragging techniques and the options on the Format menu to size, position, and align the buttons to your liking. Figure 22.8 shows our dialog box after creating and formatting all three buttons, and tidying up in general. Table 22.2 lists the names and captions assigned to those buttons.

Print, Save, and Close the Form

With the controls in place we can now name and close the form, and optionally print up some "technical documentation" that will help us develop the macros in the next step. Here are the steps to follow:

1. Choose File ➤ Close ➤ Yes and enter a name such as Print-DialogBox. The new dialog box name appears in the database window along with any other forms, as in the example shown in Figure 22.9.

2. If you want to print the technical documentation, choose Tools ➤ Analyze ➤ Documentor.

FIGURE 22.8

Three command buttons added to our custom dialog box

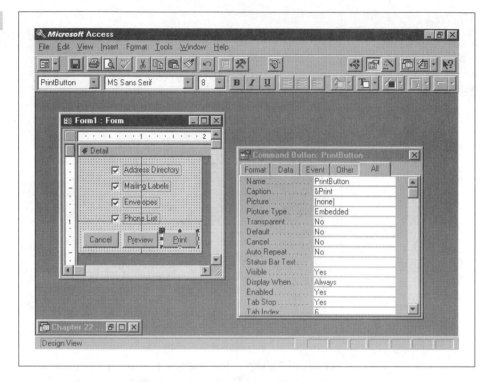

FIGURE 22.9

Once closed and saved, the new dialog box is listed right along with any other forms in the database window.

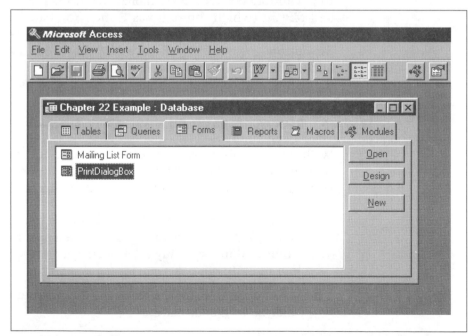

TABLE 22.2: Names and Captions for the Three Command Buttons Shown in Figure 22.8.

NAME	CAPTION
CancelButton	Cancel
PreviewButton	P&review
PrintButton	&Print

3. Under Object Type choose Forms, and click on the name of the form that you want to document (PrintDialogBox in this example, as shown below):

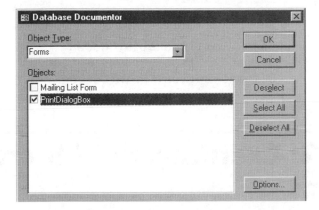

4. We don't need a whole lot of detail in this particular case. So click on the Options button and limit the display to the options shown below.

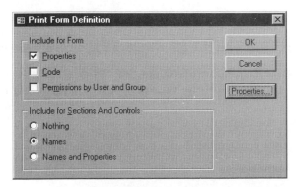

5. Choose OK (twice) and wait for the Object Definition window to appear.

You can then use the Print button in the toolbar to print the documentation. Then just click on the Close toolbar button to close the Object Definition window. You're back at the database window.

We'll use the printed documentation to help us remember the exact names we gave to each of the controls in the dialog box. The names of the controls appear near the end of the printout and will look something like this:

```
Command Button: CancelButton
Check Box: DirectoryChosen
Check Box: EnvelopesChosen
Label: Label1
Label: Label7
Label: Label9
Check Box: LabelsChosen
Check Box: PhoneListChosen
Command Button: PreviewButton
Command Button: PrintButton
```

Step 2: Creating the Macro Actions

Next we need some macros to define what will happen when the user makes selections from the dialog box. We need to start with a blank macro sheet:

1. Click on the Macros tab in the database window.

2. Click on the New button to get to a new, blank macro sheet.

3. Open the Macro Names and Condition columns using the appropriate options on the toolbar or the View menu. You should see all four column headings listed across the top of the columns as below.

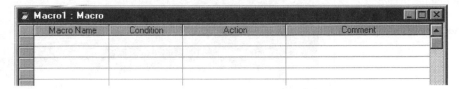

Now we're ready to start creating the individual macros. You can start off by typing just a comment into the first row(s) of the macro sheet, as I've done below.

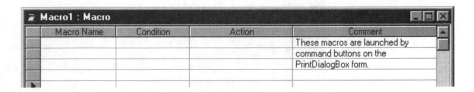

The Macro to Cancel Printing

One of the buttons on our PrintDialogBox form lets the user just Cancel, and bail out without doing anything. The macro we assign to that button need only close the form. So follow these steps to create that macro:

1. In a blank row beneath the comments you typed, enter a name such as CancelPrint in the Macro Name column.

2. Leave the Conditions column empty.

3. In the Action column, choose Close.

4. Fill out the action arguments as follows:

Object Type:	Form
Object Name:	PrintDialogBox
Save:	Yes

5. Optionally, fill in the Comments column to describe what this macro does.

Figure 22.10 shows how this first macro looks when completed.

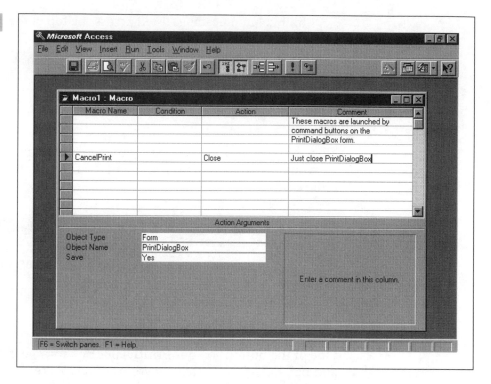

The Macro to Preview Reports

The next macro in our macro group is a little trickier than the first, because it needs to say, "If the DirectoryChosen check box is checked, then preview the Address Directory report," and then, "If the LabelsChosen check box is checked, then preview the Avery 2163 mini-sheet labels report"... and so on. So we need to explain one thing about the check boxes before we do that.

A check box is a control that can contain any one of two values, either True (checked) or False (unchecked). We don't actually use the check boxes to launch an action. Instead, we decide whether to perform some action based on whether a check box is checked or not. The "decision" part takes place in the Conditions column of the macro. As you may recall from Chapter 20, the Conditions column must contain an expression that evaluates to True or False. Since the value of a check box is inherently True or False, we really only need to use the name of the check box in the conditions column of the macro. For example, if I put *DirectoryChosen* as the condition in a line, then *DirectoryChosen* proves True if the check box is checked, and proves False if the check box is unchecked.

With that little tidbit in the back of your mind, let's go ahead and create the next macro in this sheet. We'll name this new macro PreviewReports. Here's how to proceed:

1. Leave one blank row beneath the CancelPrint macro, and type the name PreviewReports into the Macro Name column of the new row.

2. In the Conditions column, type *[DirectoryChosen]*.

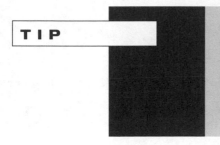

TIP

The printed documentation for the form lets you easily look up the exact spelling of the check box controls on the form. That's how I "remembered" the *DirectoryChosen* name. In lieu of using printed documentation, you can use the Expression Builder (...) to locate names of controls on forms.

3. In the Action column, choose OpenReport and fill in the action arguments as follows:

   Report Name: Address Directory
   View: Print Preview

4. Optionally, type a description into the Comment column.

At this point our macro sheet looks like Figure 22.11.

Next we need to repeat steps 2–4 to add three more rows to the macro. But we need to refer to different controls and report names. The Condition and Action columns, and the action arguments for these next three rows, are summarized below. Figure 22.12 shows how the macro looks when completed.

Table 22.3 shows the condition, action, and action argument for each row in the PreviewReports macro.

FIGURE 22.11

Getting started on the second macro, which we've named PreviewReports

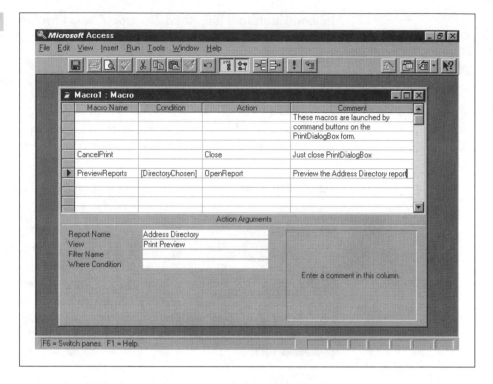

FIGURE 22.12

The PreviewReports macro defined in our macro sheet

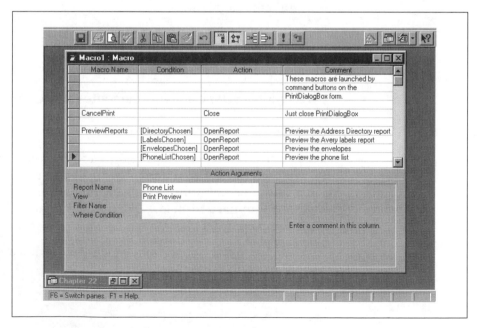

TABLE 22.3: Conditions, Actions, and Action Arguments for the Macros Shown in Figure 22.12

CONDITION	ACTION	ACTION ARGUMENTS
[LabelsChosen]	OpenReport	**Report Name:** Avery 2163 mini-sheet labels
		View: Print Preview
[EnvelopesChosen]	OpenReport	**Report Name:** Envelopes
		View: Print Preview
[PhoneListChosen]	OpenReport	**Report Name:** Phone List
		View: Print Preview

The Macro to Print Reports

Next we need a macro to print reports. This macro is virtually identical to the PreviewReports macro, except that the View action argument for each OpenReport action needs to be changed from Print Preview to Print. To create this macro quickly and easily, follow these steps:

1. Hold down the Ctrl key and click on each of the four rows in the PreviewReports macro, so that all four rows are selected.

2. Choose Edit ➤ Copy or press Ctrl+C to copy those rows to the Clipboard (nothing happens on the screen.)

3. Leave a blank row under the Preview Reports macro, click in the Macro Name column, and choose Edit ➤ Paste (or press Ctrl+V.) An exact copy of the PreviewReports macro appears.

4. Change the macro name from PreviewReports to PrintReports.

5. Change the View action argument in the first row of this new macro from Print Preview to Print.

6. Change the comment to reflect this change.

7. Repeat steps 5 and 6 for the remaining three rows in the PrintReports macro.

Figure 22.13 shows how the macro sheet looks at this point (though you can only see the action arguments for the last row in the macro.)

You may now save and close the macro in the usual manner. That is, choose File ➤ Close ➤ Yes, type in a name such as PrintDialog-BoxMacros, and choose OK. The macro name appears in the database window whenever the Macros tab is selected, as below.

FIGURE 22.13

The PrintReports macro added to the macro sheet

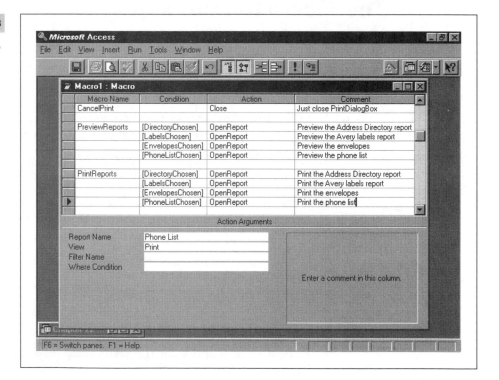

Step 3: Assign Macros to Dialog Box Buttons

Next we need to assign each of those macros to the three command buttons in the PrintDialogBox form. Here's how to do that:

1. In the database window, click on the Forms tab, click on the PrintDialogBox name, and then click on the Design button to open that form in design view.

2. Open up the property sheet, and click on the Events tab.

3. Click on the Cancel button.

4. In the property sheet, click on the On Click property, and then use the drop-down list button to choose PrintDialog-BoxMacros.CancelPrint as the macro to run when the user clicks that button, as in Figure 22.14.

FIGURE 22.14

The PrintReports-Macros.CancelPrint macro assigned to the On Click property of the button captioned Cancel

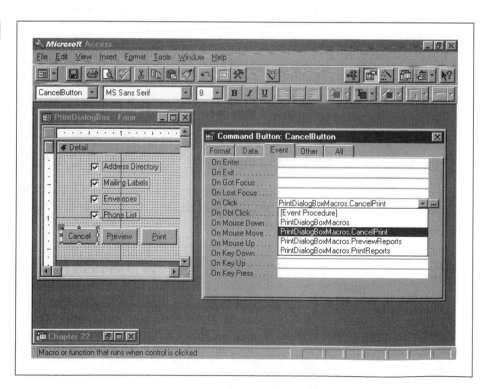

5. Click on the button captioned P&review, and assign the macro named PrintDialogBoxMacros.PreviewReports to that button, as below:

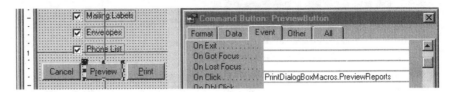

6. Click on the button captioned <u>P</u>rint and assign the PrintDialog-BoxMacros.PrintReports to the On Click property of that button, as below.

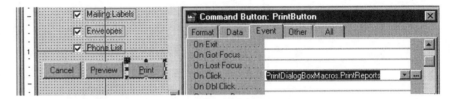

7. Close and save the form (choose <u>F</u>ile ➤ <u>C</u>lose ➤ <u>Y</u>es).

You're returned to the database window. The dialog box and its macros are complete. Assuming you had created the four reports mentioned at the start of this chapter, you could test the dialog box right now simply by opening it in form view and making selections.

As you may recall from earlier in this chapter (see Figure 22.3) we actually assigned this dialog box to the Print button on a form we had created earlier. The simple way to do this would be to open that form, in design view. Then open the toolbox, and turn on the Control Wizards. Create the Print command button and when the Control Wizard asks for actions, choose Form Operations ➤ Open Form ➤ PrintDialogBox. The caption for the button would be &Print.

Putting on the Finishing Touches

There are some finishing touches you can put on your dialog box to refine its appearance and behavior, as we'll discuss in the last few remaining sections in this chapter. As always, these "features" are actually properties or specific controls that you assign to the form using the property sheet in the form design screen.

Modal and Popup Properties

You may have noticed, in your day-to-day use of Windows, that most dialog boxes are "sticky." By that I mean that once the dialog box is on the screen, you can't just shoo it away by clicking on some other window. You need to specifically complete the dialog, or close the dialog, or choose the dialog box's Cancel key to get rid of the dialog box.

The technical term for "stickiness" is *modal*. That is to say, most dialog boxes are actually modal windows. By contrast, most "regular" (i.e., application and document) windows are *modeless*, meaning that you can do work outside the window even while the window is on the screen.

A second characteristic of dialog boxes is the fact that they are *popup* forms. That is to say, once the window is on the screen, no other window can cover it. You might already be familiar with the Always On Top feature of Windows help screens. When you activate that feature, you are, in essence, making the Windows help window a "popup" window.

If you want to give your own custom dialog boxes the modal and popup characteristics, follow these steps:

1. Open the custom dialog box in form design view.

2. Choose <u>E</u>dit ➤ Select Fo<u>r</u>m to select the entire form.

3. Open the property sheet, and click on the Other tab.

4. Set the Modal and Pop-up properties to Yes, as below.

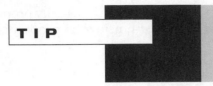

TIP

To learn more about modal and pop-up properties, and ways to combine them, just press F1 while the cursor is on either property within the property sheet.

5. Close and save the form normally (File ➤ Close ➤ Yes).

To test your efforts, open the dialog box in the normal form view. When you click outside the dialog box, nothing will happen (except, maybe, you'll hear a beep). The only way to get rid of the dialog box is to specifically close it using one of its command buttons, or the Close (×) button in its upper-right corner.

The Dialog Box Border Style

Another characteristic of many dialog boxes that make them different from other windows is their border. Many dialog boxes have a thick, black border which cannot be sized. If you want to give your own custom dialog box that kind of border, follow these simple steps:

1. Open the custom dialog box in form design view.

2. Choose Edit ➤ Select Form to select the entire form.

3. Open the property sheet, and click on the Format tab.

4. Set the Border property to Dialog, as below.

TIP To learn more about border styles, just press the Help key when the cursor is in the Border Style property box.

5. Close and save the form normally (File ➤ Close ➤ Yes).

To see the effects, open the dialog box in form view. Then try sizing the dialog box by dragging one of its edges or corners. Can't be done! If you try to "trick it" by using commands in the control menu (in the upper-left corner of the dialog box), no go. The menu will now offer only the Move and Close options, as illustrated below.

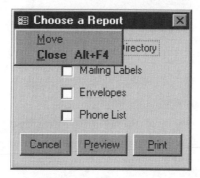

Default and Cancel Buttons

Two last features that many dialog boxes share are cancel and default buttons, as defined below:

- **Cancel button** The button that gets pushed automatically when the user presses the Escape key.
- **Default button** The button that is automatically selected when the user presses ↵. This button will also have a darker border than other buttons on the same form.

You can make one (and only one) button in your dialog box the default button, and any other single button the cancel button. Here's how:

1. Open your custom dialog box in design view.

2. Open the property sheet.

3. Click on the Other tab.

4. If you want to make a button into the Cancel button, first click on that button to select it. Then set its Cancel property to Yes, as below.

5. If you want to make some other button the default button, first click on that button to select it. Then set its Default property to Yes, as below.

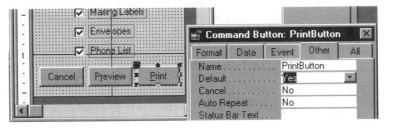

6. Close and save the form normally (File ➤ Close ➤ Yes).

When you reopen the dialog box in form view, the only visual difference you'll see is the darker border around the default button (the Print button in the example below). You can test out the new properties by pressing the Escape or ↵ key while the form is on the screen.

So what we've learned here is the big secret to custom dialog boxes: They're really just forms that aren't bound to any particular table or query. You use the toolbox in form design to add controls to that form. And then you create macros (or Visual Basic code) to define the actions that the dialog box will perform. You can even make your dialog box behave like the dialog boxes in bigger Windows applications by setting Modal, Pop-Up, and Border Style properties to the form as a whole. You can also assign the Cancel and Default properties to any two command buttons on the form.

Where to Go from Here

In the next two chapters we'll look at techniques for creating custom toolbars and menus. Those two features will add even more professional polish to your custom Access applications. Other chapters you might want to explore include:

- If you need a refresher on the mechanics of creating macros, see Chapter 20 "Using Macros to Create Custom Actions."

- To see a custom application with lots of custom dialog boxes, try the Fulfill sample database on the CD (see Appendix C).

- To learn about exploring custom applications behind the scenes, see Chapter 28.

What's New in the Access Zoo?

For those of you familiar with earlier versions of Access, here's what's new in creating custom dialog boxes:

- You can make any one command button on a form the "default" button. When you do, the button will have a dark border, and the user need only press ↵ to select that button. The property setting is in the Other tab of the property sheet.

- You can also make any one command button on a form the "cancel" button, which is pushed automatically when the user presses Esc. Set the Cancel property in the Other tab of the property sheet to Yes.

CHAPTER

23

Creating
Custom Toolbars

HANNA Barbera got it right in *The Jetsons*; most of us have ended up with "push-button" jobs. Microsoft's toolbars are a perfect example, because they let you do virtually *anything* with the click of a button.

Access's Toolbars

Microsoft Access comes with 19 built-in toolbars. Fifteen of them are tied to specific views, and are named accordingly:

Database	Table Design
Table Datasheet	Filter/Sort
Query Design	Query Datasheet
Form Design	Form View
Report Design	Print Preview
Relationships	Formatting (Form/Report Design)
Visual Basic	Formatting (Datasheet)
Microsoft	

There are also four built-in toolbars that aren't attached to a specific view. They are:

- **Utility 1** and **Utility 2 toolbars**   For creating your own custom toolbars.

- **Microsoft toolbar**   Provides quick access to other Microsoft applications.

- **Toolbox**   Offers buttons for creating controls in form design and report design. It's generally free-floating, but can be docked like any other toolbar (see the next section).

Hiding/Displaying the Built-In Toolbars

You can hide or display any number of toolbars at any time. Just follow these procedures:

- **To enable or display *all* the built-in toolbars,** choose View ➤ Toolbars. Then, check each toolbar that you want displayed in the Toolbars dialog box. Choose Close when you are finished.

- **To hide or display a specific toolbar,** right-click on a toolbar and choose Toolbars. Or choose View ➤ Toolbars (or File ➤ Toolbars if there is no database open). Then check or uncheck the toolbar you want to hide or display. Choose Close when you're done.

- **To move a toolbar,** move the mouse pointer to any blank space in the toolbar, and drag the toolbar to wherever you want to put it.

- **To dock a toolbar,** drag it to the edge of the screen until its outline expands to the width or height of the screen, then release the mouse button.

- **To undock a toolbar,** so that it becomes free-floating, just move it away from the edge of the screen.

TIP

You can quickly dock or undock a toolbar by double-clicking on any blank space in the toolbar. To hide a floating toolbar, click on the small close button in the toolbar's upper-right corner.

Controlling the Size and Appearance of Toolbars

You can control the size of the buttons and the appearance of any toolbar by following these steps:

1. Right-click on any toolbar and choose Toolbars, or choose View ➤ Toolbars (or File ➤ Toolbars if no database is loaded).

2. Choose any combination of appearance features from the lower part of the dialog box:

    Color Buttons   Clear this check box if you have a monochrome monitor and want to see the toolbar buttons in monochrome.

    Large Buttons   Choose this option to make the buttons larger (handy on small laptop-sized screens, or on screens with resolution that's higher than VGA).

    Show ToolTips   Clear this option if you don't want your toolbar to display ToolTips. (A ToolTip is that little message that appears on the screen after you've rested the mouse pointer on a button for a few seconds.)

3. Choose Close after making your selection(s).

Modified vs. Custom Toolbars

As an application developer, you need to be aware of the difference between a modified built-in toolbar and a custom toolbar:

*   **Modified existing toolbar**   If you modify an existing toolbar, that version of the toolbar will appear in *all* your databases.

*   **Custom toolbar**   When you create a new custom toolbar, it appears only in the database in which it was created.

NOTE The built-in Utility 1 and Utility 2 toolbars are initially blank. When you add buttons to those toolbars, that counts as modifying an existing toolbar—not as creating a new, custom toolbar. In other words, the Utility 1 and Utility 2 toolbars are accessible from all your databases.

Empowering/Limiting Your Users

As an application developer, you can use custom toolbars to determine what the user of your application can and can't do. For example, if you want your user to be able to create and change objects, you can include design buttons on your toolbars. On the other hand, if you don't want the user to be messing around with your objects, you can prevent them access to the design screens by excluding design buttons from your application's custom toolbars.

NOTE You'll need to create custom menus, discussed in the next chapter, to determine exactly how much freedom your user has.

Creating a Custom Toolbar

It's very easy to create a new custom toolbar:

1. Make sure that the database you want to put the toolbar into is the currently open database.

2. Right-click an existing toolbar, choose Toolbars, then choose New. Or, choose View ➤ Toolbars ➤ New.

3. Enter a name (up to 64 characters) for your new toolbar, then choose OK.

4. Choose Customize from the Toolbars dialog box.

A tiny (and sometimes hard to see) empty toolbar appears on the screen, as does the Customize Toolbars dialog box shown in Figure 23.1.

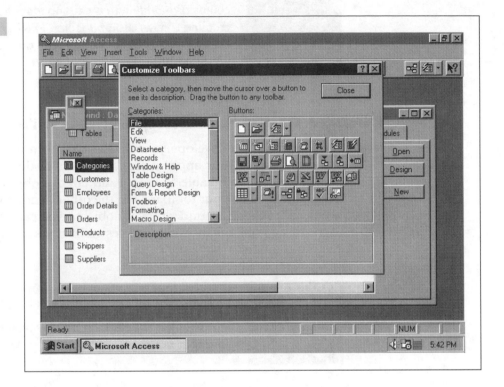

Adding and Deleting Buttons

Once you get to the Customize Toolbars dialog box, the rest is even easier:

1. Choose a category of button type from the Categories list (just click on any category name).

2. Under Buttons, move the mouse pointer to whichever button you think you might want to add to your toolbar. Check the ToolTip and description that appear to make sure you know what the button will do (see below).

3. If you want to add that button to your toolbar, just drag it over to your custom toolbar.

Figure 23.2 shows an example where we've already dragged a couple of buttons over to our custom toolbar, and are currently exploring buttons in the File category.

FIGURE 23.2

Here we've just dragged two buttons to our custom toolbar and are browsing the Customize Toolbars dialog box for more buttons to add.

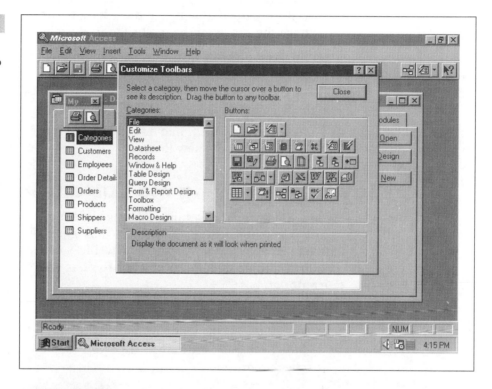

WARNING

If you inadvertently drag a button to a blank area of the screen, Access creates another new toolbar, and gives it a unique name (such as Custom Toolbar 2). This can be confusing. If you want to see the name of the toolbar you're currently adding buttons to, move the mouse pointer to a blank space around any button on the toolbar, and take a look at the status bar.

You can use any of these techniques to refine your custom toolbar while you're viewing the Customize Toolbars dialog box:

- **To remove a button,** drag it off of your custom toolbar.

- **To move a button to a new location on the toolbar,** just drag the button to its new location.

- **To add space between buttons,** drag the button slightly to the right (a distance a little less than half the width of the button). (Closing the dialog box and docking the toolbar allows you to have the space on the toolbar to undertake this operation.)

- **To delete space between two buttons,** drag one button slightly to the left.

- **To position a button exactly,** dock the toolbar horizontally, by dragging it to the top or bottom of the screen until it expands to full-screen width. Then hold down the Shift key while dragging the button to its new location.

Saving/Modifying the Custom Toolbar

When you've finished adding buttons to your custom toolbar, just choose Close from the Customize Toolbars dialog box. You can then use any of these techniques, at any time, to view, hide, or change your custom toolbar (but don't forget, your custom toolbar will only be available in the current database):

- **To hide or display a custom toolbar,** right-click on any toolbar, then click on the name of the custom toolbar that you want to hide or display. Currently displayed toolbars are indicated with a check mark.

T I P   If no toolbars are visible, choose <u>V</u>iew ➤ <u>T</u>oolbars (or <u>F</u>ile ➤ Tool<u>b</u>ars), double-click on a toolbar name, and choose Close.

- **To change a custom toolbar,** first display that toolbar, right-click on it, and choose Customize to return to the Customize Toolbars dialog box. There you can make changes using the same techniques that you used to create the custom toolbar.

- **To delete a custom toolbar,** choose <u>V</u>iew ➤ <u>T</u>oolbars, scroll down to the name of the custom toolbar you want to delete, then click on the <u>D</u>elete button in the Toolbars dialog box, and choose <u>Y</u>es.

- **To rename a custom toolbar,** choose <u>V</u>iew ➤ <u>T</u>oolbars, scroll down to the name of the custom toolbar you want to rename, and click on the Rena<u>m</u>e button. Type a new, unique name for your toolbar and choose OK.

N O T E   The <u>D</u>elete and Rena<u>m</u>e buttons aren't visible in the Toolbars dialog box when the highlight is on a built-in toolbar, because you can't delete or rename those toolbars.

- **To move/dock/undock a custom toolbar,** use the same techniques you'd use with a built-in toolbar, as described earlier in this chapter.

Creating Your Own Buttons

You're not limited to creating buttons that perform built-in Access tasks. You can create your own buttons to run macros, open tables, preview reports, and more. The general procedure is the same as for "regular" buttons. You just need to choose your buttons from the categories that start with the word *All*. Here are the steps:

1. Display the toolbar to which you want to assign a custom button.

2. Right-click on that toolbar and choose Customize.

3. Scroll down to and select one of the last few categories (beginning with the word *All*.) The <u>O</u>bjects list shows the names of all the

objects in the current database that fall into that category (see below).

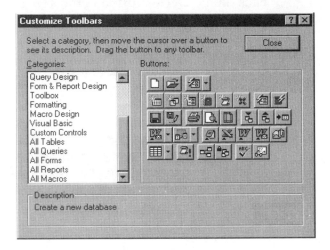

4. Drag the name of any object to your toolbar.

5. Repeat steps 3 and 4 to add as many buttons as you like, then choose Close.

A default button for that type of object appears on your toolbar. (You can change the button, as you'll see in the next section.)

When you move the mouse pointer to the custom button, the status bar and (in a couple of seconds) the ToolTip describe what the button will do, as illustrated below.

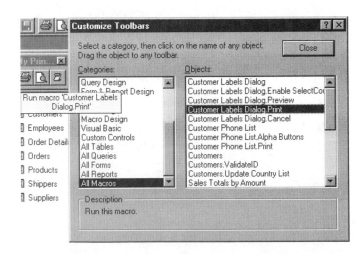

TIP You can also drag the name of any object from the database window into the toolbar to instantly create a button that displays that object.

Changing a Button's Face/Description

You can change the face of any button in any toolbar. And, you can change the description of any custom button you create. Here's how:

1. Right-click on the toolbar that contains the button you want to change, then choose Customize.

2. In the toolbar, right-click on the button that you want to change, and select Choose Button Image. You'll see the Choose Button Image dialog box shown below. (You can also copy, paste, and reset button images using other items on this right-click menu.)

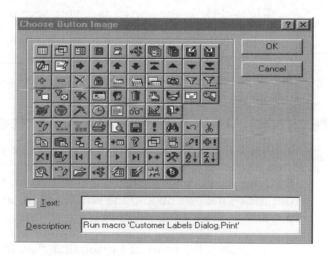

3. Now you can do any of the following:

   • **To pick a new picture for the button,** just click on whatever button picture you want.

   • **To display text,** rather than a picture, on the button face, choose Text, then type the text you want to appear on the button.

• **To change the ToolTip and status bar description of the button,** choose <u>D</u>escription and type in a new description.

Remember, you can only change the Description on custom buttons—not the built-in buttons.

4. Choose OK.

5. Repeat steps 2–4 to choose a face and/or description for as many buttons as you wish. Then choose Close when you're done.

Resetting a Button Face

If you change a button face on a built-in button, then decide to go back to the original button face:

1. Right-click on the button face you want to reset, and choose Customize from the shortcut menu.

2. Right-click on the button again, and choose Reset Button Face.

3. Choose Close from the Customize Toolbars dialog box.

Creating Your Own Button Face

So what do you do when you want to create your own button image? Once you have added a button to the toolbar, with the Customize Toolbars dialog box open, right-click on the button. Select Edit Button Image from the context menu and the button editor appears (see Figure 23.3). To create your own button image, follow these steps:

1. To change the color of a pixel, first click on the color in the Colors frame, then click on the box on the Picture grid that represents the pixel. (Select the Erase color box to erase a pixel.)

2. To scroll the Picture grid (not all of it appears in the box), click on the arrows below the grid.

3. To see what your new button image looks like, check the Preview frame.

FIGURE 23.3

The button image editor included in Access

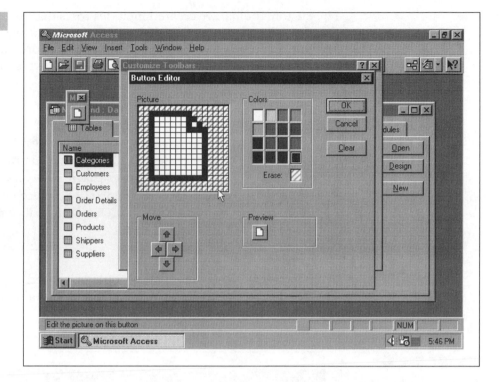

4. To clear the button face, click on the Clear button.

5. To save the button image, click on OK.

Adding Toolbars to Your Custom Application

As an application developer, you'll want to control exactly *which* toolbar appears *when*. First, create a database with the Database Wizard or open a database that you have already created so that you can work through a couple of examples. (We will use the Northwind Traders database included with Access for the examples in this chapter.) Create a custom toolbar and add the buttons to it that you use most often when you work with a database.

The custom toolbar we created includes tools that switch to our other applications. It reflects the fact that much of the time we are working in Access and switching to other applications to perform less frequent tasks. Figure 23.4 shows this custom toolbar, which we creatively named My Applications.

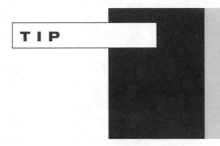

TIP

Since we obviously use Microsoft applications, we could have just used the Microsoft toolbar. However, most users have other applications. If Access doesn't provide a button for your application, you can use Visual Basic for Applications to launch it and attach that code to a button on the toolbar.

We then created a second custom toolbar, named My Printing Preview. This toolbar is shown in Figure 23.5, and contains icons for printing, print preview, and page setup.

FIGURE 23.4

The custom toolbar My Applications displayed in the Northwind Traders database

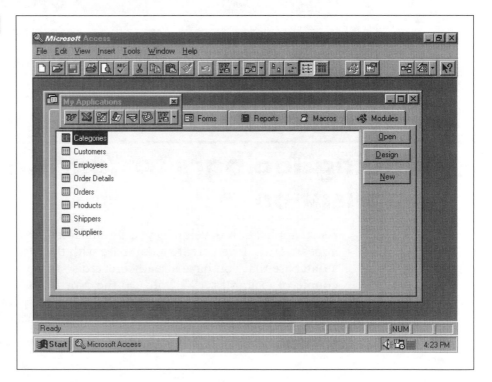

FIGURE 23.5

The custom My Printing
Preview toolbar

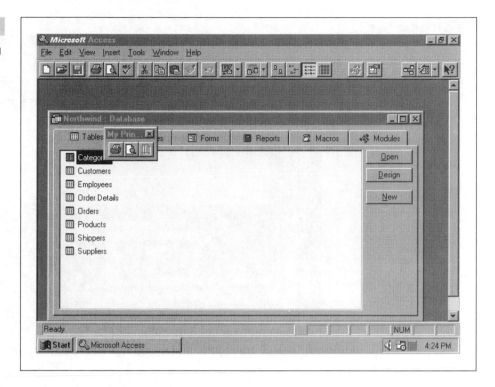

Creating Macros to Show or Hide Custom Toolbars

After you've created your custom toolbars, you need to create macros to show and hide them. In the Northwind Traders application, we put all those macros into a single macro group named Global Macros, as shown in Figure 23.6.

Table 23.1 shows the name, action, and action argument of each macro. (Notice that there is no Conditions column in this macro group.) Basically, each macro uses a single ShowToolBar action. The action arguments for each action name the toolbar to show or hide, then use Yes to show the toolbar, or No to hide that toolbar.

FIGURE 23.6

Our macro group named Global Macros contains the macros that show or hide the custom toolbars.

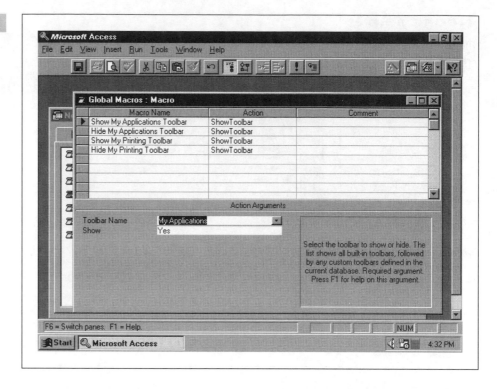

TABLE 23.1: Sample Macros to Hide and Show Custom Toolbars

MACRO NAME	ACTION	ACTION ARGUMENTS
Show My Applications Toolbar	ShowToolBar	**Toolbar Name:** My Applications
		Show: Yes
Hide My Applications Toolbar	ShowToolBar	**Toolbar Name:** My Applications
		Show: No
Show My Printing Toolbar	ShowToolBar	**Toolbar Name:** My Printing
		Show: Yes
Hide My Printing Toolbar	ShowToolBar	**Toolbar Name:** My Printing
		Show: No

Attaching Toolbars to Forms

In order to attach a toolbar to a particular form, you need to execute, from an event on the form, the macro that displays (or hides) the toolbar. To do that:

1. Open, in design view, the form that you want to display a custom toolbar.

2. Open the property sheet, select Event Properties from the property sheet's drop-down list, and choose Edit ➤ Select Form.

3. Assign the macro that *shows* the toolbar to the On Activate property.

4. Assign the macro that *hides* the toolbar to the On Deactivate properties of that form.

Figure 23.7 shows an example using the Northwind Traders application, in which we display the My Printing toolbar when the form appears, and

Form event properties for the Northwind Traders customer phone list form. The macro to display a custom toolbar is assigned to On Activate. The macro to hide the toolbar is assigned to the On Deactivate and On Unload properties.

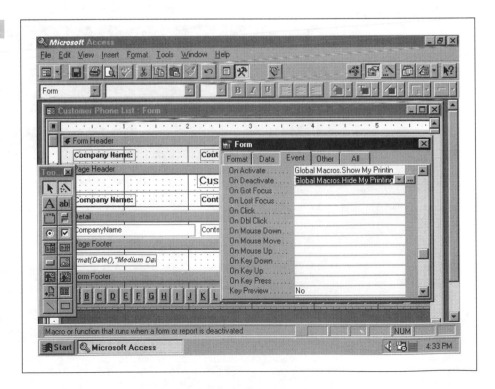

we also want to hide that toolbar when the user is done with the form. By using the On Activate and On Deactivate properties, we can make sure the toolbar is visible whenever the user is working with this form, and hidden whenever she moves the focus to another form.

Attaching a Custom Toolbar to Print Preview

If you want your application to display a custom toolbar during print preview, you need to open the report in design view, open its property sheet, and choose Edit ➤ Select Report. Assign the macro that shows the toolbar to the On Activate event properties. Assign the macro that hides the toolbar to the On Deactivate event properties. Figure 23.8 shows an example, using one of the reports from the Northwind Traders application.

 ➤ By the way, we know that all these form and report event properties can be confusing. For help while assigning macros to these properties, just press F1. Or, search help for *Order of Events*.

Macros to hide and display a custom toolbar when the user looks at the report named Alphabetical List of Products in print preview.

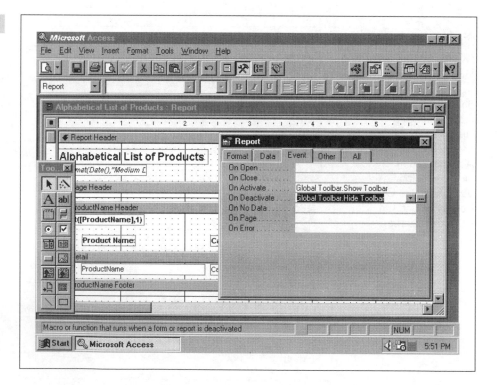

Macro to Hide the Built-In Toolbars

When creating an application, you might decide to hide all the built-in toolbars from the user. As you know, you can turn off the built-in toolbars manually through the Startup dialog box. If you want your application to turn off those toolbars, have your AutoExec macro send the necessary keystrokes at startup. You can use a SendKeys action to have the macro press the appropriate keys, as in the following example.

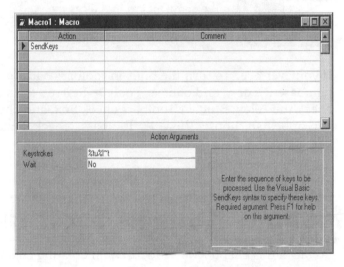

Notice the Keystrokes entries in the action argument for the SendKeys action:

%t	Presses Alt+T to open the Tools menu
u	Types **u** to choose Startup
%l	Unchecks the Allow Built-in Toolbars check box
~	Presses ↵ to choose OK.

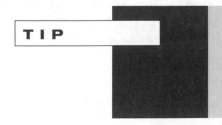

TIP

When defining the arguments for a SendKeys action in a macro, press F1 for help. Then click on the green underlined *SendKeys* jump word, and scroll through that help screen to find the codes you need to represent various keystrokes.

Redisplaying the Built-In Toolbars

If you want your application to redisplay the built-in menus when the user quits the application, have your "quit" macro execute a SendKeys action to turn the built-in toolbars back on. You might also want to have that macro redisplay the database window.

TIP The same macro that turns the built-in toolbars off will turn them back on.

If you ever need to turn the built-in toolbars back on manually, go to the database window, and choose Tools ➤ Startup from the menu bar. Then check the Allow Built-in Toolbars check box, and choose OK. If no toolbar appears, choose View ➤ Toolbars, check Database, then choose Close.

Modifying a Built-In Toolbar

So far in this chapter we've focused on creating custom toolbars for your custom applications. But you may also want to modify Access's built-in toolbars to better suit your own needs. As mentioned earlier, when you modify a built-in toolbar, that toolbar becomes accessible in all your databases.

NOTE A custom toolbar is stored in the database it was created in; so it is available only in that database. Built-in toolbars (modified or not) are stored in the Access workgroup information file, and are therefore available to any database.

To modify a built-in toolbar:

1. Display the built-in toolbar that you want to modify.

2. Right-click on that toolbar and choose Customize.

3. Make changes using the techniques described under "Adding and Deleting Buttons" earlier in this chapter.

4. Choose Close when you've finished.

That modified version of the built-in toolbar will appear in all your databases.

Resetting a Built-In Toolbar

If you want to reset a built-in toolbar to its original self, right-click on a toolbar and choose Toolbars. Click on the name of the built-in toolbar that you want to reset. Then click on the <u>R</u>eset button, choose <u>Y</u>es, then click on Close on the Toolbars dialog box.

Where To Go from Here

Adding custom toolbars can make your applications much more functional for users. They are truly a convenience feature in any application. However, toolbars need to be backed by menus. The next chapter explains how to create the custom menus that are necessary to back up custom toolbars.

What's New in the Access Zoo?

Toolbars have been seriously enhanced in this release of Access. Several new toolbars are available, and several new features make working with toolbars easier. These features include:

- A button editor for creating your own button images.
- The ability to copy and paste images from button to button.
- A new formatting toolbar available in design view, which makes formatting forms and reports easier.
- Buttons that support drop-down list boxes and palettes.
- The ability to prevent modification of a toolbar by disabling shortcut menus.

CHAPTER

24

Creating
Custom Menus

WHEN developing an application, you'll probably want to give your application its own custom menus. As with custom toolbars, you can use custom menus to determine exactly what the user of your application can and can't do.

Two Ways to Display Custom Menus

There are two ways to display custom menus in your application:

With a particular form   You can attach a custom menu to a form, so that the menu bar is displayed only while that form is on the screen.

Globally   A global menu is one that appears throughout your application, though it will be replaced by any custom menus that you attach to forms.

You can use the Access Menu Builder to create either type of menu. We'll talk about how you attach each type of macro to your application a little later in this chapter. For now, just keep in mind that you can use the Menu Builder to create any number of custom menus for an application.

Starting the Access Menu Builder

The Menu Builder is the easiest way to create a custom menu. Follow these steps to get started.

1. If you haven't already done so, open the database that you want to add the custom menu to.

2. Choose <u>T</u>ools ➤ Add-<u>I</u>ns ➤ <u>M</u>enu Builder.

3. To create a new menu, choose <u>N</u>ew.

4. Choose one of Access's built-in menu bars to use as a template in creating your own menu. For example, if your menu bar will be displayed with forms, you can choose the Form or Form Datasheet menu bar as a template. Alternatively, you can choose <Empty Menu Bar> to create a new menu from scratch.

5. Choose OK. You'll be taken to the Menu Builder dialog box, shown in Figure 24.1.

FIGURE 24.1

The Menu Builder dialog box using the Access Form menu bar as a template

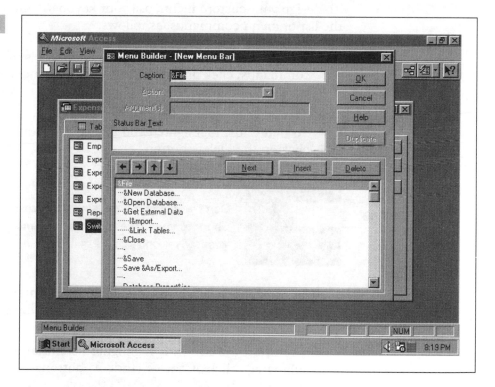

What the Menu Builder Shows

The trick to using the Menu Builder is being able to envision how the menu will look when you're done. Each little symbol and indentation in the lower half of the window symbolizes how the final menu will look:

&	Precedes the letter that will be the command's hotkey.
---	Indicates a pull-down menu command.
---_	Indicates a separator bar.
------	Indicates a submenu command.

As an example, Figure 24.2 shows how a sample menu looks in the Menu Builder, and how the actual menus will look to the user.

Designing Your Custom Menu

To design your custom menu, use your keyboard and the tools just above the list of menu commands, as follows:

- **To move through** (and highlight commands in) the list of menu commands, click on the list and use the ↑ and ↓ *keys*, or click on the button labeled <u>N</u>ext, or click on the command you want to highlight.

- **To delete** the highlighted command from your custom menu bar, click on the <u>D</u>elete button.

NOTE Don't worry about messing up Access's built-in menus. Changes you make to the menu template have no effect whatsoever on Access's built-in menus.

- **To outdent** the currently highlighted command (move from a submenu to the next higher level), click on the ← (Outdent) button.

- **To indent** the currently highlighted command (move down to a submenu), click on the → (Indent) button.

- **To move a command up or down** in the list, without changing its level, click on the ↑ or ↓ button.

FIGURE 24.2

An example of a menu
and submenu (top)
and the same menu as
specified in the Menu
Builder (bottom)

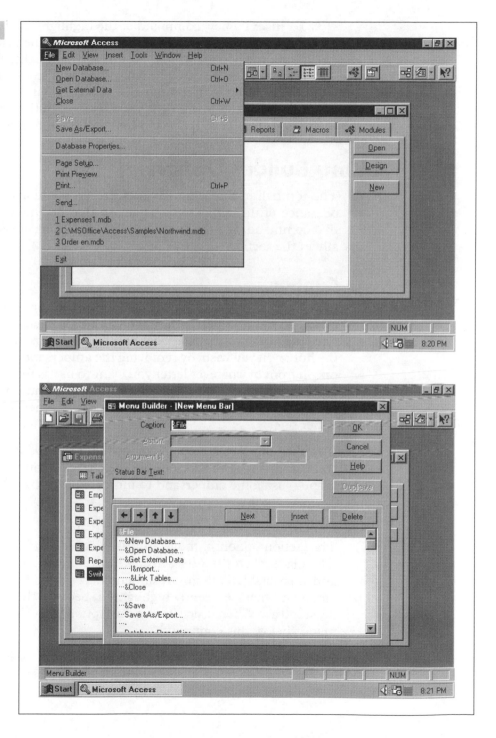

- **To insert** a new command at the highlighted position, click on the Insert button. The new command will be inserted directly above the command that is currently highlighted. Initially, a blank command appears. Optionally, click on the → (Indent) or ← (Outdent) button to determine the new command's level. Then define the command by filling in the Caption, Action, Argument(s), and Status Bar Text options in the upper half of the dialog box.

Menu Builder Options

The top half of the Menu Builder presents options for defining the appearance of the command, the action that occurs when the user selects that command, and the status bar text. We'll look at each option individually in the sections that follow.

Caption

The Caption box shows what will appear on the menu, with the hotkey preceded by an ampersand. When you're using a menu template, the caption and hotkey are already defined for each command. You can change the hotkey, if you wish, by removing the ampersand and then typing a new one in front of whatever letter you want to use as the hotkey. If you should accidentally repeat a hotkey within a single menu, that key will highlight the two potential commands one after the other, but it won't execute either one.

If you're not using a template, or if you inserted your own command, then you can just type in the command exactly as you want it to look on the menu—using the ampersand to indicate the hotkey.

Action

The Action option in the Menu Builder lets you define what action will take place when the user selects the command. That action is dimmed and unavailable if there are indented commands appearing below the command that's currently highlighted, because the action is already understood as "When users choose this option, show 'em any indented commands below this command."

Action is also dimmed and unavailable if the cursor is on a separator line, because the separator line is just for looks—you can't assign an action to it.

You can assign any one of the following three actions to the current menu command:

DoMenuItem   When the user selects the command, it will choose one of the options from the (invisible) built-in menus. (This is the default setting for commands you create from a menu template.)

RunCode   When the user selects the command, it will run a custom Access Basic procedure you've created.

RunMacro   When the user selects the command, it will run a macro you've created.

Argument(s)

The Argument(s) box lets you define the action: that is, which menu items will be selected, or which macro or procedure will run. If the action is DoMenuItem, you can click on the ... button and choose which menu bar, menu name, command, and (if appropriate) which subcommand will run. For example, in the following DoMenuItem Arguments dialog box, we've told the Menu Builder, "When the user picks the currently highlighted command, we want you to choose File ➤ New Database from Access's Form menu."

DoMenuItem Arguments	⊠
Menu Bar: `Form` ▾	OK
Menu Name: `File` ▾	Cancel
Command: `New Database...` ▾	
Subcommand: ` ` ▾	

If you choose RunMacro or RunCode, you'll need to type in the name of the macro or procedure you want to have the command run. If you're specifying a macro within a macro group, be sure to include the macro group name, followed by a period, and the name of the macro to run (for example, type **Orders.Close.**).

Status Bar Text

The Status Bar Text option lets you determine what appears in the status bar when the user highlights the menu command. Type a description of what the command will do, or instructions to the user, in plain English.

Saving a Custom Menu Bar

When you've finished defining all the commands and actions on your custom menu, follow these steps to save and name it:

1. Choose OK, then type in a name of your choosing. We suggest you include the word Menubar in whatever name you assign, so you can more easily identify the resulting macros later. For example, we named the custom menu bar for an Expenses application, generated using the Database Wizard, Expenses Menubar.

2. Choose OK.

Menu Macros

When you save your custom menu bar, the Menu Builder creates a macro for it, and a macro for each pull-down menu on that menu bar. You can see the names of those macros in the database window whenever the Macro object button is selected, as in the following example.

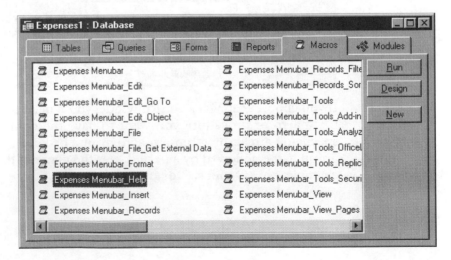

In that example, Expenses Menubar is the macro for the menu bar itself. Expenses MenuBar_Edit is our custom Edit menu, Expenses MenuBar_File is our custom File menu, and so forth. The next step, of course, is to get the custom menu to appear on the screen. As mentioned, you can have the macro appear *globally* (whenever your application is running) or just have it appear along with certain forms or reports. Or you can do both. The global menu will be visible at all times *except* when a custom menu that's attached to a form or report replaces it.

Displaying a Global Menu Bar

If you want your custom menu to replace the built-in menus as soon as the user starts your application, you need to set your application's MenuBar property to the name of your custom menu bar. To do that, open (or create) your AutoExec macro. Then add a SetValue action with the Item action argument set to Application.MenuBar. Then set the Expression action argument to the name of your custom menu bar, enclosed in quotation marks.

For example, in the Expenses application, we added the SetValue command shown below to the end of our AutoExec macro. When the user starts the Expenses application, the menu bar named Expenses MenuBar will instantly replace the built-in menu bar.

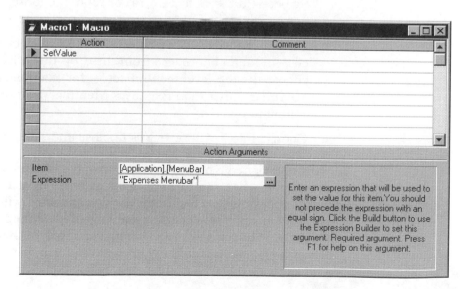

To test the new menu bar, first save the modified AutoExec macro. Then close the entire database, and reopen it. Your custom menu bar will appear exactly where the built-in menu bar normally appears.

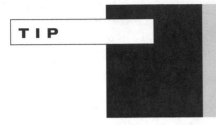

T I P If you have trouble returning to the normal built-in menus, close the database. Then hold down the Shift key, and reopen the database. Holding down the Shift key tells Access to ignore the Startup Properties; hence your custom menu won't appear.

Attaching a Custom Menu to a Form or Report

If you want a custom menu bar to appear whenever the user opens a particular form or previews a particular report, follow these steps:

1. Open, in design view, the form or report you want to attach the custom menu bar to.

2. Open the property sheet (View ➤ Properties), and select the form (choose Edit ➤ Select Form) or report (choose Edit ➤ Select Report). Select the Other tab in the property sheet.

3. Choose the Menu Bar property, and then select the name of your custom menu bar macro from the drop-down list. Be sure to choose the top-level menu macro—for example, choose Expenses Menubar rather than Expenses Menubar-Edit or any of the other submenu macros.

4. Choose File ➤ Close ➤ Yes to close and save the form or report.

If you've assigned a menu bar to a form, the menu bar you specified will appear only when the form is open in form view. If you've assigned a menu bar to a report, the menu bar you specified will appear only when the report is open in print preview. If you've defined a global menu bar for your application, the menu bar you attached to the form or report will replace the global menu bar whenever the form or report is open. When the user closes the form or report, the application's global menu will reappear.

Editing a Custom Menu Bar

If you need to change a custom menu bar that you've created:

1. Choose Tools ➤ Add-Ins ➤ Menu Builder.
2. Click on the name of the macro that contains your custom menu bar (for example, we would choose Expenses Menubar in the Expenses application), then choose Edit.

N O T E   The macro you open must contain only Access AddMenu actions. If you try to open a macro that contains more than that, Access will refuse to run the Menu Builder.

3. Make your changes using the same techniques you used to create the menu bar.
4. Choose OK when you're done.

Copying a Menu Bar

If you want to create several custom menu bars that are similar, though not exactly the same, your best bet will be to create one menu bar, make duplicates of it, and then edit the copies. Here's how:

1. Choose Tools ➤ Add-Ins ➤ Menu Builder.
2. Click on the name of the macro that contains the custom menu bar that you want to duplicate, then choose Edit.
3. Choose Duplicate and enter a name for the copy of this menu bar.
4. Choose OK.

The copied menu bar appears in the Menu Builder ready for editing. If you get confused about which menu bar is which, just look at the menu bar name in the title bar at the top of the Menu Builder dialog box.

Creating Shortcut Menus

A *shortcut menu* is a menu that appears when you right-click on an object. The object can be a control on a form or a report. It can also be the form or report itself. In fact, any object that contains a Shortcut Menu Bar or Shortcut Menu property on its property sheet can take a shortcut menu.

You can create either a global or a context-specific shortcut menu. The next two sections explain how. A prerequisite, however, is to have built a menu with the Menu Builder that can serve as the shortcut menu, or a group of macros that Access can use to build the menu.

Building a Global Shortcut Menu

To set a global shortcut menu, the one that displays when a form or object does not display its own shortcut menu, set the Shortcut Menu Bar property in the Startup dialog box (shown in Figure 24.3). To set this property, take these steps:

1. Select Tools ➤ Startup.

2. Use the Shortcut Menu Bar drop-down list box to select the shortcut menu you want to be global.

3. Choose the OK button.

Building a Contextual Shortcut Menu

To add a shortcut menu to a particular control on a form or to a form itself, follow these steps:

1. Open, in design view, the form you want to attach the custom menu bar to.

2. Select the object you want to display the menu, or select the entire form.

FIGURE 24.3

FIGURE 24.3

Creating a global
shortcut menu by
setting the Shortcut
Menu Bar property in
the Startup dialog box

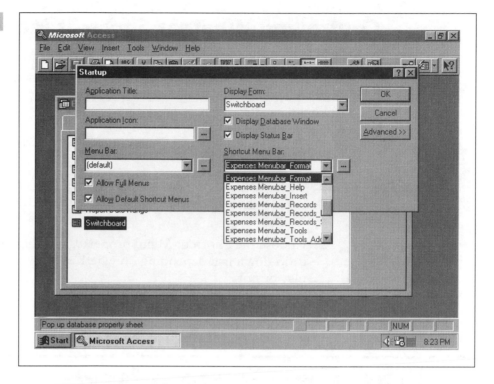

3. Open the property sheet (View ➤ Properties). Select the Other tab in the property sheet.

4. Choose the Shortcut Menu Bar property, and then select the name of your custom menu bar macro from the drop-down list.

5. Choose File ➤ Close ➤ Yes to close and save the form.

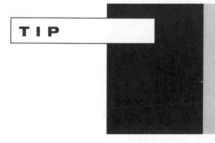

TIP

You can create a shortcut menu by specifying a macro group rather than a menu in the Shortcut Menu Bar property. In this case, Access builds the menu items from the macro names. You can also use the AddMenu action in your macros to add menu items other than those Access creates automatically.

Controlling Whether Shortcut Menus Appear

You determine whether a shortcut menu can appear for items on a form by setting the Shortcut Menu property for the form. To set this property, follow these steps:

1. Open, in design view, the form you want to display or not display shortcut menus.

2. Open the property sheet (View ➤ Properties), and select the form (choose Edit ➤ Select Form). Select the Other tab in the property sheet.

3. Choose the Shortcut Menu property, and then Yes or No from the drop-down list, depending on whether you want the menu to display or not.

4. Choose File ➤ Close ➤ Yes to close and save the form.

Where to Go from Here

Creating custom menus can make your databases function like a stand-alone application. So can the custom toolbars we discussed in Chapter 23. To begin building more complex applications, you need to use the more powerful programming features of Access for Windows 95. The next three chapters show you how to take advantage of Visual Basic for Applications, Access's new programming language.

What's New in the Access Zoo?

Custom menus can add a great deal of specialized functionality to your database applications. Access's menu capabilities give you some new options. These features include:

- Improved menu editing.
- The ability to create Windows 95-style context menus.
- Support for submenus.

PART FIVE

Refining a Custom Application

CHAPTER

25

Introducing Visual
Basic for Applications

JUST when you thought you had mastered everything there was to master about Access Basic and macro programming, Microsoft has changed the game. Access for Windows 95 scraps the old Access Basic engine and swaps in the Visual Basic for Applications engine. Why make this change? The main reason is that Visual Basic for Applications, now shared by Visual Basic 4.0, Excel 7.0, Project 4.5, and Access 95, offers you greater capabilities than Access Basic. If you want your database applications to be easy to maintain, highly portable, and exceptionally interoperable, you need to make the transition to VBA.

Why Use VBA?

Access provides you with macros that are easy to use and properties that can be set to run macros. A legitimate question is why you would need to program in Visual Basic at all. In Chapters 20 through 24, for example, we showed you how to accomplish lots of tasks with macros. Can't you do everything you need with a macro?

The answer to that question is both yes and no. Yes, many Access users will never have to go beyond macros to accomplish what they need to do. However, no, you can't do everything with macros. Macros have some bad habits that prevent them from being ideal for every purpose. In general, you should use macros under the following conditions:

- When your focus is simplicity. Macros provide an extremely visual programming style. You do not have to learn syntax. You simply select from among the options provided and the action you desire is programmed.

- When you want to create a toolbar or menu. Visual Basic does not provide an alternative way of creating these objects.

- When you want to undertake an action at the time the database opens using the AutoExec macro. In this circumstance, you must use the macro.

- When the built-in error messages from Access are insufficient in case of trouble.

You should use Visual Basic for Applications when you have these goals in mind:

- When your focus is ease of maintenance. Unlike macros, Visual Basic procedures can be a part of the forms or reports that contain them. When you copy a form or report from one database to another, all of the Visual Basic procedures stored with the object are copied with it.

- When Access does not provide a function that you need. If there is no built-in function to perform a calculation that you need done, you can write your own function in Visual Basic.

- When you want to respond to error messages creatively. Using Visual Basic, you can create your own error messages or take an action that corrects the error without user intervention.

- When you need to check the state of the system. Macros will allow you to run another application, but they don't provide access to system level information. You cannot check, for instance, whether a file exists using a macro. Visual Basic, however, allows you access to system level information and actions.

- When you need to work with records one at a time. Macros perform actions on sets of records. Visual Basic allows you to step through records and perform actions on each single record while it is in focus.

- When you need to pass arguments between procedures. You can set the initial arguments for macros, but you can't change them while the macro runs. You can make such changes, or use variables for arguments, using Visual Basic.

What Is the Shape of Visual Basic?

So where does Visual Basic for Applications hide within the overall structure of Access? How do you use all of its wonderful features? To find Visual Basic, you need only look behind the Code button on the Form Design or Report Design toolbar. Clicking on this button opens the code window for the form or report in focus (see Figure 25.1). Using this window, you write your custom procedures and functions.

The code that you insert into a form or report applies only to that form or report, or the objects contained within it. While you can call these procedures from any other procedure included in your database, the code still applies only to the form or report and the objects contained therein. For code that needs to be accessible to any object in your database, create a module using the New button on the Modules tab in the database window. Place your global procedures and functions in this code window.

FIGURE 25.1

The code window for the Contacts form in the Contact Management database generated by the Database Wizard, where you write Visual Basic procedures for the form

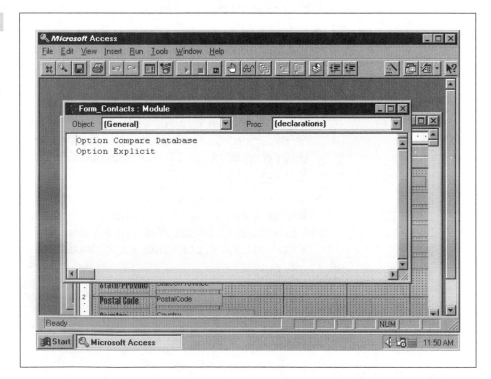

Visual Basic and Objects

Visual Basic is an object-oriented programming environment. An *object* has a set of procedures and data associated with it. Some objects also have a visual representation, though others are available only in Visual Basic code. A good example of an object is a form. You draw the form on the screen. There are a set of procedures associated with the form. And there is data that is displayed in the form.

Given this definition, reports are also objects, as are any of the controls that you use to build both forms and reports. (Technically, tables and queries can also be considered objects.) Each object has associated with it *properties,* which govern the appearance and behavior of the object. Each object also has a set of *methods* defined for it, which are actions the object can take. Some objects, including forms, reports and controls, also respond to a set of *events.*

You are already familiar with properties for objects. They are the same properties that you have been setting for forms, reports, and controls as you have worked with databases throughout this book. Methods should also be familiar, since you have used the methods (such as Recalc, Go-ToPage, and SetFocus) associated with forms. Events are very similar to event properties, into which you could insert a macro, except you can write code that responds to each event instead of relying on predefined macro actions.

Visual Basic and Events

Visual Basic uses event procedures to respond to events. By default, VBA never does anything when an event occurs. If you want an object to respond to an event, say a button click or the activation of a form, you have to write the code for the procedure. Your code overrides the default action, allowing the action you define to take place in response to the event.

Each object defines the events to which it responds. If you look in the code window for the Calls form in the Contact Management database, you can get a sense of how these events are made available to you as the database developer (see Figure 25.2). The form contains several objects. The Object drop-down list box in the upper-left corner of the window lists all the objects associated with the form. The (General) object represents code that affects all the objects in the list. Each object, including the form itself, is designated by a name, which is one of an object's properties.

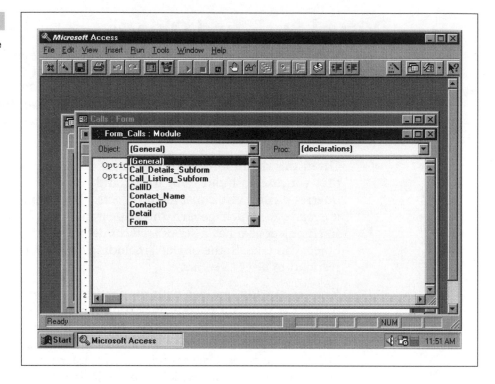

FIGURE 25.2

The list of objects in the code window for the Calls form in the Contact Management database

The Proc drop-down list box in the upper-right corner of the code window lists all of the events to which an object responds, as shown in Figure 25.3. Each event is given a descriptive name, such as Click. When you select an event from the list, the code window displays the frame of the event procedure, consisting of a **Private Sub Calls_Event (Arguments)** statement and an **End Sub** statement. These two statements are required to frame the code responding to the event. They frame the block of code known as an *event procedure*, the set of statements that causes an action in response to an event.

Visual Basic and Statements

In order to build an event procedure, you have to use Visual Basic statements and functions. If you are not familiar with programming, you may feel overwhelmed by the number of statements available to you. Visual Basic provides flow control statements, like **If ... Then ... Else ...** , which govern the order in which other statements execute. (The two statements that frame an event procedure are in fact flow control statements.) VBA

FIGURE 25.3

The Proc list and the event procedure for the Click event associated with the Calls object on the Contacts form

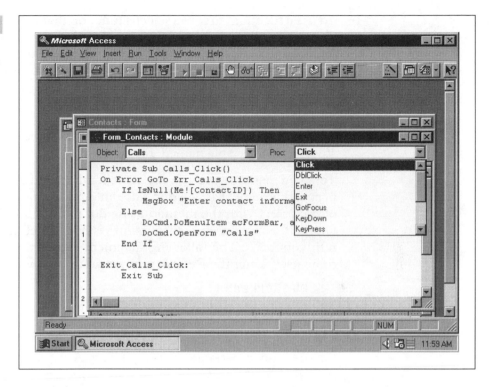

also provides statements which cause an action to take place, like **Beep** (which causes the system to send a beep to the speaker) or **ChDir** (which changes the current folder or directory). In total, 81 such statements are used in VBA. (Help contains a complete reference for them.)

TIP The next chapter covers flow control in more detail.

In addition, you can write statements that set an object property, assign a value to a variable, use a function, or use a method. To assign a value to an object property, you write a statement in the following form:

```
Set Object.Property = Value
```

To assign a value to a variable, you use a statement of this form:

```
Set Variable = Value
```

To use a function, first you select a function that calculates something that you need calculated or takes an action that you need taken. Typically, functions return the value they calculate or a code indicating success for your program to use. As a result, you often assign the value of a function to a variable for future use, as in the following:

```
Today = Date()
```

This statement uses the Date function to collect the system date and stores it in a variable named Today.

To use a method, you use the same kind of syntax that you use to set a property, except that you don't use an equal sign. You combine the name of the object with the method using dot notation to form the statement. One of the most useful object names is Me, which names the object currently in focus. The following statement causes the current object to redraw itself using the Refresh method associated with it:

```
Me.Refresh
```

Visual Basic and Variables

We mentioned variables just in passing. A *variable* is a name you give to Access. Access sets up an area of memory for storing items and gives it that name. A variable is said to have a *type*, which describes the nature of the item that can be stored in it. By default, Visual Basic creates variables of the *variant* type, which means that anything can be stored in it. To create a variable name, you simply use it. Or you can explicitly name it in a statement called a declaration at the beginning of your procedure, like this:

```
Dim strDialStr As String
```

This statement says to create, or "dimension" (hence the Dim statement), a variable named strDialStr as type String. StrDialStr can therefore contain only strings of characters. Attempting to assign data of some other type to it will cause an error. Visual Basic supports the following variable types:

- **Integer** Whole numbers between −32,768 and 32,768
- **Long** Whole numbers between −2,147,483,648 and 2,147,483,647
- **String** Text up to approximately 65,500 characters in length

- **Currency**   Numbers with up to four decimal places between −955,337,203,685.5808 and 955,337,203,685.5807

- **Single**   Real numbers in the range $\pm 1.40 \times 10^{-45}$ to $\pm 3.40 \times 10^{38}$

- **Double**   Real numbers in the range $\pm 4.94 \times 10^{-324}$ to $\pm 1.79 \times 10^{308}$

- **Variant**   Can contain any of the preceding data types

When you name a variable, you should include the first three letters of its type in its name, as shown above. The reason for including the type in the name is that you can always tell what can be stored in a variable by looking at its name. Late at night on a long project, or coming back to maintain code after two months away from it, you will appreciate this convention.

N O T E   To make a variable available to all procedures and functions in your application, place it in a global code module and precede it with the keyword Public.

Visual Basic and Procedures

Event procedures are not the only procedures you can write in Visual Basic. You can also write a procedure as a part of a global code module or at the General level of any form or report, and you can call that procedure any time you need to perform the action undertaken by the procedure. The Contact Management database uses this type of procedure to handle the button clicks in the switchboard. At the General level in the Switchboard form is the procedure HandleButtonClick. This procedure receives the button number as its argument and takes action based on the button number received. One function can therefore service several buttons. The OnClick property of each button is set equal to the name of this procedure. When a click takes place, the procedure is called to perform its task.

There are two things to remember about event procedures. First, event procedures cannot return values for the rest of the program to use. You cannot set a variable equal to the value of the event procedure. Second, when a procedure is a part of a form or report, it has reference only to that form or report. Place your procedures in global code modules if you want to be able to use them anywhere in your database application and precede them with the keyword **Public** rather than **Private**.

Visual Basic and Functions

Functions are procedures that return a value for use by other statements in the program. The return value is set using the function name as a variable, as shown in the following function generated by the Database Wizard for the Contact Management database:

```
Function IsLoaded(ByVal strFormName As String) As
Integer
' Returns True if the specified form is open in
  Form view
' or Datasheet view.

    Const conObjStateClosed = 0
    Const conDesignView = 0

    If SysCmd(acSysCmdGetObjectState, acForm,
      strFormName) <> conObjStateClosed Then
      If Forms(strFormName).CurrentView <>
        conDesignView _
          Then
          IsLoaded = True  ' Set the return value
                           ' using
                           ' the function name as a
                           ' variable.
      End If
    End If

    End Function
```

Don't worry about the statements that seem like Greek in this function right now. Wait till you have some experience with Visual Basic before you try to start interpreting them. The main thing to remember about building a function is to set the return value and to use the **Function** and **End Function** statements to frame it.

N O T E Both functions and subs can take *arguments*, variables whose values are made available to the function for use. These variables are named in the parentheses following the function or subroutine name. When you name them, you use the As keyword to name their type, just as you do when declaring a variable. If you do not want the function or procedure to modify the value stored in the variable, precede the name of the variable with ByVal.

Building a Sample Procedure

Speaking of getting some experience with Visual Basic, here's your chance. In this section, we build a real VBA procedure! While this procedure will be simple, it will give you the basics. The next two chapters undertake some more complex actions. (Remember, we've got three chapters to get you started programming with a language that you can write whole books about. Be patient, give yourself some time, and study the Help files and sample code. You'll be an expert in no time!)

Having read the preceding sections, you have enough background to understand how a procedure is built. We have a surprise for you about how Access builds procedures. In many cases, you don't have a great deal of code to write—because a Wizard writes it for you. (Convenient, no?) As an example, we are going to add a command button that prints a copy of the data entry form we built for the database used by our client who runs a nonprofit corporation. You can practice on any database form that you want. Visual Basic works the same no matter what form you use.

To add the button, take these steps:

1. Open the form in design view.
2. Make sure the Control Wizards button is "in."
3. On the toolbox, select the button that draws the command button.
4. Drag with your mouse to draw the button on the form.

5. In a few minutes, the Command Button Wizard appears (see Figure 25.4). Select the class of action you want to take in the Categories list. Since we want to print a form, select Form Operations. Select the specific action in the Actions list, in this case, Print Current Form. Click on the <u>N</u>ext button.

6. Select whether you want a picture or text to appear on the button face using the option buttons provided. If you choose text, enter the text as you want it to appear. If you choose a picture, you can use the browse button to select a graphic. Click on the Next button.

7. Enter a meaningful name for your button in the text box on the last Wizard page. Make the name a mnemonic for the button's function. Then click on the <u>F</u>inish button.

When the Wizard finishes, it has built the click event procedure for you. You can see the procedure by right-clicking on the button and selecting

FIGURE 25.4

The first page of the Command Button Wizard allows you to select the type of action the event procedure performs.

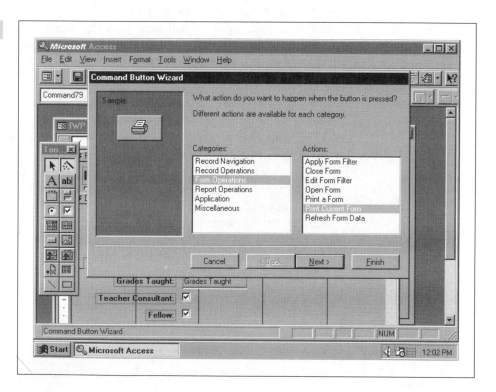

Build Event from the menu that appears. The procedure created appears below:

```
Sub PrintButton_Click()
On Error GoTo Err_PrintButton_Click
    DoCmd.PrintOut
Exit_PrintButton_Click:
    Exit Sub
Err_PrintButton_Click:
    MsgBox Err.Description
    Resume Exit_PrintButton_Click
End Sub
```

Congratulations! You've just programmed your first procedure, and using excellent programming form, we might add. This procedure is very straightforward. The first statement turns on error handling (more about that in the next chapter). The second statement uses the PrintOut method of the DoCmd object to print the form. (The DoCmd object contains all the actions you can invoke using macros.) The next program line is a *label*, which is a string of text that carries out no action but can serve as a jump destination. Labels end in colons. The line following the colon causes the procedure to end. The remaining three lines are a label and error handling code. (Again, more about that in the next chapter.)

The greatest thing about writing procedures for common objects in Access is that you have a Wizard for each one. You do not have to be an expert programmer to get lots of work done in Visual Basic.

Converting Macros to Visual Basic

If you want, you can convert macros you already have written into Visual Basic code. To convert macros associated with a form or report, open the object in design view and select Convert Macros to Visual Basic from the Macros submenu on the Tools menu.

To convert global macros, click on the Macros tab in the Database dialog box. Then click on the macro you want to convert. Open the File menu, select Save As/Export, and click on the Save As Visual Basic Module option button in the Save As dialog box. Then click on the OK button.

Learning More about Visual Basic for Applications

 ➤ Visual Basic for Applications is obviously a large topic, one that we can only begin to discuss as a part of a book on Access in general. To find more information about how to exploit the features of Visual Basic, take a look at these sources:

- The topic *Writing Visual Basic Code in the Module Window* in the Access Help file. This is the basic primer on using Visual Basic in Access applications.

- Any of the excellent books available on using Visual Basic for Applications in Access, including the *Microsoft Access 95 Developer's Handbook* from Sybex.

- The Visual Basic documentation that comes as a part of the Microsoft Developer Network CD-ROM product. All the latest documentation on Visual Basic comes on this CD every quarter.

- The code that the Database Wizard generates whenever it creates a database of a specific type. You can learn a lot about how Microsoft programmers use Visual Basic by studying these examples.

- Two magazines, the *Visual Basic Programmer's Journal* and the *VB Tech Journal*, both of which bring you monthly discussions of how to use Visual Basic to accomplish specific tasks.

- The *Access/Visual Basic Advisor*, a newsletter from Advisor Publications, or Pinnacle Publication's *Smart Access* and *Visual Basic Developer*.

Where to Go from Here

Having introduced you to Visual Basic in this chapter, we show you in the next two chapters how to do some interesting work with this programming language. Chapter 26 shows you how to create your own error messages, and Chapter 27 shows you how to use OLE Automation to control other programs.

What's New in the Access Zoo?

You've just taken a look at the major new feature of Access for Windows 95, Visual Basic for Applications. The most exciting features of this addition to the Access environment are the following:

- The ability to write database programs using a full-featured programming language.

- The ability to leverage objects provided by Access and other programs in writing your own code.

- The ability to attach your code directly to your database objects.

- The ability to make a suite of applications work in concert with your database to perform complex tasks.

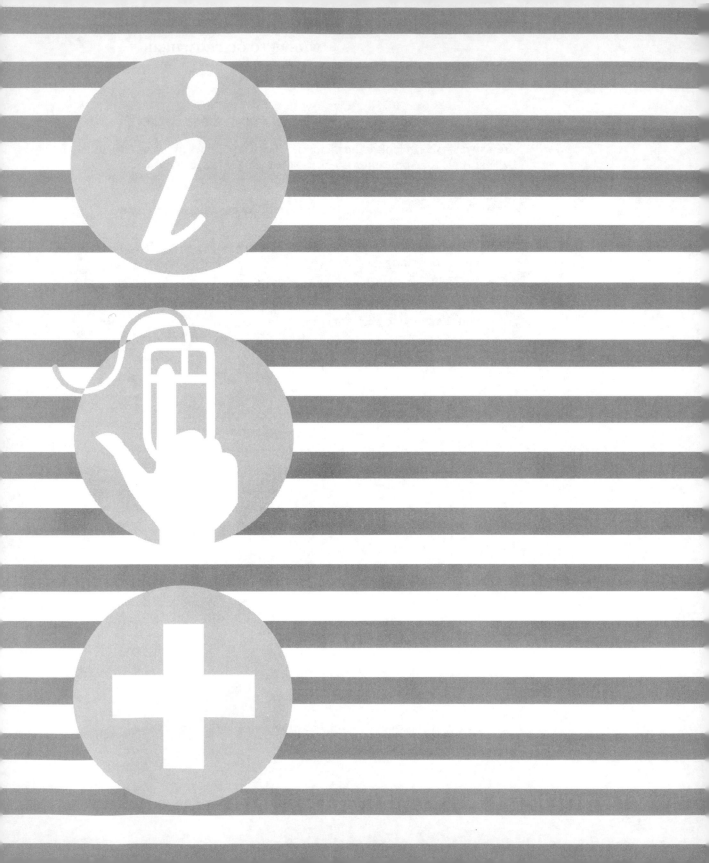

CHAPTER

26

Creating Custom Error Messages

EVEN the best planned application occasionally screws up. When that happens in Access, an error is generated. You have two options in handling errors: let Access and Visual Basic do it for you, or respond to the errors yourself. The first option is *very* convenient. You don't have to do anything. However, the result of an error is that your application stops executing. The user is presented with a dialog box and whatever was happening stops. While the default error handling is convenient for you, it is rather rude for users of your application.

The second option, handling errors yourself, is less convenient for you, but makes your application much more user friendly. When you respond to the errors, instead of the cryptic error descriptions provided by Access, you can interpret the error for your user and provide a suggestion about what to do. In many cases, you do not even have to inform the user that an error has occurred. You write code to correct the situation and restart the execution of your code.

This chapter teaches you how to handle errors yourself, and in the process shows you a couple of ways to go beyond the Wizard-written code that you learned how to create in the last chapter. To learn how to handle errors, you need to learn about flow control in Visual Basic programs. But first, we need to focus on the two ways to create custom error messages in an Access application, one for macros and one for Visual Basic.

WARNING

There is one time when error trapping is absolutely necessary: when you use the Access Developer's Toolkit (ADT) to create a "run-time" version of your application. In this case, any untrapped error causes your application to quit completely.

Building Custom Error Messages with a Macro

When you are using macros, you can create a custom error message using the MsgBox action. To do so, create a new macro by clicking on the New button in the Macros tab of the database window. On the macro sheet, select MsgBox as the action and fill in the properties. Figure 26.1 shows a completed error macro.

When you fill in the arguments, you can create a formatted message in the Message box using the @ character. Format your message in the following way:

```
Data Entry Form@This form does not support double-
clicking. @Use the buttons at the bottom of the form
to scroll to the record you want.
```

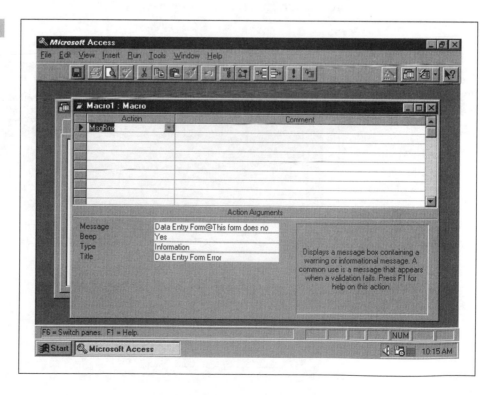

The first third of the message, to the left of the first @ symbol, appears in boldface at the top of the message box window. The second third of the message, between the two @ symbols, appears just below. Access supplies the word **Solution** in boldface, and the remainder of your message appears below this word, as shown in Figure 26.2.

The remaining arguments for the MsgBox action govern additional features of the message box. The Beep argument determines whether a warning beep is played when the message box appears. The Type argument determines which icon is displayed in the message box, either Information (as in the example in Figure 26.2) or Critical, Warning?, Warning!, or none. The Title argument contains the text string displayed in the title bar of the message box window.

To display such a custom error message, you assign the macro to an appropriate event argument of the object to which it refers. In the case of a data entry form, we would assign this macro to the On Dbl Click event property for each object on the form. If your custom error message were intended to respond to an error generated by Access, you would assign it to the On Error event property.

FIGURE 26.2

A custom message displayed using the MsgBox action

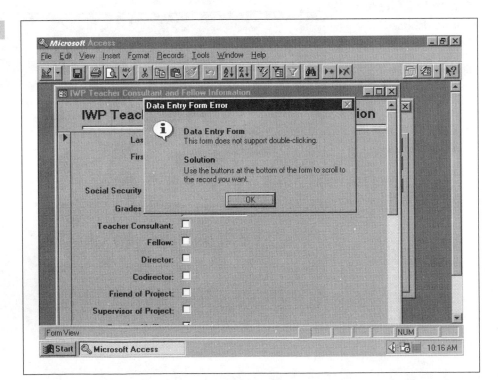

Building Custom Error Messages in Visual Basic

To create a custom error message in Visual Basic for Applications, you need to learn a little more about VBA programming. You need to learn how the flow of execution is controlled in a Visual Basic program, and you need to learn how to handle the flow of execution when an error occurs.

Flow Control in Visual Basic

Typically, Visual Basic executes a procedure by either copying the arguments into the variables made available to the procedure or (for **ByVal** arguments) giving the function access to the variable named in the argument. After arguments are made available, Visual Basic starts at the first statement in the procedure and executes each statement in line until it reaches the **End Sub** or **End Function** statement. If an error occurs, Visual Basic stops executing the code and displays an error message. It does not resume executing the code after the user dismisses the error message from the screen.

You can change the order in which statements are executed in three ways. For our purposes in explaining error handling, we will refer to these as using flow control statements and invoking flow control on error.

Flow Control Statements

To build effective custom error handling in Visual Basic procedures, you have to know how to control the flow of execution. The reason you have to know is that you might want to respond to several possible types of errors. We'll show you how as this section progresses.

N O T E   You can use flow control anywhere in your program. We are discussing it in relationship to errors because, given the way Access builds code for you, you are most likely to use flow control in building your own error handlers.

Conditionals Probably the most common way of controlling the flow of execution is a conditional statement. You set up a condition using an **If** statement. If the condition is true (and all conditions must evaluate to either true or false logically), you execute the statement following the **Then** statement. If the condition is false, you execute the statement following the **Else** statement. You can express alternate conditions using an **ElseIf** statement. The whole conditional ends with an **EndIf** statement. Such a block of code looks like the following:

```
If ErrorNumber = 10 Then
    ' Code lines that execute if the ErrorNumber
    ' equals 10 go here.
ElseIf ErrorNumber = 100 Then
    ' Code lines that execute if the ErrorNumber
    ' equals 100 go here.
Else
    ' Code lines that execute if the ErrorNumber
    ' is equal to some other value go here.
End If
```

Loops Loops allow you to repeat a set of statements over and over again. In handling errors, you will find loops most useful when you are correcting an error condition. For example, in response to a *File Not Found* error, you might want to loop through the list of controls on a form to make certain that those used to represent the file name have valid values. When you find the control that needs correction, you could prompt the user to enter a valid value.

You have four different ways of looping available to you. A **Do** loop executes the statements that appear between the **Do** statement and the **Loop** statement until a condition, expressed in either the **Do** or **Loop** lines, is false or while a condition is true. (You determine whether the loop executes until or while by using the **While** or **Until** keywords.) You can exit such a loop at any time by using an **Exit Do** statement. Such loops look like the following:

```
Counter = 0
Do While Counter < Me.Controls.Count
    If Me.Controls(Counter).Text = "" Or
IsNull(Me.Controls(Counter).Text) Then
        Me.Controls(Counter).Text = InputBox("Enter _
        a proper filename")
```

```
        End If
        Counter = Counter + 1
    Loop
```

This example assumes that a form has several text controls on it, each holding a file name. The user has asked Access to open the files, and one of the controls is blank. An error occurs, and to handle it, you choose to check the text of each box to make certain none of them are blank. (You might also check for invalid characters as well.) Every form has associated with it a collection of controls. **Me** is an Access keyword referring to the form which the code is directly attached to. You can access each control using the notation shown. The collection is named Controls, and each control can be identified by an index number. By using the variable Counter, you can start at the first control in the collection (Control(0)), and repeat the action for each control until the last one on the form (Control(9)). If we encounter a blank control, we use an **InputBox** statement, which displays the text in the argument and a text box in a dialog box, collects input from the user, and returns the text to be stored in the variable Me.Controls(Counter).Text, which is also the text property of the control. If you wanted to exit the loop when you found the first blank text control, you would place an **Exit Do** statement immediately before the **End If** statement.

TIP You could accomplish the same task using the statement Do Until Counter = 10. The expression can also be placed on the last line, as in Loop Until Counter = 10.

You could accomplish the same error handling task using a counted loop. These loops begin with the keyword **For** and execute a fixed number of iterations named in the first line. These loops have the following form:

```
    For Counter = 0 To 9
        If Me.Controls(Counter).Text = "" Then
          Me.Controls(Counter).Text = InputBox("Enter _
          a proper filename")
        End If
    Next Counter
```

In **For** loops, the counter is incremented for you automatically. In this case, it starts at the value 0 and increments to 9 automatically. The **Next** statement marks the end of the loop code. While the name of the counter variable is optional on the last line, it's a good idea to use it. If you have loops within loops, you can tell which **Next** goes with which **For**.

Visual Basic provides you with a loop to use with collections of objects that simplifies the task of looping. These loops have the following form:

```
For Each Control In Me
    If Control.Text = "" Or IsNull(Control.Text)
      Then
         Controls.Text = InputBox("Enter _
         a proper filename")
      End If
Next
```

This form of the **For** loop allows you to avoid having to manage a counter. What if you aren't sure how many controls are on the form denoted by **Me**? Access knows, and this loop simply makes use of Access's internal count to increment a counter that is hidden from you.

> **TIP**
>
> You can exit a For loop at any point by using the Exit For statement.

The last type of loop executes a set of statements while a condition remains true. It has this form:

```
Counter = 0
While Counter < 10
    If Me.Controls(Counter).Text = "" Or
IsNull(Me.Controls(Counter).Text) Then
        Me.Controls(Counter).Text = InputBox("Enter _
        a proper filename")
      End If
      Counter = Counter + 1
Wend
```

This form of loop is very like a **Do** loop with some simplification of form. It is bounded by **While** and **Wend** statements, and once again you must increment your own counter.

N O T E

To learn more about any statement used in Visual Basic, load the Visual Basic Reference Help file from your Access disks or CD. You may need to use Add/Remove Programs to do so, because this file is not included as part of a Typical install. Once it is installed, it appears in the list of Access help topics.

Branches Branches are critical to error handling code, as you will see in the next section. Understanding them is therefore essential to learning how to make Visual Basic handle errors elegantly.

The concept of branching goes back to the days when each line in your program was numbered. If you knew the flow of execution had to skip from one line to another distant line, you could use a **GoTo** statement to jump to the appropriate line number.

While you can still use line numbers in Visual Basic, the practice is not recommended. (Eventually you have to renumber all the lines because of additions or changes to the program, and then all your line-number-based jumps have to be adjusted by hand.) Instead, you jump to labels, which are strings of text used as bookmarks in the code. A label is any string of text ending in a colon. Visual Basic keeps track of where they are, and can move to them when you use a **GoTo** statement to request a jump.

The **GoTo** statement has the following form:

```
GoTo Label
```

And the label would appear in your program code in a line as the following:

```
Label:
```

When Visual Basic encounters the **GoTo** statement, it moves to the text string Label: and resumes execution with the first line following.

A variant of the **GoTo** statement allows you to return the flow of execution to the line after the statement that caused the jump to take place. The variant form looks like this:

```
GoSub Label
'Other program lines go here
```

```
Label:
     If Me.Controls(Counter).Text = "" Then
        Me.Controls(Counter).Text = InputBox("Enter _
        a proper filename")
     End If
Return
```

The **GoSub** statement works exactly like **GoTo** in that the jump occurs to the text string **Label:** and the **If** statement is executed. However, when Visual Basic encounters the **Return** statement, execution returns to the line following the **GoSub** statement. You can jump out, execute some code, and return to where you were.

Another variation of both these statements begins with the keyword **On**, as in the following lines:

```
On ErrorCode GoTo Label1, Label2, Label3
On ErrorCode GoSub Label1, Label2, Label3
```

In each of these statements, ErrorCode can be a variable or an expression that evaluates to a value ranging from 0 to 255. If the value is 0, execution resumes with the next statement. If the value is 1, execution jumps to Label1. If the value is 2, control jumps to Label2. If the value exceeds the number of items on the list of labels, execution resumes with the next statement. If the value is negative or greater than 255, an error occurs. These variations are just ways to have a single jump statement branch to several labels.

NOTE

You must remember that Visual Basic ignores a label when it encounters one in the normal flow of execution. As a result, if you have several labels at the end of a procedure for handling errors, you need to have a means of stopping your program before it gets to those labels in the event no error occurred. We'll show you how in the next section.

The most effective branching statement, however, is the **Select Case** statement. It allows multiple branches, and it allows you to respond to discontinuous values of an expression or variable. As a result, you can collect an error number (patience, that information is coming!) and branch to the statements that handle the error appropriately. You can even specify what to do in case there is no match for the values you specify. The **Select Case** statement looks like this:

```
Select Case ErrorNumber  'Evaluating the error number
Case 1, 2, 3  'Error numbers 1 through 3
    Debug.Print "I have mapped these error numbers
        to the same message"
Case 5 To 8  'Error numbers 5, 6,  7, and 8
    Debug.Print "Error numbers 5, 6, 7, and 8
        receive this message through Debug.Print"
Case Is > 8 And ErrorNumber < 20 'Error numbers
    between 8 and 11
    Debug.Print "I have demonstrated how to trap
        error numbers within a range, specifically
        between 8 and 20"
Case Else  'What to do when there is no match
    Debug.Print "All other error numbers get this
        message"
End Select
```

This example shows that you can use various expressions to form the matching statements. Each **Case** statement represents one possible match. The **Case Else** statement marks the code that will execute if no match is found. When a **Case** or **Case Else** statement executes, the code lines following it execute, and the flow of execution jumps to the statement following the **End Select** statement.

Flow Control On Error

We're sure that seems like a lot about flow control, but error handling in Visual Basic depends on flow control. You use an **On Error** statement to determine the flow control when an error occurs. If you don't have an **On Error** statement in your procedure, execution stops when an error occurs. If you want the opportunity for your user to be able to correct the error, or if you want execution to continue at all for any reason, you need to use one of these three variations of the statement:

- **On Error GoTo Label** This version causes control to jump to the specified label when an error occurs. At the end of the error handler at that label, a **Resume** statement causes execution to resume with the line after the one that caused the error.

- **On Error Resume Next** This version causes the error to be ignored and execution to continue normally.

- **On Error GoTo O**   This version causes the current error handling to be canceled. You can then use another form of **On Error** to redirect flow control in a different way.

It's time to look again at the click event procedure you created for the print button in the last chapter. Here is the procedure:

```
Sub PrintButton_Click()
On Error GoTo Err_PrintButton_Click
    DoCmd.PrintOut
Exit_PrintButton_Click:
    Exit Sub
Err_PrintButton_Click:
    MsgBox Err.Description
    Resume Exit_PrintButton_Click
End Sub
```

Notice the **On Error** statement at the beginning of the procedure. When an error occurs anywhere in the procedure, it redirects execution to the label Err_PrintButton_Click. This label leads to code that handles the error. The **Resume** statement includes the label Exit_PrintButton_Click as an argument, which causes the resumption of execution at that label. The first statement following this label causes the event procedure to exit.

Notice the logic of building the procedure. If no error occurs, the statements execute sequentially until the **Exit Sub** statement causes the procedure to end. If an error occurs, execution jumps beyond the **Exit Sub** statement to the error handling code. After the errors are handled, execution jumps back to the **Exit Sub** statement. This procedure provides an excellent template for developing error handling routines.

You might recognize the MsgBox function in the error handling code and guess that it performs the same function as the macro of the same name. It does. But what is that Err.Description argument? Visual Basic provides an Err object. When an error occurs, it makes the Err object, with its properties and methods, available to you. The Description property is the text string that describes the error. The MsgBox function builds a message box that announces that an error of this type has occurred.

The Err object also has a Number property. This property can be used with branching statements to allow you to handle any of several errors that might occur in your procedure. (The **Select Case** statement is especially useful for this purpose.)

➤ For more information about the Err object, search Help for *Err*.

Building the Error Message

So, having been drilled in the basics of Visual Basic error handling, you might have guessed already how to provide a custom message to your users: Use the MsgBox function and use your own text string rather than the one stored in Err.Description. Congratulations! You've mastered some of the mysteries of Visual Basic coding.

You might wonder why we say *MsgBox function* rather than *MsgBox statement*. The reason is that MsgBox returns a value. It has some subtleties, therefore, that you should know about.

First, MsgBox has three critical arguments, which must occur in the order specified. (Although you can omit the Buttons and Title arguments, you will almost always wish to supply them, since they provide information to your users.):

- **Prompt**   The text string to display as the message.
- **Buttons**   A number that determines which buttons are displayed in the message box. These numbers are represented by constant expressions maintained by Visual Basic for your use. As a result, you should use the constant names, as shown here.
- **Title**   The text string to display in the title bar of the message box.

You can use the @ symbol to format the message string exactly as you do when you use the MsgBox macro to display a custom message.

TIP   If you want to learn more about the arguments for MsgBox, search the Help file for the function name.

The Buttons argument can take the following values:

- **vbOKOnly**   Show OK button only.
- **vbOKCancel**   Show OK and Cancel buttons.
- **vbAbortRetryIgnore**   Show Abort, Retry, and Ignore buttons.

- **vbYesNoCancel**   Show Yes, No, and Cancel buttons.
- **vbYesNo**   Show Yes and No buttons.
- **vbRetryCancel**   Show Retry and Cancel buttons.
- **vbCritical**   Show Critical Message icon.
- **vbQuestion**   Show Warning Query icon.
- **vbExclamation**   Show Warning Message icon.
- **vbInformation**   Show Information Message icon.
- **vbDefaultButton1**   First button is default.
- **vbDefaultButton2**   Second button is default.
- **vbDefaultButton3**   Third button is default.
- **vbApplicationModal**   Only the Access application is suspended until the user responds to the message box.
- **vbSystemModal**   Suspend all applications until the user responds.

To combine any of these attributes to determine what is displayed and how, simply add these constants together using the plus sign.

The following code fragment shows how to build the same custom message that you built using the macro earlier in this chapter:

```
strMsg = "This form does not support " _
& "double-clicking.@Use the buttons at the bottom of "
& "the form to scroll to the record you want."
intResult = MsgBox (strMsg, vbOkOnly +
    vbInformation, "Data Entry Form")
```

The variable intResult collects the return value of the function, which allows you to determine which button in the message box the user clicked on. The possible return values are the following:

- **vbOK**   OK button clicked
- **vbCancel**   Cancel button clicked
- **vbAbort**   Abort button clicked
- **vbRetry**   Retry button clicked
- **vbIgnore**   Ignore button clicked

- **vbYes**   Yes button clicked
- **vbNo**   No button clicked

Obviously, you can use flow control statements to test the return value and take appropriate action in response to the user's click.

Where to Go from Here

Now that you have a grasp of flow control and error handling, we would like to use the next chapter to introduce you to controlling other applications from inside your Access application. This is a slick trick, so be prepared to see some real magic.

What's New in the Access Zoo?

Microsoft Access for Windows 95 provides new features for creating your own error messages. You gain the following capabilities:

- The use of Visual Basic On Error statements.
- The use of Visual Basic flow control statements to correct error conditions.

CHAPTER

27

Interacting with
Other Programs

ONE of the greatest features of Access for Windows 95 is its support for OLE automation, a technology that allows you to control other programs from within your database applications. To make use of this feature, you need to be able to program in Visual Basic for Applications code. You also need to be aware of some quirks associated with OLE objects and their automation. In this chapter, we will explain those quirks and provide you with a basic template for using automation in your own applications.

What Is OLE Automation?

OLE automation is a way of treating any application on your system as an object that belongs to Access. Imagine being able to treat Word or Excel as though they behaved exactly like a command button that you draw on a form. You could carry out any command in either application using the *object.method* notation. And you would have access to every command. You could reliably start the application from within an Access application, and direct the application to do exactly what you wanted it to do.

OLE automation allows you this kind of flexibility, but there are a couple of hitches:

- The application you want to control has to be an OLE automation server. In other words, it has to be designed to allow itself to be automated.

- When you automate an object, you get access only to the commands to which the designers allow you access. The set of commands available may change depending on whether the data object you intend to use is embedded in your database. An embedded Word document, for instance, does not allow you to use the Save <u>A</u>s command to save a copy of the data under a different file name.

- You have to know something about the command structure of the program you are automating. In automating Word, for example, you have to use WordBasic commands. Even when you automate a program such as Excel, which shares Visual Basic for Applications with Access, there are program-specific extensions to Visual Basic that you have to master.

You can work your way around most of the limitations you might encounter. Quite obviously, you would not try to automate a program that cannot be automated. And there are workarounds for limited functionality. In Word, for example, you can select the entire document, copy it to the Clipboard, open a new document, and save that document using a new file name. Lastly, Access provides an object browser to allow you to see the automation objects available and the methods you can use. You will see both workarounds and the object browser in use in this chapter.

Creating the Basic Object

To use automation, first you have to make an object out of the application you intend to automate. In this example, we will automate the creation of an Excel worksheet. You must do two things as preliminaries to prepare to automate this action. First, you must create an Excel template for the worksheet. Assume that the members of our nonprofit corporation, whose database you have seen from time to time in examples, want to build an Excel worksheet to track the fees their educational consultants earn. Open Excel, create a worksheet containing the boiler-plate text, and save it as a template using <u>F</u>ile ➤ Save <u>A</u>s. (Be sure to set the Save as <u>T</u>ype to Template.) A simple worksheet of this sort is shown in Figure 27.1.

The second step is to open the data entry form for the database in design view and to add a button to the form. When you draw the button, select Application and Run MS Excel in the Wizard, as shown in Figure 27.2. Name the button AutomateExcel and finish the Wizard. You won't be using the actual code generated, but the Wizard will generate a useful event procedure template for you.

FIGURE 27.1

A sample Excel template for tracking consultant fees

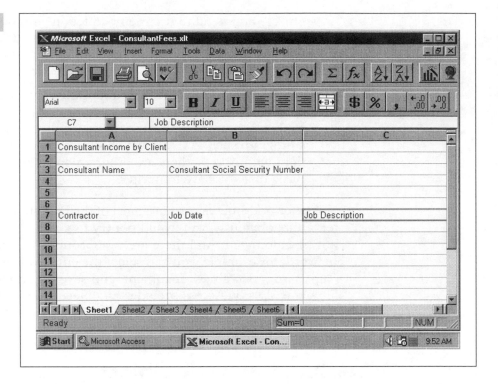

Now it is time to create an object for Excel. Right-click on the button, and follow these steps:

1. Select Build Event from the context menu.

2. In the code window, open the Object drop-down list and select (General).

3. Open the Proc drop-down list and select (declarations).

4. Enter the following lines in the code window:

```
Dim xlObject As Object    ' Declare variable to
                          ' hold the
                          ' reference to the
                          ' Excel Object.
```

5. Open the Object drop-down list and select AutomateExcel. You will be taken to the Click event procedure that Access generated for you automatically.

FIGURE 27.2

Entering the correct information in the Command Button Wizard to get ready to automate Excel

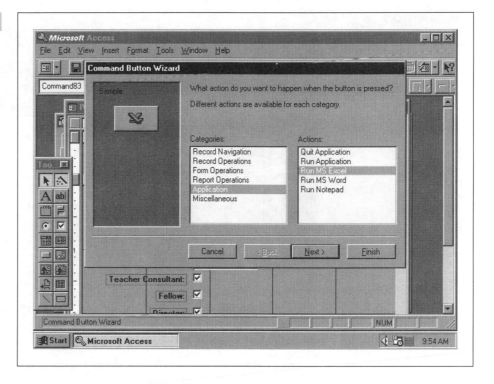

6. Replace the two lines of code following the On Error statement with the following lines of code:

```
' Create an object for Excel
Set xlObject = CreateObject("excel.application")

' Make the Excel application visible
xlObject.Visible = True
```

Your Click event procedure should look like Figure 27.3. At this point, close the code window, take the form to form view, and try out the button. Excel should start and become visible.

What have you done so far? A pretty neat trick, actually. The **Dim** statement you added declared a variable that can hold a reference to an object. Whenever you want to use the object whose reference is stored there, you can use the variable name as the object name. You created the object variable at the form level so that it would remain available while the form was in use. If you created it in the event procedure itself, as soon as the event procedure terminated, Access would deallocate the variable's memory,

FIGURE 27.3

The click event so far

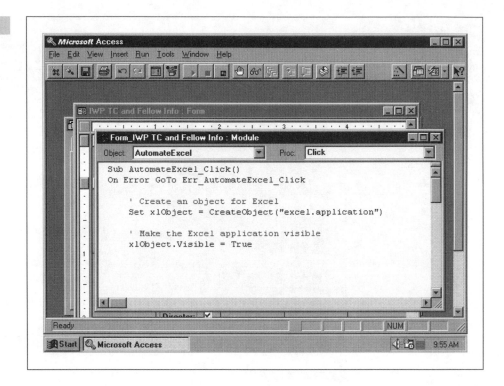

effectively removing it from use until the event procedure was run again, when the variable would be recreated.

The **Set** statement in the Click procedure sets the variable equal to the return value of the CreateObject function. The CreateObject function—you guessed it—creates objects out of whatever item you provide as its argument. In this case, we asked it to create an Excel application object. OLE automation-enabled applications provide strings that you can use as arguments to CreateObject to make objects out of them. CreateObject creates the object and returns a reference to the object. The reference is now stored in xlObject for later use.

Immediately after creating the object, you used it. Excel was started automatically by virtue of the fact that you created an object out of it. But Excel does not become visible until you decide to show it. The next line in the Click procedure sets the xlObject's Visible property to true, causing Excel to show itself to you on the screen.

Working with the Basic Object

Now that you have created an Excel object, you might like to do something with it. First, having started Excel, you need to create a workbook. Return the form to design view and open the code window. Place the cursor in the code window where the next statement should appear, open the Object Browser (press F2), select the Excel Object Library in the Libraries/Databases drop-down list, select Workbooks in the Modules/Classes list and Add in the Methods/Properties list. A description of this method associated with workbook objects appears in the help area of the dialog box (see Figure 27.4). Click on the Paste Text button, and the text you should type to insert the method in your code is inserted for you. Well, almost all the text. You need to make the line read as shown below:

```
Set xlBook = xlObject.Workbooks.Add _
("C:\MSOffice\Templates\ConsultantFees.xlt")
```

FIGURE 27.4

Using the Object Browser to paste code into your application

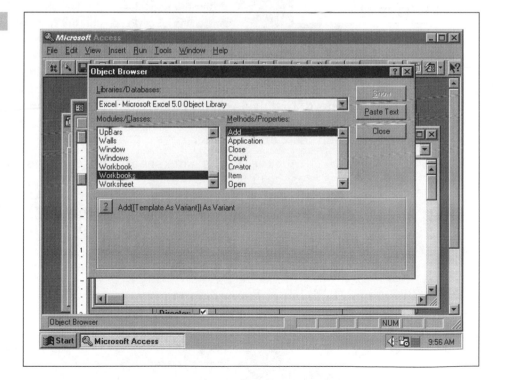

WARNING

If you don't see Excel in the Libraries/Databases list, you need to add a reference to this class library. Open Tools ➤ References, check off Excel in the Available References list, and click on OK.

There are a couple of reasons for making these additions. First, Access would not know to what object to attach the Add method unless you told it. You tell it by adding xlObject.Workbooks in front of Add. In other words, you say in Excel, using the Workbooks object, "add a new workbook." You add the name of the template to use to create the workbook in the parentheses, and you save a reference to the workbook in a variable because you will want convenient access to the workbook later.

NOTE

While the Object Browser is useful, it does not insert the entire line of code for you under many circumstances.

Having created the workbook using the last few lines of code, we want to insert the appropriate information from the database into the Excel worksheet. To do so, you have to activate the worksheet, select the cell using Excel's Range function, and activate the cell. To accomplish these actions, add these lines of code:

```
' Activate the worksheet, select the range, activate
' a cell in the range.
    xlObject.Worksheets("Sheet1").Activate
    xlObject.ActiveSheet.Range("A4").Select
    xlObject.ActiveSheet.Range("A4").Activate
```

In these lines, you use the Worksheets object to activate the worksheet, and the ActiveSheet object to work with the cells on the worksheet you activated.

TIP

You can use the Object Browser to add most of these lines if you want to.

To actually insert information from Access into the Excel worksheet, you have to set the focus to the control containing the information on the Access form. You do so using the SetFocus method for the control. You can then set the value for the ActiveCell object in Excel. Insert these lines of code:

```
' Set the focus to the Last_Name control on the
' Access form.
Last_Name.SetFocus
' Place the last name in the active cell.
xlObject.ActiveCell.Value = Last_Name.Text
```

Next, you repeat the same process for the social security number cell using these lines of code:

```
' Repeat the process for the social security
' number cell.
xlObject.Worksheets("Sheet1").Activate
xlObject.ActiveSheet.Range("B4").Select
xlObject.ActiveSheet.Range("B4").Activate
Social_Security_Number.SetFocus
xlObject.ActiveCell.Value =
    Social_Security_Number.Text
```

To complete the operation of creating the spreadsheet, set the focus to the Last_Name control once again, since the last name of the consultant will be the file name for storing the workbook. Then use the Workbook's SaveAs method to save the spreadsheet, as in the following lines:

```
' Set the focus to the Access Last_Name control
' and save the workbook.
Last_Name.SetFocus
xlBook.SaveAs (Last_Name.Text + ".xls")
```

Now take the form to Form View and click on the button. Watch as Excel opens and builds the worksheet, completely under your control from Access.

Closing Your Automation Session

Having learned how to automate Excel and do some work with it, you might want to know how to stop Excel when you want to. Otherwise you might have lots of copies of Excel starting, and eventually your system would crash from lack of memory, even if you have a lot of memory. To automate the close of Excel, you do two things. Use the Excel object's

Quit method, and set the value of any variables you used to store object references to the built-in value Nothing. The following lines of code do the trick:

```
' Quit Excel and clear the object variables.
xlObject.Quit
Set xlBook = Nothing
Set xlObject = Nothing
```

Now when you click on the button, Excel creates the spreadsheet, then closes itself. (The assumption is that you create these worksheets infrequently, otherwise it would make more sense to keep the workbook open until you were finished and to set the name of each sheet to the last name of the consultant.)

Where to Go from Here

OLE Automation offers you exceptional possibilities. You can conduct complete spreadsheet analyses, build documents, chart graphs, print presentations, etc., all from within Access. If you so desire, you can work from within Word or Excel as well.

The main question you might have is how you can learn more about using these Access features. Take these steps:

- Use the Object Browser to explore different applications to see which objects, properties, and methods are available to you.

- Check the documentation for each of your applications to learn the fundamentals of their macro languages. In Excel, you can use VBA as well.

What's New in the Access Zoo?

Interacting with other applications has always been possible under Access. But Access now gives you these additional features to make such interaction easier:

- The Visual Basic for Applications programming language.
- The ability to use objects provided by other applications.
- The ability to allow other applications to use Access's own objects.

CHAPTER

28

Pulling It All Together

CHAPTERS 1–27 have, for the most part, been about creating individual objects in Microsoft Access. Needless to say, there are *a lot* of tools available for creating tables, queries, forms, reports, macros, and Visual Basic code.

But as with any endeavor, knowing how to create a finished product requires more than just knowing how to use the individual tools. For example, you might well know how to use a hammer, nails, saw, drill, and similar tools. But knowing how to build a house is yet another matter. Maybe you can pick up a guitar and play any note or chord with ease. But how do you go about creating a song? Likewise, perhaps you know every tool and technique your word processor has to offer. But then, how do you go about creating a novel?

You might think of this latter transition as going from "toolmaster" to "artist." And for most people that transition is sort of the second brick wall in the learning process. That is to say, there's the first brick wall of learning what tools are available and how to use them. Then there's the second brick wall of learning how to *apply* those tools to actually create something useful.

Many people get past the second brick wall by doing some "reverse engineering" from other peoples' work. In the fine arts, we take this for granted, even though we use a different terminology. We talk about the artist's "influences." That is to say, the artist has mastered the tools of his trade. But in learning to apply those tools to create, the artist has no doubt observed and borrowed from other artists. The artist has "reverse engineered" the existing work to see what makes it tick.

This is not to say that all works are plagiarism. To the contrary, anything the artist creates is uniquely his or her own creation. But in virtually every work of art or product that a human being creates, you can find some influences from the artists that preceded him or her.

So what does any of this have to do with Microsoft Access? Well, granted, Access is a tool for managing data. But it is also a tool for creativity. You can't create songs, novels, or houses from Access's tools. But you certainly can create Windows 95 applications.

A good way to make the transition from being an Access toolmaster to an Access applications artist is to reverse-engineer other peoples' applications to see what makes them tick—to see how more experienced Access developers have applied Access's tools to create their own unique applications. For the rest of this chapter (and book) we want to give you some tips on how to learn by example (i.e., by reverse-engineering existing applications).

What's Available to You

Microsoft has provided three complete applications with Microsoft Access for you to explore. They are named Northwind.mdb, Orders.mdb, and Solutions.mdb. You can typically find them in the c:\msoffice\access\samples folder after you've installed Microsoft Access.

NOTE   If any of the sample databases are missing from your Samples folder, you can install them from your original Office 95 CD-ROM or Access 95 floppy disks. From the Windows 95 desktop, click on the Start button and choose <u>S</u>ettings ➤ <u>C</u>ontrol Panel ➤ Add/Remove programs. Click on Microsoft Access 7.0, then click on <u>A</u>dd/Remove. Follow the instructions on the screen to add just the Sample Databases.

We've also included a sample application named Fulfill 95 on the CD-ROM that comes with this book. We'll refer to that application as the example to explore throughout this chapter. To install and learn about Fulfill 95, see Appendix C.

Opening and Using an Application

Keep in mind that an Access database application is an Access database (.mdb file) with macros and code to make it perform like a standalone product. So you can open any Access application by using the standard File ➤ Open Database commands within Access. You can also just double-click the name of the .mdb file in the Windows 95 Explorer, Find, or My Computer icon to launch Access and load the application.

To *use* the application, you just interact with the command buttons, menus, and toolbars that appear on the screen. If you want to go spelunking behind the scenes to see what makes the application tick, you need to get to the application's objects. The general term we use for all the behind-the-scenes stuff is *source code*. That term is sort of a leftover from the days when all there was "behind the scenes" was program code. Nowadays, especially in an Access application, there are lots of objects—tables, queries, forms, reports, and macros, as well as code behind the scenes. But Access developers still use the term *source code* anyway.

Getting to the Source Code

Before we describe how to get into source code, we first need to tell you that it isn't always possible to get to the source code! If an Access developer sells his or her product for a fee, he or she might have secured the database to prevent you from getting to the source code, using the techniques we covered in Chapter 18. We respect their right to do that and have no complaints about it. You might, however, be able to purchase the source code (for an extra fee) from the developer.

Many applications, like the four we mentioned at the start of this section, are wide open to exploring behind the scenes. All you need to do is get past the forms and get to the database window. In the Fulfill 95 application, this is simple to do:

1. Choose Exit from Fulfill's main switchboard. You'll come to this little dialog box.

2. Choose To Fulfill's Database Window.

You're taken to the database window for all of Fulfill's objects. All the standard Access menus and toolbars are intact, so you can explore to your heart's content.

To go behind the scenes with the Northwind, Orders, or Solutions sample databases, you may just have to close any custom form that appears, by clicking on its Close (×) button. If you don't see the database window, typically a simple press on the F11 key will bring it into view.

If an application gives you access to its database window, chances are you can also modify its startup options as well. Doing so will allow you to get right to the application's database window, as well as the standard built-in menu bars and toolbars, as soon as you open the application. To change the startup options:

1. With the application's database window showing on your screen, choose Tools ➤ Startup.

2. In the Startup dialog box that appears, select (check) the various Display... and Allow... options to give yourself access to all the normal Access tools, as in Figure 28.1.

3. Choose OK.

4. To activate the new settings, reopen the database. That is, choose File ➤ Close. Then choose File and click on the database's name in the File menu to reopen with the new startup settings.

FIGURE 28.1

The Startup options determine how much access you'll have to built-in Access tools when first opening a database.

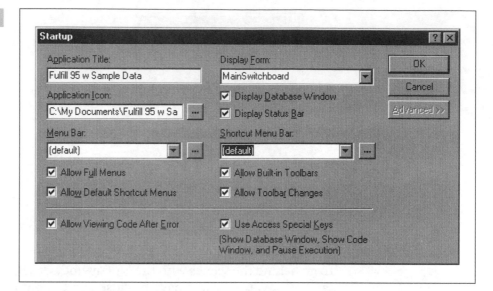

Why No Custom Menus in Fulfill 95?

We've intentionally left custom menus and toolbars out of Fulfill 95 on the CD-ROM, because its main purpose in life is to act as an example for aspiring application developers to explore. If we were to turn Fulfill 95 into a "real product" we'd have to do some more work.

For starters, we would create all custom menus and toolbars. Then, we would use the Access Developer's Toolkit (ADT) to round out the application even further. We'd use the ADT (or some other commercially available tool) to create a standard Windows 95 help system for Fulfill. And then we'd use the ADT to generate a *runtime version* of Fulfill 95 so that we could distribute the application to people who don't own Microsoft Access. (The Microsoft Access Developer's Toolkit (ADT) is a separate product that must be purchased separately.)

Then we'd probably give away a few copies to interested parties to get some feedback and to find any weaknesses and bugs we didn't catch the first time through. We'd fix any remaining problems before actually selling the product.

Finding What Makes It Tick

Once you get to an application's database window, and have all the standard menus and toolbars in place, you're free to explore to your heart's content. Just click on the type of object you want to explore (i.e., Tables, Queries, Forms, and so on), click on the name of the object you want to explore, and then click on the Design button.

The bulk of the "meat" in most applications is in its forms. You can discover a lot about what makes an application tick by exploring its forms. Here's an example. Suppose you open, in design view, the form named AddressBook in Fulfill 95. Your screen might initially look something like Figure 28.2.

Now suppose you want to find out where this form gets its data. Well, you need to look at the form's property sheet so you choose Edit ➤ Select Form. Then you open the property sheet, click on the All tab, and take a look at the Record Source property. There you'll see that the form is based

FIGURE 28.2

Fulfill's AddressBook form open in Design view

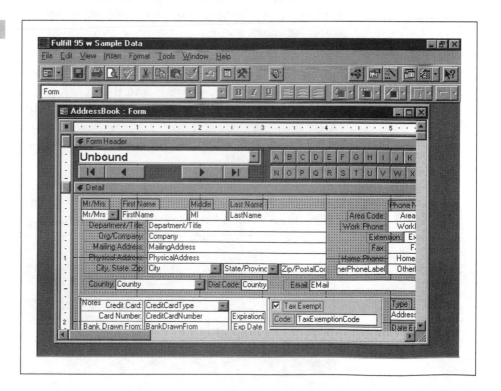

on a query named AddressesAlphabetized, as below.

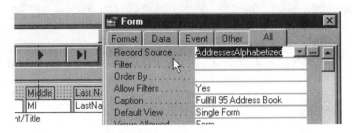

To see what makes that query tick, you just need to click on the Build (…) button next to the query's name.

In virtually all applications, most of what makes the application behave the way it does are the *event procedures* assigned to the form and individual controls. To see the events assigned to a form, as a whole, you choose Edit ➤ Select Form, open the property sheet, and click on the Event tab. In this example, we've created four custom event procedures for the Address-Book form, as you can see in Figure 28.3.

Many of the individual controls on a form will also have one or more custom event procedures assigned to them. To see a control's event procedure, just click on the control you're interested in, and take a look at the Event tab in the property sheet.

In some cases, you may see the name of a macro in an event property. You can click on that macro name, and then click on the Build (…) button to explore the macro. But in most cases, you'll probably see [Event Procedure] as an event's property. The Event Procedure is Visual Basic code that's stored right along with the form, and is accessible only through the form's design view.

Let's take a "for instance." Suppose we click on the big "Unbound" control in the AddressBook form. The property sheet informs us that 1) this control is a combo box, 2) its name is AlphaNameList, and 3) there's a custom event procedure assigned to this control, as you can see below.

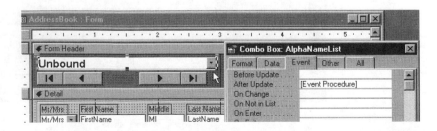

FIGURE 28.3

The AddressBook form's behavior is controlled by four event procedures.

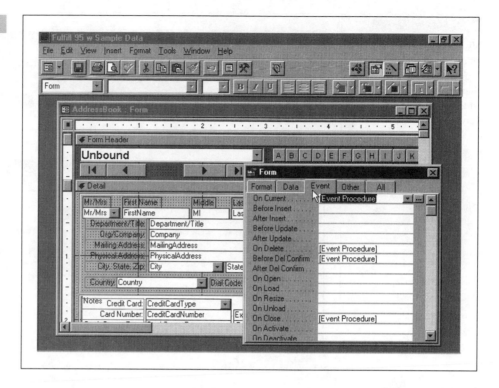

So, how do we go behind the scenes and see the Visual Basic code? Easy—just click on [Event Procedure] in the property sheet, then click on the Build (...) button. The underlying code appears in a module window, as in Figure 28.4.

So unless you happen to be a Visual Basic expert, your reply to this finding might be, "Great, but I have no idea what any of that code means." One of the cool things about Microsoft Access is that the online Help is linked to "keywords" in the code. So you can start learning what all the various Visual Basic commands do just by exploring Help right from this screen.

For example, to find out what the heck *recordsetclone* is all about, you could drag the cursor through that command to select it, as below.

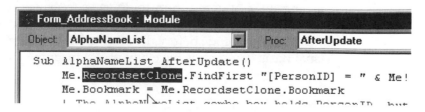

FIGURE 28.4

Visual Basic code attached to the After Update property of the AlphaNameList control in the AddressBook form

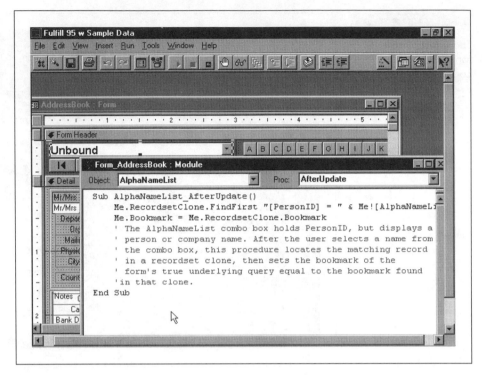

 ➤ Then you press Help (F1) and lo and behold, a help screen appears telling you what RecordsetClose is all about, as in Figure 28.5.

What Good Is This Information?

Now you might look at that so-called help screen back in Figure 28.5 and think, "But it's so *technical*, it really doesn't help me at all." If that's the case, you're reading all of this much too early in your application-development apprenticeship.

There's a reason why we're telling you this in Chapter 28. The information does you no good until you know how to do all the stuff in Chapters 1 through 27! This kind of exploration is only useful when you're in the learning stage of going from toolmaster to artist. You have to know the "mechanics" of creating tables, queries, forms, controls, reports, macros, and Visual Basic code before the nitty-gritty technical details of individual Visual Basic commands have any useful meaning to you.

FIGURE 28.5

Information about
RecordsetClone on the
screen

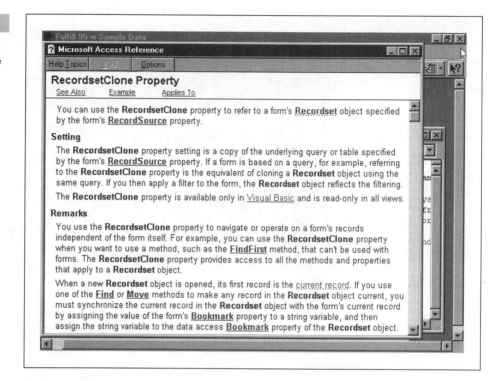

Printing Technical Documentation

Pointing and clicking on individual objects is just one way to explore existing Access applications. You can also print all the technical behind-the-scenes stuff. Here's how:

1. If you haven't already done so, open the application you want to explore, and get to its database window.

2. Chose Tools ➤ Analyze ➤ Documentor to get to the dialog box shown in Figure 28.6.

3. Choose the type of object you want to explore, then choose the specific objects. Be aware that any given object can produce a whole lot of documentation, so you may want to just document one or two objects at a time.

FIGURE 28.6

The Database Documentor dialog box lets you view and print technical behind-the-scenes information on any object in a database.

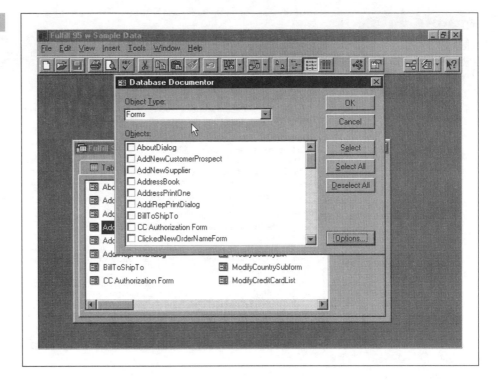

4. Optionally, click on the <u>O</u>ptions button and specify exactly what you want to print. Then choose OK after setting your options.

5. Choose OK, and give Access a few minutes to prepare the documentation.

6. When the documentation is ready you'll be taken to the report preview screen showing a window named Object Definition (Figure 28.7.)

7. To print the documentation, just click on the Print button in the toolbar.

When you've finished you can just click on the Close (×) button in the Object Definition window to return to the database window.

FIGURE 28.7

The Object Definition window displays technical information about one or more objects in a database.

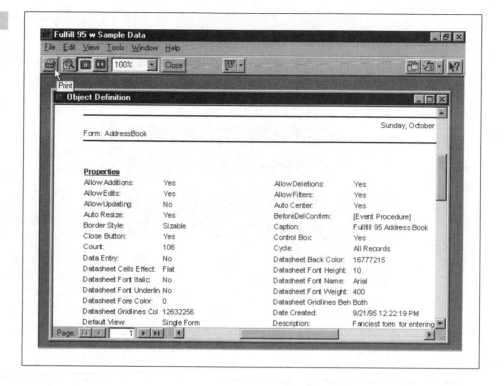

Modifying Existing Applications

Once you get to the source code (i.e., database window) of an Access application, the temptation to start tweaking it to better meet your own needs will be strong. In fact, if you can *get* your hands on the source code for an application, the implication is that you're doing this so that you *can* modify the application. We have some advice to give you on modifying existing applications.

Modifying an existing application is a terrific way to help ease the transition from toolmaster to artist. However, if you try to customize an existing application before you've become an Access toolmaster, then you're very likely to find yourself in deep yogurt very quickly. Just the simple act of deleting or renaming a single object—even one little field in a table—can wreak havoc throughout the rest of the application. Here's why.

Let's suppose we have a field named AddressLine2 in a table in an application. You decide you don't need that field, so you delete it from the table. Or, you just change its name to PhysicalAddress. You save the change and all seems fine.

But then as you start using the application, you keep coming across little *#Name?#* and *#Error#* messages. Or you keep seeing a little window like this popping up on the screen:

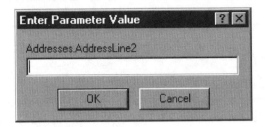

The problem is that other objects—queries, forms, reports, macros, and modules—might "expect" to find a field named AddressLine2 in that table. When you delete or rename that field in Access's table design view, *that change does not carry over to any other objects in the database.* So when you use one of those objects, it just flat-out doesn't work.

Where to Go from Here

Exploring existing applications is just one way to make the transition from Access toolmaster to Access artist (a.k.a., *application developer.*) There are also plenty of books that pick up where this one leaves off, to help you. We can definitely recommend *The Microsoft Access for Windows 95 Developer's Handbook* by Access gurus Ken Getz, Paul Litwin, Greg Reddick and Mike Gilbert. An excellent book on macros is *Automating Microsoft Access Databases with Macros,* by Susann Novalis. Both books are also published by Sybex, the publisher of this book.

There's also the *Access/Visual Basic Advisor* magazine, a great resource for information, add-on products, training, and more. For information and pricing contact *Access/Visual Basic Advisor* at P.O. Box 469030, Escondido, CA 92046-9918. (Phone (619) 483-6400 or (800) 336-6060; or fax: (619) 483-9851.) Or you can reach them at CompuServe 70007,1614 or 70007.1614@compuserve.com on the Internet.

As for us, the authors of *Mastering Access for Windows 95*, we thank you for reading, and wish you all the best in your endeavor to become a full-fledged Windows 95 application developer. We know, from experience, that it takes a heck of a lot of time, patience, and brain cells to master this tool. But the creative prowess that mastery buys you is well worth the suffering. So hang in there. If you need to get in touch, our addresses are in the Introduction at the beginning of this book.

APPENDICES

APPENDIX

A

Installing Microsoft Access

YOU must install Microsoft Access for Windows 95 before you can use it to manage your data. This appendix briefly explains how to install Access on a single-user computer.

NOTE The single-user installation procedures might differ slightly, depending on whether you're installing Access as part of Microsoft Office Professional, and whether you're installing from floppy disks or a CD-ROM disk.

 It's best to check the materials that come with your Access program for specific installation instructions, late-breaking news, and more details than we can provide in this appendix. For general information about installing Access, check the *Getting Results with Microsoft Access for Windows 95, Version 7.0* book that comes with Access. For late-breaking news, see the Acreadme file on your setup disk.

If you're planning to install Access on a network, see the network.txt file on your setup disk for an overview of the steps. For detailed network installation instructions, you'll also need a copy of the book *Microsoft Office For Windows 95 Resource Kit*, available in many computer bookstores and from Microsoft Press (call 1-800-MS PRESS).

Checking Out Your Hardware

Before you install Access, you need to find out if your hardware meets these requirements:

- A PC with at least a 486 DX2 or DX4 processor.

- For Windows 95, we strongly recommend at least 16MB memory (RAM). For Windows NT, we recommend 32MB memory.

- About 42MB of hard disk space available for a full installation (about 33MB for a Typical install and about 14.8MB for a Compact install). Of course, you'll need extra space for your databases.

- Windows 95 or Windows NT 3.51 (either Server or Workstation).

- A VGA or higher monitor.

- A Microsoft Mouse or compatible pointing device.

Yes, we know the box states lower memory and processor requirements, but those more modest recommendations may lead to sluggish performance when you use Access.

N O T E   If you're installing Microsoft Access on Windows NT, you must be the *Administrator* or have *Administrator* privileges.

Preparing Your 1.x and 2.x Databases

Please read this section if you have old Access version 1.0 or 1.1 (1.*x*) or version 2.0 databases. If you're installing Access for the first time and do not have any old databases, feel free to skip ahead to the next section.

There are two ways to use old databases in Microsoft Access for Windows 95:

- **Convert the old databases to the new format.** Doing so allows you to take full advantage of all the new features in Access. However, you should *not* convert your databases if others must use them with Access 1.*x* or 2.0.

- **Use the old databases *without* converting them to the new format.** This method, called *enabling* the databases, allows people to view and update the databases with older versions of Access.

However, it does not let you change database objects or create new ones in Microsoft Access for Windows 95. In secure databases (see Chapter 18), you also can't change or add permissions unless you convert the old database to the new format.

> **WARNING**
>
> In general, databases will work more efficiently if you convert them to Microsoft Access for Windows 95 format. Remember, however, that if you do convert your databases, they can't be used with Access 1.*x* or 2.0, and they can't be converted back to the old versions. Of course, you *can* restore the old databases from backup copies you made before you converted.

Regardless of whether you decide to convert or enable your old databases, you must do these quick preparation steps *before* removing your previous version of Access.

1. Back up any databases you plan to convert. *Do not skip this step!*

2. If you're using Access 2.0, skip to step 3. If you're using Access 1.*x*, you should be aware of and compensate for the following:

   - **Backquote character (`) in object names**. Backquotes aren't allowed in Microsoft Access for Windows 95 object names, and they'll prevent you from converting your database or opening the object in Access for Windows 95. You must use Access 1.*x* to rename such objects before converting or using them in Access for Windows 95.

   - **Indexes and relationships.** Microsoft Access for Windows 95 tables are limited to 32 indexes each. You won't be able to convert your databases if any tables exceed that limit. If necessary, delete some relationships or indexes in complex tables before converting the database.

   - **Modules named DAO, VBA, or Access.** Modules named *DAO, VBA,* or *Access* will prevent a database from converting, because they are names of "typelibs" that Access references automatically. You'll need to change these module names before converting any databases that use them.

3. *Using Access 1.x or 2.0* (as appropriate), open your database, and then open all of your forms and reports in design view. Click on the Module tab of the database window. Next, open any module in design view, and then choose Run ➤ Compile Loaded Modules. If your database doesn't contain any modules, click on the New button to create a blank module, and then choose Run ➤ Compile Loaded Modules. This step will ensure that all of your modules are fully compiled.

4. Close and save all of your forms, reports, and modules, and then close your database. Repeat steps 2–4 for each database you want to convert.

5. Back up your databases again to preserve your work in steps 3 and 4.

Now you're ready to install Microsoft Access for Windows 95. After installing Access, you can convert or enable your databases, as explained later in this appendix under "Enabling and Converting Access Databases."

For more information about conversion issues, please see Appendix A of the *Building Applications with Microsoft Access for Windows 95* manual that comes with Access, and look up topics under *Converting* in the Microsoft Access Answer Wizard. You also may want to search the Microsoft Knowledge Base for late-breaking information on conversion issues. The Knowledge Base is available on CompuServe (GO MSKB), the Microsoft Network (use the Find tools to search for "Knowledge Base"), and the Microsoft Internet servers at www.microsoft.com and ftp.microsoft.com. Chapter 4 offers more details about the Microsoft Knowledge Base and other sources of technical information about Access and other Microsoft products.

Installing Access on a Single-User Computer

Installing Access for use on a single computer is quite easy. Here are the basic steps:

1. Start Windows 95, and make sure other programs are not running.

W A R N I N G

When installing Access, be sure to do so on a "vanilla" system. Exit any nonstandard Windows shells or memory managers, any terminate-and-stay-resident (TSR) programs, and any virus-detection utilities. Check the Windows taskbar and close any programs that are running. If any programs are started from your autoexec.bat and config.sys files, restart your computer by choosing Start ➤ Shut Down ➤ Restart The Computer ➤ Yes. Then, when you see the message "Starting Windows 95," press F8, and choose Step-By-Step confirmation. You'll be asked whether to run each command in config.sys and autoexec.bat. Press Y to run the command or N to bypass it.

2. Insert the Microsoft Access Setup Disk 1 into floppy drive A or B of your computer. Or insert the Microsoft Office Professional CD-ROM disk into your computer's CD-ROM drive.

3. Click on the Start button on the Windows taskbar, and then choose Run.

4. In the Command Line text box, type the name of the drive you put the setup disk in (for example, **a:** or **b:** or **d:**), followed by **setup** (or use the Browse button to search for the Setup program). For example, if you put Setup Disk 1 in drive A, type

    a:setup

5. Click on OK or press ↵.

T I P

As an alternative to steps 2–5, you can choose Start ➤ Settings ➤ Control Panel, double-click on Add/Remove Programs, and then click on the Install button to start the Install Program From Floppy Disk Or CD-ROM Wizard. When the Wizard starts, follow the instructions on the screen.

6. Follow the initial instructions that appear on the screen. Among other things, you'll be asked to supply your name and serial number, and given a chance to choose an installation folder for Microsoft Office. In most cases, you can fill in a dialog box (if necessary), and then press ↵ or click on OK to go to the next dialog box.

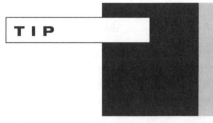

TIP

To learn more about which components an installation option will set up or what an installation button will do, click on the ? button at the upper-right corner of any Microsoft Access For Windows 95 Setup dialog box, and then click on the place you're interested in.

7. When asked to choose the type of installation you want, click on one of these buttons:

Typical Installs Access with the most common options. This is the default choice. Requires about 33MB of available disk space.

Compact Installs Access with the bare-bones components needed to run the program. This is useful if you're using a laptop computer, or if your hard disk is very short of available space. Requires about 14.8MB of available disk space.

Custom Allows you to select the installation options you want to use. Choose this option if you want to install all of Access, or if you're short on disk space and want to install only certain components of Access. A full Custom install requires about 42MB of available disk space.

After choosing the Custom option, you can click on the Select All button to check all components, or you can select (check) or deselect (clear) components as needed. When you're finished choosing components, click on Continue. Figure A.1 shows a Microsoft Access For Windows 95 - Custom dialog box that's similar to the one you'll see. Table A.1 briefly describes the main components you can select.

TABLE A.1: Microsoft Access Components That You Can Install with the Custom Option

COMPONENT	DESCRIPTION
Microsoft Access	The Access program and minimum utilities needed to run it. This option is required for an initial installation of Access.
Help Topics	Online Help and language reference files. To get the most out of Access, be sure this option is selected.
Wizards	The easy to use question-and-answer tools that help you create tables, forms, reports, queries, and so on. It's best to leave this option checked so you're sure to get all the built-in Wizards. You can use the Add-In Manager (described in Chapter 15) to install or uninstall Wizards that you've purchased separately from Access.
Developer Tools	Tools that let developers build custom menus, convert macros to Visual Basic code, document databases, and complete other advanced tasks.
Data Access	Drivers that let you import and attach tables created by other database management programs including Excel, Text, xBASE (dBASE and FoxPro), Paradox, Lotus 1-2-3, Microsoft SQL Server ODBC, and Microsoft Desktop ODBC.
Sample Databases	The sample databases and applications that Microsoft supplies with Access, including Northwind and Solutions.
Tools	The Microsoft Info program that provides information about your system configuration when you choose <u>H</u>elp ➤ <u>A</u>bout Microsoft Access from the Access menu bar.
Microsoft Graph Version 5.0	An embedded program that lets you create charts in forms and reports (see Chapter 14).
Microsoft Brief-case Replication	The feature that lets you keep different copies of databases in sync (see Chapter 17).
Calendar Control	The OLE custom control and associated help files that let you create fully programmable calendars in your forms and reports (see Chapter 13).

TIP

It's best to select (check) *all* the components listed in Table A.1 if you have room for them on your hard disk. The check mark options are toggles: simply click on a check box to select or deselect it. If necessary, you can install omitted components or remove unwanted components later, as described under "Running Setup to Add or Remove Components."

Run From CD or **Run From Network**   Installs only those files needed to run Access from the CD-ROM or from the network.

8. If you're installing from floppy disks, feed the appropriate disk into the floppy disk drive whenever Access Setup asks you to, and then press ↵ or click on OK to continue with the installation.

9. Answer any additional prompts that appear.

FIGURE A.1

The Custom installation option lets you choose which Access components to install. If you have enough disk space, it's easiest to click on the Select All button in the Microsoft Access For Windows 95 - Custom dialog box to install everything at once.

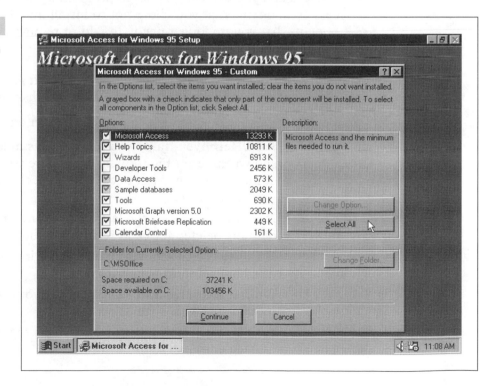

10. After copying all the needed files to your computer, Setup will take several minutes to update your system. Wait patiently for this task to finish, and *don't* restart your computer (the computer isn't really dead, it's just thinking). When Setup is finished, you'll see a message indicating that the setup completed successfully. Click on the <u>O</u>K (or Online <u>R</u>egistration) button to finish the job.

After installing all the files you need, Setup will create a Microsoft Access option on the Start ➤ <u>P</u>rograms menu. When you've completed the installation, go to Chapter 1 of this book, where you'll learn how to start Microsoft Access and get around in it.

Running Setup to Add or Remove Components

If necessary, you can run the Setup program again to add Microsoft Access components that you chose not to install initially or to delete components that you no longer need. To add or remove components, follow these steps:

1. Start the Setup program from the Microsoft Access Setup Disk 1 or Microsoft Office Professional CD-ROM disk, as explained earlier.

2. In the dialog box that appears next, click on one of these buttons:

> **<u>A</u>dd/Remove** Takes you to a screen similar to the one shown earlier in Figure A.1. From here you can select components you want to add or deselect components you want to remove.
>
> **<u>R</u>einstall** Repeats the last installation, replacing any accidentally deleted files and restoring initial settings.
>
> **Re<u>m</u>ove All** Removes all previously installed Access components from your hard disk.
>
> **Online Registration** Lets you use your modem to register your software with Microsoft.
>
> **E<u>x</u>it Setup** Lets you exit the Setup program without making any changes.

3. Follow any instructions that appear on your screen to complete the installation or removal of components.

Enabling and Converting Old Access Databases

As mentioned earlier, you can convert your old Access 1.*x* and 2.0 databases to the new Access for Windows 95 database format, or you can just *enable* the databases for use with Access for Windows 95 without converting them.

Enabling a Database

To enable a database that was created in an older version of Access, start Microsoft Access for Windows 95 and open the database (see Chapter 1 if you need details). You'll see a Convert/Open dialog box that explains your options, as shown in Figure A.2.

1. Choose Convert Database to convert the database to the new format, or choose Open Database to enable the database (leaving it in the old format).

2. Click on OK and follow any instructions that appear.

Your database will either be converted or enabled, depending on your choice in step 1.

Converting a Database

To convert a database, you can open it and choose the Convert Database option described above, or you can follow these steps:

1. Close all open databases. If you're using a network, make sure that no one else has opened the database you want to convert.

2. Choose Tools ➤ Database Utilities ➤ Convert Database.

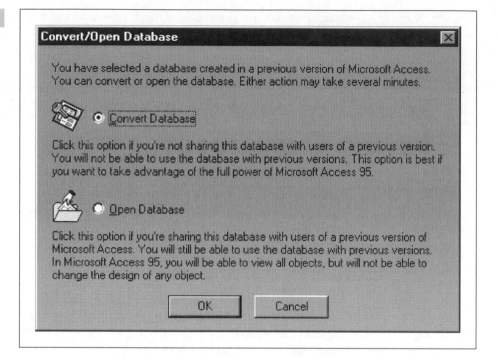

3. In the Database To Convert From dialog box, locate and click on the database you want to convert. If you also want to convert any old-style OLE objects (such as Graph 3.0 objects), select (check) the Convert OLE option below the Advanced button. Click on the Convert button.

4. In the Database To Convert Into dialog box, type a new name for the database, or just select a different directory location if you want to keep the same name. Click on Save.

5. Respond to any prompts that appear while Access converts your database. When conversion is complete, you can open the new database and use it normally.

After converting (or enabling) your old database, you may discover some changes in the way database objects behave, and you may need to tweak your applications to make them work more smoothly.

WARNING

Once you convert a 1.*x* or 2.0 database to Access for Windows 95 format, you can't open that database in version 1.0, 1.1, or 2.0, and you can't convert it back.

TIP

If your database is very large, the conversion steps given above may fail (it's rare but possible). If that happens, create a new blank database, and then try using the Import procedures discussed in Chapter 7 to import just a few objects (about 20–30) at a time. The Import process will convert the objects as needed.

 ➤ The steps given above apply to the simple case of converting an unsecured database without linked tables on a single-user computer. For more information about conversion issues, see Appendix A of the *Building Applications with Microsoft Access for Windows 95* manual that comes with Access, and look up topics under *Converting* in the Access Answer Wizard.

Setting Up ODBC Support

The Open Database Connectivity (ODBC) drivers that come with Access let you connect to SQL database servers and use SQL databases from Access. (If you're not interested in using SQL databases, you needn't bother to set up ODBC support and you can skip the rest of this appendix.)

Getting your machine ready to use SQL database servers and to use the data in SQL databases involves the two main steps given below. These steps assume you want to work with databases stored on a Microsoft SQL Server; if your databases are stored on another vendor's server, you'll need to use an ODBC driver from that vendor.

1. **Install the Microsoft SQL Server driver that comes with Access.** If you performed a Custom setup and checked all the options, the ODBC drivers will be installed for you automatically. If you did a Typical or Compact setup, or you cleared the *Microsoft*

SQL Server ODBC Driver option under *Data Access* in the Custom setup, you must re-run Setup and do a Custom setup to install those drivers.

2. **Set up data sources using the ODBC Manager (or the ODBC Administrator for Windows NT).** After starting one of these ODBC management programs, you can define a new data source for a currently installed driver, or change the definition of an existing data source. (A data source is a set of instructions that tell ODBC where to get the data you're interested in.)

 For more information about installing ODBC support and setting up data sources using the ODBC Manager, look up *ODBC* in the Access Answer Wizard, and then double-click on *Install ODBC Drivers And Setup ODBC Data Sources* under *How Do I*. Or, start the ODBC Manager or ODBC Administrator and then click on its <u>H</u>elp button.

APPENDIX

B

About the CD-ROM

THE CD-ROM that comes with this book contains sample databases, shareware, freeware, demos, and a multimedia catalog for you to enjoy. To see the contents of the CD-ROM, follow these steps:

1. Put the CD in your CD-ROM drive.

2. Close any open applications so that you're just at the Windows 95 desktop.

3. Double-click on your My Computer icon.

4. Double-click on the icon for your CD-ROM drive (typically D:).

The contents of the CD are displayed in a My Computer window, looking something like Figure B.1.

TIP

If you don't see the Large Icons view, you can just choose <u>V</u>iew ➤ Large Icons from the menu bar in the "Masteringac" window. To show or hide file name extensions, choose <u>V</u>iew ➤ <u>O</u>ptions, click on the View tab, then either clear or check the Hide MS-DOS file <u>e</u>xtensions… option.

Opening an Access Database

Most of the files on the CD-ROM are Microsoft Access for Windows 95 databases, as indicated by the Access icon, shown below.

FIGURE B.1

The contents of the CD-ROM disk displayed in a My Computer window, with Large Icons view

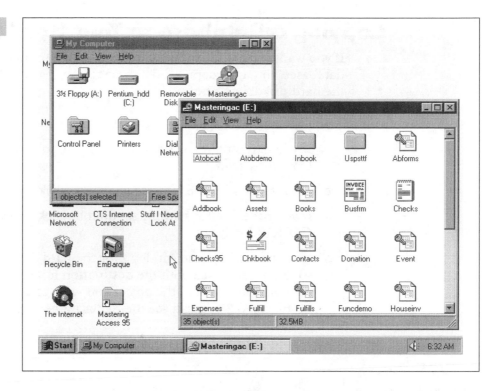

Assuming you've already installed Microsoft Access for Windows 95 on your PC, exploring one of those databases is simple. Just double-click on the icon for the database you want to open. Because you're opening the database from a CD-ROM, you'll initially see a message that looks something like this:

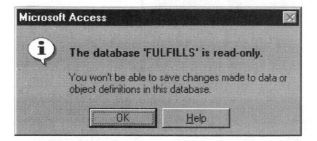

Just choose OK to proceed and open the database in Read-Only mode. You won't be able to add, change, or delete anything in this mode. But that's OK if you're just exploring. You can scroll around through options, view the sample data in the forms, and print and preview reports.

Copying a Database to Your Hard Disk

If you want to be able to add, change, and delete data in one of the sample databases, you must copy the database to your hard disk, then run it from the hard disk. Here's how:

1. If you're in Microsoft Access, exit out to the Windows 95 desktop.

2. If you haven't already done so, open (double-click on) your My Computer icon.

3. Double-click on the icon for your hard disk (typically C:).

4. If you haven't already done so, double-click on the icon for your CD-ROM drive.

5. Size and position the windows for the hard drive and CD-ROM so that you can see both the destination folder (the folder you want to copy *to*), and the object you want to copy. For example, in Figure B.2 you can see the folder named My Document on

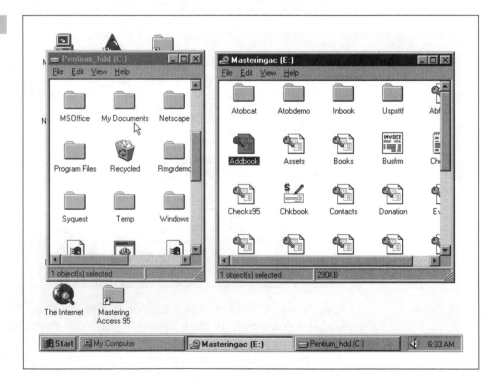

drive C: (where I want to copy to), and several databases from the CD-ROM disc.

6. Drag and drop the icon for the database you want to copy from the CD-ROM drive's window over to the destination folder's icon.

That's all there is to it. To run the database from your hard disk:

1. Open (double-click on) the folder on your hard drive that contains the database (My Documents in this example).

2. Double-click on the icon for the database you want to open.

You won't get the Read-Only message this time, because you've opened the database on a "normal" read-write disk.

NOTE Remember that the ROM in CD-ROM stands for "Read-Only Memory." You cannot change anything that you open directly from the CD-ROM. You can only change items that you copy to, and run from, your hard disk.

In the sections that follow we'll describe what's in each of the databases.

Abforms and Checks95

The Abforms and Checks95 databases are freebies from Cary Prague Books and Software. You can run either from the CD. If you want to actually use the Checks95 database, we suggest that you copy both the Checks95 (or Checks95.mdb) file, and the Chkbook (or Chkbook.ico), using the basic technique described under "Copying a Database to Your Hard Disk" earlier in this appendix.

For more information, see "Cary Prague Books and Software" later in this appendix, or the file named Checks (Checks.txt) on the CD.

Fulfill and FulfillS

The databases named Fulfill and FulfillS contain a sample data-entry database application that you're free to use, abuse, ignore, explore, and tinker with at will. The difference between the two is as follows:

FulfillS (or FulfillS.mdb) The Fulfill database application with some fake data already entered. Explore from the CD, or copy it to your hard disk if you want to add, change, delete data.

Fulfill (or Fulfill.mdb) Same as FulfillS but without the fake names and addresses, products, and orders. To use this version, first copy it to your hard disk.

Appendix C contains lots more information about using Fulfill 95 with its many special bells and whistles. Chapter 28 offers techniques that you can use to explore Fulfill 95 "behind the scenes" to see what makes it tick, and to learn some tricks for your own custom applications.

ZipDemo and FuncDemo

The ZipDemo (or ZipDemo.mdb) database illustrates a Microsoft Access *event procedure* that does something very useful: After you type in a Zip Code, it auto-fills the City, State, and Area Code fields on the same form. The Fulfill databases use the same technique to do the same job.

The FuncDemo (or FuncDemo.mdb) database illustrates a couple of sample *function procedures* (also called *user-defined functions*) written in Visual Basic:

- **NumWord( )** Converts a number, such as *123.45*, to words, such as *One hundred twenty three and 45/100*. Cary Prague's Check Writer application uses this function to print checks.

- **Proper( )** A function that Access forgot. Converts any case (i.e., *alan simpson, ALAN SIMPSON, aLaN SiMpsOn*) to proper noun case (i.e., *Alan Simpson*).

You can open and explore the ZipDemo and FuncDemo databases right from the CD—there's no need to copy either to the hard disk.

The Inbook Folder

The Inbook folder contains some small sample databases used in examples throughout the book:

- Lessons (or Lessons.mdb) used in the hands-on lessons at the start of this book.

- OrdEntry (or OrdEntry.mdb) used heavily throughout the first few chapters.

- StarSrch (or StarSrch.mdb) illustrates the use of photos in a database.

- Chap 22 (or Chap22.mdb), a small custom dialog box.

The Other Database Files

The rest of the database files are all samples generated from the Database Wizards that come with Access. Feel free to explore them from the CD, but don't bother to copy these to your hard disk. If you find one you like, and want to use it for "real" data, just recreate it from scratch using the Database Wizards. That way, you can start with your own data, and also choose a style for your forms and reports.

To create a "clean" copy of one of those databases:

1. Start Microsoft Access for Windows 95 in the usual manner.
2. Choose Database Wizard, then choose OK.
3. Click on the Databases tab to get to the Database Wizards (Figure B.3).
4. Choose the Database Wizard you want, and follow the instructions on the screen.

Table B.1 lists the names of sample databases that appear on the CD, and the Wizard used to create each one.

FIGURE B.3

The new Database Wizards available in Microsoft Access for Windows 95

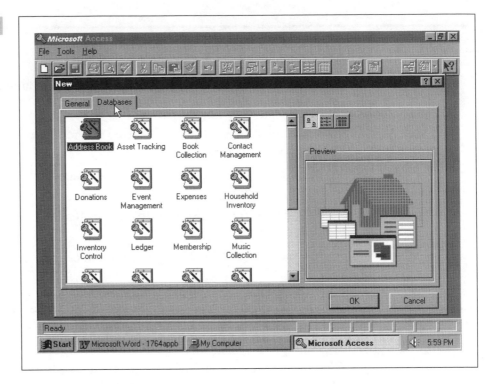

TABLE B.1: Wizards Used to Create Sample Databases on the CD-ROM Disc

FILE NAME	DATABASE WIZARD USED
Addbook	Address Book
Assets	Asset Tracking
Books	Book Collection
Contacts	Contact Management
Donation	Donations
Events	Event Management
Expenses	Expenses
Houseinv	Household Inventory
Inventry	Inventory Control
Ledger	Ledger

TABLE B.1: Wizards Used to Create Sample Databases on the CD-ROM Disc (continued)

FILE NAME	DATABASE WIZARD USED
Members	Membership
Music	Music Collection
Orderent	Order Entry
Photos	Picture Library
Recipes	Recipes
Schedule	Resource Scheduling
School	Students and Classes
Service	Service Call Management
Timebill	Time and Billing
Videos	Video Collection
Wines	Wine List
Workout	Workout

Access to Business Multimedia Catalog

Access to Business offers great products for Access users and is a valuable resource for everyone from beginner to seasoned pro. We've included their multimedia catalog of Access-related products on the CD.

Using the Multimedia Catalog

The Access to Business catalog is your direct path to ready-to-run Microsoft Access databases for a variety of industries and applications. To view

the multimedia catalog there is no need to install anything on your hard drive. Instead, just do the following:

> **WARNING**
>
> You must set your screen resolution to 800 x 600 or better *before* you start the catalog. To do so, right-click your Windows 95 desktop and choose Properties from the pop-up menu. Click on the Settings tab and set the Desktop Area option to 800 x 600 or higher. Choose OK and follow any instructions that appear on the screen.

1. Close any open applications so that you're at the Windows desktop.

2. Put the CD-ROM that came with this book into your CD-ROM drive.

3. Click on the Start button, and choose <u>R</u>un.

4. Type *d*:**\AtoBCat\AtoBCat** as below, but replace *d*: with the drive letter of your CD-ROM drive. For example, our CD-ROM drive is E:, so we would type the entry shown below:

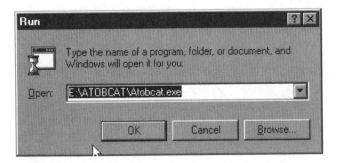

5. Choose OK.

It might take a minute for the catalog to load from the CD. But when it does, you'll be taken to the opening screen. Work your way through to the Contents screen shown in Figure B.4.

We (the authors of *Mastering Access for Windows 95*) strongly suggest that once you get the catalog going, you *just* use the catalog. That is to say, click

The opening screen for
the Access to Business
multimedia catalog of
Microsoft Access-
related products

on any graphic to get somewhere, and use these arrows and buttons
within the catalog to navigate.

NOTE   If you forgot to increase your screen resolution, and
can't see the navigation buttons, you can easily shut
down the catalog and try again. Press Ctrl+Alt+Del,
click on Quest, then click on the End Task button.

We also recommend that you *avoid* using these options:

We know this sounds like strange advice, so let us explain our reasoning here.

Windows 95 and Access for Windows 95 are *very* new products. The vendors of the products that the demos and slide shows illustrate have not had enough time to prepare the true 32-bit versions of their products. Nor have they had time to prepare 32-bit demos and slide shows for those products.

We've all seen the commercials that say that Windows 95 can run all the cool new (i.e., 32-bit) stuff, as well as existing (i.e., 16-bit) stuff. But sometimes reality dictates otherwise. A demo or slide show that runs as smooth as glass under Windows 3 and Access 2.0 won't necessarily be quite so smooth under Windows 95 and Access 95.

If you stay in the catalog and don't install any demos or slide shows to your hard disk, you won't have to worry about any bumpy roads or disappointments. Furthermore, you'll probably get enough information from the catalog to determine whether or not you're interested in a particular product.

We're certain that Access to Business will make the 32-bit products, demos, and slide shows available to you as soon as possible. Should you have any questions or comments, please direct them to Access to Business at:

Access to Business
16903 SE 39th St.
Bellevue, WA 98008-5825

Telephone: (206) 644-5977
Fax: (206) 641-9271
CIS: 72774,3523
E-mail: atob@nwlink.com
World Wide Web: http://www.troubador.com/atob

The remainder of this section was contributed by Access to Business.

About Access to Business

Access to Business markets and develops Microsoft Office and Microsoft Access-related products for all business types. We have over 60 applications, including accounting, point of sale, developer tools/utilities, special Wizards and controls, as well as products geared toward specific industries such as auto repair shop, health care, and real estate.

With our quarterly multimedia CD catalog you can keep up with all the latest software (most can be customized) for Microsoft Office and Access, whether you are an end-user, developer, or consultant. The catalog includes live working demos of over 15 products, such as Contacts Unlimited, a total information manager (contact manager). All demos can be copied and given to anyone who might be interested in purchasing that software.

Inside the product catalog you'll also find a multimedia newsletter, free games, shareware, and other resources. A yearly subscription (four issues) to the multimedia CD can be purchased for only $29.95. Fax and e-mail orders are accepted. The subscription pays for itself after installing only one demo—plus all the resources and information you receive make the $29.95 price a bargain. We accept Visa, MasterCard, American Express, and company checks.

Access to Business is also a full service graphic design company offering these services:

- Company office stationary designed and printed
- Product and company logo design
- Product package design and production
- Disk label design and production
- Disk duplication
- Product manuals, brochures, newsletters
- Multimedia product demos

Marketing support includes:

- Possible partnership with us or others to bring your product to market
- Assisting in producing online help
- Advising on marketing strategies
- Designing and producing PowerPoint and interactive demos

We already have an international partner in Australia and Canada, and are negotiating with several other countries. We are looking for national and international partners to sell some or all of our product line. These are available to qualified resellers, consultants, and developers.

Some of our products are available for developer vertical licenses. You can use these products as an engine to develop an entirely new product with a new name and purpose. Contact us for more details and pricing.

The Access to Business name and logo are trademarked.

Cary Prague Books and Software

Cary Prague Books and Software is another valuable resource for Access users, and the company has graciously given us the rights to distribute their Check Writer database application free of charge. Also provided are some examples of their pre-designed business forms.

Using the Check Writer Database

To try out Check Writer in read-only form, just double-click on Checks95 (or Checks95.mdb) in My Computer, as discussed earlier in this appendix. To actually use Check Writer, copy Checks95 (or Checks95.mdb) and Chkbook (or ChkBook.ico) to the My Documents folder, or some other folder of your choosing, on your hard disk. Then run Checks95 from your hard disk rather than the CD.

When Check Writer starts up, just follow the instructions on the screen to get around. Figure B.5 shows one of the sample screens from Check Writer.

From the Check-Writer Readme File

Check Writer for Microsoft Access 95 © 1995 Cary Prague Books and Software.

The main Check Writer switchboard offers four basic functions:

- **Check Writer/Register**   Add, change, delete, or print checks, deposits, and adjustments, or display the check register.

FIGURE B.5

Cary Prague Books
and Software's Check
Writer database
application

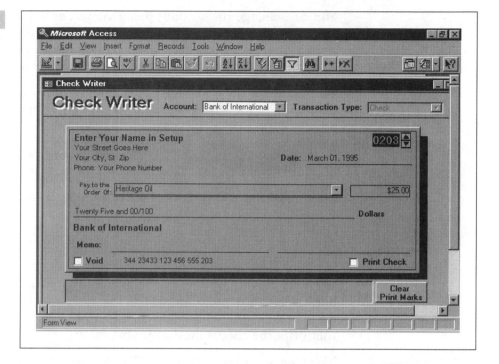

- **Check Reconciliation**   Display the Check Reconciliation system.

- **Bank Accounts**   Add, change, or delete Bank Account
  information.

- **Setup**   Enter your company information, recurring payees, and
  default bank account number.

The Check Writer comes with two sample bank accounts and a selection
of transactions to get you started. You can practice with those and then
create your own accounts.

You start by creating your own bank account (Bank Accounts icon) and
then make that bank account the default bank account (Setup icon).
Once you have done that you can open up the Check Writer and enter
transactions.

Use the buttons at the bottom of the form to navigate from record to record or between functions. Click on the Register icon to display the check
register. In the register, click on the Check icon to return to the check
writer form to enter or edit checks.

You can change the account being viewed at any time using the combo box at the top of the Check Writer form. You can only change the transaction type for new checks and can choose between checks, deposits, and a number of adjustments that you can add to by using the Setup icon.

You can enter the payee for a check or select from the combo box in the payee line of the check. You can add more recurring payees in the Setup screen.

When you mark a check as void, a void stamp will appear on the check and it will not be counted in the check register or check reconciliation.

The area below the check is the voucher stub and anything you enter is printed when you select certain types of checks.

Press the Find… button to display a dialog box showing five ways to find a check, deposit, or adjustment.

Press the Print… button to display a dialog box allowing you to print the current check/deposit/adjustment, marked checks, a range of checks by date, or a range of checks by check number. You can modify the reports that print the checks for custom paper.

The Check Writer is normally $79.95. Mention *Mastering Microsoft Access for Windows 95* and you can buy the documentation for only $49.95. To order full documentation or purchase tech support call us at (860) 644-5891, fax us at (860) 648-0710, or e-mail us at 71700,2126 or send mail to CARYP on the Microsoft Network, or CaryP@msn.com from the Internet.

Sample Business Forms

Cary Prague Books and Software has also provided some samples of their pre-designed business forms. To view them:

1. Double-click on abforms (or abforms.mdb) in the My Computer window for the CD, as discussed near the start of this appendix.

2. When you get to the database window, click on the Forms tab.

3. To view a sample form, just double-click on its name in the database window.

The purpose of the abforms database is simply to show you a small sampling of ready-to-use business forms that you can purchase from the vendor. The section that follows was contributed by the vendor, Cary Prague Books and Software.

More from Cary Prague Books and Software

We also have fully customizable Payroll for Microsoft Access for only $129.95. You can also purchase our fully customizable business accounting product named *Yes! I Can Run My Business* at $50–$200 off of our regular prices:

Single User Edition: $299.95 Only $249.95

Unlimited Multiuser: $399.95 Only $349.95

Royalty Free Developer: $999.95 Only $799.95

You can also request a free catalog of all our products and services including books, videos, and add-on software for Windows 95, Microsoft Access 2.0 and 95, Visual FoxPro, and Visual Basic 4.0.

Cary Prague Books and Software
60 Krawski Drive
S. Windsor, CT 06074

Telephone: (860) 644-5891
Fax: (860) 648-0710
CIS: 71700-2126
Internet: 71700,2126@compusrv.com
Microsoft Network: CARYP

United States Postal Service Barcodes

TAZ Information Services has generously donated their shareware True-Type font for printing PostNet bar codes. (TrueType™ Font copyright © 1993 TAZ Information Services, Inc. All Rights Reserved.)

The shareware TrueType font for printing PostNet barcodes is contained in the file Uspsttfs.ttf. This font must be installed using the Windows 95 Control Panel. (Do not install the Uspsttfs.fon file.) To install the font:

1. Insert the CD-ROM that comes with this book into your CD-ROM drive.

2. At the Windows 95 desktop, click on the Start button and point to Settings.

3. Click on Control Panel.

4. Double-click on the Fonts folder.

5. Choose File ➤ Install New Font from the Font window's menu bar.

6. Make sure the Copy fonts to Font Folder check box is checked.

7. Under Drives choose the drive letter for your CD-ROM drive.

8. Under Folders, double-click on the USPSTTF folder.

9. Under List of Fonts, click on USPSTTF (TrueType), as below.

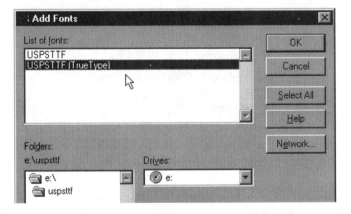

10. Choose OK and follow the instructions on the screen.

Once installed, you can use the font as you would any other TrueType font. For example, when creating a report in Microsoft Access's design view, you can choose any control on the report. Then use the Formatting (Form/Report Design) toolbar to choose the USPSTTF font for that control.

From TAZ Information Services

The remainder of this section was supplied by TAZ Information Services. If you have any questions about their products, please contact them directly at:

TAZ Information Services, Inc.
PO Box 452
Linthicum, MD 21090-0452

Telephone: (800) 279-7579
America Online: TAZ INFO

Specifications

To meet the U.S. Postal Service (USPS) specifications, the barcodes must be set in 16 point and the FIM pattern must be set in 72 point.

The frame bar that begins and terminates the POSTNET is generated by the keyboard character "s" or "S." The barcoding of the Zip Code itself follows USPS formats for 5-, 9-, or 11-digit Zip Code information by simply typing the numbers. The FIM patterns are obtained by typing the character of the desired pattern (either "a" "A," "b" "B," or "c" "C" for FIM A, FIM B, or FIM C, respectively).

Following are the three formats defined and an example of the keyboard input necessary to generate the proper POSTNET. In these examples, the address P.O. Box 452 and Zip Code 21090-0452 is used.

Five-Digit Zip Code (A Field)

Frame Bar	5-digit ZipCode	Correction Character	Frame Bar
S	21090	8	S

Keyboard = s210908s

Zip + 4 Code (C Field)

Frame Bar	5-digit ZipCode	+4 Code	Correction Character	Frame Bar
S	21090	0452	7	S

Keyboard = s2109004527s

Delivery Point Barcode (DPBC) (C Prime Field)

Frame Bar	5-digit ZipCode	+4 Code	Delivery Point	Correction Character	Frame Bar
S	21090	0452	52	0	S

Keyboard = s210900452520s

The generation of the Correction Character is accomplished by adding the digits in the Zip Code to be used (either 5, 9, or 11 digits). The correction character is the number that must be added to this sum to produce a total that is a multiple of 10. In other words,

Correction Character = $10 - (X(\bmod 10))$,

where X is the sum of the digits.

For example $2 + 1 + 0 + 9 + 0 + 0 + 4 + 5 + 2 = 23$. The next highest multiple of 10 is 30. Thus, the Correction Character is 7, $30 - 23 = 7$.

The generation of a Delivery Point is, generally, to append the last two digits of the address line (street address, P.O. Box, rural route, etc.) to the Zip +4 Zip Code number. The Correction Character is then generated on this number, i.e., sum of digits (21090045252) = 30. Thus, the Correction Character is zero (0).

However, because of the wide variation of address line numbers, such as fractional streets, letter suffix, etc., no complete rule can be given here. A publication titled *Letter Mail Barcode Update* and dated May 1992 is available through your postmaster and contains all the rules for the generation of the delivery point.

CASS Certification

Pre-printing the POSTNET barcode on your mail can improve delivery through the USPS. By obtaining a CASS Certification of your mailing list, you can substantially reduce your postage costs. TAZ can perform the CASS Certification of your mailing list required for reduced postage rates via disk or online file transfer. See the file Cass.txt in the USPSTTF folder for further information.

Disclaimer

TAZ Information Services, Inc. makes no warranties on this trial copy of the USPS Barcodes and FIM Patterns TrueType font. In no event shall TAZ Information Services, Inc. be liable for any damages whatsoever arising out of the use of or inability to use this sample product.

Registering Your Fonts

Thank you for trying the USPS Barcodes and FIM Patterns TrueType Font. If you have any questions about these fonts, please contact TAZ Information Services, Inc. TAZ will attempt to answer all questions; however, support is only guaranteed for registered users.

To register your fonts, please print and complete the form titled REGIS-TER.TXT in the USPSTTF folder on the CD-ROM that came with this book.

To check with Better Business Bureau of Greater Maryland, call (900) 225-5222.

APPENDIX

C

Installing and Using
Fulfill 95

FULFILL 95 is a sample order-entry database application that you can use and explore freely. It's especially designed for what we call "SHMOOP" users (where SHMOOP is sort of an acronym for *S*mall Office, *H*ome Office, *M*obile *O*ffice, and Home *P*C.) Which, as you may know, is the same group of users that Windows 95 itself is geared to. You can use Fulfill to manage a mail-order, or similar business.

Fulfill 95 is a completely custom Access application. We didn't use Database Wizards to create it. Fulfill offers many more bells and whistles than the Wizard-generated order-entry application and is, in our opinion, much easier to use. Even if you don't need an order-entry database, you might still want to try out Fulfill. You'll probably discover some neat tricks that you can incorporate into your own custom Access databases.

There are two versions of Fulfill 95 on the CD-ROM disc that comes with this book:

- **FulfillS.mdb**   This version of Fulfill already contains some hypothetical data that will make it easy to get a feel for how Fulfill works.

- **Fulfill.mdb**   This version comes with most of Fulfill's tables empty, so you can add your own data from scratch.

We suggest that you try the FulfillS version first, to play around and get a feel for how Fulfill works. If you then decide you can use Fulfill in your "real work," you're welcome to copy and use the Fulfill.mdb version. Just be sure to read this disclaimer first.

WARNING

While every effort has been made to prevent bugs and errors, Fulfill 95 has never actually been tested in the field. If you plan to use Fulfill 95 to manage "real data," we strongly suggest that you run it in parallel with your existing manual or automated order-entry system for a while, to see if it performs as you expect. Address any problems or errors to the author, whose address appears in Fulfill's Help ➤ About ➤ Author screen.

The focus in this appendix is on how to *use* Fulfill 95. If tinkering with Fulfill makes you curious about what makes it tick, you're more than welcome to peek under the hood. Chapter 28 discusses techniques for exploring Fulfill 95 and similar open applications behind the scenes.

Copying Fulfill 95 to Your Hard Disk

Fulfill 95 is an Access database, and therefore will only work on a computer that has Microsoft Access for Windows 95 installed. All you need to do is copy FulfillS.mdb (or Fulfill.mdb) from the CD-ROM onto your hard disk. You can use any copying technique you want. And you can copy Fulfill to any folder you want. Here are some step-by-step instructions to copy FulfillS.mdb to the My Documents folder on drive C:

1. Close any open applications to get to the Windows 95 desktop.

2. Insert the CD-ROM disk that came with this book into your CD-ROM drive.

3. At the Windows 95 desktop, double-click on the My Computer icon.

4. Double-click on the icon for your C: drive, then move and size the window so you can see the icon for the destination folder (the folder you'll be copying *to*), My Documents in this example.

5. Go back to My Computer and double-click on the icon for your CD-ROM drive (typically drive D:).

6. Size and position the window so you can see both the destination folder and the FulfillS.mdb file in Figure C.1.

7. Drag the FulfillS.mdb file (or Fulfill.mdb file) from the CD-ROM drive to the My Documents folder, and then release the mouse button.

You'll probably see an indicator showing the progress of the copy. When the copying is complete, you can close the windows for the C: drive and your CD-ROM drive.

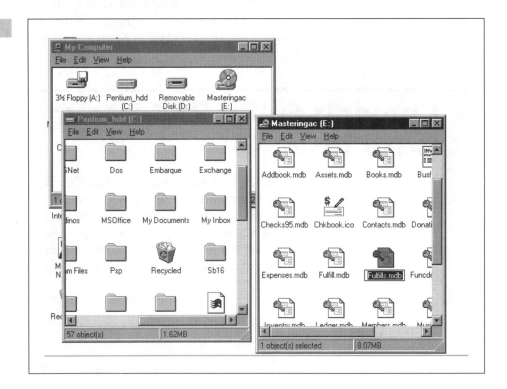

Starting Fulfill 95

Once you've copied FulfillS.mdb (or Fulfill.mdb) to your hard disk, you can use either of these techniques to start Access and load the Fulfill 95 database:

- Open the folder in which you've stored the database, and double-click on the FulfillS.mdb file icon, as below.

     .doc   FulfillS.mdb Gwsh.

- Or, start Microsoft Access, and use the File ➤ Open Database commands to browse to and open FulfillS.mdb (or Fulfill.mdb).

Microsoft Access for Windows 95 will start up, with the main switchboard for Fulfill 95 displayed, as in Figure C.2.

FIGURE C.2

The main switchboard for Fulfill 95

N O T E   When Fulfill 95 starts up, you still have access to the standard Access menus and toolbars. Normally, we would have created custom menus and toolbars for an application such as this. But we want you to be able to explore "behind the scenes" easily, so we left all the standard Access tools in place.

Entering Information About Your Business

The first time you use Fulfill 95, you need to tell it about your business. You only need to do this once, of course, not every time you start Fulfill. To enter information about your business:

1. Click on the My Biz Info button in the main switchboard.

2. Fill in the blanks as instructed on the screen, then click on the Click Here When Done button. You're returned to Fulfill's main switchboard.

If you're using FulfillS 95 you'll see some data already filled in, as in Figure C.3. You can leave that information as-is. Or change it, if you prefer.

Using Fulfill's Address Book

An important part of any order-entry system is the ability to manage names and addresses of customers, prospects, and suppliers. Fulfill 95 comes with a handy address book that makes it very easy to do so. To get to Fulfill's Address Book, just click on the Address Book button on Fulfill's main switchboard. You'll be taken to the Address Book form shown in Figure C.4. If you're using FulfillS, you'll see the address for a hypothetical company on the screen.

FIGURE C.3

The form for filling in
information about
your own business in
Fulfill 95

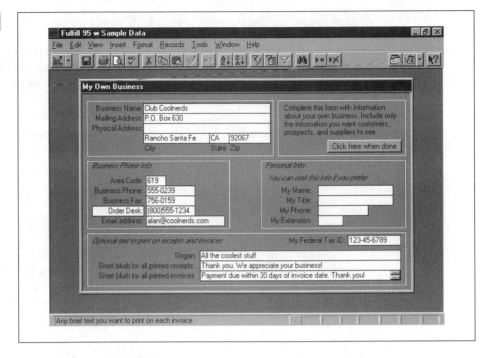

FIGURE C.4

Fulfill's Address Book
form with a sample
company address
displayed

Adding a Name and Address

Adding a new name and address to Fulfill's address book is simply a matter of clicking on a button and filling in the blanks. But, there are lots of little time-savers and shortcuts available that you might miss if you don't read the sections that follow. To get started:

1. Click on the <u>A</u>dd button near the bottom of the Address Book form.

2. Now you can start filling in the blanks for a new name and address as discussed in the sections that follow.

Entering the Name and Company

The first few blanks in the Address book are for typing a person's name and affiliation. If there is no particular person's name for this address (just a business name), you can leave these fields blank and skip right down to Department/Title or Org/Company. If you do have a person's name to type in:

- Type in an honorific (Ms., Mr. Etc.), or choose one from the drop-down list under Mr/Mrs as shown below. You can leave this blank if you want.

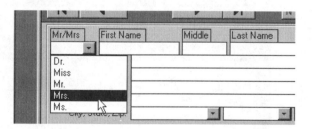

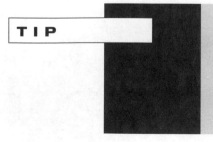

TIP

If you want to open a drop-down list without taking your hands off the keyboard, just press Alt+↓. Then you can use the ↑ and ↓ keys to point to a selection, and press ↵ to select it. Also, if you want to change the Mr/Mrs drop-down list, just double-click on the Mr/Mrs blank and follow the instructions on the screen.

- Press Tab to move to the next field, or just click on the next field you want to fill.

- Type in a middle name or initial. If you enter a single character, such as *C*, Fulfill will automatically add the period for you (*C.*).

- Type in a Last Name.

TIP If you're not sure how to fill in a blank on a form, try right-clicking and choosing <u>I</u>nfo from the shortcut menu that appears.

- If there is a department, title, organization, or company name affiliated with the address you're entering, type that information into the Department/Title and/or Org/Company blanks. You may also leave either, or both, fields empty.

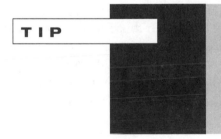

TIP Tips for aspiring developers: The custom shortcut menu is assigned to the Address Book form's Shortcut Menu Bar property. Macros named AddressBookShortcut and AddressBookShortcut_Shortcut display the menu. The Info help is handled by a module named ShortcutMenuInfo.

Entering the Street Address

Now you need to type in the mailing address:

- If the blinking cursor isn't in the Mailing Address field yet, click on the field, or press Tab until the cursor gets there.

- Type in the mailing address (required) then press Tab or Enter. The cursor jumps to the Zip Code field, for reasons we'll describe in a moment.

- If you need to type in a second address line, do so in the Physical Address line. You can just backtrack to that field at any time, by clicking on it or by pressing Shift+Tab.

NOTE Pressing Tab or Enter *always* moves the blinking cursor forward to the next field in the form. Pressing Shift+Tab always moves the cursor back to the previous field. You can move the cursor to any field on the form simply by clicking on that field.

Entering the City, State, Zip, and Area Code

After typing in the mailing address and pressing Tab or Enter, the cursor lands in the Zip Code field. This is because Fulfill will try to fill in the City, State, and Area Code automatically for you after you enter a Zip Code. Note that when entering a U.S. Zip+4 code, you can omit the hyphen, and Fulfill will add it for you. For example, if you type 920671234 as a Zip Code, Fulfill will automatically change that to 92067-1234. Anyway, here's how to proceed:

- Type the Zip Code and press Tab or Enter.

- If you *don't* hear a beep, Fulfill has made a "best guess" on the City, State, and Area Code, and filled in those fields. *But you still need to check, and perhaps correct, Fulfill's guess, because the Fulfill doesn't always get it right!* The cursor lands on the Work Phone field.

- If you *do* hear a beep, that means Fulfill doesn't know that Zip Code. You'll have to type in the City, State, and Area Code yourself.

Fulfill will not change the City, State, or Area Code if you've already filled it in. Fulfill assumes that if you've already filled in the field with some information, it shouldn't try to second-guess you with it's own information!

Fulfill is pretty accurate when filling in the City, State, and Area Code for a particular Zip Code. But it's not 100 percent accurate because some Zip Codes cover multiple townships and Area Codes. (Not to mention the fact that Zip and Area Codes get re-mapped all the time!)

TIP Tips for aspiring application developers: The Zip Codes are stored in a table named ZipLookup. The event procedure that looks up the Zip Code and fills in the City, State, and Area Code is attached to the After Update property of the Zip/PostalCode field in the AddressBook form.

Making Fulfill 100 percent accurate on filling in the City, State, and Area Code from the Zip Code would require storing a huge collection of data that would eat up disk space and slow things down. As it stands, Fulfill contains a list of about 44,000 Zip, City, State, and Area Code combinations that make it accurate enough to be worth including.

If Fulfill doesn't find a Zip Code you type in often, you can add that Zip Code to the list. Just double-click on the field where you type in the Zip Code, and then follow the instructions on the screen.

Optionally, you can add the City, State, Zip, and Area Code combination to the City drop-down list, as we'll discuss next.

Using the City Drop-Down List If most of the addresses that you type in are within your own vicinity, you can pre-enter the City, State, Zip, and Area Code, so you don't have to type in *any* of that information in the future. To do this, just double-click on the City field. You'll come to the dialog box shown in Figure C.5. (If you're using FulfillS you'll see some examples already typed in.)

Just follow the on-screen instructions to add, change, or delete any City, State, Area Code, and Zip Code combination(s) that you would otherwise need to type in often. Click on OK to return to the Address Book form.

In the future, you'll be able to choose any City, State, Zip, Area Code from your custom drop-down list. After typing in the mailing address for an address in your own vicinity, click on the drop-down list button in the City field. Your custom list will appear, as in the example below. Just click on

FIGURE C.5

Double-clicking on the City field takes you to a dialog box for modifying the City drop-down list.

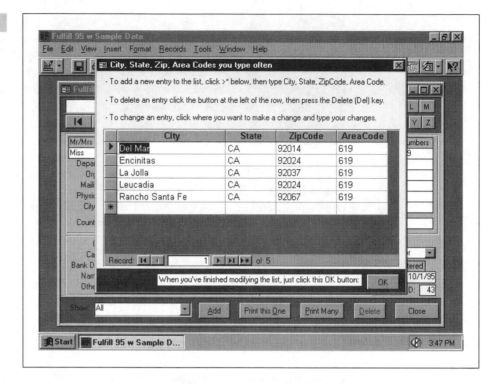

the one you want, and Fulfill will fill in the City, State, Zip, and Area Code fields for you.

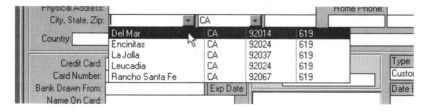

Note that there's also a drop-down list button for the State field. You can use that to fill in the two-letter abbreviation for any state in the United States.

Entering the Country

If you are entering an address that's within the United States, leave the Country and Dial Code fields empty. Blanks in those fields mean USA. If you are entering an address from a foreign country, you can type in the country name and dialing code, or choose a country from the Country field's drop-down list. You can also customize the Country drop-down list to better suit your own needs, using the standard "Fulfill" technique: Just double-click on the Country field, and follow the instructions that appear on the screen.

Entering the Area Code, Phone Numbers, and E-mail Address

When filling in the phone numbers, enter the Area Code only once at the top of the list. Unless, however, one of the phone numbers uses a different Area Code, such as 800, in which case you *do* want to type in the Area Code, as in the Toll Free example below:

You can leave any field blank if you don't have the appropriate information. Also, note that you can add a label and phone number for the last number in the list. For example, we typed in a Toll Free: label next to the phone number in the example shown.

When typing the phone number, you can omit the hyphen. For example, if you type 5551323, Fulfill will convert that to 555-1323 after you move to another field. If you do need to type in an area code with a particular phone number, you can omit the parentheses. For example, if you type 8005553323, Fulfill will convert that to (800)555-3323.

There are no shortcuts for the E-mail field. If the person you're entering has an e-mail address, just go ahead and type it into the E-Mail field.

Entering Credit Card Information

If you're entering the name and address for a customer who regularly pays by credit card, you can record that credit card information in the Address Book. Choose a credit card from the Credit Card drop-down list. If you accept a credit card that isn't in the list, you can add it to the list. Just double-click on the Credit Card field and follow the on-screen instructions.

WARNING

There is no security built into Fulfill 95 to prevent unauthorized users from seeing credit card info. If security is a concern, you should either omit the credit card information Or, at the least, omit the expiration date.

You can leave any of the Credit Card fields blank if you prefer. When typing in the expiration date, you should use the standard mm/yy format. But you can omit the slash and leading zero. For example, if you type 1296 Fulfill will convert that to 12/96. If you type 196 Fulfill will convert that to 01/96 (after you move to another field.)

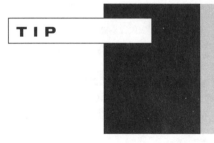

TIP

More tips for application developers: Most of the underlying fields in the AddressBook table are of the text data type, which makes it easier to create these little custom conversion routines. The conversion routines themselves are attached to the After Update properties of the various Phone fields and ExpirationDate field.

Entering Tax Exempt Information

The Tax Exempt fields are for those rare customers that are in a state where you normally charge sales tax but who are, for whatever reason, exempt from sales tax. If you acquire such a customer, you can just select (check) the Tax Exempt option. And, optionally, record the account number or whatever information that customer offers to justify their tax-exempt status. When entering orders for this customer later, Fulfill will not charge them sales tax.

NOTE

Fulfill only charges sales tax to customers in areas where you are required to charge sales tax. If a particular customer is in a region where you don't charge sales tax, it's not necessary to mark that person as tax exempt. Fulfill won't charge them sales tax anyway. You set up your sales tax rates in the Orders form, as we'll discuss later in this appendix. You don't need to concern yourself with that right now.

Entering Customer Notes

The empty white space under the Tax Exempt fields is for entering optional notes. The notes can be as long as you want them to be. Now you might be thinking "Yeah, but the box is so small." Here's a little trick for you:

- Double-click on the Notes field to make it larger, as below:

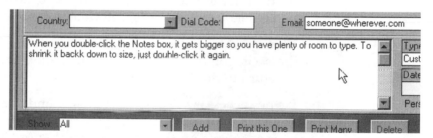

- Double-click on it again to shrink it back down to size.

TIP

Tip for aspiring application developers: The AddressBook form contains two controls bound to the Notes field, one named Notes, and an invisible one named BigNotes. The event procedures that make BigNotes visible/invisible are attached to the On Dbl Click property of the Notes and BigNotes controls.

Address Type, Date Entered, and Person ID

The final step in entering a person's name and address is to identify the addressee as a customer, prospect, or supplier. You can use the drop-down list button under Type, as shown below, to do so:

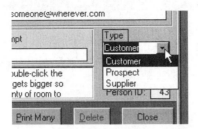

You can't change the Type drop-down list, so double-clicking on it does nothing. Fulfill uses the information in the Type field when printing information about customers, and *must* be able to identify the address as belonging to either a customer, prospect, or supplier.

The Date Entered and Person ID fields in the Fulfill's Address Book are filled in automatically, and cannot be changed. (In general, a yellow-tinted field on a form is for information only and cannot be changed.)

When you've finished typing in all the information for one name and address, click on the Add button to enter another address. Or click on Close to return to the Main Switchboard.

It's not necessary to enter every name and address through the Address Book form. As you'll discover, you can enter customer, prospect, and supplier addresses on the fly while entering orders and information about your products. But if you're not using FulfillS, and you want to try out some of the navigation and printing techniques discussed in the sections that follow, you should add at least a few names and addresses so you have some data to work with.

Navigating with the Address Book

The tools across the top of the address book are for navigation—finding a particular address to change or print. The address book is automatically kept in alphabetical order, based on the following rules:

- If there is an entry in the Last Name field, then the address is listed in alphabetical order by name.

- If a particular address has no entry in its Last Name field, then the entry is listed in alphabetical order by Company name.

So for example, suppose you have the following addresses in three records of the Address Book:

TABLE C.1: Sample Data in FirstName, LastName, and Company Fields of the AddressBook table

FIRST NAME	LAST NAME	COMPANY
		Sybex, Inc.
Levanthal	Sylvia	A & B Furniture
Andy	Adams	

Because the last two rows have Last Name entries, they are listed in alphabetical order by name. Since the first entry has no Last Name contents, it will always be listed in alphabetical order by company. Thus, the three entries would be alphabetized as:

Adams, Andy

Levanthal, Sylvia

Sybex, Inc.

TIP

Tip for aspiring developers: The tricky alphabetization scheme is handled by a calculated field in the query named AddressesAlphabetized.

Navigating around in Fulfill's Address Book is pretty easy, once you understand those rules. You just use the tools at the top of the form to zero in on the name you're looking for. Here are the exact steps:

- Click on one of the letters in the Rolodex button area to jump to that part of the alphabet. (If nothing in the alphabetical list starts with the letter you clicked, you'll just hear a beep, and nothing will change.)

- The drop-down list box to the left of the Rolodex buttons shows the first address entry that starts with that letter.

- Use the drop-down list button to view nearby names, as shown below. To jump to one of those names, just click on it in the drop-down list.

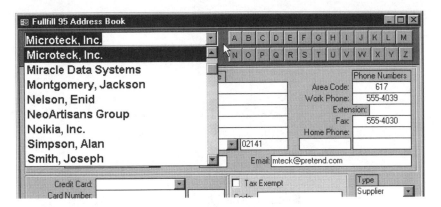

You can also use the navigation buttons surrounding A...Z buttons to move from record to record. To see where one of those buttons will take you just rest the mouse pointer on the button for a couple of seconds, and wait for the ToolTip to appear, as below.

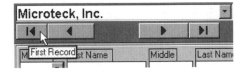

Searching the Address Book

If you're sure you've entered a particular name and address, but can't seem to find it using the navigation buttons, perhaps you've just forgotten the exact spelling of the person's last name or the company name. You can search for any text in any part of an address by following these steps:

NOTE

If you use the Show option to limit the display of address to Customers, Prospects, or Suppliers, and want to include *all* addresses in your search, set the Show option back to All before you begin the search.

1. If you want to search a particular field, right-click on that field. If you want to search all the fields in all the records, right-click on any field on the form.

2. Choose <u>F</u>ind from the shortcut menu that appears. You'll come to the Find dialog box shown below.

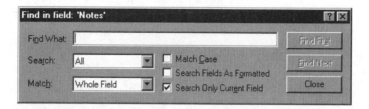

3. In the Fi<u>n</u>d What box, type the text you're looking for.

4. Set other options in the Find dialog box as follows:

- **Search**   Choose Up to search up from your current position, Down to search down from your current position, or All to search the whole address book (broadest search, most likely to find a match.)

- **Matc<u>h</u>**   Choose Whole Field, Start of Field, or Any Part of Field. The last option provides the broadest search and has the best chance of finding a match.

- **Match <u>C</u>ase**   Select this option only if you want to locate an exact uppercase/lowercase match to the text you typed. Leaving this option cleared provides a better chance of finding a match.

- **Search Fields As Formatted**   Looks for a specific format match rather than just an informational match. Leave this cleared to increase your chances of finding a match.

- **Search Only Current Field**   If you select (check) this box, only the field that you right-clicked on will be searched. The name of that field appears in the Find dialog box's title bar. To broaden the search and increase your chances of success, you can clear that check box.

5. Click on the Find Fir<u>s</u>t button to begin the search.

If Fulfill finds a match, the first matching record will be displayed. If you can't see the information behind the Find dialog box, just drag the dialog box out of the way (by its title bar.) If the found record is not the one you're looking for, you can click on the Find Next button to locate the next record that matches your request. When you find the record you're looking for (or are ready to give up), just click on the Close button in the Find dialog box to close that dialog box.

If you can't find the record you're looking for, perhaps you misspelled something in the entry. You might want to print a directory of all the names and addresses you've entered to see how everything is spelled. We'll talk about printing in a moment.

Limiting the Address Book Display

If you have lots of addresses in your address book, and want to limit the display to Customers, Prospects, or Suppliers, just choose an option from the Show drop-down list near the bottom of the form (see below.)

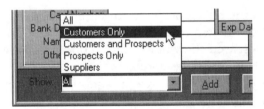

Any addresses that aren't of the type(s) you specified will be virtually invisible until you set the Show option back to All.

Printing from the Address Book

You can print information from the Address Book in a variety of formats at any time. If you want to print only the address currently showing on your screen, click on the Print This One button. You'll be taken to the dialog box shown in Figure C.6.

Just click on the format you want to print. Then click on the Preview button if you want to see how the address will look when printed. To actually print the address, prepare the printer and click on the Print button. When you've finished printing, just click on the Close button in the Quick Print One Address dialog box to return to the Address Book form.

FIGURE C.6

Options for printing
one name and
address from Fulfill's
Address Book

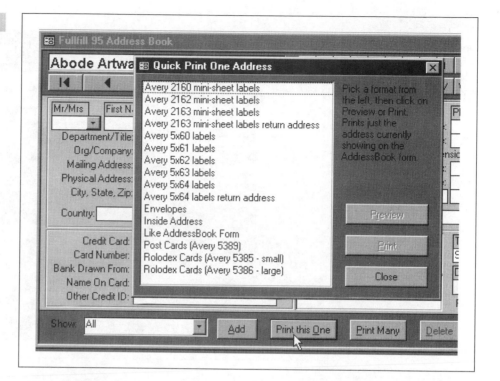

NOTE

The various label and card formats available in the Print
dialog boxes are standard Avery labels for laser and
inkjet printers. You can purchase those labels at most
office-supply and computer stores. The mini-labels
(Avery 2x6x) are for very small print runs (usually one
or two labels), and work properly only with certain
printers.

If you want to print several addresses, click on the Print Many button.
You'll be taken to the dialog box shown in Figure C.7.

To use this dialog box, first select a format from the drop-down list box.
After you do, you'll see more information on the screen. And, depending
on the format you selected, additional options in the dialog box will become available. For example, suppose you choose the Address Directory
format, as in Figure C.8.

FIGURE C.7

Options for printing several names and addresses from Fulfill's Address Book

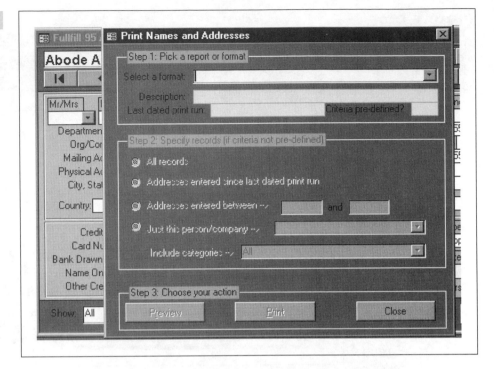

FIGURE C.8

Options for printing several names and addresses from Fulfill's Address Book

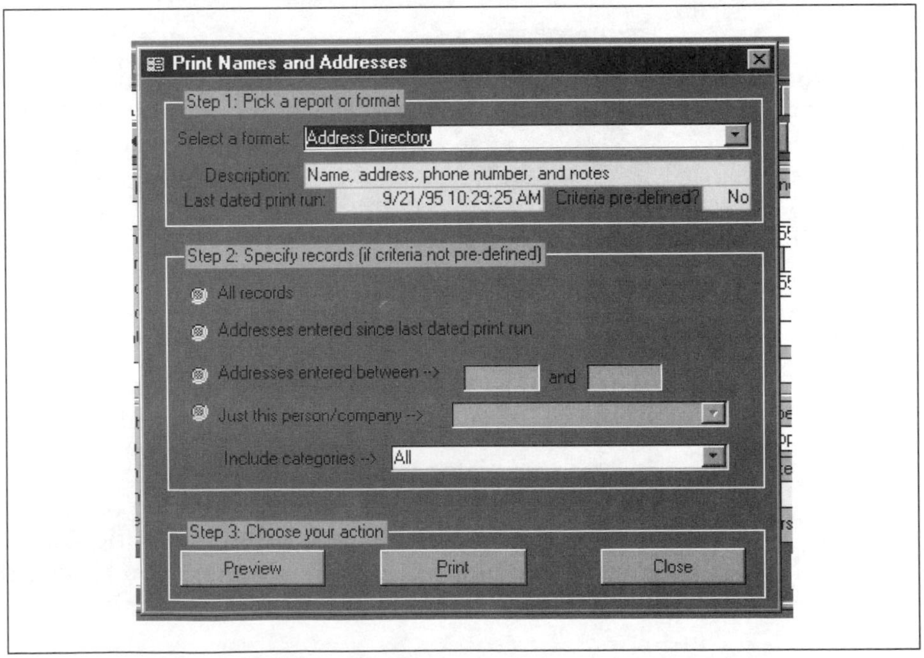

The yellow-tinted fields tell you some things about the format you've selected:

- **Description** Describes the format you've selected.

- **Last Dated Print Run** The date and time of the last time you printed in this format using the second option under step 2 (described in a moment).

- **Criteria Pre-defined?** If set to Yes, you cannot choose Criteria under step 2 because the criteria are already defined for this format. (The Categorized Address Summary and Possible Duplicates reports are the only two with pre-defined criteria.)

After selecting a format that allows you to specify your own criteria, you can choose options under Step 2 in the dialog box to specify which records you want to include in the printout:

- **All Records** All names and addresses within the selected category will be printed.

- **Addresses Entered Since Last Dated Print Run** Only new entries—those addresses entered since the date and time shown in the yellow Last Dated Print Run box will be printed. For example if you print Rolodex cards of your addresses, and want to print Rolodex cards only for addresses that you've never printed Rolodex cards for before, you would choose this option.

- **Addresses Entered Between**... If you choose this option, you can specify a range of dates to include. Initially the option will suggest "today" by setting both the start date and end date to today's date. But you can type in any range of dates you wish.

- **Just This Person/Company** You can pick a single person or company to include in the printout.

The Include Categories option lets you limit the printout even further. For example, if you choose Customers and Prospects from the Include Categories drop-down list, only addresses for those two categories will be printed. Suppliers will not be included in the print run.

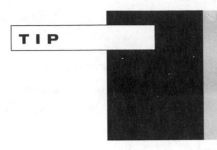

T I P

Tips for aspiring developers: The print dialog boxes are forms named AddressPrintOne and AddrRepPrintDialog in Fulfill. Visual Basic code attached to the Print and Preview buttons handle much of the work of setting up an appropriate query and previewing/printing the reports.

If you select All next to Include Categories, then all types of addresses—Customers, Prospects, and Suppliers—will be included in the print run.

Once you've made your selections, you can click on the Preview button to see how the printed report will look. Once you're in the Preview mode you can click on the document, or use the various Zoom tools on the toolbar to change magnification. When you're done previewing, just click on the Close button in the toolbar.

To print the addresses, click on the Print button. If you requested labels or cards, you'll hear a beep and see a message reminding you to load the proper stock into the printer. Load the paper, and then choose OK to start printing.

Managing Your Product List

Before you start filling orders, you should type in information about some (or all) of the products you sell. You can add products on the fly while entering orders. But you need at least a few products in the list to get the benefits of Fulfill's order form.

If you're using FulfillS, there are already several products and product categories entered for you. But you may want to follow along in the sections that follow, just to get a feel for the Products component of Fulfill.

Adding New Products

When you want to add a product to the list of products that you sell, just follow these steps:

1. In Fulfill 95's Main Switchboard, click on the <u>P</u>roducts button. You'll come to the form shown in Figure C.9.

2. Click on the Add New Product button near the bottom of the form.

3. Fill in the blanks for a single product, using techniques summarized in the sections that follow.

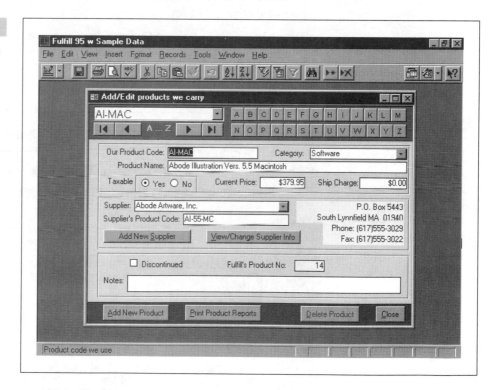

Typing In Product Information

You can assign whatever code or abbreviation you like to each product you carry. However, each product must have its own unique identifying code. (That is to say, no two products can have the same ID code.) Later, when you're entering orders, Fulfill will present products in alphabetical order by code. So you should try to come up with a code that will be easy to remember.

You also need to assign the product to a product category. Choose a category from the Category drop-down list. Or, if you need to create a new category, double-click on the Category field. You'll come to a screen like the one in Figure C.10. Just follow the on-screen instructions to add, change, or delete a product category, then choose OK to return to the Products form.

Type in the rest of the information as follows:

Product Name   Enter a name or description that specifically identifies this product.

Taxable   Choose Yes if this product is taxable in the region(s) in which you charge sales tax. If the product is not taxable, choose No.

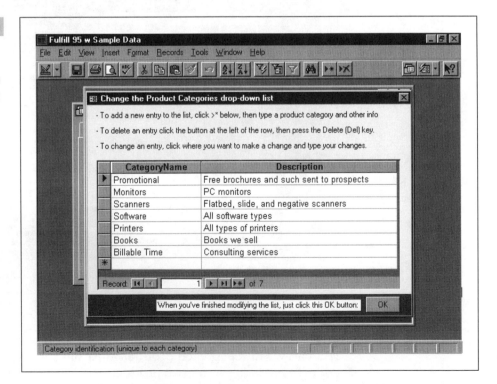

FIGURE C.10

Double-clicking on the Category drop-down list in the Products form takes you to this dialog box, where you can add/change product categories.

Current Price   Type the current selling price of the product.

Ship Charge   If this product carries its own special shipping charge, type in that amount. Otherwise, leave at $0.00. (Example: You might tack an extra shipping charge onto especially large or heavy products that are costly to ship.)

Entering Product Supplier and Other Info

If the product you're describing here is one you purchase wholesale from a supplier, then use the drop-down list button to choose that supplier. If you haven't already entered the supplier's name and address into Fulfill's Address Book, click on the Add New Supplier button, and follow the instructions on the screen to fill in the new supplier's name and address.

TIP   If you are the supplier as well as the seller, enter your own name and address into Fulfill's Address Book as a Supplier. Then choose your own business as the Supplier when entering information about the product.

The yellow-tinted supplier information comes from Fulfill's Address Book, and cannot be changed on this form. You may, however, click on the View/Change Supplier Info button if you need to make a quick change to the supplier's info while in the Products form. Use the Supplier's Product Code field to store the product code that the supplier uses to identify this product.

Finally, you can use the Notes field to type any other descriptive information about this product. The yellow-tinted Fulfill's Product Number code is assigned automatically. You can select (check) the Discontinued box should you stop carrying this product at some time in the future.

NOTE   Once you start entering product information, you should complete the whole form. Otherwise, Fulfill might not save the entry when you close the form. Or, you might get stuck, at which point you'll need to either complete the form, or choose Edit ➤ Undo... from the menu bar to cancel out the entry.

Navigating in the Products Form

You can also use the Products form to look up and change existing information. Your product list is kept in alphabetical order by your Product ID. So to quickly locate a product in your product list:

- Use the Rolodex-style buttons to click on a part of the alphabet (where you're looking to match the first letter of a product's ID code.)

- If you don't land on the appropriate product at first try, select a nearby product ID from the drop-down list, as shown below.

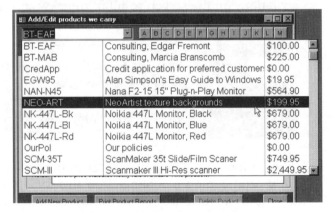

- You can also use the VCR-style buttons to move from product to product.

Printing Product Information

To print your product list,

1. Click on the Print Product Reports button near the bottom of the Products form. You'll be taken to this dialog box.

2. Select (check) the report(s) you want to print.

3. To preview the reports, click on the P̲review button. To print the report(s), click on the P̲rint button.

Entering Orders

After you've entered some data into the My Biz Info, Address Book, and Products portions of Fulfill (or have copied FulfillS, which contains the sample data), most of your work with Fulfill will center around the Order Forms. To add, view, change, or print orders, you start with this simple step:

- In Fulfill's Main Switchboard, click on the O̲rders Central button.

You're taken to the Orders Central switchboard shown in Figure C.11.

FIGURE C.11

The Orders Central switchboard is where you'll do all your work with orders.

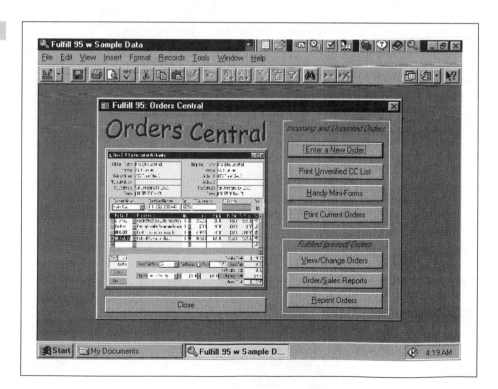

Entering a New Order

When you are ready to take an order, you need to get to a blank order form, and start filling in the blanks. To get started, click on the Enter A New Order button in the Orders Central switchboard. You're taken to the form shown in Figure C.12.

- If a new customer or prospect (one whose name isn't already in Fulfill's Address book) is placing the order, click on the New Customer/Prospect button. Then see Adding a New Customer/Prospect on the Fly below.

- If an Existing Customer/Prospect (one whose name is already in Fulfill's address book) is placing the Order, click on the Existing Customer/Prospect button, and continue below.

After you choose Existing Customer/Prospect you're taken to the dialog box shown in Figure C.13. The navigation tools at the top of this dialog box work exactly as they do in the Address Book form discussed earlier

FIGURE C.12

Step 1 in filling an order is identifying whom the order is for.

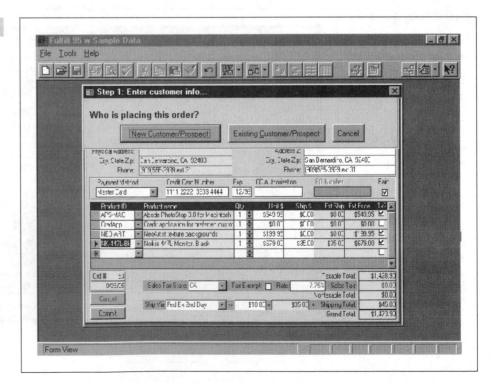

FIGURE C.13

Use the navigation tools at the top of this form to locate the customer/prospect who is placing the order. Then click on the To New Order Form button.

in this appendix. All you need to do is locate the Customer/Prospect who is placing the order, and then click on the To New Order Form button.

At this point, you can skip down to the section titled "Filling in the Rest of the Order Form" below.

Adding a New Customer/Prospect on the Fly

If you choose New Customer/Prospect in response to the question "Who is placing this order?", you'll be taken to the dialog box shown in Figure C.14.

When entering the customer's (or prospect's) name and address, you can use some handy shortcuts and techniques that the Address Book offers to speed your data entry. (If you skipped all that, see "Adding a Name and Address" earlier in this appendix.) After you've filled in as many blanks as you can, click on the To New Order Form button to move onto the order form.

FIGURE C.14

Use this form to enter a new customer (or prospect's) name and address before moving on to the order form.

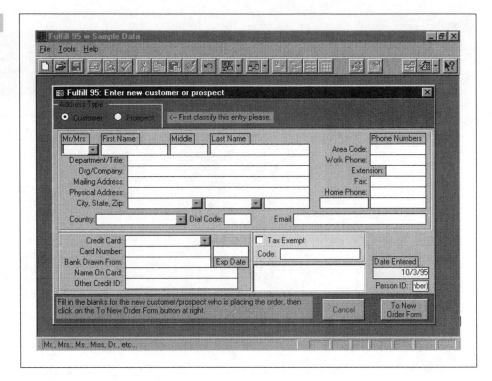

Filling In the Rest of the Order Form

After you've clicked on the To New Order Form button, you're taken to the actual order form, which is shown in Figure C.15. Notice that much of the order form is already filled in for you:

- The Bill To name and address is already filled in with the customer's name and address. These yellow-tinted boxes cannot be changed here on the order form.

- The Ship To name and address are, initially, the same as those in "Bill To." But you can change any of that information simply by clicking where you want to make a change and typing in the new information.

- If you've stored credit card information for this customer, the Payment Method is set to that credit card and the credit card number and expiration date are filled in automatically.

FIGURE C.15

After you click on the To New Order Form button, you're taken to the actual order form with many of the blanks already filled in for you.

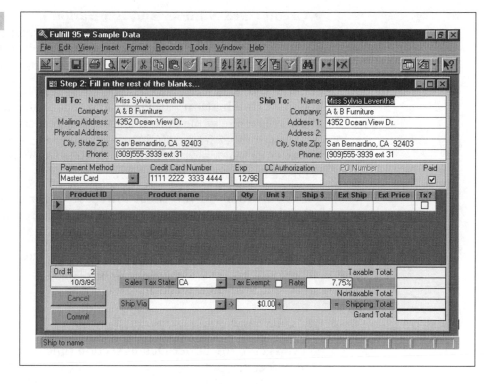

Filling In the Payment Information

When filling in the payment method section of the form, you can use these handy techniques and shortcuts:

- **Payment Method** Choose any payment method from the Payment Method drop-down list shown below. If you need to add a new payment method to the list, just double-click on the Payment Method field and follow the instructions on the screen.

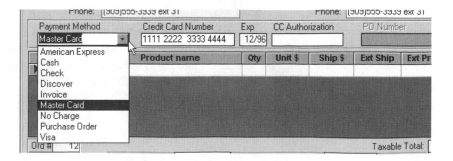

- **Credit Card Number and Expiration Date**   Fill in the Credit Card Number box only if the customer is paying by credit card. If you choose the credit card that you entered into the Address Book for this person, the card number and expiration date will be filled in automatically.

- **CC Authorization**   If you have some means of verifying a credit card purchase while entering an order, you can fill in the authorization number in the CC Authorization box. Optionally, you can leave this blank and fill it in at any time in the future, as we'll discuss a little later in this section.

- **PO Number**   If you chose Purchase Order as the Payment Method for this order, you can type the customer's Purchase Order number into the PO Number field.

- **Paid**   If you select (check) the Paid box, the order is marked Paid and Fulfill will print a receipt. If you leave the Paid check box empty, Fulfill will print an invoice.

Filling In the Order Details

When you get to the Order Details section (line items) of the form, here's how to proceed:

- **Product ID**   Click on the Product ID field, then click on the drop-down list button that appears to see your list of products (as shown below.) You can type the first letter of the Product ID you're looking for to quickly jump to that section of the list. When you see the Product ID you're looking for, click on it to select it. The Product Name appears, and the cursor jumps to the Qty (quantity) field.

NOTE

To add a new product to your product list on the fly, double-click on the Product ID or Product Name field. Then choose Add A New Product. Fill in the blanks and choose Close. When you get back to the order form, use the Product ID drop-down list button to select the new product.

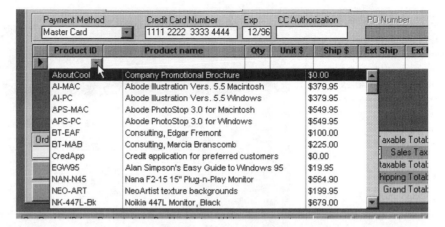

- **Qty**　The default quantity is one (1). If you need to enter a different value, just type it in. You can type in fractional numbers, such as 2.5 (for 2.5 hours of billable time, for instance).

- **Unit $** (Unit Price) and **Ship $** (per-unit shipping charge) fields are "suggestions" based on the contents of the Products field. But you can change either value for the current order. The Extended shipping charge (Ext Ship) and Extended Price (Ext Price) are calculated automatically.

You can add as many line items as necessary.

Sales Tax and Ship Via

The sales tax rate for an order is based on the values you put into the drop-down list. To change the sales tax you charge in any given state, double-click on the Sales Tax State field. You'll come to the dialog box shown in Figure C.16.

You should also check the Sales Tax State entry to make sure that Fulfill has typed in the correct state, tax exempt status, and rate for you. If any one of those is incorrect, just type in the corrected value. The sales tax amount is calculated automatically from your entry.

You can also choose a shipping method from the Ship Via drop-down list. If you need to add a shipping method, or change its dollar amount, double-click on the Ship Via field and follow the instructions on the screen.

FIGURE C.16

Use this list to specify the sales tax rate you charge in states where you do charge sales tax. Leave the rate at 0.00% in states where you don't charge sales tax.

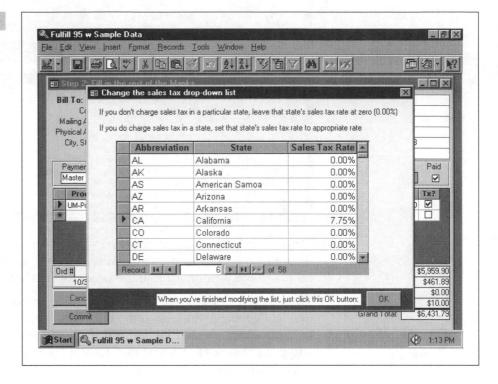

Note that the Shipping Total is based on the shipping charge of your Ship Via selection, plus the total per-unit ship charge from the Ext Ship column of the line items.

Cancel or Commit

Once you've completed one order, take a look at the form to check for any errors (it's always easier to correct errors *before* you save your work). Figure C.17 shows a sample completed order on the screen.

When you're finished, click on the Commit button to save the order. Or, if you don't want to save this order, click on the Cancel button. You'll be returned to Orders Central. From there, you can either enter another new order (by clicking on Enter A New Order again), or return to the Main Switchboard (by clicking on the Close button), or start printing information about the current order(s), using the buttons beneath the Enter A New Order button.

FIGURE C.17

Use this list to specify the sales tax rate you charge in states where you do charge sales tax. Leave the rate at 0.00% in states where you don't charge sales tax.

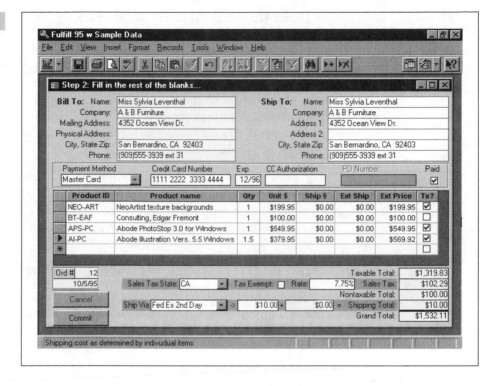

Tools for Managing Current (Unprinted) Orders

Other buttons in Orders Central give you some quick tools for managing current orders (*current orders* being orders that have been typed into Fulfill, but not yet printed as invoices, receipts, and so forth.) Those buttons are:

- **Print Underlined CC List**   Prints a list of credit card orders and expiration dates, to make it easier for you to call in for verification on those cards.

- **Handy Mini-Forms**   Offers three small forms that make it easy to 1) fill in credit card verification numbers (after you've called in for authorization using whatever means you have available), 2) mark unpaid orders as Paid (after you've received payment), and 3) change any addresses currently marked as Prospect to Customer (after the prospect has actually made a purchase).

- **Print Current Orders**   Prints packing slips, invoices, receipts, and labels for current orders.

You can print current orders at any time. For example, you might want to take in orders for the entire day, then perhaps verify the credit card purchases and fill in the verification numbers using the Handy Forms described above. Then, at the end of the day, use the Print Current Orders button to print the day's invoices, receipts, packing slips, mailing labels, and shipping labels.

Once you have printed current orders, they are no longer considered "current." Rather, they're considered "printed" (or "fulfilled") orders. If you need to review, change, or reprint those printed orders, you can use the last three buttons in Orders Central, as discussed next.

Tools for Managing Printed Orders

The lower three buttons in Orders Central let you work with all orders in Fulfill. That is, you're not limited to current (unprinted) orders. We'll discuss each of those buttons in the sections that follow:

View/Change Orders

The View/Change Orders button takes you to an order form that's used strictly for viewing, changing, and printing orders. When you click on the View/Change Orders button, you come to an order form that has navigation tools. You can turn those navigation tools on or off simply by clicking on the Navigation Tools On/Off button in the toolbar. Figure C.18 shows the View/Edit Orders form with the navigation tools turned on.

To locate a specific order, you can use the same basic techniques you use to navigate the Address Book. That is to say, orders are organized in alphabetical order by Bill To name. So to look up a specific order, you first look up the name of the person or company that placed the order. So the procedure goes like this:

- Click on one of the Rolodex-Style buttons to jump to a section of the alphabet (where you're looking for the name of the person or company that placed the order).

- Click on the drop-down list button just to the left to see nearby orders. There may be more than one order for any customer, but the

FIGURE C.18

The View/Edit
Orders form with
the navigation tools
turned on

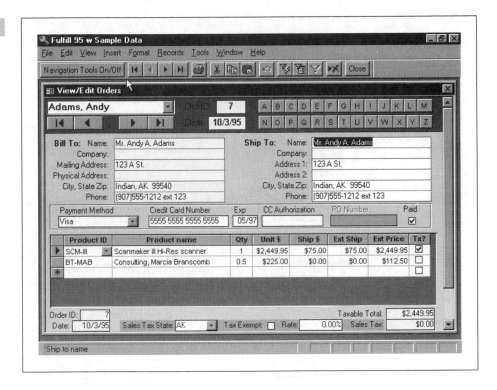

drop-down list also shows the Order ID and Order Date (see below.) So you should be able to zero in on a specific order easily.

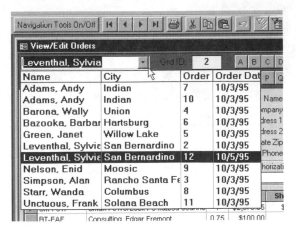

- You can use the VCR-style navigation buttons to scroll through orders as well.

On a 640 × 480 monitor, the navigation buttons make it hard to see the bottom of the order form. So once you find the order you want to work with, click on the Navigation Tools On/Off button in the toolbar to hide those tools, and see the entire order form.

WARNING

Canceled orders do show in View/Change Orders, with a check mark in the Canceled box. But canceled orders are never printed, and are never used in calculating sales, sales tax, or any of the other reports available from the Order/Sales Reports button.

If you change an order, and need to reprint it, you can just click on the Print This Order Now button in the toolbar. When you've finished viewing/changing orders, click on the Close button to return to Orders Central.

Orders/Sales Reports

The Orders/Sales Reports button lets you print information about all orders, or just a range of orders you specify. When you click on the Orders/Sales Reports button you're taken to the dialog box shown below.

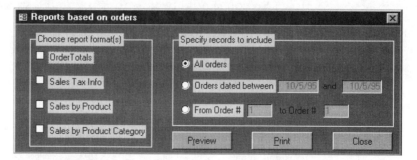

You can select any combination of reports simply by clicking on their check boxes. You can also include All Orders, Orders within a certain range of dates, or a range of orders by Order ID. Then choose the Preview button to preview the reports on the screen, or choose Print to actually print the reports. When you've finished with this dialog box, click on the Close button to return to Orders Central.

Reprint Orders

If you need to reprint any invoices, receipts, or labels for orders that you've previously printed using the Print Current Orders button, then just click on the Reprint Orders button. You'll be taken to this dialog box:

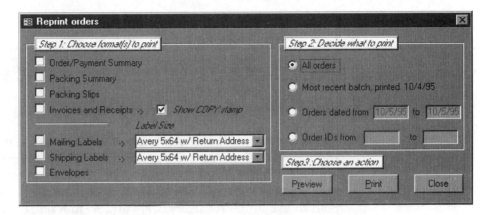

As instructed on the screen, select a format (or formats) to print. Then decide what to print, and click on the Preview or Print button. Click on the Close button to return to Orders Central.

Exiting Fulfill 95

To exit Fulfill 95, get back to the main switchboard and click on the E<u>x</u>it button. You'll come to the dialog box shown below. Choose any one of the following options:

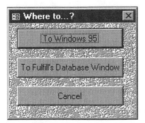

- **To Windows 95**   Closes Fulfill and Microsoft Access, and takes you back to the Windows 95 desktop.

- **To Fulfill's Database Window**   Keeps Fulfill and Access open, and takes you to Fulfill's database window where you can explore behind the scenes (see Chapter 28).

- **Cancel**   Neither of the above, takes you back to Fulfill's main switchboard.

Questions, Comments, Snide Remarks

As mentioned earlier in this appendix, we've made every effort to make Fulfill 95 bug-free and accurate. But a freeware product such as this does not have the benefit of beta testing (i.e., testing in the field), so bugs and mistakes can slip by. The copy you have is named version 1.0. But if you plan to use Fulfill for real work, you *are*, in a sense, the beta tester!

We will try to keep up with Fulfill and release additional versions with bug fixes and improvements. But we need your feedback to do that. If you find a problem, or have a suggestion for improvement, feel free to contact the author, Alan Simpson, whose addresses are listed in the Help ➤ About ➤ Author box in Fulfill, as well as in the introduction to this book.

To see if there are any post-1.0 versions of Fulfill out there, or to see a list of FAQs (Frequently Asked Questions), check out Alan's Web site at http://www.coolnerds.com/coolnerds. TIA (Thanks In Advance) for taking the time to do that. :-)

GLOSSARY

THIS glossary contains common terms that you're likely to run into when you work with Access. Here you'll find short definitions, along with references to chapters where you can learn more about the topic.

Of course, lots of online information about Access is just a few mouse clicks away:

1. From the Access menu bar, choose Help ➤ Microsoft Access Help Topics (or press F1). Or, if you're already using the online Help, click on the Help Topics button in any Help window.

2. Click on the Index tab.

3. Type **glossary** in the first text box, and press ↲.

4. Click on the alphabetical buttons to go to any part of the alphabet. Then click on any word to see its definition.

5. When you've finished reading the definition, click on the definition (or on any part of the Help window).

Also remember that any time you see a word underlined with dots, in any Help screen, clicking on that word will take you to a definition (or to a screen where you can make a more specific selection). See Chapter 1 for more information on using Access's built-in help.

Action The basic building block of a macro. An action is a task the macro performs, such as opening a table or sounding a beep. You can assign actions to a macro by dragging and dropping an object from the database window to the macro window's Action column. Or you can click in the Action column and choose an action from the drop-down list (Chapter 20).

Action query A type of query that takes an action on your data. This category includes Append, Delete, Make Table, and Update queries. Delete and Update queries change existing data; Append and Make Table queries copy existing data. See Chapter 10; see also *Select query*.

Append To add records from one table to the bottom of another table (Chapters 8 and 10).

Application A program designed to do a specific job. Microsoft Access, Microsoft Word, and Microsoft Excel are all examples of Windows applications. An Access application is a database that's designed to do a specific job, such as manage orders, juggle names and addresses, manage accounts receivable—whatever. You can design switchboards, dialog boxes, and data entry forms to make it easy for people who know little about Access to use your application (Chapter 3 and Chapters 19 through 28).

Argument The part of an action or expression that defines what to operate on. For example, in Sqr(81), Sqr( ) is a function (square root), and 81 is the argument (the value that Sqr( ) will operate upon). (Chapters 20 and 25.)

Attach See *Link*, which is the new name for the Access 2.*x* Attach feature.

Autonumber field A field in a table that automatically numbers each new record entered into a table. Autonumber fields can be incremental or random (Chapter 6).

Bitmap A graphic image stored in bitmap (.bmp) format (Chapters 8 and 13).

Bound control A control on an Access form or report that displays data from the underlying table (Chapter 13).

Bound object frame A control on an Access form or report that displays an OLE object stored within the underlying table (Chapter 13).

Bound OLE object An OLE object that's stored in an Access table (Chapters 8 and 13).

Calculated control A control on a form or report that gets its value by performing some calculation on data in the underlying table (Chapter 13).

Calculated field A field in a query that computes a value based on data in the table. Access will refresh the value in a calculated field automatically, whenever you change values of fields used in the calculated field. You could, for example, define a query field with the expression [Quantity]*[UnitPrice] to calculate the extended price of an item (Chapter 10).

Case-sensitive In a case-sensitive search, text must match uppercase and lowercase letters exactly. A *case-insensitive* search, by contrast, matches any combination of uppercase and lowercase text. When you ask Access to find or replace text values in a table, you can search with case-sensitive matching on or off (Chapter 9).

Cell The intersection of a row and column in a datasheet or grid. Each cell in the datasheet stores a single piece of data. (Chapters 6, 8, 9, 10, and 20.)

Chart A graphical representation of data in a form or report. Charts can summarize large amounts of data graphically, so the data is easier to understand (Chapter 14).

Check box A control that shows whether you've selected or cleared an option. A check mark (✓) appears in the box when you've selected it. Check boxes on forms make it easy to assign a Yes or No value to Yes/No fields in a table (Chapter 13). Some Windows dialog boxes also use check boxes to let you turn an option on or off.

Clipboard A general storage area used by all Windows programs, mainly for copying and moving things from one place to another. For example, selecting an item and then pressing Ctrl+C copies that item to the Clipboard.

Code Instructions for the computer to follow, expressed in a written language such as Visual Basic. The act of creating programs is sometimes called "writing code" or "coding" (by people who do that sort of thing). (Chapter 25.)

Column The visual presentation of a field in a datasheet, query, or filter window. A relational database stores data in tables that you can display in horizontal rows (records) and vertical columns (fields). (Chapters 2, 8, 9, and 10.)

Combo box A control that works like a combined text box and list box. Combo boxes on forms or datasheets make it easier to enter values into fields, because you can either type in the value or select it from a drop-down list. Some Windows dialog boxes also use combo boxes to let you choose options (Chapters 6, 9, and 13).

Command button A control that opens a linked form, runs a macro, or calls a Visual Basic function. You simply click on a command button on a form to open the linked form or start the macro or function. Command buttons work like the pushbuttons in many Windows dialog boxes and programs (Chapters 11 and 13).

Comparison operator An operator that compares two values, such as > (greater than), < (less than), and so on (Chapters 9 and 10).

Control An item on a form, report, or dialog box. Controls typically display data, provide decoration, or let the user make choices. For instance, a command button in a dialog box is a control (Chapter 13).

Control menu Activated by the tiny icon in the upper-left corner of a window, this standard Windows component lets you close, restore, and otherwise manipulate the window it controls. (For these jobs, however, many people prefer to use the Minimize, Maximize/Restore, and Close controls at the upper-right corner of a window, instead of the Control menu.)

Crosstab A query that computes summary totals based on values for each row and column. Crosstab queries answer questions such as "What are my monthly sales by region?" and "Who has ordered each of my products, and how many items of each product did they order?" (Chapter 10).

Current Record The record that currently holds the focus. See Chapter 8; see also *Focus*.

Data type The kind of information that will be stored in a field, such as Text, Number, or Date/Time. You define data types in table design view (Chapter 6).

Database A collection of all the objects—tables, queries, forms, reports, macros, and modules—related to a particular topic or subject (Chapter 2).

Database window The container window that shows all database objects. This window often appears first when you open a database. Usually, you can display the database window by pressing the F11 key (Chapter 1).

Datasheet view (or datasheet) The view that lets you see several records in a table or query result at a time, as opposed to form view, which generally shows only one record (Chapter 8).

DBMS An abbreviation for Database Management System. Popular database management systems include dBASE, Paradox, and of course, Microsoft Access (Chapter 2).

Default A setting that is assumed, and used, unless you change it. For example, the default margin on a report might be 1 inch.

Delete query An action query that deletes whatever rows match criteria that you specify. Delete queries provide a fast, automatic way to delete a certain set of records from a table without disturbing other records that don't match the criteria (Chapter 10).

Delimited text file A text file that contains values separated by commas, tabs, semicolons, or other characters. You can import delimited text files into new or existing Access tables (Chapter 7).

Design view The view that lets you create an object or change its appearance. Clicking on an object name in the database window and then clicking on the Design button takes you to the design view of that object (Chapters 6, 10, 13, 20, and 25).

Detail section The part of a form or report that displays records from your table or query. Also called the *detail band* (Chapter 13).

Developer (application developer) A person who uses Access to create specialized, user-friendly applications for less sophisticated computer users to work with (Chapters 19–28).

Dialog box A window that lets you select options or provide more information so that Access can carry out a command. Many dialog boxes include an OK button (that continues the command) and a Cancel button (that cancels the command).

Duplicate key A value that already exists in a table's primary key field or in an index field that doesn't allow duplicates. Access won't let you enter duplicate key values into a table (Chapters 6 and 8).

Dynaset The results of running a query or filter, which shows only the set of records requested (Chapters 9 and 10).

Embed What you do when you insert an object into a form or report. You can embed objects in these ways:

- Use drag-and-drop techniques (Chapters 4 and 8).
- Use the Insert ➤ Object command (Chapter 8).
- Use Copy and Paste options on the Edit menu (Chapter 8).
- Use Insert ➤ Chart or the Chart Wizard toolbox button to embed a chart in a form or report (Chapter 14).
- Use the PivotTable Wizard to embed a Microsoft Excel PivotTable into a Microsoft Access form (Chapter 14).

Equi-join See *Inner Join.*

Event An action, taken by the user, that Access can recognize. For example, a mouse click is an event (Chapter 19).

Expression A calculation that results in a single value. An expression can contain any combination of Access operators, object names (identifiers), literal values, and constants. You can use expressions to set properties and action arguments; to set criteria or define calculated fields in queries, forms, and reports; and to set conditions in macros. You also can use expressions in Visual Basic (Chapters 6, 10, 13, 20, and 25).

Field One column, representing a category of information, in a table. Also refers to one "blank" on a form (Chapters 6, 8, and 13).

Field list A small window or drop-down list that shows all the fields in an underlying table or query. You can display field lists in tables, filters, forms, reports, and queries (Chapters 8, 9, 10, and 13).

Field name The name that you assign to a field. A field name can have up to 64 characters (including letters, numbers, spaces, and some punctuation characters), and must be unique within the table (Chapter 6).

Field properties Characteristics of a field in a table, as defined in the table design view (Chapter 6).

Filter A type of "mini-query" that isolates specific records by filtering out unwanted records (Chapter 9).

Focus A general term for the insertion point, cursor, highlight, or whatever is indicating where your next action will take place. For example, if you click on a person's name, and the cursor jumps there, we say that the person's name "has the focus."

Foreign key When there's a one-to-many relationship between tables, the field that uniquely identifies each record on the "one side" of the relationship is called the *primary key*. The corresponding field in the table on the "many side" of the relationship is called the *foreign key* (Chapter 6).

Form properties Properties assigned to an entire form, as opposed to a section or control on a form. To change form properties, you open the form in design view, open the property sheet, choose Edit ➤ Select Form, and then choose your properties (Chapter 13).

Form view A way of viewing data in a table one record at a time, similar to a printed fill-in-the-blank form (Chapters 8, 11, and 13).

Function A procedure that returns a value. For example, in Sqr(81), Sqr( ) is the square-root function. (The expression *returns* 9, the square root of 81.) For a list of built-in Access functions, search the Help Index for *References, Functions* (Chapter 25).

Group *In a secure network system,* you can use groups to identify a collection of user accounts, each with its own group name and personal identification number (PID). Permissions assigned to a group apply to all users in that group (Chapter 18).

In a report, you can sort records and organize them into groups based on field values or ranges of values. You also can display introductory and summary data for each group (Chapter 13).

In a query, you can use groups to categorize data and perform summary calculations (Chapter 10).

I-Beam Another name for *mouse pointer.* The I-Beam appears when the mouse pointer is on some text. To position the cursor with your mouse, move the I-Beam to where you want the cursor to appear, and then click the left mouse button.

Index A feature that speeds up sorting and searching for data in a table. Access maintains each index in sorted order and keeps it in memory for quick retrieval. Primary key fields and certain other fields are indexed automatically. You can define additional index fields in table design view (Chapter 6).

Inner join A join that combines records from two tables that have matching values in a common field. Suppose two tables—Customers and Orders—each have a CustomerID field. An inner join of these tables would match customers and the orders they placed. No information would appear about customers who haven't placed orders (Chapter 10).

Insertion point The blinking vertical bar on the screen that indicates where any characters you type will appear. More generally referred to as the *cursor* or even *the focus.*

Join A query operation that combines some or all records from multiple tables. Access supports three types of joins: *inner join, outer join,* and *self join* (Chapter 10).

Key field The field in a table that uniquely identifies each record in that table, such as a product code or SKU in a products list (Chapter 6).

Label A control on a form or report that displays descriptive text such as a title, caption, or instructions (Chapters 11, 12, and 13).

Link (object) A connection between a source document and destination document. A link inserts a copy of the object from the source document into the destination document, and the two documents remain connected. Thus, changes to the linked object in the source document are also reflected in the destination document. Links provide a powerful and convenient way to share objects among Windows programs (Chapter 8). You also can link main forms or reports with subforms and subreports, so that the data on the subform/subreport is in sync with the corresponding data on the main form/main report (Chapters 11, 12, and 13).

Link (table) You can link tables from other database programs (Paradox, dBASE, FoxPro, and ODBC), from text files and spreadsheets, or from closed Access databases. The linked tables will appear in your open database window. After linking tables, you can add, delete, and change their records, just as if you were using "native" Access tables (Chapter 7).

List box A control that displays a list of values to choose from. List boxes on forms or datasheets make it easier to enter values into fields. Some Windows dialog boxes also use list boxes to let you choose options (Chapters 6, 9, and 13).

Lookup Field A field that displays and stores values looked up from a field in another table or another part of a form. You can display a lookup field as a *combo box* or *list box* (Chapters 6 and 13).

Macro A series of actions that can be played back with a single action (Chapter 20).

Make Table query A query that creates a new table from the results (the dynaset) of a previous query. Make table queries provide a handy way to create copies of tables that you want to edit, print, chart, or crosstabulate. They're also helpful when you need to export data to a nonrelational program such as a spreadsheet (Chapter 10).

Many-to-many relationship A relationship in which many records in one table might refer to many records in another, and vice versa. A classic example is an Orders and Products relationship, in which an order can include many products, and each product can appear on many orders. Often we set up a third table as a go-between, so that we end up with two one-to-many relationships. For instance, if we use an Order Details table as the go-between, Orders would have a one-to-many relationship with Order Details and Order Details would have a one-to-many relationship with Products.

Memo field A field that can store a large amount of text (Chapter 6).

Modal Describes a form that keeps the focus until you explicitly close the form. Most dialog boxes are just modal forms (Chapter 22).

Module An Access object that contains one or more custom procedures, each written in Visual Basic. A global module is one you create. A form or report module is one that Access creates automatically (Chapter 25).

Move handle A square that appears at the top left edge of a control when you draw or select it in form design or report design view. You can drag a move handle to move the control. See Chapter 13; see also *Sizing handle*.

Null An object that has no value. An empty field (Chapter 8).

Null propagation The tendency for a blank (as opposed to zero) numeric value to cause any calculations that rely on the calculation to be null (blank) as well.

Object Any element of a database system. Access recognizes these types of objects:

- Controls and database components, including tables, queries, forms, reports, macros, and modules.
- Special system objects used in Visual Basic programming.
- Linked or embedded objects such as a chart, drawing, spreadsheet cell, PivotTable, table, and so forth.

ODBC An acronym for Open Database Connectivity, a standard created by Microsoft for allowing a single user to access many different databases (Chapter 7).

OLE (Pronounced *olay*) A technique that allows multiple Windows programs (for example, Access, Excel, or Word) to share objects (such as pictures, sounds, or charts). (Chapters 8, 13, and 14.)

OLE client A program that can hold an object that was initially created by some other program (the *OLE Server*). (Chapter 8.)

OLE server A program that can "serve up" an object to an *OLE client*. For example, Paint can serve up pictures to put in your Access database. Sound Recorder can serve up sounds to put in your database (Chapter 8).

One-to-many Describes a natural relationship between two types of information where for every single item on one side of the relationship, there may be many items on the other side. For example, any *one* customer might place *many* orders with a particular business (Chapter 6).

One-to-one Describes a relationship between two tables in which each record in the first table can be associated with exactly one record in the second table. A one-to-one relationship usually suggests a poor database design (Chapter 6).

Operator A character (or characters) used to perform an operation or comparison. For example, + is the operator used for addition (Chapters 9 and 10).

Option group A control on a form that frames a set of check boxes, option buttons, or toggle buttons. You can use option groups to provide a limited set of alternative values to choose (for example, Cash, Check, or Credit Card). The selected option will store a number in the underlying table field. Therefore, if you select the first button in an option group, Access will store the number 1 in the field; if you select the second button, Access stores 2; and so forth. You can use the stored number to make decisions in a macro or Visual Basic program (Chapter 13).

Page

1. The portion of the database (.mdb file) in which Access stores record data. Each page may contain more than one record, depending on the size of the records.

2. A screen of data in a form or a page in a report (Chapters 11, 12, and 13).

Parameter query A query that asks for specific information before doing its job (Chapter 10).

PivotTable A special type of Microsoft Excel worksheet that's embedded within an Access form. Like Crosstab queries, PivotTables let you quickly summarize large amounts of data in a tabular format. But they're more flexible because they let you rearrange rows and columns interactively, and filter out unwanted data on the fly (Chapter 14).

Primary key The field in a table that contains information unique to each record in that table. Your Social Security Number is the primary key on the IRS's database; nobody else has the same Social Security Number as you (Chapter 6).

Property A characteristic of an item. Typical properties include size, color, screen location, whether you can update a control, and whether a control is visible (Chapters 6, 10, and 13).

Property sheet A window that lets you define the properties (characteristics) of a database, a database object, or its individual controls. To display the property sheet for objects other than the database, choose <u>V</u>iew ➤ <u>P</u>roperties from any menu in which it's available. To display database properties, choose <u>F</u>ile ➤ Database Properties (Chapters 5, 6, and 13).

Query An Access tool that lets you ask questions about your data, such as "How many customers live in New York?" You use filters (Chapter 9) and/or queries (Chapter 10) to structure such questions.

Query By Example (QBE) The query technique used by Access and many other modern database management systems. With QBE, you create an *example* of the fields to show, calculations to perform, and sort order to use (Chapters 9 and 10).

QBE grid The part of the query design window in which you enter the field names and other example elements to construct the query (Chapters 9 and 10).

Read-only A property of a field, record, or database that allows you to view data but not change it.

Record A collection of related data (fields) that describes a single item (row) in an Access table (Chapter 2).

Referential integrity A set of rules that prevent you from inadvertently deleting, adding, or changing data in one table if that change would cause problems in another table (Chapter 6).

Report A formatted display of Access data that you can print or preview on the screen (Chapters 12 and 13).

Report properties Properties assigned to an entire report, as opposed to a section or control on a report. To change report properties, you open the report in design view, open the property sheet, choose Edit ➤ Select Report, and then choose your properties (Chapter 13).

Row The visual presentation of a record in a datasheet, query, or filter window. A relational database stores data in tables, which you can display in horizontal rows (records) and vertical columns (fields). (Chapters 2, 8, 9, and 10.)

Row selector A small box or bar that you can click on to select an entire row when you design a table or macro. (Also called a *field selector*.) (Chapters 6 and 8.)

Section Part of a form or report, such as the header, footer, or detail section. (Chapter 13.)

Select query A query that asks a question about your data and returns a *dynaset* (result) without changing the data. See Chapter 10; see also *Dynaset* and *Action query*.

Self join A table that's joined to itself in a query. For example, if a part consists of other parts, you could identify the "parts of a part" using a self join on a Parts table (Chapter 10).

Sizing handle A tiny square that appears around a control when you draw or select it in form design or report design view. To resize the control, drag one of its sizing handles vertically, horizontally, or diagonally (depending on which handle you choose). See Chapter 13; see also *Move handle*.

Sort To put into some meaningful order, such as alphabetical (A–Z) or numeric (smallest-to-largest). (Chapter 9.)

SQL An acronym for Structured Query Language—a standardized language for asking questions about data in a database. In Access, you set up questions by designing queries. Access converts your query to an SQL statement before it answers your question (Chapter 10).

Status bar The bar along the bottom of the screen that displays the current status of things. To hide or display the Access status bar for a specific database, choose Tools ➤ Startup, and then either select (check) or deselect (clear) Display Status Bar. To control the default status bar setting for all Access databases, choose Tools ➤ Options ➤ View, and then either select or deselect Status Bar (Chapters 1 and 15).

String A computer buzzword for "a chunk of text." For example, "Hello there" is a string (as opposed to 123.45, which is a number).

Subform A form that's inside another form or report. You can use subforms to combine (or *link*) data from multiple related tables onto a form (Chapters 11 and 13).

Subreport A report that's inside another report. You can use subreports to combine (or *link*) data from multiple related tables onto a report (Chapters 12 and 13).

Table The Access object that holds the data you want to manage (Chapters 2 and 6).

Text box A control in a form or report that lets you view or enter text (Chapter 13).

Title bar The bar across the top of a window that describes what's in the window.

Toggle A menu command or setting that can have only one of two possible values: On or Off (or Yes or No).

Toolbar A bar or box that offers buttons as shortcuts to specific features. To turn the default Access toolbars on or off, choose Tools ➤ Startup, and then select (check) or deselect (clear) Allow Built-In Toolbars. You also can turn individual toolbars on and off by right-clicking on any visible toolbar or by choosing View ➤ Toolbars and selecting or deselecting the toolbars you want to show or hide (Chapters 1, 15, and 23).

Toolbox A toolbar in the form design and report design windows that lets you place controls on your design. You can hide or display the toolbox in those windows by choosing View ➤ Toolbox (Chapter 13).

ToolTip A short description that appears beneath a toolbar or toolbox button if you rest the mouse pointer on the button for a couple of seconds without clicking. To turn ToolTips on and off, choose Tools ➤ Options ➤ View, and then either select (check) or deselect (clear) Show ToolTips (Chapter 15).

Unbound control A control on a form or report that isn't tied to the underlying table (Chapter 13).

Unbound object frame The container for an object that's displayed on a form or report, but isn't tied to the underlying table (Chapters 13 and 14).

Update query An action query that lets you change data in all or selected records in a table (Chapter 10).

User The person who uses an application.

Validation rule A rule that defines whether data will be accepted into a table or form. You can define validation rules in the table design window's field properties (Chapter 6) or in the form design property sheet (Chapter 13). Forms automatically inherit rules defined in the table design. Validation rules defined in a form are active only when using the form to enter and edit data. Those validation rules are used in addition to any validation rules defined in the table structure.

Value The contents of a field or control. For example, if you type *Smith* into the Last Name field in a table, "*Smith*" is the value of Last Name in that particular record. If you say "X=10" then X has a value of 10.

View A way of looking at an object. In Access, you often can pick a view from the database window, the <u>V</u>iew menu, or a toolbar button. When the focus is on an expression, you can zoom in by pressing Shift+F2.

Visual Basic for Applications (VBA) The optional programming language that comes with Microsoft Access, to give knowledgeable programmers more control over the custom applications they develop (Chapter 25).

WHERE clause An SQL statement that isolates specific records in a table. WHERE clauses are created automatically when you design a query. Not to be confused with BEAR CLAWS or SANTA CLAUS (Chapter 10).

Wizard A tool that asks you questions and creates an object according to your answers. For example, you can use Wizards to create databases, tables, queries, forms, and reports with just a few mouse clicks. Wizards are available throughout Microsoft Access, Microsoft Office, and Windows 95 (Chapters 3, 6, 10, 11, 12, 13, and 14).

Zoom An expanded text box that lets you enter expressions or text more conveniently. You can press Shift+F2 to open a zoom box in property sheets and in the grid in various Access windows (Chapter 10).

You can zoom in Print Preview to change the magnification of the report page, anywhere from a close-up view to a full-page view (Chapters 9 and 12).

Finally, OLE and picture objects have a Size Mode (or Picture Size Mode) property called Zoom that grows or shrinks the object to fit its frame, but keeps the proportions the same (Chapters 8 and 13).

INDEX

Note to the Reader: Throughout this index **boldface** page numbers indicate primary discussions of a topic. *Italic* page numbers indicate illustrations.

G

N

S

X

Y

Z

FOR EVERY COMPUTER QUESTION,
THERE IS A SYBEX BOOK THAT HAS THE ANSWER

Each computer user learns in a different way. Some need thorough, methodical explanations, while others are too busy for details. At Sybex we bring nearly 20 years of experience to developing the book that's right for you. Whatever your needs, we can help you get the most from your software and hardware, at a pace that's comfortable for you.

We start beginners out right. You will learn by seeing and doing with our **Quick & Easy** series: friendly, colorful guidebooks with screen-by-screen illustrations. For hardware novices, the **Your First** series offers valuable purchasing advice and installation support.

Often recognized for excellence in national book reviews, our **Mastering** titles are designed for the intermediate to advanced user, without leaving the beginner behind. A **Mastering** book provides the most detailed reference available. Add our pocket-sized **Instant Reference** titles for a complete guidance system. Programmers will find that the new **Developer's Handbook** series provides a more advanced perspective on developing innovative and original code.

With the breathtaking advances common in computing today comes an ever increasing demand to remain technologically up-to-date. In many of our books, we provide the added value of software, on disks or CDs. Sybex remains your source for information on software development, operating systems, networking, and every kind of desktop application. We even have books for kids. Sybex can help smooth your travels on the **Internet** and provide **Strategies and Secrets** to your favorite computer games.

As you read this book, take note of its quality. Sybex publishes books written by experts—authors chosen for their extensive topical knowledge. In fact, many are professionals working in the computer software field. In addition, each manuscript is thoroughly reviewed by our technical, editorial, and production personnel for accuracy and ease-of-use before you ever see it—our guarantee that you'll buy a quality Sybex book every time.

To manage your hardware headaches and optimize your software potential, ask for a Sybex book.

FOR MORE INFORMATION, PLEASE CONTACT:

Sybex, Inc.
1151 Marina Village Parkway
Alameda, CA 94501
Tel: (510) 523-8233 • (800) 227-2346
Fax: (510) 523-2373

SYBEX

Sybex is committed to using natural resources wisely to preserve and improve our environment. As a leader in the computer books publishing industry, we are aware that over 40% of America's solid waste is paper. This is why we have been printing our books on recycled paper since 1982.

This year our use of recycled paper will result in the saving of more than 153,000 trees. We will lower air pollution effluents by 54,000 pounds, save 6,300,000 gallons of water, and reduce landfill by 27,000 cubic yards.

In choosing a Sybex book you are not only making a choice for the best in skills and information, you are also choosing to enhance the quality of life for all of us.

GET A FREE CATALOG JUST FOR EXPRESSING YOUR OPINION.

Help us improve our books and get a ***FREE*** full-color catalog in the bargain. Please complete this form, pull out this page and send it in today. The address is on the reverse side.

Name _____   Company _____

Address _____   City _____ State ____ Zip _____

Phone (____) _____

1. How would you rate the overall quality of this book?

❑ Excellent
❑ Very Good
❑ Good
❑ Fair
❑ Below Average
❑ Poor

2. What were the things you liked most about the book? (Check all that apply)

❑ Pace
❑ Format
❑ Writing Style
❑ Examples
❑ Table of Contents
❑ Index
❑ Price
❑ Illustrations
❑ Type Style
❑ Cover
❑ Depth of Coverage
❑ Fast Track Notes

3. What were the things you liked *least* about the book? (Check all that apply)

❑ Pace
❑ Format
❑ Writing Style
❑ Examples
❑ Table of Contents
❑ Index
❑ Price
❑ Illustrations
❑ Type Style
❑ Cover
❑ Depth of Coverage
❑ Fast Track Notes

4. Where did you buy this book?

❑ Bookstore chain
❑ Small independent bookstore
❑ Computer store
❑ Wholesale club
❑ College bookstore
❑ Technical bookstore
❑ Other _____

5. How did you decide to buy this particular book?

❑ Recommended by friend
❑ Recommended by store personnel
❑ Author's reputation
❑ Sybex's reputation
❑ Read book review in _____
❑ Other _____

6. How did you pay for this book?

❑ Used own funds
❑ Reimbursed by company
❑ Received book as a gift

7. What is your level of experience with the subject covered in this book?

❑ Beginner
❑ Intermediate
❑ Advanced

8. How long have you been using a computer?

years _____
months _____

9. Where do you most often use your computer?

❑ Home
❑ Work

❑ Both
❑ Other _____

10. What kind of computer equipment do you have? (Check all that apply)

❑ PC Compatible Desktop Computer
❑ PC Compatible Laptop Computer
❑ Apple/Mac Computer
❑ Apple/Mac Laptop Computer
❑ CD ROM
❑ Fax Modem
❑ Data Modem
❑ Scanner
❑ Sound Card
❑ Other _____

11. What other kinds of software packages do you ordinarily use?

❑ Accounting
❑ Databases
❑ Networks
❑ Apple/Mac
❑ Desktop Publishing
❑ Spreadsheets
❑ CAD
❑ Games
❑ Word Processing
❑ Communications
❑ Money Management
❑ Other _____

12. What operating systems do you ordinarily use?

❑ DOS
❑ OS/2
❑ Windows
❑ Apple/Mac
❑ Windows NT
❑ Other _____

13. On what computer-related subject(s) would you like to see more books?

_____

_____

_____

_____

14. Do you have any other comments about this book? (Please feel free to use a separate piece of paper if you need more room)

_____

_____

_____

_____

- - - - - - - - - - - PLEASE FOLD, SEAL, AND MAIL TO SYBEX - - - - - - - - - -

SYBEX INC.
Department M
1151 Marina Village Parkway
Alameda, CA
94501

Let us hear from you.

 Talk to SYBEX authors, editors and fellow forum members.

 Get tips, hints and advice online.

 Download magazine articles, book art, and shareware.

Join the SYBEX Forum on **CompuServe**®

If you're already a CompuServe user, just type **GO SYBEX** to join the SYBEX Forum. If not, try CompuServe for free by calling 1-800-848-8199 and ask for Representative 560. You'll get one free month of basic service and a $15 credit for CompuServe extended services—a $23.95 value. Your personal ID number and password will be activated when you sign up.

Join us online today. Type **GO SYBEX** on CompuServe. If you're not a CompuServe member, call Representative 560 at **1-800-848-8199**.

 SYBEX

(outside U.S./Canada call 614-457-0802)

On the CD

The CD-ROM for this book contains:

Fulfill 95   The world's easiest order-entry system. Prints invoices and receipts, and keeps track of customers. Illustrates fancy new techniques such as auto-fill City, State, and Area Code from Zip Code entry!

Check Writer   *Cary Prague Books and Software* provides a complete Check Writer program. Prints checks, manages accounts, and simplifies reconciliation of bank statements.

Multimedia Catalog   *Access to Business* provides a multimedia catalog of professionally designed Access applications that you can purchase separately. Purchase ready-to-run Access databases for Auto Repair and Towing, Bid Tracking, Chiropractic, General Accounting, Human Resources Task Management, Job Costing, Legal Evidence, Medical Patient Records, Merchant Point-of-Sale, Real Estate and Realty Management, Time and Billing, and more.

USPS TrueType Font   *TAZ Information Services* provides a shareware TrueType font that can print POSTNET bar codes on labels and envelopes.

Sample Access Databases   All Microsoft Access Database Wizard databases are ready to run. So are the Order Entry database and many other databases we used as examples for this book.

...and much more!